The
Farm Management Guide
Fifteenth Edition

DOANE WESTERN

Published by Doane-Western, Inc.
8900 Manchester Road / St. Louis, Missouri 63144

Table of Contents

Introduction

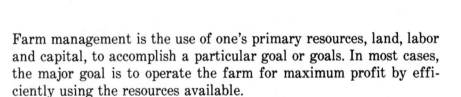

Farm management is the use of one's primary resources, land, labor and capital, to accomplish a particular goal or goals. In most cases, the major goal is to operate the farm for maximum profit by efficiently using the resources available.

Management is making decisions. A manager is constantly faced with decisions of many kinds—immediate, short term and long range. He must decide what to do and how, when and where to do it. Then he must take the necessary action to carry out that decision. Success depends on the soundness of one's decisions.

Alert farm managers are aware of the rapid changes taking place in agriculture. They are quick to reap the benefits of these changes by shifting and allocating the use of their resources to capitalize on new farming methods.

Regardless of your goals or inborn ability, you can greatly improve your farm management know-how by applying the tested principles found in this guide.

Chapter 1

Types of Farming

Modern farming is a competitive business and to compete effectively, you need to know who your competitors are and where they are located. Understanding why certain areas have become important in the production of specific crops and classes of livestock can help you select those enterprises which are most likely to be profitable under your conditions. You can also benefit from the experience of others.

FACTORS AFFECTING TYPES OF FARMING

Through years of experience, farmers have learned that they can raise certain crops and livestock in their area more profitably than others. For example, the wheat areas of the Plains states can generally produce wheat more economically than the Southeast. In the Southeast, other crops can be more profitably produced. In the Plains, the number of alternative crops which can be profitably produced is limited, especially under dryland conditions. Economists call this the "law of comparative advantage."

Some of the factors which influence where certain crops or livestock are produced are as follows:

- Soils and Topography—Cultivated row crops require reasonably level, fertile soils. Pasture, hay crops and timber, on the other hand, are well adapted to rolling, hilly, less fertile land. Livestock is produced to utilize these crops. The productivity of the land and its adaptation to mechanization have a tremendous effect on crop profits.
- Climate—The amount and distribution of rainfall over the year, the temperature, its range by seasons, the number of frost-free days or length of growing season and even day lengths are vitally important.
- Market—Demand for the product and nearness to sizable markets influence production areas. Milkshed location near major population centers is a good example.
- Transportation—Available transportation facilities and type of product, whether perishable or bulky to handle, play a definite role.

Many other factors influence what particular commodities are produced in certain areas. One of these is land value, which is determined in part by competition from industrial and suburban development. Farmland near urban areas is usually devoted to intensive cropping and livestock programs. Also the ability and skills, together with likes and dislikes of the people of an area, have effects on the type of farming that the area will adopt. Basically, there are eight major types of farming in the United States:

- Fruit, truck, special
- Feedgrains and livestock
- Wheat and small grains
- Tobacco and general
- Dairy
- Range
- Cotton
- General

FLEXIBILITY IN TYPES OF FARMING

Regardless of the types of farming limitations within a certain area, it should be recognized that there is a certain amount of flexibility in what a farmer can produce on his farm. Thus, each farmer has some leeway for adjusting his crop and livestock production to achieve maximum returns from his enterprises. Often this is learned through experience and trial and error. This is where management becomes important.

Although resources in an area are generally channelled to produce the most profitable crop or class of livestock, this does not necessarily mean that a farmer should produce only one crop or class of livestock. Other crops usually are grown to make more efficient use of available labor, power and machinery and to meet conservation requirements.

MAJOR TYPES OF FARMING IN THE UNITED STATES

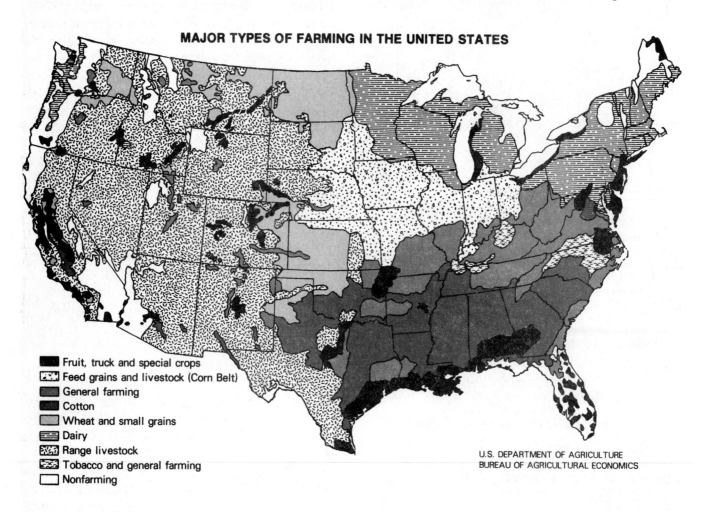

Fruit, truck and special crops
Feed grains and livestock (Corn Belt)
General farming
Cotton
Wheat and small grains
Dairy
Range livestock
Tobacco and general farming
Nonfarming

U.S. DEPARTMENT OF AGRICULTURE
BUREAU OF AGRICULTURAL ECONOMICS

CORN BELT

Favorable climate, soils and markets have made the Midwest (Corn Belt) the corn production center of the world. Differences in topography and soils have resulted in three major types of farming within the central portion of this region.

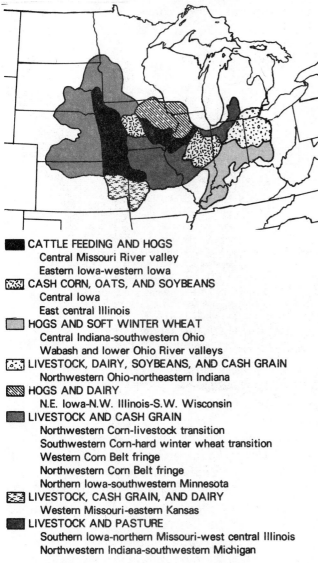

■ CATTLE FEEDING AND HOGS
  Central Missouri River valley
  Eastern Iowa-western Iowa
▨ CASH CORN, OATS, AND SOYBEANS
  Central Iowa
  East central Illinois
▨ HOGS AND SOFT WINTER WHEAT
  Central Indiana-southwestern Ohio
  Wabash and lower Ohio River valleys
▨ LIVESTOCK, DAIRY, SOYBEANS, AND CASH GRAIN
  Northwestern Ohio-northeastern Indiana
▨ HOGS AND DAIRY
  N.E. Iowa-N.W. Illinois-S.W. Wisconsin
▨ LIVESTOCK AND CASH GRAIN
  Northwestern Corn-livestock transition
  Southwestern Corn-hard winter wheat transition
  Western Corn Belt fringe
  Northwestern Corn Belt fringe
  Northern Iowa-southwestern Minnesota
▨ LIVESTOCK, CASH GRAIN, AND DAIRY
  Western Missouri-eastern Kansas
▨ LIVESTOCK AND PASTURE
  Southern Iowa-northern Missouri-west central Illinois
  Northwestern Indiana-southwestern Michigan

Cash corn and soybeans are grown on a major acreage of the level, fertile land in central Iowa and east central Illinois. Acreage planted to oats is declining. There is insufficient hay and pasture for beef cattle enterprises. Income is derived mainly from the sale of grain crops.

Cattle feeding and hogs is a system of livestock farming that has developed in areas where the land is mostly rolling. The sloping cropland is subject to erosion. Therefore, the cropping system includes grasses and legumes to protect the soil from erosion and to maintain soil organic matter. Even with the large number of hogs, a surplus of corn is produced on many farms in this area each year. Beef cattle are fed to use up large supplies of hay, pasture and corn.

Hogs and soft winter wheat represent a principal type of farming in the eastern part of the central Corn Belt. Conditions are favorable for the production of winter wheat as well as corn and soybeans. Production of corn on many farms is often limited to the acreage needed to produce the necessary feed for a hog enterprise.

Outside the central Corn Belt, corn and soybean production is not as dominant as it is in the central section. Less favorable soils and climate are the chief influencing factors.

Livestock, dairy, and cash grain are the major enterprises in northeastern Indiana, and northwestern Ohio. Crop acreages consist of corn, soybeans and small grain, with hay and pasture occupying a large portion of the farmland. Nearness to large cities and a favorable cropping system provide a market and plentiful feed for fluid milk production.

Hogs and dairy are commonly combined in northeastern Iowa and northwestern Illinois because of the existing favorable feed situation. Corn is an important crop, but large amounts of hay and pasture are produced in proportion to concentrate feeds.

Livestock and cash grain production are predominant in the western Corn Belt. This is a transitional area between corn and livestock feeding to the east and wheat and range livestock to the west. The low productivity of hay and pastureland results in fewer cattle and the smaller quantity of corn produced results in fewer hogs. Proportionately more grain, particularly corn, is sold from this part of the border region.

Livestock, cash grain and dairy are important enterprises in western Missouri and northwestern Kansas. Large acreages of hay are combined with the production of corn or grain sorghum and wheat. Soils are best suited to a grassland type of farming in this area.

Livestock and pasture is a principal type of farming along the southern edge of the Corn Belt. More pasture relative to feedgrains is produced. Because of the scarcity of good cropland and the low yields produced on available cropland, grazing is more important than the feeding of cattle. Hog production is limited.

COTTON BELT

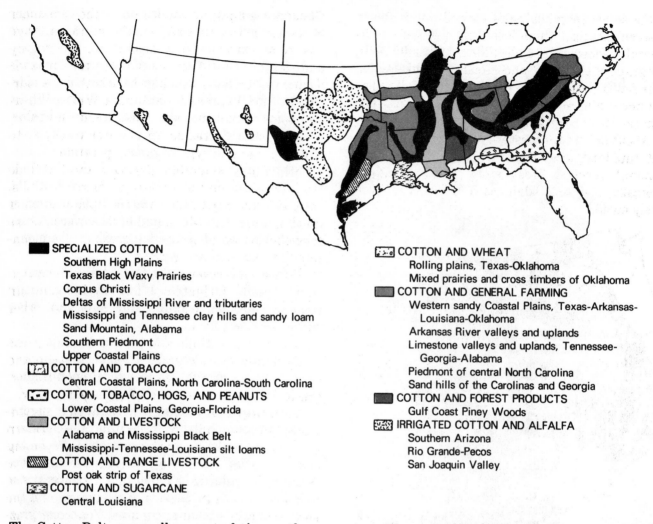

■ **SPECIALIZED COTTON**
Southern High Plains
Texas Black Waxy Prairies
Corpus Christi
Deltas of Mississippi River and tributaries
Mississippi and Tennessee clay hills and sandy loam
Sand Mountain, Alabama
Southern Piedmont
Upper Coastal Plains

▨ **COTTON AND TOBACCO**
Central Coastal Plains, North Carolina-South Carolina

▨ **COTTON, TOBACCO, HOGS, AND PEANUTS**
Lower Coastal Plains, Georgia-Florida

▨ **COTTON AND LIVESTOCK**
Alabama and Mississippi Black Belt
Mississippi-Tennessee-Louisiana silt loams

▨ **COTTON AND RANGE LIVESTOCK**
Post oak strip of Texas

▨ **COTTON AND SUGARCANE**
Central Louisiana

▨ **COTTON AND WHEAT**
Rolling plains, Texas-Oklahoma
Mixed prairies and cross timbers of Oklahoma

▨ **COTTON AND GENERAL FARMING**
Western sandy Coastal Plains, Texas-Arkansas-
Louisiana-Oklahoma
Arkansas River valleys and uplands
Limestone valleys and uplands, Tennessee-
Georgia-Alabama
Piedmont of central North Carolina
Sand hills of the Carolinas and Georgia

■ **COTTON AND FOREST PRODUCTS**
Gulf Coast Piney Woods

▨ **IRRIGATED COTTON AND ALFALFA**
Southern Arizona
Rio Grande-Pecos
San Joaquin Valley

The Cotton Belt covers all or most of nine southern states and a portion of four others. Cotton is also grown in irrigated areas of California, Arizona, and New Mexico. The northern boundary of the Cotton Belt closely follows the line of 200 frost-free days. Except where cotton is irrigated, the western boundary closely parallels the 20-inch rainfall line.

Specialized cotton production areas are located in the High Plains and around Corpus Christi, Texas and the Delta of Arkansas, Louisiana, Mississippi and Missouri. One-third to one-half of the cropland is planted to cotton. In these areas and in the irrigated areas of the West, farms are large, and cotton production is highly mechanized.

In Texas, grain sorghum is important. In the Delta, soybeans, oats and corn are grown with cotton.

Other specific enterprises in various areas throughout the Cotton Belt are combined with cot-

ton. The soils are well adapted to peanut and tobacco production in parts of the coastal plains of Georgia, South Carolina, and North Carolina.

Pasture and livestock production are combined with cotton in the Black Belt of Alabama, Mississippi and Louisiana.

In central Louisiana, sugarcane and rice are important, but cotton occupies more cropland than either of these crops.

In the low, rolling plains of Texas and central Oklahoma, wheat, grain sorghum and range livestock are important.

Cotton and general farming areas are found in parts of several southern states. Some specialty truck crops such as tomatoes and sweet potatoes are grown in the western sandy coastal plains of Texas, Arkansas and Louisiana.

Highly specialized farms are found in the limestone areas of Tennessee, Georgia and Alabama.

RANGE LIVESTOCK

Cattle or sheep ranching is carried on in eleven western states, though sheep production is generally viewed as a declining industry. Soils, topography, elevation and climate of this region offer few alternatives to ranching. Rainfall is low and uncertain, making crop production impossible or hazardous except under irrigation.

About half of the western range area is federal and state land, most of which is public domain and national forests. Most stock farm areas of Nebraska, Kansas, Oklahoma and Texas are privately owned.

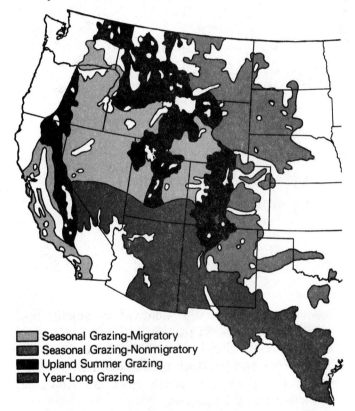

- Seasonal Grazing-Migratory
- Seasonal Grazing-Nonmigratory
- Upland Summer Grazing
- Year-Long Grazing

Year-long range grazing is generally practiced in the Southwest, extending northwest from the Rio Grande plains of Texas to southwestern Nevada. Winters are mild except at high altitudes. Range feed is usually short in late winter and early spring. Considerable supplemental feeding is necessary in dry years and some cottonseed cake is commonly fed in winter.

Little or no crop production is practiced on most livestock ranches. The small areas under irrigation in the region supply very little livestock feed. Cattle ranching is the chief enterprise in the Rio Grande plains area. Goats are a major enterprise on the rougher and brush-covered range in the Edwards Plateau of Texas.

Seasonal grazing is carried on in the remainder of the range livestock region. The northern range has great extremes in temperature, topography and rainfall. Cattle are moved into the lowlands during winter. Some ranchers have both dry and irrigated land. In areas bordering the Winter Wheat Belt some stock is moved to wheat fields in winter.

The seasonal grazing areas differ widely as to season of use and type of ranch operation.

Migratory seasonal grazing areas include the intermountain region plus the Sierra foothills, the California coast range and the upland summer grazing areas. Grassland and brush-covered areas furnish winter and spring-fall grazing. The mountains furnish summer grazing.

Public lands cover about 80% of the intermountain region. Irrigated lands and mountain meadows furnish pasture and hay and other winter livestock feed.

The Sierra foothills and the coast range areas in California provide grazing for both sheep and cattle. These areas are comprised of open timber, brush, forage grasses and adequate stock water.

Nonmigratory seasonal grazing encompasses the sandhills of Nebraska, the western parts of the Dakotas and northeastern Wyoming and Montana. Farther south, this area includes the Osage-Flint Hills in Kansas and Oklahoma, the Canadian breaks in Texas and Oklahoma, and the north central Texas grazing area. Year-long grazing is possible in some areas, but two to four months of winter feeding is usually necessary.

Combination wheat and cattle ranches are found in the Great Plains. Most ranchers grow at least part of their winter feed supply.

Upland summer grazing is predominant in the higher altitude areas of the Rocky Mountains and associated ranges and the Sierra Nevadas and the southern Cascade Mountains. The summer grazing areas surround a number of large important irrigated farming areas; and scattered farming areas are found which produce hay, grain, and other crops. Otherwise, the areas generally are unsuited for use other than grazing.

The climate is rigorous. All livestock kept within the area must be fed some during the winter. Hay is the universal feed. The hay comes largely from mountain meadows, irrigated land near ranch headquarters, or from irrigated farms. The location of home ranches is governed chiefly by land suitable to produce hay.

DAIRY BELT

■ SPECIALIZED DAIRY
North Pacific Coast
Eastern Wisconsin-northeastern Illinois
Central Northeast
Boise Valley and Star Valley
San Joaquin Valley
Los Angeles milkshed

▨ DAIRY AND LIVESTOCK
Minnesota cut-over fringe
Southeast Minnesota-west central Wisconsin

▤ DAIRY, HAY, AND POTATOES
Lake States cut-over

▦ DAIRY AND CASH CROPS
East central Michigan
Western New York

▦ DAIRY, POULTRY, AND MIXED FARMING
Puget Sound-Willamette Valley
Southern New England
Hudson River Valley
Central Maine

▢ DAIRY AND GENERAL FARMING
Central Wisconsin
Central Pennsylvania
Northern Piedmont
Lake Erie border
Northern New England
Allegheny Plateau, Pa.

Dairy farming is concentrated in the Northeast, in the Lake States, along the North Pacific Coast and in the smaller areas adjoining large cities.

Specialized dairy operations are found in the central Northeast, in eastern Wisconsin and northeastern Illinois and in the Pacific Coast areas. Family-sized dairy farms predominate. Farmers produce part of their concentrate feed, but a major share is shipped into these areas.

Dairy farming enterprises can be found combined with poultry, fruit and truck-crops in central Maine, southern New England, the Hudson River Valley of New York, around Puget Sound in Washington, and in the Willamette Valley in Oregon. Other cash crops are important in local areas.

Dairy and other enterprises are predominant in other Dairy Belt areas, with dairying being the most important single enterprise. In east central Wisconsin and southeastern Minnesota, produc-tion of feedgrains, hay and pasture is generally adequate for both dairy and hog enterprises. This is the center of creamery butter production.

Butter production extends into the northern cutover sections of each of the Lake States. The cold climate, the scarcity of good tillable land and the small farms limit the production of feed crops.

South of the cutover area in Michigan and in western New York, the soils and climate are favorable for production of several cultivated crops in rotation with hay and pasture.

Dairy and general farming areas are central Pennsylvania, the upper Piedmont and the Allegheny Plateau in Pennsylvania and in most of northern New England.

In northeastern Ohio and northwestern Pennsylvania, dairying is combined with production of wheat, oats, hay and pasture.

In central Wisconsin, farming systems range from specialized dairying to a combination of dairying, hogs, potatoes or canning crops.

WHEAT AND SMALL GRAINS

Wheat is grown commercially throughout most of the United States, except in dryland areas with less than 12 to 15 inches of rainfall and parts of the deep South where rainfall is excessive. The major wheat regions include much of the Great Plains and an area centering in the Columbia Basin of the Pacific Northwest.

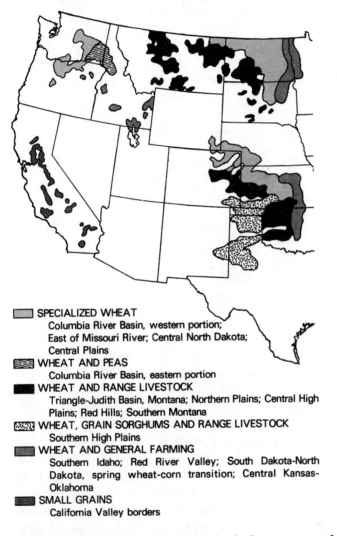

■ SPECIALIZED WHEAT
   Columbia River Basin, western portion;
   East of Missouri River; Central North Dakota;
   Central Plains
▨ WHEAT AND PEAS
   Columbia River Basin, eastern portion
■ WHEAT AND RANGE LIVESTOCK
   Triangle-Judith Basin, Montana; Northern Plains; Central High
   Plains; Red Hills; Southern Montana
▨ WHEAT, GRAIN SORGHUMS AND RANGE LIVESTOCK
   Southern High Plains
■ WHEAT AND GENERAL FARMING
   Southern Idaho; Red River Valley; South Dakota-North
   Dakota, spring wheat-corn transition; Central Kansas-
   Oklahoma
■ SMALL GRAINS
   California Valley borders

Hard winter wheat region includes areas of central and western Kansas, southwestern Nebraska, eastern Colorado and northwestern Texas and Oklahoma. Hard winter wheat is grown in combination with grain sorghum. Acreage of summer fallow increases from east to west. Corn acreage grown under irrigation is increasing.

Limited acreages of alfalfa and sweet clover are grown on the eastern portions and along streams of the region. Wheat production and summer fallow are alternated in dryland areas. Grain sorghum and corn are grown under irrigation.

Livestock is found where topography is rough, where the soils are tight and where sorghum is grown.

Spring wheat region, second in importance in wheat and small grain production, comprises areas of western Minnesota, North and South Dakota and Montana. Rainfall distribution throughout the year is especially suited to wheat, flaxseed, barley and rye. Winters are too long and severe for winter wheat. An exception is the Triangle-Judith Basin area of north central Montana. Here the growing season of 120 to 140 days permits winter wheat production.

In the Red River Valley and in northeastern South Dakota and southeastern North Dakota where precipitation is highest, farms are smaller and less specialized. Wheat is grown in combination with barley, oats, flaxseed and some corn. Special crops such as potatoes and sugar beets are also grown in the Red River Valley. Livestock is more numerous than farther west where yields are lower and supplies of feed are less dependable.

The production of wheat is more specialized from this area westward to the banks of the Missouri River in North Dakota and in northeastern Montana. Generally, the crop is grown along with other small grains. Farms are larger and more acreage is in summer fallow.

Farming operations are most extensive in Montana and in North Dakota west of the Missouri River. Rainfall is limited and much of the land is too rough for anything but range livestock. Much of the wheat is grown on summer fallow. Barley, flaxseed and some corn are grown and native hay is harvested for livestock feed.

Pacific Northwest (Palouse) region of the Columbia River Basin produces soft red and soft and hard white wheats. Precipitation ranges from about 20 inches in the Palouse area of eastern Washington and northern Idaho to a low of little more than 10 inches in the Big Bend area immediately east of the Columbia River. Both spring and winter wheat are grown.

In the western, drier Big Bend area, wheat is grown exclusively on summer fallow. Dry, edible peas are the major crop besides wheat. Barley, oats, seed peas and hay are also grown. Production of livestock is important. The number and type depend on rainfall and available feed supplies.

TOBACCO AND GENERAL FARMING

This region, located in the east central part of the United States, is divided into four subregions. Each subregion grows a different type of tobacco.

The chief differences in the farming systems of the four subregions are the nature and importance of supplemental enterprises.

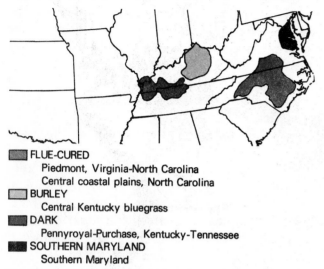

■ FLUE-CURED
   Piedmont, Virginia-North Carolina
   Central coastal plains, North Carolina
□ BURLEY
   Central Kentucky bluegrass
■ DARK
   Pennyroyal-Purchase, Kentucky-Tennessee
■ SOUTHERN MARYLAND
   Southern Maryland

Tobacco farmers in the flue-cured areas of the Carolinas and Virginia depend almost entirely upon cash crops for their income. Southern Maryland also approaches the cash-crop economy of the South. Tobacco is produced in combination with livestock in the burley region. Farming systems are varied in the dark air-cured tobacco region. The importance of livestock depends mainly on the quality of pasture and feed crop yields.

Tobacco is also produced in small areas outside the main tobacco regions, mainly in the Connecticut River Valley, southeastern Pennsylvania, southern Ohio and Indiana, Wisconsin, southeastern Georgia and northern Florida.

Flue-cured tobacco subregion includes a section of the Piedmont in south central Virginia and north central North Carolina, and a section of the central coastal plains in North Carolina.

The "Old Belt" tobaccos grown on Piedmont soils have a heavier body and a darker color than the "New Belt" types that are grown on the light sandy soils of the coastal plains.

Tobacco, corn and hay are the principal crops in the Piedmont area. Wheat is the only important small grain, but barley is grown to supplement corn. A small acreage of cotton is grown in the eastern Piedmont counties. Tobacco cannot be grown in combination with many kinds of legumes.

Commonly, two rotations are followed—a large acreage of tobacco land is left idle.

Cotton is the major supplementary crop in most of the central coastal plains area. Most farmers grow some cotton along with tobacco in a highly intensive farming system. Peanuts are produced along the northeastern border.

Burley tobacco subregion of the bluegrass area of north central Kentucky has a livestock-tobacco farming system. The fertile soils support good yields of high-quality burley tobacco and excellent bluegrass pastures which occupy about half of the farmland.

Bluegrass is important in rebuilding the soils depleted by tobacco production. It also furnishes pasture for livestock enterprises. Tobacco is seldom grown two years on the same land. Acreage of hay is about double that of tobacco. The combined acreage of tobacco and hay is about the same as that of corn. Small grains are not widely grown.

Livestock enterprises include dairy, beef, cattle, sheep, hogs and poultry. Most of the hogs are sold as feeder pigs.

Dark tobacco producing region of southwestern Kentucky and northwestern Tennessee is varied. White burley has replaced the dark types in the eastern part of the area. Production of livestock is restricted by limited feedgrain production and low quality pastures.

About a third of the farmland is in crops and a somewhat higher percentage is idle or in rotational pasture. Corn occupies the largest acreage. Some cotton is grown in the southwestern Jackson Purchase counties. In some localities, truck crops, fruits, potatoes and dairying are important. Production in the Pennyroyal Purchase area consists largely of field crops, including tobacco, corn, wheat and hay.

Southern Maryland subregion produces Maryland leaf tobacco. The region lies within five southern Maryland counties that are bordered by the Chesapeake Bay and the Potomac River. The air-cured type of tobacco grown is light in body and color and has good blending qualities.

Only a small proportion of farmland is in crops. Tobacco and corn occupy about equal acreages. Minor crops include small grains, hay, potatoes and vegetables.

GENERAL AND SPECIAL CROP FARMING

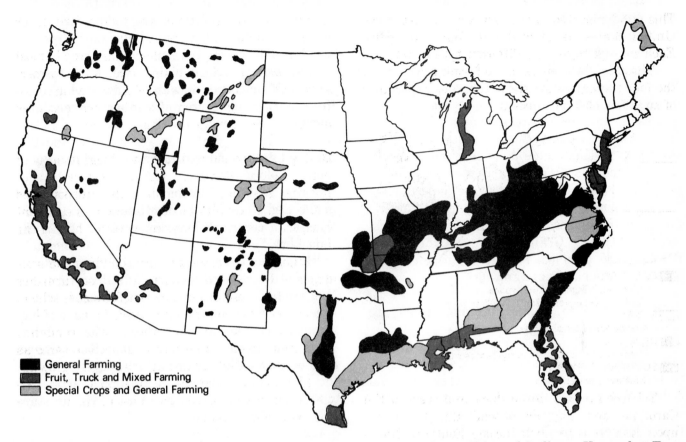

General Farming
Fruit, Truck and Mixed Farming
Special Crops and General Farming

Farms that produce several crops, classes of livestock, or both, are found in nearly all parts of the country. They are most common in areas where the three major farming regions merge—Corn Belt, northeastern Dairy Region and the Cotton Belt.

On most general farms, the acreage suited to cultivation is limited. Much of the land cannot be cropped intensively and livestock can utilize available forage and pasture.

Income from farms of this type is usually lower than from more specialized farms. However, since the income is derived from several sources, it may be more stable.

Eastern general farming areas are located where the climate and soils support many different enterprises. Corn, wheat, oats, hay, soybeans, tobacco, fruit, and truck crops are grown. Much land is in pasture because of the broken topography.

Farming centers around dairying, livestock and poultry in the St. Louis milkshed, the Ozark Mountains and on southern Illinois gray land. In the highland rim of Tennessee, livestock and dairying are important. Livestock, dairying and fruit prevail in the Shenandoah Valley.

In southern Ohio and Indiana, Kentucky, Tennessee, and Virginia, livestock, tobacco, small grains, truck crops, hay, and fruit are important crops. In the tidewater area of Virginia and North Carolina, truck crops, tobacco and livestock are the chief enterprises.

Small scale general farming predominates in Ozark, Ouachita and Appalachian Mountain areas and in the flatwoods area along the Atlantic and Gulf Coasts. Livestock, truck crops, and cotton are the chief sources of income.

Western general farming areas are usually small and often widely separated. Irrigated areas in western Nevada produce hay, dairy products, livestock, potatoes and poultry. The lower Snake River area in Idaho and Oregon produces hay, potatoes, sugar beets, dry beans, seed crops, some fruit and small grains. It has some dairying, livestock and livestock feeding operations. The central Utah and southeastern Idaho areas produce hay, sugar beets, potatoes, fruit, truck crops, grain, some dairy products and livestock.

Western Montana and the upper Arkansas Valley produce sugar beets, hay, feedgrains and livestock; the San Luis Valley—hay, livestock,

15

potatoes, dry beans and some truck crops; the San Juan Basin in eastern Colorado and northwestern New Mexico—livestock, hay, cash grain, potatoes, dairying and fruit. The southern Yakima Valley has a few specialized fruit and potato farms.

In the irrigated general farming area of Nebraska, corn, sugar beets, popcorn, potatoes, truck crops and hay are grown. Some dairying, beef cattle and feeder cattle are found. The northern Rocky Mountain cutover area has chiefly livestock and small scale dairy farming on nonirrigated land. Small grain and potatoes are the principal crops. Forest products are important.

Other small nonirrigated general farming areas are in northeastern New Mexico and northwestern Texas. Grain sorghum, wheat and livestock are principal sources of income. Some corn, oats and barley are grown.

Fruit, truck crop, mixed farming areas are localized and widely dispersed.

The principal specialized deciduous fruit areas are located in intermountain valleys and on protected mountain slopes. These areas include central Washington, southern Oregon, the Sacramento and San Joaquin Valleys in California, the Colorado west slope, the Ozark Plateau and the Shenandoah and Cumberland Valleys in Pennsylvania, Maryland, Virginia and West Virginia.

Other important deciduous fruit and truck crop areas are located on the eastern shore of Lake Michigan and the southern shores of Lake Erie and Lake Ontario.

Dairying and poultry generally are combined with fruit and truck crop farming in the lake-shore areas.

Citrus fruit and truck crop areas are the central California coast, southern California, southwestern Arizona, and lower Rio Grande Valley.

Highly specialized truck farming areas are in southern Florida where winter vegetables are grown for the early season market. Areas of specialized truck and mixed farming are the Gulf Coast and the Atlantic sandy coastal plains.

Special crops consist mainly of potatoes, sugar beets, sugarcane, peanuts, rice, tobacco, and dry beans. Generally these crops are grown commercially in small, definitely outlined areas where soil and climate are especially favorable. Sometimes they are the main crop grown and in other instances they serve as a supplementary cash crop.

Potatoes are a seasonal crop. The late crop areas are located in the northern third of the United States. The intermediate and early crop areas are in the South, and the southern coastal areas of the East and West.

The principal late crop areas are Aroostock County, Maine, and the western irrigated areas—the Klamath Basin area of southern Oregon and northern California, the Snake River area, the southern Yakima Valley in Washington, and the San Luis Valley and part of the South Platte River area in Colorado.

Crops are grown in combination with potatoes in the Red River Valley of Minnesota and North Dakota, in central Wisconsin, parts of Michigan, Ohio, New York, Pennsylvania and New England.

Sugar beets are a major crop on irrigated land in the Yellowstone River and Milk River areas in Montana, the Big Horn Basin and North Platte River areas in Wyoming and Nebraska and in northeastern Colorado. Sugar beets are grown with other crops in the upper and middle Snake River area of Idaho, the Sacramento Valley and along the central California coast. Important irrigated areas are the lower Snake River area, central Utah and southeastern Idaho, western Montana, and the upper Arkansas Valley in Colorado.

In the Midwest, sugar beets are grown in rotation with potatoes and small grains. They are included in the cropping programs of some dairy or livestock operations in the Red River Valley, east central Michigan and northwestern Ohio.

Sugarcane is grown chiefly in the lower Mississippi River Delta of Louisiana, with some produced in other parts of the state, and in Florida.

Dry beans are primarily grown under dry land or irrigation in the western states of Idaho, Colorado, Nebraska, California, North Dakota and Washington, with lesser states being Wyoming, Utah, Montana and Kansas.

In the East, the major producing states are Michigan and New York, with some also grown in Minnesota.

Rice is produced primarily in the Gulf coastal prairies in southwestern Louisiana and southeastern Texas, the prairies in Arkansas and parts of the California Central Valley.

Peanuts are commercially concentrated in three intensive areas. Virginia-type peanuts are produced in the North Carolina-Virginia coastal plains. The southern coastal plains of Georgia and Alabama is the largest area. The third area is the western part of the Cotton Belt.

WEATHER AND CROPS

Adaptation of crops and their performance is dependent on temperature, rainfall and length of growing season.

Summer temperatures are generally high enough throughout the United States to support crop production. Short growing seasons in some sections limit the type of crop that can be grown, but moisture usually determines what crops will yield well in an area.

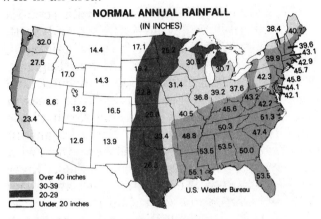

NORMAL ANNUAL RAINFALL
(IN INCHES)

U.S. Weather Bureau

Over 40 inches
30-39
20-29
Under 20 inches

Total annual rainfall tends to diminish from east to west across the country, with the exception of the West Coast.

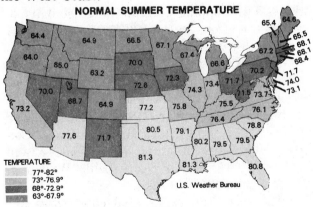

NORMAL SUMMER TEMPERATURE

TEMPERATURE
77°-82°
73°-76.9°
68°-72.9°
63°-67.9°

U.S. Weather Bureau

The effectiveness of rainfall is dependent on more than the total rainfall received during the year. The efficiency of rainfall use is associated with its distribution, intensity and evaporation. While the total rainfall on the West Coast approaches or equals that of some eastern areas, most of it occurs during winter. In the central plains most of the rain falls during the growing season, but in the western plains drouth is frequent.

Heavy downpours are less effective than a steady, prolonged rain since more is lost to runoff. Further, a larger amount of moisture is required to produce a given crop yield in arid areas compared with more humid regions because greater quantities are lost through evaporation.

Growing season refers to the period from the last killing frost in the spring to the first killing frost in the fall. For any given crop, a minimum number of growth days are required.

Production of most crops usually requires a frost-free season of at least 125 days, but as few as 100 days are required by small grains. Cotton requires a growing season of about 200 days; corn, 150 days. Small grains require fewer frost-free days than corn or sorghum and they can be safely sown two months before the average last spring frost. Soybeans, on the other hand, are usually sown after the average frost-free date.

The short growing season which prevails in much of the West is a result of the high altitude and the dry air which permits rapid cooling at night. The Pacific Ocean exerts a powerful influence on the frost-free dates of the West Coast. However, the Atlantic Ocean has only a slight influence in lengthening the growing season along the East Coast since the prevailing winds are from the West. No part of the country is entirely free from frost.

The first average killing frost of fall determines the practical limit as to how late a crop can be planted. When emergencies arise, such as flooding or poor germination due to extremely dry weather, late planting may be necessary, or double cropping may be practiced in some areas. Whatever the reason, it may be necessary to select a shorter season variety or make provisions to use the crop in a way that will reduce an early fall frost hazard.

Frequently, a large mass of cool, but not frigid air, will settle over a locality in the fall. It brings with it fair, sunny days and windless, cloudless nights. These are frost danger signs. As a service to growers of perishables, the Weather Bureau issues special frost warnings.

Growing degree days (GDD) is a measure used to check the relative progress of crops at any given time during the season. Plants grow and produce best within certain limits of air temperature and there is a direct relationship between temperature and speed of development. For corn and soybeans, the limits are approximately 50 and 86 degrees; small grains, 40 and 90 degrees. Each degree above the minimum contributes toward the development of the crop and is called a Growing Degree Day.

In 1969, USDA and U.S. Department of Commerce started calculating and publishing GDD's. The GDD accumulation for a given day is calculated as shown in the formula. Maximum temperatures above 86 degrees are entered as 86°—additional heat does not contribute to crop development. Minimum temperatures below 50° are equal to 50°—lower temperatures do not reverse the development.

$$GDD = \frac{Daily\ Max.\ (86°) + Daily\ Min.\ (50°)}{2.0} - 50°$$

GDD, though a measure of crop progress, is not an accurate predictor of crop progress under such conditions as heavy weeds, inadequate fertility or especially low soil moisture.

Once a crop is planted, GDD's give you an idea of how it is doing. For example, assume that 350 GDD's had accumulated at planting. If on July 1, 1,200 GDD's have accumulated, 850 of these will have contributed to the development of your crop. If the variety requires 2,400 GDD's to mature an additional 1,550 GDD's are needed before the crop will be free from frost damage.

Weather requirements vary by crops. These are briefly listed for some of the major crops.

Corn requires relatively high temperatures both day and night, with the region of greatest production having a mean summer temperature of 70 to 80 degrees. This crop requires a plentiful supply of moisture, well distributed throughout the growing season. Maximum moisture requirements occur during silking and tasseling.

Soybeans need a five-month growing season with warm temperatures and fairly heavy rainfall during summer, especially during the bloom and pod setting periods.

Small grains, except rice, are generally grown where the annual precipitation is 15 to 45 inches. Annual rainfall is as low as 15 inches in the northern Great Plains and 17 inches in the southern Great Plains. Production in these low rainfall areas is possible because of the favorable rainfall distribution and climatic conditions. Summer fallowing also allows the moisture falling in two or more years to be stored for one crop.

Extensive production of small grains is limited generally to areas with a frost-free period of 100 days or more. The temperature preceding harvest is important. The northern limits of fall-seeded grains are largely determined by winter temperatures.

Rice is grown only in sections where the growing season is relatively long, the summer temperatures are relatively high and the supplies of water for irrigation are abundant.

Sorghum can be grown in areas where the average annual precipitation is fairly light, the average frost-free period 130-140 days and the average July temperature 70 degrees and above.

Cotton grows best where conditions consist of a mild spring with light, but frequent showers, a moderately moist summer, warm both day and night (over 50-60 degrees with plenty of open, sunny weather), and a dry, cool and prolonged autumn. Normally, cotton is not grown north of the 200-day growing season area.

Tobacco needs an average growing season temperature which ranges from 70 degrees in the North to 77 degrees in the South. Too much rain in late winter and spring makes seedbed preparation difficult. Moderate rain is needed during seedling growth. Sufficient rain at transplanting time is especially important. For normal, rapid growth in the field, tobacco requires liberal, well-distributed rainfall or its equivalent in irrigation water.

Citrus must be grown where temperatures do not drop below 55 degrees. About 35 inches of water is needed annually. Rain is most needed from February to November. Supplemental moisture is supplied through irrigation.

Deciduous fruits require a winter dormant period for proper development and fruit production is limited to regions having a sufficiently cold winter to break the natural rest period. At least 600 hours of below 45 degree temperatures are needed. However, prolonged temperatures below 20 degrees will cause injury to the trees.

For best growth and production, these fruits require ample available moisture in their root zone soil throughout the growing season.

Sugar beets require temperatures of 45 to 48 degrees or above for germination. The sugar beet is most sensitive to cold during emergence, then it becomes very hardy. Summer temperatures around 70 degrees speed growth. Fall temperatures should be cool. Well distributed rainfall or irrigation is needed throughout the growing season.

Chapter 2

Acquiring the Farm

Acquiring a farm demands a lot of thought and requires far-reaching decisions. Decisions made at this point will greatly affect your future success.

The initial step in renting or buying a farm is to choose a type and area of farming. Then, select a farm that offers the greatest potential for your proposed investment. Thoroughly examine those factors which control your decision. They may be classified in two major categories.

PERSONAL RESOURCES

● Your likes and dislikes are vital to your success. Choose the type of farming that you like most. Carefully consider your goals. Do you want to farm for the rest of your life or for a short period of time? Do you plan to move to another farm later, or to expand the initial farm?

● Your capital position will impose certain limitations. Take inventory of the money you have available, the amount of credit you can obtain, and the extent of debt you are willing to assume.

● Available labor (including family labor), plus the degree of skill, should be analyzed. Your experience and ability to operate a farm are definitely controlling factors. Technical and practical knowledge, from both past experience and schooling, need to be balanced against any weaknesses you have in this area. Choose an operation you can handle well; it should present a continuing challenge, to allow growth and development.

19

FARM AND AREA RESOURCES

• Knowing the types and sizes of farms available and how well they are suited to your goals is important. Note any changes or improvements which may be necessary and estimate the costs involved.

• Inventory such things as machinery, livestock and buildings. Compare the present inventory with what is needed and estimate how long it will take to acquire the additional resources.

• Environmental factors, supply of labor in the area, roads and railroads plus location in respect to towns, churches and schools should be carefully examined.

STEPS IN ACQUIRING A FARM

A farmer may take several approaches to acquiring a farm. These are outlined as follows:

Leasing offers a way to get started in farming with limited capital. Both crop and livestock sharing arrangements are available in various areas. When drawing up any form of lease, remember that income should be shared in the same proportion as expenses and risks. With agriculture changing rapidly, it is important to review leasing terms each year. A lease that is fair one year may become unfair if drawn up under the same terms the following year.

Father-son and other partnerships are arrangements in which each party shares in the management, profits, losses and ownership of the farm business. In setting up any partnership arrangement, consider the legal aspects. Understand your rights and liabilities. In a partnership, for instance, you may be held responsible for the damages inflicted on a third person by your partner, if he fails to settle damages.

For any partnership arrangement to be successful, mutual trust between partners must exist. Otherwise, the arrangement will be one of constant disharmony and eventual failure.

Part-time farming is a method used by some beginning farmers to gain full farm ownership. Through outside employment, they hope to accumulate sufficient capital for building their farm business into an eventual full-time operation. However, this method of acquiring farm ownership has a number of limitations.

Limited capital often forces you to buy a farm too small to support yourself and your family. You may be unable to expand your business unless rental land is available.

With continually rising costs of production, a large farm and considerable capital are necessary to operate an efficient business. Accumulating land and capital through off-farm employment is a long and laborious road.

Attractive off-farm wages may discourage you from breaking away from your other employment and devoting your attention to full-time farming. As a result, you may be forced to continue operating your farm in an inefficient manner. Consequently, the farm never pays a high return, and eventually it may be given up in favor of your other endeavors.

Purchasing a farm becomes the final goal of most farmers. Before buying a farm, work out a budget to determine if you have sufficient capital and decide how that capital can best be used. Don't overlook your day-to-day operating expenses and the living requirements of your family.

Determine how much capital can be borrowed from your farm earnings. The amount of capital you can safely borrow depends to a large extent on how much cash you can put into the business, your character and credit rating, and your farming experience. As a young farmer, your potential and proven managerial ability are major assets.

In many areas, acquiring sufficient land to operate an efficient farming operation can be a problem under any circumstances. Competition for good agricultural land is keen and land usually becomes available only when a farmer retires or dies and has no one in his family to take over.

There is also strong competition for agricultural land for purposes other than farming, particularly in areas adjacent to an urban community. Many look favorably on agricultural land as an investment. The price of land has been bid up rapidly in recent years.

Adjusting Crop Share Leases

Because of changes in farming methods and higher input costs, there has been a shift from customary lease agreements to leases that are custom tailored to the operation.

Customary or traditional crop-share leases have gradually become obsolete in many areas. The reason is that farming inputs have changed so drastically.

There are many points that should be bargained out each time a lease is written, or merely renewed. The adjusted lease should be the result of weighing each party's inputs against the traditional leasing terms used in the community.

Adjust input shares. The only way to determine if the traditional crop sharing arrangement is equitable now is to total up each party's contributions as accurately as possible and then make a comparison. Here too, some negotiation may be required to set an agreeable rate of return to use for land and for labor and/or management. If the sharing of inputs doesn't match the sharing of crops, usually the inputs should be adjusted.

The following discussion of lease terms does not spell out the normal as much as it lists the modifications that are found in crop-share leases in the Corn Belt, South, and Great Plains. In other regions, and even in these regions, you'll find wide variations both in the crop sharing and in the way various production inputs are handled. Use these examples as a guide to making your own lease adjustments.

50-50 LEASES

Normally the owner and the tenant each pays half of the fertilizer, seed and chemical costs. Then each receives half of the crops to market as he wishes. However, even these standard items are subject to negotiation.

Fertilizer to build up rundown soil may be the owner's expense, while annual maintenance applications are shared. Or cost of bringing soil up to the average productivity of the community may be shared with a provision in the lease for a prorated tenant payback over three or five years if his lease is terminated sooner.

Lime usually is the owner's expense though it, too, may be partially paid for by the tenant on a payback basis. A recent development is the application of some lime every second year—then the cost may be shared.

Herbicide costs are split, usually. In some cases the tenant pays two-thirds or all of the costs because herbicides reduce his labor or he pays a higher share when he makes a broadcast application, since he uses more chemical and eliminates cultivation. However, with the shift to 30-inch rows, this provision has been dropped from many leases as there is less difference in the amount of chemical used when banding and broadcasting; and better weed control will improve yields for both parties.

If a farm has a specific weed problem, such as Johnsongrass, initial herbicide treatments to clean it up may be at the owner's expense.

Cost of custom applying chemicals may be shared, but in a majority of cases, the tenant pays all costs of application, regardless of how chemicals are applied.

The same arrangements apply to insecticides and fungicides—usually the cost of chemicals is split and the tenant applies them or pays the custom applicator.

Grain handling changes have forced more lease modifications on landowners and tenants than perhaps any other factor. The shift is still in progress, but field shelling of corn and on-farm drying of grains and soybeans have become more the normal practice than the innovative. As a result, special provisions for corn combining or grain drying are less often written into leases now.

With a 50-50 lease, the trend is toward the tenant owning the equipment and harvesting the whole crop—corn, soybeans, wheat, etc., at no additional cost to the owner. However, there still are many leases written that charge the owner an amount equal to the custom shelling rate for his share of the corn crop when the tenant combines or field shells it. That shelling charge should reflect the sharp increase in energy and other costs.

Hauling depends on distance—often the tenant agrees to deliver the owner's share to the nearest elevator or to the farm bin. When

	TENANT SHARES IN NORTH DAKOTA**					
	Tenants on a 50-50 Lease That Paid			Tenants on a 1/3-2/3 Lease That Paid		
Expense	All	1/2	None	All	2/3	None
	(percent)					
Fertilizer	6	90	4	58	40	*
Seed	7	14	79	97	2	*
Gasoline	96	3	*	99	*	*
Herbicide	21	68	9	76	22	0
Custom weed spraying	30	68	*	85	14	0
Swathing	72	25	*	96	3	*
Combining	25	64	0	95	3	0
Grain hauling	73	23	*	97	2	0
Crop insurance	33	65	1	58	39	*
Machinery repair	97	2	*	99	*	0
Building repair	31	6	63	73	1	25
Fence repair	72	5	23	92	0	8
Hired labor	98	1	*	99	0	0

*Less than 1%.
**Based on a 1973-74 survey of 1,300 leasing arrangements in six widely separated North Dakota counties.

grain goes to a more distant market, to a river terminal or inland grain terminal, the tenant receives the going hauling rate. In other cases, more often on less productive land, the tenant is paid for hauling grain off of the farm. When the owner's grain is sold from farm bins, the buyer usually picks it up.

Grain drying arrangements still are highly variable. Most consistent lease terms seem to be with in-bin drying systems owned by the landlord. Bins are usually furnished by the owner at no storage charge to the tenant whether drying is involved or not—in some cases the tenant pays an agreed upon per bushel per month storage fee.

If the landlord does not provide storage, he may pay a harvesting fee for his share of the crop. Usually, too, the owner installs the bin dryer, motor, fuel tank, electrical hookup, bin unloading auger and he may furnish the filling auger. Fuel and electricity are split evenly in most cases. The tenant is expected to provide all management and labor.

When the tenant owns a portable dryer, he may charge the landowner a minimum drying fee, often about 2¢ under the going elevator rate. If the landowner furnishes the portable dryer, he should charge the tenant at about the same rate, since the tenant furnishes the labor. That would apply to drying of grain grown on other land, too. Maintenance and repair of equipment may be paid for on a 50-50 basis.

Major equipment investments. When a more elaborate setup is desired by the tenant, or cost of the installation is shared by both parties, special payback arrangements can be included in the lease. For example, the landlord and tenant might share the investment in a portable dryer with the provision that should the tenant move within a certain number of years, he would pay the landlord his share of the undepreciated value and remove the dryer from the farm.

Or the tenant might install an elevator leg to farm owned storage. In that case he should arrange to be

repaid a pro rata share of his investment if his lease is terminated in less than, say, 10 years.

This same type of payback arrangement can be used with other permanent facilities such as machine storage or irrigation systems or with portable equipment desired by the tenant, but paid for by both parties. Payback period normally is shorter than the period of depreciation on items with a long life such as buildings, i.e., eight years on a machine shed.

40-60, 1/3-2/3, 1/4-3/4 LEASES

Customarily, the landowner furnishes very little under these arrangements, but that, too, is changing as farming changes. High costs of labor and the big investments made by tenants in machinery, fertilizer and chemicals often have resulted in bargained concessions from the owner. But again, rising land values have tended to counterbalance the tenant's increased contributions.

Fertilizer usually is split as the crops are split under the 40-60 and 1/3-2/3 leases. Sometimes chemicals are included. In regions where the owner gets only one-fourth of the crop, he normally expects to furnish only the land.

In the South, where the 1/4-3/4 split is common in cotton and some soybeans, the owner usually pays his share of the fertilizer bill for cotton, but if fertilizer is applied to soybeans, then that's the tenant's expense. The owner may pay for half of the lime, or the tenant will pay all under a five-year reimbursement agreement. Sometimes the owner will agree to bring the pH up to normal, then the tenant pays for lime applied in later years.

The landowner usually does not share the cost of herbicides unless there is some special weed problem. He then may furnish the chemical and the tenant must apply it, or the bill is split 50-50. Where soil fumigant is needed to kill nematodes, that's usually a 50-50 deal.

The tenant pays for cotton insecticides, but in some cases the owner

will pay one-fourth toward the services of a scout.

The landlord commonly receives one-third to one-half of the rice crop and pays a comparable share of the fertilizer and chemical costs. If he gets only one-fourth of the crop, he pays his share of the fertilizer, but no chemical costs.

Irrigation equipment. On rice and other irrigated crops in the South, the landowner usually furnishes the well and the tenant furnishes the pump and motor and pays the fuel and electricity bills.

In the Plains regions, under 40-60 leases for row crops, the owner typically is expected to furnish the well, pump and motor and 40% of the fuel and electricity bills. The tenant furnishes the irrigation equipment and labor. Cost of water from an irrigation district is usually shared as the crops are shared. Irrigated wheat often is grown under a 1/3-2/3 lease with the owner supplying only the well.

In many cases the irrigation equipment is a negotiation point in the lease. Gated pipe is sometimes supplied by the owner, sometimes shared and sometimes the property of the tenant. With center pivot systems, the leasing arrangement may be changed to 50-50 with cost of the pivot and all cash inputs shared equally.

Grain storage is often furnished by the landlord, but he seldom contributes a dryer. As a result, the tenant will charge the owner a fee for shelling and drying his share of the crop and for hauling it off of the farm. In some cases the tenant is charged for storage.

Elevator and commercial hauling rates are commonly charged. However, lower fees are used, too, such as 2¢ under elevator rate for shelling and drying and ½¢ per bushel per month for storage. These are equitable since the tenant is expected to furnish all labor.

Under a 1/4-3/4 lease, a cotton grower usually delivers the owner's share of the cotton crop as baled cotton and seed and soybeans are delivered to the local elevator. The owner pays no harvesting or ginning costs.

Family Farm Business Organization

The form of business organization you use—sole proprietorship, partnership or corporation—should depend on your goals for operating the farm and for orderly transfer of your estate.

There is no one best form of farm business organization. The size of your operation, your family situation, your enterprises, your objectives—all are important in determining the best way to organize your farm business.

First: define your objectives. Since more than one person is usually involved, you can expect conflict. But planning ahead will help to iron out differences before they can cause difficulty. The consequences of death in the family should be thoroughly explored. (A reluctance to do this is the most common reason for inadequate planning.) Children, too, should be encouraged to voice their real feelings if they don't agree with other members of the family.

You should consider the business as both an operating unit and as property to be transferred at the death of one of the parties.

From an operational standpoint, these questions should be discussed:

• Is expansion of the operation possible and desirable?

• Would reorganization allow more capital to be brought in, raising profits?

• Are there tax advantages to be gained from the business reorganization?

• Could reorganization help reduce risks or liability?

From an estate planning aspect, some points to consider are:

• Should the farm be kept in the family? Is there a son or son-in-law who is able to carry on? Is the farm big enough to provide ample opportunity for an heir?

• How can income security for the parents be best provided.

• How can a reasonable degree of security be given to a son operating the farm? He should have a reasonable degree of independence and some assurance of his future equity.

• How can fair treatment be assured for children who are engaged in other businesses and do not have a direct interest in the farm?

• Can reorganization minimize the effect of death taxes and probate costs? This should not be the principal reason for business reorganization. Financial security, opportunity and equity should come first.

• Will the business reorganization help maintain the farm on an efficient basis during transfer to another generation? Will it make the transition smoother and more equitable?

Once you have established your goals, a definite plan should be set up. Consult your legal counsel to insure a properly drawn up agreement. The plan should be in writing and legally binding to avoid misunderstandings.

There are three basic forms of business organization: (1) the sole proprietorship, (2) the partnership, and (3) the corporation. Each has advantages and disadvantages.

THE SOLE PROPRIETORSHIP

Most farms are sole proprietorships. This doesn't mean that this form is the best, but with no other form of organization, it naturally results.

Under this form of business, one man controls all the assets used in the operation. He has sole management and control, though this may be delegated somewhat through rental agreements.

Basically, the sole proprietor has a right to all profits and must take all losses.

From an operational standpoint, the sole proprietorship is more limited than other forms of organization. It may be more difficult to acquire new capital for expansion.

For estate planning, the individual proprietorship is not as flexible as other business forms. Renting a farm to a son is one way to provide retirement income for the parent, but not much can be done to provide continuity and keep the present business as a unit.

PARTNERSHIP

A partnership is two or more persons who, as co-owners, operate the business.

The successful partnership must be big enough

to use the available time, abilities and assets of the partners with a suitable return.

A partnership is a way to bring in a son, while keeping the father in active participation. A partnership with a managing partner may preserve the farm as a unit for the benefit of heirs if a physical distribution is not practical.

Partnership advantages:

Combining resources: This often increases returns from the operation. Too, one partner may contribute labor and management instead of capital, making it easier to bring a son, who is short on capital, into the business.

Equitable management: Unless agreed otherwise, all partners have equal rights, regardless of financial interest. Any limitations should be a written part of the agreement. Differences are decided by majority vote, but the partnership agreement cannot be violated without the consent of all the partners.

Tax advantages: The partnership pays no tax on its income, although it must file an informational tax return. The tax is paid as a part of the individual tax returns of the partners, usually lowering the tax rates.

Flexibility: Normally, the partnership does not need outside approval to change its structure or operation.

Partnership disadvantages:

Unlimited liability: Each partner is liable for all the debts and obligations of the partnership, except in a limited partnership.

Uncertainty of length of agreement: A partnership ceases on the death or withdrawal of any partner, unless the partnership agreement provides for continuation or by common agreement of partners.

Value of partner's interest: Since a partner owns a share of every individual item belonging to the partnership, it's often hard to judge value. This tends to make transfer of a partnership interest difficult. Market values should be determined regularly to minimize this disadvantage.

LIMITED PARTNERSHIP

This is a special kind of partnership with one or more "general" partners and one or more "limited" partners. The general partners are like partners in a regular partnership, but the limited partner has only limited liability. He cannot contribute services or management and his name cannot appear in the partnership name.

CORPORATIONS

A corporation is an artificial entity with its own rights and duties. It can make contracts and hold property. It pays taxes as an entity. One form, subchapter S, can be taxed as a partnership, escaping the corporate tax.

The owners' interests in a corporation are represented by shares of stock. The shareholders elect the board of directors who, in turn, elect the officers. The officers are responsible for the day to day business operation. In a close family corporation, shareholders, directors and officers can be the same persons.

The procedures and regulations governing the corporation are determined by state laws. The state must approve any amendments to the articles of incorporation.

Corporation advantages:

Limited liability: Unlike the partnership, the corporation stockholder is liable only to the extent of the value of his stock. Creditors, however, may require a shareholder to assume additional liability as a condition of a loan.

Continuity of operation: The corporation does not cease when a shareholder dies. Long-range planning is more certain.

Higher credit status: The continuity of operation may be more attractive to lenders.

Employee benefits for owners: Under the corporate form, the owners can be employees. As such, fringe benefits such as group life insurance, medical insurance, retirement plan and sick leave are possible. Most of these benefits are deductible as business expenses.

Ease of transfer: Shares of stock rather than property make an orderly transfer of interest much easier. As in a partnership, the value of a share of stock is sometimes difficult to determine.

Corporation disadvantages:

More red tape: The federal and state governments keep tighter control on corporations than on other forms of business organization. More complete operational and tax records must be kept.

Initial and annual costs: A corporation has special fees and taxes to pay that are not required under other business forms. These are not usually large enough to alter a decision to incorporate.

Family farm partnerships

A father-son partnership is the easiest answer when a son decides on a farming career, but it might not be the right answer. Personal and financial aspects should be carefully studied.

The formation of a father-son partnership is normally the first step toward passing ownership and management of a farm or ranch operation from one generation to the next. This eventual goal can be accomplished through other forms of business organization, such as a corporation. However, where one or two sons are to be involved in the farm business, a partnership offers a great deal more flexibility in tailoring the business organization to the situation.

If it is practical to do so, the working relationship of the parties should be tested before a formal partnership agreement is drawn up. Typically, father and son have worked together while the son completed his schooling, and in many cases, that is trial enough. For others, a year or two with the son devoting full time to the operation, and paid a salary plus a percentage of the farm profits, has several advantages. (1) The experience helps the young man decide for certain if he wishes to farm or pursue some other occupation. (2) Both parties can see whether or not they can work together on a business as well as a personal basis. (3) The trial period allows time for consideration of features of the partnership agreement to fit the individual situation.

If a trial period is set up, a date should be set for evaluating the arrangement and/or creation of a formal partnership agreement—or dissolution of the arrangement, if that be the case. Otherwise, temporary arrangements tend to outlive their purpose.

There are other important considerations which should be closely examined before a father and son enter a partnership agreement. The most important and most frequently ignored is the capacity of the farm business to provide enough income to support two or more families. A farm might provide a good standard of living for one family and an unmarried partner son (or sons) living with his parents. It is a quite different situation when the son marries, has children and a separate household to maintain. Marriage brings another factor into the equation—a daughter-in-law (or son-in-law) who might have different ideas on what is an adequate standard of living or what is a fair arrangement between partners.

Thus, the question must be asked and answered at the outset: "Will the business provide a satisfactory income for all partners and their families?" If not, what is required to increase income to the required level, can it be done, and is there potential for business growth beyond that level sufficient to meet the increasing needs of the younger partner as his family needs grow? If these questions cannot be answered affirmatively, the partnership probably should not be formed.

Another situation which is not conducive to a partnership is one in which there are other children in off-the-farm occupations. Since they would not contribute labor or management to the partnership, their inclusion as partners would result in an unfair division of profits. Also, as partners they would be personally liable for debts and obligations of the partnership, which would be undesirable from their standpoint. This is where a corporate form of business organization or possibly a limited partnership may be advantageous. Operating under either of these forms, the off-the-farm members would have no legal liability for the business.

Under corporate organization, transferring shares in the ownership of the business from parents to children is easily done; the children staying in the business share the management of the business with the father as officers of the corporation and are paid salaries by the corporation.

With a limited partnership, the management of the business is handled by one or more general partners, the father and son(s) in the business. The limited partners (other children) would share in profits to the extent of their investment, which would be a portion of the ownership transferred to them by their parents.

PARTNERSHIP RULES

The statutory law under which partnerships operate is detailed in the Uniform Partnership Act adopted by most states. This act provides the basic rules that govern the partnership, but it allows considerable flexibility in permitting partners to adopt additional rules as part of the partnership agreement.

While an oral partnership agreement can be

valid, it is best put in writing. This helps avoid misunderstanding and gives all partners a basis for knowing what to expect. An attorney should draft the partnership agreement.

Unless stated otherwise in the agreement, each partner has an equal voice in management control, regardless of the amount of capital he contributes. The sharing of profits and losses should be spelled out in the partnership agreement; otherwise, profits are shared equally by all partners.

The partnership itself pays no taxes. It files an informational tax return and each partner reports his share of partnership profits or losses on his personal income tax return. Each partner is subject to liability for all debts and obligations arising in the partnership business.

Property may be owned in the name of the partnership or it may be owned in the name of one or more of the partners. In addition to ownership rights in specific property used by the partnership, each partner also has an interest in the partnership. This interest, which in reality is the partners' share of profits and surplus, is personal property.

It is important that in all partnerships some determination be made as to the ownership of items contributed for the use of the partnership. Under general law, property brought into the partnership or acquired with partnership funds becomes partnership property. In states where partnerships operate under the Uniform Partnership Act the partnership itself can own property, but in some other states there is no provision for the partnership to own property.

Termination of a partnership. Unless otherwise provided in the partnership agreement, the partnership is automatically dissolved upon the death of any partner. Dissolution also occurs in the event of incapacity of any partner, by bankruptcy of the partnership or by any event which makes continuation of the business unlawful. Partnerships can also be terminated by agreement between the partners or by the terms of the partnership agreement.

When a partnership is terminated, its liabilities must be discharged and assets distributed. Debts and obligations to creditors outside the business have first call on the assets, followed by loans by partners, capital investments in the business by partners and finally, the assets remaining are distributed on the basis of the agreement for sharing profits. If the partnership is insolvent at termination, the debts of the business can be satisfied from the personal sources of the individual partners. Debts are satisfied among partners at termination in accordance with the agreement for sharing losses.

Generally, when a partnership is terminated, the remaining partners will buy out the interest of the withdrawing partner (in the case of his death, from the heirs). The partnership agreement should specifically spell out the terms of settlement at termination including rates, payment period, number of payments or cash settlement. An inventory and appraisal to establish current values is usually necessary. A determination must be made of any increase or decrease in inventory value from the time the partnership began until time of termination. Once these steps are taken, property must either be transferred to the remaining partners or sold, and the proceeds divided among all partners.

Partners' authority. An important aspect of partnership operation is that each partner is an agent of the partnership for the purposes of its business. Thus the act of any partner binds the partnership when he is carrying on the partnership's business, unless he has no authority to act and unless the person with whom he is dealing knows that the partner is exceeding his authority.

Specifically, no partner acting without the consent of all partners has any authority to: (1) Assign the partnership property in trust for creditors or on the assignee's promise to pay the debts of the partnership; (2) dispose of the good will of the business; (3) do anything which would make it impossible to carry on the ordinary business of the partnership; (4) confess a judgement; or (5) submit a partnership claim or liability to arbitration. If all partners authorize one partner to do any of the above acts they are binding on the partnership. However, if some partners abandon the business, one or more of the remaining partners may act in the above capacities.

Hire an attorney to advise you on details of partnership law in your state. The above listed partnership rules are general and based on the Uniform Partnership Act, but in some states the law may be different. If a partnership seems to be right for your situation, visit with other farmers in your area who operate under partnerships. They can tell you from experience some of the features that should or should not be in the partnership agreement, what has worked well for them and what has not.

Family Farm Partnership Arrangements

Once it is decided that a partnership is feasible, the situation and goals of the partners determine the type of partnership needed.

At the outset, figure that you are going to need the assistance of two skilled people when you set up a partnership: an attorney and an accountant. Your attorney can prepare the following documents for you: (1) the partnership agreement, (2) buy and sell agreements to provide for the continuation of the business beyond the death of a partner or the mutual agreement for the discontinuation of a partner, (3) any I.O.U.'s or promissory notes that are necessary, (4) wills for all parties, (5) any bill of sale necessary for the sale of personal property.

The accountant comes in during the creation of the partnership, but his main function is to handle the often complicated accounting procedures and tax management of the business on a continuing basis. Unique tax rules apply to partnerships which are beyond the scope of this publication and beyond the knowledge of most people who are not accountants. You do the farming; let the accountant do the accounting.

Most often the primary goal of a family partnership is to help the younger man get established in farming or ranching. In conjunction with this goal is the intention to pass ownership of the operation from one generation to the next. For others, the more immediate purpose is the expansion of the business.

Contributions to the partnership may include land, buildings, equipment, livestock, feed and operating capital. The labor contribution includes the labor input of each partner. A decision must be made at the time of establishing the partnership as to whether the property is to become partnership property or retained by the contributing partner and its *use* contributed to the partnership by lease or other arrangement.

No capital gain or loss is realized when assets are contributed to the partnership. The basis of the contributed asset to the partnership is the same as it was to the partner. However, where title to property is held in the partnership name, any of the partners may convey title to that property to another person if it is done in the partnership name. Usually, the partnership agreement specifically prohibits assignment of such property, but if one partner does, in fact, transfer property to an unsuspecting buyer, the partner's act can bind the partnership.

While this might not often be a problem in a family partnership, keeping title to land outside of the partnership makes for a cleaner deal. The same is true of machinery and equipment owned by one of the parties prior to formation of the partnership. To avoid the possibility of recapture problems upon ultimate sale of assets contributed in kind, it is often better for the partner owning the asset to retain ownership until it is traded; the partnership then buys the replacement. When this happens, adjustments are necessary to allow for the unrecovered cost to the owner of the trade-in. This can be taken care of by sale or gift of the unrecovered cost.

Where a father and one or more children form a partnership and there are other children with no farm interests, a farm operating partnership with land ownership left in the father's name works better from an estate planning standpoint than if the land is put into the partnership name. In this type arrangement, the partnership could lease the land from the father under a crop-share, livestock share or cash lease. This system makes it easy for the father to give each of his children—those in the partnership and those outside of it—a share of the land. The father likewise could retain title to equipment and other depreciable assets previously owned, then replacement equipment and additional land can be purchased in the partnership name. Equipment owned by the father could be leased to the partnership until it is replaced.

A partnership arranged in this fashion gets away from problems of lopsided sharing of profits according to capital input and from income tax problems relating to investment credit and depreciated value. Profits could then be shared by all partners evenly or according to labor input.

SHARING OF PROFITS

The method by which profits are shared is the guts of the partnership agreement. Unless otherwise specified, partners share equally in profits of the business. But by written agreement, profits can be shared in any way desired—no set percentages need be adhered to and the partners may decide on or before the due date of the tax return to divide income or losses in a different manner than was previously agreed upon. This flexibility is probably the biggest advantage to a partnership over other types of business organization.

If it is desired to share income according to a set procedure based on contributions of capital, labor and management, a method to measure such contributions is needed. A set sharing agreement is advisable where there is a father-son partnership with more than one son and in other family partnerships such as brother-brother, brother-brother-in-law, etc. The following preliminary steps can be used in establishing income sharing procedures.

1. Establish a mutually agreeable wage rate for contributed labor and an interest rate for contributed capital. Example: Wage rate - $4 per hour; interest rate on land - 10%; interest rate on capital other than land - 12%.

2. Determine the amount and value of each partner's capital and labor contributions.

Example:

AMOUNT OF CONTRIBUTION

	Partner 1	Partner 2	Total
Capital (land)	$300,000	—	$300,000
Capital (other than land)	$ 50,000	$ 50,000	$100,000
Labor	500 hrs.	2,000 hrs.	2,500 hrs.

VALUE OF CONTRIBUTION

	Partner 1	Partner 2	Total
Capital at 10%	$ 30,000	—	$ 30,000
Capital at 12%	6,000	$ 6,000	12,000
Labor at $4/hr.	2,000	8,000	10,000
Total	$ 38,000	$ 14,000	$ 52,000
Percent contribution	73%	27%	100%

3. Each year calculate net profit as gross receipts minus operating expenses. If shared proportionate to partners' contribution of capital and labor, multiply each partner's percent of total contribution by net profit.

Example:

```
Gross receipts ............................. $105,000
Operating expenses ......................... 73,000
Net profit ................................. $ 32,000
```

Partner 1: $32,000 x 73% = $23,360
Partner 2: $32,000 x 27% = $ 8,640

The problem that most often develops with sharing profits according to contributions is that income is not high enough for the partner with the least capital contribution. With continued upward appreciation of land, the share gets more unbalanced.

Several things can be done to alleviate this. If the land is to be in the partnership name, the father or partner with the capital sells half interest in the capital asset to the son—or one-third interest to each of two sons, etc. Payment can be by a series of notes maturing over several years. This effectively isolates capital contribution from the sharing of profits and it gives the younger man an asset most likely to appreciate in value. Depending on basis for the land and other factors, the transaction might be a gift, an installment sales contract or a mixture of the two with some or all of the maturing notes forgiven as gifts within the $3,000 annual gift tax exclusion.

If the land is to be held out of the partnership and its use contributed to the partnership or it is to be rented to the partnership, the same transfer of equity to partners, as well as off-the-farm children, can be made.

RECORDKEEPING

Recordkeeping is more important for a partnership than a sole proprietorship and in many cases more involved than under the corporate form of business organization. An important use of records in a partnership is in making the annual settlement among partners. A complete summary and analysis should be made at the end of each business year. While an accountant should be retained to handle accounting procedures and tax management, the everyday income and expense entries are usually done by one of the partners or one of their spouses.

Normally, each partner has a drawing account in the partnership which he uses for personal expenses during the year. At the end of each year, partners' shares of profits are calculated and the balance between each partner's share of profits and the amount he has drawn during the year is paid out to him. He may leave it in the partnership which increases his equity in the business or, if he has drawn more than his share of profits, his equity in the partnership is reduced. Each partner pays income taxes on his share of profits, regardless of the amount he has drawn. Often a partner falls into the trap of drawing in excess of his share of profits year after year. This reduces his partnership equity—and often total partnership equity as well. A partnership that continues to operate in this fashion has a problem. It should be recognized and, if possible, alleviated. Either the partner is living higher than his means or his share of profits is not large enough. One or the other must be changed or the partnership will eventually cease to function as a business.

Farm Incorporation

As your farm or ranch grows larger and increases in value, the advantages of incorporation merit careful consideration.

Not only is it possible to reduce income taxes by incorporating, estate transfers may be simplified when farm assets are represented by shares of stock. These are the main advantages of incorporation. Among the other often-noted advantages are the ease of arranging group insurance, retirement plans and other fringe benefits for employees (including the operator) and continuity of the farming operation from one generation to the next.

While limited liability and the ease of securing additional credit are characteristics of large corporations, they are of minor importance in the farm setting, since most farm lenders are quick to recognize the individuals behind the corporations and nearly always require their personal signatures on corporate notes. The corporation does provide the machinery to bring in capital and other resources from outside the immediate family.

Family farms account for most farm corporations. Some are groups of farmers—only a few could be classed as "big business." Except in a few states, any farmer or rancher can incorporate. There is no reliable rule of thumb on how big you should be. In most cases, it is unwise to incorporate a farm business for just one of the advantages above.

According to farm law specialists at Purdue University, only larger family farms, with two generations participating or with above average income, are likely to benefit from incorporation.

The running of a corporate farm business necessarily involves certain formalities such as annual meetings, corporate minutes, annual reports to the state and other special records, all of which become routine with the aid of competent legal counsel. But day-to-day farm operation is similar to that of a partnership.

If you consider going the corporate route, work closely with a lawyer experienced in both corporate law and farm estate planning. Your corporation should fit the needs of your business, estate plan and tax situations.

Incorporation procedure in most states is similar to the following:

1. A notice of intent to incorporate is filed with the Secretary of State, reserving a proposed name for the corporation.

2. The incorporators draft and file their Articles of Incorporation with the Secretary of State and pay the initial incorporation fees. If the Articles conform to law, they are approved and a Certificate of Incorporation is issued which, together with a copy of the Articles, is filed with the recorder in the corporation's home county.

3. The subscribers exchange assets for shares of stock according to the terms of a previously drawn preincorporation agreement and thus become shareholders.

4. The directors are elected by the shareholders at an organizational meeting.

5. The directors meet to elect officers and adopt bylaws, after which the farm can start doing business as a corporation.

Transfer of farm assets to a corporation for stock will qualify as a tax-free exchange if those transferring property to the corporation own at least 80% of its stock immediately after the exchange. Transfers to most farm corporations will qualify. Since there is no gain or loss, the tax basis of all property transferred remains the same as it was before the transfer, and the stock received takes the same basis as the property exchanged.

Dissolving a corporation is not always tax free, however, and complications arise if property has appreciated in value. Liquidation of corporate property, whether by cash sale to outsiders or by exchange for shareholders' stock, may result in a capital gain taxable to the shareholders based on any increase in the fair market value of corporate property. It is as if the stock were sold back to the corporation for the fair market value of the property received. Thus, you should not consider incorporation unless you intend to continue with that form of organization indefinitely.

Tax benefits to be derived from an ordinary incorporation become significant when the farmer's personal income is high enough to place him in a high tax bracket. Federal income tax rates for corporations in 1983 are scheduled to be 15% of the first $25,000 of taxable income, 18% of the next $25,000, and 30% of the next $25,000. With these figures in mind, it is possible to distribute income among employees' salaries, shareholders' dividends and corporate retained earnings in such a way as to result in tax savings.

By adjusting salaries, small corporations are able to keep earnings within lower tax brackets. However, the IRS requires that salary levels be set at the beginning of the year, before the corporate earnings level is known. This problem can be somewhat overcome through the use of a salary plan which provides for a base salary plus an end-of-year bonus equal to a percentage of corporate income. However, IRS has challenged some plans of this type for various reasons, so work it out carefully with your attorney or tax specialist.

Dual taxation results when corporate earnings, taxed once to the corporation, are passed on to shareholders as dividends and thus are taxed again as personal income to the shareholders. While the problems may be avoided by not paying dividends, nonsalaried shareholders will usually demand dividends as their only source for return on their investment. As an alternative the Subchapter S corporation, often called the "tax option" corporation, is selected by many farming operations since it provides most of the advantages of corporation operation without "dual taxation."

Subchapter S corporations differ from regular corporations only in the eyes of the Internal Revenue Service. They are formed and managed in much the same way as a regular corporation, but pay no income tax—like partnerships, only the individual owners (shareholders) pay tax on earnings. This aspect may be an advantage or disadvantage depending on your situation. The Subchapter S election should thus be made only with the advice of your attorney.

Special requirements must be met before a corporation will qualify for this election. It must be a domestic corporation with only one class of stock. A Sub-S corporation can have no more than 15 shareholders, all of whom must be individuals, estates or certain kinds of trusts. Husband and wife are counted as one shareholder. The corporation can have only one class of stock and no stock can be owned by another corporation or partnership. A Subchapter S corporation must not be a member of an affiliated group. No more than 20% of the corporation's gross receipts can be from rental income, interest, dividends, and gains from sale of stock or securities.

Under this election, each shareholder must pay income tax on his share of the corporate income and also on his pro rata share of the undistributed income. This can be a hardship to some shareholders who end up paying tax on income they do not receive. When such income is later distributed, it is not taxed. If it is invested in the corporation, it increases the basis of the stock. A corporation's long-term capital gains and also its losses automatically "pass through" to the shareholders just as regular income.

State and local taxes imposed upon corporations may more than offset tax breaks at the federal level. While this is usually not the case, their effect deserves careful study.

Initial cost of incorporation and annual fees vary widely from state to state. Some states charge flat fees while others base charges on value of capital stock. Attorney fees depend upon the complexity of the situation.

A shareholder's income from a Subchapter S corporation (not his salary) is not considered to be self-employment income, thus does not contribute to his earnings for social security. After retirement, it will not reduce social security benefits.

What Should You Pay for Farmland?

Two important questions must be answered before you decide to buy farmland:
1. What is the land worth to you? 2. What are you able to pay for it?

You can start to answer the first question above, by capitalizing the earning power of the land into a cash value. Prepare a budget of gross income and expenses for the land, using the best records, averages and estimates you can obtain.

If you are looking at a complete farming unit, you'll need to work up a whole-farm budget including all variable and fixed costs. Allow a reasonable wage rate for your own and family labor which will cover family living expenses, income taxes, life insurance, personal savings, etc.

A simpler method is to calculate rental income, on the theory that the rent share is the return to land ownership. Budget the gross income for the land you propose to buy. Then calculate net rent by deducting from the landlord's share of the crops, his share of farm expenses plus property taxes. This is somewhat less complicated than working up a complete budget for the farm and automatically allows, in the renter's share, for your labor from which family expenses and income taxes can be paid. The result may vary somewhat from that of the whole-farm budget, but both are rough estimates, at best.

The net return determined by either of these methods may be somewhat less than the return you can budget for a tract of land that will be added to your existing farming unit. If you are adding land, then a partial budget can be used, including only those costs which are directly attributable to the added acreage. Charges for labor and machinery repairs, depreciation, and interest on investment may be low if existing labor and machinery can be used.

CAPITALIZATION FORMULA

Once you have estimated net return per acre, you can make a simple calculation to capitalize that earning power into an estimated land value. Divide annual net return or net rent by a reasonable percent return on your investment.

$$\frac{\text{Annual net income}}{\text{Capitalization rate}} = \text{Land value}$$

For example, assume net return budgets out to $60 per acre and you hope for a 7% annual return on your investment. $60 ÷ .07 = $857 per acre.

The capitalization rate or percent return on investment used in this calculation should be chosen with care. It can be the local farm loan interest rate or a rate you think provides a reasonable long term return on your money.

This capitalized value will probably be somewhat below the current price of farmland because it is based only on the expected productivity of the land. To that value you should add whatever you feel is a reasonable allowance for personal satisfaction from owning the land, for location, and most important, for expected appreciation in land value over the years.

CALCULATE MAXIMUM DEBT

Once you have determined the value of the land to you, you then must determine whether or not you will be able to pay for it. That depends on four factors--the debt remaining after making a down payment, the interest rate on the debt, the repayment term of the loan and finally, the size of the annual payments you will be able to make.

The Maximum Debt tables on the back of this page will help you to determine if you can handle the debt required to purchase the land. In these tables you can start with the maximum payment you think can be made, then find how much debt that payment will amortize (pay off) at a given interest rate and loan term. Or you can start with the price of the land, subtract your down payment, then find the approximate size of annual payment you'll have to make to repay the loan.

Size of the annual payments you can make will depend on the net return expected from the land being purchased, the amount of income you can count on from other sources--both farm and off-farm, and your need to draw on such net income for family and personal expenses. If you have budgeted income from the land as net rent, these non-business expenses are accounted for in the tenant's share.

If annual payments must be larger than the net return from the land, you'll have to decide if the excess can come from earnings from other land and off-farm employment, or can be picked up through superior management, reduced consumption, or failure to replace depreciating capital.

31

10% ANNUAL INTEREST RATE

Annual Payments	Years of Repayment				
	10	15	20	25	30
500.00	3072	3803	4257	4539	4713
480.00	2949	3651	4087	4357	4525
460.00	2827	3499	3916	4175	4336
440.00	2704	3347	3746	3994	4148
420.00	2581	3195	3576	3812	3959
400.00	2458	3042	3405	3631	3771
380.00	2335	2890	3235	3449	3582
360.00	2212	2738	3065	3268	3394
340.00	2089	2586	2895	3086	3205
320.00	1966	2434	2724	2905	3017
300.00	1843	2282	2554	2723	2828
280.00	1720	2130	2384	2542	2640
260.00	1598	1978	2214	2360	2451
240.00	1475	1825	2043	2178	2262
220.00	1352	1673	1873	1997	2074
200.00	1229	1521	1703	1815	1885
180.00	1106	1369	1532	1634	1697

12% ANNUAL INTEREST RATE

Annual Payments	Years of Repayment				
	10	15	20	25	30
500.00	2825	3405	3735	3922	4028
480.00	2712	3269	3585	3765	3866
460.00	2599	3133	3436	3608	3705
440.00	2486	2997	3287	3451	3544
420.00	2373	2861	3137	3294	3383
400.00	2260	2724	2988	3137	3222
380.00	2147	2588	2838	2980	3061
360.00	2034	2452	2689	2824	2900
340.00	1921	2316	2540	2667	2739
320.00	1808	2179	2390	2510	2578
300.00	1695	2043	2241	2353	2417
280.00	1582	1907	2091	2196	2255
260.00	1469	1771	1942	2039	2094
240.00	1356	1635	1793	1882	1933
220.00	1243	1498	1643	1725	1772
200.00	1130	1362	1494	1569	1611
180.00	1017	1226	1344	1412	1450

14% ANNUAL INTEREST RATE

Annual Payments	Years of Repayment				
	10	15	20	25	30
500.00	2608	3071	3312	3436	3501
480.00	2504	2948	3179	3299	3361
460.00	2399	2825	3047	3162	3221
440.00	2295	2703	2914	3024	3081
420.00	2191	2580	2782	2887	2941
400.00	2086	2457	2649	2749	2801
380.00	1982	2334	2517	2612	2661
360.00	1878	2211	2384	2474	2521
340.00	1773	2088	2252	2337	2381
320.00	1669	1965	2119	2199	2241
300.00	1565	1843	1987	2062	2101
280.00	1461	1720	1854	1924	1961
260.00	1356	1597	1722	1787	1821
240.00	1252	1474	1590	1650	1681
220.00	1148	1351	1457	1512	1541
200.00	1043	1228	1325	1375	1401
180.00	939	1106	1192	1237	1260

16% ANNUAL INTEREST RATE

Annual Payments	Years of Repayment				
	10	15	20	25	30
500.00	2417	2788	2964	3049	3089
480.00	2320	2676	2846	2927	2965
460.00	2223	2565	2727	2805	2842
440.00	2127	2453	2609	2683	2718
420.00	2030	2342	2490	2561	2594
400.00	1933	2230	2372	2439	2471
380.00	1837	2119	2253	2317	2347
360.00	1740	2007	2134	2195	2224
340.00	1643	1896	2016	2073	2100
320.00	1547	1784	1897	1951	1977
300.00	1450	1673	1779	1829	1853
280.00	1353	1561	1660	1707	1730
260.00	1257	1450	1541	1585	1606
240.00	1160	1338	1423	1463	1483
220.00	1063	1227	1304	1341	1359
200.00	967	1115	1186	1219	1235
180.00	870	1004	1067	1097	1112

FIND TOP LAND PRICE

The tables show the maximum debt that can be amortized with certain annual payments. By including your downpayment, you can approximate the highest price you can pay for the land.

For example, suppose you have $20,000 available for a downpayment and 80 acres of land have been offered to you on a 15-year installment contract. You determine that the maximum annual payment you are certain you can make is $200 per acre. The table shows that at the 12% rate of interest demanded by the seller, your payment would amortize a debt of $1,362 per acre. Adding your downpayment of $250 per acre ($20,000 divided by 80 acres) makes a maximum price of $1,612 per acre that you would be able to pay.

If the seller insists on a 10-year contract, the maximum you could pay would be $1,380 per acre ($1,130 from the 12% table plus the $250 available downpayment).

If you financed through a commercial lender at 14% interest with 30 years to repay, your $200 per acre annual payment would amortize a $1,401 debt. Add your $250 downpayment, and the maximum you could pay would be $1,651.

When your farm loan is to be set up on a variable interest rate basis, you should probably base your repayment calculations on an interest rate toward the top of the expected range and allow some additional margin of safety in the annual payment used in determining what you can pay. Here's why: A $200 annual payment will retire a debt of $1,569 per acre in 25 years at 12% interest. When interest rate is increased to 14%, an annual payment of about $230 is required to pay off the same debt.

The accompanying tables can be used to approximate alternate financing arrangements, too. For example, if the asking price of 80 acres is $2,750 per acre, a $1,250 downpayment will leave $1,500 to be financed by credit. From the tables you can determine that at 10% interest and a $220 per acre annual payment, it would take about 12½ years to amortize $1,500. At 12%, it would take about 15 years, and at 14%, about 25 years.

If a table does not go high enough, divide your higher annual payment by the top payment shown in the table, then multiply by the top debt shown in the proper column of the table. If the figure does not go low enough, divide the bottom payment shown in the table by your lower annual payment, then divide this figure into the bottom debt shown in the proper column of the table. For other repayment periods and interest rates, refer to similar available tables.

New Installment Sale Law

Now, virtually any sale of farmland or other property with payments in a future year will postpone reporting of gain until the future installment is received.

Frequently, a landowner finances the purchase of his farm by agreeing to take payments from the buyer over a period of years. An installment sale has long offered special tax benefits because the seller can spread the gain on the sale over the period the payments are made. However, there were some highly technical rules that often made it difficult to qualify for installment sale treatment. Now the rules are much easier.

The new Installment Sales Revision Act of 1980 contains good news and bad news. The good news is the elimination of the old finicky rules. The bad news is that there are some traps in sales between family members or businesses.

Changes from old law. The new law makes these changes:

1. Any amount can be received in the year of sale. Old law required that less than 30% of the selling price be paid in the year of sale.

2. A single lump-sum payment can be postponed until a later year. Old law required payments in at least 2 years.

3. Sales of personal property for any price will qualify. Old law required a purchase price of $1,000 or more.

4. There is no election to qualify for the installment sale; it is automatic. In fact, a taxpayer who does not want to report on the installment method must elect *out*.

5. The gain from "boot" on a tax-free exchange can be reported on the installment method if boot is paid in installments. Under the old law, this was almost impossible.

6. The installment method can be used even if the sale price is contingent, e.g., based on production or sales. The old law did not allow it.

7. Guarantees or standby letters of credit are not treated as payments. Under the old law, these were often treated as payments in the year of sale.

New rules. The new law has some tricky rules that will be important to farm family sales:

1. If the sale is to a family member or business, and the buyer resells the property within 2 years, the seller must immediately report all of the postponed gain.

2. If the seller forgives the buyer a payment or all of the payments, the seller will recognize the postponed gain.

3. If the seller dies and forgives the obligation of the buyer, the seller's estate will have to report all of the postponed gain.

4. If the seller sells depreciable property to a spouse or to an 80% controlled corporation or partnership, *all* gain must be reported in the year of sale, and it is *ordinary* income, not capital gain.

Installment sale defined. An installment sale is any sale in which any part of the price is paid in a tax year after the year of sale. This includes any sale of real estate or personal property that is not required to be included in inventory. Since a farmer on the cash basis does not have to inventory farm products, a deferred payment sale of raised grain should postpone reporting of income until the payment is received.

A taxpayer may elect *not* to have installment treatment. The election must be made on the tax return for the year of sale.

Reporting gain. Installment treatment applies only to sales that produce a gain. A pro rata part of the total gain is reported as each payment is received by the seller.

The portion of each installment to be treated as gain is the ratio of "gross profit" to "contract price." The gross profit on the sale is the selling price less the basis of the property and the expenses of the sale.

The contract price is the cash that the seller will be paid. It is the selling price less any debt or mortgage on the property that the buyer will pay to someone other than the seller. Dividing the contract price by the gross profit gives the "gross profit ratio," the percentage of each installment payment that is gain.

Example: Farmer A sells his farm for $150,000, agreeing to take annual principal payments of $15,000 for 10 years. Interest on the unpaid price is 12%. A's basis for the farm is $100,000. His gross profit is $50,000 ($150,000 minus $100,000). The total contract price is $150,000 (the selling price), and the gross ratio is $50,000:$150,000, or 33⅓%.

Of each annual payment, $5,000 (one-third of $15,000) will be reported as gain from the sale.

Example: If, in the above example, the property was subject to a $25,000 mortgage that the buyer agreed to pay, the gross profit is still $50,000. The contract price is the selling price less the assumed debt ($125,000), which is the amount to be paid to the seller. The gross profit ratio is $50,000:$125,000, or 40%. Six thousand dollars of each payment (40% of $15,000) is treated as gain.

If the debt is more than the seller's basis for the property, the excess of debt over basis is treated as a payment in the year of sale.

Contingent price. Sometimes the price is calculated in such a way that the total price or the installment payments are not fixed amounts, e.g., a price based on production. Usually, however, there is a stated maximum amount due under the contract or a maximum period over which payments are to be made. If the contract price has a stated maximum, the profit ratio is calculated using the maximum price. If payments will continue for a fixed period but there is no maximum price, profit is computed each year by allocating basis equally to each year for the stated period. If there is neither a maximum price nor a fixed period for payment, basis is allocated equally each year over a 15-year period.

Sales to related parties. Under prior law, if a spouse sold property to the other spouse on the installment basis, the seller-spouse realized gain only when payment was made, but the buyer-spouse had a basis equal to the full purchase price for the computation of gain on a later sale.

For example, if a husband sold to a wife using the installment method, the wife could resell the property for cash to an outsider. The couple would have the cash, but no tax would be incurred until the wife actually paid the husband on the installment note. The new law eliminates this gimmick.

If property is sold to a related purchaser, the seller is treated as receiving any payment that the buyer receives upon resale of the property within 2 years of the first sale. (The 2-year cutoff does not apply to sales and resales of marketable securities.) If the related buyer does not sell the property but gives it away or otherwise disposes of it, the seller is treated as receiving the full fair market value of the property. If IRS can be convinced that the sales had no tax-avoidance purpose, the resale rule will not apply.

For the resale rule, the related purchasers are spouses, children, grandchildren, or parents (not brothers or sisters), and corporations, partnerships, trusts, or estates in which the seller has a 50% interest.

A new, harsh rule applies to a sale of depreciable property to a spouse or to an 80% controlled corporation or partnership. All of the gain must be reported in the year of sale as *ordinary* income.

Cancellation of installment debt. The 1980 changes eliminate another tax advantage sometimes sought by farm families. Suppose a parent sold a farm to a child on an installment sale. Thereafter, the parent might forgive an installment or, in his will, forgive the remainder of the outstanding debt. There could be a gift or estate tax on the gift or bequest, but, under the old law, the parent did not report the postponed gain in the forgiven installments.

The 1980 law provides that a cancellation or forgiveness of an installment obligation will require recognition of the postponed gain by the parent. A similar rule applies if the cancellation results from a bequest to the buyer or if he inherits his own installment note at death. The postponed gain is recognized to the parent's estate.

Deferred payment sales of farm produce. The 1980 changes were intended to apply to deferred payment sales of farm produce by farmers. In the past, IRS has challenged a farmer's postponement of income reporting on sales where payment is deferred to a year following the sale. The new law treats these deferred payment sales as installment sales, so gain should not be included in income until the payment is made. The statute says that the new installment provisions do not apply to property "*required* to be included in the inventory." A cash-basis farmer is not required to inventory crops, livestock, or other produce.

Purchase price guarantees. The new law also provides a special rule that a guarantee of the obligation to pay the price does not convert the obligation into a payment. A seller can require the buyer to put up a standby letter of credit and still not have to pay tax until payment is received. On the other hand, an arrangement that requires that the buyer put the purchase price in escrow with payments to the seller in installments from the escrow account is likely to draw the disapproval of the Internal Revenue Service.

34

Land Description and Measurement

There are two methods of describing real property; by metes and bounds and by reference to an official map on which land is divided into townships and sections.

The rectangular survey system was set up in 1784 as the United States System of Surveying Public Lands and requires that public lands "shall be divided by north and south lines, run according to true meridian and by others crossing them at right angles, so as to form townships six miles square; also that the townships shall be divided into 36 sections, each of which shall contain 640 acres, as nearly as may be, by a system of two sets of parallel lines, one governed by true meridian and the other by parallel of latitudes, the latter intersecting the former at right angles at intervals of a mile." This survey includes 30 states located principally west and south from Ohio.

States that lie outside the rectangular survey and special cases such as small irregular tracts within the survey are described by metes and bounds. Metes and bounds means a description of the boundaries. This was the system used in the eastern United States before the system of rectangular survey was inaugurated.

METES AND BOUNDS

The description of a tract of land defined by metes and bounds always starts at a given point called the "point of beginning." The outline of the tract is then followed by using certain measurements and reference points such as trees, stakes, stones, roads and rivers until you arrive back at the "point of beginning."

In plotting metes and bounds descriptions, all directions are oriented from either north or south. There are four quadrants. Any direction from 0 to 90 degrees and 270 to 360 degrees is referred to as being so many degrees either east or west of north. Conversely, any direction that you would normally think of as being between 90 degrees and 270 degrees is referred to as being so many degrees east or west of south. Here is a typical example of a metes and bounds description showing how it would be plotted:

"Beginning at the maple tree on the property line of the old Jones Farm and its intersection with the Summer Creek road; thence S 67 degrees W 593', thence N 24 degrees W 642'; then N 15 degrees E 265'; thence S 35 degrees E 490'; thence S 66 degrees E 500' to the point of beginning, con-

taining 5.46 acres more or less."

The readings given can be used to draw the tract. The reading S 67 degrees W means the line runs 67 degrees west of the North-South line in the southwest quadrant.

The figure below is the plat drawn from the metes and bounds description. The dotted lines are for computing acreage by the use of triangles.

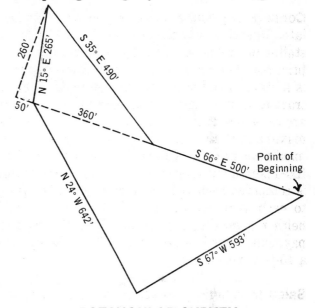

RECTANGULAR SURVEY

In areas where rectangular survey is used, land is divided into townships, sections, quarter sections, and quarter-quarter sections. The starting points are meridians and base lines. Meridians used in survey or legal descriptions of land are arbitrarily chosen north and south lines from which measurements are made to the east or west. Base lines are arbitrarily chosen lines running east and west from which measurements are made to the north or south. Each meridian has its own base line intersecting it.

The map on the back shows the area covered by rectangular survey and the names of some principal meridians. The heavy lines bound the areas measured from each principal meridian.

Legal descriptions of property identify the location in relation to meridian and base line, measured in units of one township or one range. A township is six miles square. The term **range** is used to represent the distance east or west from the meridian, one range equaling the width of one township. In a legal description, the word township represents the distance north or south from the base line, each township being equal to approximately six miles.

A legal description of a farm might read in part "...township 9 north, range 12 east of the Black Hills meridian." This would mean that it is 12 ranges or about 72 miles east of the meridian and 9 townships or 54 miles north of the base line.

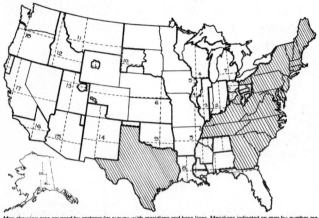

Map showing area covered by rectangular survey with meridians and base lines. Meridians indicated on map by number are identified as follows: 1-First; 2-Second; 3-Third; 4-Fourth; 5-Fifth; 6-Sixth; 7-Michigan; 8-Louisiana; 9-Indiana; 10-Black Hills; 11-Principal; 12-Boise; 13-Salt Lake; 14-New Mexico; 15-Gila and Salt Rivers; 16-San Bernardino; 17-Mt. Diablo; 18-Willamette; 19-Copper River; 20-Fairbanks; 21-Seward. Metes and bounds are used in the shaded areas.

TOWNSHIPS AND SECTIONS

A regular township is divided into sections of one square mile or 640 acres. Certain sections in each township are normally fractional, that is, they contain more or less than 640 acres. They occur because it is impossible for two lines to run due north and remain parallel. The north end of a township is narrower than the south end.

Each section in a township is numbered with section 1 in the northeast corner, section 6 in the northwest corner; immediately below section 6 is section 7 and the numbering continues back and forth across the township to section 36 in the southeast corner.

Because of convergence, some sections will not be precisely 640 acres. It was decided early that all excesses and deficits would be thrown to the sections on the north and west boundaries of the township. Likewise, within each section, the deficit is thrown to the north or west 40 acre tracts, depending on which boundary of the township the section is on. If section 1 of a township is short 20 acres, each of the four 40 acre tracts along the northern boundary contains only 35 acres.

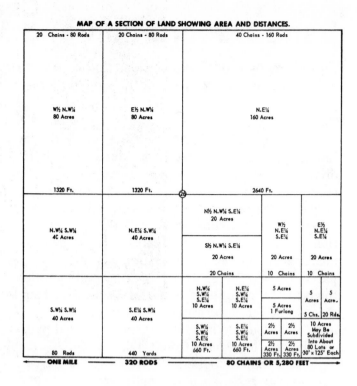

MAP OF A SECTION OF LAND SHOWING AREA AND DISTANCES.

LEGAL DESCRIPTIONS

A typical description might read: SW1/4 SW1/4 sec. 4, township 45 north, range 25 west of the fifth principal meridian. Work backward when reading rectangular survey descriptions. First find the fifth principal meridian. From the map you can see that it is a north and south line running through Arkansas, Missouri, and Iowa.

Continuing to read backward from the description the phrase "range 25 west" indicates that the farm is 25 ranges or roughly 150 miles west of the fifth principal meridian. Next in the description is "township 45 north." This means it is 45 townships or about 270 miles north of the base line which runs east and west through Arkansas.

Once the township is found in west-central Missouri, locate section 4 along the northern boundary of the township. Reading backward again "SW1/4 SW1/4" means the southwest quarter of the southwest quarter of the section. The southwest quarter of the section will contain 160 acres and the southwest quarter of it will contain 40 acres. The location of this 40 acres will be in the extreme southwest corner of the section. If the tract were not a full 40 acres, the description would have been SWfr. 1/4 SW1/4, the fr. denoting a fractional unit. Often, the legal description will give the acreage at the end such as "containing in all, 38 acres more or less according to government survey."

Chapter 3

Records, Planning and Financing

The office work of farming may earn you a greater return per hour of labor than any other phase of your farming operation. The farmer who underrates the value of records is probably overrating himself and his business.

Good records serve many functions in the successful operation of a farm. By helping you plan a more efficient operation, they keep you "on track" toward accomplishing your long term goals. They are also the best way to determine what enterprises are the most profitable for you.

Records form the basis for filing and managing income taxes. Good records permit you to adjust your business to save on taxes. They provide you with the proof that might be necessary should you ever be audited by the Internal Revenue Service.

Establishing yourself as a good credit risk can be made easier with a complete set of records. Records also provide the basis for formulating a sound management plan, which is often required by creditors. Profit sharing arrangements can be properly set up from good records.

Cropping history in relation to various governmental programs can be supplied by well-kept field records.

Most records and accounts kept on the farm can be classified into three categories: Income and expenses, inventory (to show your financial position at one particular time), and crop and livestock records. This last category includes data on land use, crop yields, livestock production, pasture, and feed use.

Records are also necessary to meet Social Security requirements for information on hired labor. To receive gas tax refunds, records must be kept of the gasoline used on the farm. Other records can include information on machinery use and products used in the household.

IMPORTANCE OF PLANNING

The kind of job you do in planning your farm business shows up in the profit and loss column of your farm record books. Planning centers around thoroughly understanding and evaluating the amounts available and the quality of each of the four factors of production.

Land — Know how much can be farmed or ranched, and its limitations (fertility, topography, cost of improvements and the products for which it is best adapted).

Labor — Information needed is the amount available from the family or hired sources, its cost, and the suitability and skill of the workers being considered. Know the labor demands, total and seasonal, of various enterprises in your farm program.

Capital — Consider the amount of money available for immediate use, anticipated funds, your credit rating and position, interest rates or cost of money and capital requirements of various enterprises.

Management — This vital factor is determined by the owner's and/or operator's ability to plan, organize and operate the farm, including his capacity to make decisions quickly and wisely.

Combine your resources, after thoroughly evaluating them, into enterprises that will return maximum profit. Concentrating too much land, labor or capital on one enterprise and not enough on another can lead to inefficiencies. Some factors to consider in combining enterprises into an efficient farming operation are:

● Select enterprises which will distribute the use of labor throughout the year and make optimum use of your land.

● Select those enterprises which use the same equipment and machinery to avoid excessive investment. Some enterprises go together better than others.

● Plan your operation around existing facilities as much as possible.

Though a number of enterprises may be adapted to your area, you will want to select those which are best suited to your farm. Make use of various tools to decide which enterprises and what size of each will best combine your available resources. Study records of your farm and those in your area. Make complete cost and return budgets for each enterprise and secure aid from your agricultural college and county agent.

Many planning considerations must be taken into account when managing a farm other than which enterprises and systems of management will be most profitable. Here is a list of only a few things you must consider and plan for in your business. Although a number of them are not important when you first start farming, they become important as your business grows and develops.

● Plan your financial needs and establish the necessary credit.

● Determine insurance needs and spend what you can afford to pay in premiums to get the best possible protection.

● Decide if incorporation would be advantageous. This is not a problem until you have built up a large net worth.

● Lay out buildings, equipment and the farmstead for maximum efficiency.

● Understand government programs. They place definite limitations on management decisions and affect long range plans.

● Plan for good labor relations with employees and provide them with necessary incentives to get the job done.

YOUR FINANCIAL PROGRAM

It's easier to borrow when you can show why you need the money, and how, where and when you'll use it. This planning requires:

● Enterprise analysis. This will show those enterprises that should be expanded and those that perhaps should be eliminated. Records for enterprise analysis should include complete inventories of your assets, such as livestock and equipment, and of your liabilities, such as existing debts and mortgages.

● The long-range and short-run plans for your farm should be well established.

● Plans for the expected use of the borrowed money should be well formulated. Show how and when you expect to pay off the loan. Review these plans with your lender.

● Repayment plans. These should be drawn up so the improvements will pay for themselves by the time the final payment is made. To permit some degree of flexibility, a loan should carry rather liberal prepayment privileges without having to pay penalties. Such a loan privilege allows a farmer to make advance payments on the principal during higher income years. In addition, it allows you to refinance. Refinancing is important if interest rates drop considerably after you acquire a loan or mortgage.

Farm Computers

The microcomputer is fast becoming a necessary piece of farming and ranching equipment. These guidelines should help you to ease into this new technology.

Computers in agriculture have become a reality. Rapidly rising costs and major price swings of farm products have prompted many producers to look to these affordable new tools to help them in day-to-day operations. The microcomputer can add considerable power to the thinking side of farming. However, without the right instructions or programs, it is useless.

Computer applications range from farm records to budgeting to day-to-day decisionmaking. Some farmers are using their computers for gathering market information and for assistance in marketing.

Applications are limited only by your vision and ability to make the computer perform. Given the right instructions, it can take much of the day-to-day drudgery out of decision-making and recordkeeping. Given the wrong instructions, it will frustrate and confuse you, making mistakes at a record pace.

Computer systems have two main components–hardware, or the computer equipment, and software, or the programs to control the equipment. Your farm computer will be no better than the weaker of these two components. Unfortunately, hardware development is 2 to 5 years ahead of the software needed to take advantage of the system's capability. Keep this timelag in mind when you are purchasing a computer. You may well outgrow the programs before you outgrow the computer. Thus, you should spend 90% of your time looking for the right programs.

Dealer support is as important as the hardware and software. Few farmers would buy machinery for fieldwork without a competent dealer to stand behind it. The same should be true of a computer system. Some farmers have been forced to change computers simply to find better dealer support.

Support is probably more important for software than for hardware, at least during the startup phase. Computers are very disciplined. They do only what they are told to do by the programs. A slight error or an incorrect assumption can be confusing. (A common one is whether interest rates should be input as decimals or whole numbers.) Unless you can go back to the author for advice, you can't be certain the conclusion the computer has reached is correct.

A common complaint among farmers using computers today is a lack of program support and shoddy or sloppy programming. Since development of software is lagging hardware, there's a push by developers to release programs as soon as possible. Unfortunately, errors in the programs are often not found. This is where a strong dealer helps by keeping you informed of current releases of new programs, or by helping you to understand the output from your computer.

A farm computer setup will usually include computer terminal, video display, two disk drives, and printer.

Program documentation is one of the simplest, yet most often overlooked, forms of program support. Documentation is simply an owner's manual for a program.

Some of the better programs available will be documented through a reference manual and other means, such as cassette tapes or training sessions. Some vendors may sponsor a newsletter or users' group to assist users of a particular program. These are the quickest ways to keep up with new additions and applications for a program. It's also helpful to be able to discuss your particular problems in a meeting with other farm users.

Purchasing a system may take upwards of a year, depending on your particular needs and applications. One vendor of farm record systems suggests taking 6 months or more to look at different systems. Then, when you have found the system you feel will meet your needs, buy it and test it for another 3 or 4 months. Use the program along with your normal bookkeeping system. This will give you a check on the program and what it is and is not providing. Then, you can go back to the software vendor to have the changes you need incorporated into a customized version.

An important warning is in order: Computers will not make a recordkeeper out of you. If you don't have an understandable record system now, it's unlikely a computer will help you. You must have a good idea of the type of records you need before buying a computer.

Determining your needs is the first step in deciding on a computer system. What do you want the computer to do? Keep herd records? Prepare income taxes? Do word processing? Budgeting? Enterprise analysis? Ration balancing? Management programs, such as land purchase analysis or sprayer calibration? Decide your most important need, and shop first for that need. Often it will be some type of recordkeeping system for income and expenses. Most farmers want the system to write the checks, so data has to be entered only once. Limited tax records and enterprise analysis of competing crops are also wanted in the system.

Livestock herd record and production analysis programs are very popular with computer users. They organize the records in a usable, understandable form. Many farmers have justified a computer solely for this purpose, even with a relatively small herd.

If you get a computer that will handle the major need, the secondary needs will fall in line. It's a mistake to try to computerize everything at once. A slow, gradual approach will pay off in the longrun.

Start locally when beginning a program search. A check with area farmers and land grant universities may turn up some vendors of programs. In addition, some local computer dealers in farm areas are doing an excellent job of supplying both hardware and software for farm use. Ask around in your area to locate the better dealers who are working with farmers.

Finally, you may decide to go in with a neighbor or two and have the programs you need custom developed. However, this is expensive, with programming costing $15 to $25 per hour.

Expand your search out of state if necessary to locate programs. However, try to limit your search radius to adjoining states first. Slight differences in taxes, soils, growing conditions, and other factors may be considered by various programs. Make sure these assumptions will hold for your area. If not, they will need modification.

Off-the-shelf programs for general business have been used with good success by some farmers. Data base management programs are being used for recordkeeping. Word processors are being used for mailings and herd books. Programs such as VisiCalc electronic ledgersheet have gained wide acceptance by farmers for budgeting and planning purposes.

Which computer should you purchase? This will be determined by two factors–the software you have been able to locate in the first

step of the search, and local computer availability. Computers will vary by area, depending on the systems being supported by local dealers and land grant universities.

Radio Shack and Apple computers are the most popular computers with farmers, followed by Commodore, Vector Graphics, IBM, Texas Instruments, Heath, and Ohio Scientific, to name a few. No one computer can be considered "better" than a competitive model. The power and suitability of the particular computer you choose will depend on the software and applications you purchase or program for that computer.

Regardless of the brand or model of computer you purchase, it will need certain components for satisfactory farm use. Typically, these will include the computer processor itself, a terminal with keyboard for inputting and outputting information, two floppy disk drives, and a printer for hard copy of the computer output.

Computer capacity is another major consideration. This capacity usually refers to storage, commonly called "K". "K" is a unit of measure representing about 1,000 characters of information, or about one typewritten page. (Actually, 1K equals 1,024 characters.) The minimum processor memory suitable for farm purposes will be about 32K, and preferably 48K. This refers to the internal storage of a computer available for instant access from programs.

You'll also need storage outside of the computer for programs and data. This storage is typically on floppy disks– small, round flexible disks which store magnetically

Typical Floppy Diskette

encoded information, similar to recording tapes. Storage on these disks will vary widely from 100K to 500K or more, depending on the system. For a typical farm, one disk holding roughly 200K should be adequate for 1 year's worth of records.

Printer selection will usually be based on characters per line (CPL) and characters per second (CPS). CPL refers to the number of characters the printer can print on one line. Eighty characters per line is standard, though 132 characters is preferred for multicolumn accounting statements. The CPS rating of printers refers to the speed of the printer. If you'll be doing much computer work with printed output, a printer with 100 CPS output or higher should be selected. For situations where printed output is not as important, printers as slow as 40 CPS will be adequate.

System price will depend on the model and size of computer you select. However, for the typical farm, a system costing about $4,000 is adequate for most purposes. For larger applications, cost of a complete system could approach $8,000.

These prices are for hardware only. Programs for farm purposes will range from free to $3,000 or more. Typically, you get what you pay for. In some cases you may purchase a turnkey system–both hardware and software from one dealer.

What's on the horizon for farm computer use? Within 5 years, specialists foresee the farm computer accessing large networks for information exchange. Much of the printed material you now receive may be transmitted electronically. Some farmers are now accessing networks for market information and advice, as well as specialized programs and data.

Specialists in several states are working to adapt the computer to an on-farm weather station. The computer will be able to monitor sensors, giving continuous forecasts of weather and disease incidence. A similar system may be developed to monitor insects. You'll also see computers put to use in monitoring livestock facilities, from daily milk production records to environmental control in livestock houses.

No doubt, much of the day-to-day recordkeeping and risk analysis will be more easily and efficiently handled by farm computers.

Farm Recordkeeping

There are many reasons why a farmer should keep good records.
The primary objective is to operate the business more profitably.

Today's commercial farmer or rancher has several reasons for keeping good records. He must have the necessary information for filing income tax returns. Furthermore, he wants to be able to measure his own progress in terms of net worth increase and annual operating profit or loss.

Records help you maintain management control over the business. Creditors will often examine your management skills and repayment ability in addition to your collateral. Cash flow projections are frequently requested by creditors, as well as profit and loss statements.

Tailor your recordkeeping system to your own particular set of circumstances, so that it is as simple as possible and still supplies the information you need. There is a point where the time and cost of maintaining accounting information surpasses the benefits obtained.

An inventory of all items involved in the business—and perhaps each enterprise—is the first step in setting up a recordkeeping system. This includes those items which are normally thought of as assets: land, buildings, improvements, machinery, equipment, livestock, feed, etc. This beginning inventory should be credited to the proper accounts and enterprises where enterprise accounts are maintained.

The charges to the various enterprises will consist of depreciation taken in the case of items such as buildings and equipment or the use of the asset in the case of items such as feed and gasoline. A number of items may be used in more than one enterprise. These items may be handled in one of three ways: Charge to an overhead, or undistributed account with no attempt to break down further; charge to an overhead account and then distribute the costs to the respective enterprise on a use basis using standardized rates; distribute the costs, as they are incurred, to the enterprises on an arbitrary basis.

A net worth statement or balance sheet is a listing of all farm property owned (assets) and money owed (liabilities). It is important in setting up any system of records. The difference between what the operator owns and owes is net worth. The inventory and the net worth statement may be completed anytime. However, January 1 or near that date is probably best, since it is the start of the calendar year. Farm work may also be less pressing.

Beginning and succeeding annual net worth statements give helpful information for planning the year-ahead operation. A comparison of net worth at the beginning and at the close of a given year shows a farmer's financial gain or loss.

Farmers who report taxes on the cash basis will not need these records for income tax purposes. However, they are needed for proper analysis of the farm operation.

BASIC RECORDS

Basic records required in any farming operation, regardless of your particular system, include the following:

A cash disbursement sheet should be used to record all cash expenses, except payments for labor. By spreading each item to the appropriate columns, all disbursements may be classified into the various expense categories for income tax and financial statement purposes. Also, by using an additional set of column headings, all disbursements may be placed in the proper enterprise for management information purposes. In this case, each disbursement will be placed in at least two columns for the proper expense and for the proper enterprise, such as "Livestock feed" and "Cattle."

The normal period covered before the disbursements are totaled is one month, but any period may be selected to best suit your needs. At the end of the period, all columns are totaled and posted in the profit and loss statement and the enterprise record.

When you receive your bank statement and cancelled checks, the checks which cleared should be checked off. This way, you can determine which checks are still outstanding and reconcile the bank statement with your records.

Income records pull together all cash receipts or sales of farm products and/or services. You need no separate column headings for enterprises, since each income category is an enterprise as well as an income tax item.

This record should also be totaled at the end of the period (same as disbursement period), and the column totals posted to both the profit and loss statement and the enterprise record. Also, assuming that all receipts are deposited in the bank, each entry in the income record should be checked against the bank statement for reconciliation.

Labor distribution record sheets enable you to compute gross and net pay for hired help, as well as distribute the labor charges to the proper enterprises. The period covered by this record may or may not be the same as for the disbursement and income records, depending on the payroll period. The normal period would probably be a week. For each payroll period, the record should be totaled and posted to the particular enterprise record.

A month's payroll distribution should be summarized. Make only one posting for the month to the profit and loss statement. The cancelled checks received with the bank statement should also be checked off on this record.

Earnings records enable you to keep track of all wages paid to each employee. It contains information necessary for completing withholding reports to the federal and state governments.

Depreciation schedules provide a convenient record of all depreciation taken for each depreciable asset.

Profit and loss statements are summaries of all income and expenses for the period covered, usually the calendar year. The period should coincide with your income tax filing year. The form for this statement is on a following page.

Balance sheets show the financial condition of the farm at any one point in time. This statement is normally prepared on December 31 of each year in order to measure progress on the farm from year to year. It might also be prepared for your banker at various times during the year as part of the loan procedure.

ADDITIONAL RECORDS

Aside from the basic records described, other supplemental ones are often necessary to develop more detailed information.

Enterprise records accumulate the income and expense involved in one particular endeavor, such as corn, hogs, wheat or cattle, etc. When properly completed, it will enable you to determine the amount of profit or loss incurred for each enterprise. This record could be kept on each field of a particular crop or on each lot of cattle.

Use of electronic recordkeeping systems enables you to effectively engage in more detailed enterprise accounting without the burdensome work involved. To minimize the cost, keep only those records and analyses which will be helpful in your business.

Fuel usage records enable you to charge fuel consumption to each piece of equipment and to distribute it to the various enterprises. It also is helpful in a maintenance program since excessive fuel consumption is easy to spot. At the end of each month, the enterprise columns should be totaled and posted to the corresponding enterprise record. The totals of the gallons used simplify the keeping of a fuel inventory.

Repair records show all necessary repairs made to a particular piece of machinery or equipment. It is helpful in evaluating the equipment's useful life for trade-in purposes and in spotting recurring repairs.

Production, performance and farm practice records help in analyzing the business. Among these are dairy and egg production records, livestock performance records, acreage and yield summaries, and field records including herbicides and fertilizers applied and their rates.

Farm Financial Statements

A major responsibility for the success of your farming operation rests on sound financial management. Good records are essential, but they are useful only when properly analyzed.

You must know where you are before you can develop sound future operating plans and arrange for your credit needs.

The most useful coordinated financial statements to use for summarizing your farm's financial position and demonstrating your managerial ability are the balance sheet, income statement and cash flow projection. These financial statements force you to systematically analyze your financial progress, plan operations for the year ahead and demonstrate credit worthiness to your lender. To be most useful these statements should be compared over time. If not available from previous years, there is no better time to start keeping these statements than now.

The statements shown are for illustration only—each is one of many varied forms available through many sources including banks and PCAs, record associations and state universities.

BALANCE SHEET

The balance sheet, also referred to as a net worth statement, is a summary of all assets and liabilities in the farming operation at a specific point in time (normally the last day of each year). The difference between total assets and total liabilities represents the owner's equity (net worth) in the business. Stated another way, the total capital in the business equals the sum of debt and equity capital. By comparing your current balance sheets with those of past years, you can determine the rate of net worth growth or decline from year to year.

Major purpose of the balance sheet, therefore, is to show the overall liquidity and solvency position of the business.

Assets should be categorized, as shown in the sample statement, into current, intermediate and fixed or long term. Current assets include all cash or assets that can be easily converted to cash or used within a 12 month period—livestock to be sold, feed, grain, supply inventories, and notes and accounts receivable.

Intermediate assets usually cannot be converted to cash within a 12 month period, but as a rule have a productive life of 1 to 10 years. These assets contribute to the productivity of the business over several years--breeding livestock, machinery, equipment, etc.

Fixed (long term) assets also are needed to produce income, but they are not usually liquidated for the life of the business or at least for a period of 10 years or longer—usually land and buildings.

BALANCE SHEET (Net Worth Statement)			
Year			
ASSETS			
Cash on hand			
Notes, accounts receivable			
Securities			
Feed, crop inventory			
Supply inventory			
Livestock held for sale			
Life insurance cash value			
Other current			
Total current			
Dairy, breeding stock			
Machinery, equipment			
Major household items			
Other intermediate			
Total intermediate			
Farmland			
Farm improvements			
Other long term			
Total long term			
TOTAL ASSETS			
LIABILITIES			
Notes, accounts payable			
Liens, past due items			
Rent, taxes, interest due			
Loan payments due this year			
Other current liabilities			
Total current			
Dairy, breeding stock debts			
Machinery, equipment debts			
Other intermediate debts			
Total intermediate			
Farm real estate debts			
Other long term debts			
Total long term			
TOTAL LIABILITIES			
NET WORTH			
Increase from previous year			

Liabilities are divided into the same categories as the assets. Current liabilities are debts payable within the year. These include personal property, real property and income taxes; interest on outstanding loans; charge accounts; operating notes due within the year; and annual payments on intermediate and long term loans.

Intermediate liabilities are usually payable in 1 to 10 years. Most commonly these liabilities represent the outstanding balances owed on loans or sales contracts for breeding livestock, equipment, farm buildings, and machinery.

Long term liabilities are those obligations that have a repayment period exceeding 10 years. Most common items within this category are outstanding amounts owed on land mortgages and contracts and on farm improvements.

Valuation of assets is probably the most difficult problem you'll encounter in constructing the balance sheet. The question arises as to whether book value (cost less depreciation, if any) or current market value should be shown for such assets as machinery and land. Illinois economists recommend that there are sound reasons for using both and suggest using a double column balance sheet with cost or basis shown in one column and current market value shown in the other column.

The same approach, they say, can be used for liabilities, thus showing the contingent capital gain-tax liability associated with current market valuation on land and other assets that are worth more than their original value. Using the two values, the effects of inflation on a changing net worth can be evaluated–it also aids in evaluating potential estate tax problems.

For management purposes, where the manager wants to measure only financial performance of the business, Wisconsin specialists say the following valuation scheme would be helpful: land at cost; buildings, depreciable real estate, machinery and equipment at adjusted tax basis; breeding livestock at conservative market value; resale livestock, feed, seed, supplies, and other current assets at market value. Further, to make valid comparisons from year to year, breeding livestock value should not be changed materially. This avoids paper profits and losses. However, current assets will change in value and, since they are converted to cash within the next 12 months, should be valued at expected market value. Using this scheme, changes in net worth reflect the earning capacity of the farm better than investment strategies or changes in values of fixed assets.

Uses of balance sheet other than to show your equity in the business at a given point in time are:
1. Shows how critical a financial loss would be to the equity and leverage position of your business.
2. Indicates the amount of collateral (such as machinery, land or inventory assets being held for later sale) available to support loan requests.
3. Provides an annual inventory of assets and liabilities to aid you in preparing your income statement and cash flow projections.

Remember that a balance sheet does not show how you arrived at your present financial position. That is why it is so important to construct and compile a series of balance sheets over successive years. Then you are able to chart your financial progress or growth in equity. Use care to differentiate between the growth in equity that was due to inflation and that due to the acquisition of more assets in the operation.

OPERATING OR INCOME STATEMENT

While the balance sheet provides a financial picture of the business at a given point in time, the income statement reflects its profitability or success over a period of time, usually from the beginning to the end of the tax year. It is a summary of all farm receipts and financial gains during the year minus expenses and financial losses. An income projection for the year ahead can therefore aid in planning and budgeting, provided you properly take into account changes in management and in expected prices.

While the income statement may show a good profit situation for the year, it does not give the full financial picture. Though reasonable profits and generation of cash are indicated by this statement, the business could be in an unhealthy financial condition. Overall financial situation can be determined only through coordinated use with the other two statements discussed.

Net income earned for the year, as reflected by this statement, is divided into two major sections–net cash income and net farm income. Most farmers report income tax using the cash-basis method, as reflected in net cash income–the difference between gross cash farm income and cash farm expenses. This figure alone does not completely measure the total earnings of the farm business. The task of the income statement is to convert cash-basis income to an accrual basis, reflecting the real net earning capacity of the farm.

Primarily the cash-basis method does not take changes in inventory values into account. For instance, in a year in which a farmer may sell a large volume of crops stored from the previous year his income would be much higher for that year than the farm actually could produce over time. The opposite would be true for the previous year when crops were stored rather than sold. Without records from previous years, the profitability figures for the farm would be misleading.

Net farm income corrects for the shortcomings of net cash income and more closely portrays the true earnings of the farm through the following important adjustments.

1. Changes in inventory values during the year—the difference between values at the start and end of the year. Inventories represent commodities produced or purchased for resale but not yet sold, or expenses incurred but not yet used. Inventory items include accounts receivable, feed and grain on hand, farm supplies, feeder livestock, accounts payable, accrued taxes and interest, and unpaid rent outstanding.

2. Depreciation claimed—any investment that lasts longer than a year is a capital expenditure. Depreciation allows you to recover your investment in depreciable assets as an expense against the farm business over the useful life of the assets. Depreciation represents the annual loss in value of capital assets, and must be taken into account in determining true farm income.

3. Adjust land or machinery sold if price received is different from that which existed on the books (book or depreciable value). Any sale value above its depreciable value must be added to net cash income; if below, it must be subtracted.

This net farm income figure most accurately reflects the profitability of your farm for the past year. It represents the return to unpaid labor (family and operator), management and equity capital invested in the business.

CASH FLOW PROJECTION

Unlike the balance sheet and income statement, which focus primarily on an analysis of the past or present, a cash flow projection is directed toward planning and budgeting for the coming year. Essentially, cash flow is the connecting link between the profitability of a business as shown in the income statement and its liquidity or solvency as revealed in the balance sheet.

Simply, a cash flow statement or projection is a listing of all anticipated cash inflows for the year ahead, farm and nonfarm, and all projected cash outflows, including farm operating expenses and capital outlays, along with family living expenses and tax payments. The annual projection for each of these items is spread to appropriate months. Existing debt repayment commitments are included in the monthly breakdown. The difference between cash inflow and outflow allows you to anticipate cash shortages or excesses month by month.

A cash flow projection demonstrates to your lender when and how much credit is needed and when it can be repaid. With any loan request, repayment ability is a prime consideration. A cash flow also helps you plan sales and purchases to minimize your credit needs and shows when cash surpluses are available for capital investments

OPERATING STATEMENT (Profit and Loss) YEAR_____	Projected	Actual
INCOME		
Raised livestock sold		
Crops sold		
Other		
Purchased livestock sold		
Total current income		
Dairy, breeding stock sold		
Other capital asset sold		
Total capital asset sales		
Total cash income		
EXPENSES		
Hired labor		
Repairs-machinery		
Interest, rent		
Feed		
Seed, chemicals		
Fertilizer, lime		
Machine hire, trucking		
Farm supplies		
Livestock expenses, veterinary		
Gasoline, fuel oil		
Taxes, insurance		
Other		
Other		
Livestock purchased for resale		
Total current expenses		
NET CASH INCOME		
Market livestock inventory change		
Feed, crop inventory change		
Supply inventory change		
Total inventory change		
Accounts receivable		
Accounts payable		
NET OPERATING PROFIT		
Machinery, equipment value change		
Dairy, breeding stock value change		
Buildings, improvements value change		
Total capital asset change		
PROFIT OR LOSS FROM OPERATION		

and/or purchases, as well as for making repayments on outstanding loans.

Records of cash flow from previous years can provide a history of how cash moves in your business and aids in preparing your year-ahead projections. Further, by comparing actual with projected cash flow during the year, you will be able to monitor actual with planned performance. It can alert you to problems, allowing you to make adjustments wherever possible.

Preparing a cash flow projection budget isn't easy unless few changes from the previous year are anticipated–then minor adjustments may be adequate. However, more detailed planning is increasingly required, according to Illinois specialists. They say this involves generating a field crop plan, complete with yield projections, as well as plans for the use of seed, fertilizers, herbicides and insecticides, including estimates of amount and timing of costs. Production must be estimated and combined with beginning inventories in order to arrive at figures for total feed and grain available. Next, livestock plans must be developed, showing purchases, production and marketing plans, as well as feed required and expected nonfeed costs. Then, salable feed and grain can be determined and a marketing program established.

Detailed plans are rounded out by carefully estimating other income and expenditures for the year. Figures from these budgets are summarized and transferred to the cash flow form.

Actually, it is useful to prepare more than one cash flow projection in order to take into account variables in prices and production costs. This helps to identify the financial range within which your business can reasonably operate.

The task of putting together a cash flow projection may appear laborious and time consuming, but once it is completed, it can ease your management problems for the year ahead. Since it forces you to thoroughly think through and plan your production and business plans, it is in fact a blueprint for the year's operation, helping to eliminate hit and miss snap decisions that could prove costly. You'll have a much better picture of how major changes or expansion plans will affect your credit needs, the repayment ability of your operation and setting up repayment schedules that will more closely match the inflow of your income.

Further, the cash flow projection will allow you to plan your credit needs and make the necessary arrangements well ahead of time, allowing you to concentrate on production during periods when your time is at a premium.

CASH FLOW PROJECTION	YEAR		
	Jan.	Feb.	Mar.
INCOME			
Raised livestock sold			
Crops sold			
Other income			
Other income			
Other income			
Purchasd livestock sold			
Current income			
Dairy, breeding stock sold			
Capital assets sold			
Asset income			
Total cash income			
EXPENSES			
Hired labor			
Repairs-machinery			
Repairs-buildings			
Seed, chemicals			
Fertilizer, lime			
Interest			
Other			
Other			
Livestock for resale			
Current expenses			
Dairy, breeding stock			
Other assets			
Asset expenses			
Total expenses			
CASH BALANCE			
Loan payments (Principal)			
Loan payments (Principal)			
Total principal paid			
BUSINESS CASH BALANCE			
CUMULATIVE CASH BALANCE			
Family living needs			
Life insurance payments			
Total family expense			
NET CASH BALANCE			
NET CUMULATIVE BALANCE			

Farm Business Analysis

Time spent in analyzing your farm business can pay big dividends.
The analysis provides a guide for future planning.

The balance sheet completed at the end of each year provides an accurate measure of annual financial progress and supplies information for the farm business analysis worksheet. This worksheet will help you analyze farm earnings and business performance, based on information taken directly from your federal income tax forms and an annual net worth statement.

Net farm income (line 6). Note that inventory change includes only raised livestock. If total livestock is used, the impact of the deduction of the purchase of livestock in the tax return is doubled.

Capital earnings (line 12) and rate of return on capital (line 15) show how competitive earnings from capital used in farm business are with alternative investments and with current interest rates. If allowance for operator and family labor covers both living expenses and income tax, then capital earnings represent what is available for interest and reinvestment.

Net farm production (line 22) and rate of capital turnover (line 25) are the best volume of business measurements for a farm. High rate of capital turnover is good, if you can control costs, too, but it will vary widely depending on the operation. Turnover rate could range from 50% for a tenant grow-

ing corn and feeding it all to hogs, down to near 20% for a dairy operation with a lot of equipment substituted for labor.

Production per $1 expense (line 28) is a valuable indicator of your ability to control costs, or to increase production faster than costs. The range of $1.50 to $2 of production per $1 expense is considered normal with the lower figure being the high risk one.

Cost per acre for machinery, power and facilities (line 40) lumps all such costs together as they are in Schedule F, which on today's farms and ranches gives a better overall picture of cost trends than crop machinery costs alone.

Investment per acre for machinery and power (line 43) and net production per man (line 48) should advance together. If investment increases without an increase in production per man, farm business growth and dept repayment capacity can deteriorate. Volume of business per man is more closely related to net income and capital earnings than any other single financial analysis factor. Growth here is essential for success.

After you have completed this worksheet and studied the results, file it for comparison with a similar analysis in succeeding years.

FARM BUSINESS ANALYSIS WORKSHEET*

Year

1. Net Farm Income
2. Net farm profit, Schedule F, Form 1040. . . . . $_____
3. Plus gain or loss on sale of breeding stock, Form 4797 . . . . $_____
4. Plus value of all feeds, crops and raised livestock from
    financial statements (end of year) $_____ minus
    same assets (beginning of year) $_____ (+ or −). . . . . $_____
5. Plus value of all raised breeding stock from financial
    statements not included in line 4 above (end of year)
    $_____ minus same assets (beginning of year)
    $_____ (+ or −) . . . . $_____
6. Equals NET FARM INCOME. . . . . $_____

7. Capital Earnings
8. Net farm income, line 6 above . . . . $_____
9. Plus interest paid, Schedule F . . . . $_____
10. Less operator labor_____ month at $_____ . . . . $_____
11. Less family labor_____ month at $_____ . . . . $_____
12. Equals CAPITAL EARNINGS . . . . $_____

13. Rate of Return on Capital
14. Capital earnings, line 12 above $_____ divided by total
    assets, financial statement (beginning of year)
    $_____ x 100
15. Equals RATE OF RETURN ON CAPITAL .... _____ %
16. Net Farm Production
17. Gross profit, Schedule F... $_____
18. Less feed purchased, Schedule F.................................... $_____
19. Plus sale of breeding stock, line 3 above........................... $_____
20. Plus inventory change, line 4 above (+ or −)...................... $_____
21. Plus inventory change, line 5 above (+ or −)...................... $_____
22. Equals NET FARM PRODUCTION .... $_____
23. Rate of Capital Turnover
24. Net farm production, line 22 above $_____ divided by total
    assets from financial statement (beginning of year)
    $_____ x 100
25. Equals RATE OF CAPITAL TURNOVER .... _____ %
26. Production Per $1 Expense
27.   Net farm production, line 22 above $_____ divided by
        (expenses, Schedule F, "Total Deductions" $_____ less feed
        purchased, Schedule F, $_____) $_____
28. Equals PRODUCTION PER $1 EXPENSE .... $_____
29. Machinery, Power and Facilities Cost per Acre
30. Repairs, maintenance, Schedule F.................................... $_____
31. Plus machine hire, Schedule F...................................... $_____
32. Plus gasoline, fuel, oil, Schedule F................................. $_____
33. Plus utilities, Schedule F .... $_____
34. Plus auto expense, farm share, Schedule F.......................... $_____
35. Plus other machinery and facility expenses (if any) Schedule F ...... $_____
36. _____ $_____
37. Plus depreciation, Schedule F, (except breeding stock) .... $_____
38. Equals total machinery, power and facilities cost .... $_____
39. Machinery, power and facilities cost $_____, line 38
    above, divided by total acres _____ A.
40. Equals MACHINERY, POWER AND FACILITIES
    COST PER ACRE.. $_____
41. Machinery and Power Investment per Acre
42. Value of machinery, equipment, tractors, trucks and auto
    from financial statement (beginning of year) $_____
    divided by total acres _____A.
43. Equals MACHINERY AND POWER INVESTMENT PER ACRE................. $_____
44. Net Farm Production per Man
45. Months of operator labor, line 10 above, _____ month
    plus months of family labor, line 11 above, _____
    month plus months of hired labor (labor hired, Schedule F.
    line 29 $_____ ÷ $_____ average monthly wage),
    _____month equals total months labor _____
46. Total months of labor, line 45 above _____ ÷ 12 equals
    man-years _____
47. Net farm production, line 22 above $_____ divided by
    man-years, line 46 above _____
48. Equals NET FARM PRODUCTION PER MAN.............................. $_____

*Prepared by H.B. Howell, Iowa State University.

Farm Financial Ratios

Just as there are a number of ways to measure and evaluate production efficiencies of your farming operation, financial ratios can be used for a similar purpose on the business side.

A financial ratio is simply a comparison of two measurements of a business. These two measurements are expressed in terms of a ratio or one as a percentage of the other. Each ratio is designed to highlight some particular phase of the financial condition of your business.

Primary function of financial ratios is to permit you to keep track of the financial side of your business without having to devote a lot of time to detailed study of individual records. They aid you in understanding your accounting figures. Since the financial ratios to be discussed can be obtained from figures contained primarily on the balance sheet and operating statement, they can be calculated in a matter of minutes.

Ratios provide the needed insight into the financial strengths and weaknesses of your business. Then production plans and credit projections can be directed toward building on these strengths and shoring up the weaknesses.

Because of the growth in farm credit needs, a well developed set of financial statements and their accompanying ratios are particularly important tools for demonstrating your managerial ability to your lender and obtaining the necessary credit to conduct a profitable operation.

Maximum value of financial ratios comes from comparing them over a period of years. Otherwise, you have no way of measuring how well you have progressed. These ratios provide an early warning of potential financial problems. By studying past ratios of your business as well as comparing them with standard guidelines set by your lender, any changes from expected ratio values can signal certain areas that need attention.

Many ratios can be used for analyzing your business, but outlined here are those that are especially meaningful and most frequently examined by lenders. These ratios measure adequacy of capital and profitability.

ADEQUACY OF CAPITAL

The ratios in this category are obtained from the balance sheet and reflect the financial soundness of the business.

Current ratio is one of the most used of all ratios. It measures the liquidity of your business—the shortrun ability of your operation to service debt.

$$\text{Current ratio} = \frac{\text{Total current assets}}{\text{Total current liabilities}}$$

Current assets are those that turn over during a normal year's operation. Examples are crops, feed, or livestock held for sale and cash on hand. Current liabilities are debts that will come due within the year. Since this ratio compares total current assets with total current liabilities, it demonstrates the adequacy of current assets, if liquidated, to pay off annual debts as they come due.

A ratio of 2:1 would be considered good by most lenders. It indicates that there are $2 worth of current assets to cover each $1 of current debt. A farm business with a ratio of less than 1:1 could be in serious financial trouble. Your interpretation of this ratio depends a great deal on how you value current assets. You should value crops and livestock for sale at near current market price.

Current debt ratio is another measure of liquidity showing the debt structure between current and total liabilities. It indicates the portion of your total debt that must be paid within the year.

$$\text{Current debt ratio} = \frac{\text{Total current liabilities}}{\text{Total liabilities}}$$

A ratio of 1:3, for instance, means that 33% of the total farm debt must be paid within the next year. The higher the ratio, the greater will be the drain on cash flow and the more the risk of being unable to repay current debts on time. A high ratio of current to total liabilities may indicate a need to refinance some short term debts.

Current debt to worth ratio compares current liabilities to net worth rather than to current assets as is the case with the current ratio.

$$\text{Current debt to worth} = \frac{\text{Total current liabilities}}{\text{Net worth}}$$

This ratio recognizes that the ability of the operator to pay current debts depends on equity in the business—his ability to pay debts either through the use of current assets or by borrowing on equity. A business may show a poor current ratio, yet be in a secure financial position if net worth is high relative to current debts.

Leverage (debt to worth) ratio is similar to the preceding ratio, except that it relates total debt to net worth. It reflects soundness of your business.

$$\text{Leverage (debt to worth)} = \frac{\text{Total liabilities}}{\text{Net worth}}$$

This ratio compares creditors' contributions of capital (total liabilities) to your own contributions (net worth). A ratio of 2:1 means that creditors have $2 invested for every $1 you have put into the business. The higher the ratio, the larger the share creditors have in your farm's assets and the greater the risk exposure to both your creditors and you.

Equity-value ratio, being a measure of your net worth in relation to total assets, shows the portion of total assets paid for and owned by you, clear of financial claims.

$$\text{Equity-value ratio} = \frac{\text{Net worth}}{\text{Total assets}}$$

A ratio of 1:2.5 means that you own 40% of all your total assets, while your creditors have a 60% claim to them. Increases in this ratio over time reflect an improved financial situation.

Net capital ratio is a measure of the solvency position of the business—ability of your business to pay off all debts if it were forced to liquidate. It tells your lender if there are potential problems in recovering the loan if the business should fail.

$$\text{Net capital ratio} = \frac{\text{Total assets}}{\text{Total liabilities}}$$

A ratio of 3:1 means that there are $3 of assets to cover each $1 of debt. A ratio of less than 1:1 would mean that your business is insolvent and cannot cover all its debts.

PROFITABILITY

These ratios are obtained from information contained in both the balance sheet and the operating statement. These ratios become increasingly important as profits narrow in relation to volume.

Profit to gross income ratio relates volume of business to profit.

$$\text{Profit to gross income} = \frac{\text{Profit (net income)}}{\text{Gross income}}$$

Profit is defined as net farm income and gross income (the measure for volume of business) is total receipts of the business less purchased feed and livestock. This ratio shows the dollars (gross income) required to produce $1 in profit.

Profit to net worth measures return earned on the farmer's equity capital investment in the business. Profit is again defined as net farm income.

$$\text{Profit to net worth} = \frac{\text{Profit (net income)}}{\text{Net worth}}$$

This ratio demonstrates the profitability of investing equity capital in the farm business.

INTERPRETING FINANCIAL RATIOS

We have purposely avoided suggesting what financial ratios should be, since there is no best ratio for all farms.

Interpret ratios as they relate to each other—don't pay undue attention to any one ratio independent of the others. Some lending institutions, farm operators and farm advisors have a selected group of ratios that they believe give a composite picture of the farm business. These ratios are interpreted as a group rather than individually.

For example, a young farmer may have a current debt to worth ratio that is much higher than an older farmer of similar ability. However, this same young operator may show a much more desirable profit to net worth than the older farmer, again due to the lower net worth base.

Type of enterprise and amount of capital relative to labor required to produce income is another reason why ratios vary among farms.

The prevailing conditions can affect how critical a certain ratio may be when evaluated. A tight current ratio, for example, would be further jeopardized when farm prices are declining. Though the relation of net worth to total liabilities might be suitable when land values are rising sharply, the same ratio could be considerably less favorable if land prices leveled out or declined. The way assets are valued, conservatively or liberally, can make a difference in how you interpret ratios.

Planning Procedures

Long range planning enables you to take an overall look at your available resources and to organize them into an operation that permits maximizing returns.

A long run farm plan should be based on a sufficient time period to permit making changes or adjustments in the basic resources of land, labor, capital and management. This type of planning may be done with conventional budgeting procedures or through the use of computer linear programming, which is available through various sources.

Regardless of which tools are used, certain procedures should be followed in the planning process. They aid in developing a plan which will contribute to the needs and objectives of the farm family. The procedures outlined by Pennsylvania farm management specialists are as follows:

Goals of the family are a consideration in any farm plan. Emphasize the major goals first, but their achievement may also contribute to the fulfillment of lesser goals. Family goals may include a new home, providing income for retirement, vacation trip, dairy herd with a 600 pound butterfat average and college education for the children.

Some of these goals may require more income than the farm is presently capable of producing. Some ways to boost income may be to increase the physical size, use more capital, and add more labor. Other ways may include doing things right at the right time and reorganizing enterprises.

List available resources so you can accurately define what inputs can be included in your farm plan.

● Land resource includes not only the acres in the farm or available through rental, but the kinds of land and what it is capable of producing–its yield capabilities, what crops it will profitably produce, possible need for irrigation, etc.

● Labor resource includes hours of family labor available, if you should consider hiring outside labor, cost of labor and if custom operators might be obtained to perform some of the jobs on the farm.

● Management is a difficult resource to measure, but relates to the ability of the operator to organize his resources and to properly execute a plan from start to finish. Some measures might include get-

ting crops planted and harvested on time and comparing yields with neighbors' and standards for the area. Is livestock performance and production average, above average or below average? How well are commodities marketed? Does the operator financially analyze his business at the end of the year? Is he willing to consider new enterprises? Does he shop around before be buys? Does the operator make an annual plan of his crops, fertilizer needs, seed? Is machinery inspected and repaired to prevent costly breakdowns.?

Develop enterprise budgets. This is an absolute essential for any successful farm plan. The enterprise budgets are the source of input and output data. In effect, they indicate the efficiency of resource use and distribution of the basic resources (land, labor and capital) among the various alternative activities to be considered in the farm plan. The budgets are effective in providing comparisons among the different activities. Example enterprise budgets are given at the end of this discussion.

Labor required and its distribution is critical to an effective operation. If available family labor is short in some periods of the year, some other arrangements must be made to fill in during those periods when it is needed. Certain jobs might be performed by a custom operator.

When figuring labor requirements, it is important to include all labor such as time to prepare equipment for field work, putting fuel in the tractor, etc. In livestock production, labor for repairing buildings and equipment, preparing feed and observing animals, are all part of total labor needs.

Capital investment required. Not all farm plans to boost income may require additional capital. Many farm operators are able to accomplish this objective by reorganizing their crop and livestock enterprises. However, if this does not produce the desired results, additional capital will need to be considered.

When employing capital, the manager should keep two items in mind. First, he should consider what rate of return is desired from the capital and how much risk is attached to making the additional investment. If risk is involved, set the rate of return sufficiently high to provide some margin of protection.

Secondly, is the rate of depreciation properly charged? For example, a building depreciated over 40 years no longer makes sense, even though the building may be structurally sound for that period of time. There is a high probability that the functional value will be obsolete long before the 40 years is up.

Therefore, set depreciation rates to reflect functional value of the item and the fact that changing technology could make it obsolete in a much shorter period of time. This could mean that an investment will need to pay for itself in a much shorter time than might otherwise be the case.

Alternatives to the farm business. Though planning provides a guide to assist the farm family in reaching its goals, constraints sometimes may prevent development of the business to the point where it provides the necessary income. When this happens, the operator must carefully examine possible alternatives. Some questions are: Should the farm operation be continued as is, curtailed or closed out? Could the business be sold and a larger farm purchased to provide more income? Would the operator and perhaps other members of the family consider off-farm employment?

Compare new plan with present plan. Even though a written plan may not be available for the present operation, one should be made to determine the resources used and the income produced. This plan can then be compared with a new one, item by item or activity by activity.

Being able to compare the two plans is helpful to the farm manager. He can determine what resource reorganization is involved and evaluate how the new plan may affect the operational procedures of the farm business. Does the new plan call for greater specialization? Are fewer or more purchased inputs used in the new plan? Will the new plan require more attention to marketing—both buying and selling?

Farmstead and field rearrangement may be desirable, but not necessarily practical or important enough to implement a new plan. These should not be undertaken unless they contribute significantly to efficiency, which could in turn produce greater returns.

Example Enterprise Budgets

Costs and Returns per Acre of Corn

Budget item		
Land value per acre	$1,150.00	
Yield (bu)	135.00	
Fertilizer (lbs)		
N-P_2O_5-K_2O	170-50-90	
Direct cost per acre		
Fertilizer cost	$ 49.80	
Limestone	1.70	
Seed	12.00	
Herbicides & insecticides (materials)	13.00	
Machine operation	19.50	
Interest on operating capital & miscellaneous costs	8.00	
Total direct cost	$104.00	
Indirect costs per acre		
Machinery & equipment	$ 25.00	
Grain storage cost	12.00	
Taxes & land maintenance	10.50	
Interest on land at 8%	92.00	
Labor at $4 per hour	16.00	
Total cost except management	$259.50	
Summary		
Estimated price per bushel	$ 2.00	$ 3.00
Gross return per acre	270.00	405.00
Income over direct cost	166.00	301.00
Management return	10.50	145.50
Labor & management return per acre	26.50	161.50
Labor & management return per hour	6.60	40.40
Land & management return per acre	102.50	237.50

Costs and Returns per Sow (15 Pigs—2 Farrowings/yr)

Budget Item	High investment facilities; farrow 6 times per year
Income	
Market animals (31.9 cwt at $34)	$1,085.00
Breeders (2-1/8 cwt at $30)	64.00
Gross income	$1,149.00
Direct costs	
Feed	
Corn (197 bu at $2)	$ 394.00
Purchased feed (2,550 lbs at $10)	255.00
Total feed	$ 649.00
Veterinary and medicine	10.00
Breeding	6.00
Marketing	27.00
Power, fuel and equipment repair	50.00
Miscellaneous (bedding, supplies)	15.00
Total direct cost	$ 757.00
Direct cost w/o home-grown feed	$ 363.00
Income over direct cost (rounded)	392.00
Overhead expense	
Investment overhead	$ 206.00
Total labor (28 hrs at $3.50)	98.00
Total overhead	$ 304.00
Total cost	$1,061.00
Per cwt of market hog	31.25
Summary	
Net return to management	$ 88.00
Returns to labor and management	186.00
Rate earned on investment	18.3%

52

Farm Business Planning—
Preparing Unit Budgets

Business profits hinge on effectively using all your resources.
A unit budget can help you properly allocate the resources you have.

Each farm has different resources. Total acres, the number of tillable acres, soil types, buildings and facilities will vary from one farm to another. There are also wide variations in the amount of labor, operating capital and investment capital that are available to a farmer. The effectiveness of farm management will change depending on the abilities of the individual in charge. These varying factors can cause farms that are the same size and type to end up with entirely different overall management plans.

Good records, either your own or those of the previous operator, are the basis of the highest profit plan. If these are not available, you must turn to college research information, your county agent, and your ASCS office. The first two can give you average costs and income for your size and type of farm. The ASCS office has crop production information on your farm.

A budget based on one unit, an acre of land or a livestock unit, is a good place to start when considering a new farm plan. Going through all the costs and income on this basis gives you the net return per acre or animal unit.

Include all items of cost and return which are applicable in your unit budget. Use accurate figures that apply to your situation. A budget is no better than the information from which it is prepared. Averages from research can't be as accurate for your operation as your own figures.

Each unit budget should stand on its own. All costs and returns should relate directly to the enterprise. When budgeting a unit of livestock, include feed costs at their market value in your area. If you enter crops into the livestock end of an operation at cost of production, you could actually be making money on crops and losing it on livestock—yet the budget might show a livestock profit. These results could mean a low profit plan.

Make a unit budget for each crop you can grow. Some crops may not be very popular in your locality. However, if the crop is marketable and will grow and you feel you might make it a part of your operation, go ahead and budget it. Individual preference usually has more to do with the livestock enterprises which are budgeted.

Your unit budget will be misleading, if you don't include all applicable costs. Interest rates should only vary between long and short term rates. Use the same value per hour of labor throughout the budgets. Costs may not be exactly correct in absolute terms, yet your results will be good in comparative terms. Since the unit budget is used primarily to compare various alternatives, values and rates must stay the same throughout.

Fixed costs include interest on the investment or rent, taxes, insurance and depreciation. These items should be included in each budget. Don't include an interest charge on one budget and forget it on another. This would make your results misleading. Depreciation on buildings is applicable where crops are stored rather than sold at harvest. The increased capital use in farming makes it essential to include accurate fixed costs.

The livestock budget involves insurance, depreciation, interest and taxes on the buildings used, but not on the cropland. This allows the livestock and crop budgets to stand on their own.

Variable costs include seed, fertilizer, herbicides, insecticides, lime, oil, fuel, repairs, maintenance, depreciation, interest and taxes on equipment. Insurance on equipment and crops should be included, as should interest on the money tied up in the crops.

The livestock budget should include feed at market value, animal depreciation if applicable, interest on the animal investment, interest on the feed inventory to be used, breeding, veterinary and medicine costs, electricity and water costs, supplies, testing and trucking expenses. Taxes and insurance on the animals should be included. Labor is a cost, too.

MAKING THE BUDGET

When you have all these figures, you are ready to prepare the unit budgets for your farm plan. Ordinarily you should start with the crops and then go on to livestock enterprises. The following unit budget is used only to illustrate the procedure. You won't use the figures shown—perhaps not even the crop, but the budget outline will help you include all costs associated with the enterprise. All you need is some lined paper so you can keep the budget as neat as possible while allowing room to include all items of income and expense.

Crop unit budgets are quite detailed and complete. Anything less will not show you the true net profits per unit. Your records may allow you to break down the budget figures even more. You may have the figures for each step in the production of crops such as plowing, harrowing, planting, etc. If you have these figures use them, because they will allow for easier and better comparisons later on.

ONE ACRE OF HAY (alfalfa)

Costs		
Fixed		
Interest on land investment	$14.00	
Taxes on land	6.00	
Total fixed costs		$ 20.00
Variable - growing		
1.4 tons manure at $5	7.00	
131 lbs. fertilizer at $170/ton	11.14	
Seed	5.00	
All other	2.60	
Total growing		25.74
Variable - harvesting		
6.3 hrs. labor at $2.50	15.75	
3.5 hrs. tractor work at $2.30	8.05	
Equipment costs.	13.40	
All other	2.09	
Total harvesting		39.29
Variable - storing and selling	8.94	8.94
Total cost per acre		93.97
Income		
3 tons at $40	120.00	
Value of aftermath pasture	3.50	
Total income		123.50
Net profit per acre		$ 29.53

You might raise some questions about the budget example. Why storing and selling costs on hay? This applies if you store hay or other crops to take advantage of higher prices later. If sold from the field, this cost would not be included. If the hay is fed to livestock, these costs will commonly be expensed in the livestock unit budget. These costs may even be part of the building which houses the livestock and may be a direct part of housing costs.

The labor costs used could be the hourly rate paid by small companies in the area or the actual rate paid for hired farm labor. The tractor cost per hour is the amount directly related to the tractor for the hay crop. The equipment cost includes interest, depreciation and repairs on all hay equipment. The fixed interest and tax costs are those paid on the land. They don't include taxes paid on buildings, except in the case of crop and machinery storage facilities. The latter may be part of equipment costs.

Livestock unit budget shows the profit per animal or animal unit, just as the crop budget shows the profit per acre for the crop. In this case we used one sow and two litters as a unit.

Again, try to use figures applicable to your situation. If you don't have much invested in buildings and equipment for livestock, your figures should reflect this. Your variable costs may be quite different too. A highly automated farrowing setup could mean only seven to eight hours labor per sow, so labor costs should be adjusted. Production and prices must relate to your particular situation too.

ONE SOW AND TWO LITTERS FEEDER PIGS

Costs		
Fixed		
$120 investment at 12%	$ 14.40	
$600 total capital at 8%	48.00	
Total fixed costs		$ 62.40
Variable costs		
36 bu. corn at $2.50	90.00	
500 lbs. protein at 8¢	40.00	
18 hrs. labor at $2.50	45.00	
Veterinary and medicine	13.00	
Power, fuel and equipment	10.00	
1 acre pasture	5.00	
Taxes on livestock and feed	3.00	
Other costs	5.00	
Total variable costs		211.00
Total costs per sow		273.40
Income		
13 pigs (40 lbs.) at $30	390.00	
1 sow, 400 lbs. at 30¢	120.00	
Total income		510.00
Net profit per sow		$236.60

COMBINING UNIT BUDGETS

Now that you have budgeted each of the crop and livestock enterprises that should be considered in the final farm plan, you are ready to combine them into an operation which nets the most profit. A procedure is outlined on the pages that follow. The object is to allocate limited resources to enterprises with the greatest return for each unit of that resource used. More enterprises can be evaluated by use of a computer and what is referred to as linear programming.

Include as many high profit enterprises in your operation as possible. Total acres, tillable acres, labor available, etc., will set certain limitations. However, specifying the limitations relative to the units budgeted will allow you to proceed, with the final plan being most profitable.

Farm Business Planning—
Enterprise and Resource Analysis

Resources need to be properly balanced between enterprises. Total acres, soil type, weather, buildings, available capital and your management ability all need to be considered.

The following procedure is important if you are considering more than two enterprises in your farm plan. Try to stay below 10 enterprises or the paperwork will be too much. If you have this many to consider, you probably should seek outside help.

This procedure of farm planning may seem long and laborious at first, but the most difficult part is getting good information to use in the unit budgets. If you have them prepared, the rest of the work is primarily arithmetic.

On the previous page we prepared unit budgets. Without them we would not be able to take these next steps. The more detailed your unit budgets, the easier these steps will be. The operating capital figure, labor requirements and net profits are the most significant.

Resources available and the amount required per unit of each enterprise should be prepared as shown in Table 1. The net return per unit as derived from the unit budget is included. If there are any reasons why acreage or number of livestock should be limited in a given enterprise this should be noted, so that a larger enterprise will not be budgeted.

Break down your available labor seasonally, quarterly, or monthly so it reflects availability during crucial labor periods. Be sure to include family labor, if applicable. Notice that 1,800 hours of family labor are available during the summer in the example. Usually about 3,000 hours of operator labor are available during the year, but if other interests demand time, limit your labor accordingly.

You may have more tillable acres than you wish to plant to the highest profit crop. Specify this as a limit, too. In the example, the farmer does not want to plant corn on all tillable acres due to soil type and weather. He feels the risk is too great; therefore corn was limited to a maximum of 125 acres.

Don't forget the operating capital limit. This should include the cash you have available for your needs, plus the loan limit from your creditor.

Hired labor is a variable expense and requires operating capital. Family labor is a fixed expense, not requiring operating capital. Be sure this is correct in your unit budgets so it will be right when you figure the operating capital used per unit.

If you want to include enterprises that would require additional investment capital, include a capital investment limit. Set this limit according to your equity, personal funds available and the amount you can borrow for this purpose.

Most agricultural colleges publish farm management manuals which might help you. This is especially true for the amount and timing of labor requirements. Contact the agricultural economics department at your state university, or check with your county agent or creditor.

Maximum units which can be included in each enterprise while staying within your resource limitations are shown in Table 2. The maximum net returns possible from each enterprise are also developed and entered into this table.

To find the maximum units you can include, divide the amount of the resource available by the requirement per unit of each enterprise. For instance, from Table 1 we take the 1,800 hours of May-August available labor and divide it by the three hours required per acre of corn. This farmer could grow 600 acres of corn with labor available during that period. Carry out this procedure for each enterprise and resource. All figures are based on Table 1 and entered in Table 2.

The bottom row in Table 2 is maximum returns to management. To get this figure, go down the columns in Table 2 and find the smallest number for each enterprise. This number represents the maximum number of units of the enterprise which you can include in your farm plan. The resource to the left of the number is the limiting factor. Multiply this smallest number under each enterprise by the net return per enterprise unit in Table 1. The result is the maximum returns to management.

For example, corn with a 125-acre limit is the smallest number in that column. This times the $52 net return per acre from Table 1 means a maximum return of $6,500. Do this for each of the enterprises. Enter the answers in Table 2.

Resource returns per unit are calculated as shown in Table 3. All computations are based on information in Table 1. Divide the amount of resource required per unit of each enterprise into the net returns per unit of the enterprise. Enter the answer in its proper place in Table 3.

During the May-August period, one acre of corn requires three hours of labor. Dividing three into the $52 net return per acre of corn means a $17.33 net return per hour of labor.

All these tables are important in step 4, which will follow later. As we complete the "linear programming" process we must consider the maximum returns to management, the net return per unit of enterprise, and the net return per unit of resource. Table 2 shows us the enterprise that will net the most returns. Since we have limitations we must also consider the returns to both resource and enterprise units. Thus, Tables 1 and 3 help us make the highest profits while staying within our limits.

If no limits exist, you would need only the unit budgets. Whatever enterprise shows the highest net return would be the entire farm operation. But since limitations do exist in most farm situations, you need all three tables. This procedure allows you to arrive at the most profitable final farm plan.

If you are considering an organizational change, it would be quite beneficial to follow this procedure. Even if you aren't figuring on a change, it would be worth your effort. Various possibilities for change will come to mind as you go through the process. It may confirm your ideas or present possible future problems in time to take corrective action.

What has been produced thus far will be used to arrive at a final farm plan on the following page. Though it is "simplified linear programming," the results can be just as good as when a computer is used—the only difference is that you don't include as many alternative enterprises.

Table 1   Enterprise Resource Requirements and Limitations

Resource	Amount available	1 acre corn	1 acre soybeans	1 acre wheat	1 sow and 2 litters
Land:					
Row crop acres	200	1.00	1.00	--	--
Acres for corn	125	1.00	1.00	--	--
Other row crop acres	75	--	1.00	--	--
Total acres	240	1.00	1.00	1.00	--
Labor:					
Jan.—Apr.	1,000	1.00	.75	.30	22.50
May—Aug.	1,800	3.00	2.75	1.50	12.50
Sept.—Dec.	1,000	2.50	1.50	1.20	15.00
Operating capital	$7,000	$45.00	$20.00	$25.00	$150.00
Return to management	--	$52.00	$32.00	$ 7.00	$ 86.00

Table 2   Maximum Amount of Each Enterprise Possible

Resource	Amount available	1 acre corn	1 acre soybeans	1 acre wheat	1 sow and 2 litters
Land:					
Row crop acres	200	200	200	--	--
Acres for corn	125	125	--	--	--
Other row crop acres	75	--	--	--	--
Total acres	240	240	240	240	--
Labor:					
Jan.—Apr.	1,000	1,000	750	3,333	44
May—Aug.	1,800	600	654	1,200	144
Sept.—Dec.	1,000	400	666	833	66
Operating capital	$7,000	$155.50	$ 350	$ 280	$ 46
Maximum return to management	--	$6,500	$6,400	$1,680	$3,784

Table 3   Net Return Per Unit of Resource

Resource	1 acre corn	1 acre soybeans	1 acre wheat	1 sow and 2 litters
Land:				
Row crop acres	$52.00	$32.00	--	--
Acres for corn	52.00	32.00	--	--
Other row crop acres	--	32.00	--	--
Total acres	52.00	32.00	$ 7.00	--
Labor:				
Jan.—Apr.	52.00	42.66	23.33	3.47
May—Aug.	17.33	11.63	4.66	6.88
Sept.—Dec.	20.80	21.33	5.83	5.73
Operating capital	$ 1.16	$ 1.60	.28	.57

Farm Business Planning—
Combining Resources Into Enterprises

The final step in planning the farm business involves bringing the facts from the resource and enterprise analysis tables together.

On the previous pages, enterprises which could make the most profits individually were determined. Enterprises which would return the most profit per unit of input used were also calculated. Further, the maximum amount of each enterprise which could be included in the farm plan, considering the resources (land, labor, capital, etc.) was resolved. Now these analyses must be put together to arrive at the final farm plan.

Prepare a table similar to the one shown below. Make a column for each resource listed in Table 1 on the previous page. At the end put a column for returns to management. Under each heading, enter the total amount of each resource available—this comes from Table 1 on the previous page. The rest of the table will be completed using simple arithmetic.

Now look at Table 2 on the previous page for the enterprise that will yield the most total profits. It's shown in the bottom row of Table 2. In the example, we see that corn will return the greatest profits as an enterprise. Notice also that corn returns the highest net per acre and pays the most per hour of labor. Remember that the limit on corn acres has previously been set at 125 acres.

Taking the 125 acres of corn and multiplying the resource requirement per acre given in Table 1 gives the resources used by the corn enterprise. Enter these amounts under the unused row in the new table. Subtract the amount of resources used in the corn enterprise from the total available. This gives the amount of resources available for other enterprises. Also enter the total profits from corn in the return to management column.

Now look for the next most profitable enterprise. Soybeans look best. However, the production of soybeans will use all the remaining row crop acreage that can be farmed, so you should first check to see if some other enterprise will yield higher profits per acre. According to Table 3 on the previous page, returns per acre from soybeans are greater than from wheat. Soybeans also produce greater returns per hour of labor and return more per dollar of operating capital.

The unused row in the new table tells us that there are 75 row crop acres available for soybeans. Multiplying this acreage by the resources required per acre of soybeans grown will give the total resources soybeans will use. Comparing resource requirements for 75 acres of soybeans shows that there are plenty of resources left over from the corn to support the 75 acres of soybeans, except for operating capital. Because there is only $1,375 of operating capital left to produce soybeans, the acreage grown must be cut back to less than the 75 acres available. In our example, the remaining operating capital will limit soybean production to 69 acres and the remaining 46 acres will have to go uncropped. You'll also notice that we have some remaining unused labor.

Add up the returns to management from the enterprises. The farmer in the example will get about $8,708 return from his farm business—provided we used the right information for his situation. It also assumes the correct decisions were made each step of the way.

Upon completing the farm plan, you should go back and check the unit budgets. Also be sure your figuring was correct. If you feel that wrong figures were used, correct them and start over.

THE FINAL FARM PLAN

Enterprise	Row crop acres	Acres for corn	Other row crop acres	Total acres	Jan.-Apr. labor (hrs.)	May-Aug. labor (hrs.)	Sept.-Dec. labor (hrs.)	Operating capital	Return to management
Unused	200	125	75	240	1,000	1,800	1,000	$7,000	--
Corn	125	125	0	125	125	375	313	$5,625	$6,500
Unused	75	0	75	115	875	1,425	687	$1,375	--
Soybeans	69	0	69	69	52	190	104	$1,380	$2,208
Unused	6	0	6	46	823	1,235	583	$ -5	--
TOTAL									$8,708

Filing Systems for a Farm Business

These suggestions and the indexing guide may be helpful to you in setting up a workable, easily maintained file of farming records and management information.

A handy, simple filing system can be a big help in management of a farming or ranching operation. The expense mainly depends on the size and quality of filing cabinet you use, plus the nominal cost of dividers and file folders. If the file is for farm records, it's a deductible business expense.

A suggested index for an agricultural file is shown. It's set up both alphabetically and numerically and includes a wide variety of subjects which should be adaptable to almost all types of farming or ranching operations. You can add to it or simplify it as you prefer.

Follow the index of subjects shown or prepare your own subject list, as you file material. You may want to shift some sections from the back to the front of a drawer if they are used frequently. Put the file number or subject on each item, so another member of the family can do the actual filing.

Determine from the list whether each item to be filed will fit logically under one of the headings. If not, add new headings to your index where necessary and remove those not used. Numbers have been omitted in the index to permit you to add headings, and you can add decimals where needed.

After you have started your filing system, you may want to prepare a revised list of subjects for quick reference when filing material.

10. Accounts and Records
10.1 Farm Account Records
10.2 Home Account Records
10.3 Income Tax Returns
10.4 Inventories
10.5 Net Worth Statements

11. Addresses
11.1 Farm Business
11.2 Home Business
11.3 Personal

12. Agricultural Economics
12.1 Budgets
12.2 Credit Information
12.3 Farm Plans
12.4 Leases
12.5 Property Transfer Info.
12.6 Reference Material
12.7 Tax Information

13. Bank
13.1 Deposit Slips
13.2 Notes on Valuable Papers
13.3 Statements

14. Bills Paid —Receipts
14.1 Crop Expenses
14.2 Feed Bought
14.3 Improvements
14.4 Labor
14.5 Machinery
14.6 Taxes

15. Bills—Unpaid
15.1 Unpaid Bills

16. Correspondence
16.1 Farm Business
16.2 Home Business
16.3 Personal

17. Crops and Soils
17.1 ASC Material
17.2 Chemicals Applied
17.3 Farm Maps
17.4 Fertilizer & Lime Use
17.5 Reference Material
17.6 SCS Material
17.7 Soil Tests
17.8 Yield Records

18. Dairy
18.1 Breeding Records
18.2 Feeding Records
18.3 Herd Health
18.4 Production Records
18.5 Registration Papers
18.6 Reference Material

19. Farm Buildings
19.1 Landscaping
19.2 Plans
19.3 Reference Material

20. Fruit and Vegetables
20.1 Production Records
20.2 Reference Material

21. Home Business
21.1 Equipment Guarantees
21.2 Equipment Instructions and Manuals
21.3 Food-Canned, Frozen, Stored
21.4 Garment Care
21.5 Health Records
21.6 Household Inventory
21.7 Household Records
21.8 Magazine Subscriptions
21.9 Vegetable Garden

22. Home Reference Material
22.1 Clothing
22.2 Crafts
22.3 Family Living - Child Development
22.4 Food
22.5 Health - Safety
22.6 Home Furnishings
22.7 Home Management
22.8 Insurance
22.9 Remodeling - Bldg.

23. Insect & Disease Control
23.1 Reference Material
23.2 Spray Materials

24. Livestock
24.1 Breeding Records
24.2 Feeding Records
24.3 Livestock Health
24.4 Reference Material
24.5 Registration Papers

25. Machinery and Equipment
25.1 Car Records
25.2 Guarantees
25.3 Manuals
25.4 Reference Material
25.5 Tractor Records
25.6 Truck Records

26. Organizations
26.1 Church
26.2 Extension Groups
26.3 4-H Clubs
26.4 Farm

27. Personal
27.1 Birthday Dates
27.2 Christmas Card List
27.3 Gift Suggestions
27.4 Reading Book List
27.5 Service & Veteran
27.6 Special Interest

28. Poultry
28.1 Feeding Records
28.2 Flock Health
28.3 Production Records
28.4 Reference Material

29. Supply Catalogs
29.1 Farm
29.2 Home

30. Valuable Papers
30.1 Abstracts
30.2 Birth Certificates
30.3 Deeds
30.4 Government Bonds
30.5 Insurance Policies
30.6 Marriage Certificates
30.7 Notes & Mortgages
30.8 Stock Certificates
30.9 Wills

31. Inactive Business Records
31.1 Record Books
31.2 Receipts & Income Records
31.3 Cancelled Checks & Deposit Slips
31.4 Income Tax Reports

Partial Budgeting

This shortcut budgeting procedure can be used to determine if an investment or change in some portion of your business will be profitable.

Many management decisions concerning an investment or change in your farming or ranching operations can be made rather easily and quickly using partial budgeting.

Some examples of decisions that can be made by partial budgeting are whether or not to irrigate a particular crop, expand an enterprise, purchase a new machine, custom hire or own a combine or some other piece of equipment, and graze wheat or harvest it for grain.

Analysis and computations are held to a minimum with partial budgeting. Only those costs and returns that change as a result of adjustments in one segment of your business are considered. Credits from a proposed change (added income and/or reduced cost) are weighed against the debits (added cost and/or reduced income).

A partial budget tells you only if a proposed change or investment will be more or less profitable than the present situation with which it is compared. It doesn't indicate if the change will be the most profitable use of the resources. However, this can be determined by comparing a series of partial budgets using your resources in several different ways.

A partial budget worksheet shown on the back provides a format for making your own partial budgets. Note that the worksheet has columns headed profitability and repayment capacity. The profitability analysis considers the income generating ability of a change or investment on the accrual basis. Then if the adjustment appears profitable, a repayment capacity analysis is made. It deals only with the cash generating ability of the change. Finally, if the repayment capacity analysis is favorable, a financial analysis is made to determine the return per dollar of added investment and the years required to pay off debt.

To demonstrate the partial budget procedure, the worksheet has been filled in using an example (for illustrative purposes only) provided by Wisconsin farm management specialists, with some modifications. The business change being considered is whether to drop a five sow, two-litter-per-year feeder pig enterprise in favor of adding 10 milking cows to the dairy herd, with a premise being that the operator wants an additional $1,000 for family living in addition to a profit. Here is a step-by-step discussion of the example.

Profitability analysis (first column of the worksheet) considers both cash and non-cash (accrual basis) annual costs and returns from the proposed change or investment.

● **Credit** side of the worksheet consists of added income and reduced costs as a result of the proposed change. Added annual income includes the sale of milk from 10 cows averaging 15,000 pounds, 2.5 cull cows, and 4.5 calves. Reduced costs (operating) include homegrown and purchased feed and other costs associated with the feeder pig enterprise. Homegrown feed is charged at market price. Total credits ($28,615) is the sum of total annual added income and total annual reduced cost. Enter this figure at the bottom left of the worksheet.

● **Debit** side of the worksheet consists of three categories–added investment costs, added operating costs, and reduced income. Added fixed investment costs in the example include an annual charge for depreciation, interest, repairs, taxes, and insurance on the investment for remodeling the barn (20% of the remodeling cost was used) and interest (charged at 15%) on the investment of 10 dairy cows. (Though not included in the example, consideration should be given to possible income tax savings on interest costs. Also, where applicable,

consider investment credit on eligible machinery and other investments.) Added operating costs are listed, including a charge of $1,000 for family living. In the example, the operator will be putting in 400 hours of additional labor annually. He wants this labor income for family living expenses. Reduced income is the loss of income from the sale of feeder pigs and cull sows.

Total debits ($16,395) is the sum of added annual investment costs and reduced income from the proposed change. Enter this figure at the bottom left of worksheet to obtain the change in net income (total credits minus total debits) recorded in the line below ($12,220).

Repayment capacity analysis is the next step if the profitability analysis turns in a positive net income figure. The same steps, using the same categories as in the previous analysis, are used; the difference is that only cash costs and returns are considered. The significance of this analysis is that it deals only with the cash generating ability of the proposed change. It reflects whether the proposed change is able to pay its own way.

● **Credit** side of the worksheet, under added income from the proposed change, remains the same as in the previous analysis. All returns are cash in this particular example. Reduction in cost figures is lower. Whereas homegrown feed was charged at market price in the profitability analysis, the cash cost of producing it is used in this analysis. Also, the operator's labor is omitted since it is not a cash cost.

● **Debit** side of the worksheet deserves special attention since annual investment costs may or may not be cash costs. For instance, cash interest cost will depend on how much of the investment money is borrowed. Also, actual cash interest cost will decrease as the debt is paid. Perhaps the best way to handle this is to use an average annual cost. Taxes and insurance are cash costs; depreciation is not. Under added operating costs, homegrown feed once again is charged at the cash cost of producing it, not at what it will sell for on the market. Reduced income is all cash in the example, so it remains the same as in the profitability analysis.

Credits and debits are totaled. These are entered at the bottom right of the worksheet. Total debits ($12,675) are subtracted from total credits ($27,365) to arrive at the change in cash income figure which is ($14,690).

Financial analysis is made if the net income figure from the repayment capacity analysis is positive. The total investment figure in this example is $27,000–barn remodeling, $15,000 and purchase of 10 milk cows, $12,000 (shown under new investment on the debit side of the worksheet). The return per dollar of added investment (45%) is obtained by dividing the change in net income derived from the profitability analysis ($12,220) by the total added investment ($27,000). Since a 15% charge to capital was made in the profitability analysis, the total return to the investment is 60% (15% + 45%). Years required to pay back or generate investment capital (1.8 years) are obtained by dividing total added investment by the net income figure derived in the repayment capacity analysis ($14,690). This indicates time required to repay borrowed money and whether depreciation is slower or faster than repayment ability.

Be practical when reviewing your budget. If the profit from the change is not greatly improved from the existing situation, be especially careful that prices, costs, livestock production, and crop yields are reasonable and attainable. A small variation in any of these could mean a loss rather than a profit. It may be particularly helpful to prepare several budgets using different yields and production figures, prices, and costs.

Select prices that you think will prevail for at least the years required to pay back the investment. Use as much information as you can from your own farm records. Fill in gaps with averages from state record summaries.

Decision to make a change or a new investment should include consideration of factors other than a sufficient profit and cash for family living and debt retirement. These factors should include risk associated with the change, markets, effect on management, availability of capital, and personal preferences.

PARTIAL BUDGET: _____

(Proposed Plan)

CREDIT
Added Return and/or Reduced Cost

Added Return	Profitability Annual Return	Repayment Capacity
Added income		
15,000 # milk sold @ $14 x 10 cows	$21,000	$21,000
2.5 cull cows sold @ $800	$2,000	$2,000
4.5 calves sold @ $150	$675	$675
Total annual added income	$23,675	$23,675
Reduced Costs *Purchased $1,200*		
Feed – Homegrown $2,800	$4,000	$3,150
Supplies, interest, machine, electricity, taxes, etc.	$540	$540
Operator labor (100 hrs.) @ $4	$400	$0
Total annual reduced cost	$4,940	$3,690
TOTAL CREDITS	$28,615	$27,365

FINANCIAL ANALYSIS

Total added investment . . . . $ 27,000
Returns/$ added investment
(Change in net income ÷ added investment). . 45%
Years required to pay back
(Added investment ÷ change in cash income) 1.8 yrs.

$ 28,615 minus $ 16,395
Total Credits   Total Debits

CHANGE IN NET INCOME $ 12,220

DEBIT
Added Cost and/or Reduced Return

Added Cost	Profitability Annual Costs	Repayment Capacity
New investment & added investment costs		
Barn remodeled $15,000	$3,000	$1,500
Cow investment $12,000 (interest) *15%*	$1,800	$900
	$	$
Total annual added investment cost	$4,800	$2,400
Added operating costs *purchased $800*		
Feed – Homegrown $4,400	$5,200	$3,880
Supplies, electricity, death loss, insurance, taxes, etc.	$2,490	$2,490
Operator labor (wants $1,000 for family living)	$1,000	$1,000
Total annual added operating costs	$8,690	$7,370
Reduced Income		
Feeder pigs 75 head @ $35	$2,625	$2,625
Cull sows 2 head @ $140	$280	$280
Total annual reduced income	$2,905	$2,905
TOTAL DEBITS	$16,395	$12,675

$ 27,365 minus $ 12,675
Total Credits   Total Debits

CHANGE IN CASH INCOME $ 14,690

Budgeting Farm Machinery Costs

By budgeting each planned machinery purchase, you'll bring together all the significant costs, fixed and out-of-pocket, needed to make a sound analysis of your needs.

Budgeting the costs of machinery and equipment before purchase is necessary to prevent uneconomical investments. At the same time, it's necessary to avoid possible higher costs for custom hiring or equipment rental. Under-equipping your farm can easily cut your profits by a greater amount than over-equipping adds to costs.

Machinery and equipment involve both fixed and variable costs. Farm records from Kansas show annual equipment costs amount to about 25% of the new cost of the machinery line. About 20% of the annual costs are for fuel, oil and lubrication; 25% cover repairs; and 55% to 60% are fixed costs. So budgeting is important.

FIXED COSTS

Depreciation accounts for over half of the fixed costs. A crude rule of thumb, according to Kansas researchers, is that depreciation will amount to 10%, interest to 3%, and taxes, insurance and housing, 3% of new cost annually.

There is some question about figuring annual depreciation—the problem is which depreciation method, useful life and salvage value to use. Practically speaking, you should use the market "as is" or "trade-in" value depreciation rather than book value. Normally you should take rapid depreciation on machinery—it corresponds closely with the actual market value drop.

The table shows the market value of used farm machinery based on new cost. Consider your normal trading policy and check the years of use. You can get annual depreciation rate by subtracting the figure in the table from 100 and dividing by the number of years used. For instance, if you trade tractors every five years, the market value loss is 57% (100 - 43%). Dividing by five gives an 11.4% annual depreciation rate, based on new cost.

During periods of strong demand for machinery, the used market may be much higher than these figures indicate. However, over the long run it is sound to stick with the more conservative valuations. Rarely will you be able to "luck out" by being in a position to move used equipment on the exceptionally strong market.

Interest. The interest on your investment must be considered a part of machinery costs. Figure 3% of new cost as annual interest cost. If you are short on capital, you may want to use a rate to reflect the higher capital value.

To avoid confusion, use the current rate charged on your machinery loans and half the new cost of the implement. Use the correct interest rate—some loans are made at 8% or 9% simple interest while others are made using add-on interest. A loan quoted at 7% but using the add-on approach may actually be costing you almost 14% simple interest. Use the simple interest rate on half the original cost. If add-on interest is involved, use the stated interest rate but use full new cost.

Taxes, insurance and housing. This group of costs is a small part of total costs, only 3%, but it should be included. Using the thumb rule will put these costs very close to actual. Housing costs will be the same each year—about 1.5% of new cost. One percent will cover your property taxes and .5% will take care of insurance. Include insurance even if you don't buy it.

VARIABLE COSTS

Kansas farm management records show variable costs will range from 40% to 45% of your annual

USED MACHINERY VALUES AS % OF NEW PRICE

Age in Years	Tractors*	Other Equipment*	Tractors, Balers, Forage Harvesters and Combines**	
	"As Is" or Trade-in Values			Dealer Price Reconditioned
1	--	--	70	85
2	59	53	62	76
3	53	47	57	70
4	47	41	51	63
5	43	36	46	56
6	38	32	42	52
7	35	28	40	50
8	31	25	37	46
9	28	22	--	--
10	25	19	--	--

*University of Missouri
**Kansas State University

machinery costs, and 10% to 12% of new cost. Repairs and maintenance account for half of this while operating costs such as fuel, oil and grease make up the rest.

Repair and maintenance costs. Along with reduction in "as is" value, repair and maintenance costs are the most critical to machinery cost analysis. Research in Illinois shows a very wide range in repair costs stated as a percent of new cost for tractors. An Ohio study shows wide differences on self-propelled combines.

Amount of use and fuel type are important factors in your repair costs. Just as important is the care and treatment given the machinery by the owner and operator. These are conclusions of the Illinois study. It found wide variations even within tractor sizes and models. The table shows what portion of new cost will have been spent on the tractor at the end of ten years, depending on the type of fuel and the hours of annual use.

10-YEAR TRACTOR REPAIR COSTS
PERCENT OF NEW COST

Fuel Type	Hours Used Annually			
	400	600	800	1,000
Gasoline	31	43	55	66
Diesel	31	43	55	66
LP-gas	27	37	47	56

The above figures can be divided by 10 years to get the average annual repair cost for tractors. Repair costs increase rapidly—a reverse sum-of-the-years digits calculation gives you a close estimate of annual costs for a particular year.

SUGGESTED VALUES TO USE IN CALCULATING ANNUAL
REPAIR COSTS FOR VARIOUS FARM MACHINES

Machine	Annual Repairs in Percentage of First Cost of Machine	Machine	Annual Repairs in Percentage of First Cost of Machine
Baler, hay, with engine	3.0	Lister	5.0
Blower, forage	2.5	Mower	3.5
Combine, engine-driven	3.0	Picker, corn	3.0
Combine, self-propelled	3.0	Planter, corn	2.0
Combine, power take-off	3.0	Plow, one-way	5.0
Cultivator, duckfoot	3.5	Plow, moldboard	7.0
Cultivator, listed corn	3.5	Plow, tractor mounted	7.0
Cultivator, shovel	3.5	Sprayer, field	5.0
Drill, grain	1.5	Spreader, manure	1.5
Field forage harvester	4.0	Rake, hay, side-delivery	2.0
Grinder, feed, burr	3.0	Tractor	3.5
Grinder, feed, hammer	2.0	Truck	5.0
Harrow, disk	3.0	Wagon	1.5
Harrow, drag	1.0	Weeder, rod	2.0

KANSAS STATE UNIVERSITY

The nature of repair costs will enable you to reduce costs by keeping track of accumulated use.

It will allow you to repair or trade prior to the likely time of breakdown. Maintenance costs depend on the operator, but a rigid maintenance schedule will save on repairs. The table above gives annual repair rates for most machinery.

Fuel, oil and lubrication. These cost items depend on annual equipment use and the operator's lubrication schedule. Fuel costs vary by type of fuel, machine size and difficulty of the job. The table shows Illinois fuel consumption figures.

AVERAGE FUEL CONSUMPTION
GALLONS PER HOUR

Fuel type	Horsepower		
	40	65	90
Diesel	1.6	2.6	3.6
Gasoline	2.3	3.6	5.0
LP-gas	2.85	4.5	6.1

You'll need to figure the number of hours the machine will be used and multiply that number by the gallons per hour and the price per gallon of fuel in your area. Larger units burn more fuel per hour, but the cost per acre usually varies only slightly among sizes of units, so be sure hours used is relatively correct or you will throw the comparison by size of unit out of line.

Engineers at Minnesota say you can figure your annual fuel consumption by using the following formula:

$$\text{Gallons fuel per year} = \frac{\text{maximum drawbar hp} \times \text{hours operated} \times 0.6}{\text{hp-hours per gallon}}$$

The denominator in the equation, horsepower hours per gallon, is as follows:

gasoline -- 9.2 hp hours per gallon
propane -- 7.3 hp hours per gallon
diesel -- 13.0 hp hours per gallon

One of these two methods can be used to arrive at a fairly close fuel use figure, but you need to estimate your annual use for both. Nebraska tractor test reports found elsewhere in this Reference Volume list fuel consumption for various tractor models under various conditions.

Lubrication for tractors and self-propelled machinery, including engine oil, grease, transmission oil and hydraulic fluid, will be approximately 15% of fuel cost.

Labor costs should also be figured in some budgets—the value will depend on your own situation. It's particularly important when comparing equipment sizes and is critical to ownership-custom hiring comparisons.

Comparing Farm Loan Charges

Even when two lenders quote the same interest rate on a loan, the dollar cost may vary substantially. The difference arises in the way the interest is charged.

Loan cost will often be your foremost consideration in choosing among available lenders. The yardstick too often used to compare loan charges is the quoted interest rate. But without knowledge of how that rate is applied, it is meaningless. In addition there may be other charges such as loan service fees, stock investment requirements and minimum deposit requirements. Each of these will affect the true cost of the money you borrow. The actual dollar cost of the loan should be used to compare lenders.

Simple interest is what you pay to borrow money that you agree to repay in a lump sum. The basic formula for determining the dollar cost of such a loan is as follows:

$$\text{Cost} = \text{Principal} \times \text{Interest Rate} \times \text{Time (in years)}$$

By transposing the same formula, the annual interest rate can be computed from the dollar cost:

$$\text{Interest Rate} = \frac{\text{Cost}}{\text{Principal} \times \text{Time (in years)}}$$

Using these formulas, notice how the dollar cost can change depending on when the interest is paid. Straight interest, as it is sometimes called, is paid at the end of the loan period. If you borrow $2,000 for one year at 9% and repay the $2,000 plus interest at maturity, the interest will come to $180 ($2,000 x .09 x 1 = $180). If, instead, your lender *discounts* interest, you pay interest in advance. Thus, if that same loan were discounted at the same 9% rate the interest charge would be the same $180, but you'd only have the use of $1,820 during the year, rather than $2,000. The actual simple interest rate would be almost 10%:

$$\frac{\$180}{\$1,820 \times 1} = .099$$

The difference arises because you lose the use of that $180 during the loan term. If you really need the entire $2,000 and your lender discounts interest, you will need to borrow and pay interest on $2,197.80.

Notice from the formula that simple interest is figured in terms of an *annual percentage rate*. If money is repaid in three months your interest bill is only one-fourth as large as it would be if you were to keep the money for a full year. Some loans, however, are made on the basis of a flat interest charge on the original balance. Usually these are short-term loans for no more than a few months. Suppose you need $500 for three months. An 8% loan charged at a flat rate, without reference to the time involved, would cost $40 interest (.08 x $500 = $40). That translates into a 32% annual rate.

$$\frac{\$40}{\$500 \times .25} = .32$$

At an annual 8% rate, the three month loan would cost only $10.

Add-on interest is used on most consumer installment loans and is an extension of the flat-rate idea. Assume that you obtain an automobile loan at a quoted rate of 10% and that you finance $1,800. The dollar interest charge is computed by multiplying the 10% times the *original* loan amount times the number of years you'll take to pay for the car. In terms of an annual percentage rate, that comes out to more than 19-1/2%. Why? Because again you didn't borrow the full amount for the full term. To buy the car you need to repay the original loan of $1,800 in 36 monthly installments. The amount of your monthly installments is easily figured if you "add-on" to the $1,800 the total interest charge of $540,

$$\$1,800 \times .10 \times 3 = 540$$

for a total of $2,340, and then divide by 36 payments. Each payment is $65.00. Actually you borrowed the full $1,800 for only one month. If monthly payments to principal and interest were to remain constant over the life of the loan, each payment would reduce the borrowed amount—from $1,800 to $1,750 the second month; $1,700 the third month, etc. For this reason, the simple interest formula will not reveal the true annual rate.

To make your own comparisons on installment loan rates, plug your figures into the following formula. It will give the true annual percentage rate on installment loans where payments are equal and evenly spaced.

$$\frac{\text{Total Finance Charges}}{\text{1/2 the Original Loan}} \times \frac{\text{No. of Payments}}{\text{No. of Years}} \times \frac{1}{\text{No. of Payments} + 1} = \text{Annual Percentage Rate}$$

By comparison, if you could have gotten the same installment loan at an annual percentage rate of 10%, the total finance charges would have been only $360. Compute this figure by using this transposed version of the above formula:

$$\text{Annual Percentage Rate} \times \text{1/2 the Original Loan} \times \text{No. of Payments} + 1 \times \frac{\text{No. of Years}}{\text{No. of Payments}} = \text{Total Finance Charge}$$

In this formula be sure to use as "one-half the original loan," one-half the amount of money *actually received*, not necessarily the amount applied for. Loan fees, stock charges and other costs taken out of loan proceeds must be deducted.

Stock purchase requirements and compensating balances have the effect of slightly increasing the annual percentage rate on usable loan proceeds. For example, Farm Credit Associations require a stock investment of $5 per $100 or fraction thereof, of the loan amount. Assuming you need $10,000 and cost of stock is to come out of the loan, you will actually borrow and pay interest on $10,530. You have use of only $10,000 and at 9% interest, your true annual rate on usable dollars is 9.48%.

The result is the same when a commercial bank imposes a minimum deposit requirement commonly called a compensating balance. For example, if you are required to keep at least $100 of a $1,000 loan on deposit with the bank, you have $900 available while paying interest on $1,000.

Application of payments will also affect the interest cost to you. Most annual farm operating loans are made with the understanding that payments will be made as crops and livestock are sold. Depending on the lender's policy, however, such payments may be applied first to principal or first to pay interest.

Suppose that on January 15 you borrow $50,000 operating money for the year and expect to pay back $15,000 on August 15; $20,000 on November 15; and the balance on January 15 of the following year. Further assume you have a choice of whether to borrow from "Lender A" who applies payments first to reduce principal and "Lender B" who pays interest first, and both charge 8% interest. If you take the entire $50,000 on January 15 and make payments as anticipated, your interest charge will be $88 more from "Lender B" than from "Lender A." The difference arises because after the first payment, your principal loan balance is always greater with "Lender B." This table should clarify that fact:

Date			Lender A		Lender B	
			Principal	Interest Accrued	Principal	Interest Paid
Jan. 15						
	7 months		$50,000		$50,000	
Aug. 15			15,000	$2,333	12,667	$2,333
	3 months		35,000		37,333	
Nov. 15			20,000	700	19,253	747
	2 months		15,000		18,080	
Jan. 15			15,000	200	18,080	241
Total Interest Bill				$3,233		$3,321

Prepayment penalties. Often overlooked is the possible cost of getting rid of that loan sooner than expected. Use of a prepayment penalty varies among lenders and in different areas of the country. It is most commonly used with long-term real estate loans.

Borrowers are inclined to think they will never pay off a loan ahead of time and so ignore the penalty clause. Yet real estate lenders' records show that only a minority of their loans are paid to maturity. Most often the land is sold. At other times a borrower may want to refinance his debt at a lower rate. Occasionally an inheritance will enable him to pay the loan in advance.

In any case where you anticipate borrowing again in the near future, check with the lender. He might waive the penalty if you agree to borrow from him when you buy another farm.

Loan service charges. In addition to interest, some lenders charge a loan service fee which is usually added to the loan. As a result, you not only pay the fee, but interest on the fee as well. Such fees may be imposed to offset the administrative cost of setting up the loan, investigating your credit history, etc. Whatever the stated purpose, these costs add to the total finance charge, thus allowing the lender to quote a lower interest rate.

Chapter 4

Taxes, Insurance and Law

Income tax management is more than just an end-of-the-year job. You should keep income taxes in mind when managing your farm throughout the year. It's possible to reduce income taxes by timing the sale of farm commodities or selecting a method of depreciation that is best suited to your situation. The use of sales contracts and prepayment of expenses in years of high income helps to level income from one year to another.

Social security taxes, according to present laws, must be withheld and wages reported for any farm employee who earns at least $150 from one employer or works more than 20 days during the year for one employer. Before doing this, however, you are required to establish an employer identification number by filing Form SS-4. As soon as you owe $200 in social security taxes, you are required to submit this amount by the fifteenth of the following month.

As an employer, you must pay tax if you net more than $400 per year. Consider the benefits you will get in later life from social security when planning your life insurance needs.

Spend insurance dollars wisely. The importance of insurance is growing with the ever-increasing investment required in capital assets, and insurance helps you protect these large investments. A major catastrophe might easily cause you to lose

your farm or wipe out your savings unless you're adequately insured. On the other hand, carrying larger amounts of insurance than necessary can be costly.

It's impractical to insure against all possible risks. Therefore, you must carefully study your situation and determine which risks are most serious. Once you decide what risks to insure, shop around to get as much protection as possible with each dollar you can afford to spend. Premiums will vary, depending upon the coverage and clauses included in a given policy. The more coverage you get, the more your insurance will cost.

Seek advice on legal problems. No one can keep up on all the legal angles involved with running a farm business. Farmers need to concentrate on doing a good job with crops and livestock. In fields where their knowledge is limited, they should not hesitate to call on tax experts, lawyers, engineers and other specialists.

Locate a lawyer who has some knowledge of agriculture and work with him on all of your legal problems. Contracts should be drawn up by a lawyer or you should use a form that has been prepared especially for the situation. Contracts should not be signed without reading the so-called "fine print." Your lawyer can advise you on any matters regarding contracts.

Like all businessmen, farmers frequently enter

into contracts or agreements with other people. They need a basic understanding of the uses of contracts and of the conditions which make a contract legal and binding.

A contract should provide some benefit to each party involved, otherwise there is no advantage to be gained. It is agreed that you will do something or provide a certain amount of specified product under a definite financial arrangement. The contract should be in writing, but oral agreements can also be binding. The time of the contract's expiration should be set or a method agreed upon for cancelling it. All terms of the contract should be set forth as carefully as possible and each person involved should sign it.

Some examples of various contracts commonly used by farmers are: farm leases, sale of land by contract, livestock or poultry feeding contracts, grain sales contracts, feeder cattle contracts, and hired labor agreements.

Contracting or integrating may be advisable under some conditions. Entering into some form of contract arrangement or becoming a part of an integrated operation does offer advantages in some situations.

An integrated operation is one in which two or more links in production are tied together under the same management. For example, one company may own poultry breeding flocks, a hatchery, a feed mill and a processing plant. In turn, this company might contract with individual producers to grow their broilers.

Contracting is a way to obtain necessary credit, but there are several other reasons why this method of operation might prove beneficial for some farmers.

● Expert management and know-how become available through many contracts. In many situations, the contracting company will make many of the management decisions. Their wide experience and research may provide a sound background for making wise decisions. They will help you to incorporate the latest equipment and know-how into your business.

Under such arrangements you lose part of your independence and freedom to manage your business as you see fit. You may not make as much profit in a year with a contract. However, contracting may help to even out the good and bad income years, giving you a more stable income.

● Higher quality products may be the result of using latest scientific know-how and expert management advice which may be available to you through a contract. Thus, you may command a higher price for your product.

● Contracting permits you to reduce much of your market risk. You are assured of a market for your product. In turn, the company with which you contract is assured a supply. You are not faced with uncertain markets and prices.

● A more efficient operation may be possible. You will have more assurance of a market for your product, a source of credit and available management know-how. This permits you to organize your enterprise at its most profitable size.

Income Tax Accounting Procedures

You have a choice of the accounting procedures that can be used for reporting income tax. Once you select a method, permission from IRS is required before a change can be made.

All taxpayers must keep good records in order to prepare accurate income tax returns and to insure that the proper tax is paid. Paid bills, cancelled checks and other records to substantiate your entries on the tax form should be filed in an orderly manner and stored in a safe place.

In addition to adequate and accurate records, you must have an accounting period and establish an accounting method. The calendar year is the accounting period most commonly used by farmers. However, income may be reported on a fiscal year basis—a period of 12 consecutive months ending on the last day of any month other than December. Once the accounting period is established, it must be followed in future years unless it is changed in accordance with the law.

Accounting methods that accurately reflect income and expenses are satisfactory for income tax reporting purposes. However, the same accounting method you use for keeping your records must be used for filing your tax return. The cash and accrual methods of accounting are commonly used.

A farmer makes his choice when he files his first tax return. If he is a part of a newly organized farm partnership or corporation, or files for a newly purchased farm operated as a separate business, he may file on the same basis or may change to another method. Once a method is chosen, written consent from the Internal Revenue Service Commissioner is required for a change.

Cash method of accounting is the most widely used by farmers. It simplifies recordkeeping for income tax purposes. Gross income on your tax return includes: Income actually or constructively received from the sale of all crops and market livestock produced on the farm; profits (selling price less cost) on livestock and other items purchased for resale; and other farm income actually or constructively received.

Income is constructively received when it is credited to your account or unconditionally set apart so that you may draw upon it at any time. The receipt of a check is constructive receipt of money, even though you may not deposit or cash the check during the tax year in which you receive

it. Income credited to your account at the bank, store, etc., is taxable in the year it is credited.

The sale of a farm product through a valid contract that calls for payment in the following year is not constructively received in the year of sale and need not be reported as income in that year. However, if the contract terms give you the right to collect from the buyer any time after delivery of the product, you must report the sale as income in the year the arrangement was made, regardless of when you actually received payment.

Allowable deductions for cash basis farmers include farm operating expenses paid during the year, regardless of when they were incurred and depreciation expense allowable on farm improvements, machinery, equipment and purchased dairy, breeding, sporting and work stock.

There are certain tax planning advantages in filing on the cash basis:

It is a simple method of reporting. Fewer records are neccessary since inventory accounts don't need to be kept.

Taxes are postponed for the farmer who is in a period of year-to-year increases in inventory. He then has a tax advantage, particularly if tax rates remain constant or decrease. The advantage is less if tax rate increases are in prospect as his farm business moves toward maturity and cash sales of products accumulated during years of lower taxes materialize.

More flexibility is provided to adjust income from year to year when wide variations may occur in prices and production rates.

For example, when using the cash method, part of the crop or livestock production in a good year may be held over for sale in years of lower production. Sales can be speeded up in years of low production and/or prices. You may also delay expenditures and postpone payments. Conversely, certain cash purchases can be made before needed, depending upon the year's net income situation.

Deductible ordinary expense items such as feed, seed, fertilizer and repairs may be purchased in the latter part of the year, even though they are not used until the next taxable year. However, in making these purchases, care must be exercised. Livestock feeders may purchase needed feedgrain in late fall when prices are generally lowest. Advantages would depend on price, cost of storage and cost of money.

Fertilizer, feed or other annual operating supplies purchased should be actually acquired and preferably delivered. Expenditures will not be allowed until the obligation is paid.

Sales of raised breeding, dairy, sporting and work stock, treated as capital assets, result in a lower tax liability if the cash method is used. This is because these animals have a zero cost basis when sold, while under the accrual method the cost basis for determining gain is the last inventory value if left in inventory (or salvage value plus remaining depreciation if capitalized). In addition, if animals are capitalized under the accrual method, any depreciation taken must be recaptured as ordinary income.

Accrual method more clearly reflects the income from ordinary farming operations than the cash method does. Farm income is included in the year it is earned, regardless of when payment is received. Gross farm income includes all income from sales made during the year, regardless of when payment is received; all miscellaneous income regardless of source; and the inventory value of all livestock, crops and supplies on hand and not sold at the end of the year.

To arrive at net income, subtract: The inventory value of livestock and products on hand at the beginning of the year; the cost of livestock or products purchased during the year (except livestock held for draft, breeding, dairy or sporting purposes, unless they are included in inventory); all operating costs or expenses incurred during the taxable year; and depreciation—same as allowable under the cash method.

Costs of purchased feeder livestock are subtracted in the year purchased and then are included in the inventory at the end of the year if not sold. With the cash method, these costs are not deductible until the year the animals are sold.

Some advantages of the accrual method include the following:

Farmers who store some crops and sell them in the next year level out their income to some extent by including the production of a given year in the closing inventory of the year in which most of the costs of production were incurred. They may thus avoid having to pay income tax on the sales of more than one year's production in one year.

Livestock feeders who have heavy expenses in the latter part of one year, but sell the livestock early in the following year may prefer the accrual method in order to count the increased value of the animals in their ending inventory and offset costs which may already be paid.

Farmers who report on the accrual method have their income tax paid more "up to date" than farmers who use the cash method, especially if the latter deduct all expenses but hold back unsold production from one year to the next. This generally results in a more even year-to-year taxable income.

Young farmers starting with a small operation or with inadequate financing may desire to use the accrual method in order to keep their income and their taxes on a more current basis, rather than postpone taxes until the year in which production is sold. They may need to count the increase in the values or unsold production as income to offset cash farm operating expenses, allowable non-business deductions and personal exemptions, or to avoid showing a net operating loss.

A significant difference between the cash and accrual method of computing income is illustrated in the following example. A farmer purchases and takes delivery of feed for $500 on December 15 and charges the purchase. He is billed for it January 2 and pays the bill in January. With the cash method, it is a farm expense in January when the bill is paid. With the accrual method, the $500 expense is a deduction in December when the obligation to pay was incurred or "accrued." Any feed on hand at the end of the year would be included in the ending inventory and the $500 debt in accounts payable.

Increases in inventories are included in the income of the accrual method farmer. For example, a farmer raises and feeds livestock during the year, but does not sell any. With the cash method he has no income until the livestock is actually sold. With the accrual method there is income in the amount of any increase in the value of livestock and crops on hand at the end of the year compared to value at the beginning of the year.

Investment Credit Rules and Limits

Provisions of the Economic Recovery Tax Act of 1981 have further enhanced the benefits available to farmers and ranchers through this tax credit.

You should consider the effect of the investment credit when the purchase of equipment, livestock, and some farm buildings is planned. The investment credit is a rebate on the purchase price of property that is paid by the Federal Government in the form of a reduction in income taxes. Generally, it is 10% of the qualified investment in the business property.

The amount of the qualified investment is 60% of the cost of 3-year property and 100% of the cost of 5- and 10-year property under ACRS (the new depreciation system), enacted by the Economic Recovery Tax Act of 1981. Thus, the amount of the credit for 3-year property is 6% of its cost, and for 5- and 10-year property, 10% of its cost.

The investment credit is earned by purchasing either "new" or "used" property. The credit must be taken and is allowed in the year when the qualified property is placed in service.

New or used property. The credit is allowed on all purchases of new property, but no more than $125,000 of used property may qualify for the credit in any 1 year. (In 1985, the limit on used property will increase to $150,000.) If your purchases of used property exceed the limit, you may choose the assets that will earn the credit. Since only 60% of the cost of 3-year property is qualified investment, you should choose to apply the credit to 5- or 10-year property if possible.

A property is "new" property only the very first time that it is placed in service. For example, if a cow is first used for dairy purposes and then sold for breeding, it would be "new" to the first owner but "used" to the second owner. A reconditioned or rebuilt machine is "used" when purchased. But, if you rebuild a machine already owned, the cost of reconditioning is treated as a "new" purchase.

Qualifying property. Eligible property includes depreciable livestock (except horses) and almost all other tangible property (except most types of buildings) that is used in farming and can be depreciated. Purchased breeding and dairy livestock, specialized livestock structures, grain storage facilities, and machinery are the big items.

Livestock (other than horses) purchased for breeding or dairy purposes is eligible, but the tax credit is allowed only on the excess of the cost of purchased animals over the sale price of any "substantially identical" animals sold within 6 months before or after replacements are acquired—unless the investment credit was recaptured on the sale. This rule prevents a farmer from selling raised livestock on which no credit was allowed and buying similar animals to get the credit.

The rule does not apply if replacement is caused by an involuntary conversion, such as loss by drouth or disease. Animals are likely to be considered "substantially identical" if they are nearly the same age and held for the same purpose.

Most buildings and their structural components do not qualify for investment credit. However, there are two major exceptions. Single-purpose agricultural structures and enclosures are eligible for the investment credit. These include confinement hog buildings, cattle finishing facilities, milking parlors, poultry houses, etc., if built specifically to house, raise, and feed a particular type of livestock. Also, such a structure must house equipment necessary to feed and care for the livestock. If use of the structure changes, the credit could be recaptured.

Workspace used in caring for livestock is allowed, but other uses—such as selling of produce or storage of feed, supplies, and machinery—would be disqualified.

Greenhouses specifically designed, built, and used for the commercial production of plants also qualify for the tax credit.

Storage facilities qualify, even though they would otherwise be classed as buildings. The principal requirements include the following: (1) the structure must be used in farming, (2) any workspace within the structure must be quite small in relation to storage space, and (3) the structure must be used for the bulk storage of fungible commodities, such as grain. Most grain bins and silos will qualify.

Other depreciable property that qualifies, if it is used for crop or livestock production, includes:

● Fences, gates, and corrals to confine livestock or keep them out of cultivated areas.

● Drain tiles to irrigate or drain cultivated fields and pastures.

● Paved barnyards to keep livestock out of mud and to facilitate loading on trucks.

● Water wells and water systems for livestock, poultry, and irrigation—if outside of buildings. However, a water system in a single-purpose livestock structure would qualify.

● Depreciable parts of dams and drainageways.

● Special lighting, signs, and other identity symbols.

● Gravel or paved roads, bridges, and culverts essential to farming.

● Replacement parts, machinery overhauls, and shop tools placed on a depreciation schedule.

● Business portion of depreciable property put to both personal and business use.

Exchange property. The rules vary on a trade-in, depending on whether the property purchased is new or used. On new property, the credit applies to the basis of the property acquired (adjusted basis of the property traded plus any boot paid). For example, a machine with an adjusted basis (undepreciated cost) of $4,000 is traded for a new one priced at $18,000, and cash boot paid in addition to the trade-in is $11,000. The credit is figured on the new machine's basis of $15,000 ($4,000 basis of used machine plus $11,000 boot).

When you trade used property for used property, the investment credit applies only to the cash boot. If, in the above example, the machine received in the trade was used property, only the $11,000 cash boot would be eligible for the credit.

Disqualifying transactions. You cannot sell property, then reacquire it and claim an investment credit. The problem arises under a sale and leaseback, or any other type of transaction where the same person uses the property before and after the acquisition.

Also, no investment credit can be taken on property acquired from a related person, which means a spouse, parent, or child, but not a brother or sister.

New "at-risk" rules. Beginning in 1981, there is another limit on the amount of the investment qualifying for investment credit. The basis of property that supports an investment credit is limited to the amount which the owner of the property is "at risk." Generally, a farmer is "at risk" for the amount of cash and the basis of property invested in the activity and debt for which he has personal liability.

If the property is financed by a financial institution or a government agency, a farmer can be at risk for only 20% of the property and still get a full investment credit.

Generally, if any financing is on a nonrecourse basis or if financing is provided by family members, the "at risk" rules should be checked.

Rehabilitation costs. While buildings do not generally qualify, the rehabilitation of a farm building can lead to an investment credit. The credit is 15% of the rehabilitation cost if the building has been used more than 30 years and 20% if it has been used more than 40 years.

To qualify, the expenditures must exceed $5,000 or be more than the adjusted basis of the building on the date the rehabilitation commenced. At least 75% of the external walls must be retained in the rehabilitated building. An example of rehabilitation is replacement of partitions and electrical wiring in a barn. A farmhouse does not qualify. Many other details should be checked with your tax advisor.

Reforestation expenses. Forestation or reforestation expenditures up to $10,000 per year qualify for a 10% investment credit and, in addition, the expenditures may be amortized over 7 years.

Energy investment credit. A business energy credit of 10%, in addition to any regular investment credit, may be allowed on certain energy-saving properties. They include equipment that uses a fuel, other than oil or gas; special energy conservation devices, such as a heat exchanger; and equipment to recycle solid wastes. The credit is 15% on solar and wind equipment.

This credit arises under a complex section of the 1978 Energy Tax Act, and regulations pertaining to its application to farming and other businesses should be forthcoming. It applies generally to energy property acquired after September 30, 1978, and before January 1, 1983.

Commuter vans. New vans are eligible for the full 10% investment credit if used to transport employees. A van must seat at least eight passengers and at least 80% of the use must be to transport employees to and from work.

Recapture of credit. If property (for which an investment credit was allowed) is disposed of, the tax in the year of disposition will be increased by the amount of the credit that was not fully "earned." For 3-year property, one-third of the credit is earned for each full year of use. For 5- and 10-year property, 20% of the credit is earned by each full year of use.

For example, if 3-year property having a cost of $10,000 was purchased in 1981 and thus earned a credit of $600, two-thirds of the credit, or $400, would be recaptured if the property was sold in 1982 after it had been used more than 1 full year. If it was not used a full year, all of the credit would be recaptured. If the property was 5-year property, which earned a credit of $1,000, disposition after 1 full year of use would lead to a recapture of $800.

(The rules are slightly different for property purchased before 1981. In the year of sale, the credit must be recalculated for the actual years of use and, if shorter than the useful life originally claimed, any unearned credit must be repaid. If the property was sold in less than 3 years, no credit was earned. If sold after 3 or 4 full years of use, $3\frac{1}{3}\%$ credit was earned, and after 5 or 6 years of use, $6\frac{2}{3}\%$ credit was earned. If more than those percentages were claimed in an earlier year, the difference must be repaid. If the property was used 7 or more years, there would be no recapture.)

Recapture is forgiven if the credit did not reduce tax in the year of purchase or in some other year to which the credit has been carried. In such cases, the amount of the carryback or carryover is adjusted.

The amount of the recaptured credit is simply added to your tax in the year of the disposition of the property. The tax that results from the recapture may not be reduced by investment credits earned in the year of the disposition.

Limitation on credit. The investment credit that can be claimed in any 1 year may not exceed $25,000 plus 90% of the tax liability over $25,000.

Any credit that is not used under this limitation may be first carried back to the 3 years before the year of purchase. Also, if there is any investment credit remaining after this carryback, it may be carried forward and used in succeeding years for up to 15 years or until it is exhausted.

Cost Recovery–The New Depreciation

Before 1981, many farm assets could be depreciated. Now the technique for recovery of cost of most assets is the cost recovery allowance.

Massive changes from the old, familiar depreciation rules were made by the Economic Recovery Tax Act of 1981. They apply to acquisitions made in 1981 or later.

Our tax jargon is changed by the new law from "depreciation" to "cost recovery" if "recovery property" is involved. If recovery property is not involved, the old rules for depreciation remain applicable.

Under the new rules, a cost recovery deduction is allowed for the exhaustion, wear and tear of tangible property used in the trade or business or held for the production of income, and that deduction will be used for more than 1 year. Inventories, stock-in-trade, and land are not subject to cost recovery as they are not depreciable assets under old or new law. Dirt dams, terraces, drainage ditches, and similar improvements to land also do not qualify, but their costs may be deductible soil and water conservation expenses. No cost recovery applies to assets held for personal use, such as the family residence and car, because they are neither income producing nor business assets.

What Is Recovery Property?
Recovery property includes most tangible, depreciable property acquired after 1980. There are several exceptions, though.

Property acquired in certain transactions from persons who used it in 1980 is not recovery property and must be depreciated under the old rules. Tangible, depreciable personal property (called "Section 1245 property") acquired in 1981 or later may not be treated as recovery property if it:

(1) was used or owned at any time in 1980 by a related person,

(2) was acquired from a 1980 owner in a transaction in which the user did not change,

(3) is leased by the taxpayer to a person who used or owned the property in 1980 (or to a person related to the 1980 owner or user), or

(4) was acquired in a transaction in which the user of the property did not change and the property was not recovery property to the transferrer because of (2) or (3).

Real estate (called "Section 1250 property") is not recovery property if it:

(1) was used or owned at any time in 1980 by a related person,

(2) is leased by the taxpayer to a person who used or owned the property in 1980 (or to a person related to the 1980 owner or user), or

(3) was acquired in a tax-free exchange as replacement property after condemnation or other involuntary conversion or in a repossession of real property, but only to the amount of the carryover basis that represents the adjusted basis of property owned in 1980.

A related person is a spouse, a sibling, an ancestor, or a lineal descendant. Corporations and partnerships at least 10% owned by the taxpayer are related persons. So are partnerships or proprietorships under the control of the same person and members of a group of corporations with 50% ownership.

Property acquired in other tax-free transactions does not qualify as recovery property to the extent that the property's basis is carried over from property owned before 1981. This includes transfers to controlled corporations, corporate reorganizations, liquidations of a corporate subsidiary, and other corporate transactions where there is a carryover basis, transfers from partners to partnerships, and from partnerships to partners.

These rules were enacted to prevent the churning of property, i.e., a transfer that would have allowed the transferee to treat the property as recovery property.

How Is Property Classified?
Your property will fall into one of four classes, depending on the class life of the property under the old ADR (Asset Depreciation Range) depreciation rules and whether it is Section 1245 property (tangible personal property) or Section 1250 property (real estate).

If the ADR class life of Section 1245 property is 4 years or less, the property is 3-year recovery property. Section 1245 property that is not 3-year property is 5-year recovery property. Section 1250 property that has an ADR class life of less than 12.5 years is 10-year recovery property. Section 1250 property that is not 10-year property is 15-year real property.

The table below illustrates the recovery classes for most depreciable farm property.

Some property is specifically classified by the statute. Single-purpose agricultural or horticultural structures are 5-year recovery property. Race horses that are 2 years old or more when placed in service are 3-year recovery property. So are other horses that are 12 years old or more when placed in service. Mobile homes are 10-year recovery property.

What Is the Annual Recovery?
Once the property is classified, the statute prescribes the percentage of

COST RECOVERY CLASSES FOR FARM PROPERTY		
Asset	ADR class life	Kinds of property under ACRS
Machinery, equipment, grain bins, and fences	10 years	5-year property
Cotton ginning assets	12 years	5-year property
Cattle, breeding or dairy	7 years	5-year property
Horses, breeding or work	10 years	5-year property
Hogs, breeding	3 years	3-year property
Sheep and goats, breeding	5 years	5-year property
Farm buildings	25 years	15-year real property

cost to be recovered each year. The statutory percentage is applied to the full adjusted basis; there is no longer a salvage value computation. In the years 1981-84, the recovery percentages are determined from the following table:

COST RECOVERY PERCENTAGES

If the recovery year is:	The applicable percentage for the class of property is:		
	3-year	5-year	10-year
1	25	15	8
2	38	22	14
3	37	21	12
4		21	10
5		21	10
6			10
7			9
8			9
9			9
10			9

The recovery amounts in the early years of ownership will be increased in 1985 and again in 1986.

For 15-year real property, the cost recovery deduction is calculated under tables promulgated by the Treasury Department. Unlike the cost recovery deduction on tangible personal property, the deduction for real estate recovery is adjusted to reflect the number of months that the property is used in the year of acquisition. Component depreciation is not allowed. The table below is for all real estate except low-income housing.

Electing Slower Recovery.
If you think foregoing schedules will produce faster depreciation than is necessary or wise, you may choose one of several options that will slow down the recovery deductions. The optional deduction must be computed on the straight line method, but the taxpayer has a choice of periods over which the deduction may be taken.

Except for 15-year real property, each option requires the use of the "half-year convention," i.e., each property is treated as placed in service on the first day of the last half of the first year of use, regardless of the month of acquisition.

Except for 15-year real property, the election to use one of the optional periods must be made for all acquisitions of that particular class of property in the tax year. The election for 15-year real property may be made on a property-by-property basis.

The optional cost recovery periods available are:

In case of:	You may elect a recovery period of:
3-year property..........	3, 5 or 12 years
5-year property..........	5, 12 or 25 years
10-year property.........	10, 25 or 35 years
15-year real property.....	15, 35 or 45 years

The Expensing Option.
Before 1981, taxpayers could elect to take a bonus depreciation allowance equal to 20% of the cost of new equipment, but the deduction could not exceed $2,000 ($4,000 on a joint return). This allowance was intended primarily as tax relief to small business, although in fact, it was available to all taxpayers. Debate in the Congress while the 1981 Act was pending frequently characterized this provision as inadequate. It was repealed for 1981 and later years. A provision allowing the immediate deduction of the cost of some assets was substituted for bonus depreciation. This new deduction is not available until 1982. Neither 20% depreciation nor the expense option applies to 1981 acquisitions.

The expense option is limited in amount. In 1982 and 1983, the limit is $5,000; in 1984 and 1985, $7,500; and thereafter, $10,000. For partnerships, the limit applies to a partnership as well as to each partner.

No investment credit is allowed on the cost of property that is expensed under this election. If the property is disposed of, the full expensed amount is recaptured in the year of sale even on an installment sale.

The expense option applies to purchases of tangible personal property that qualifies for the investment credit; but no investment credit is allowed on the expensed portion of the cost.

The property must be purchased for use in the trade or business; the option does not apply to inherited property or property which has a basis determined by reference to the basis of other property, such as in a tax-free exchange. Property acquired from related parties does not qualify. Related parties are spouses, ancestors, descendants, and 50% controlled corporations. Noncorporate lessors who do not qualify for the investment credit may not use this option.

Conclusion.

The new rules apply to recovery property which is acquired in 1981 or thereafter. The old rules apply to farm properties acquired before 1981 and to farm assets which do not qualify as "recovery property," primarily assets purchased from related parties. Thus, for the foreseeable future, a farmer will have to be alert to the two sets of depreciation rules.

ACRS Cost Recovery Tables for Real Estate
The applicable percentage is:

If the recovery year is:	(Use the column for the month in the first year the property is placed in service)											
	1	2	3	4	5	6	7	8	9	10	11	12
1	12	11	10	9	8	7	6	5	4	3	2	1
2	10	10	11	11	11	11	11	11	11	11	11	12
3	9	9	9	9	10	10	10	10	10	10	10	10
4	8	8	8	8	8	8	9	9	9	9	9	9
5	7	7	7	7	7	7	8	8	8	8	8	8
6	6	6	6	6	7	7	7	7	7	7	7	7
7	6	6	6	6	6	6	6	6	6	6	6	6
8	6	6	6	6	6	6	5	6	6	6	6	6
9	6	6	6	6	5	6	5	5	5	6	6	6
10	5	6	5	6	5	5	5	5	5	5	6	5
11	5	5	5	5	5	5	5	5	5	5	5	5
12	5	5	5	5	5	5	5	5	5	5	5	5
13	5	5	5	5	5	5	5	5	5	5	5	5
14	5	5	5	5	5	5	5	5	5	5	5	5
15	5	5	5	5	5	5	5	5	5	5	5	5
16	—	—	1	1	2	2	3	3	4	4	4	5

How to Determine "Basis"

How much gain or loss occurs when property is disposed of? How much depreciation is allowable? "Basis" is the starting point in answering both questions.

Basis is the amount of your investment for tax purposes and more important, it's the amount you can recover tax-free when you dispose of the property.

Basis for depreciation is the same as the basis for computing gain on sale or disposition of property. The only real exception has to do with property converted from personal to business use. Qualified investments for purposes of investment credit should not be confused with basis for depreciation, though in some instances they may be the same.

ORIGINAL BASIS

Original basis is the amount of your initial tax investment. "Adjusted basis" is the original basis as adjusted either up or down to reflect, on any given date, the amount you can recover tax-free. However, the basis of an item of property depends first upon the manner in which it was acquired.

Purchased Property. The original basis of property you buy is the purchase price or the cost to you. Cost includes the amount paid either in cash or other property plus commissions, legal fees and other expenses which may have been connected with the purchase. The cost likewise includes the amount of debts assumed in connection with the purchase. For example, if in buying a farm you pay $25,000 and assume a mortgage with $65,000 still owing, your basis is $90,000.

The original basis of property purchased from a farmer cooperative is the cost less the amount of any patronage dividend received as a result of the purchase.

Apportioning Basis. Very often the sale of a farm will involve not just the land, but the buildings and machinery, as well as livestock and growing crops. Ideally, the contract for sale will have set a unit price for the land, another for each building and so on. The price allotted to each item would likely be accepted by IRS as proof of the basis.

More often however, contracts list only the lump-sum sale price. Thus, bases must be assigned by allocating the cost to each item in proportion to its fair market value at the time acquired. If farm buildings are worth $20,000, that amount must be allocated to the buildings collectively. Then it must be further allocated among the several buildings in proportion to their relative values.

Assessed valuation and insurance values can be helpful in allocating basis. IRS will likely agree to reasonable allocations, so long as the amount left allocated to land is consistent with current bare land values.

Gifts. When property is acquired by gift, the basis is generally the same as it would have been in the hands of the donor. There are exceptions. If the donee disposes of the property at a loss, then for purposes of figuring that loss, the basis is the fair market value at the date of the gift, not the donor's basis. If property is received by gift and a gift tax paid on it, its basis to the donee is increased by the gift tax paid on the appreciation in value.

Inherited Property. If you inherit property your basis will generally be its fair market value at the date of the decedent's death. If a federal estate tax return is filed listing the property, your basis will generally be the value shown. Though Congress recently considered changing the manner by which basis would be determined, legislation in this regard failed to pass.

Trades. If you take property for other property in a "taxable exchange," the basis of the property received is its value at the time of the trade.

Like-Kind Exchanges. If property that is used in the farm business or for capital investment purposes is traded for property of a "like-kind," any gain is included in income only to the extent of "boot" received in cash or "unlike property."

Property of like-kind must be of the same nature and used for the same general purpose. A farm tractor for a farm truck would be a like-kind exchange. Though not identical, both are used in the farm business. Farm machinery for farmland would NOT be a like-kind exchange. Farmland and city rental property are of a like-kind—both are business investments. Livestock must be of the same sex to be like-kind.

The rule to be followed with like-kind exchanges says that the basis of the property acquired is the same as the adjusted basis of the property that was traded, minus the amount of money received, plus the amount of gain included in income and the cash paid.

Example: Under this rule, if you swap bulls with your neighbor and no money changes hands, the basis of your new bull is the same as the adjusted basis of your old bull. If in the deal you get two bulls, their total bases will be the same as the adjusted basis of your old bull which must be prorated between them according to their respective values.

Example: Assume your old farm pickup truck originally cost $3,500 and allowable depreciation on the truck amounts to $2,800. Now in a trade for a new truck costing $5,000, you are allowed $1,400 for the old truck and pay $3,600 cash difference. The basis of the new truck is computed as follows:

Cost of truck traded (basis)	$3,500
Less: Depreciation allowable	2,800
Adjusted basis of truck traded	$ 700
Plus: Cash paid	3,600
Basis of new truck	$4,300

Example: Farmland bought for $30,000 is traded for another tract worth $45,000 plus $5,000 cash. Your gain is $20,000, but because it is a like-kind exchange, only the cash received is recognized as income at the time of the trade. The other $15,000 is "deferred into" the basis of the new tract as follows:

Basis of land traded	$30,000
Less: Cash received	5,000
	$25,000
Plus: Gain recognized	5,000
Basis of land acquired	$30,000

Example: If instead, that same tract of land were traded for another parcel worth $25,000 and you receive $10,000 boot, your gain on the deal is $5,000 ($25,000 + 10,000 - 30,000). All of that gain is includible as income at the time of the exchange. Now the basis of the new tract is figured as follows:

Basis of land traded	$30,000
Less: Cash received	10,000
	$20,000
Plus: Gain recognized	5,000
Basis of new tract	$25,000

Example: If in the above example, you get only $3,000 boot, you have a loss of $2,000 ($30,000 - 25,000 - 3,000). Since losses on like-kind exchanges are not recognized, the basis of the new farm would be simply the $30,000 (basis of the land traded) minus $3,000 (cash received) or $27,000.

Conversion to Business Use. Some special rules apply where non-business property, such as a farmhouse, is converted to rental property or otherwise put to an income-producing use. The basis for depreciation and also for determining a loss is either the cost (original) or the fair market value at the time of conversion, whichever is less. In computing a gain, however, the general rule is followed and the original cost is its basis.

Business-Personal Property. If you devote a portion of your family car to farm business, computing basis of the new car is basically the same as for a like-kind exchange.

Example: Assume your old car cost $3,600 and is used 50% for farm business. With a useful life of six years and a salvage value of $600, the annual depreciation allowance for one-half the car comes to $250. After four years it is traded for a new car with a price of $4,800 and $3,400 cash difference is paid in the deal. The basis of the new car will equal adjusted basis of the old car plus the cash paid:

One-half cost of old car	$1,800
Less: 4 years depreciation	1,000
Adjusted basis of ½ old car	$ 800
Plus: Boot paid for ½ new car	1,700
Cost basis of ½ new car	$2,500

If you expect the new car to have a salvage value of $800, the basis for depreciation of one-half the new car would then be $2,100 ($2,500 - ($800 ÷ 2).

ADJUSTED BASIS

To determine adjusted basis the original basis of the property is adjusted by adding:

Cost of Improvements or Additions to the property. Before adjusting basis upward, though, be certain that the "improvement" actually increases the value of or prolongs the life of the property. If it doesn't, it probably can qualify as a repair deductible in full in the year of the expenditure.

Basis can then be further adjusted by subtracting these allowances:

Depreciation as allowed or allowable—whichever is greater. If you took less depreciation than the amount allowable under the method you use, you must deduct the full allowable amount under that method. If the property was eligible for depreciation, but you neglected to depreciate it, then the adjustments to basis for depreciation allowable are made using the straight line method.

Casualty Losses. Basis must be reduced by the amount of casualty insurance proceeds recovered where property was partially or totally destroyed. If the casualty results in a deductible loss, the basis of the property must be further reduced by the amount of that loss deduction.

Severance damages arising from condemnation awards.

Easement proceeds. Basis of real estate must be reduced by the amount received from the sale or granting of an easement.

Negligence and Liability

Your responsibility for the well-being of persons coming onto your farm or ranch is changing as more states adopt the "reasonable care" standard.

While the law generally favored the landowner and occupier in the past, such is not necessarily the case now. More and more lawsuits are filed each year. The fact that a person is your friend today may not keep him from suing you tomorrow. You have duties to those who come onto your land and you must be aware of those duties. The area of law most frequently involved when someone is injured on your property is a question of your negligence, if any.

Negligence. The term "negligence" is generally the failure to use ordinary care. It can be doing something that you should not have done (comission) or failing to do something that you should have done (omission). Except in the case of strict liability, discussed later, you are liable for someone's injuries if you (1) owed that person a duty, (2) breached that duty, (3) the person was hurt, and (4) your negligence was the main or proximate cause of the injury.

Traditional law. In the past, and in many cases still today, the courts made fine distinctions between categories of people on your property as to what duty you owed to them. These visitors were referred to as trespassers, licensees, and invitees.

Trespassers are those who come onto your land without permission for their own purposes. It makes no difference whether or not the land is "posted." The trespasser may only expect that he will not be intentionally injured on your property.

You may forcibly remove trespassers from your property, but you may only use that force which is reasonably necessary and no more. You will be liable for the use of excess force. You may not use dangerous weapons or threaten injury to or the life of the trespasser.

Once you have discovered the trespasser on your property, many states hold you to a higher degree of care.

Licensees are those who come onto your land with your permission, but for their own benefit. Examples would be hunters, fishermen, etc., who ask your permission to be on your property or are there with your permission. Most invited guests fall into this category.

Traditionally, you had no duty to make your property safe for licensees nor even to inspect the property for dangers of which you were unaware. The licensee had to accept the property as he found it. Since you knew the licensee was on your property, you had to make a reasonable effort to point out the known dangers which were otherwise hidden.

Note, however, that you may owe a higher duty to a trespasser who becomes a licensee by, for instance, your knowing that he always cuts across your property without asking your permission.

Invitees are the people who visit your property with your permission for a business purpose which benefits you. They are owed the highest duty of care. Examples are fishermen and hunters who pay you a fee for using your property, livestock buyers (perhaps), plumbers, veterinarians, repairmen you call in, etc.

Most states applying the traditional laws require you to make a reasonable inspection of your property to discover dangerous conditions. Once discovered, they must be either corrected or called to the attention of the invitee in order to avoid potential liability.

New trend. Today, however, a growing number of states are less likely to look to the technicalities of the law to determine which duty you owed to a person injured on your land. The recent trend has been to adopt a single standard of "reasonable care" owed to all users of your land, regardless of the classification.

As a recent New York court said, "...if a property owner knows or has reason to know of a dangerous condition on his land, then the property owner must exercise reasonable care to remove the risk of injury to anyone coming onto the land, whether they be trespasser, licensee, or invitee, child or adult; ..."

Violations of law. Violations of local, state, and federal laws and regulations can be indications that you were negligent or breached the reasonable care owed to the injured person, i.e., environmental protection laws, OSHA, licensing requirements, and the like. A law is presumably passed where there is a need for regulation. Although the need for the regulation is important, the reason for the law may become lost once it is shown that you violated the law and someone was injured, when that person might not have been injured had the law been obeyed.

Custom and practice. Violations of custom and practice within your community or industry can be of vital importance in showing that you were negligent. For instance, if it is shown to a court that it is the custom or practice in your area or state to keep bulls in pens with one-half inch steel rods for fencing, the fact that your fencing is only three-eighths inch steel rods can show that you were negligent if your bull broke through your fence and injured someone. On the other hand, the fact that your fence was also of one-half inch steel rods does not automatically prove you were not negligent. It is, though, one factor to be considered in determining whether or not you were negligent.

Practical jokes. Intentionally hiding dangers from a visitor, for whatever reason (practical joke or otherwise), is very dangerous from a liability standpoint. If you let a guest who is not familiar with horses ride your "wild bronc" without telling him of the dangers involved, you will in all likelihood be liable when that guest is injured by being thrown from the horse.

Strict liability. You will be strictly or completely liable for injuries to persons from those things you may have which are inherently dangerous, such as wild animals (pet fox), explosives (dynamite), many chemicals, setting trap guns to shoot or scare trespassers and thieves (man or animal), and the like. This may be true even though you can show that you were not at all negligent.

Attractive nuisances. Many courts have held that children are not normally capable of detecting hidden danger. This lack of judgment, coupled with their natural curiosity, entitles them to special care when they wander onto your land. As a result, the "attractive nuisance doctrine" has been created for situations which might lure children into dangers. Attractive nuisances could include unattended machinery, ponds and lakes, rundown buildings, piled lumber, open cisterns, and so forth. When injuries to children involve such items, you are judged on whether you used a reasonable standard of care in eliminating what could be considered a dangerous condition.

Caution. When you work around dangerous conditions all day, there is a tendency to become accustomed to them and forget that there is actually a danger. You should warn any visitor of all machinery, trap doors, holes in the floor, pulleys, augers, "frisky" livestock, low pipes overhead, and similar conditions.

Contributory negligence. The injured person may have been doing something negligent himself, which helped to cause his injury. In some states, his own negligence may keep him from recovering anything from you. In other states, it may reduce the amount he wins against you. In any event, his own negligence may not excuse you in the strict liability cases.

Damages. If you are found liable for someone's injuries, you are liable for the reasonable consequences, or extent, of those injuries. This would include all proven reasonable medical and other expenses, loss of wages, pain and suffering, loss of the use of the limb or body part injured, loss of future wages, future medical and other related expenses, future pain and suffering, as well as other damages.

Ounce of prevention. The best way to avoid accidents is to prevent them. Periodic inspections of your farm or ranch are imperative, for your safety as well as that of others. When you find a dangerous condition, immediately stop and repair it. If, for some reason, it cannot be corrected right then, mark it in such a way that a guest will clearly see it is dangerous, and make certain to warn your guests of the condition. Pay particular attention to dangerous or potentially dangerous livestock, machinery, buildings, materials storage areas, equipment, electrical wiring, doorways, overhead and underfoot obstructions, and holes.

Review your liability insurance policy and coverage with your insurance agent. Take him on a tour of your farm or ranch. Increase, if necessary, your coverage and the amounts of insurance you have. Most farms and ranches are grossly underinsured against liability claims.

Meet with your attorney and discuss with him your particular situation. Take the time now to find out where you stand legally as to possible liability for injuries to others sustained on your property. Perhaps incorporation of your farming or ranching business would be helpful in reducing your exposure to liability claims.

Federal Gift and Estate Taxes

Significant changes in federal taxation of gifts and estates have resulted from passage of the Economic Recovery Tax Act of 1981.

Although the value of an estate that is exempt from federal estate tax will increase through 1987, this doesn't eliminate the need for an estate plan. For one thing, much of the increased exemption could be offset by inflation. Further, most of the changes in the federal estate tax law provide greater flexibility in setting up an estate plan. Whereas a smaller portion of an estate may be taxable under the new law, careful planning may enable a farmer to further reduce or, in many cases, completely avoid estate taxes.

Estate and Gift Tax Rates

A "unified" tax rate schedule applies to all taxable gifts made during life and to the taxable estate. Also, there is a single "unified credit" that must be used by each individual or estate to reduce the taxes on gifts and estate transfers. The credit is intended to shield smaller estates from tax and to reduce the tax bite on larger estates. The phase-in of this credit started in 1977. The 1981 law continues the yearly increases to 1987 when the full credit will reach $192,800, exempting from tax the first $600,000 of taxable gifts and estate. This progressive credit is listed in the table along with the equivalent exemption. No estate tax return need be filed unless the value of the gross estate exceeds the tax-free amount shown.

TAX CREDIT AND EXEMPTION

Year of death	Unified credit	Amount passing tax free
1981	$47,000	$175,625
1982	62,800	225,000
1983	79,300	275,000
1984	96,300	325,000
1985	121,800	400,000
1986	155,800	500,000
1987 and later	192,800	600,000

The next table lists the estate tax rates for 1982. The unified credit of $62,800 in 1982 will offset all federal estate taxes up to the 32% level. In 1987, the fully phased-in credit of $192,800 will offset all taxes up to the 37% bracket.

The 1981 tax legislation also started a progressive reduction in the top estate tax brackets. The top rate drops yearly from 70% in 1981 to 50% in 1985 and thereafter. Thus the top bracket, for taxable estates over $2,500,000, will be 50% in 1985. The tax rates below the 50% level will not change.

UNIFIED GIFT AND ESTATE TAX SCHEDULE FOR 1982

If tentative tax base is more than:	but not over:	tentative tax is:	of excess over:
0	$10,000	18% of such amount	
$10,000	20,000	$1,800 + 20%	$10,000
20,000	40,000	3,800 + 22%	20,000
40,000	60,000	8,200 + 24%	40,000
60,000	80,000	13,000 + 26%	60,000
80,000	100,000	18,200 + 28%	80,000
100,000	150,000	23,800 + 30%	100,000
150,000	250,000	38,800 + 32%	150,000
250,000	500,000	70,800 + 34%	250,000
500,000	750,000	155,800 + 37%	500,000
750,000	1,000,000	248,300 + 39%	750,000
1,000,000	1,250,000	345,800 + 41%	1,000,000
1,250,000	1,500,000	448,300 + 43%	1,250,000
1,500,000	2,000,000	555,800 + 45%	1,500,000
2,000,000	2,500,000	780,800 + 49%	2,000,000
2,500,000	3,000,000	1,025,800 + 53%	2,500,000
3,000,000	3,500,000	1,290,800 + 57%	3,000,000
3,500,000	4,000,000	1,575,800 + 61%	3,500,000
4,000,000	—	1,880,800 + 65%	4,000,000

Unlimited Marital Deduction

Starting in 1982, there is no tax (with a few minor exceptions) on transfers of property between spouses, either by gift, will, formation of a joint tenancy, as life insurance beneficiary, as life tenant with a power of appointment, or in any other manner. The 1981 amendments also remove provisions of the old law which limited the marital deduction for transfers of community property between spouses.

Thus the entire estate of the first spouse to die, regardless of its total value, may be passed to the surviving spouse tax free. This may not be desirable from a planning standpoint, however, as such a transfer may substantially increase the surviving spouse's estate, creating an unnecessarily high tax liability.

A simple life estate qualifies for the marital deduction under the new law. Property left to a spouse in which he or she has only a life interest may be treated as part of the marital deduction and thus avoid taxation. The property will be taxed on the death of the surviving spouse, however, but the tax will be collected from the person who receives it, not from the spouse's estate. This provides added estate planning flexibility.

Joint tenancies. There is no gift tax due on the creation of a joint tenancy (or tenancy by the entirety) between husband and wife starting in 1982, regardless of when or how the property was acquired. The 100% gift and estate tax marital deduction covers such a transfer.

Estate tax application is very simple. On death of the first spouse joint tenant, after 1981, half of the value of the property will be included in the gross estate for tax purposes; but since the interest passes to the surviving spouse, it qualifies for the marital deduction–thus it passes tax free. It no longer matters which spouse provided the original consideration for the joint tenancy property.

This new rule does not apply to joint tenancies between persons other than husband and wife, however. For example, if Father creates a joint tenancy with Son in ownership of the family farm, worth $500,000, Father owes gift tax. Father has made a gift to Son of $250,000. If, when Father dies, the property is worth $800,000, the full value of the farm will be included in his estate for tax purposes, although a credit will be allowed for the gift tax paid previously.

Annual Gift Exclusions

Gifts of up to $10,000 per year per donee may be made tax free in 1982 and later years. The prior law limited the tax exclusion to $3,000 per gift. Gifts of $20,000 per donee may be made by a married couple if each agrees to treat half of the gift as made by him or her. This means that a farm couple with three children could gift up to $60,000 worth of property each year to their children. This exclusion may now be large enough to make annual gifting of real estate practical. Payments of school tuition and medical expenses are not considered to be gifts, whether the person benefiting is related to the donor or not.

As mentioned earlier, gifts to a spouse after 1981 may qualify for the unlimited marital deduction. Thus the $10,000 per year exclusion need not be considered.

Gifts within 3 years of death, with a few exceptions, will be treated like gifts made prior to that period. This new simplified treatment is effective for deaths in 1982 or later. However, any gift tax paid on gifts made within 3 years of death will be added to the estate for purposes of determining the estate tax.

There is one important exception to this new rule–life insurance policies. If ownership of a policy is given away within 3 years of death, the full proceeds of the policy will be included in the donor's gross estate.

All taxable gifts made within 3 years of death are added to the decedent's gross estate for such purposes as determining whether interest in the farm business is great enough to qualify the estate for 15-year installment payment of estate tax and/or special use valuation of the land and for corporate stock redemption after death.

Gift tax returns for gifts made after 1981 need to be filed only on an annual basis on April 15 of the year following the year of the gift. If the donor dies in the year the gift is made, the gift tax return is due with the federal estate tax return. Generally, no gift tax return is required for transfers of property to a spouse after 1981.

Installment Payment of Estate Tax

Normally, the estate tax is due 9 months after death. For deaths occurring in 1982 or later, a 15-year installment plan is available in many cases. This installment provision may be very beneficial. (The previous extension for up to 10 years is no longer available.)

If more than 35% of the decedent's adjusted gross estate is an interest in a closely held business, the executor may elect to pay the estate taxes in up to 10 equal annual installments, the first installment deferred for 5 years. Only interest need be paid during the first 5 years. For the entire 15-year period, the interest rate on the tax due for the first $1,000,000 of the estate attributable to farm or other closely held business property is only 4%. For the remainder of the tax, the interest rate is equal to the average predominant prime rate adjusted annually.

Closely held business properties would include proprietorships, partnerships with no more than 15 partners and where 20% or more of the partnership assets are included in the gross estate, and corporations with no more than 15 stockholders and where 20% or more of the corporation's voting stock is included in the estate. All deferred tax must be paid immediately if 50% or more of the interest in the business is transferred to someone outside of the family.

Late payment of interest or tax will not cause acceleration of all unpaid installments unless more than 6 months late. The late payment loses its eligibility for the 4% interest rate, though, and is subject to a 5% per month penalty.

Estate Planning for Farmers and Ranchers

A will is basic in every estate plan, but a comprehensive plan goes far beyond the drafting of your will.

One problem that is common among farm estates is the lack of liquidity. The assets of the estate, which may be considerable, are in the form of land, equipment, livestock, and buildings. These assets cannot be readily converted to cash to pay estate taxes and other death costs. Very often dying without an estate plan results in the mortgage or sale of the farm by the heirs to pay these costs. This problem can be alleviated to an extent by permitting deferral of payment of estate taxes for up to 10 years at a low interest rate, but there is still a debt.

Some farmers still assume they will not have to worry about estate taxes because the values of their farms can be set at the prices they paid for them. Unfortunately that is not true. For estate tax purposes, the decedent's estate is the fair market value of all assets owned at death. This includes the face value of life insurance policies owned at death by the decedent.

Estate Taxes. What size estate is taxable? Depending on whether taxable lifetime gifts have been made and other factors, estates in excess of $225,000 could be subject to tax for persons dying in 1982. The amount that will pass tax free increases to $275,000 in 1983, $325,000 in 1984, $400,000 in 1985, $500,000 in 1986, and $600,000 in 1987 and thereafter.

You can reduce your taxable estate by the property left to a surviving spouse (regardless of amount). Thus, a married person can avoid all estate tax by leaving all of his or her property to a spouse or by leaving to the spouse all property in excess of the tax-free amount. There is a "marital deduction" for property left to a spouse.

This does not solve the estate tax problem, however. When the surviving spouse dies, there is no marital deduction available (unless he or she remarried). The federal estate tax will fall on all of the spouse's property in excess of the amount allowed to pass tax free.

Estate Settlement. The other costs at death include such items as expenses of the last illness, funeral, and burial; probate costs, including fees to the estate's executor or administrator; attorney's fees; and various filing and notice fees. In most states, the executor's and attorney's fees are determined by a schedule under state law. In some states, the attorney's fee is set as a percentage of the entire estate's value, or it may be based on the attorney's regular per hour charge. Estate settlement costs should run from 6% to 10% or more of the net assets of the estate.

All debts of the deceased must be discharged and moneys owed him collected before the estate can be settled. This is the duty of the executor and the estate attorney. The balance of the assets, after debts and obligations are discharged and other estate settlement costs paid, is the amount available for distribution to the heirs and beneficiaries. For federal estate tax purposes, deductions are claimed for gifts to a spouse and to charities. The remainder is the taxable estate upon which the tax is computed. The tax is reduced by the unified estate and gift tax credit, and any excess is the amount of tax due.

State death taxes, while normally less than federal estate taxes, can be considerable. Many states have an inheritance tax that is levied on the heirs or beneficiaries receiving property from the estate. Some states have an estate tax, similar to the federal estate tax, that is levied on the decedent's estate.

The estate settlement process can take 1 year or longer for moderate-sized estates. Large estates might take 2 years or more to settle. Small estates with assets of a few thousand dollars may avoid the full probate procedure in states which have "simplified probate" laws.

Estate Planning Objectives. Reduction of taxes is only one of the objectives of estate planning. Very often the more difficult objective is the division of a limited amount of assets among several heirs. Most farmers and ranchers have one property and more than one child. For many farmers and ranchers, the primary consideration is support for a surviving spouse who may have had limited experience with business and finance.

Few people consider the question of when the estate plan should take effect and probably assume that it takes effect after death. But the astute planner puts his plan into effect at the time he begins accumulating significant property assets. In this way, the property is owned in the best form for eventual disposition. For example, joint tenancy ownership with rights of survivorship might be the best form of ownership for some types of property, such as a residence. But, generally, it is not the best tax method of holding assets such as farmland, equipment, livestock, or stock in a family-owned business.

Estate planning is not a one-time job. It should be a continuing process, periodically reviewed. The earlier planning is started, the better. There are several tools that can be used to carry out the plan for your estate. Since each situation is different, any of the following might be used. Often, several of the tools work in tandem.

The Will. Both husband and wife should have wills. For families with minor children, the naming of a guardian is important and this is done in the will. Otherwise, the state will name a guardian for the children in the event of the deaths of both parents, and the appointed guardian might not be the person the parents would have chosen.

Another reason for a will is to name an executor for your estate. It is the executor's duty to see to the proper disposition of your assets at your death. Unless an executor is named in the will, the probate court will appoint an administrator to carry out this function. The will contains your written directions as to what shall be done with your assets. Certain estate requirements are mandatory: payment of probate court costs, state and federal estate taxes; the payment of all valid claims against the estate; the filing of income tax returns; and payment of taxes due.

Without a will, the distribution of your assets is controlled by the state under what is known as intestate succession. In some states, the statutes provide for a division of the assets between the surviving spouse and the children—one-half to each. Other states differ. Intestate succession laws are geared for a theoretical person who failed to write a will. Thus, the state has a will for you if you do not take the time to write your own. But the state's will would probably handle things differently than you would prefer.

Don't attempt to write your own will. Knowledge of law and tax and technical accuracy in the language used are necessary to assure that the willmaker's desires are achieved. The cost of a will ranges from $50 to $100 for a simple will to several hundred dollars for wills which include trust instruments.

Trusts are used increasingly in estate plans. The individual making the trust (trustor) transfers property to a trustee (bank, corporation, or individual) who manages the property according to a written trust instrument for the benefit of the designated beneficiaries—a surviving spouse, children, or others. Trusts can be created during the trustor's lifetime and can be revocable or irrevocable. If a trust is revocable, it can be changed by the trustor. If it is irrevocable, it cannot be changed, because the trustor has given up all ownership rights to the property.

A testamentary trust is established in a will and takes effect after death of the trustor. The trust directs the trustee manager of the property as to how and when to distribute income and principal to the trustor's beneficiaries.

A popular use of testamentary trusts is to obtain estate tax savings. One common plan is to place in one trust assets equal in value to the amount of property that will pass tax free under the estate tax credit. A second trust holds property qualifying for the marital deduction for the benefit of the surviving spouse. The first trust is tax free because it passes under the tax-free allowance, and the second is tax free because it qualifies for the marital deduction. On the death of the spouse, the property in the marital trust will be taxed to the extent that the value exceeds the spouse's tax-free allowance.

The spouse must be entitled to all of the income from the marital trust, and the principal will pass on the death of the spouse as the spouse directs or as the first spouse directed in his or her will.

The income from the other trust can be used for the spouse and/or children or others. The principal passes at the spouse's death to the remaindermen, usually the children, named by the first spouse's will. This trust will not be taxed at the spouse's death, and the property passing to the children will not be taxed until they die.

Trusts can be very flexible. The trustee may be authorized to make principal payments to the surviving spouse during his or her lifetime. Principal payments may be made from the nonmarital trust to other beneficiaries. It is also possible to permit a spouse or other beneficiary to withdraw some or all of the trust assets during life.

Trust instruments are technical, and tax consequences depend on careful wording. The trustee—whether it be a bank, trust company, or individual—receives a management fee, often a percentage of the trust income. By law, the trustee is required to practice conservative, nonspeculative management of the trust assets.

Gifts made during life can reduce your gross estate. Each person may make tax-free gifts of $10,000 per year to any number of beneficiaries. If the donor's spouse agrees, the tax-free gifts to each beneficiary can be $20,000 a year. Amounts paid for another's education or medical care are also tax-free gifts. All of these amounts will not be subject to gift taxes during the donor's life or to estate taxes at his or her death. In addition, the appreciation in the value of the gifted property after the date of the gift is not subject to gift or estate taxes.

Any gift made to a spouse (regardless of amount) is free of gift taxes and estate taxes, if it qualifies for the marital deduction.

Tax rates on taxable gifts in excess of the $10,000 (or $20,000) exclusions and the marital deduction are calculated from the same schedule as estate taxes, and the same credit against tentative taxes applies to both. Furthermore, taxable gifts made during life are totaled with transfers made after death in calculating estate taxes, with a credit applied against estate taxes for prior gift taxes paid.

Life Insurance can be used to solve liquidity problems where much of the estate is in assets difficult to convert to cash. In all estates, there is a need for cash to pay estate settlement costs as well as estate taxes. Life insurance proceeds are immediately available after the insured person's death. If the insurance policy is owned by the decedent, it is part of the gross estate and subject to estate taxes. This may not present a problem when the beneficiary is the spouse, since exemption can be claimed through the unlimited marital deduction. However, life insurance proceeds will be subject to estate tax if the beneficiary is someone other than the spouse, unless the beneficiary is the policy owner.

Other Tools, such as family annuities, buy-sell agreements, charitable gifts, and the various forms of ownership and business organization, can be used in estate planning. Where grown children are self-sufficient and the estate is large, you can reduce estate taxes by simply spending the money.

Buy-and-Sell Agreements in Estate Planning

Here's a means of equitable estate transfer which assures that those heirs
who wish to continue the operation of your farm or ranch will be able to do so.

One good way a farmer or rancher can care for his family and keep his farm business from falling apart following his death, is to create a market for the farm before death. Usually, he will want his child or children to take over his farm. At the same time, he must be certain that his widow is well provided for, and that other children, who may not wish to farm, receive an equitable inheritance.

Frequently, a farmer's entire worth is tied up in the farm property. Over the years, the business, with its land, livestock and machinery, has been built up as a single, economical unit. Selling part of the farm to divide an estate would likely leave the child who prefers to continue farming with an unprofitable operation. To strap him with notes payable to his mother, or brothers and sisters, might have the same effect.

A buy-and-sell agreement funded with life insurance is one suitable way of overcoming these problems. It is a contract in which one party (usually the father) agrees that his property is to be sold for a specified price to the other party (often a son). The father's life insurance can be used to fund the purchase. At the time of the father's death, the buy-and-sell agreement is triggered and the funds are provided to carry it out.

The life insurance policy will be on the life of the father, with the son as owner of the policy and payer of all premiums. The son names himself as beneficiary. At the death of the father, the son collects the insurance proceeds, and uses them to pay for the farm. In effect, the farm has been sold for a fair price at the death of the farmer, the proceeds go to his estate, and his will provides for the distribution of his estate as he wishes. The farm remains in the family as a profitable business.

Paying the premium for the insurance policy is often a problem for the employee son. Thus, it may become necessary to increase his salary, increase his percent of the profits, or arrange for the father to loan him the money to pay the premium. However, the father himself should not be the owner of the policy, as the proceeds at his **death** would then be counted as part of his estate for federal estate tax purposes.

USES IN PARTNERSHIPS

Buy-and-sell agreements have broader usage in farm partnerships than in the sole proprietorships discussed above.

A partnership results from two or more persons, such as a farmer and his son or two sons, contracting with each other to operate a farm; to own the farm in proportion to what each has contributed in terms of money, property, and expertise; and to share in the profits and losses of the farm business in the same proportion as they own the farm. The death of a partner legally dissolves a partnership. At that point, the business must either be liquidated or reorganized. There are at least four possible forms of reorganization that may be considered:

(1) Heirs may become partners.

(2) Someone who purchases the heirs' interest may join the business organization.

(3) The remaining partner or partners can buy out the interest of the heirs, and continue to operate the farm.

(4) Heirs can buy all shares.

A buy-and-sell agreement set up before the death of any partner can avoid liquidation and determine the form of reorganization mutually agreeable to all partners. Embodying price and terms, the agreement would be binding on both heirs and surviving partners, no matter which partner died first.

As with a sole proprietorship, life insurance is one of the best methods of providing cash to carry out the agreement. There are two basic types of partnership buy-and-sell agreements: the cross-purchase plan and the partnership entity plan.

Cross-purchase plan is an agreement by two or more partners that if one of them dies, the survivors will purchase his business interest. To fund the purchase, each partner applies for a life insurance policy on the life of each of the other partners in the amount he would be obligated to pay for his share of the insured partner's interest, should that partner predecease him.

Usually, if there are only two partners in a cross-purchase plan, each partner is owner and beneficiary of the policy on his partner, and pays the premium.

Partnership entity plan is an agreement between the partnership business and the partners individually. It is agreed that if a partner dies, the partnership will purchase his business interest on behalf of the surviving partner or partners. The partnership takes out a policy on the life of each partner for the full amount of the purchase price, or for whatever portion is being insured. The partnership business itself is owner, beneficiary and premium payer of these policies. The premium payments are not deductible expenses for income tax purposes. The cash values of the policies are assets of the business, just as though the premiums were the cost or price of some other investment.

Fair market value. To establish fair market value of a farm partnership, the buy-and-sell agreement must be "at arm's length"—a negotiated agreement between two knowledgeable independent parties, without collusion, striving to arrive at fair market value.

The price or formula for calculating the sale price must represent the fair market value at the time the agreement is drawn. Fair market value is the price a willing buyer would pay a willing seller for the property.

The same price determination that would apply at death can be applied during life as well. If a partner wishes to sell during his lifetime, the agreement must bind each partner to offer his interest to the other partners or to the partnership itself, before he offers it to anyone else.

In some cases, it may be desirable to have a qualified independent trustee administer the farm purchase agreement. To accomplish this, the trustee would be named as beneficiary of the funding policies and the policies deposited with him. The trustee's specific duties would be set out in a business insurance trust agreement. Upon the death of a partner, the trustee would collect the proceeds, determine the value of the interest according to the terms of the agreement, apply the proceeds toward the purchase of that interest, and then turn the money over to the deceased partner's estate.

No provision in the agreement is more vital than the one that sets forth either an agreed upon price or method for determining the price at death. If an exact amount is set out, the agreement should be subject to periodic review with an eye for modification. An alternative is to have the value of the interest set by mutually acceptable independent appraisers. Another possibility is for the surviving partners and the estate of the deceased to select a three-man board to set the price at the death of a partner.

FARM CORPORATIONS

While a corporate form of business frequently has advantages over sole-proprietorships and partnerships in the transfer of the farm business from one generation to the next, problems revolve around control of the farm and the value of the deceased's business interests. It is important to shareholders and heirs that these areas be thought out and dealt with while all shareholders are living. With a buy-and-sell agreement, the parties are bound by contract to exchange the deceased's stock for a price stated in the agreement or determined by a prescribed formula.

In addition, the agreement should require any associate who withdraws from the corporation during his lifetime, to offer his stock to the remaining shareholders or to the corporation at the stipulated price per share.

In other respects, buy-and-sell agreements for corporations are approximately the same as for partnerships.

LEGAL COUNSEL

As with any important contract, a buy-and-sell agreement should be drawn up by an attorney who is fully acquainted with your business. Depending on your situation, financial condition and other factors, he may advise that a buy-and-sell agreement is not needed; or that special terms be included in it. While buy-and-sell agreements are frequently useful in smoothing the transfer of property, they are not a panacea for all problems. Rather, they should be viewed as one of many tools available in estate planning.

Land Condemnation Procedures

Any government agency using federal funds to acquire land for public use must follow specific procedures when dealing with property owners.

The purpose of the Uniform Relocation and Real Property Acquisition Policies Act of 1970 (Public Law 91-646) is to assure that uniform and equitable procedures for land acquisition are followed by all federal agencies and by any state agency that has received federal money or grants.

The law also provides for relocation and resettlement payments to the property owner under certain conditions. This provision for payments is most often used in highway construction through urban areas, but it also has implications for farmers and ranchers.

REAL PROPERTY ACQUISITION

Here's what the taking agency must do when acquiring land under condemnation where federal funds are used in the project. These steps are discussed in detail since they often are unfamiliar to property owners or are misunderstood.

When real property is acquired, the taking agency must, to the greatest extent possible:

(1) Make every reasonable effort to acquire it expeditiously through negotiation.

(2) Before initiation of negotiations, have the real property appraised and give the owner or his representative an opportunity to accompany the appraiser during the inspection of the property.

(3) Before the initiation of negotiations, establish an amount believed to be just compensation for the real property and make a prompt offer to acquire the property for that amount. In line with this provision the taking agency must, before requiring the owner to surrender the property, pay the agreed purchase price, or deposit with the court for the benefit of the owner, an amount not less than the agency's approved appraisal of the fair market value of the property, or pay the amount of the award of compensation in a condemnation proceeding.

(4) If the taking agency must exercise power of eminent domain, it must not intentionally make the owner institute legal proceedings to prove the fact of the taking of his real property.

(5) If the acquisition of only part of a property would leave an uneconomic remnant (remainder),

the taking agency must offer to acquire that remnant. Caution: it's often a better idea to keep control over these remnants. Studies have shown they often increase in value.

MAKING THE OFFER

At the time the taking agency makes its offer to purchase the property, the agency must provide the owner with a written statement of the basis for the amount estimated to be just compensation. The following information must be included:

(1) An identification of the real property and the particular interest being acquired.

(2) A certification, where applicable, that any separately held interest in the real property is not being acquired in whole or in part.

(3) An identification of buildings and other improvements that are considered to be part of the real property for which the offer is made.

(4) An identification of real property improvements not owned by the owner of the land.

(5) An identification of the type and approximate quantity of personal property that is not being acquired, but is on the premises.

(6) A declaration that the agency's determination of just compensation is based on the fair market value of the property; isn't less than the approved, appraised value of the property; disregards any decrease or increase in fair market value caused by the project for which property is being acquired; and where interests in the real property are separately held, includes an apportionment of the total just compensation for each of those interests. Finally, the amount of damages to any remaining real property must be shown.

ATTORNEY'S FEES

There's a little trap here. You may have heard that if you fight a valuation and are awarded a larger amount than the taking agency's offer, the appraisal fees and other costs incurred by the owner are paid by the taking agency. This is not generally true. Only if you successfully prove that the government cannot acquire the property by condemnation, or the proceeding is abandoned by the taking agency, are costs borne by the government. In cases of inverse condemnation, you get the costs paid by the agency, if you prove your case. This is not a normal situation of land condemnation and would rarely apply in typical condemnation proceedings.

ACQUIRING THE PROPERTY

A taking agency must to the greatest practical extent do the following when acquiring property:

(1) They should not schedule construction or development that would require the lawful occupant of the property to move from a dwelling or to move his business or farm operation without giving that person at least 90 days written notice of the date he must move.

(2) They should not, if possible, advance the time of condemnation.

(3) They shouldn't defer negotiations, condemnation, the deposit of funds in court for use of the owner or take any coercive action to compel an owner to agree to a price for his property.

As soon as possible after real property has been acquired, the displacing agency shall reimburse the owner for recording fees, transfer taxes and similar expenses incidental to conveying the real property to the agency.

They shall also pay penalty costs for prepayment of existing recorded mortgages entered into in good faith. The pro rata portion of any prepaid real property taxes, which are allocable to a period subsequent to the date of vesting title in the agency, must also be paid by the taking agency.

MOVING OR RELOCATION EXPENSES

The act also provides reimbursement for certain expenses of moving a farming business and residence. Listed here are those expenses that are most apt to occur when an entire farm is taken and the owner is forced to move elsewhere and start over. Payments are also possible when residences are taken, and under certain conditions, tenants are eligible for reimbursement. These situations will crop up most often in urban areas.

A farm operation that is discontinued or relocated is entitled to actual reasonable expenses for:

(1) Transporting personal property from the displacement site, but only a distance of less than 50 miles, unless the farming operation can't be relocated within that distance.

(2) Packing, crating, insuring, installing and reinstalling equipment, etc.

(3) Searching for a replacement farm operation. Under this provision, usually the cost of travel, meals and lodging is covered. Time spent searching can be charged provided it doesn't exceed a specified maximum charge per hour. Cost of a broker or realtor may be borne by the displacing agency if they feel it is needed.

FIXED PAYMENTS

The law provides a method of determining fixed payments to cover moving and related costs. If a farmer elects to receive a fixed payment in lieu of actual moving expenses, he's entitled to an amount equal to the average annual net income of the farm operation, but it can't be less than or more than specified amounts.

The average annual net is the annual net earnings before federal, state and local income taxes during the two years immediately preceding the tax year in which the farmer is displaced. If these years aren't representative they can be changed.

There are additional procedures that cover corporate, partnership and joint type operations. Proof of earnings is required.

APPLICABLE DATE, DEFINITION

Definition of the actual time of taking is complex and often has different meanings depending on the circumstances.

A farm operation is defined as a lawful activity conducted solely or primarily for the production of one or more agricultural products or commodities to the extent that they provide one-third of the operator's income. However, where the operation is obviously a farming operation, it need not meet this requirement.

Chapter 5

Soils and Crop Production

A good crop manager is able to evaluate his soil's productive capacity and to plan his production program to achieve this potential. He should not try to cut costs too close or to push production beyond his soil's capabilities.

Some production costs cannot be reduced without seriously affecting yields and profits. Plant high quality seed and apply required fertilizer rates. Don't overlook proper cultivation and pesticide treatment.

There are some costs, on the other hand, which can be reduced without limiting yields. With today's high labor costs, many farmers are reducing their labor requirements by investing in more and larger equipment, laying out fields for maximum efficiency, growing crops to level out labor requirements and using less expensive tillage methods.

Crop production practices should be performed on time if weather and other factors permit. Planting late or letting weeds get a headstart will seriously trim your potential yields and profits.

Various crops require different amounts of labor, machine work and other resources. Try to set up a cropping system which will spread labor requirements over the year. Owning machinery can be costly, so plan your program to make as much use of a given piece of equipment as possible. For some producers, this may mean specialization. In other instances, it may be desirable to expand your operation or use a double cropping system.

Certain crop rotations may make more complete year-round use of land and reduce weed, disease and insect problems. Although high fertilization rates may allow such practices as continuous corn growing, good rotations still have a definite place on the farm. They help you build up and maintain soil tilth and prevent erosion. This is especially true for irregular land and less fertile soils. Highest returns are normally possible by cropping as intensively as your soil's fertility permits, as long as good conservation practices can be maintained.

The application of sound conservation principles and practices is necessary if soil fertility is to be maintained at satisfactory levels. Cropping programs which minimize soil erosion include contouring, strip cropping, terracing and mulching.

Minimum tillage practices include any method of land preparation and planting which eliminates one or several operations normally performed when conventional tillage systems are used. Yields can usually be maintained using minimum tillage where the land is suited to this practice. However, this is possible only through good management. Desired stands and effective weed control are more difficult to achieve. These tillage methods may reduce production costs, but some of the savings in tillage may be offset by the need to place greater reliance on herbicides in order to obtain effective weed control.

Reduce harvest losses by getting the crop under cover as quickly as possible once it reaches maturity. Combining at high moisture levels can permit you to harvest corn and similar crops with a minimum of field losses and risk from adverse weather, which is more likely with later harvest. However, this will increase the cost of drying and the required capacity of your drying system. Drying can be eliminated or supplemented on livestock farms by storing all or part of your feedgrain as high moisture in airtight or conventional silos.

A knowledge of soils is fundamental for developing a sound cropping and fertilization program. Determine the specific limitations of your soils and develop programs which will fully utilize their potential. Base fertilizer rates on crop requirements, soil structure and drainage and the particular soil's productive capacity.

Soil testing is a valuable tool for monitoring and managing your soil's fertility. Soil samples should be taken in a systematic manner and tested by an approved laboratory. Soil tests estimate the amount of nutrients available for crop growth. Know the nutrient requirements for various crops. Nutrient removal by a given crop is directly related to its yield. Then use soil test results and a record of your past fertilizer applications to develop a fertilization program for each crop.

Observe growing crops. Plant analysis can be used to supplement soil test results. Regardless, you should observe growing crops throughout the season for any signs of specific nutrient shortages. Then confirm your observations by taking a plant tissue sample for testing. Deficiency of one element can restrict the effectiveness of other elements present in the soil in sufficient amounts.

You may want to set up small plots in your field to test the effect of certain types and various rates of fertilizer.

Forms and types of fertilizer are varied. Fertilizers are available in solid (fine and granular), liquid and gaseous forms. These materials can be applied in several ways: broadcast (dry, liquid), drill (dry, liquid), band (dry, liquid), knifed-in (gaseous, liquid), foliar (liquid sprays), and irrigated (soluble forms put on with water).

Commercial fertilizer mixtures are available in varying analyses. Elements essential for plant growth are classified into three groups:

Major plant nutrients include nitrogen (N), phosphorus (P), and potassium (K).

Secondary plant nutrients are comprised of calcium (Ca), magnesium (Mg), and sulfur (S).

Micronutrients are those plant food elements which are required in minute quantities by growing crops. They are nevertheless important for high yields. These nutrients include boron (B), copper (Cu), iron (Fe), manganese (Mn), molybdenum (Mo), zinc (Zn), and chlorine (Cl).

Soil Origin and Formation

Many factors interacting over a long period of time have produced the soil types found in your area.

The wide variation in kinds of soils found throughout our country is the result of the differing conditions under which they were formed. The characteristics of a soil have been determined by five major factors—parent material, age or degree of weathering, climate, topography and vegetation. If these factors in two different areas are identical, the resulting soils will be alike or nearly so. But vary any one or more of them and differences occur.

Parent material is paramount to soil formation. Constant exposure to the atmosphere subjects various rock material to the forces of weathering. The action of water, including freezing and thawing, oxygen, carbon dioxide and acids over time give rise to soil as we know it. These underlying parent materials are classed as either residual (those which remain where formed) or transported by water (alluvial), glacier or wind.

Glaciers gave rise to a wide variation in parent materials throughout the northern portion of our country. Parent material was picked up, carried, mixed and redeposited. This wide variation in parent material, combined with differing topography, drainage and other soil forming factors, has given rise to many soil types across the country.

Tremendous amounts of water carrying large amounts of sediments were released along the frontal edge of the glaciers. Water deposited materials resulted, including outwash plains, glacial lake soils, valley fills and river alluvial deposits.

With the retreat of the ice sheets there were periods of low rainfall. This subjected much of the fine material, earlier carried and deposited by the melting ice, to severe wind erosion. As a result, large areas of loess (wind blown material) were deposited across the central section of the U.S.

Age or development of soils varies widely, depending on the other factors of soil formation. Nevertheless, all soils undergo definite stages of maturity. Rock and minerals are broken into smaller particles, some to clays. Soil acidity increases and water permeability decreases. Soils tend to develop rapidly at first. Sufficient nutrients are released for plant growth and organic matter accumulates. Later, the process slows and nutrient removal exceeds its release.

Some soils weather and develop faster than others. Those having good underground drainage, receiving excessive rainfall, and located in a slight depression, weather faster than the average soil. Such soils will likely be more acid and lower in productivity than soils located on higher slopes or having a higher water table. Soils having a sandstone origin also weather rather rapidly. They also decline in productivity faster and usually don't achieve the fertility that is possible from limestone soils.

As soils mature, a pronounced layering occurs in the profile, particularly in a soil that is well drained and located in the temperate zone. Three distinct layers known as horizons develop. The surface is the zone of maximum leaching, whereas the subsoil is basically a zone of maximum accumula-

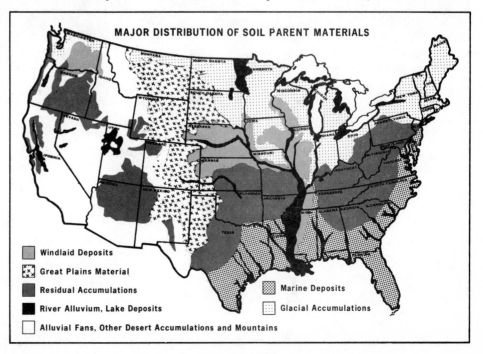

MAJOR DISTRIBUTION OF SOIL PARENT MATERIALS

Windlaid Deposits

Great Plains Material

Residual Accumulations

River Alluvium, Lake Deposits

Alluvial Fans, Other Desert Accumulations and Mountains

Marine Deposits

Glacial Accumulations

tion from materials leached from the surface. Underlying is the parent material.

Climate, a term which includes rainfall, sunlight, temperature changes and air movement, greatly influences the intensity, nature and sequence of soil development. In the initial stages of development, most of the soil characteristics are inherited. But as a soil matures, more of its characteristics are acquired through the influence of climate. Climatic differences over an extended period tend to produce varying soil profiles, even though they may have originated from the same parent material.

Vegetation, closely associated with climate, supplies the organic matter or living portion of our soils. Native vegetation consists primarily of conifers, hardwoods, various grasses and desert shrubs. While trees produce substantially more organic debris, it all remains near the soil surface, much of which is lost through oxidation and decay.

Grasses, on the other hand, contribute more to soil organic matter. The bulk of the organic matter is incorporated within the upper one to two feet of soil through their fibrous root systems. Naturally, the production of organic matter is more profuse in high rainfall areas. Also, organic matter is more difficult to maintain under higher temperatures.

Topography, along with soil permeability, proportions the amount of rainfall which percolates through the soil. The more level the soil, the greater the profile development is likely to be. On steep slopes, due to erosion, soils are generally young and shallow.

Topography also influences depth of water tables. In low areas where drainage is imperfect, the water table is near the surface. Poor aeration gives rise to a predominance of dull, gray soils. On moderate slopes, where the water table may fluctuate, soil will likely show a mottling of gray. On steeper slopes with a deep water table, oxidation produces yellowish or reddish-brown soils.

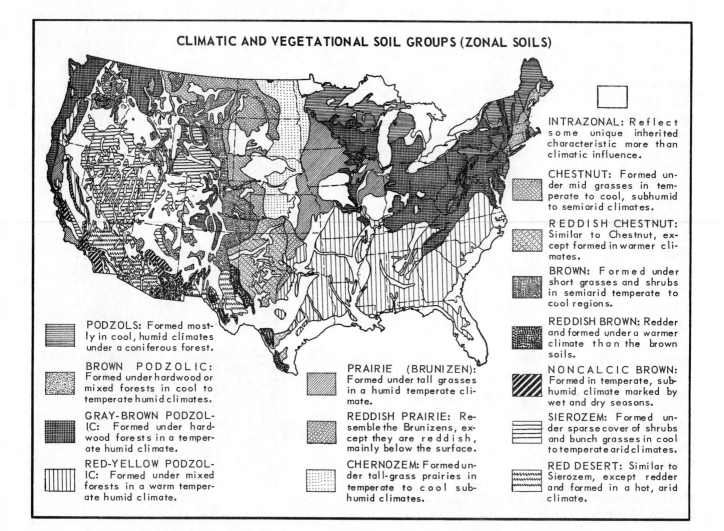

CLIMATIC AND VEGETATIONAL SOIL GROUPS (ZONAL SOILS)

INTRAZONAL: Reflect some unique inherited characteristic more than climatic influence.

CHESTNUT: Formed under mid grasses in temperate to cool, subhumid to semiarid climates.

REDDISH CHESTNUT: Similar to Chestnut, except formed in warmer climates.

BROWN: Formed under short grasses and shrubs in semiarid temperate to cool regions.

REDDISH BROWN: Redder and formed under a warmer climate than the brown soils.

NONCALCIC BROWN: Formed in temperate, subhumid climate marked by wet and dry seasons.

SIEROZEM: Formed under sparse cover of shrubs and bunch grasses in cool to temperate arid climates.

RED DESERT: Similar to Sierozem, except redder and formed in a hot, arid climate.

PODZOLS: Formed mostly in cool, humid climates under a coniferous forest.

BROWN PODZOLIC: Formed under hardwood or mixed forests in cool to temperate humid climates.

GRAY-BROWN PODZOLIC: Formed under hardwood forests in a temperate humid climate.

RED-YELLOW PODZOLIC: Formed under mixed forests in a warm temperate humid climate.

PRAIRIE (BRUNIZEN): Formed under tall grasses in a humid temperate climate.

REDDISH PRAIRIE: Resemble the Brunizens, except they are reddish, mainly below the surface.

CHERNOZEM: Formed under tall-grass prairies in temperate to cool subhumid climates.

On-Farm Crop Testing

Determine what crop varieties or practices seem to have the most merit on your farm. Then use this guide to set up a test to further evaluate their suitability under your conditions.

The alert manager evaluates new developments in crop production before adopting them for his own operation. Test results from agricultural experiment stations furnish valuable information. By comparing these test findings with your own experience, you can often determine the merits of a new variety or practice. At least you can sift out the most promising prospects and test under your own farming conditions before committing yourself to a major change or investment.

In setting up any test, decide what is to be specifically tested. Your current variety, practice or treatment should be included as a yardstick for comparison. Hold all conditions except the one being tested as constant as possible.

TESTING PROCEDURE

Success of any crop test, whether it be variety or fertilizer rate depends on careful planning, test area selection, management and interpretation.

Selection of test site should be given serious consideration. The soil should be as uniform as possible to insure comparable test results. If you cannot restrict the test plot to one soil type, try to plant rows so they cross the different soil types.

If possible, select a location that has received essentially the same fertilizer treatment for several years. Avoid sites that have received manure recently. Manure applications aren't usually even enough to give uniform results. Soil drainage, drainage ditches, fence rows, dead furrows and slope of the field should also be kept as uniform as possible. Avoid having one or more of the treatments fall in a dead furrow or drainage ditch. Don't locate the test plot near a fence. Experience has shown that rows bordering a fence turn out different than those within the field.

Size of test plot needs to be large enough to permit using your equipment and to give reliable results. Test rows the length of the field are usually most practical. They are easier to plant and harvest along with the rest of the field.

Don't plant excessively large plots hoping to increase the accuracy of the test. The opposite may be true. More variables may creep into the test.

Number of rows or width of plot should be about double your equipment. If you own a two-row corn picker or sheller, plant at least four corn rows to a given treatment; for soybeans, small grain, etc., double the width of the combine. Adjoining rows of different treatments influence each other. Only the middle rows of the plot should be harvested for comparison.

Plant trial plots at the same time you seed the complete field. This will save you both time and labor. Normal cultural methods shouldn't be changed unless they are being tested. In planting for a varietal trial, put in the hoppers only what seed you think it will take. Clean out the planter or drill between varieties—easiest way is to drill out the excess in a roadway or waste area.

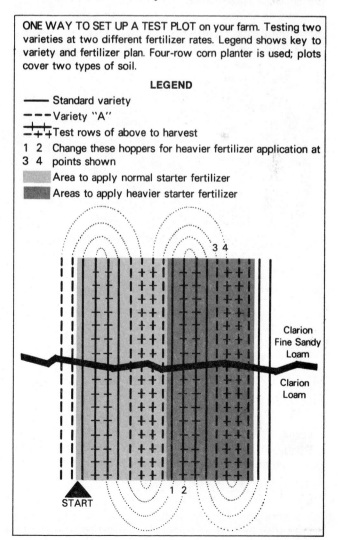

ONE WAY TO SET UP A TEST PLOT on your farm. Testing two varieties at two different fertilizer rates. Legend shows key to variety and fertilizer plan. Four-row corn planter is used; plots cover two types of soil.

LEGEND

—— Standard variety

- - - Variety "A"

╫╫ Test rows of above to harvest

1 2 Change these hoppers for heavier fertilizer application at
3 4 points shown

▨ Area to apply normal starter fertilizer

▩ Areas to apply heavier starter fertilizer

Clarion Fine Sandy Loam

Clarion Loam

3 4

1 2

START

Harvest of test plots is probably most easily accomplished by harvesting a complete strip across the entire field. Harvest the middle section for reasons previously given. If a combine is used, let it run out between treatments. Another method is to use a watch and let it run the same length of time between treatments. Rows at the head of the test plots should be harvested ahead of time to give room for clearing equipment and to avoid mixing this grain with the test.

Weigh grain from each plot carefully to the smallest possible unit. A small error can make a big difference when per acre yields are figured.

Figure yields of row crops by first multiplying the length of the field or test plot in feet by the number of rows harvested. The part of an acre the plot represents can be calculated using total row length in feet. Refer to the number of feet in an acre for different row widths shown in the table below. For row widths not shown, use the formula for figuring feet of row in an acre.

You can also measure row crop test yields by measuring off 1/100 of an acre and then picking and weighing grain from that row length. Length of row in 1/100 of an acre is shown.

GUIDE FOR PLANNING A FARM TEST

Row Width (inches)	Feet of Row to Equal an Acre	Feet of Row to Equal 1/100 Acre
22	23,800	238.0
24	21,780	217.8
26	20,074	200.7
28	18,695	187.0
30	17,424	174.2
32	16,314	163.1
34	15,392	153.9
36	14,520	145.2
38	13,741	137.4
40	13,081	130.8
42	12,446	124.5

To figure feet of row per acre for other row widths, use the following formula:

$$\frac{43,560}{\text{Width of row (feet)}} = \text{Feet of row per acre}$$

For figuring small grain or forage yields multiply length x width of plot in feet. Divide the resulting square footage by 43,560 to obtain the percentage of an acre the plot represents.

If you know what part of an acre is contained within the plot, you can find the yield in bushels per acre as follows:

$$\text{Lbs. harvested} \quad x \quad \frac{\text{Part of acre harvested}}{\text{Lbs. per bushel}} = \text{Bu. per acre}$$

Variation in treatment or a noticeable difference in maturity between varieties calls for making a moisture test. Seal a small sample in a glassine bag and take it to your local elevator for a test. Correct yields for moisture as follows:

Harvested yield x (100 — field moisture percentage) = Bu. dry matter/A.

$$\frac{\text{Bu. dry matter/A.}}{\text{(100—desired moisture percentage)}} = \begin{array}{c}\text{Bu. per acre (corrected to}\\\text{desired moisture)}\end{array}$$

Complete crop test records are essential for comparing results both in the season they were made and historically. Record the location of the plot on the map and within the field. Count the number of rows from the edge of the field to where planting of the test rows was started. Then there can be no dispute about where the testing area is, even if the stake is lost. In addition, mark a piece of lath and weave it in the fence at the end of the rows.

Weather, disease, insect problems, standability, health of plant and root development should be recorded throughout the season. Prior to harvest, a final recording of information will help in evaluating final yields. An example of harvest-time notes is shown.

HARVEST RECORDS OF A CORN VARIETY TEST
(from 65-1/2 feet of row)

Variety	Total Plants	Erect Plants	Down Plants	Barren Stalks	Dropped Ears	Sample Weight (lb.)	Moisture Percent	Yield Bu./A	Yield Corrected For Moisture Bu./A
A	64	53	7	3	1	45.75	20.0	130.7	123.8
B	63	39	24	2	0	50.50	18.5	144.3	139.1
C	66	57	9	1	0	49.00	18.0	140.0	135.8
D	61	49	12	1	0	42.00	16.0	120.0	119.3
E	54	45	9	4	0	39.00	16.5	111.4	110.1
F	64	60	4	0	0	45.00	16.0	128.5	127.7
G	69	61	8	0	0	55.00	16.0	157.1	156.2

Although each variety or treatment is planted at the same rate, insects, stalk rot or some other problems can make a difference in harvest stands. Final stand can affect yields. This may warrant some consideration if the difference arose from a factor other than those being tested.

Yield differences between treatments or varieties need to be viewed with a certain amount of discretion. Yield variations can occur from outside influences. Small yield disparities should not necessarily be interpreted as being affected by the varieties or treatments tested.

Several years of testing may be needed. Don't draw conclusions on the basis of one year's tests alone. Keep tests up to date. Treatments definitely showing no promise should be eliminated from further testing.

Soils and Fertility Management

Many factors affect the crop yielding ability of a soil.
Each soil should be managed to make the most of its production capability.

Soil testing is the single most important guide to profitable fertilizer application. A basic understanding of soils can help you interpret and apply soil test results to your specific soils and management practices. Though soils may look alike and test the same, required fertilizer rates and crop response may be substantially different.

Yield producing capability of soils and their response to fertilizer vary with their physical, chemical and biological makeup. Many soil characteristics can be altered by fertilizer and lime, drainage and good soil management practices. However, basic limitations must be recognized when establishing attainable, profitable yield goals and the fertilizer rates to achieve them.

PHYSICAL SOIL PROPERTIES

Effective rooting depth is dependent on the nature of soil as well as pH and nutrient availability. Limited root penetration prevents a crop from making fullest possible use of available nutrients throughout the soil profile. Root penetration is more restricted on soils having a shallow profile, high clay subsoils, natural or plow pans, and those which are compacted, poorly drained or inadequately aerated.

An effective fertilizer program can help you make the most of restricted root penetration. On Huey, a problem Illinois soil, corn rooting, when unfertilized, is restricted to about 2-1/2 feet; 3-1/2 feet when fertilized.

Water holding capacity of highly productive soils is usually substantial. Except for soils that are irrigated, those having a higher water holding capacity exhibit greater ability to supply necessary moisture and nutrients during drouthy periods. Silty soils hold up to two to three inches of available moisture per foot of soil, whereas a sandy soil may hold only a little over an inch. A silty soil having an effective rooting depth of five to six feet for corn, for example, will allow much better crop performance and use of nutrients during dry seasons than a sandy soil or one that limits root growth to the top two or three feet of the soil.

Topography affects the yield goal you can reasonably expect from a particular soil. Normally, yield predictions for a given soil are lowered as slopes exceed 6% to 12% and as erosion becomes severe. A larger amount of rainfall runs off rather than being absorbed by the soil. Good management practices such as reduced tillage, which leaves the residue on the surface to limit erosion and increase water infiltration, can permit you to set higher yield goals and fertilize accordingly.

BIOLOGICAL ACTIVITY

While organic matter comprises only a small portion of the soil, it plays an important function in soil productivity. Microbial activity and resulting by-products stabilize the soil through improved granulation and quality, increased moisture retention, better aeration and reduced surface crusting. Nitrogen, phosphorus, sulfur and other nutrients are also released for crop use.

More important than the actual amount of soil organic matter is the nature of the material and stage of decomposition. Major benefit is derived when the material is being decomposed. Returning crop residue may not increase organic matter for any length of time, but the biological activity during decomposition improves the physical condition of the soil. In addition, released nutrients reduce the amount of required fertilizer.

Return as much residue as your cropping program permits, particularly on heavier soils. Using modern cropping and fertilizer practices, the more intensively and profitably a soil is farmed, the more productive it will likely become.

CHEMISTRY OF THE SOIL

Agronomists are giving greater weight to soil type and chemical makeup in soil test interpretations and fertilizer recommendations.

Nutrient-supplying power is defined as the capacity of a soil, both topsoil and subsoil, to provide nutrients for crop needs. Within the topsoil, both mineral composition and organic matter affect nutrient content. The parent material and degree of weathering determine nutrient availability in the lower rooting zone. Some soils have a much larger nutrient reservoir than others.

Though nutrient-supplying power of soils differs greatly, other factors must also be considered in determining how effectively crops may be able to use available nutrients. Soil characteristics which affect root growth and development play an important role in use of subsoil nutrients. Compactness of the soil, its drainage, aeration, water holding capacity, depth to bedrock and pH all enter the picture.

The rooting habit of the crop and period of greatest nutrient uptake need to be taken into account, too. Corn and alfalfa, for example, root to a much greater depth than small grains. Likewise, differences in uptake exist between nutrients. In corn, major uptake of potassium occurs soon after silking and before the root system has reached maximum development and depth. Therefore, the potassium available in the plow layer and upper subsoil is more important than that in the lower subsoil. Conversely, subsoil phosphorus is extremely important because corn takes up substantial amounts after roots are fully developed and right through grain formation.

Cation exchange capacity affects the liming and fertilizer program, too. The base or cation exchange capacity of a soil is its ability to hold, by absorption, various nutrients including potassium, manganese, magnesium, calcium, iron, copper, zinc and others. Ability of a soil to absorb and provide nutrients to growing crops is partially a function of soil organic matter and mineral content referred to as the colloidal complex. Soil colloids are minute particles of clay and humus which carry a negative charge and have the capacity to trade or exchange one base nutrient for another. Soils containing much sand, but little organic matter or clay of the Kaolin type, have a low exchange capacity.

Leaching and crop use deplete the nutrients held by soil. They are replaced by hydrogen and aluminum ions. But the soil's fertility potential can be realized by applying fertilizer and reversing the process.

Calcium and magnesium account for some 80% or more of the exchangeable nutrients in most soils, with potassium totaling some 1% to 5%. Consequently, liming is important to maintain both required calcium and magnesium in the soil and a pH most suitable for optimum production. The higher the exchange capacity of a soil, the heavier the liming rate will need to be to raise the pH.

Aside from applying proper amounts of lime and fertilizer to maintain soil pH and base exchange cations, it is important that calcium, magnesium and potassium be supplied in the proper balance. Though a rather wide range is generally acceptable, the balance usually falls within this range: calcium, 70% to 75%; magnesium, 10% to 15%; and potassium, 2% to 5%. Where the balance between calcium and magnesium may fall out of the desired range, limestone recommendations will call for a low or high magnesium limestone (calcitic or dolomitic).

Because lower exchange capacity soils, such as sands, have a lower capacity to supply nutrients, fertilizer rates need to be somewhat higher to support a given yield, unless the soil's fertility has been built to the recommended test level.

MANAGEMENT SUGGESTIONS

● Larger applications of phosphorus and potassium every two or three years, once soil is built to desired fertility, may be more economical than annual applications. Major exception is for potassium on sandy soils.

● On higher testing soils, it is doubtful that depth of fertilizer application will affect yields. Where no-plow tillage is used, plowing every four or five years may be necessary to incorporate the fertilizer through the plow layer.

● Make sure you know the plow depth on which your state's fertilizer recommendations are made. If you plow 10 inches deep and fertilizer recommendations are based on a 6-2/3 inch depth, you are turning 50% more soil and further diluting the fertilizer.

● Improved practices which raise crop yield require increased rates of nitrogen. Not so for phosphorus and potassium. A soil test level that produces 99% of maximum yield at the 100 bushel level for corn will do likewise for 175 bushels. The higher the yield, the larger the root system and its contact with nutrients.

Soil Testing for Top Yields

*The soil test is an important, reliable tool for
determining the most profitable fertilizer application rates.*

Soil tests measure the available plant foods in a soil. The methods used and elements tested vary from state to state. Research and practical field work indicate little need for certain tests in some states, but as they become necessary, they will be added.

Micronutrients are one case in point. Research is proceeding along these lines but many soil testers feel we are not yet at the point where routine laboratory tests can accurately predict the need for many of the micronutrients. As yields climb the need will grow. Some states are making extensive tests for micronutrients.

Tests most commonly run by your state laboratories include those for phosphorus, potassium, soil acidity or pH and calcium. Nitrogen is sometimes estimated by amount of organic matter present. Phosphorus may be measured by either a P_1 or P_2 test, depending on the soil pH and form of phosphate fertilizer to be applied.

Soil acidity or pH contributes directly to the efficiency with which crops can use the nutrients in the soil. Alfalfa, red clover and other legumes, in particular, will not grow successfully unless the soil pH tests close to neutral. Calcium tests are also used in many areas in addition to the acidity test. Apart from raising pH, calcium is essential for plant growth.

Various tests can be made for nitrogen including its content in organic matter. However, the usefulness of these tests is limited since soil nitrogen content changes rather rapidly.

VALUE OF SOIL TESTS

Benefits from soil tests depend on properly translating them into sound fertilizer recommendations. Available soil nutrients must be compared with the needs of a given crop to produce the desired yield. But the soil test alone cannot simply be used to determine how much fertilizer is required to make up the difference.

A given fertilizer rate can often result in widely variable crop yields even for the same set of soil test values. The crop response depends on much more than just the availability of nutrients in the surface soil as revealed by a soil test. The soil type and the crop to be grown are two important factors to be considered when making any fertilizer recommendation.

Soil type greatly affects crop response to fertilizer. For example, crop response to phosphorus application varies between different types of soil within the same state, even when P_1 soil tests are the same. Variation is thought to be due in part to depth of rooting and amount of available phosphorus in the subsoil.

Crop grown affects the yield response you can expect from soil with a given soil test reading and the amount of nutrients to be supplied through use of a fertilizer.

In Illinois, test readings have been correlated with the yield response for various crops. Shown in the chart below is the relationship between percent of maximum yield and the P_1 (phosphorus) test, provided other nutrients are not limited. Notice that with a P_1 test of 30, 97% of the maximum obtainable yield is possible when growing corn. At the same test level, wheat, oats, alfalfa and clover will produce only about 70% of their maximum yield. They need sharply higher amounts of phosphorus for maximum yield.

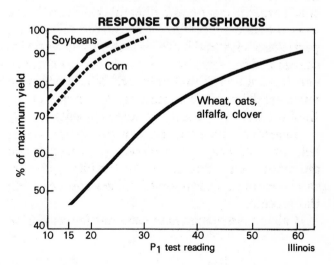

RESPONSE TO PHOSPHORUS

Soybeans

Corn

Wheat, oats, alfalfa, clover

% of maximum yield

P_1 test reading

Illinois

Management, both past and present, has a big influence on fertilizer rates. Previous cropping practices, residual fertilizer effects, manure applied, previous and present methods of fertilization, plant population and weed, insect and disease control all should be considered. That is why most states provide crop and soil information forms to accompany soil samples. Complete records will help supply accurate information to match recommended fertilizer rates with your situation.

Combining all factors into one equation that can be used to make fertilizer recommendations is not easy. Electronic computers can help. Progress is being made in this direction. Principal problem lies in obtaining adequate field data essential for developing the desired relationships for different soils and crops. Even then, soil tests cannot be looked upon as a cure-all. Unusual moisture and temperature conditions can alter expected results.

Accurate calibration of fertilizer need is the basic foundation of useful soil tests. States develop soil test correlation data through extensive experimental testing. For this reason, it is often best to use laboratories set up in your area. By comparing past crop responses with a given soil test value they know about what fertilizer rate is needed to achieve a particular yield. Field studies need to be continuously updated to match modern cropping practices and yield goals.

TAKING SOIL SAMPLES

Soil chemists have developed sound and reliable testing procedures. But your soil tests will be no better than the sample you take. They must be representative of the soil in your fields.

Methods of sampling vary between states, but here are some general points to keep in mind.

Divide field according to soil type or condition and take samples from each area large enough to manage separately. A uniform area will seldom be larger than five to 10 acres—so sample accordingly. In most areas, 12 to 15 individual samples

Suggested Sampling Procedure
(For 10 acre sampling area)

```
        X X
(1)      X
        X X
                    X X
                     X (3)
                    X X
        X X
(2)      X
        X X
                    X X
                     X (4)
                    X X
```

should be taken and mixed together to form a representative sample from that area. One approach is shown here.

On fields where there is only one kind of soil and/or recent cropping and fertilizer and lime treatments have been the same throughout, follow the pattern illustrated. Select four major sample locations as suggested and make five individual samplings at each location. Taking five small samples at each location will assure that the whole sample doesn't come from a fertilizer band applied previously. Where fields have different soils, problem areas, or have been cropped, fertilized or limed differently in the past five to 10 years, take enough samples to represent the variation.

Representative samples can be better assured by adhering to these suggested sampling procedures:
● A soil map can help you select uniform areas to sample. You may be able to combine similar soil areas so they can be sampled as one, provided treatments, etc., have been the same.
● Avoid sampling unusual areas such as dead furrows, back furrows, old fence lines, eroded spots, old hay stack bottoms, field depressions and manure piles. Don't take any samples from an unusual area in the field unless you wish to test it separately.
● Individual samplings can be taken with an auger, sampling tube or spade. Whichever you use, be sure to collect a sample that represents soil from the surface to plow depth on cultivated land—5 to 7 inches on pastures. Most fertilizer recommendations in the past have been based on a 6-inch plow depth. Plowing to 8 inches will increase the lime requirement by one-third. Broadcast recommendations for phosphorus and potash in a buildup program need to be adjusted too.
● Mix subsamples from each area thoroughly in a clean pail and take your sample from it.
● Record on a map the locations from which you took samples and outline low spots, knolls and draws. This will help you or the soil tester to interpret the tests and suggest the proper treatment. If you plan to treat areas individually, you must know where each sample came from.
● Pay strict attention to handling and shipping advice of the laboratory. Iowa, for instance, now tests undried samples, so it is important to send them to the laboratory as soon as possible after collecting. Place samples in a clean container, preferably the soil sample boxes obtainable from many county extension agents.

Frequency of testing will vary with farms and soils. To assure proper balance and fertility, fields should be tested at least every three to five years. This usually means once every rotation. Since subsoils are not treated, they do not change as much. One sampling may be used for many years. Missouri recommends a retest of subsoil at least once every 10 years.

Plant Analysis Detects Fertility Problems

It's a useful supplemental tool for monitoring soil nutrients available to the growing crop and for avoiding deficiencies before they occur.

Plant analysis by itself does not provide all the answers for planning a fertilizer program and producing top yields. Perhaps with more refinement in the future, it will come much closer to filling this role. But for the present, plant analysis can serve as a valuable tool to supplement soil testing.

Primary tool by which to judge the overall fertility status of the soil and upon which to base fertilizer recommendations continues to be soil testing. Plant analysis cannot measure soil nutrient reserves or determine a precise need for fertilizer.

Farmers who can benefit most from plant analysis are those who soil test regularly and apply fertilizer according to recommendations. Of the many plant tissue samples taken each season, a majority of the nutrient deficiencies can be traced to failure to follow these practices. Only when the soil tests up to desired levels can you be reasonably assured of getting top yields as permitted by adequate plant nutrient composition.

Complete program of plant analysis combined with soil testing should be considered if yields have leveled out or are suspected of being low despite having adhered to soil test recommendations. This signals that it is time to look at the growing crop from the inside.

The program now being recommended by some states and various companies is to begin with a soil test and apply the necessary fertilizer and lime. Then make periodic visual observations throughout the season and take plant tissue samples at the appropriate time as a double check on how well the program is faring. The plant analysis serves as a guide in planning or altering fertilizer applications in the seasons to follow. Combining the results of both soil tests and plant analysis can help to nail down what is often referred to as a prescription fertilizer program.

Monitoring feature of plant analysis serves the important function of avoiding future deficiencies or excesses. Though you may have supplied the nutrients to the soil, you have no assurance that they are being taken up in adequate amounts by the crop. The balance or relationship among nutrients can determine sufficiency or deficiency in a crop, too. One nutrient being taken up by the plant in limited or excessive quantities can prevent the full use of another. For example, the ratio of potassium to calcium; magnesium to phosphorus; and iron to magnesium or zinc can prove valuable when diagnosing suspected deficiencies of these nutrients.

Usefulness of plant analysis for correcting existing deficiencies in the growing crop is limited. In a majority of cases the sample is taken too late in the season to permit effective treatment, but there are exceptions.

Importance of plant analysis is increasing. The push for higher yields, and the fertilizer applications required to achieve them, is prompting a closer check on plant nutrient balance. Heavier rates of fertilizer and lime, though necessary, can alter the concentration of nutrients within the plant and may cause a deficiency or a toxicity of one or more nutrients. Plant analysis can detect nutrient disorders within a crop that a soil test may not predict. Once a deficiency symptom is recognized, it must be assumed that the field has not been producing top yields for several years.

Increasingly, micronutrients are being recognized for their importance in promoting efficient use of the major nutrients. Soil tests are available for micronutrients, but they are not as reliable as for the major nutrients. Besides, their level within the soil can change appreciably with soil conditions. Further, micronutrient levels in growing tissue may exceed those found in the soil. Best measure of their availability appears to be where the greatest quantities exist.

The range between deficiency and toxicity of some micronutrients in crops is rather narrow. Just as more micronutrient deficiencies are showing up, so are toxicities. So application should be made discriminately. In some situations, a plant analysis may be the only means of evaluating the nutrient status of the soil-plant environment.

Careful interpretation is as much or more important than the plant analysis itself. Recognizing that plant analysis has its limitations, interpretation of the results by an expert is required if you are to benefit most from the use of this tool. Considerable research and testing have gone into establishing desirable nutrient levels or sufficiency ranges for various crops.

These sufficiency ranges vary within a crop. For instance, it is known that certain genes can control the uptake and accumulation of certain nutrients in some crops. As a result, a particular variety may turn in a top performance at a different nutrient level than another variety of the same crop.

Nutrient content in a plant can vary widely from the sufficiency range for a number of reasons, so the cause needs to be checked out. Aside from nutrient availability in the soil, weather, soil compaction, root growth, disease, insects, plant stand, weeds and many other factors can affect plant nutrient composition. This is why it is extremely important to accurately provide all the information requested in the questionnaire which is submitted with the tissue sample.

Where soil nutrient availability is the cause for several nutrients testing above or below the sufficiency range, it is necessary to track down the primary deficiency. Usually, correction of that deficiency will pull the other nutrients back in line.

Correct sampling procedures are essential. Be sure to follow the detailed instructions prescribed by the laboratory which will be doing the analysis. Sampling is usually advised when a deficiency first appears. But for routine sampling of normal plants, a definite time for sampling is suggested.

Nutrient composition varies between plant parts at a given stage of growth and within a particular plant part throughout the season. So both the stage of plant growth and part for sampling of normal plants need to be prescribed and followed. As yet, standards for nutrient levels for varying stages throughout the growth of the plant have not been well established. Especially during early growth or after seed set, the normal growth pattern is interrupted. Nutrients may become concentrated or diluted in various plant parts.

Suggested Plant Sampling Procedure For Plant Analysis

Crop	Stage of growth	Plant part	Number of plants to sample
Corn	Prior to tasseling	Whole plant or fully developed leaf below whorl	15-25
	At silking	Ear leaf	
Sorghum		2nd leaf from top just as head is fully emerged	15-25
Soybeans		1st bloom, select 1st fully developed trifoliate leaf below top of plant. Remove and discard stems. Submit leaves only.	35-50
Cotton		When bolls start to set, most recently matured leaves	35-50

Where a deficiency is apparent, it is advised that two samples be sent to the laboratory for comparison. One sample should be taken from several normal plants; the other from deficient ones. That way everything is essentially the same except for the deficiency, including variety, stage of growth, plant part and soil moisture. Also, some laboratories will not accept tissue samples without an accompanying soil sample. More meaningful information may be obtained by comparing readings of the different samples taken at the same time.

Select your sample distribution to represent a soil area and avoid taking samples from plants obviously damaged by disease, insects, chemicals or machinery. Sampling is not recommended when plants are under extreme weather stress and when stands are poor or excessively weedy.

Because type of season can affect plant composition, several years of sampling and testing may be necessary.

Samples can easily become contaminated. Wherever possible avoid sampling dusty or soil contaminated plants—this can affect the test. If absolutely necessary dust the sample off. Do not collect samples in a galvanized bucket. Before sending samples, air dry them to prevent molding. Send the sample in a recommended sampling bag, not a plastic or polyethylene bag.

Liming Soils for Profitable Crops

Applying lime to raise the soil pH to the proper level improves the availability of soil nutrients to growing crops.

On acid soils use of lime is required to achieve a well balanced fertility program.

Benefits of lime are reflected in improved crop yields and income. Many of the benefits accrue over several years, so the results are often less dramatic than with fertilizer.

• **Availability of plant nutrients** for crop growth is generally improved by raising the soil pH to the desired level. Maximum availability of most nutrients is attained when the pH falls within the range of 6.0 to 7.0. With increasing concern for minor elements this pH level could become even more important. Furthermore, the solubility of manganese, aluminum and iron is lower within this range, reducing the possibility of toxicity in some crops.

• **Lime adds calcium and magnesium** to the soil—both essential secondary nutrients.

• **Nodulation of legumes** is improved. A near-neutral soil is most conducive for the growth of nitrogen-fixing bacteria.

• **Decomposition of crop residue** occurs under more desirable conditions. Bacterial soil organisms thrive best when the soil is properly limed. They aid humus formation and nutrients are retained for the following crop.

• **Better soil structure** often results, especially on heavier soil types. Higher crop yields return more residue to the soil.

Most desirable soil pH from both a crop production and economic standpoint varies with soil type and crops to be grown. For mineral soils a pH of 6.5 to 7.0 is generally most suitable. Organic soils may not benefit from liming unless the pH of the root zone (a minimum of two feet) is below 5.0.

As for crops, legumes perform best at a pH of around 6.8 to 7.0. On the other hand, to avoid scab, pH for potatoes should range from 5.3 to 5.5. Most liming recommendations call for raising soil pH to near 6.5 for most crops except where legumes are included in the rotation. However, Iowa research indicates that maximum yields for corn following a legume on manured plots occur at pH 6.9; corn

following timothy, 7.0; and alfalfa, 6.9. But lime costs money. Discounting future returns from an initial investment in limestone, Iowa agronomists conclude that liming to 6.9 can be profitable over, say, a 10-year period, provided lime costs permit.

Ohio recommendations list lime requirements for both a 6.5 and 7.0 pH. When corrective lime applications are desired to correct subsoil acidity, liming to a pH of 7.0 is recommended. Under these conditions, the topsoil pH needs to be 7.0 or above to provide for downward movement of lime to the 14 to 21 inch depth. Again, this takes years, so a question of economics is involved.

With the shift from use of rock phosphate to the other forms, there is not the need to hold pH near 6.0 to aid the breakdown of the rock. However, the higher the pH the greater the loss of nitrogen through denitrification under those situations where it occurs. Denitrification may be more than twice as rapid at a pH of 7.0 compared with 6.0. So, on poorly drained soils, particularly where nitrogen is applied ahead of planting, it may be desirable to lime to about 6.5 rather than 7.0.

FACTORS AFFECTING LIME RATE

Recommendations for liming received with your soil test results are based upon a number of factors. An understanding of the assumptions behind the recommendations is necessary so you can make adjustments for your particular situation.

Soil type is an important factor taken into account by the laboratory technician. Fine textured soils have a higher base exchange capacity than coarse ones—a larger amount of lime is required to raise the pH a given amount.

Liming recommendations are ordinarily stated in terms of the amount of lime required to raise the pH to a specific reading. It may be 7.0, 6.5, both or some other specified amount. You'll need to alter the liming rate if some other level is desired.

Plow depth makes a big difference in the amount of lime required. Many states base their recommendations on a 6-2/3 inch plow depth. Other states, recognizing the shift to deeper plowing to effectively turn under residues, have gone to a 9-inch plow depth.

Take any difference in your plowing depth into account. The deeper you plow, the more the lime is diluted. For example, the furrow slice using a 9-inch plow depth contains 35% more soil than a plow setting of 6-2/3 inches. So a given amount of lime is only 74% as effective. The reverse is true with topdressing pasture or a hay crop.

FIT LIME APPLICATION TO PLOWING DEPTH

Soil Depth (inches)	Percent of Lime Requirement to Use	Effectiveness According to Soil Depth (%)	Pounds of Lime to Apply Per Ton Recommended
3*	50	200	1,000
6-2/3**	100	100	2,000
8	120	83	2,400
9	135	74	2,700
10	150	67	3,000

*Recommendation for topdressing permanent pasture.
**Base figure for soil test recommendations.

OHIO STATE UNIVERSITY

Adjust liming rates if you have previously applied limestone. Iowa suggests the following:

Time Since Last Application	Amount of Previously Applied Limestone to Deduct from Recommended Application
6 months	full amount
1 year	deduct half
2 years	deduct one-fourth
More than 2 years	use recommended rate

Quality of limestone, as measured by purity and fineness of grind, noticeably influences its effectiveness. Purity varies widely by area and, as a result, lime recommendations by states are based on different standards.

Iowa has taken steps to remedy this situation. Lime requirements in that state are given as pounds of effective calcium carbonate equivalent (ECCE) instead of tons of average quality limestone. It considers both the calcium carbonate equivalent (CCE) of the limestone and its fineness. Using this method permits you to compare the relative worth of various limestones.

The amount of calcium carbonate equivalent (CCE) or total neutralizing power (TNP) is usually available from the producer. To demonstrate what neutralizing value can mean, suppose a farmer's soil test calls for five tons of lime having 90% calcium carbonate equivalent or neutralizing

value. Using one rated at 80% will require 5-1/2 tons; 100%, 4-1/2 tons.

Effectiveness related to fineness is demonstrated in the table below. Multiplying the percentage available, based on fineness, with the percent of calcium carbonate equivalent contained in the limestone gives ECCE.

EXAMPLE CALCULATION OF PERCENT OF LIMESTONE AVAILABLE BASED ON FINENESS

Screen Size	Percent of Material Passing Each Screen	Factor	Percent Available Based on Fineness
4 mesh	100	x 0.1	10
8 mesh	90	x 0.3	27
60 mesh	55	x 0.6	33
		Total	70

Value placed on fineness of limestone needs to be evaluated in terms of your cropping program. For example, Illinois recommends that if you are liming a strongly acid soil just before seeding alfalfa or clover, it is important to have plenty of fine, quick acting lime. The figures for one year given in the table below are probably the best guide. But if you apply lime on sod before plowing corn, the four-year value may be satisfactory. Where fields have been previously limed and only a maintenance application is made, the eight-year value may be sufficient.

RELATIVE EFFECTIVENESS OF LIMESTONE OF VARYING FINENESS OVER PERIOD OF TIME

Size Fraction	Time After Application		
	1 year	4 years	8 years
Through 60 mesh	100	100	100
30 to 60 mesh	50	100	100
8 to 30 mesh	20	45	75
Over 8 mesh	5	15	25

To compare several limestones on the basis of fineness, Illinois suggests you select the number of years most applicable to your situation. Multiply the percentage of each limestone in each of the screen sizes and total the products as shown. Dividing the value of 94.5 for limestone B by 69.5 for A, B is worth 136% more than A. Assume a price of $4 per ton for limestone A. Limestone B is therefore worth 136% of $4 or $5.44 per ton.

EFFECTIVENESS OF TWO LIMESTONES OF DIFFERENT FINENESS

Screen Sizes	Limestone A	Limestone B
Through 60 mesh	30% x 100=30	80% x 100=80
30 to 60 mesh	20% x 100=20	10% x 100=10
8 to 30 mesh	40% x 45=18	10% x 45= 4.5
Over 8 mesh	10% x 15= 1.5	0 0
	69.5	94.5

Fundamentals of Fertilizer Application

*Many factors influence the rate of fertilizer application
required to produce a profitable crop and maintain soil fertility.*

Soils vary widely in the amount of available nutrients they contain for crop production. This becomes readily apparent when you survey the wide variation in soil test results available. But even at high soil test levels some nutrients must be supplied from a fertilizer source, whether it is legume, manure or commercial fertilizer, to insure an optimum crop production and to maintain the fertility of the soil.

Nutrient deficit, which exists between the amount of nutrients required by a crop and those supplied by the soil, largely determines the rate at which fertilizer needs to be applied. Fertilizer recommendations are made on a simplified version of this principle.

Crop nutrient requirements, as shown in the table, aren't used alone in figuring fertilizer needs, but they serve as a guide. The table suggests the difference which exists between crops. Nutrient requirements vary with yield.

Fertilizer recommendations made in accord-ance with soil tests are derived from rather exhaustive fertilizer tests conducted by state universities. Over the years crop response at various fertilizer rates has been measured on each of the given soil types at different test levels.

On the nutrient supply side, soil tests measure the amounts available in the soil for crop use. A fertilizer rate is determined by comparing the soil test level with the optimum crop yield a given soil type will support.

Fertilizer recommendations need to be interpreted in view of factors other than soil test results alone. Such factors as fertilizer carryover from previous crops, use of manure and inclusion of legumes in a rotation should be considered. The plant nutrients contributed by these sources should be credited to or subtracted from the fertilizer requirements when determining the actual rate to apply.

Legumes contribute fertility to the following crop in the form of nitrogen. Nodule bacteria utilize

PLANT FOOD REMOVED BY CROPS — POUNDS PER ACRE

Crop		Acre Yield	N	Phosphorus[1] P_2O_5	P	Potassium[2] K_2O	K	Crop		Acre Yield	N	Phosphorus[1] P_2O_5	P	Potassium[2] K_2O	K
Grains					Pounds			**Fruits and Vegetables**					Pounds		
Corn	(Grain)	150 bu.	135	53	23	40	33	Apples		500 bu.	30	10	4	45	37
	(Stover)	4.5 tons	100	37	16	145	120	Beans, dry		30 bu.	75	25	11	25	21
Barley	(Grain)	40 bu.	35	15	7	10	8	Cabbage		20 tons	130	35	15	130	108
	(Straw)	1 ton	15	5	2	30	25	Onions		7.5 tons	45	20	9	40	33
Oats	(Grain)	80 bu.	50	20	9	15	12	Oranges (70 lb. boxes)		800 bx.	85	30	13	140	116
	(Straw)	2 tons	25	15	7	80	66	Peaches		600 bu.	35	20	9	65	54
Wheat	(Grain)	40 bu.	50	25	11	15	12	Potatoes		400 bu.	80	30	13	150	124
	(Straw)	1.5 tons	20	5	2	35	29	Spinach		5 tons	50	15	7	30	25
Sorghum	(Grain)	60 bu.	50	25	11	15	12	Sweet potatoes		300 bu.	45	15	7	75	62
	(Stover)	3 tons	65	20	9	95	79	Tomatoes		20 tons	120	40	18	160	133
Rye	(Grain)	30 bu.	35	10	4	10	8	Turnips		10 tons	45	20	9	90	75
	(Straw)	1.5 tons	15	8	4	25	21	**Other Crops**							
Rice	(Rough)	80 bu.	50	20	9	10	8	Cotton (seed and lint)		1,500 lbs.	40	20	9	15	12
	(Straw)	2.5 tons	30	10	4	70	58	(stalks, leaves and burs)		2,000 lbs.	35	10	4	35	29
Hay															
Alfalfa[3]		4 tons	180	40	18	180	149	Tobacco (leaves)		2,000 lbs.	75	15	7	120	100
Bluegrass		2 tons	60	20	9	60	50	(stalks)		--	35	15	7	50	42
Coastal Bermuda		8 tons	185	70	31	270	224	Sugar beets (roots)		15 tons	60	20	9	50	42
Cow pea[3]		2 tons	120	25	11	80	66	Sugarcane		30 tons	96	54	24	270	224
Peanut[3]		2.25 tons	105	25	11	95	79	Peanuts (nuts)		1.25 tons	90	10	4	15	12
Red clover[3]		2.5 tons	100	25	11	100	83	Soybeans (grain)		40 bu.	150	35	15	55	46
Soybean[3]		2 tons	90	20	9	50	42								
Timothy		2.5 tons	60	25	11	95	79								

[1]P X 2.3 = P_2O_5, P_2O_5 X 0.44 = P   [2]K X 1.2 = K_2O, K_2O X 0.83 = K   [3]Legumes get most nitrogen from air.   NATIONAL PLANT FOOD INSTITUTE

both carbohydrates and minerals from their host plant in fixing nitrogen from the air. This nitrogen in turn is used by the legume and other plants growing nearby. Later, the nitrogen may be released through decomposition after the legume is plowed under. The amount of nitrogen legumes contribute to the succeeding crop is shown in the table.

FERTILITY VALUE OF LEGUMES

Stand*	Pounds N Per Acre
Straight legume	80
Legume 75% - grass 25%	60
Legume 50% - grass 50%	40
Legume 25% - grass 75%	20
Soybeans (harvested for grain)	20

IOWA STATE UNIV.

*Legumes include both green manure and sod crops. Good to excellent stands are assumed.

Farm manure is a source of plant nutrients which shouldn't be overlooked. Content of various livestock manures is shown in the table. Many factors influence what portion of these nutrients will reach the field and be used by the growing crop.

NUTRIENT CONTENT OF MANURE

Kind of Manure	Pounds Per Ton		
	N	P_2O_5	K_2O
Dairy	10	5	10
Beef	14	9	11
Hog	10	7	9
Sheep	28	10	24
Poultry	25	25	12

Substantial nutrient losses from manure can occur through failure to save the liquid portion, runoff losses from winter applications, loss of nitrogen and potassium by leaching, and the loss of nitrogen by volatilization. As a result, only about one-third of the potential fertilizing value of manure is realized through improved crop yields.

Your particular manure handling system and amount of liquid preserved make a big difference in the nutrients contributed to the soil by manure. The liquid portion contains only 5% of the phosphorus, but it contains 50% of the nitrogen and 85% of the potassium contributed by manure.

Converting Spreader Capacity in Bushels to Tons of Manure

Bushel Rating of Manure Spreader (heaping full)	Approx. Tons of Manure Per Load
75	1¾
100	2½
125	3
150	3¾

Therefore the importance of conserving this part of the manure is obvious. Remember also that some nutrients are not readily available for crop use, but remain "tied up" in the organic matter and are released over a number of years. Only about one-third of the nitrogen and phosphorus in manure and half of the potassium become available the first year.

Fertilizer carryover from one crop to the succeeding one varies among the nutrients and depends on a number of factors, including rate, time and method of application, crop yield and type of crop grown. Of the major plant foods nitrogen is least likely to be carried over. Phosphorus exhibits the greatest carryover effects. In fact, phosphorus added through fertilizer frequently furnishes only a small portion of the nutrient taken up by a crop, but it is recovered by following crops.

Generally crops remove a higher portion of applied fertilizer at a low rate of application. Spring applications won't carry over as much as summer or fall ones. The larger the yield the higher the percentage removed during the first cropping season.

Iowa State University estimates of phosphorus and potash carryover are given in the following table. These estimates are based on normal rainfall and crop response the previous year. "Total pounds applied last year" means the sum total of the nutrients applied as fertilizer plus that portion considered as carryover from the previous year. Begin computations of carryover from the first corn crop in the rotation and discontinue with the final meadow crop. Carryover from final meadow crop usually is insignificant.

FERTILIZER CARRYOVER

Total Pounds of Nutrient Applied Last Year					Carryover Credit In Pounds Per Acre			
							K	
N	P_2O_5	P Equiv.	K_2O	K Equiv.	N	P	Crop Residue Left on Field	Crop Residue Removed
40	40	17.6	40	33.2	6	7	20	10
60	60	26.4	60	49.8	12	13	32	17
80	80	35.2	80	66.4	18	21	46	27
100	100	44.0	100	83.0	25	27	61	36
120	120	52.8	120	99.6	32	34	76	46
140	140	61.6	140	116.2	41	40	90	56
160	160	70.4	160	132.8	48	47	106	66

Nitrogen is the most leachable of the major elements, but several conditions can affect the amount of carryover. On a nitrogen deficient, sandy soil, there is little likelihood of carryover. On an adequately fertilized silt loam or heavier soil type, carryover may give a response equal to one-third that of the original application. Crop grown can influence this response. Deep-rooted corn can make better use of residual nitrogen in late summer than shallow-rooted oats.

Nutrient uptake by crops falls considerably short of the amount available. The relative effectiveness of these various nutrient sources during the first year is shown in this table. Note that these figures only approximate crop use and will vary according to specific conditions.

Approximate Nutrient Percentage Used By The First Crop

Source of nutrient	Percent used by first crop		
	Nitrogen	Phosphorus	Potash
Soil	40	40	40
Manure	30	30	50
Fertilizer	60	30	50

Effective Use of Fertilizer

Tailor your nitrogen, phosphorus, and potash applications
to achieve maximum response from each pound of nutrient applied.

Fertilizer is a major ingredient in any profitable crop production program. The most profitable yields are usually those produced on soils testing medium to high in phosphorus and potassium. Most long-range plans should be based on building and maintaining soil fertility at this level.

With the higher cost of fertilizer, though, more attention should also be given to practices that allow you to make maximum use of applied fertilizer. This is especially true in the shortrun if you are pinched for high-cost operating capital, or if you are operating with a short term lease. Then it becomes important to make effective use of fertilizer, without rates needed to build up the soil's fertility.

An effective fertilizer program should include a soil test at least every 3 years so you can measure and monitor changes in the soil's fertility level. This helps you avoid overfertilizing some soils, while underfertilizing others. You may be able to boost production on your total acreage, while applying the same or possibly less fertilizer.

The yield response curves shown in the graph demonstrate why you need to manage the program to get the most from applied rates, particularly in a season when your fertilizer budget may be limited. The higher a soil's fertility, the less fertilizer you will need to apply. Crops respond little to fertilizer once the available P has been built to 30 to

45 pounds per acre, and the exchangeable K tests around 300 or a little above.

The major reason for applying fertilizer to these higher-testing soils is to replace nutrients removed by the crop. You will need to apply fertilizer regularly for this purpose, but you have considerable flexibility in the way you do it. You can concentrate on lower-fertility fields in years when operating funds are limited. For instance, you might omit application on high-fertility soils for 2 or 3 years, then compensate by applying a higher rate. Or you may want to limit annual application to a starter rate in years when you don't broadcast.

Fertilizer application should be tailored to a given field, particularly if there are major soil differences. Even though you don't see much variation in crop growth throughout a field, correction of minor problems in certain areas of the field may boost overall yield by 10% or more.

Soil should be sampled to determine the range of fertility in a field, not its average fertility. This probably means taking more samples to represent various areas of a field. As a guide, use soil survey maps and colored or infrared photographs whenever possible. For best results, you may need to double the application rate in some parts of a field or apply fertilizer only every other year to other parts of the field. Or it may mean applying a combination

of broadcast and starter grades in order to achieve best results.

Balanced fertilization is required to obtain maximum returns from your fertilizer dollars. The results of an Illinois test, shown in the graph, compare the response of corn to nitrogen and potassium rates. It demonstrates that you can't expect to get maximum yield response from nitrogen unless you also apply a sufficient amount of potash. In this instance, a producer would need to apply about 120 pounds of potassium, along with 180 pounds of nitrogen, to produce 130 bushels of corn per acre. Without the potassium, the corn would yield only about 70 bushels per acre. A similar relationship exists between nitrogen and phosphorus.

EFFECT OF POTASSIUM APPLICATION ON RESPONSE TO NITROGEN

120 lb K/A

K 80

K 40

No K applied

Soil K = 100

Corn yield-bu/A

N-lb/A

Band application, or some form of application other than broadcasting and plowing or disking fertilizer into the soil, offers a way to improve yields from a given rate on soils that test relatively low in P and K, or on acid and alkaline soils that tie up large quantities of phosphorus. Banding can be beneficial on fertile soils, too, especially for early planted crops in northerly areas or on poorly drained soils that warm up slowly in the spring.

Using a more efficient method of application doesn't mean you

EFFECT OF SOIL FERTILITY ON CROP YIELDS

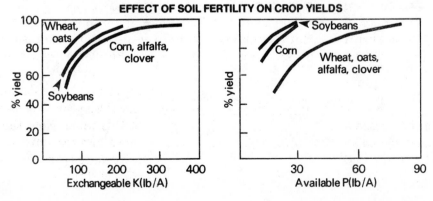

Wheat, oats

Corn, alfalfa, clover

Soybeans

% yield

Exchangeable K(lb/A)

Soybeans

Corn

Wheat, oats, alfalfa, clover

% yield

Available P(lb/A)

should cut back on rates, though. In most cases, it is more economical to increase yields than to reduce costs by using less fertilizer. And, in the case of the operator with a short term lease, it offers him the alternative of boosting yield, while perhaps pulling back on rate–at least to a slower buildup rate.

Time, equipment, labor, crop grown, and tillage system used need to be considered before deciding whether or not to apply fertilizer in a band. But there are instances where banding may work quite well. For instance, subsurface banding and dual injection methods look promising for some areas, especially some western-wheat states. By adapting standard chisels and sweeps on minimum-tillage equipment, you may be able to save a trip over the field, while placing fertilizer where it can be used more effectively. Dual application is made by equipping each shank with two lines or using one line and a flow divider to deliver the correct proportion of anhydrous ammonia and ammonium poly-phosphate to the band.

Wheat yields in some tests have been as much as 10% to 20% higher, compared with broadcasting phosphorus and potassium, disking it in, and injecting the anhydrous ammonia. The phosphorus is placed deeper in the soil, where more moisture is available. Also, the phosphorus is more available since less is fixed by the soil; especially beneficial to wheat, which makes most of its growth during the early, cooler portion of the season.

Fertilizer rates should be based on normal weather conditions. Yields lost will cost you far more in the longrun than you will save on fertilizer. You may spend more for fertilizer in a dry year than the crop uses, but the phosphorus and potassium will be carried over for the next crop. If soil fertility level is already high, you can cut back the rate by the amount of the carryover and still maintain yields. But where fertility is low, you probably should maintain your normal rates.

Where yields fall substantially short of what your fertilizer rate would support in a normal season, you can estimate the amount of P_2O_5 and K_2O carried over. Estimate the difference between your actual and normal yield. Multiply this yield difference by the amount of nutrients that each bushel, ton, or bale would have removed, as indicated in the table.

NUTRIENTS REQUIRED

Crop	Unit	P_2O_5	K_2O
		(Pounds per unit)	
Corn (grain)	bushel	.44	.28
Corn (silage)	ton	2.67	7.00
Milo	bushel	.43	.25
Wheat	bushel	.90	.30
Soybeans	bushel	.87	1.30
Cotton	bale	20.00	14.00

If you wonder how much the additional carryover would contribute toward buildup of the soil, figure that roughly 9 pounds of P_2O_5 will raise the P_1 soil test about 1 pound per acre; 4 pounds of K_2O will raise the K test 1 pound per acre.

You can't rely on nitrogen carryover from one season to the next, since it is subject to leaching and denitrification losses. Under normal rainfall conditions, and on soils not subject to leaching or denitrification, though, some nitrogen will be carried over. Most grains use about 1 pound of N per bushel produced. A corn yield of 90 bushels, for example, would remove about 90 pounds of N. Assume, though, that you had applied 160 pounds of N, expecting a yield of around 135 or 140 bushels. Illinois agronomists advise that the maximum carryover you can expect, even under near ideal conditions, would be about half of the difference between the amount applied and that used by the crop, or in this instance, 35 pounds of N.

Reduced tillage practices, especially no-till, may require some adjustments in your normal fertilization methods. From a fertilizer standpoint, it's best to build soils to a relatively high fertility before switching to a no-till system. Continued surface application of P and K leads to high fertility in upper few inches of soil. This tends to encourage shallow rooting of crops on low-fertility soils, making them more susceptible to moisture stress.

This isn't a problem in most seasons. A good residue cover on the surface will maintain favorable moisture and an adequate uptake of nutrients near the soil surface. However, serious crop stress can occur in a dry season.

Fields that have been in continuous no-till for several years should be tested. Sample the soil at various depths. Consider plowing to distribute phosphorus and potassium if the concentration is 2½ times higher in the upper 2 inches than at 4 to 6 inches.

Where possible, knife in a nitrogen solution or anhydrous ammonia rather than make a surface application on soil with a heavy residue cover. You may be able to do this by adding rolling coulters to cut trash and sealing wings to close the knife slot. The residue tends to tie up nitrogen applied to the soil surface. Also, denitrification or volatilization losses may be greater, especially if the soil is wet. If you do apply the nitrogen to the surface, it may be advisable to increase the rate by 15% to 20%.

Liming is often shortchanged in many fertilization programs, yet acid soils can seriously limit yields. Though farmers have increased nitrogen rates, most haven't boosted lime applications to compensate for the acidity created by the nitrogen. About 4 pounds of lime are needed to neutralize the acidity caused by 1 pound of nitrogen applied as ammonia or urea; 9 pounds of lime are needed if the nitrogen is applied as ammonium sulfate. For most soils, a pH of around 6 should be maintained–up to 6.5 if a legume is grown in the rotation.

Some reduced tillage systems may create special problems with soil acidity. If anhydrous ammonia is knifed in over a period of time without an occasional plowing, soil acidity may build up in the 7 to 9-inch soil zone. Where nitrogen is surface applied, pH in the top 3 inches may drop rapidly if no tillage or very shallow tillage is practiced. Aside from reducing yields, an acid soil surface can reduce the effectiveness of some herbicides.

Nitrogen Fertilization

Nitrogen fertilizer effectively used and properly applied to nonlegume crops often returns more per dollar invested than any other single production input.

Nitrogen is the most elusive of the major plant nutrients. Unlike unused applied phosphorus and potassium, which generally remain in the soil for succeeding crops, nitrogen is subject to loss through several escape routes—leaching, denitrification, and volatilization. Although it is important to apply enough nitrogen to attain optimum yields, it is wasteful to apply more than enough or to apply it in a fashion that will lead to excessive losses. Also, there is a growing concern about nitrates in our water sources.

A nitrogen program should be established by setting your yield goals, determining how much nitrogen will be needed to achieve this yield, then deciding on a nitrogen rate to apply.

Recommended rates for various crops vary widely among areas, so you will want to use those suggested by your own state as much as possible. Illinois tests under a varying range of soil and climatic conditions demonstrate that the average economic optimum nitrogen rate for corn is around 1.2 to 1.3 pounds of N per bushel produced. However, rates for various crops should be adjusted for several factors, including those outlined.

● Many soils release around 50 to 60 pounds of N per acre each season, and recommendations normally take this into account. However, clay soils having only 1% organic matter may release as little as 15 pounds; conversely, clay soils with 4% organic matter or sandy soils with around 2% organic matter may release more than 100 pounds of N. These wide departures from normal should be reflected in your nitrogen application rates, particularly for crops such as corn, sorghum, and cotton. Their greatest need for nitrogen occurs during summer when the bulk of the nitrogen is released in the soil. For small grains, more growth occurs in fall and/or early spring.

● Previous crop is a major consideration. Use the Indiana suggested adjustments given in the table as a guide for corn. As with soil release of nitrogen, considerably less credit should be given to the previous crop when selecting the application rate for small grain-about one-fourth as much.

NITROGEN RATES FOR CORN

Previous crop	Yield levels (bu/a)		
	100-110	126-150	176-200
	Pounds N per acre		
Good legume	40	100	150
Average legume	60	140	180
Soybeans	100	150	220
Corn, small grain, grass sod	120	170	230

● Manure contains about 10 pounds of N per ton, but only about half of that is available to crops in the season when it is applied. Further, much of the nitrogen in the ammonia form may volatilize before it can be used by the crop, especially if it is spread and left on the surface rather than incorporated into the soil shortly after application. In most instances, you shouldn't allow for more than 2 to 4 pounds of N per ton of manure.

● Irrigation water doesn't normally contain more than 10 ppm of nitrate, but if it does, adjust N rates accordingly. For example, if you apply a net of 6.5 inches of water and the nitrate test is 10 ppm, you can deduct 15 pounds of N per acre from the normal rate.

● Though some nitrogen may be carried over from one season to the next in humid areas, the amounts are unpredictable. The greatest chance of significant quantities being carried over is in a drouthy season. In many western areas, though, nitrogen accumulates, and these quantities can be determined by testing the soil for nitrate. In most instances, this quantity can be subtracted from the required rate, as demonstrated by these Nebraska recommendations:

NITROGEN RECOMMENDATIONS FOR CORN

lbs/A, Nitrate (depth) 3 feet	Relative level of NO₃N	Yield goal (bu/acre)				
		100	120	140	160	180
		(lbs/acre of nitrogen to apply)				
0-40	L	125	150	180	210	240
41-78	M	100	125	150	175	200
79-117	H	60	85	110	135	160
118-156	VH	—	25	50	75	100
157-195	VH	—	—	—	20	40

● Time of planting can also affect nitrogen rate. For example, Illinois agronomists suggest that for each week's delay in corn planting beyond the optimum date, the nitrogen rate can be reduced by 10 pounds per acre, down to a minimum of 80 to 90 pounds. As a reference, the optimum planting date for southern Illinois is April 10 to 15; central Illinois, April 20 to May 1; and northern Illinois, May 1 to May 10.

● In no-till situations where the nitrogen is applied to the soil surface, some states recommend that the rate be increased to 15% to 20% above normal, especially if urea-based nitrogen fertilizers or nitrogen solutions are applied. The increased residue on the soil surface tends to tie up more nitrogen. Also, the nitrogen may be subject to more denitrification and/or leaching, particularly on poorly-drained soils. In the case of urea-based fertilizers, volatilization may occur. One way to avoid this problem is by injecting nitrogen as anhydrous ammonia. When heavy residue presents an application problem, a solution may be to equip the applicator with rolling colters to cut the trash and sealing wings or packer wheels to close the knife slot.

Efficiency of Various Fertilizers

Since crops can effectively use either ammonium or nitrate nitrogen, there is little difference in the efficiency of various fertilizer formulations, as long as each is used properly. However, the characteristics of various forms must be taken into account when deciding what time and method of application are best. While the cost per pound of N varies rather widely among formulations, consideration should also be given to convenience of using a certain fertilizer and cost per pound of N applied.

Method of Application

Each nitrogen fertilizer form is subject to loss under its own set of conditions, with method of application playing a major role in minimizing losses. Ammonium forms of nitrogen are held by soil-clays and organic matter, so as long as nitrogen remains in this form, it is not subject to leaching. Also, unlike nitrate nitrogen, this form is not susceptible to denitrification. For these reasons, ammonium forms are best suited to fall application or to preplant use on sandy or poorly-drained soils.

On the other hand, ammonium nitrogen in the form of anhydrous ammonia needs to be knifed in some 6 to 8 inches and the slots properly sealed to prevent gaseous losses. Use of the Cold-NPN method of applying anhydrous, though, allows putting it on as shallow as 4 inches due to reduced pressure. This gives you somewhat more flexibility in application, allowing you to apply it in conjunction with a tillage operation such as disking or field cultivation. Also, aside from the fact that anhydrous precipitates out and clogs the nozzles, it should not be applied through sprinkler irrigation systems because large volatilization losses will occur. Nitrate forms are well suited to injection into the water of sprinkler systems, though.

Nitrate forms are most efficiently used when applied as close as possible to the time when needed by the crop.

There is still another set of circumstances under which urea nitrogen is most efficiently used. When it is applied to soil or crop residue, the urea is converted to ammonia, and unless it is readily moved into the soil by rainfall or incorporated by tillage, it will escape into the air. For this reason it is not well suited to no-till where it is applied and left on the surface. However, loss of urea applied as a topdress to small grains in the early spring will probably not be significant. Chances are that the urea will be carried into the soil before much loss occurs at the temperatures which prevail at that time of year.

Time of Application

Given in the table are Nebraska ratings of nitrogen efficiency, based on the time and method of application.

EFFICIENCY OF APPLIED NITROGEN

Time & method of nitrogen application	Relative percent of nitrogen required for a specific yield
Preplant	100
Preplant plus inhibitor	95
Preplant plus 20% through irrigation	95
Sidedress	90
Sidedress plus 20% through irrigation	85
All through the irrigation system	80

Where preplant nitrogen is put on in the fall, it's important to limit use to ammonium nitrogen and delay application until the soil at the 4-inch level cools to around 50°F. Conversion to nitrate nitrogen is much slower at that temperature. Further, avoid application on sandy or poorly-drained soils-wait until spring. Although sidedress application should be superior to fall or spring applied nitrogen, it isn't always best. Where moisture is limited, the nitrogen will not be moved into the active root absorption zone. Also, unless weather permits sidedressing early, excessive root pruning may occur.

Nitrogen fertilization of grass pasture should be timed according to your needs for the forage. For early grass production, put it on in early spring; late spring for mid-season use; and early August for fall grazing. Where fairly uniform grazing is desired, apply about two-thirds of the nitrogen in the early spring and the rest around June. However, applications need to be gauged according to your own area and the type of grass (whether it's a cool or warm season grass).

Nitrification Inhibitors

Nitrate inhibitors offer another way to improve the effectiveness of nitrogen. Although ammonium forms are not lost through leaching and denitrification, they quickly convert to nitrates when soil temperatures exceed about 50°F. Inhibitors slow the conversion of ammonium to nitrate nitrogen. Consequently, they can significantly reduce losses and increase yields under soil and weather conditions that are conducive to leaching and denitrification. For instance, midwestern research has shown that corn yields might be boosted by 10 to 20 bushels per acre when inhibitors were applied to poorly-drained or coarse-textured soils in years with excessive rainfall. In one experiment, inhibitors that were properly applied in the fall with anhydrous ammonia held as much as 42% of ammonia in the ammonium form through the early part of the growing season. Without an inhibitor, only 4% remained in the ammonium form.

The farther north or south you are located, the faster or slower the conversion of ammonium to nitrate nitrogen and the more or less you will benefit from an inhibitor.

Presently, N-Serve is fully labeled for use on corn, milo, cotton, and wheat, and full clearance is expected this year for Dwell on corn, wheat, and cotton. Recommended rate is one-half pound per acre, at a cost of $5.50 to $6 per acre. From a strictly economic point of view, possible nitrogen loss must be weighed against the cost of the inhibitor. In some instances, it may be cheaper to apply nitrogen at a somewhat higher-than-recommended rate. However, under conditions where inhibitors work best, the pendulum swings to the use of an inhibitor. Its value will increase if nitrogen prices rise appreciably over the next several years.

Unlike N-Serve, Dwell is not soluble in anhydrous ammonia. But for this nitrogen formulation, procedures are being developed that will allow direct injection into the anhydrous line during application. Similar procedures are being developed with N-serve.

Fertilizer Application and Placement

Best method of applying fertilizer depends on required rate, equipment, time, labor and your own particular fertilizer program.

Efficiency of fertilizer use by crops will often vary with the application method. If soil fertility is high and a good fertilizer maintenance program is followed, there is usually very little yield difference between banded and broadcast applications. Indiana test results with phosphorus demonstrate this extremely well. The same relationship would apply to potassium. As shown in the graph, no additional yield response was achieved by banding phosphorus at planting when a high soil test level was maintained with broadcast phosphorus. If the soil is low in phosphorus, band applications can give good yield response.

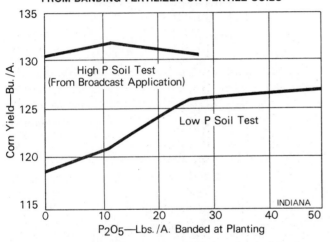

NO PARTICULAR ADVANTAGE IS GAINED FROM BANDING FERTILIZER ON FERTILE SOILS

On soils testing low to medium in phosphorus and potassium Illinois agronomists have demonstrated that a given rate of banded fertilizer can give more yield response than the same rate broadcast. On Cisne soil, which tests low in potassium, 25 pounds of K per acre (30 pounds K2O) when banded produced 112 bushels of corn, 32 bushels more than when broadcast. A rate of 50 pounds K (60 pounds K2O) banded produced 125 bushels of corn—21 bushels more than when broadcast. The higher yield from banding is due to reduced fertilizer contact with the soil. The nutrients remain more available.

Overall fertilizer program therefore influences the best placement method, particularly for phosphorus and potassium. If you're interested in correcting or building up soil fertility, broadcast application is usually best even though you need more fertilizer and a greater cash outlay to achieve a given yield on low to medium testing soils in the year applied. Nutrients not removed by the crop are carried over to raise the soil fertility level.

If a lower rate is used, a band application will probably produce the highest yield from a given amount of fertilizer applied. But it won't contribute as much to raising the fertility level for following crops. Notice from the graph that it is difficult to achieve top yields on low fertility soils through band application alone. Using annual maintenance applications on fertile soils, choice of application method becomes more a matter of which best fits your operation since there is little difference in effectiveness.

Most profitable method of fertilizer placement may not necessarily be the most efficient. While band application may be most efficient on low fertility soils, it may not permit top yields. Furthermore, many farmers are shifting to broadcasting all or most of their fertilizer to save on labor and time at planting, even when following a maintenance program. If you fall plow you must broadcast beforehand so it can be turned under unless it is to be injected later. Besides, this gets the job out of the way, permitting earlier planting. Broadcasting also allows application of bulk or straight goods which may be somewhat lower priced.

Starter effect from planter-applied fertilizer should not be overlooked. This can be particularly advantageous in northern areas or on heavier soil types in a wet season. This fertilizer provides readily available nutrients to get the germinating crop off to a fast start, even on fertile soils. On fertile soils in southern areas—central to southern Corn Belt and on south—starter effect becomes less pronounced. It will vary with the soil type, season and date of planting.

Problems of plant injury from fertilizer applied by the planter were practically erased when the sideband applicator replaced the old split boot attachment. Placing fertilizer two inches to the side and two inches below the seed permits putting on substantial amounts with the planter.

Only small amounts of plant nutrients are needed to achieve starter effects alone. Amounts applied over and above this requirement must be viewed in relation to broadcast—relative efficiencies, cost, time involved at planting, etc.

Pop-up method of planter application permits applying enough fertilizer to achieve the starter effect. But because fertilizer is placed directly in contact with the seed, rates must be held to amounts to achieve this purpose only. Otherwise, germination injury can occur. Since it appears impractical to apply both pop-up and a band with the planter, the use of pop-up would seem to best fit those situations where most of the fertilizer is broadcast.

The University of Minnesota recommends that the combined total of N and K_2O in pop-up applications be held below 10 pounds per acre on sandy soils and under 20 pounds on fine textured, wet soils. Experience with pop-up in drier areas, such as Nebraska, has been rather variable. Under dryland conditions, of course, injury may be a problem. A band application may be safer unless the crop is irrigated.

Broadcast fertilizer can be spread ahead of plowing and turned under, disked in after plowing or topdressed. Crops grown and mobility of the element influence most desirable depth of placement. Phosphorus stays where it's placed and movement of potassium in the soil is slow. Nitrogen is considerably more mobile. Depth of placement is less critical, except for anhydrous ammonia and pressure solutions.

For deep-rooted crops such as corn and sorghum, it may be beneficial to occasionally plow under phosphorus and potassium. Disking in may be sufficient for more shallow rooted crops such as small grains and soybeans. Forage crops have the ability to absorb available nutrients at or near the soil surface.

Need for plowing under fertilizer may not be as essential when minimum tillage systems are used. Residue left on the soil surface helps to retain sur-

face moisture and crop roots are better able to take up nutrients in the top few inches of the soil. Still, periodic plow-down application may help.

Sidedress applications are generally restricted to nitrogen. With heavy spring rainfall, putting nitrogen on as a sidedress may prevent denitrification losses, especially on poorly drained fields where water is likely to stand. Also, with heavy rainfall on light soils considerable leaching of nitrate forms might occur from fall or early spring applications. To hold root pruning to a minimum, anhydrous application should be made down the center of the row middles. And for the same reason, the sooner it's done the better. Roots soon close in the row middles and can make good use of the nitrogen applied there.

Preplant anhydrous ammonia application is finding increasing acceptance. Some farmers, to reduce compaction, want to hold trips over the field to a minimum after planting.

Skips in corn rows have been observed where anhydrous ammonia was preplanted. This may happen where the corn row is directly over the anhydrous band. Such a condition is most likely to occur in a dry, sandy soil; soil with a low exchange capacity; or where deep planting followed shallow placement of anhydrous. To avoid this, the University of Illinois suggests holding N rates to around 150 to 200 pounds per acre when knifed in at a 40-inch spacing on medium textured soils; 125 pounds under ideal conditions on sandy soils. With higher rates, space knives 20 inches apart. Other precautions include injecting the anhydrous five inches below planting depth and putting it on one to two weeks ahead of planting.

Nitrogen solutions can be applied in combination with a herbicide and/or insecticide to replace water as the carrier. Non-pressure solutions may either be worked into the soil or left on the surface. You may get better control of soil insects when solutions are incorporated into the soil. The same is true for some herbicides in dry years, especially those with low solubility. Not all pesticides are suited to the same placement as fertilizer, however, so you need to be careful which ones are used with a nitrogen solution.

Fluid Mixed Fertilizers

Liquid fertilizers are about equal in value to dry forms, but they offer other advantages you may want to consider.

Several developments have led to the rapid increase in the use of commercial fluid mixed fertilizers. Fluid fertilizers have always been more convenient to handle and apply, but some drawbacks had to be overcome.

Polyphosphates, highly complex phosphate compounds, have permitted the formulation of higher nutrient-containing fluid fertilizers. These compounds help dissolve what have been troublesome impurities. Further, it is possible to use some hard to dissolve, less expensive fertilizer materials. Another benefit has been the lowering of salting-out temperatures, permitting application during cooler weather.

Research also has paved the way for introduction of suspension type fluids as well as clear solutions. These products, in which some fertilizer is carried as suspended solids, can be made in grades containing about as much plant food as dry fertilizer.

Effectiveness of fluid fertilizer is essentially equal to dry materials when applied on an equivalent plant nutrient basis. Major exception may be instances where polyphosphates show some additional yield advantage over other phosphorus forms. The claim that polyphosphates are universally superior has not been verified by research, according to Purdue agronomists, but they agree there may be some conditions under which polyphosphates give greater crop responses.

All phosphorus sources perform well when conditions are good, but they may not do so under more adverse situations. Conditions or reasons for additional response from polyphosphates are not well defined. However, as a polyphosphate, the phosphorus is 100% soluble and contains a combination of both ortho and polyphosphates. This may provide a phosphorus source which performs more consistently over a wide range of soils, climate and cropping conditions, particularly where row crops are planted early in cold soil. Sequestering action of polyphosphates may increase micronutrient availability, too.

In order for the phosphorus in polyphosphates to become usable by crops, it must take up water and be converted to orthophosphate. This is not a problem, however, since about half of the phosphorus is already present in the ortho form. Having half the phosphorus in the poly form may prove beneficial in some instances. Polyphosphate may remain available in the soil longer without being rendered insoluble. The conversion takes place rapidly in acid soils, but at a slower rate in neutral or alkaline soils.

Cost of fertilizer on a per unit of plant food basis is normally higher when purchased in fluid form compared with dry bulk blends. However, the higher analysis and lower cost materials now being used in formulations are helping to hold down the cost. It is necessary to compare the cost of the two forms on the basis of cost per pound of plant food applied, not purchased. Convenience and savings in time and labor, along with any yield benefits which might result from greater timeliness, should be considered.

Chances are that fertilizer will be chosen more and more on the basis of the form which permits one man to cover the most acres per day, rather than on cost per pound of nutrient.

Labor and time savings can be substantial. Liquid starters can be loaded into planters in about one-sixth the time required for dry forms. For broadcasting, giant flotation liquid spreaders with wide booms can cover a larger acreage in a short time over wet, muddy fields with a minimum of soil compaction.

Fluid fertilizers can be advantageous when their versatility fits your particular situation. Fluids are particularly adapted to the addition of micronutrients, herbicides, and insecticides. This can eliminate one or several trips over the field. It frees the operator's time for other field operations and, where the fertilizer is custom applied, reduces the cost of combining operations.

The uniformity of liquids permits applying

crop protection chemicals and micronutrients evenly with no segregation resulting. Segregation isn't particularly a problem where only major nutrients are applied in dry bulk blends, but it can be when pesticides and micronutrients are added. Low per acre application rates require greater precision in application.

Though there have been some problems with the compatibility of certain pesticides and fluid fertilizers, these have been largely overcome. Many types of compatibility agents and surfactants are available to reduce these problems. Proper procedures should always be followed in matching the correct pesticide with the right suspension or liquid formulation.

Combined application of fertilizer and pesticide is not always practical. When deciding whether or not to mix and apply chemicals with fertilizer, several factors should be considered: optimum time of application for each chemical; physical compatibility; adequacy of equipment for making uniform application; possible synergistic or antagonistic effects of mixing chemicals; and distribution accuracy requirements of the pesticides.

Most fertilizers should be mixed with the soil while some herbicides do not perform well when incorporated. While deep incorporation is satisfactory for fertilizer, incorporating a herbicide too deeply will dilute its effectiveness. Compromising one requirement may limit the usefulness and safety of the mixture.

Starter fertilizer applied as fluid offers advantages in addition to saving time. Though high solubility has been said to be beneficial, this may not always be the case. High solubility does not necessarily mean the fertilizer will be more readily available to the plant, especially if the material is broadcast well ahead of planting. It can become tied up by reactions which take place in the soil. The most value from high solubility is achieved through starter application, especially when crops are planted early. Release and movement of phosphorus and potassium in the soil is very slow in cold wet soils. A starter application provides a readily available source of nutrients.

Fluid starters may be somewhat safer than some dry forms, particularly if applied as a pop-up in direct contact with the seed. Normally, fluid fertilizers have a lower salt index than dry starters. Excessively high concentrations of soluble salts in the fertilizer can force the sap to flow from plant roots into the soil causing dehydration, permanent injury or death of the plant. Water contained in fluid fertilizer lowers the salt index by dilution. Fluids that contain low nitrogen, high phosphate and low potash make an ideal combination for a pop-up or starter. This formulation has a low salt index, permitting placement with or near the seed without injury so long as rates are held within reasonable limits.

Minimum tillage systems may be adapted to fluid fertilizer use. A drawback of zero or reduced tillage systems has been the inability to incorporate fertilizer throughout the rooting zone. As a result, fertilizer tends to remain concentrated in the upper few inches of soil when broadcast on the surface. When broadcast nutrients are plowed under every several years, this is no great problem. But, the injection or knifing-in of liquid fertilizer, especially phosphorus and potassium, combined with the use of a starter, offers an alternative.

Fertigation, using water soluble fertilizers injected into the irrigation water, can be an effective application method. Present day injection equipment is very accurate and the amount applied can be calculated within a few pounds. Liquid proportioning systems provide a completely automatic and continuous system for injecting fertilizer and eliminating labor.

Application of fertilizer solutions in irrigation water is as effective as applying fertilizers with a ground rig in medium or fine soils and it is more effective on sandy soils. Possible advantages of fertigation over ground-rig application include reduction in field operations, improved distribution, lower probability of ground water pollution and yield increase from improved nitrogen efficiency.

Fertigation requires that fertilizer must be compatible with the irrigation water. An interaction can occur between some water and polyphosphates causing precipitation of the fertilizer. An easy test can be made to determine compatibility by using a graduated cylinder and eye dropper and adding the correct proportion of fertilizer to water. If incompatible, the solution will turn cloudy.

Micronutrients for Crops

Applying major nutrients and lime at recommended rates will often alleviate micronutrient deficiencies. If not, crops will show a marked response to applied micronutrients.

Though only trace amounts are required to "round out" the nutritional needs and balance of the plant, micronutrients are no less important than the major and secondary nutrients.

Basic approach to micronutrient fertilization should be to test your soil regularly and then apply the major nutrients (N, P & K) according to recommendation. Also, adequate major nutrient and lime levels will establish the foundation for top yields, the point where micronutrients are especially essential.

Where micronutrient deficiencies are suspected, it is advisable to follow a program of plant analysis in conjunction with regular soil testing. Since micronutrients are required in such small amounts, they may be sufficiently available within the soil, but for some reason may not be adequately taken up by the crop. Though soil tests are available, a plant analysis is more reliable for detecting micronutrient disorders within the crop. While the analysis may be too late to permit correcting a deficiency, it can signal future needs.

Essential micronutrients for crop growth, their functions and crop response are outlined below.

Those crops most susceptible to certain deficiencies are the ones you should test for possible hidden hunger or watch for deficiency symptoms. If symptoms are evident, you are already suffering yield reductions.

Nutrient balance within the soil, including the major, secondary and micronutrients, is extremely important in minimizing and correcting micronutrient deficiencies. In many instances, micronutrient deficiencies have been corrected by "pulling" the major nutrients and soil pH to the proper level and into balance within the soil. A soil pH of six to seven normally provides the best balance in availability of the essential micronutrients while holding others which may be toxic to acceptable levels.

Given in the top portion of the table on the next page are various deficiencies caused by soil nutrient imbalances. Where some major or secondary nutrient is deficient, its addition may correct a micronutrient deficiency. On the other hand, when a major or secondary nutrient tests high in the soil, the addition of a micronutrient may be necessary to offset plant uptake interference or possible nutrient imbalance. Sometimes, deficiencies of one

MICRONUTRIENT FUNCTIONS, SOIL CONDITIONS CONTRIBUTING TO DEFICIENCIES AND CROPS MOST SUSCEPTIBLE

Micronutrient	Functions	General soil type and condition	Crops most likely susceptible
Boron (B)	Essential to actively growing tissue in growing point; necessary for pollen viability and good seed set.	Acid leached soils, coarse textured sandy soils, peats and mucks, drouth conditions, over-limed acid soils. Also, alkaline or low organic matter soils.	Alfalfa, apples, beets, clovers, citrus, cotton, cauliflower, celery, corn, sweet potatoes, tomatoes, tree crops and sugar beets.
Copper (Cu)	A part of a necessary photosynthesis enzyme.	Sandy soils, peats and mucks, over-limed acid soils.	Small grains, vegetables and tree fruits.
Iron (Fe)	Promotes formation of chlorophyll.	Alkaline soils, particularly, calcareous when cold and wet; excess phosphate.	Beans, soybeans, corn, sorghums, tree fruits, ornamentals.
Manganese (Mn)	A part of important enzymes which are involved in respiration and protein synthesis.	Sands, mucks and peats, alkaline, particularly calcareous, over-limed soils.	Soybeans, small grains, tree fruits, cotton, leafy vegetables.
Molybdenum (Mo)	Transforms inorganic to organic nitrogen. Essential for nitrogen fixation by nodule bacteria in legumes.	Highly weathered acidic leached soils, acid soils.	Cauliflower, citrus, all legumes.
Zinc (Zn)	Important as a catalyst and regulator in the plant's use of other nutrients.	Calcareous soils after leaching and erosion, acid leached soils, after heavy phosphate, coarse sands.	Beans, soybeans, citrus, corn, sorghum, onions, potatoes, tree fruits, flax, and sugar beets.

or more nutrients may occur where another nutrient is excessively available.

Other causes for deficiencies are summarized in the lower portion of the table. Weather and soil conditions contribute to micronutrient needs. Generally, cold, wet soils tend to aggravate a deficiency. The trend to earlier planting can create deficiencies which might not otherwise occur.

FACTORS WHICH AFFECT MICRONUTRIENT AVAILABILITY

Mn	Fe	B	Cu	Zn	Mo	Cause of Deficiency
Deficiency Observed						
Soil Nutrient Imbalances						
	X		X			High Nitrogen
	X		X	X		High Phosphorus
	X					Low Potassium
	X					Low Calcium
	X					High Calcium
			X			High Magnesium
	X		X		X	High Manganese
X						High Iron
X	X				X	High Copper
			X			Low Zinc
X	X		X			High Zinc
X						Low pH
X	X	X	X	X		High pH
					X	High Sulfur
X						High Sodium
	X					High Bicarbonates
	X					Iron: Copper: Manganese Imbalance
Other Soil Conditions						
	X	X	X			Low Organic Matter
X			X	X		High Organic Matter
X						Poor Drainage
X		X				Drouth
X	X					Cold, Wet Soils
					X	Following Sugar Beets or Sweet Corn
	X					Poorly Aerated Soils
				X		Exposed Subsoils
	X					Heavy Manuring
			X			Heavy Rainfall
X	X		X	X		Light and Sandy Soil

Methods of application include soil treatment by either banding or broadcasting, foliar spraying or injecting the micronutrient into a sprinkler irrigation system.

Ideally, where a deficiency is known, it may be best to apply the micronutrient to the soil at or ahead of planting, depending on the particular micronutrient. But, if the crop shows a deficiency, the fastest way to correct it is by foliar spray followed by soil application the next season. Stage of growth needs to be early enough to allow sufficient crop response from foliar treatment.

Following is a brief summary regarding application of micronutrients as reviewed at a recent TVA micronutrient symposium:

Boron - Deficiencies are commonly corrected with soil application. While sprays are often beneficial, soil applications remain effective longer; because of boron immobility in plants, several sprays may be necessary.

Copper - More frequently applied to the soil than as a foliar spray. Chelated materials are particularly adapted for foliar application.

Iron - Soil application with either inorganic or synthetic organic sources has been extremely variable in effectiveness due to iron's reaction with the soil. Economics favor spray application using chelates. Foliar applications also provide more rapid response.

Manganese - While soil application is most common, broadcasting is not generally recommended. Soluble manganese readily reverts to unavailable forms.

Molybdenum - Generally, deficiencies are corrected with a soil or seed application. However, a foliar spray can be used to correct a deficiency during the growing season.

Zinc - Soil application is by far the most common and generally successful method of application for a number of crops. Broadcast applications are acceptable and when combined with mixed fertilizers or nitrogen materials their uptake may be improved. Band applications can be efficient but should be placed beside and below the seed. Foliar spray should be viewed only as an emergency treatment.

Recommended rates for the various micronutrients should be obtained from your state extension service agronomists for the specific crop in question. However, to give you some idea of the rates required for each of the micronutrients, the ranges shown in the table are recommended in areas where deficiencies have occurred.

MICRONUTRIENT RATES

Micronutrient	Pounds/Acre (elemental)
Boron	0.22- 8.9
Copper	1.07-22.3
Iron	0.45- 8.9
Manganese	0.71-17.8
Molybdenum	0.02-0.36
Zinc	0.31-17.8

Tillage Management

No one tillage method is best for all situations–select the one that offers the most benefits while minimizing the problems.

Many farmers have changed tillage methods to cut costs, save time and fuel and reduce erosion. However, most recognize that there is no one best method for all seasons, crops, and soil conditions and they have remained flexible, even though it usually has meant greater investment in equipment.

Savings in time are generally more significant than the cost reduction realized by switching tillage methods. A comparison of tillage systems by Ohio agronomists shows that time and fuel used can be significantly decreased through reduced tillage. Machinery and labor costs usually can be reduced, too, but the additional cost of herbicide and insecticide required often will offset these savings.

Time and Fuel Requirements Per Acre

Tillage system	Time (minutes)	Diesel fuel (gallons)
Plow-disk-plant	37	3.15
Chisel-plant	30	1.55
Disk or field cultivate-plant	23	1.10
No-till	15	0.40

Choice of tillage system has recently centered on selecting one that will effectively manage crop residue to control erosion and conserve moisture.

The relative effectiveness of various tillage systems in controlling erosion is demonstrated by Illinois research using a rainfall simulator to apply 2.5 inches per hour on a silt loam soil having a 5% slope that had previously been planted to corn. Soil loss following crops which leave less residue such as soybeans under the same conditions, may be more than double that shown in the graph.

A residue cover also helps to conserve moisture. In research conducted in northwestern Iowa, average yield increases of 14 bushels of corn per acre resulted from the tillage system that most effectively conserved moisture.

While reduced tillage can aid in erosion control, it may require more management to control disease, insects and weeds, especially under continuous cropping.

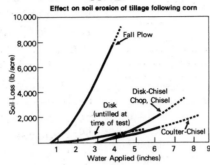

Effect on soil erosion of tillage following corn

Soil type and previous crop are major factors that influence which primary tillage method will work best. In many areas, for instance, the chisel plow and the large disk are replacing the moldboard plow on an increasing acreage, but each method should be carefully evaluated in terms of soil conditions and previous crop.

Fall tillage can often help you spread your workload and get crops planted earlier in the spring. While moldboard plowing can surpass all other tillage implements in loosening the soil; incorporating crop residue, manure, fertilizer and lime; reducing weeds, insects, and disease; the soil is left completely exposed to erosion. So it is desirable to limit moldboarding in the fall to nearly level, relatively heavy, poorly drained soils. Where moldboarding is to be done, it is especially beneficial to plow these soils in the fall, since freezing and thawing during winter will help break up clods and slabs.

Even on these soils, moldboard plowing is most beneficial following a crop such as corn, rather than soybeans which loosen the soil and make it more susceptible to erosion when plowed. One or two secondary tillage passes over soybean ground in the spring are often sufficient to achieve a good seedbed.

Following corn, some 3 to 4 tons of residue may remain. Turning under at least a part of it will aid soil warmup and drying in the spring, particularly in more northerly areas of the country. Illinois agronomists have found soil temperatures to be 3 to 5 degrees warmer in fall plowed fields than in fields having a surface mulch. The effect of residue on early plant growth is more pronounced in a wet year than a dry one. Again, the crop to be planted can affect your choice of primary tillage. An early planted crop such as corn will be affected more by early growth problems on wet, slow to warm up soils than will a later planted crop such as soybeans.

Fall moldboard plowing on soils with low organic matter will tend to puddle or run together over winter, so the early drying benefit that might otherwise be gained on some soils in the spring could be lost.

Fall chiseling or disking should be considered on poorly drained soils not suited to moldboard plowing. The roughened surface will dry out and warm up faster in the spring than when left untilled over winter. However, herbicide carryover from a previously dry season or volunteer corn following a fall with heavy field losses could be more serious than if the field were plowed. Further, you will have to rely more on herbicides to control weeds where crop residue is heavy.

Both the chisel plow and the large disk can increase your tillage capacity over that of a moldboard plow. Either of these tools permits you to cover more acres per day–as much as 60% more. When a field has a slope in excess of 2% it is desirable to chisel or disk on the contour. However, the disk tends to pulverize the soil more than a chisel, leaving a smoother surface which may cause more erosion.

The heavier, large disks having wider spacings are designed to increase soil penetration and to do a better job of handling large quantities of surface residue.

There's a wide range of chisel plows available, so you can select one to fit your conditions. Trash clearance is governed by shank length and spacing. The sharper, narrower points produce the lowest draft and greatest operating depth. Ridging and covering of ridge residues to speed warming and drying of soils can better be achieved using twisted shovels. For shallow cultivation, sweeps provide maximum coverage. Where residues are heavy, the modified chisel which has disk cutters mounted ahead of the chisels will partially cut the residue and prevent plugging of the shanks. It can save a trip over the field to chop the stalks or disk them in ahead of chiseling.

Iowa researchers have noted that on clay loams and other fine textured soils, more spring secondary tillage may be required following fall chiseling than following a moldboard plowing. However, this is less likely where corn follows soybeans than when corn follows corn.

Since a chisel relies on shattering action to break up the soil, somewhat drier conditions are required to achieve satisfactory results than when a moldboard is used. However, this problem can be partially overcome by substituting "duckfoot" sweeps for chisel points and operating shallower.

Indiana agronomists have found that disking or shallow spring chiseling will compete favorably with spring plowing on poorly drained soils, provided comparable plant stands can be obtained. Where crop residues are heavy, you will probably have to disk twice or chisel and disk. In some instances, it may be necessary to chop the residue first. Use only a disk opener type planter. Minnesota agronomists have found that on soybean ground with no fall tillage, disking frequently gives superior seedbeds compared with spring moldboard or chisel plowing on poorly drained, finer textured soils.

On medium to coarse textured soils that are well drained, disking or other secondary tillage, till planting or no-till can produce yields comparable to those obtained from fall or spring plowing or chiseling. Regardless of the primary tillage used, similar seedbeds can be achieved by varying the amount of secondary tillage, except where no-till is used.

No-till system is best suited to well drained soils. No-till can be superior to plow systems on soils with limited water holding capacity. In Ohio studies, no-tillage of well or moderately well drained soils with low organic matter has produced 10% to 20% higher yields if there is a good mulch cover. On soils devoid of residue, tillage is necessary for highest yields.

On poorly drained soils, tests conducted in Ohio and Indiana suggest that substantial yield reductions can occur using no-till, particularly where corn follows corn. However, much of this yield loss can be prevented by rotating corn with other crops or by occasionally plowing ground in continuous corn.

No-tillage can provide a bail-out system when soils are too wet in the spring to permit other tillage.

As with chiseling or disking, no-tillage results in less mixing of lime and fertilizer throughout the rooting zone, leaving the nutrients concentrated near the surface. This situation generally has not reduced yields substantially, but it appears desirable to distribute the nutrients by occasionally plowing.

Soil compaction is of increasing concern, so any tillage practices you can use to reduce this problem can be beneficial. Research indicates that compaction won't greatly affect crop yields when adequate topsoil moisture is available, but yields can be reduced substantially in a dry year.

Indiana engineers say these practices can help to prevent soil compaction in the topsoil and the formation of hardpans: Don't work the soil too wet. Avoid plowing to the same depth each year, especially if the tractor tire runs in the furrow. Remove tractor weights when they are not really needed for traction. Use moldboarding and chiseling in alternate years, at varying depths.

Work ground only as many times as necessary for good stand establishment. Incorporate residues in the topsoil. Use a crop rotation that includes a deep rooted legume.

Eliminating existing compaction is a separate problem, according to the Indiana engineers. Deep tillage with subsoilers is being used by more farmers with most reporting satisfactory results. Many have noted a drying up of wet spots. There is very little research to document the effects of subsoiling in the Midwest, especially on the heavier soil types that are naturally compacted. It is thought that subsoiling is more beneficial on the lighter soil types and/or those that are compacted by machinery, since the compacted layer may be less extensive and more easily penetrated.

Subsoiling is more generally accepted in the South and West. Louisiana test results on lighter soil types show that subsoiling of compacted sandy type soils can greatly improve cotton yields, especially in dry years.

Effect of subsoiling on yield of cotton grown on silt loam

Subsoiling regime	Yield 6-yr. avg.
	(lb/a)
Check—no subsoiling	1,564
Subsoiled in fall	1,792
Subsoiled in spring	1,756
Subsoiled in fall and spring	1,812
Subsoiled in spring, 20 in. apart*	1,681

*In water furrow before and after rebedding.

While much is not known about subsoiling, a couple of things are certain. To maximize the possible benefits of subsoiling, it should be done when the soil is dry. The hardpan or plow sole is more likely to shatter when the soil is dry. Under moist conditions, the slot formed by penetrating the hardpan may melt back together fairly soon.

Even under dry conditions, a shank spacing-depth relationship must be recognized. For instance, shanks spaced 20 inches apart may have to be operated only a few inches below the hardpan to insure good breakup. Spaced at 40 inches, shanks may need to be set several inches deeper.

Soil Conservation Practices

Soil conserving practices help to maintain soil productivity and to preserve the nation's water quality. They may permit more intensive cropping, while achieving high yields.

Effective management of residue from crops produced on fertile soil provides a basis for a sound soil conservation program on many farms. The return of large quantities of crop residue to the soil through good cropping and fertilization practices contributes to good soil condition. It provides a reservoir for plant nutrients; increases soil aeration, water holding capacity, and permeability; reduces erosion; maintains good soil structure and ease of tillage; reduces soil compaction; and acts as a source of energy for soil organisms.

Conservation tillage methods are those that leave crop residue on the soil surface. Tillage is performed without a moldboard plow. Implements used include tandem and offset disks, chisel plow, field cultivator, harrow, and no-till planters. These tillage methods, aside from contour farming, terracing, and the production of forage crops, provide a farmer with the best means for controlling soil erosion. Though some soils are not adapted to row crop production, tillage systems that leave a high portion of the residue on the surface can broaden a soil's suitability for intensive cropping.

USDA estimates place average annual soil loss from U.S. cropland at 9 tons per acre. This, say specialists, is about two times the level that can be sustained without decreasing soil productivity and is much too high if water quality is to be improved.

Water pollution occurs primarily through sedimentation arising from soil erosion, so major emphasis in maintaining and improving water quality will be on reduction of runoff from cropland. Under Section 208 of the Federal Water Pollution Control Act Amendment of 1972, states and their local agencies are required to develop what are termed as Best Management Prac-

tices for reducing non-point pollution of streams, rivers, and lakes. These practices may include conservation tillage, terraces, rotations, etc. States are in the process of developing these plans. Those suggested for a particular area probably will vary considerably, depending on cropping practices being used and the susceptibility of soils to erosion. Unless producers voluntarily initiate some possible changes in farming practices on soils subject to erosion, they may eventually be required to do so through government regulation.

Protection of soil from erosion by crop residue left on the surface is demonstrated by Indiana test results shown in the table. Tests were conducted on silt loam soil with a 5% slope. These soil losses resulted from a simulated 6.5 inch rainfall.

Effect of Surface Residue on Soil Erosion and Water Infiltration

Mulch (T/A)	% surface cover	Runoff (in)	Infil-tration (in)	Soil loss (T/A)
0	0	2.8	3.4	12.4
1/2	77	1.6	4.7	1.4
1	95	0.3	6.0	0.3
4	100	0	6.1	0

The tie-in between tillage system and surface residue left to control erosion and to increase water infiltration is demonstrated by an Illinois test on soil with a 5% slope.

Tillage and Soil Loss on 5% Slope with 10 Inches of Simulated Rainfall

Tillage System	Soil Loss-T/A
Fall plow-spring disk-plant	8.3
Fall chisel-spring disk-plant	3.2
Spring disk-plant	1.7
No-tillage	1.1

In the Great Plains where stubble mulching of wheatland is the most widely used conservation practice, the approximate amounts of residue needed to hold wind and water erosion losses to an acceptable level of 5 tons per acre annually are given in the following table. You can estimate the amount of wheat or rye residue present before tillage at

about 100 pounds per bushel of grain produced; barley and flax, 80 pounds; and oats, 60 pounds.

Ecofallow, another soil management practice that is receiving attention, though still limited in practice, is the use of herbicides in place of tillage to control weeds in a fallow rotation.

Approximate Amounts of Flattened Wheat Residue Needed to Minimize Erosion

Soil	Protection from Erosion	
	Wind	Water
	lb/a	
Silts	925	1,450
Clay and silty clay	1,600	1,850
Loamy fine sand	2,125	900

No particular tillage tool is best for all conditions, and in some instances a combination of tools may be required. However, choice of equipment and tillage sequence, as much as possible, should be based on amount of residue present at harvest and the amount needed at seeding time, taking into account the weed situation and possible herbicide use. Given in the table is the average amount of residue left on the soil surface after a trip over the field using different pieces of equipment. The same percentage reduction can be used for each trip over the field.

Residue Left on Soil Surface

Implement	Residue remaining after tillage
	Percent
Moldboard plow (7" deep)	0-5
Chisel plow 2" wide points (7" deep)	75
Oneway (18" to 20" disks)	60
Oneway (24" to 26" disks)	50
Heavy tandem or offset disks	60
	50
Field cultivator (12" to 18" sweeps)	80
V-sweep (20" to 30" wide)	85
V-sweep (over 30" wide)	90
Mulcher treader (spade tooth)	75-80
Rodweeder (with semi-point chisel or shovel)	85
Rodweeder (plain rotary rod)	90-95

Choice of a tillage system should include many considerations. Primarily, you should weigh conservation tillage benefits of reduced erosion against the costs and yields relative to more conventional tillage methods. Consider where this method of tillage is best suited and use good management to make it work. Evaluate the method relative to soil type, slope, drainage, soil temperature, timeliness, fertilizer distribution, and weed, insect, and disease control.

Production costs of various conservation tillage methods relative to more conventional systems have been estimated by Illinois engineers, taking into account the size of machinery that best fits a farm and available labor, as well as the importance of achieving best results through timely operations.

When one system is directly compared with the other, there may be little difference in total cost per acre. Conservation tillage tends to reduce labor, fuel, and other variable machinery costs, but more reliance usually must be placed on the use of pesticides to control weeds, insects, and diseases. Decreased costs for some items may be about offset by increases in others.

Where conventional tillage equipment is owned and occasionally used with other than a conventional tillage system, then costs per acre will naturally be increased.

Estimated Costs of Machinery and Pesticides with Different Tillage Systems

Tillage system	Machinery related*	Pesticides	Total
	Dollars per acre		
Fall plow	33	8-22	41-55
Spring plow	36	8-22	44-58
Chisel	31	8-22	39-53
Disk	28	8-22	36-50
No-till	22	18-32	40-54

*Machinery-related costs include fixed and variable machinery costs, labor at $5 per hour, and timeliness.

Crop yields using conservation tillage methods generally compare favorably with conventional systems on reasonably well-drained soils if adequate stands are achieved and weeds and other pests are adequately controlled. However, yields usually are consistently higher on poorly drained, fine textured soils when conventional tillage is used.

Yield response to various tillage systems on different Illinois soil types is given in the table to demonstrate how soil affects your choice of tillage. Symerton silt loam is a dark prairie soil that has good internal drainage and is free of root restricting layers in the top 40 to 48 inches. Note that yields are nearly identical, regardless of tillage used, except for no-till and in this instance, the lower yield was due to poorer weed control.

Corn Yields Achieved with Various Tillage Systems

Tillage system	Symerton silt loam	Drummer silty clay loam	Claypan Cisne silt loam
	Bushels per acre		
Moldboard plow	112	165	87
Chisel plow	110	159	114
No-till	99	144	108

Lower yields from conservation tillage of poorly drained Drummer silty clay loam are due largely to slower early growth. Wet soils are especially slow to warm up in the spring when residue is left on the surface. This can slow early growth of a crop such as corn, that is planted early. Cisne silt loam is a poorly drained claypan soil with a subsoil that restricts root development and water use by crops. Because crop residues left on the soil surface help to reduce evaporation and conserve water, conservation tillage methods on this kind of soil often produce higher yields than clean tillage. This is especially true in drier seasons.

Weed control programs require greater reliance on herbicides to achieve effective control. Though secondary tillage in the spring can aid weed control, it also reduces the residue on the soil surface to a point where its ability to control erosion is essentially lost during the growing season. More attention should be given to specific herbicides to control the existing weed problem. Combinations help to broaden the spectrum of weeds controlled. Cropping system may be more crucial, too. Weeds not controlled with herbicides used on one crop may be held in check by rotating to another crop and using different herbicides.

Conservation tillage leaves clods and crop residue on the surface. Since this can interfere with distribution and incorporation, it may be necessary to use the upper rate given on the label. Where a spray is used, up to 60 gallons of water per acre may be needed to achieve adequate coverage for no-till in a dense sod. Follow the label for specific planting depth, properly adjust the planter, and avoid planting in soil that is too wet to allow the furrow to properly close. If the crop seed is not properly covered, a herbicide sprayed at or just after planting may kill the germinating seed.

Insect and disease problems may be increased, but this should not necessarily limit usage. You will want to monitor possible problems more closely, but generally these can be handled through soil insecticides applied at planting, or through properly timed sprays and/or crop rotation.

Crop fertilization practices should fit the tillage system used. Research has shown that surface applied fertilizer tends to remain in the upper 2 inches of soil with no-till; the top 3 to 4 inches with chisel plowing or disking; and uniformly throughout the plow layer when a moldboard plow is used.

Though fertilizer is concentrated in the upper few inches of soil when using conservation tillage, this is not particularly detrimental to yields if soil test values have been raised to recommended levels. Sufficient amounts of crop residue on the soil surface during the growing season will keep the surface soil moist and aid crop uptake of nutrients close to the soil surface. However, Wisconsin tests indicate that yields will probably be boosted by applying at least part of the fertilizer in a band at planting. Also, it may be beneficial to moldboard plow every 3 to 4 years or so.

With conservation tillage, nitrogen can be applied either to the surface or injected as anhydrous ammonia or a low pressure solution. Use a coulter mounted ahead of the applicator knife when injecting into heavy residue.

Growing Corn for Maximum Profit

While systems of corn production have become somewhat standardized, each grower still must tailor production practices to fit his own situation.

Many practices contribute to optimum corn yields and top profits. The right combination for one grower is not necessarily correct for another. Since each practice is dependent on the others for maximum response, any change in one practice may require adjustments in several.

Select those hybrids, within the maturities adapted to your area, which will yield best under your management system. A hybrid that yields well at one population level may not do so at another planting rate. Some hybrids respond more to high fertility. Others are more resistant to certain diseases or insects. Some newer hybrids are better able to withstand harvest delays without much additional field loss.

Though single and special crosses may have a somewhat higher yield potential under top management than double crosses, their uniformity also makes them more susceptible to certain adverse conditions. For example, extreme heat and cloudy conditions during silking can seriously reduce yields. By planting two or three hybrids of different silking dates, you can spread these and other risks.

While each company can tell you the relative silking dates of their own hybrids, they may not be able to compare them with those of other companies, especially the newer hybrids. Days to maturity is not always a guide to silking dates.

Wise choice of hybrids may mean as much as 10, 20 or 30 more bushels per acre. Use all possible sources of information when making your selections. In the final analysis, setting up your own farm tests may provide the most reliable basis for choosing hybrids.

Early planting can boost yield potential. The corn plant develops better when vegetative growth occurs primarily during the cooler, higher rainfall period of May and early June. By silking earlier, the risk of moisture stress during the silking stage is reduced. Further, the earlier growth helps the crop use available moisture more effectively. Plants are deeper rooted by the time greatest moisture stress occurs. More shading reduces evaporation. While corn planted in early to mid-April improves yield potential in the southern Corn Belt and further south, it may yield no more than corn planted in early May through the central and northern Corn Belt.

Planting as much corn as possible in April does, however, improve your chances of finishing within the first week of May. Yields can drop rather sharply with each day planting is delayed beyond this period. When planting in April, use soil temperature as a guide. You can plant if soil temperature reaches 50 degrees at the two-inch level at 7:00 a.m., 55 degrees at the four-inch level at 1:00 p.m., according to Illinois agronomists.

Planting depth of two inches has consistently produced the highest yields for most soil types in tests conducted by Pioneer Seed Company. Planting another two inches deeper can reduce yields as much as 30 bushels per acre, except under ideal conditions. Deeper planted corn takes longer to emerge; silking is delayed, and vigor and stand are reduced. When planting early, especially in heavier soil types, hold planting depth to 1-1/2 inches. This keeps the growing point below the soil for frost protection while minimizing the distance for emergence. On light, dry soil, it may be advisable to plant three-inches deep to place the seed in more moist soil.

Optimum plant stand is dependent on rainfall, soil moisture reserves, fertility, row width, date of planting, and the hybrid grown. The push to higher populations several years ago has evolved into heavier stands today, but they have settled back from the extremes some farmers were planting.

Experience has shown that high plant stands much in excess of 24,000 plants per acre are profitable only for some of the more tolerant hybrids in extremely good seasons on deep, well drained, fertile soils when the corn is planted early and weeds are effectively controlled. Also, the yield advantage of higher stands may be offset by more susceptibility to lodging.

Indiana agronomists say that most hybrids attain 90% of their yield potential at a harvest stand of 18,000 to 20,000 plants per acre. Their tests on highly productive soils show that yields increase sharply as harvest populations are boosted from 16,000 to 20,000 plants per acre. The yield increase slows from 20,000 to 22,000; is very slight from 22,000 to 24,000; and essentially ceases above 24,000 plants per acre. Yield of many hybrids declines as stands approach 28,000 plants per acre.

In dry years, maximum yields will occur at the lower harvest populations. In years of ample moisture, maximum yields will be attained with the higher stands.

Hybrid response to plant stand also varies with the average rainfall of an area. Optimum plant stand in the western Corn Belt, for example, will be somewhat below the Indiana test results.

When planting early, planting rate should be about 15% higher than the desired stand; normal planting time, 10% higher.

Narrow rows result in more uniform spacing of plants and more efficient use of sunlight, fertility and moisture. But, the pull back in plant population has slowed the trend to substantially narrower rows. Few producers have narrowed rows below 30 inches. Except under extremely high level management and high planting rates, it appears that the major advantage from narrow rows is reached at the 30 inch width.

Tillage systems ranging from conventional to no-till planting have proven satisfactory. A comparison of several systems under Indiana conditions is shown in the first table. Choice of a tillage system hinges on many factors -- soil type, susceptibility of fields to erosion, costs and management. Where adapted, reduced tillage systems can be used without appreciable sacrifice in yield. Weed control is critical to their success, particularly no-till planting. Getting the desired stand is often difficult. Best results are obtained by using planters equipped with fluted coulters or some type of equipment that tills ahead of seed placement.

CORN YIELDS COMPARED USING VARIOUS TILLAGE METHODS

| Tillage Method | Poorly Drained Soils | | | Well Drained Soils | |
	Runnymede loam	Blount silt loam	Pewano clay loam	Tracy sandy loam	Bedford silt loam
	(Bushels per acre)				
Fall plow	158	116	97	128	--
Fall chisel	145	113	102	142	104
Spring plow	141	108	101	133	87
Disk	143	100	92	140	94
No-till	125	59	37	136	91

Fertilizer program for optimum yield should be based on building or maintaining the level and balance of potassium and phosphorus to recommended soil test levels. A P_1 test of 40 and a K test of 300 will normally produce about 98% of maximum yield. Shown in the bottom table are rates recommended by Indiana, based on soil test readings of a 7-inch plow layer of medium textured soils.

NITROGEN FERTILIZATION GUIDELINES
(Medium Textured Soils)

| Previous Crop | Yield levels (bu/A) | | | | |
	100-110	111-125	126-150	151-175	176-200
	pounds N per acre				
Good legume (Alfalfa, red clover sweet clover)	40	70	100	120	150
Average legume (Legume-grass mixture, or poor stand)	60	100	140	170	180
Continuous corn (Desired yield obtained)	100	120	160	190	220
Corn, soybeans, small grain, grass sod	120	140	170	200	230

Nitrogen rates need to be adjusted for a number of factors including moisture, date of planting, soil organic matter, preceding crop, and stand. The Indiana recommendations shown above take these variables into account.

RECOMMENDED FERTILIZATION RATES FOR MEDIUM TEXTURED SOILS

| Soil test level | Bray P_1 test | Yield levels (bu/A) | | | | | Potassium test | Yield levels (bu/A) | | | | |
		100-110	111-125	126-150	151-175	176-200		100-110	111-125	126-150	151-175	176-200
	lb P/A	pounds P_2O_5 per acre					lb K/A	pounds K_2O per acre				
Very low	0-10	100	100	120	130	140	0-80	100	120	150	180	200
Low	11-20	70	80	90	100	110	81-150	70	90	120	140	160
Medium	21-30	40	50	50	60	70	151-210	40	60	70	90	120
High	31-45	20	30	30	40	40	211-300	30	30	40	60	80
Very high	45+	*	*	*	*	*	301+	*	*	*	*	*

*Application necessary only for long-range fertility maintenance.

116

Soybean Growing Practices

Match production practices to your soil, soil fertility, cropping program and weed, insect, and disease problems.

Growing practices are becoming more refined, making it possible to put together a production package that will permit high yields.

Cropping soybeans in rotation is especially important where diseases are a problem. Many diseases can be suppressed below damaging levels by rotating soybeans out of a field for a year. Bean yields following some crop other than beans may average 10% higher.

Unless an effective disease program is followed, yields may be reduced as much as 10% to 30%. In addition to growing beans in rotation, you should plant high quality seed of varieties resistant to your particular disease problem. Where soybeans follow soybeans, it could be especially helpful to do a good clean job of plowing to bury residue and drastically reduce disease causing organisms such as pod and stem blight, anthracnose and stem canker.

With soybean cyst nematodes spreading, a conscientious rotation program with nonhost crops such as corn or grain sorghum and elimination of weed hosts may delay or prevent the pest from increasing to damaging levels.

YIELDS OF SOYBEANS FOLLOWING CORN OR SOYBEANS, 1973-76

Location	Soybeans following Soybeans	Corn
	Bushels per acre	
DeKalb	39	44
Dixon	30	35
		ILLINOIS

Soybean cyst nematode control measures should be directed toward the use of varieties resistant to the particular race present in areas, where available. In areas where resistant varieties are not available, a crop rotation and use of a nematicide must be considered. In an Illinois field experiment, yields on nematode infested land have been boosted by 6 bushels per acre following a 2 year rotation, but at least 2 years out of soybeans are necessary to significantly reduce populations. Except for when a resistant variety is grown, soybeans should never be produced for 2 years in a row. Even then, Race 4 could build up, since the Bedford variety, the only one resistant to Race 4, is just being released for seed production by certified seed growers.

Symptoms of nematode damage include stunted, yellow or chlorotic plants. However, more positive identification generally will be required. Wash the roots and you may see tiny pear shaped white or brown cysts about one-fourth the size of a pin head.

Some states are testing soil for nematode presence and to positively identify the particular race.

Insect control measures should be based on damage being inflicted. Soybeans can tolerate considerable damage without significant loss. Insects become pests only if their populations increase above the critical level at some sensitive stage of crop growth. Notice from the graph that while plants are most susceptible to damage at pod setting,

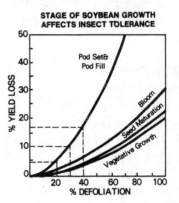

STAGE OF SOYBEAN GROWTH AFFECTS INSECT TOLERANCE

they can tolerate about 15% defoliation without yield loss. For instance, Illinois entomologists have determined that treatment for green clover worm will pay only if there are more than about 10 worms per foot of row in the vegetative stage; about 15 in bloom, pod set or pod fill stages. For the bean leaf beetle, the threshold is about 50 beetles per foot of row in the vegetative stage; 100 during bloom, pod set or pod fill.

Fertilization program to assure optimum yields requires that phosphorus and potassium be maintained near the recommended soil test level. Soybeans are good second feeders, able to effectively use nutrients remaining from preceding crops. However, if you rely on carryover nutrients, be sure to apply enough phosphorus and potassium to the prior crop. Even when fertility is high, Ohio recommends that you apply at least 30 pounds of P_2O_5 if beans are planted before May 15, in order to assure sufficient nutrients for early growth. Maintain soil pH at 6 to 6.5.

Generally a well-nodulated crop will fix sufficient nitrogen to produce at least a 60 to 70 bushel per acre yield. Added nitrogen has rarely boosted test yields, but at yields above 60 bushels per acre a re-evaluation of this practice may become necessary. Timing of nitrogen application may be especially critical for achieving response. Form of nitrogen may be a factor, too.

Manganese deficiencies sometimes occur on alkaline or sandy soils, especially when weather is wet and cool during late May and June. Suggested treatment is to spray 6 to 10 pounds of manganese sulfate in 20 to 25 gallons of water per acre when the symptoms appear (stunted plants with green veins in yellow or whitish leaves).

Tests with foliar fertilization suggest this practice has potential for increasing yields, but it's too new to be recommended. The right combination of all factors to make the practice economically beneficial has not yet been found. One major problem has been leaf burn.

Foliar fertilization shows the most promise with high fertility, to supplement rather than replace normal fertilizer practices. Theory of this practice is to supplement plant nutrition during seed development when most food is being channeled to the seeds, shorting the roots and leaves of nutrients to carry on necessary photosynthesis and food production.

Effective weed control is a major yield factor. Most weed control programs combine good cultural practices, cultivation and herbicide use. Good control during the first 3 to 5 weeks is extremely important—after that the crop can compete rather well. Use of a rotary hoe can be especially helpful to control small weeds without destroying effects of a herbicide, especially if a rain does not occur within a week or two after application to move a preemergence herbicide into the soil.

No one herbicide or combination is best—use those that fit your soil type and organic matter content, your specific weed problem, and your farming operation, without injuring the crop. Though you may select a herbicide with good crop tolerance, some conditions can cause occasional injury, but the crop will usually grow out of it with no effect on yield. However, soybeans injured by a herbicide are likely to be more susceptible to disease. Follow label directions and accurately calibrate your applicator. Where atrazine residue is likely, avoid using Sencor or Lexone on beans. These chemicals may aggravate the problem.

Fungicide application during the growing season has boosted yields as much as 10% to 15%, depending on severity of disease and location. Fungicides presently cleared are Benlate and Mertect. Diseases controlled include Septoria brown spot, Cerospora leaf blight, anthracnose, pod and stem blight and stem canker. They are most troublesome in warm, wet weather during pod filling. Most benefit has been achieved in southern and central soybean growing areas where diseases have been relatively severe.

Conditions under which you should receive the most benefit from treatment include many factors. As an aid in determing when treatment should pay, Illinois specialists have developed a checklist. Treatment should pay if you score 10 or above.

FUNGICIDE APPLICATION CHECKLIST

Risk factors	Point value if the answer is yes
Rainfall, dew, and humidity up to early bloom and pod set:	
Below normal	0
Normal	2
Above normal	4
Soybeans in the field last year	4
Chisel-plow, disk, or no-till	1
Pycnidia (small dark spots) visible on fallen petioles & Septoria blotch obvious on lower leaves	2
Early-maturing variety (not full-season)	1 to 2
Beans to be used or sold for seed	3
Yield potential better than 35 bushels per acre	2
Seed quality at planting less than 85% germination	1
Field relatively free of a weed canopy	2
Other conditions that favor disease development (weather forecast with 30-day period of greater-than-normal rainfall & disease history)	1 to 3

Double cropping, in areas where length of season permits, can be most successfully achieved by no-till planting. It saves time in preparing a seed bed and conserves valuable moisture to promote germination. Each day you gain in planting may add up to three-fourths bushel per acre to your yield. Harvesting wheat at 20% to 21% moisture and drying it down may pick up an extra 4 to 5 days. If moisture is not sufficient for germination when you are ready to plant, you'd better wait for a rain.

With no-tillage planting, existing weeds must be knocked down with a herbicide such as Paraquat. A number of preemergence herbicides are registered as tank mixes with Paraquat. Roundup is used where Johnsongrass and fall panicum are problems. Lasso and Lorox are registered as tank mixes with Roundup. No-till is not recommended under conditions where Johnsongrass or other perennial weeds are serious problems.

Grain Sorghum Production

There is a place for this crop outside the major producing areas. It can be a profitable alternative to corn in some cases.

Already a major crop of the Great Plains and Southwest, the production of grain sorghum is feasible in areas of the Corn Belt, Southeast and deep South. Though corn, soybeans and cotton are primary crops in these areas, grain sorghum is suited to drier soils or on larger farms where it is necessary to distribute labor. Success will depend on, first, determining if grain sorghum is a wise choice as an alternative crop for corn on your farm. Then, you must apply the management and cropping practices necessary to assure top yields under your conditions.

Markets are not established outside major production areas. If you will be feeding what you produce, this is no problem. Otherwise, you will want to locate a market for the cash grain before planting in the spring. Elevators in some areas have indicated they will buy, if enough farmers grow grain sorghum.

Sorghum is adapted to a wide range of soils, but the crop does best on deep, moderately well-drained soils. Many of the newer single cross sorghum hybrids have a yield potential similar to corn under good conditions, but it is better to plant the best soil to corn where conditions permit. Maryland agronomists say sorghum will yield about 70% to 80% as much as corn on many soils in their state in seasons when rainfall is adequate. Grain sorghum performs better relative to corn under more adverse conditions—on drouthier soils and those subject to spring flooding.

Select a hybrid recommended for your area. The importance is emphasized in a Missouri test of 36 varieties at four different locations, each representing a distinct weather area. Some varieties produced as much as 60 bushels per acre more than others included in the test.

Yield data are not as widely available outside major sorghum areas. But yields in southern Illinois averaged 127 bushels per acre in one season tested, with highest yields being 100 bushels per acre the following season. In another southern Il-linois location, test yields averaged 128 bushels per acre over a four-year period. Ohio tests for one season show top yields of 122 to 133 bushels per acre, depending on location.

Where birds are a severe problem, select from among recommended bird-resistant varieties when you can. Otherwise, you may want to grow a loose-headed variety in which the birds cannot perch.

Planting rate and time vary widely. Seeding rates range from 2 to 20 pounds per acre, depending on whether grown dryland, in more humid areas or under irrigation. Under favorable rainfall conditions or irrigation on fertile soils, the usual rate ranges from 8 to 12 pounds per acre. For instance, Indiana recommends 10 pounds per acre; on less fertile or drouthy soil, 5 pounds.

Soil temperature provides the best guide for planting. A temperature of 65 to 70 degrees at planting depth is required for germination. This means planting about a week or 10 days after corn in many areas. Though planting can be delayed well into June or even July, you run the risk of frost damage in the fall, but this may be necessary if you double crop.

Where situation permits, plant in rows no wider than 30 inches. Plant shallow—no deeper than one inch where moisture is adequate. A crust on the surface before emergence can reduce stands, so use a rotary hoe to break it up. Aside from using specially designed planters, seeding can be done with either a corn planter using the proper plates or a small grain drill by closing off the planting units to give desired row width.

Fertilization practices followed for corn are applicable to grain sorghum. Nitrogen rates vary from 20 to 40 pounds under less fertile, dryland conditions; 40 to 60 pounds on better soils with higher yield potential; and 100 to 150 pounds is common under irrigation. Extremely high rates of 200 or more pounds have not normally been economical under irrigation. Indiana recommends 150 pounds per acre on heavier soils; 100 pounds on sandy soils—much the same in the Southeast.

Mississippi advises 60 pounds on upland soil; 90 to 120 pounds in the Delta.

Apply phosphorus and potassium according to soil test, as recommended for corn. In the absence of a soil test, Mississippi recommends 60 pounds of P_2O_5 and K_2O; Maryland, 75 pounds of each. In areas where soil reserves are higher, rates do not need to be as high. Ohio recommendations shown below can help provide a guide.

RECOMMENDED FERTILIZER RATES FOR GRAIN SORGHUM

Soil test value	Yield goal (cwt./A.)					
	Under 56		70 to 83		98 and above	
	P_2	K_2O^*	P_2O_5	K_2O^*	P_2O_5	K_2O^*
Very low	60	70-100	80	110-160	100	150-220
Low	50	60-80	70	90-125	90	130-175
Medium	40	50-65	60	80-105	80	110-140
Recommended	30	30	50	60	70	80
High	20	20	40	30	60	50
Very high	20	20	20	20	30	30

*Lower end of range for clays and clay loams; upper end, sands and sandy loams; other soils fall in between.

Tillage requirements are similar to those of corn and cotton. Prepare the seedbed sufficiently to assure a good stand and control weeds. Because sorghum is planted later than corn and often germinates rather slowly, tillage at or just before planting to kill germinating weeds is necessary, especially in a wet spring. Sorghum does not compete strongly with weeds during the first four weeks of growth.

Herbicide choices for controlling weeds in sorghum have been broadened since the introduction of safener-treated seed. Use of a seed safener makes it possible to use Dual alone or in combination with atrazine, Milogard, and Igran; or Lasso in combination with atrazine. All are applied preemergence.

Other labeled preemergence herbicides include atrazine alone or atrazine used in combination with Ramrod and Igran; Bladex in combination with Milogard and Ramrod; Ramrod alone or with Milogard; Igran alone or combined with Milogard; Milogard alone or in combination with Lorox; Modown or Modown + Ramrod; and 2,4-D.

Postemergence herbicides include atrazine, Banvel, MCPA, soil incorporation of Prowl or Treflan, and 2,4-D.

For guidance in selecting a herbicide or herbicides to control your particular weed problem, refer to herbicide effectiveness ratings available from the extension service in many states.

Sorghum is not as tolerant of atrazine as corn. Usually, use of atrazine should be limited to the finer textured soils where leaching into the crop root zone is less likely to occur. Milogard is similar to atrazine, but sorghum is somewhat more tolerant of this chemical. Ramrod is best adapted for use on darker soils that are relatively high in organic matter. Sorghum is most tolerant of 2,4-D when it is 4 to 10 inches tall.

Insect pests can be a problem with sorghum, though the crop is generally resistant to most diseases. Sorghum midge is probably the most serious of the insect problems. Though damage by this insect is normally restricted to the southern portion of the country, it can be destructive as far north as the central Midwest. For effective control, Missouri recommends spraying within four days of 90% head emergence; Texas, 50% emergence. For this reason, planting dates and rates need to be similar throughout so stands will be uniform. Early planting will also help.

Other insect problems include the corn earworm, European corn borer, corn leaf aphids and greenbugs. The corn earworm attacks when seeds are maturing. If when shaken, 25% of the heads contain one or more larvae, it is usually economical to apply an insecticide. Control of the European corn borer is usually not warranted. Sorghum webworm is normally most concentrated in late planted fields. Check heads until seeds begin to ripen. Control is justified if 25% of the heads contain one or more larvae. Whenever greenbug infestation occurs on seedling plants, control is suggested. Only a few will kill a plant. Once crop is in the boot to heading stage, treatment should be made when more than two of the lowest leaves have been killed. Control of corn leaf aphids is questionable, since it doesn't usually raise yields.

Harvest, drying and storage can create some problems in more humid areas. Sorghum, unlike corn, does not die and dry as the grain matures. Rather, it stays green until frost and dries very slowly in the field. In a wet fall, mold can be prevalent, especially in varieties having a tight, compact head. So you need to be prepared to harvest and artificially dry as soon after a frost as moisture permits. Frost-killed plants may lodge severely. Normally, it is suggested you begin harvest at 25% to 26% moisture. You can combine as high as 30%, but the grain is hard to clean.

Modern Wheat Production Practices

Use of improved wheat varieties combined with good management has helped western producers boost yields. One practice complements the other.

Newer wheat varieties have higher yield potential for several reasons including more insect and disease resistance, winter hardiness, and tolerance to drouth. Further, being of the semidwarf type, they stand well. Thus, a grower is able to apply more intensive practices, such as increased nitrogen, without fear of excessive lodging.

More improved varieties will evolve. We have not reached a plateau, observe researchers. It is possible that wheat hybrids, introduced in the mid-70s and then shelved, may eventually help producers to boost their potential yields. Should hybrids become commercially practical on a large scale, they will be totally different in genetic makeup from their forerunners, though. It remains to be seen whether hybrids will outyield other improved varieties enough to make them pay. Breeders think they eventually will!

Select adapted varieties that are consistently high yielders for your area using your state's yield trials as a guide.

Cropping practices for wheat differ widely due to the varied areas in which it is grown, so you need to use care in adapting a practice that has been successful in another area. Discussed here, though, are tillage and fertilization practices that deserve consideration.

Conservation tillage is not new for many producers. In the Great Plains, for instance, stubble mulching has long been practiced, but refinements are evolving in the form of ecofallow and no-till systems. In the case of ecofallow, tillage trips are reduced, compared with stubble mulching. More reliance is placed on herbicides to control weeds during the fallow period. With no-till, herbicides completely replace tillage. These tillage methods are not yet widely used and their adaption will vary, depending on need to conserve moisture and number of tillage operations that might be replaced. Savings in machinery requirements, fuel, and labor need to be compared with the cost of herbicide. Also, ecofallow or no-till may boost yields over other tillage methods.

While stubble mulching helps to reduce soil erosion, these newer tillage methods conserve more moisture, as well as reduce erosion. In areas where summer and fall weeds are a problem, weed control should begin within 10 days to 2 weeks after harvest. This is necessary in order to control weeds already present and to prevent new weeds and volunteer grain from germinating. Controlling these weeds may boost potential yield as much as 10 to 15 bushels per acre in areas having an average rainfall of 18 to 22 inches.

Using herbicides rather than tillage to control weeds can often result in a decided advantage. In tests at the Central Great Plains research station, Akron, Colorado, moisture stored during fallow rarely exceeded 35% of rainfall when weeds were controlled by tillage. Each tillage pass in July and August causes the loss of as much as one-third of an inch of moisture. Where contact, postemergence, and/or preemergence herbicides were used alone, water storage averaged 52% during fallow and as high as 60% of rainfall, in some instances. Wheat yielded 41 bushels per acre when herbicides were used alone. On conventionally fallowed land, where subsurface tillage was used, yields averaged 34 bushels per acre.

In some areas of the Northern Plains, snow trapped by stubble contributes 35% to 55% of the water stored during the entire fallow period. So, where tillage is partially relied on to control weeds, subsurface tillage, as with herbicide control, leaves the stubble upright to retain snow in winter. A second pass may knock down some stubble, but this can be minimized by tilling at right angles to the first pass.

Aside from the high cost of some herbicides and possible carryover effects, the larger quantities of crop residue left on the surface have caused some planting difficulties. However, the recently introduced air seeders, large hoe drills, and large double-disk drills will help avoid this problem. But, they also have limitations, so tillage may be needed to incorporate some residue ahead of seeding. Producers generally have not encountered germination problems or increased incidence of insects or disease where large quantities of residue are present. However, as more residue is left on the soil surface, be alert to possible problems.

Effective weed control, using herbicides, during fallow or between crops is required for success with reduced or no-till systems. For maximum control with herbicides, it is important to do a good job of harvesting. Otherwise, heavy stands of volunteer grain can strain herbicide capabilities and poorly distributed straw can interfere with applying them uniformly. Spray equipment should be operated with a minimum of 30 pounds pressure when weeds are already present, and herbicide should be mixed with sufficient water to give good coverage. Straw should be allowed to settle a couple of weeks before applying the herbicide.

Check the herbicides recommended and cleared in your state for controlling weeds between crops in a reduced or no-till system. Here are some examples of herbicides that might be used in a wheat-ecofallow–wheat system in Nebraska. Where weeds are present, a contact or postemergence translocated herbicide is required. Paraquat is used as a contact herbicide to control existing weeds, but Roundup can be used as an alternative. Roundup, a postemergence translocated herbicide, should be applied for early control of existing weeds, or it can be used later in the season if growing conditions are good and weeds are not under stress. For this reason, its usage may be confined largely to controlling volunteer grain in the fall or weeds and volunteer grain in the spring.

Since Paraquat and Roundup have no residual activity, some backup is often necessary. Paraquat can be used in combination with atrazine, Bladex, or Sencor (state label) to control both existing weeds and those that germinate later. Also, a label was just granted which allows the use of Roundup in combination with either Banvel or 2,4-D amine. Either Paraquat or Roundup can be used in a system that requires use of another herbicide later. Igran can be used with atrazine to control both weeds that are present in the stubble and those that will germinate. Where only broadleaf weeds are present at application, 2, 4-D or Banvel can be substituted for Paraquat or Roundup.

Where stubble is free of weeds, atrazine and/or Bladex can be applied to control germinating weeds. A label for several states has recently been granted for use of Sencor. Atrazine should not be used within 12 months of planting the next crop of wheat, and even then, care should be observed to avoid carryover. Atrazine should not be used in many states or areas where soil pH is high, organic matter is low, or soil remains cool for a fairly long period during the year. Bladex should not be applied closer than 60 to 120 days before planting (depending on state label). Where Bladex is applied in spring, it should be put on early enough to control downy brome before it becomes too mature.

In the Pacific Northwest, Chem-Hoe is labeled for use in a fallow situation to control weeds, such as downy brome, mustards, and volunteer grain.

Fertilization practices can greatly affect yield potential in some areas. Soils having a high pH that ties up phosphorus and/or limited moisture can benefit from injecting or banding the two nutrients 4 to 6 inches deep. Kansas studies indicate this practice can boost yield as much as 5 to 20 bushels per acre, and it may save a trip over the field. Benefits are greatest on low-testing soils, where the phosphorus rate is relatively high.

Dual injection or banding helps in a couple of ways. It is believed that the N helps to reduce tieup of phosphorus, making it more available to the crop. More important, perhaps, the nutrients are more likely to be taken up by the crop when placed into the soil where moisture is more available. Consequently, subsurface banding or injection may be especially suited if no-till or minimum tillage replaces an occasional plowing which would have incorporated broadcast fertilizer.

Form of fertilizer isn't critical. Any combination of granular or liquid N and P or anhydrous ammonia can be applied, provided you have the right equipment. A variety of implements is suited for dual banding or injection, including anhydrous applicators, chisel plows, field cultivators, sweeps, and undercutters. Main requirements are that they penetrate to the desired depth and, in the case of anhydrous ammonia, seal the soil before the gas escapes. Ideally, banding should be as narrow as 10 inches and no wider than 15 to 20 inches. There are fewer equipment options for subsurface banding of granular fertilizers. However, an air seeder can double as a fertilizer applicator, and material tanks can be divided to apply two fertilizers at the same time, such as urea and granular phosphate.

In the case of liquid and/or anhydrous ammonia, dual application can be made by equipping each shank with two lines, one for anhydrous and the other for liquid phosphate. Or one line can be used if equipment combines a nitrogen solution with liquid phosphorus as they come from the tank.

Manage Soils to Avoid Compaction Problems

Intensive cropping systems, heavy tractors and harvesting equipment and rising production costs have increased the need to maintain good soil tilth.

Unless proper attention is given to a soil's physical condition, you may be unable to make the most of a well put-together package of crop production practices such as good seed, high fertility and effective weed control. Soil compaction may be no problem until it exceeds a certain point, but your objective should be to farm as effectively as you can while holding down compaction as much as your situation permits.

Poor soil tilth is natural in some soils and may be caused by rain or irrigation (surface sealing) and implement and livestock traffic on many soils. Compaction moves the soil particles closer together, reducing the soil's pore space and increasing its density. This can have an adverse effect on a soil's water holding capacity, its ability to absorb moisture, aeration of the soil and its temperature. All these factors may unfavorably affect crop establishment and growth. Compaction makes it more difficult to prepare a good seedbed and may raise tillage power and fuel needs.

Soil's susceptibility to compaction is affected by several factors. Coarse sands rarely have compaction problems whereas soils containing a mixture of sand, silt and clay may be the most seriously affected—the different sized particles will merge into closer contact with one another. Soils with a high clay content are compaction prone, too. They can be readily deformed when wet. Generally, compaction of a particular soil decreases as its organic matter content is increased. Soils are usually more resistant to compaction when a sod crop is included in the rotation compared to continuous row cropping.

Soil scientists at the National Tillage Machinery Laboratory, Auburn, Alabama report that many soils are not susceptible to compaction damage. They think that much compaction can be alleviated during winter in those areas where frost penetrates to at least 10 inches. Freezing and thawing tend to overcome undesirable soil tilth. However, it will not help to break up compaction below the frost line. Freezing depth is affected by vegetation or snow cover as well as geographic location. Also, freezing and thawing breaks up wet soils more effectively than dry soils.

Because moisture contributes to soil compaction, soils in humid and irrigated areas of the country are affected more by heavy traffic and other compaction forces than those in drier areas.

Effect of Compaction on Yields

In an Illinois study on silty clay loam, compaction was achieved by making four trips over the soil with a truck before plowing. Actually the soil was compacted more than might be expected from most tractors. This compaction increased plow draft by 92% and the soil plowed up slabby, plant emergence was delayed, germination and growth rate were reduced and yield was trimmed by 37% in the first year. In the second year yield on the previously compacted soil was cut by 13%, indicating that winter freezing and thawing can help.

In "controlled traffic" experiments, the National Tillage Machinery Laboratory has demonstrated the effects of compaction on cotton yields and how limiting implement traffic to confined areas of a plowed field can help to reduce compaction. They believe that simply reducing the trips over the field is not enough, since 75% of the compaction takes place during the first trip over the seedbed.

Soil scientist Albert Trouse says much money is wasted on plowing since a large portion of the soil is recompacted by follow-up operations. In his tests, when soil was tilled to 18 inches to break up the plow sole, cotton yields were increased by about one-third bale.

Once traffic was allowed on the seedbed, yields dropped sharply. However, by confining traffic to the skips on two by one skip row cotton, yield was 2-1/2 bales per acre compared with two bales where tractor wheels traveled between the rows.

Minnesota agronomists say that in some years compaction may not cause yield reduction. However, in three of four years of testing, it was found that when 100% of the soil surface was compacted, yields were cut by up to 54% for potatoes, 13% for sugar beets and 7.5% for wheat and corn.

Visual crop symptoms can signal soil structure problems. However, you must be careful when observing crops for these symptoms since each of them may also be associated with other causes including nutrient deficiencies, dry soil, early planting, a high water table or, in some instances, nematodes. Some symptoms to look for as outlined by Michigan soil scientists are:

- Slow plant emergence may reflect the effect of low soil temperature, wet soil, soil crust or a cloddy soil condition—all may be related to a bad soil structure. Other associated problems are variable stands and low plant populations.
- Shorter than normal plants due to slow emergence and growth may result from a cloddy seedbed produced by plowing wet soil.
- Off-colored leaves reflecting nutrient hunger or disease resulting from restricted root growth. Denitrification occurs in waterlogged soils. More fertilizer may reduce the problem but yields still will be limited.
- Shallow root systems from poor penetration. Roots should grow through soil particles, not around them; diagonally downward, not laterally. They should grow uniformly in both the plow layer and subsoil.
- Malformed roots may signal compaction problems. Sprangly roots or

dog legs in root crops such as sugar beets or a fibrous bean root system restricted to the surface few inches are common symptoms. Lodging and root rots in corn may be caused by poor soil structure.

Soil characteristics which suggest possible compaction problems are also listed by the Michigan soil specialists. They are:
● Soil crusts limit the exchange of gases between the soil and atmosphere when the pores are filled with water. When soils are dry, crusts become hard and limit plant emergence.
● Subsurface compact zones can only be observed after digging into the soil. However, it is difficult to properly identify this problem without the help of a growing crop, except in extreme conditions.
● Standing water can result from slow water infiltration rates caused by soil crusts or deeply compacted soil. This can reduce crop growth rate, fertilizer efficiency and yields.
● Excessive water erosion can result from compacted or crusted soil. When rainfall or irrigation water cannot enter the soil rapidly enough it either collects on the surface or runs off.
● Increased power requirements often are not easily recognized since most farmers now own 100 plus horsepower tractors.

Minimizing Compaction Problems

Soil management generally encompasses those cropping practices which are compatible with high yields and profits, but not always. The shift to earlier planting has put some farmers on a collision course with compaction. Culprits have been heavy equipment, careless fertilizer application practices and tillage of soils that are too wet.

Some compromises may be necessary to achieve successful, profitable crop production while holding down compaction. There are several practices that will improve soil structure or prevent further compaction.

Soil drainage, both surface and subsurface, is important since wet soils are more prone to compaction. Maintain ditches, inspect and repair tile drains, smooth the surface of fields to eliminate ponding. Consider the use of sod waterways and outlets for dead furrows.

Minimum tillage practices based on the principles of performing no more tillage than required to achieve good seed germination, an adequate stand and rapid plant growth are particularly compatible with good soil management. Combine operations if possible to reduce trips over the field and where more than one trip is necessary, try to follow the previous tracks where permissible.

Test the moisture of soil at the greatest tillage depth and postpone the operation if soil is too wet.

Where soils have to be plowed, the finer textured ones, those more susceptible to compaction, should be plowed in the fall when they are usually drier and firm enough to support heavy tractors. Then winter freezing helps to produce a friable seedbed that dries out somewhat more quickly for early planting in the spring. To avoid a plowsole, vary plowing depth from season to season and don't plow deeper than necessary.

A chisel plow can help you to break up a compacted subsoil provided you can till deep enough. You may want to start by chiseling about one inch deeper than you have been plowing and then gradually increase the depth in succeeding years as the soil becomes more loose and friable. Preferably you should chisel in the fall when soil moisture is lower, permitting more shattering of the soil. This can help you to take full advantage of your tile drains, too.

Use large disks with discretion since they tend to cause compaction, especially when soil moisture is not ideal.

Good cropping practices including adequate use of fertilizer, lime and pesticides to support high yields are beneficial in maintaining good soil tilth. Though livestock producers should return the manure to the land, recent Minnesota research

has shown that soil humus can be successfully maintained or increased with well fertilized crops. They found that well fertilized continuous corn returning four tons or more of residue per acre to the soil can maintain soil humus, whereas it may take 20 tons of wet manure to achieve the same benefit.

Research at Auburn University some years ago demonstrated that liming strongly acid subsoil to a moderately acid level could reduce soil compaction and thus provide a better rooting environment. The density of the soil was reduced and there was an increase in the number of large soil pores.

Where soils have developed severe structural problems, you may want to include a grass or deep rooted legume in the rotation.

Irrigation should be scheduled to avoid excessive compaction. As much as your situation permits, try to perform your field operations before or sufficiently after an irrigation to avoid being on the field when soil moisture is high. A properly designed and sized system will help you to avoid compaction. In a sprinkler system, for instance, try to avoid those pressures and nozzle sizes that create large water droplets—they increase runoff, compaction and surface sealing or crusting of the soil.

Machinery operations which minimize detrimental effects on soil structure include:
● Dual wheels on heavy equipment to spread the weight over more area and four wheel drive to reduce wheel slippage. This doesn't mean that you can take soil moisture for granted in field operations. The larger equipment even with duals and four wheel drive, may cause more compaction than a smaller tractor. The larger equipment may permit you to reduce the number of trips over the field, though.
● A wide wheel tractor to reduce wheel tracks from three to two.
● Flotation tires to provide a larger surface area help to limit compaction. Avoid excessive wheel weight but provide enough to hold slippage to no more than 15%.

Soil Drainage for Improved Crop Production

It may be more economical to expand crop production by improving your drainage system than by purchasing additional land.

Returns from soil drainage are usually measured in terms of higher yields and more timely field operations. These benefits can help you maximize returns from higher cost production inputs such as seed, fertilizer and herbicides.

The higher yields which are possible through proper soil drainage are demonstrated by research results (shown on graph) obtained from corn grown on lakebed soil in northern Ohio over an eight year period (1962-64 and 1967-71). Average adjusted yield was 70 bushels per acre on undrained plots; 87 bushels, surface drained; 100 bushels, tile drained; and 106 bushels for tile plus surface drainage.

In addition to higher yields, the risk of producing a crop was significantly reduced. There was less than half as much variation in yields produced on tile drained plots from year to year compared with the yields obtained on undrained and surface drained plots–about 21% compared with 48% to 50%.

Differences in corn yields between surface and tile drained plots were observed to be four times greater during the last three years of testing (1969-71) than the previous five years (1962-64, 1967 and 1968). Corn yield for surface drainage was greatly reduced in 1969 and it failed to recover as much in the following two years as

did yields in the tiled treatments. The researchers believe this yield difference was due to the progressive deterioration of the soil's physical properties (breakdown of structure, reduced permeability and poorer aeration).

The poorer soil properties resulting from improper drainage were difficult to correct, indicating that improper drainage can have a long-term effect on soil productivity. The graph shows that tiling previously undrained soil in late 1969 failed to pull yields up to the levels which were obtained on soils which had been tiled at the outset of the tests in 1962.

Timeliness of field operations

The graph to the right shows that improved drainage significantly increased the days available for tillage, especially in May.

The drainage coefficient is defined as the total inches of water that can be removed from a field per day by a combination of deep percolation and existing tile and surface drainage systems. Assuming that the normal drainage coefficient for this soil type is 0.1 inch per day, only four days are available for tillage in May. Raising the drainage coefficient to 0.5 inch would make 18 days available for tillage. In virtually all cases, available

tillage days were not increased by raising the drainage coefficient to a level above 1.0 inch.

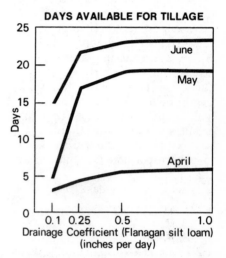

DAYS AVAILABLE FOR TILLAGE

Timeliness of tillage can also be increased by the use of high capacity equipment. In making an investment choice, factors other than available tillage days should be taken into account, including available labor and the other benefits which can result from improved drainage.

Other drainage benefits are numerous. Most contribute to the major advantages of higher yields, greater timeliness of field operations and improved soil structure and aeration. Some of these benefits are:

● Deeper, faster crop root development occurs in well drained soils. This increases the volume of soil from which crops can absorb moisture and nutrients. The effects of drouth are minimized and nutrients are more widely available to the crop. Roots will not grow in saturated soil.

● Well drained soils warm up faster in the spring and allow earlier planting.

● Crops make better use of fertilizer and native soil fertility, especially nitrogen, in well drained soils. Large losses of nitrogen can occur through denitrification on

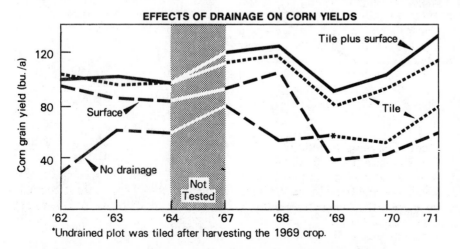

EFFECTS OF DRAINAGE ON CORN YIELDS

*Undrained plot was tiled after harvesting the 1969 crop.

Annual benefits or costs	Surface only	Tile only	Tile plus surface
Adjusted yld. (bu./a., 8 yr. av.)	87	106	108
Benefits	$34	$72	$76
Costs	$ 6	$30	$36
Benefit/cost ratio	5.7	2.4	2.1
Benefits over costs	$28	$42	$40

ESTIMATED BENEFIT—COST ANALYSIS FOR CORN LAND DRAINAGE

poorly drained soils, particularly in seasons of heavy rainfall. Also, organic nutrients are more slowly released by the action of microorganisms in poorly drained soils.

• Soil aggregation, which is destroyed on poorly drained soils, is further jeopardized when farmers begin field operations before the soil is sufficiently dry. This contributes to soil compaction.

• Free water in the soil surface is largely responsible for winter heaving of plants.

• Weeds are more easily controlled on well drained soil.

Soil drainage decisions

When you consider a soil drainage system for your field, compare possible benefits of the system with the costs and other alternatives such as buying additional land. Some soils will respond much better to good drainage than others. For example, tile drainage has not been economical for removing excess water from the Edina claypan soils of southern Iowa, according to a 15 year corn yield study. Most advantages of drainage on claypan soils can be obtained through surface drainage.

The method of drainage you select, if any, should be based on years of experience with your soils. A competent drainage engineer should be consulted to determine if drainage will pay and which system or combination of tile, surface ditches and land grading may be best for each field.

You may want to make a rough benefit—cost analysis before deciding to improve the drainage on your farm. The analysis used by Ohio researchers for the eight year test reported earlier, as shown in the table above, provides an example of the kind of procedure you might want to use. You won't have relative yields from actual tests to plug into your own analysis, but you should be able to make some fairly good estimates.

The benefits shown in the table are based on corn priced at $2 per bushel for the yield over the 70 bushels per acre produced on undrained plots. All costs were computed using a depreciation of 2% per year for the tile (50 year life), interest on the average investment at 8% and maintenance costs of $0.40 per acre for the tile and $2.00 per acre for surface drains. Cost estimates do not include fertilizer and other production costs. Initial investment costs per acre were assumed at $490 for tile and $100 for surface drains.

Relationship of tile spacing and cost per foot installed can provide you with some guidance in projecting per acre costs. Normally tile spacing is dictated by soil texture and the depth that tile is to be installed below the ground surface.

Since the water usually stands nearer the ground surface midway between drains, the depth at this point determines if the drains are adequately lowering the water table. Water moves through coarse textured soils more rapidly than it does through fine soils, meaning that tile can be spaced wider apart in coarse soils. In stratified soils, place tile in the most permeable layer, provided it is below the depth to which the water table should be lowered and within a depth that is economically justified.

TILE REQUIRED PER ACRE

Feet spacing	Feet required per acre
20	2,178
25	1,742
30	1,452
33	1,320
40	1,089
50	872
66	660
80	545
100	436
150	291
200	218

Plastic tile offers advantages and disadvantages compared with concrete or clay. When installed properly, there are no major differences. While the corrugation of plastic may reduce the flow capacity by 28% compared with a comparable size concrete or clay tile, this is not a major problem for laterals since they seldom flow full. The situation is different for main lines. Plastic is not recommended for drainage outlets since it may be damaged by rodents, by burning or by sprays used to control weeds.

Cost of installation for various tile materials will vary between areas so you'll want to check with contractors in your area and compare the relative cost of plastic, clay and concrete. Generally, there is not a great deal of difference in cost between these materials for 4- and 5-inch tile diameters. However, for larger diameter tile, the cost is significantly higher for plastic.

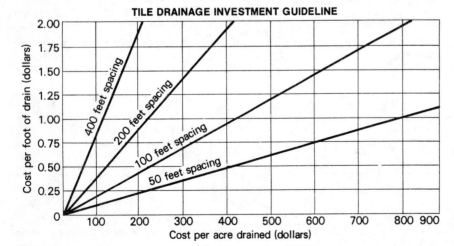

TILE DRAINAGE INVESTMENT GUIDELINE

Crop Planting and Storage Tables

A guide for estimating your seed and storage requirements and for deciding what planting rate will give optimum yield.

Planting rates for most crops shown present a range instead of a specific figure. Many factors will cause the rates to vary from one locality to another—seed size, row width, seed type, seed spacing in the row, climate, planting method, germination percentage expected, variety, soil fertility and whether or not it's irrigated. If local recommendations are more specific, these should be followed provided the source is reliable.

Soybean seed size varies greatly between varieties and within varieties depending on growing conditions. In view of this, recommendations are for number of seeds per foot of row.

APPPROXIMATE NUMBER OF CORN SEEDS PER ACRE AT VARYING ROW WIDTHS AND SPACING IN THE ROW

Row width (inches)	Seed spacing in the row - (inches)					
	6	8	10	12	14	16
20	52,168	39,126	31,300	26,084	22,172	19,563
24	43,600	32,700	26,100	21,800	18,700	16,300
28	37,300	28,000	22,400	18,700	16,000	14,000
30	34,848	26,136	20.908	17,424	14,810	13,068
32	32,700	24,500	19,600	16,300	14,000	12,300
34	30,784	23,338	18,470	15,392	13,030	11,497
36	29,000	21,800	17,400	14,500	12,400	10,900
38	27,500	20,600	16,500	13,800	11,800	10,300
40	26,100	19,600	15,700	13,100	11,200	9,800
42	24,900	18,700	14,900	12,400	10,700	9,300

Medium rounds or flats, 1,600 seeds per pound.   MICHIGAN STATE UNIVERSTIY
Large or regular flats, 1,300 seeds per pound.
Add 15% for seed and plant mortality.

CROP PLANTING TABLE

Crop	Pounds to seed per acre		Weight per bushel, pounds	Planting depth, inches	Type planting*	Recommended seeds per foot of row
Corn for grain	6-10 S & SW 10-14 Corn Belt		56	2-3	r.d.	See Table Above
Soybeans	**small seed**	**large seed**				
40-42 in. rows	30-45	45-65	60	2	r. d.	7-10
28-30 in. rows	40-55	55-85	60	2	r. d.	6- 9
20-21 in. rows	40-60	60-90	60	2	r. d.	4- 6
Sorghum (milo), grain***	2-5 (Plains states)		56	1-2	r. d.	3-6 (40 in. rows)
	8 (Humid states)		56	1-2	r. d.	10 (40 in. rows)
Wheat, winter	40-60 Plains 90-120 Humid		60	1-2	d.	
Wheat, spring or durum	60-90		60	1-2	d.	
Barley	60-96		48	1-2	d.	
Rye	56-84		56	1-2	d.	
Oats	50-80		32	1-2	d.	
Flax	42-56		56	1-1-1/2	d.	
Beans, Navy	30-45		60	2	r.	3-4 (22 in. rows)
Kidney	80		60	2	r.	3-4 (22 in. rows)
Pinto	75-90		---	2-1/2-3-1/2	r.	3-4 (22 in. rows)
Great Northern	75-100		---	2-1/2-3-1/2	r.	3-4 (22 in. rows)
Rice	90 (drill) 125-200 (air)		45	1-2	d. or airplane	
Cotton (delinted)	12-30		32	1-1/2-2	r.	
Field peas, large	120-180		---	1-2	d.	
small	90-120		---	1-2	d.	
Alfalfa**	15-25		60	1/2	b.	
Clover** alsike	4-6		60	1/2	b.	
ladino	1-2		60	1/2	b.	
red	6-8		60	1/2	b.	
Smooth bromegrass**	10-15		14	1/2	b.	
Kentucky bluegrass**	15-30		14	1/2	b.	
Tall fescue**	10-25		14	1/2	b.	
Orchardgrass**	10-20		14	1/2	b.	
Redtop**	4-6		14	1/2	b.	
Timothy**	6-14		45	1/2	b.	
Ryegrass**	10-30		24	1/2	b.	
Birdsfoot trefoil	5-8		60	1/2	b.	
Sudan grass	20-25		40	1/2	b.	
Sorghum, forage	4-8		50	1-2	b.	
Bermuda sprigs	10 bushels		---	1/2-1	Single rows	

*r. - row; d. - drill; b. - band. Increase rates 20% for broadcast.   ***For 20-inch rows use same rate but double spacing between plants.
**Rates are for solid stands. Adjust rates for mixtures.

127

ESTIMATED TONNAGE CAPACITY* OF TOWER SILOS FOR CORN OR GRASS-LEGUME SILAGE, 68% TO 70% MOISTURE

Silo height in feet	Height of settled silage in feet	Pounds per cubic foot	Inside Diameter of Silo										
			10'	12'	14'	16'	18'	20'	22'	24'	26'	28'	30'
20	20	44	33	48	66	86	—	—	—	—	—	—	—
30	29	49	56	80	109	143	180	223	270	321	377	—	—
40	38	51	77	110	150	196	248	307	371	442	520	600	690
50	47	53	—	—	193	252	320	394	477	570	668	773	886
60	56	55	—	—	—	—	392	483	585	697	818	947	1,087
70	65	56	—	—	—	—	—	574	694	827	970	1,125	1,290

*Capacity according to depth after settling.   ADAPTED FROM UNIVERSITY OF ILLINOIS DATA

(a) Silo capacity in cubic feet = r^2 x h. x 3.1416   (b) Cubic feet of settled silage = r^2 x h. of settled silage x 3.1416

(c) Silo capacity in tons of settled silage = $\dfrac{\text{Cubic feet x pounds per cubic foot of silage}}{2{,}000}$

(d) Pounds per cubic foot of unsettled silage varies from 35 to 45.

(e) Factors that cause variation from the estimated capacities include: moisture content, length of cut, speed of filling, extent of refilling, use of distributor in silo.

(f) If the crop is above 70% moisture add 5% to 10% to tonnage (corn silage in milk stage).

(g) Haylage and cornlage: deduct 25% at 60% moisture; deduct 40% at 50% moisture; deduct 50% at 40% moisture; deduct 60% at 30% moisture.

CAPACITY IN TONS PER FOOT OF LENGTH FOR TRENCH OR BUNKER SILOS

Average width, feet	Depth of silage in feet																	
	5			6			7			8			9			10		
	Cu. ft.	Tons Corn	Tons Grass	Cu. ft.	Tons Corn	Tons Grass	Cu. ft.	Tons Corn	Tons Grass	Cu. ft.	Tons Corn	Tons Grass	Cu. ft.	Tons Corn	Tons Grass	Cu. ft.	Tons Corn	Tons Grass
8	40	.70	.90	48	.84	1.08	56	.98	1.26	64	1.12	1.44	72	1.25	1.62	80	1.40	1.80
10	50	.88	1.13	60	1.05	1.35	70	1.23	1.58	80	1.40	1.80	90	1.58	2.03	100	1.75	2.25
12	60	1.05	1.35	72	1.26	1.62	84	1.47	1.89	96	1.68	2.16	108	1.69	2.48	120	2.10	2.70
14	70	1.23	1.58	84	1.47	1.69	98	1.71	2.21	112	1.96	2.52	126	2.21	2.84	140	2.45	3.15
16	80	1.40	1.80	96	1.68	2.16	112	1.96	2.52	128	2.24	2.88	144	2.52	3.24	160	2.80	3.60
18	90	1.58	2.03	108	1.89	2.48	126	2.21	2.89	144	2.52	3.24	162	2.89	3.64	180	3.15	4.05
20	100	1.75	2.25	120	2.10	2.70	140	2.45	3.15	160	2.80	3.60	180	3.15	4.05	200	3.50	4.50
22	110	1.93	2.48	132	2.31	2.97	154	2.69	3.47	176	3.08	3.96	198	3.47	4.45	220	3.85	4.95
24	120	2.10	2.70	144	2.52	3.24	168	2.94	3.78	192	3.36	4.32	216	3.78	4.85	240	4.20	5.40
26	130	2.28	2.92	156	2.73	3.51	182	3.19	4.09	208	3.64	4.68	234	4.10	5.26	260	4.55	5.85
28	140	2.45	3.15	168	2.94	3.78	196	3.43	4.41	224	3.92	5.04	252	4.41	5.67	280	4.90	6.30
30	150	2.63	3.38	180	3.15	4.05	210	3.68	4.73	240	4.20	5.40	270	4.73	6.05	300	5.25	6.75

Capacity in cubic feet = $\dfrac{\text{Top width + bottom width}}{2}$ x height x length

Capacity in tons, corn or sorghum (35 lb. cu. ft.) = $\dfrac{\text{Capacity (cu. ft.)}}{60}$ Grass silage (40 lb. cu. ft.) = $\dfrac{\text{Capacity (cu. ft.)}}{50}$

ESTIMATED BUSHEL CAPACITY, NO. 2 SHELLED CORN (15.5% MOISTURE) FOR CYLINDRICAL STRUCTURES

Diameter in feet	Height in feet												
	10	15	20	25	30	35	40	45	50	55	60	65	70
	(hundreds of bushels)												
14	12	18	25	31	37	43	49	55	62				
16	16	24	32	40	48	56	64	72	80				
18	20	30	41	51	61	71	81	91	102	112	122		
20	25	38	50	63	75	88	100	113	126	138	151	163	176
22	30	46	61	76	91	106	122	137	152	167	182	198	213
24	36	54	72	90	109	127	145	163	181	199	217	235	253
26	42	64	85	106	127	148	170	191	212	233	254	276	297
28	49	74	99	123	148	173	197	222	247	271	296	320	345
30	57	85	113	142	170	198	226	255	283	311	340	368	396
32	64	96	129	161	193	225	257	289	322	354	386	418	450
34	73	109	145	182	218	254	290	327	363	399	436	472	508
36	81	122	163	204	244	285	326	366	407	448	488	529	570
38	91	136	181	227	272	317	363	408	454	499	544	590	635
40	101	151	202	252	302	353	403	454	504	554	605	655	706

UNIVERSITY OF ILLINOIS

1. For cubic feet in a cylindrical bin use the following formula: Cubic feet = r^2 x h x 3.1416
2. For capacity of high-moisture shelled corn or ground ear corn, multiply bushels of No. 2 corn by the factors at right.

Moisture %	Shelled corn %	Ground ear corn %
15.5	100.0	64.4
20.0	96.2	61.0
25.0	91.9	57.3
30.0	86.8	54.3

Measuring Fields and Farms

Many management decisions are based on accurate land measurements. Here are some commonly used forms of measuring.

In figuring land area, the lengths of the different sides are the measurements you need. The table shows the common units used for the measurement of distance. It can also be used for converting one unit to any of the others.

DISTANCE MEASURE
1 foot = 12 inches
1 yard = 3 feet or 36 inches
1 pace = 1 yard or 36 inches
1 rod = 16½ feet or 5½ yards
1 chain = 66 feet or 4 rods
1 mile = 80 chains, 320 rods or 1,760 yards

The measuring units to be used will depend on the size of the area as well as the units most familiar to you. For example, when measuring small plots, the foot or yard may be the most convenient, but when measuring larger areas, you might use the rod, chain or even the mile.

The acre is the most common area measure used.

CONVERSION FACTORS
1 acre = 43,560 square feet
1 acre = 4,840 square yards
1 acre = 160 square rods
1 acre = 10 square chains

It is a fairly simple process to change square area measurements (square feet, square yards, square chains, etc.) into acres. The table above can be used for making these conversions.

Accurate measurements will depend on how well you follow simple basic practices. Make your measurements in a straight line and keep an accurate record of all distances, as well as corners and odd-shaped boundaries.

It's a good idea to make a rough sketch of fields before you start measuring. If this is impossible, sketch as you go along. Label each side as soon as it is measured to avoid confusion.

A number of devices can be used for determining the length or the distance around the area to be measured. It's up to you to decide which is most practical for your purposes.

The pace is a fair measure of distance and can be used when extreme accuracy is not needed. The extended step (pace) that is often used in measuring land is considered to be a yard long. It takes conscious effort to keep the pace from becoming shorter after a great distance has been measured and the person tires.

The pace should not be used unless the length of the pace is carefully checked over a measured distance to insure consistency.

The chain (66 feet long) can be used for accurate and easy figuring of large areas. The number of square chains in an area, divided by 10, gives the number of acres.

Two men are needed to carry the chain. For long distances you should tally with a set of 11 wire (No. 9) marking stakes. One stake is placed at the start. The leading man sets a stake at each 66-foot interval measured off by the chain. When the rear man has gathered up 10 stakes, the distance covered by the front man is 10 chains.

Other measuring tools may include a steel tape, or a cable or wire of an exact length. The same method of using stakes, as described for the chain, should be used to keep track of the distance covered when using these tools.

Acreage can be determined by changing field measurements into area measurements (square yards, square chains, or whatever units you may be using). For example, a field five chains long and four chains wide has an area of 20 square chains. Divide the number of square units in the field by the number of square units in an acre to determine the number of acres in a field. Formulas for determining acres for the most commonly used units are given.

$$\text{No. of acres} = \frac{\text{area in sq. ft.}}{43,560}$$

$$\text{No. of acres} = \frac{\text{area in sq. yds.}}{4,840}$$

$$\text{No. of acres} = \frac{\text{area in sq. rods}}{160}$$

$$\text{No. of acres} = \frac{\text{area in sq. chains}}{10}$$

$$\text{No. of acres} = \text{area in sq. miles} \times 640$$

Shape of field affects the method you should use for determining the square area within that field. By using one of the following examples, the area of almost any field can be determined.

Rectangular or square-shaped fields are the easiest to figure. Find the area of the field by multiplying the length times the width.

Fields that are not rectangles, but have two equal or parallel sides, can be figured in the same way as the rectangular field. Use the average of the two parallel sides for the length figure.

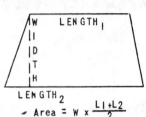

$$\text{Area} = W \times \frac{L1 + L2}{2}$$

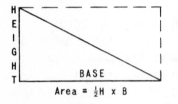

Area = $\frac{1}{2}$H x B

Right triangle fields are three-sided fields having one square corner. To find the area, figure as if it were one-half of a rectangle. Thus one-half of the length (base) multiplied by the width (height) will give you the area.

Other triangular fields not having a square corner can be figured the same way as the right triangle, but the height must be measured square

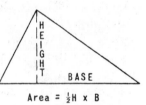

Area = $\frac{1}{2}$H x B

from the base line (at right angles to it). Thus one-half of the height times the base gives the area.

Many-sided fields with more than four sides or with four unequal sides can usually be measured by using one or more of the methods already discussed. The trick is to divide the fields into triangles or rectangles that can be easily measured. Measure from one corner to an opposite corner, dividing the field into more easily measured plots. Find the area of each of the new plots by using the formulas for rectangles or triangles. Here are some examples of how fields may be divided for easier measurement.

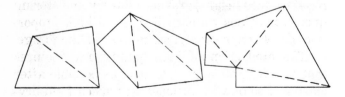

Curved boundaries are often encountered where contour farming is practiced. To determine the area, measure off a straight base line. Put it as near the center of the field as possible, but keep it straight. At equal distances take a number of measurements of the field width. Make these measurements at right angles to the base line. Find the average of these width lines and multiply this average times the length of the base line. This will give you the area of the field. If the base line does not meet the ends of the field squarely (at right angles) you will have to figure the area of the small triangles A and B separately, as shown in the figure below.

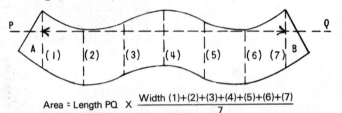

Area = Length PQ X $\dfrac{\text{Width } (1)+(2)+(3)+(4)+(5)+(6)+(7)}{7}$

When fields are too curved to permit drawing a straight base line, use the following procedure. Measure a base line down the center of the field, or as near the center as practical. Let it curve as the field curves. At equal distances measure the width of the field. Make these measurements square across (as near as possible) the base line and use the same method of figuring area as you would use with a straight base line.

Adjustments need to be made when measuring the land area of highly irregular fields. Measuring up and down hills will give a longer distance than actually exists on a level line. Consideration must be given to the slope when making surveys or appraisals. Use the table to adjust for slope.

	SLOPE CORRECTION TABLE	
Slope	Horizontal Distance for 100 Feet Surface Distance	Correction
5%	99.9	0.1%
10%	99.5	0.5%
15%	98.8	1.1%
20%	98.0	2.0%
25%	97.0	3.0%
30%	95.8	4.2%
40%	92.8	7.2%

UNIV. OF MARYLAND

Aerial photographs are used for determining land area. In most areas, photos can be checked for acreage at your local ASC (Agricultural Stabilization and Conservation) office. Measurements can be made directly from photos.

Chapter 6

Forage Production

On certain types of land, grasses and legumes grown under proper management will often return as much or more than row crops produced on the same land. Forage production makes it easier to conserve and maintain soil tilth and fertility, especially on rough land.

The success of a forage program depends on two major factors:

● It is essential that you produce top forage yields—as high as is economically feasible.

● You must have an efficient livestock operation to make profitable use of this forage.

Forages are marketed through livestock; so grassland programs must be well-balanced with livestock enterprises. There are five basic grassland programs which are either used alone or in combination.

● Pasture—this includes open or free grazing, rotational or strip grazing and temporary or emergency grazing.

● Silage or hay.

● Green chop feeding—this is sometimes called zero grazing.

● Cash crop—hay and seeds.

● Green manure or cover crop (soil building).

Forage programs should emphasize maximum production of high quality feed. Consider the following practices:

● Plant as high a portion of your forage acres to legumes or grass-legume mixtures as possible. Legumes will produce more forage per acre and maintain fertility at a higher level. However, where stands will be maintained for a number of years, it's necessary to include grasses with legumes. After a year or so many legumes begin to die out. Grass pastures can be renovated to include a legume in the mixture.

● Fertilize adequately to maintain a favorable nutrient balance in the soil. Proper fertilization will increase both the yield and quality of your forage. Carrying capacity can be increased as much as 100% to 300% through fertilization.

● Control weeds which reduce the production and quality of your forage.

● Maintain stands by rotating your pasture as much as possible. Don't graze too close or before forages have a chance to get good growth.

Harvesting forages is just as important as producing them. The quality of feed produced and the ability of plants to recover is largely dependent on harvesting at the proper stage, cutting at the recommended height, grazing properly and storing under conditions which will retain a high proportion of the original nutrient content of the forage.

The production of high quality hay requires that you dry and store it as soon as possible after cutting. Use of a conditioner will speed field drying and reduce the risk of weather damage.

The effect of early harvest on hay quality is illustrated by an analysis for digestibility, protein content and amount of crude fiber of twenty-five hay samples.

The best sample was 42% higher in digestibility than the poorest. Hay harvested before June 10 without weather damage averaged 62% digestible compared with 52% for samples harvested later. Likewise, protein content averaged 16% compared with 12% for hay harvested after June 10.

On the basis of these tests, it was concluded that a dairy cow will consume 2.2 to 2.3 pounds digestible dry matter per 100 pounds body weight from early harvested forage; 1.2 to 1.8 pounds from late harvested forage. Considering both intake and nutrient content, a cow fed late harvested forage will require 1-1/2 to 2 times more grain. The grain mixture needs to contain about 5% more protein too.

More frequent cutting should accompany earlier harvest of the first crop. While the quality of subsequent cuttings varies less with cutting date, there is a rapid decline in digestibility after six weeks of regrowth. However, yields can be boosted by harvesting more often than this—every 30 to 40 days, depending on weather. By cutting the first crop early, second growth occurs when soil moisture is more plentiful—daylight is still lengthening and regrowth is more rapid.

Harvesting forage as haylage, where your operation permits, saves on drying time and reduces risk of rain damage, especially on the first cutting. With favorable weather, forage can be put up as haylage (40% to 60% moisture) the same day it's cut. Use of a conditioner helps to speed drying, too, and may cut drying time by one-third to one-half.

Key to retaining high quality in haylage once it's ensiled relies heavily on cutting the forage while it's still young, particularly if the silo is not airtight. Young forage packs better, therefore it's easier to exclude the air.

To assure good preservation and retention of desirable quality, haylage or silage should be stored under those conditions which are conducive to the formation of desirable acids. Forage ensiled at 50% to 65% moisture produces the best feed. Forage packs well within this moisture range. Chopping the forage fine also helps to achieve good packing.

Under these conditions, normal silage fermentation temperatures usually range from 80° to 100° F. At lower temperatures, lactic acid forming bacteria can't compete with butyric acid forming bacteria. Higher than 100° F. temperatures produce a sweet, tobacco smelling, dark brown carmelized silage. It is palatable, but much of the nutrient value has been lost.

Green chop programs, which involve harvesting forage in the field and hauling it to livestock, can increase forage production and allow you to carry more livestock per acre. However, this method of harvesting forages increases your costs. Investment in feeding facilities and harvesting equipment will be higher and labor requirements are greater. Thus, the profitability of such an operation depends on how the increased production compares with the additional investment and operating costs. Generally, green chop programs are most practical for smaller farms where acreage and forage supply are limited.

Managing for Top Alfalfa Production

Alfalfa and alfalfa-grass mixtures can be profitably grown on many farms if they receive the attention and management given to row crops.

Several programs are being geared to produce 10 tons of alfalfa per acre in the Midwest, and even higher yields are possible under irrigation in the Southwest. Not all soils support these yields, but the potential for many is somewhere between 4 and 10 tons, which is far above the 2-1/2 to 3 tons per acre average.

Generally, practices required for high yields complement those that contribute to high quality. This further points out the need for combining good management practices.

Soils best adapted to alfalfa are highly fertile, well-drained, deep, open and have a soil pH approaching neutral. However, some newer varieties are bred to perform well on imperfectly drained soils. Less fertile soils will often support alfalfa when the essential nutrients and lime are applied, provided poorly drained areas are avoided.

Variety selection of alfalfa is a much more important decision now, with a larger list of good performers of several strains. The two major strains are North American and Flemish, but some are also classed as Intermediate.

Flemish varieties are exceptionally vigorous and will boost your chances of getting a good stand and top yield. Since they mature sooner, they demand earlier harvest for top quality forage. Because they bounce back rapidly, they fit well into a stepped-up cutting schedule. However, since they are more susceptible to bacterial wilt, they are not recommended for stands that are to be left down more than two years.

A variety of the North American or Intermediate strains is advised for long term stands. While less vigorous as a group, many of the newer varieties have high-yielding ability. Some exhibit much of the vigor of Flemish strains, while being wilt resistant.

Consider growing several varieties of more than one strain to spread out first cutting and insure better quality forage where a large acreage is grown. When grown in a mixture, match the maturity of the alfalfa with the grass. Under more intensive management, grasses are more difficult to maintain in the stand. When selecting a variety, take winter hardiness, wilt resistance, leaf disease resistance and quality of forage into account.

Seedbed preparation and seeding method contribute greatly to stand and yield, particularly in the first year. Top yields require a thick, uniform stand—considered to be 10 to 12 plants per square foot at the end of the first year and five well-distributed plants thereafter.

Where previous crop, available equipment and conditions permit, plowing, disking and rolling are generally preferred to create a firm, compact, level seedbed. A uniform seeding depth and close soil contact with the seed (to assure adequate moisture for the young seedling) are necessary.

Where possible, band seeding helps assure a good stand by placing the seed directly over bands of fertilizer. Press wheels should be used to firm the seedbed; if not, cultipacking before and after seeding is desired. Where seedings are not banded, double corrugated rollers or packer-type seeders are satisfactory, except on loose sands or heavy clays. Although band seeding is desirable on fall sown grains, broadcast if the soil is too wet to support equipment. Then apply the fertilizer after grain harvest.

Seed about one-half inch deep—perhaps a bit shallower on moist, heavy soils or a little deeper on sandy soils or heavier soils short of moisture. Stands will be reduced if seeds are placed much deeper than three-fourths inch.

Seeding rate of 12 to 15 pounds per acre is generally adequate when a good seedbed is prepared and an approved seeding method used. Check the rates recommended by your state. In trials where recommended seeding rates have been doubled, yields haven't been boosted significantly. When sown as a mixture, you can cut back on the alfalfa seeding rate by about one-third.

Time of seeding varies by regions. Generally, either fall or spring seedings can be successful across the northern half of the country. Fall seeding needs to be made early enough, though, to allow seedings to become established before frost. For this reason, they may be a bit more risky in upper northern regions—there seedings should be made about mid-August. Where moisture is adequate to support fall seedings, they usually encounter less weed competition than spring seedings.

In more southerly areas, late summer and fall seedings are generally preferred. Fall seedings give young plants more time to become well established before hot weather. Seedings are usually made late enough to take advantage of late summer and fall rains in many areas and to avoid extreme heat.

Need for a nurse crop to establish spring seedings has diminished. Competition of both weeds and the nurse crop can be reduced by using a herbicide. Yields of four to five tons in the first year are possible with two to three tons common.

Seeding with or without a companion grain crop depends on several factors: (1) Soil erosion hazard. A nurse crop will give quick cover. (2) Usefulness of the grain crop as hay or silage in feeding programs. (3) Comparative cost and effectiveness of weed control by mowing or herbicides.

Lime requirements should be supplied well in advance of alfalfa seedings, preferably six months, a year or even longer. If liming is made closer to seeding, disk it in after plowing so it will be within reach of young seedlings. Where rather heavy rates are required to pull the soil pH up to 6.5 to 7, plow under about half and disk in the remainder.

Fertilizer program needs to be tailored to soil test recommendations. A well-inoculated alfalfa stand, once established, will supply its own nitrogen unless the mixture drops below 50% alfalfa. Seed inoculation is cheap nitrogen fixation insurance.

Alfalfa is a heavy user of nutrients, so it's important to fulfill three major objectives for top yield. Enough phosphorus and potassium should be broadcast and plowed under to raise your soil to recommended fertility levels. Second, use a starter fertilizer to get new seedings off to a good start—around 30 pounds of phosphorus and 30 to 50

pounds of potassium. Unless soil organic matter is low, no nitrogen is required at seeding. If it is low, 15 to 30 pounds may be necessary. Third, develop an annual topdressing program based on crop removal. Be aware of the nutrient-supplying power of your soil since alfalfa is a deep feeder.

ALFALFA NUTRIENT REQUIREMENTS

Crop	Yield	N	P₂O₅	K₂O	Mg	S

Crop	Yield	Nutrient Removal-Lbs.				
		N	P_2O_5	K_2O	Mg	S
Alfalfa	10 T./A.	560*	115	500	50	60
Corn silage	40 T./A.	265	105	325	80	45
Corn grain	200 Bu./A.	180	65	45	25	20
Soybeans	80 Bu./A.	275*	65	115	15	22

*Most of the N is obtained by nitrogen fixation from the air.

AMERICAN POTASH INSTITUTE

Fertilizer can be topdressed in spring, fall or following a cutting. When only one topdressing is applied, some agronomists believe it can be most advantageously put on after the first cutting. This recommendation assumes normal rainfall. Normally, the lush spring growth tends to take up more nutrients than necessary. Applications after first cutting may give more efficient forage production and fertilizer use.

Cutting schedule should be as early and as frequent as possible. Weather and harvest system permitting, the first cutting should be taken in the bud to very early bloom stage, with a cutting every 30 to 35 days thereafter, if moisture permits. Last cutting in the fall should be made early enough to allow plants to restore their root reserves.

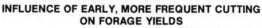

INFLUENCE OF EARLY, MORE FREQUENT CUTTING ON FORAGE YIELDS

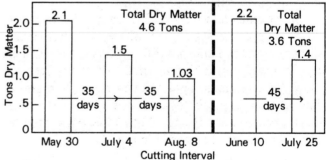

Besides increasing yields, early, frequent cuttings greatly improve the quality, digestibility and feed intake. Young alfalfa plants hold their leaves and it's the leaves which are particularly high in protein content.

Pasture Improvement and Management

Some pasture forages respond much more than others to good management. Select grasses and legumes to match your grazing and fertilization program.

A profitable pasture system requires use of productive forage species and a sound fertilization program. Where possible it is desirable to replace Kentucky bluegrass with one of the tall grasses which normally yield more and respond well to fertility and management. In the South, improved grasses such as Coastal Bermuda grass may yield twice as much as common grasses with the same amount of fertilizer and water.

RESPONSE OF TALL GRASSES TO NITROGEN RATE AND TIME OF APPLICATION

Pounds of nitrogen per acre			Tons of dry matter per acre			
Early spring	After 1st harvest	After 2nd harvest	Orchard	Smooth brome	Tall fescue	Reed canary
0	0	0	0.88	1.43	0.94	1.24
0	0	120	2.58	2.75	3.24	3.16
60	60	120	4.09	4.64	4.85	5.41
0	0	240	2.76	3.61	3.95	4.00
120	120	240	4.30	5.34	5.42	6.32
0	0	480	3.50	4.21	4.52	5.51

IOWA STATE UNIVERSITY

Annual topdress applications of phosphorus and potassium should be geared to soil test recommendations. On grasses, fall applications along with small amounts of nitrogen will stimulate fall growth and maintain vigor for spring growth. The best time to topdress legumes or mixtures may be after the first grazing, or you may want to equally divide application after the first grazing or cutting and again in early fall.

If legumes make up 30% or more of a mixture, Illinois agronomists say no nitrogen is necessary. When legumes make up 20% to 30%, they advise applying 50 pounds of nitrogen. If there are less than 20% legumes, apply 50 pounds of nitrogen in late winter or early spring and 50 pounds after first grazing or cutting. Note the rates used in straight grasses in the table above.

Legume-grass mixtures will substitute for nitrogen in straight grass pastures. Wisconsin tests show legumes produced as much beef as grass pastures receiving 120 pounds of nitrogen annually. Growth of grass-legume pastures is more evenly distributed through the season.

Missouri researchers advise that grasses and legumes sown in a mixture be similar in palatability, maturity patterns and growing vigor. It is recommended that each mixture contain only one grass and one or two legumes.

LEGUMES CAN SUBSTITUTE FOR NITROGEN IN A STRAIGHT GRASS PASTURE

Pasture Treatment	Daily gain lbs./day 1967-68	Beef gain lbs./acre 1967-69
Bluegrass, redtop, timothy (no nitrogen)	1.42	210
Bluegrass, redtop, timothy (120 lbs. nitrogen)	1.29	313
Bluegrass, redtop, timothy, birdsfoot trefoil	1.32	335
Brome, orchard (120 lbs. nitrogen)	1.24	307
Brome, orchard, alfalfa	1.08	324

N is applied 60 lbs. April and 60 lbs. June. P-K applied according to soil test. Grazed May 10 to September 5—avg. 114 days.

LANCASTER, WIS. EXPTL. FARM

Effective use of pasture must be combined with a pasture improvement program. Livestock, livestock management programs, pasture and other forage needs must all be taken into account in setting up a pasture system to fit your needs. Otherwise you'll lose much of the advantage of higher forage yields.

Fertilization does much to increase forage production, but you need to use different pasture species and management techniques to distribute production as much as possible and provide full season grazing. Seasonal availability of various pasture mixtures, along with other forage, needs to be considered when planning your pasture acreage and system.

SEASONAL AVAILABILITY OF FORAGES

Forage	Percent of annual production		
	May-June	July-Aug.	Sept.-Oct.-Nov.
Kentucky bluegrass, nitrogen added	70	13	17
Orchard grass or brome grass, nitrogen added	60	15	25
Birdsfoot trefoil grass	35	45	20
Alfalfa-orchard grass	45	40	15
Sudan grass	0	80	20
Meadow aftermath, two cuttings for hay	0	45	55
Cornstalks	0	0	Oct.-Dec. 100

STRIVE FOR FULL SEASON GRAZING

It's advisable to limit acreage of some pastures to what your livestock can use during the short period of lush growth in the spring. Properly fertilized and managed Kentucky bluegrass-white clover pasture, for instance, can be very productive, but bulk of the forage growth occurs in spring and early summer. It makes very little growth during the hot, dry summer months. Also, it does not grow tall so the excess growth cannot be satisfactorily harvested for hay or haylage.

Tall grass-legume pastures, whether rotational or renovated, as demonstrated by their seasonal availability, add some flexibility to a forage system. Aside from use for pasture these forages are also well suited for harvesting as hay, haylage or green chop. These grasses need to be renovated every three to five years, so it's desirable to confine bluegrass to areas of rougher, steeper land. Grow the taller growing grasses and legumes on fields that can be easily renovated.

Summer forage annuals help to fill in for seasonal decline in other forage growth during the hot, dry summer periods. Bulk of this forage is available during July and August, and diminishes into fall. If you use sorghum-Sudan hybrids for pasture, plan to seed relatively early. In a three-year Illinois study these forages seeded between May 10 and 20 were tall enough to graze in four or five weeks and provided three or four grazings. Seedings in late June or early July provided only two grazings and produced 28% less forage.

Stockpiling is a practice whereby forage growth is accumulated for grazing in late fall and winter. For example, fertilizing grass pastures with nitrogen and resting them during August and September can extend your grazing season one and a half to two months. Grasses work best because they hold their leaves after a killing frost—legumes do not.

In Iowa, orchard grass, tall fescue, smooth brome grass and reed canary grass were studied for their stockpiling value. Tall fescue retained its digestibility best after a frost. However, it is not extremely winter-hardy in the northern Midwest.

Another form of stockpiling is baling early growth and leaving bales in the field.

Annual forages can also be used for stockpiling.

Iowa researchers advise harvesting the early summer growth as silage or pasture and stockpiling the regrowth for grazing.

ESTABLISHING IMPROVED PASTURES

When land is suitable, it is preferable to grow semipermanent pasture mixtures in rotation with other crops. This means preparing the land as you would for other crops.

Renovation is probably your next best bet where pasture is not included in a rotation. This practice refers to killing weeds, brush and low producing grasses and establishing high-yielding grasses and legumes in existing sod.

Maryland researchers have said shallow plowing is usually better than disking and harrowing if renovation is done in early spring. But Kentucky and Missouri researchers have found plowing is not necessary to establish a new forage stand in the spring when tillage is done from November through February. They advise that you just disturb some 50% to 60% of the grass before sowing red clover or alfalfa. When pastures are renovated in late summer, disking and/or harrowing may be sufficient.

Interseeding is sowing legume and/or a more productive grass into a permanent grassland with minimum tillage of the existing sod.

While complete renovation often permits improving pastures more rapidly, many acres are rough and highly erodible or stony and must remain under present vegetation.

Special equipment is necessary. Seed must be sown shallow in a firm seedbed and competition from other plants eliminated by removing a strip of sod. A strip four to six inches wide and two or three inches deep has been adequate for alfalfa and several cool season grasses when interseeded into overgrazed bluegrass or short grass sod. A wider furrow would be required for native grasses.

Interseeding is sometimes referred to as sod seeding or overseeding in the South. A combination of small grains and rye grass can be sod seeded into permanent pastures when summer and fall grazing is finished. In permanent pasture, the sod seeded crops can be grazed in late winter and early spring, with grazing of the permanent pasture continuing into summer and fall. In cultivated areas, graze the sod seeded crop into May, then plant a silage crop or temporary summer grazing crop.

Renovation Improves Pasture Production

New seeding methods and use of herbicides to suppress competition from existing sod and weeds have renewed interest in pasture renovation.

Many benefits can be obtained by reseeding unproductive permanent pastures with higher producing grasses and legumes. This is especially true if reseeding with legumes. Renovated pastures may produce up to five times more forage than unrenovated pasture. The relative yielding ability of various grasses and legumes under Minnesota conditions is shown in the table. However, other species may be better adapted to your area or the species shown may respond differently under your conditions. Notice that legumes in a pasture will substitute for rather heavy nitrogen topdressing rates.

Legumes improve the overall quality of pasture as well as supply nitrogen to the grass. In Wisconsin tests, pastures containing legumes produced as much beef per acre as straight grass that received 120 to 150 pounds of nitrogen per acre annually. Legumes also reduce summer pasture slumps, since they are better able than some grasses to produce growth during hot, dry summer months.

In Missouri studies, a legume in the pasture mixture increased summer beef calf gains by 35 to 50 pounds, compared to gains made on straight grass pasture. A fescue-legume mixture produced 48% of its annual growth during June-August. A straight fescue pasture yielded only 10% of its total production during the same period.

Renovation, in the strict sense of the word, refers to improving an existing sod rather than completely tearing it up and reseeding to a forage mixture. Plowing or disking up the complete sod cover and reseeding is often impractical since it will lead to serious erosion. Also, complete reworking and reseeding may result in loss of production for a year.

When conditions permit, the objectives of renovation should be to seed an improved pasture species into the existing sod with as little loss of production as possible and with as little tillage as necessary to achieve a sufficient stand.

Within this definition, renovation methods range from what is referred to as frost seeding, to tearing up and destroying a portion of the sod with a disk or some other tillage tool, to interseeding in sod using minimum or no-tillage.

Frost seeding refers to broadcasting a legume in a pasture during winter or early spring so that freezing and thawing will cover the seed. In Missouri, for instance, seedings made in February have a 50% better chance of success than those made in April.

When the sod is partially torn up, it normally is recommended that some 40% to 60% of the sod be disturbed and destroyed for many legumes; as much as 80% or more for alfalfa. Seed may be either broadcast or drilled in winter, drilled later in spring or drilled in late summer.

Using the minimum tillage, sod seeding or no-tillage method, only a narrow strip is tilled and the seed is interseeded in the strip. Success depends on reducing the competition from the existing sod through use of a herbicide, severe grazing in advance of seeding or both.

Successful renovation principles, though they are refined and new tools are being used, have been long established. Regardless of the method used, considerable planning is required. A package of management practices to fit your situation should include the following:

FIELDS MUST BE SUITABLE for renovation and forage species must be properly selected to match your conditions. Most productive forage species require adequate drainage—the better drained the soil, the greater your chances of success. Soil type can affect your success. Sod seeding, for instance, is much more likely to succeed on silt loam type soils than is seeding into clay subsoil areas.

Farmers often expect too much vegetation control from the herbicide program, especially if they have a severe perennial weed problem. If such fields are to be renovated, it is advised that an intensive program of clipping and herbicide use be started a year in advance of seeding.

TEST THE SOIL and apply limestone and fertilizer to pull fertility up to recommended levels. Permanent pastures are often low in pH and phosphorus. Applications should be made six months to a year ahead of seeding, especially if a no-till or sod seeding method is to be used and the fertilizer and lime will not be worked into the soil. While most of the fertilizer probably should be broadcast, it may be beneficial to band part of it at seeding. Though limestone is typically broadcast, it also may be desirable to band some at seeding if the soil is extremely acid. Do not include nitrogen in the fertilizer mix since it stimulates the

Relative Yielding Ability of Grasses and Legumes

Grasses and legumes	Percent of yield of alfalfa or alfalfa-grass mixture
Alfalfa or alfalfa-grass mixture	100
Red clover or clover-grass mixture.	85-95
Clover (red, alsike, ladino) grass mixture	60-70
Birdsfoot trefoil.	65-75
Grass, no nitrogen fertilizer	30-40
Grass, 50 pounds N per acre per year	40-50
Grass, 100 pounds N per acre per year	60-70
Grass*, 200 pounds N per acre per year	90-100

*Tall growing grasses (bromegrass, reed canarygrass, timothy, or orchardgrass).

older grass and decreases the chances of the young seedlings becoming established.

CLOSE GRAZING and/or clipping well in advance of seeding is required to weaken and retard the grass and reduce its competition with the legume. Where perennial weeds are a problem, begin as much as a year in advance. Even when a herbicide is to be used, close grazing will reduce the vigor of the existing vegetation and improve the effectiveness of the herbicide.

HERBICIDE USE objectives are twofold—to kill broadleaf weeds and to suppress existing sod. When 2,4-D is used to kill broadleaf weeds and Paraquat is used to suppress the existing vegetation, the 2,4-D should be applied at least seven to ten days prior to the Paraquat, which should be put on just prior to or at seeding.

The difference in action of the two herbicides requires that they be applied at different times. The 2,4-D must be taken up by the broadleaf plants to give effective kill, whereas the Paraquat, being a contact herbicide, kills on contact. The 2,4-D needs time to effectively kill the broadleaves before the Paraquat is applied.

In Ohio tests, 2,4-D broadcast at the rate of one pound active ingredient per acre was necessary to eradicate the broadleaf weeds typically found in many permanent pastures. Paraquat may be applied either broadcast or band at the rate of one-half pound of active material per acre of area treated. Band treatment of half the soil surface directly over the seed placement zone has proven effective for successfully interseeding a legume into an existing sod while not severely reducing the vigor and/or total stand of the existing grass sod.

TIME OF SEEDING to assure success is related in part to the method of seeding used and to the species seeded. As mentioned earlier, frost seeding requires that seed be broadcast in winter or early spring so that freezing and thawing will occur. Using sod or no-till seeding or

tillage to partially work up the existing sod, either spring or late summer seeding can be used. However, early spring seeding offers a greater chance of success than late summer seeding. Moisture is more likely to be a critical factor with late summer seeding.

Sod or no-till seeding helps to preserve soil moisture, permitting seeding over a wider range of moisture conditions. As a result, this method may contribute to success with late summer seedings. Ohio reports equal success with seedings made in April-early May and in August. Sod seedings can be made somewhat later in the spring than is normally possible for other methods. When using Paraquat, seeding must be done during the growing season. Being a contact herbicide, it must be put on when the sod is growing.

Some forages are better adapted to late summer seeding than others. For instance, alfalfa and birdsfoot trefoil can be seeded at either time, but it is desirable to seed clovers in the spring.

WELL-MANAGED GRAZING of renovated fields is important during the year that it takes to establish a vigorous pasture seeding. Ohio recommends a light grazing or clipping or both about 45 days after seeding (when seedlings are four inches high) and infrequent rotational grazing thereafter to reduce the competition to forage seedlings. Be patient during the establishment year and manage the grazing and clipping to best suit the particular legume sown.

SEEDING EQUIPMENT that can be used for renovation varies depending on whether you seed in partially tilled sod or use the sod or no-tillage method. Regardless of equipment used, it is essential to get good seed-soil contact. Shallow seed placement of about one-fourth to one-half inch is usually optimum.

Where the sod is partially tilled, the usual seeding equipment can be used, including broadcasters for frost seedings, cultipacker seeders, and grain drills, preferably double disk drills. Grain drills can easily be

converted to band seeding by replacing the short tubes from the grass box with longer ones that will extend behind the grain-fertilizer outlet.

A major requirement of sod, no-tillage or interseeding equipment is that it be of a construction and weight that will penetrate the sod to achieve good seed-soil contact. Until recently, the most common equipment used for this purpose was the heavy duty sod seeders such as the Zip Seeder made by Midland Manufacturing Company and the Western Grassland Drill, which put seed in narrow slots 9 to 10 inches apart. The Zip Seeder was developed primarily to seed winter small grains into dormant Bermudagrass in the South.

No-tillage corn planters adjusted for 20 to 24 inch rows have also been used. By doubling back between the rows, a 10 or 12 inch row spacing can be achieved. The seed is placed in the insecticide boxes and the tubes are placed so that the seed is dropped in front of the press wheels. Some universities have experimented with modified rototillers, which prepare a tilled strip and seed a legume in one operation.

The most specialized equipment to be developed is the John Deere Powr-Till seeder. It has power-driven cutter wheels that till and prepare a mini-seedbed less than an inch wide through the sod. A packer wheel firms the soil around the seed. The unit can be used with or without a contact herbicide.

GRAZE ROTATIONALLY and fertilize annually. This will keep your pasture highly productive and maintain a balanced mixture of forages for at least three to five years. After that you will probably want to renovate again if the land is to be kept in permanent pasture. You should plan to renovate only a portion of your pasture each year, rather than the whole acreage at one time.

Remember also that you must plan to effectively utilize the increased production from renovation. Otherwise you won't profit fully from this practice.

Range Seeding and Management

In many western areas, rangeland carrying capacity can be improved significantly through stand improvement, brush control and systematic grazing.

Results of an eight year study suggest that the grazing capacity of large areas of semiarid rangeland can be increased as much as 4 to 20 times. To make this possible, researchers say reseeding is necessary. Good seedbeds, seeding with the right equipment, seeding at the right time, and using well-adapted rangeland species are required.

The rangeland study site was typical of much of that found in the Intermountain West, being a sagebrush-grassland area with an average precipitation of 8.79 inches per year.

Intensive land preparation methods gave the greatest reseeding success. These methods cost more, but they insure good establishment, earlier grazing and higher yields. The effect of different methods of land preparation on stand, rate of development, time to reach grazing readiness, and yield, are shown. Land is ready for grazing when it yields at least 300 pounds per acre.

Effect of Method of Land Preparation on Rate of Rangeland Development and Yield of a Crested Wheatgrass Mixture

Age of Stand	Seedbed Preparation				
	None	Early Burn	Late Burn	Culti-vated	Fallow
yrs.			lb./A.		
3	81	244	141	224	443
4	235	381	275	418	891
5	325	501	428	579	937
6	443	691	673	658	873
7	708	897	928	1,190	1,575
8	699	572	853	1,070	472
Average	317	473	402	530	780

Best results were obtained on land that was fallowed. The stands establish quickly and the area is ready to graze at least one year sooner than when other seeding methods are used. Competition from perennial weeds is also delayed. Plowing in the spring before cheatgrass heads, followed by one or two rod weedings is all that's required.

Next best method of land preparation was found to be heavy disking in the fall just before seeding. This can be done on land unsuitable for plowing. A good rain following disking will settle the soil before planting.

Seedings can be successfully made on rangeland which has accidentally burned, if a good ash layer remains on the ground and rains follow soon.

Direct seedings without land preparation are risky. The initial cost may be low, but because of poor stands, seedings are more likely to be invaded by unwanted vegetation and the land may require an extra year or so to reach grazing readiness.

Drilling the seed was found to be superior to broadcasting, even on fallow land. The deep-furrow-press drill and double disk drill gave consistently good results.

Average Production of a Crested Wheatgrass Mixture as Affected by Method of Seeding Made in the Fall on Fallow.

Seeding Methods	Age of stand						Ave.
	3	4	5	6	7	8	
				pounds			
Deep-furrow-press	572	891	938	873	788	472	798
Double disk	524	730	813	835	765	408	707
Broadcast	285	563	745	767	748	476	591
Alternate row with wheat	581	810	836	1,081	849	445	798
Seeded in wheat stubble	17	168	299	464	647	576	281

Seedings made in late fall, soon after mid-October and before the soil froze, produced better stands, yielded more and reached grazing readiness at least one year sooner than spring seedings on fallow and cultivated land and two years sooner than on burned-over land or land which received no preparation. If there was no effective rainfall before the late fall seeding, the seed was planted anyway. It germinated the following spring when temperature and moisture were favorable.

Five years following seeding, the crested wheatgrass mixture averaged 780 pounds per acre on fallow when it was seeded in the fall; 540 pounds per acre when seeded in the spring.

Weed and brush control are essential for maintaining productive rangeland. A new method of control developed at the U.S. Southern Great Plains Station, Woodward, Oklahoma, has increased grass production by 50% to 300%. Cost per treatment was about 20¢ per acre for the herbicide, plus application cost.

A pickup truck with a mounted mist-blower sprayer is driven at 10 mph along spray trails spaced 200 feet apart, applying a low rate of herbicide downwind. In tests, two annual sprayings thinned ragweed 70% to 90%, sand sagebrush 30% to 50%, and shinnery oak 40% to 50%. A third spraying may increase kill sufficiently to allow near maximum grass production.

Sprayer trails are 18-inch wide leveled tracks for the truck wheels. While they need not be straight they should be roughly perpendicular to the direction of the prevailing wind. Best results with a mist-blower sprayer were obtained by using two nozzles, elevated 35 degrees above horizontal with an operating pressure of less than 50 psi. This gives coarse spray droplets and limits drift largely to 100 feet and seldom more than 400 feet. Wind should not exceed 10 mph when spraying.

This method allows you to spray selectively and manage your rangeland to best advantage. Lower rates and cost permit you to spray when needed rather than go for optimum kill which is necessary with the higher cost of aerial application.

Choice of either 2,4-D or 2,4,5-T depends on the weeds or brush you need to control. A rate of one-eighth pound per acre of 2,4-D or one-sixteenth pound of 2,4,5-T will achieve effective defoliation. Where the problem is severe it may be desirable to use a maximum rate of one-fourth pound of either material the first year. By the third year you can probably cut back to the lower rates, spraying only when and where needed.

Numerous grazing systems have been tested and tried over the years, but regardless of the system used, alternate grazing and resting is essential. A well-planned system should permit range improvement while increasing livestock production. It allows plants to recover from close grazing, regain vigor and build food reserves before regrazing.

Stocking rates and rest periods are both critical in implementing any grazing system. No grazing system will compensate for overgrazing. The minimum rest period on the more humid rangelands should be three to four months, with a longer period of deferment in drier regions, perhaps as long as 12 months in arid regions.

Grazing systems that achieve optimum vegetation and livestock performance are those that do the best job of meeting both plant and livestock requirements. For example, long deferment periods allow vegetation to mature and replenish its food reserves; but during the grazing which follows, the livestock must consume mature, lower quality forage. Conversely, livestock perform best if they have access to immature forage and regrowth, but this may be harmful to the rangeland over an extended period.

Texas range specialists have found the Merrill System, shown in the chart, to be one of the more reliable grazing systems. This system has given consistent range improvement and livestock production has been 10% to 15% greater than that obtained from year long grazing at a comparable stocking rate. It allows adequate deferment for plant recovery while maintaining low stocking pressure to allow maximum selectivity by grazing livestock. This type of deferred system is optimum for the rancher with the goal of steady, but not spectacular range improvement along with maximum livestock production.

MERRILL GRAZING SYSTEM				
Grazing Period	1	2	3	4
Mar. 1 to July 1	Graze	Graze	Graze	Rest
July 1 to Nov. 1	Rest	Graze	Graze	Graze
Nov. 1 to Mar. 1	Graze	Rest	Graze	Graze
Mar. 1 to July 1	Graze	Graze	Rest	Graze
July 1 to Nov. 1	Graze	Graze	Graze	Rest
Nov. 1 to Mar. 1	Rest	Graze	Graze	Graze
Mar. 1 to July 1	Graze	Rest	Graze	Graze
July 1 to Nov. 1	Graze	Graze	Rest	Graze
Nov. 1 to Mar. 1	Graze	Graze	Graze	Rest

High-intensity, low-frequency grazing (HILF), a relatively new innovation in range management shows promise for range operations. In a Texas ranch study, a beef herd grazed single pastures intensively for approximately four weeks each. By rotating through eight pastures, each pasture was rested for six to seven months.

Since the HILF system forces animals to consume both desirable and less desirable plants, some drop in animal performance was noted. Cow weights and calf weaning weights were slightly lower than under continuous grazing.

The improved efficiency of forage production achieved by the HILF system appears to more than make up for the reduction in animal performance. Forage surveys indicated that the system may increase overall carrying capacity of a range operation by 40% to 50% in the first three years.

Regardless of the specific grazing system used, it should be set up so that pasture grazed in the summer is not grazed again in winter. Many ranchers who must depend on winter range usually include specific pastures for this use in their forage program. Since winter grazing is generally less detrimental to rangeland than summer grazing, it can help to improve range condition. Consequently, it's important to include "lowest" condition rangeland in a winter grazing sequence.

Harvesting Top Quality Forage

Harvesting forage for high protein, digestibility and palatability can help livestock producers hold down protein and concentrate costs.

Growing a good forage crop is only the first step in the production of quality hay or hay-crop silage. The way forage is harvested and stored determines how well the quality of the standing crop is preserved. The value of forage as a livestock feed depends to a large extent on preventing as much leaf loss as possible, holding weather damage to a minimum and cutting as early as practical without unduly sacrificing yield.

Method of harvest affects the amount of forage you can reasonably expect to preserve for feeding. Michigan research on the quantities of alfalfa-brome forage preserved using different harvest methods is illustrated in the graph.

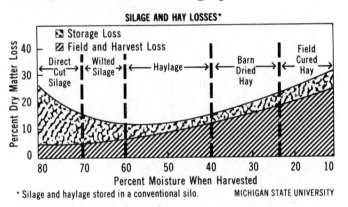

SILAGE AND HAY LOSSES*

* Silage and haylage stored in a conventional silo.   MICHIGAN STATE UNIVERSITY

Notice that harvesting forage as haylage permits you to strike the most favorable balance between harvest and storage losses. While hay storage loss is normally low (2% to 6%), harvest loss of field-cured hay may run as high as 15% to 20%. When the hay is rained on and exposed to a long curing period, loss may climb to 25% or even 50%. Direct cutting of forage and storing in a silo will hold field loss to 2% to 4%, but seepage and fermentation loss can be high. Fermentation and seepage losses were measured by Pennsylvania researchers using direct cut red clover stored in an airtight silo over three seasons. Losses ranged from 12% at 72% moisture to 30% for forage having 79.5% moisture.

Putting the same crop up as haylage in an airtight silo within a moisture range of 45% to 49%, the researchers were able to substantially reduce storage losses. Losses of an alfalfa-brome mixture stored in a conventional silo amounted to 8.6%; for alfalfa-timothy in an airtight silo, 6.2%. USDA has measured haylage storage losses from 1% to 8% in airtight silos; and 2.5% to 12% in well-sealed conventional upright silos. Missouri researchers estimate field losses at 6% when making haylage at 60% moisture. If haylage is field dried to 40%, losses rise to 13%.

High quality forage is harvested at some yield expense. A satisfactory compromise must be achieved between a high percentage of protein, digestibility and energy and the reduced yield resulting from earlier harvest. This will vary somewhat with the class of livestock to be fed.

Forage yield, in terms of dry weight, increases up to mid or late bloom. However, maximum feeding value is reached by early bloom—about 10 days before you can expect to harvest the top yield. Beyond early bloom, digestibility of forage declines about 0.5% per day. Because livestock eat less, total feeding value is reduced about 1% for each day cutting is delayed beyond early bloom.

The first cutting of forage often represents 35% to 45% of the total yield for the year, so bear that in mind when planning your harvest schedule. For top quality forage, harvest the first cutting of alfalfa at the very late-bud to first-flower stage; red clover, one-quarter bloom; birdsfoot trefoil and crownvetch, one-half bloom. The tall growing grasses should be harvested when their heads begin to show. A delay in harvesting grasses will result in a more rapid decline in feed quality than occurs with legumes.

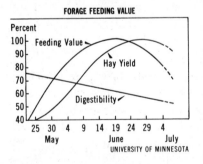

FORAGE FEEDING VALUE

UNIVERSITY OF MINNESOTA

Cutting forage earlier and more often can help to boost yield while maintaining quality. It often permits taking off an extra cutting, as shown by the following graph. When cutting is scheduled by the calendar rather than strictly by plant height or development, a 35 to 45 day interval is usually recommended for legume-grass mixtures.

However, this schedule may have to be varied according to available soil moisture and the resulting growth.

Good management must accompany early forage cutting. This practice may encourage weedier

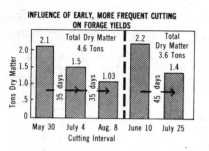

INFLUENCE OF EARLY, MORE FREQUENT CUTTING ON FORAGE YIELDS

forage fields and a higher percentage of grass may occur in legume-grass mixtures the following season. Legume-grass mixtures require annual fertilization to maintain legumes in the stand. Alfalfa stands on soils low in either phosphorus or potassium will produce lower yields and short lived stands.

Should the legume stand decline substantially, some nitrogen may help to increase the yield of the grass in the mixture. Care should be taken not to harvest a cutting in late fall when the forage is still growing. This will reduce its winter hardiness.

Minimize leaf loss as much as possible. Leaves of legumes contain a high portion of the feeding value of the plant. Alfalfa leaves, for example, contain about 70% of the total protein and 90% of the minerals and vitamins contained within the plant. Leaves also contain less fiber and are more digestible. Leaf shattering from alfalfa yielding three tons per acre can result in nutrient losses equivalent to the value of 500 pounds or more of cottonseed or soybean meal plus about 250 pounds of grain.

Best way to reduce forage leaf loss is to harvest forage as haylage or hay-crop silage, or to use a windrower to harvest hay. If hay is to be raked, try to do it while the moisture is around 55%. If it's necessary to rake hay at a lower moisture level, do it in the morning when the humidity is highest. Harvesting losses of field cured hay may be doubled by raking when it is drier than 55%.

Harvesting forage as haylage or hay-crop silage rather than hay may help to improve its quality, particularly the first cutting. A shorter drying time cuts the chances of rain damage. In contrast to one and one-half to three days needed for hay, especially for heavy crops in humid areas, haylage can be put into the silo within 24 hours after cutting. You don't have to risk harvesting a more mature crop by waiting for good drying weather.

Ground moisture tends to slow up drying of early-cut conditioned hay compared to that cut

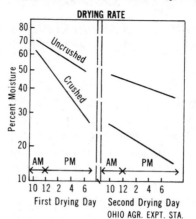

DRYING RATE

OHIO AGR. EXPT. STA.

later. Nevertheless, conditioning early-cut forage can permit putting up field-cured hay as much as one-half to one day sooner. Crushing the stems allows them to dry at a rate more closely in line with that of the leaves. Eliminating an extra night of exposure can be important because of the greater weather hazards early in the season.

Making good haylage or hay-crop silage hinges on putting it up in the proper condition to prevent heating temperatures from rising much above 100 degrees. Haylage ensiled with 50% to 65% moisture produces the best feed. At lower moisture levels, it is difficult to pack forage adequately.

Other precautions include: chopping haylage short, preferably less than three-eighths inch; keeping knives sharp and set close to the shear bar; filling the silo as fast as possible; distributing the haylage to prevent coning; and capping conventional silos with a durable plastic cover and weighting it down to minimize top spoilage.

Shown in the table are ideal forage moistures for various silos as recommended in Nebraska. Use of a preservative is not considered necessary where conditions permit wilting the forage to at least 65% to 70% moisture. Following the recommendations shown, preservatives would not be necessary for forage put into an upright silo. However, higher moisture levels are required for proper packing and air exclusion in stacks, trenches or bunkers, so the use of a preservative should be considered.

IDEAL FORAGE MOISTURE FOR VARIOUS SILOS

Type of silo	Ideal forage moisture
Gas-limiting silo	35% to 40%
Conventional upright[1]	60% to 70%
Bunker or trench[1]	
Height, 12 ft. or less	70% to 75%[2]
Height, more than 12 ft.	65% to 70%
Stack[1]	
Height, 12 ft. or less	72% to 77%[2]
Height, more than 12 ft.	68% to 73%

[1]Top 2-3 ft. should be 70% to 75% moisture.
[2]Above 73% moisture, forage may benefit from a preservative.

142

Ensiling High-Quality Corn

Feed value realized from silage depends on harvesting as close as possible to stage of maximum nutrient yield per acre while assuring good preservation and quality.

Stage of maturity is probably the most important single factor determining the nutritive value of silage. It contributes to the amount of dry matter harvested per acre, digestibility and dry matter consumed by livestock, storage losses and degree of preservation.

Dry matter yield and feeding value of corn silage both increase with maturity. Well-matured, well-eared corn may contain six bushels of grain or more per ton compared with only three to five bushels for less mature corn.

YIELD COMPARED WITH DEVELOPMENT STAGES OF CORN

	Stage of Development			
	1st Tassels	Milk	Firm Dent	Mature
Green weight, lbs./A.	27,000	42,000	40,000	30,000
Dry matter, %	12	19	30	43
Dry matter, lbs./A.	3,200	7,980	12,000	13,000
Stalks and leaves, %	100	61	43	40
Ears, %	--	39	57	60

OHIO STATE UNIVERSITY

Your ability to gear harvest to later maturity stages will, of course, necessitate selecting hybrids with the proper maturity. When a large acreage is grown it may be advisable to plant several hybrids with varying maturities. Consideration should be given to making full use of the growing season while avoiding labor distribution problems and frost damage to immature corn.

Digestibility and consumption are tied closely to the ear and grain content of silage. About 85% of the dry matter in the ears is digestible; 65% in the leaves; and 50% in stalks. Further, the digestibility of leaves and stalks changes very little from milk to hard dough stage. So, the higher the ratio of ears to stalks, the greater the digestibility up to a given point in maturity.

Digestibility increases through the full dent stage, as shown in the table. Palatability is improved as well. The lower moisture encourages production of the more desirable silage acids. However, as corn advances from hard dough to maturity there is reason to believe digestibility of the forage portion declines somewhat.

In University of Illinois studies, dairy cows fed mature silage containing 45% moisture produced as well as those fed 68.5% moisture silage. However, dry matter and protein digestibility were reduced since a greater amount of the mature silage

Digestible Energy at Various Corn Silage Maturities

Stage	% Digestible Energy
10 days pre-silk	61.6
Silk	63.0
Early milk	66.0
Full dent	69.0

PENN. STATE

was required to obtain that level of production. This suggests that dry matter digestibility for mature silage may be 6% lower.

Research with steers has given similar results. In an Ohio feeding experiment, beef heifers fed mature silage ate more silage dry matter and gained slightly faster than those fed normal silage. But they required more silage dry matter per 100 pounds of gain. Consumption of dry matter is also reduced when silage is cut late, which is beyond the point when it is fully dented.

Storage losses through seepage occur when silage moisture exceeds 70%. Above this level seepage losses may range from 5% to 20%. Using more mature silages up to full dent, Pennsylvania researchers held total dry matter losses to under 10%. Losses incurred in this case were mostly from fermentation and handling.

On the other hand, putting mature silage in conventional silos may result in poor packing and inadequate air exclusion. Molding and overheating can occur. With the right management, silage as low as 50% moisture can be stored in conventional silos. However, chances of achieving good preservation at this stage are improved with airtight silos.

Apart from greater silo losses which may occur in mature silage, some dry matter may be lost in harvesting. In University of Illinois trials mentioned earlier, silage harvested at 68.5% moisture yielded 13,985 pounds of dry matter versus 13,411 pounds at 45% moisture. The 574 pounds lost were due to some leaf loss and "downed" stalks. Both degree of maturity and the particular hybrid grown could influence this.

Best harvest stage. Evidence strongly indicates many farmers chop corn too early and sacrifice dry matter in the process. While there is some trend to putting up mature silage, the possibility of somewhat higher storage losses, except perhaps in airtight silos, and reduced digestibility need to be considered when making your decision.

Relative digestible dry matter yields expected from corn in the hard dough stage compared with mature corn, assuming given storage losses and digestibility, are shown below. While mature silage reduces the amount of water you haul to the silo, the amount of dry matter you can store in a given volume remains about constant. Though mature silage yields more dry matter per acre in the field, the total digestible dry matter may not be any higher and could be somewhat lower.

MATURE SILAGE NOT NECESSARILY HIGHER IN DIGESTIBLE DRY MATTER

Per Acre Comparisons	Stage of Maturity	
	Silage	Mature
Green weight (lbs.)	40,000	30,000
Dry matter produced	12,000	13,000
Percent storage loss (assumed)	5	10
Feedable dry matter	11,400	11,700
Percent digestibility (assumed)	63	57
Digestible dry matter	7,182	6,669

All factors considered, the most ideal stage for harvest appears to be around 60% to 65% moisture. At this stage good silo preservation is well assured and corn has reached 90% to 95% of its potential dry matter yield. If you have an airtight silo you may want to consider silage somewhat more mature to pick up the extra 5% to 10% yield while being assured of good preservation.

Hybrids vary considerably in moisture content at given stages of maturity. Some remain green longer than others. The best guide probably is to harvest from the hard dough to early glaze period. If you have a large acreage, you'll need to begin somewhat earlier.

STAGE OF HARVEST AS IT AFFECTS CORN SILAGE YIELD

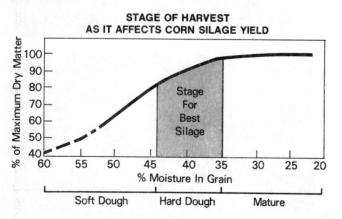

Stover silage can make good beef cattle feed. However, it lacks the energy of whole plant silage since the grain has been removed. An Indiana study indicates that it is desirable to ensile stover as soon as possible after harvesting the grain. Green corn stover ensiled at the stage when corn was dented and glazed, with leaves partly green, was compared with mature stover at the stage when ear corn was ready to crib. The mature silage required additional water when ensiling. Cattle weighing 500 pounds at the start of a 128-day feeding period and receiving 3.5 pounds of supplement gained 1.12 pounds per day when fed the mature stover silage. Those on the green stover silage gained 1.37 pounds per day.

HARVEST MANAGEMENT

Chopping is important in good silage preservation, especially in more mature corn. Finely chopped corn packs well in silos, establishing ideal conditions for rapid exclusion of air and permitting the fermentation process to get under way. It is also desirable that grain in more mature silage be finely ground. Otherwise it may pass through animals partially undigested.

A controlled length of cut from one-fourth inch to three-eighths inch is desirable with nine-sixteenths inch being about the maximum. Knives need to be kept sharp and the shear bar adjusted to proper clearance to achieve precision-cut silage with minimum power requirements.

Silage too dry to insure proper packing and preservation in conventional silos may require the addition of water. University of Minnesota agronomists recommend that you add four gallons of water per ton of silage for each 1% increase in moisture desired. You probably should add enough to pull moisture up to 60% to 65%.

There's no easy, quick test for determining silage moisture. You can make a good estimate by carefully weighing out five pounds of chopped material and placing it in a 200° F. oven for two to three hours. Then reweigh the material. If you start with five pounds, you can determine the percentage of moisture by subtracting the dry weight from five and multiplying the remainder by 20.

Silos well-sealed around doors, the walls themselves and on top are necessary to assure maximum preservation. A good coating on conventional silos improves storage.

Chapter 7

Livestock Production

Livestock production has changed greatly in recent years. Some animals now spend their complete lives inside buildings. Complex marketing techniques may determine the price of an animal months in advance. Computers can calculate animal rations with speed and preciseness, and modern slaughtering plants are models of production-line efficiency.

Livestock production fits well into many of today's different farming situations. On some farms it helps round out the farming operation by using home-grown feeds and labor left over from cropping. In others, livestock makes up the total effort, such as in ranching operations, beef feedlots and large confined hog systems. Farmers often specialize in one area of production. They may produce only weaned calves or feeder pigs, grow stocker cattle, or only finish animals for market.

Intensive methods of producing livestock have evolved. Technology and mechanization have made it possible to raise more animals in a smaller area. Today more animals per man can be produced, and they can be grown faster and marketed at a much younger age.

Perhaps the biggest difference between the modern livestock producer and his ancestors is in the amount of knowledge he needs to run a successful operation. Information about animal breeding, nutrition, health and general management has expanded rapidly. To stay competitive, stockmen must be able to use this information, which is often highly technical, in order to keep their operations running efficiently.

Reproductive efficiency often means the difference between profit and loss in livestock breeding operations. For example, if a cow does not produce a calf with the rest of the herd, she has incurred a loss for the owner. The expense of maintaining her through the year must be subtracted from profits on the rest of the herd.

On the average, about 85% of the brood cows in herds conceive and produce a calf every year. Some operators, however, consistently shoot for and get calf crops of 95% or higher. While a difference of 5% to 10% in the size of a calf crop may seem small, it can have a tremendous effect on profits.

Usually it takes around six pigs per litter in swine operations just to pay back costs. Thus, if a producer weans and sells seven pigs per litter, he is probably making some profit. But, if he could increase the average to eight pigs, profits would approximately double.

Increasingly, progressive stockmen are putting emphasis on breeding and genetics in their herds. They are selecting and breeding only the best individuals by following a systematic approach which includes recordkeeping and the use of production testing data.

145

Livestock feeding is an area which requires special attention since feed is by far the largest cost in producing livestock. Usually the cost of feed ranges from 60% to 80% of the total cost of producing the animal. Since feed makes up such a large part of overall expenses, producers can afford to spend considerable effort to assure that feeds are converted into livestock products with maximum efficiency.

The most important consideration in feeding animals is to provide a balanced ration and to supply it at the lowest possible cost. A good ration is one that supplies the five basic classes of nutrients as cheaply as possible. Energy, protein, vitamins, minerals and water must be supplied in the correct amounts to get the best gains.

Farm feeds, such as roughages and grains, provide most of the nutrients needed by livestock. However, these feeds must often be supplemented by other vitamin and mineral feeds or protein supplements to correct any nutrient deficiencies. Also, with changing prices for various feedstuffs, other feeds can often be substituted in the ration to provide the same nutrients at a lower cost.

New information on animal nutrition is being uncovered rapidly, making it difficult for producers to stay abreast of current findings. Fortunately, livestock specialists and feed manufacturers incorporate this information into standard feeding recommendations to be used by producers for various types and classes of livestock.

Livestock health programs are essential for profitable production. Diseases and parasites cost producers billions of dollars every year. It has been estimated that animal diseases may cost an average commercial livestock producer as much as $4,000 per year, measured in terms of reduced animal performance and death losses.

Actually, losses from those animals that die may be a small portion of the total losses incurred from disease. Animals that grow poorly or are unable to reproduce efficiently because of health problems, reduce profits substantially. Expenses for medical treatment and drugs mount quickly, especially when a disease outbreak strikes.

Reducing the animals' exposure to disease is the basis for a good health program. While all disease organisms can't be eliminated, good cleaning and sanitation of the animals' surroundings are fundamental. A program of vaccination and parasite control will help prevent disease and reduce the amount of stress on the animal. Once the animal has become sick, much of the damage has already been done.

While the technical advice and skill of a veterinarian is used to combat diseases on the farm, the final responsibility for managing a livestock health program rests with the stockman.

Good management in any business venture must be continually stressed . It is no less important in a livestock enterprise. Still, it is difficult to define exactly what is meant by good management.

Two producers, each with the same facilities, finances and opportunities, can achieve entirely different results. One may succeed and the other may fail. The difference lies in their ability to manage their operations.

The success of a manager rests with his ability to organize the overall operation, making the pieces fit together effectively. All of his endeavors in producing animals interlock with each other. For example, health, breeding and nutrition influence one another. Sick animals may not be able to breed, and poorly fed animals succumb to disease easily. In addition, a manager must also contend with money matters, marketing, taxes and other such factors. With the complexities of a modern livestock enterprise, it is little wonder that individual operators differ considerably in their management ability.

Livestock Space Requirements

These space requirements and design recommendations were furnished by the Midwest Plan Service and are based on currently popular types of buildings and equipment.

Beef Cattle

Feedlot, sq. ft./head

20' in barn and 30' in lot	Lot surfaced, cattle have free access to shelter
50'	Lot surfaced, no shelter
150'-800'	Lot unsurfaced except around waterers, along bunks and open-front buildings, with a connecting strip
20'-25'	Sunshade

Buildings with Feedlots, sq. ft./head

20'-25'	600 lbs. to market
15'-20'	Calves to 600 lbs.
1/2 ton/head	Bedding

Cold Confinement Buildings, sq. ft./head

30'	Solid floor, bedded
17'-18'	Solid floor, flushing flume
17'-18'	Totally or partly slotted
100'	Calving pen
1 pen/12 cows	Calving space

Feeders, in./head along feeder

All animals eat at once:

18"-22"	Calves to 600 lbs.
22"-26"	600 lbs. to market
26"-30"	Mature cows
14"-18"	Calves

Feed always available:

4"-6"	Hay or silage
3"-4"	Grain or supplement
6"	Grain or silage
1 space/ 5 calves	Creep or supplement

Bunk throat height
Up to 18" for calves, 22" for feeders and mature cows
Use 30" height only if hogs will run with cattle

Bunk width
48" if fed from both sides of bunk
54"-60" if bunk is divided by mechanical feeder
18" bottom width if fed from one side of bunk

Waterers
40 head/available water space in drylot

Corrals

600 lbs.	600-1,200 lbs.	1,200+ lbs.	
--------------- sq. ft./head ---------------			
14'	17'	20'	Holding
6'	10'	12'	Crowding

Isolation & Sick Pens
40-50 sq. ft./head
Pens for 2%-5% of herd

Mounds
25 sq. ft./head   Minimum

Hogs

Feeder and Waterer Space
Self-feeders: one space/5 pigs
Supplement feeders: one space/15 pigs
Sow feeders: 1'/sow self-feed, 2'/sow all fed at once
Waterers: one space/20 to 25 pigs

Building Floor Space
Sows and boars: 15 to 20 sq. ft.
Pigs starting thru finishing:
    12 to 60 lbs.-4 sq. ft.
    60 to 125 lbs.-6 sq. ft.
    125 to market-8 sq. ft.
    100 to market: 5 sq. ft. under roof, + 13 sq. ft. on outside paved lot
Sow and litter:
    26 sq. ft.: Slotted floor, full confinement
    32 sq. ft. inside + 42 sq. ft. outside for indoor-outdoor system

Pasture Space
10 gestating sows/acre
 7 sows with litters/acre
50 to 100 growing-finishing pigs/acre depending on fertility.

Shade Space
15 to 20 sq. ft./sow
20 to 30 sq. ft./sow and litter
4 sq. ft./pig to 100 lbs.
6 sq. ft./pig over 100 lbs.

Floor and Lot Slopes
Slotted floors: usually flat
Farrowing, solid floors:
    1/2" to 3/4"/ft. without bedding
    1/4" to 1/2"/ft. with bedding
Finishing: 1/2" to 3/4"/ft.
Paved lots: 1/4" to 1"/ft.
Paved feeding floors:
    Indoors: 1/4"/ft. minimum
    Outdoors: 1"/ft.
Building alleys:
    1/2"/ft. cross slope for crown
    1/10" to 1/4"/ft. to drain
Gutters and pits:
    1"/25' to 1"/100' to drains
    1.5% slope for flush gutters

Slot Widths, in slotted floors

New-born pigs[1]	3/8" and 1"
12 to 60 lbs.[2]	3/4" to 1"
60 to market	1"
Sows and Boars	1"-1-1/4"

[1] Cover slots during farrowing; 1" wide slots behind sows, 3/8" elsewhere
[2] 3" width preferred over wider slats

Dairy Cattle

Recommended stall barn dimensions

Alley width

Flat manger-feed alley	5'8"-6'6"
Feed alley with step manger	4'0"-4'6"
Service alley with barn cleaner	6'0"
Cross alley[1]	4'6"

Manger width

Cows under 1,200 lbs.	20"
Cows 1,200 lbs. or more	24"-27"

Gutters

Width[2]	16" or 18"
Depth, stall side	11"-16"
Depth, alley side	11"-14"

[1] Taper the end stalls inward 6" at the front for added turning room for a feed cart.

[2] Or as required for barn cleaner.

Free stall dimensions

Calves	Width x Length
6 weeks to 4 months	2'0" x 4'6"
5 to 7 months	2'6" x 5'0"

Heifers	
8 months to freshening	3'0" x 5'6"

Cows (average herd weight)	
1,000 lbs.	3'6" x 6'10"
1,200 lbs.	3'9" x 7'0"
1,400 lbs.	4'0" x 7'0"
1,600 lbs.	4'0" x 7'6"

Typical free stall alley widths

Feeding alley between a bunk and the front of a stall row	9'-10'
Feeding alley between a bunk and the back of stall row	10'-12'
Resting alley between the backs of 2 stall rows:	
Solid floors	8'-10'
Slotted floors	6'-9'

Cow stall platform sizes

Use electric cow trainers

Cow weight	Stanchion stalls		Tie stalls	
	Width	Length	Width	Length
Under 1,200 lbs.	4'0"	5'6"	4'0"	5'9"
1,400 lbs.	4'6"	5'9"	4'6"	6'0"
Over 1,600 lbs.	Not recommended		5'0"	6'6"

Slat Spacing

Elevated calf stalls: 3/4" between 1x2"s on edge
Calves, wide slats: 1-1/4" slot
Cows, wide slats: 1-1/2"—1-3/4" slot

Feeders, in./head along feeder

All animals eat at once:
  18"-22", calves to 600 lbs.
  22"-26", heifers
  26"-30", mature cows

Feed always available:
  4"-6", hay or silage

Bunk capacity:
  1—1-1/2 cu. ft./ft. of bunk length min. for animals fed twice daily.

Bunk throat height
  Up to 16" for calves, 20" for heifers, 24" for mature cows, 30" for mature cows on unscraped, flat apron.

Bunk widths
  48" if fed from both sides of bunk
  54"-60" if bunk is divided by mechanical feeder
  18" bottom width if fed from one side of bunk

Waterers
40 head/available water space in confinement. Pave at least a 10' apron around waterers.

Sheep

Feeder space
Group-fed:
  16"-20"/ewe
  9"-12"/feeder lamb
Self-fed:
  10"-12" silage, 8"-10" hay/ewe
  3"-4"/feeder lamb
Lamb creep space:
  1.5-2 sq. ft./lamb

Waterer space
Per automatic bowl
  40-50 ewes or ewes with lambs
  50-75 feeder lambs
Per ft. of tank perimeter
  15-25 ewes or ewes with lambs
  25-40 feeder lambs

Shelter space
Open-front building with lot:
  10-12 sq. ft./ewe
  12-16 sq. ft./ewe and lambs
  6-8 sq. ft./feeder lamb
Lot:
  25-40 sq. ft./ewe
  25-40 sq. ft./ewe and lambs
  15-20 sq. ft./feeder lamb
Solid floor (confinement):
  12-16 sq. ft./ewe
  15-20 sq. ft./ewe and lamb
  8-10 sq. ft./feeder lamb
Slotted floor confinement:
  8-10 sq. ft./ewe
  10-12 sq. ft./ewe and lamb
  4-5 sq. ft./feeder lamb

Lambing pens (jugs) 4'x4'x30" or 4-1/2'x4-1/2'x36"; provide grain and water

Nursery pens for 2 to 4-day old lambs before putting into group pens:
  about 16'x16' for 20 ewes and 30 lambs

Detailed construction data and livestock building plans are available through the Midwest Plan Service and Extension Agricultural Engineers at several cooperating universities. Inquiries and requests for printed material can be made directly to: Midwest Plan Service, Iowa State University, Ames, Iowa 50011.

Wire Fences

A well constructed fence will give many years of service with relatively little maintenance. Good materials and planning are important.

Do some initial planning before beginning a fencing project. If it will be a new permanent fence line, farm maps and aerial photos may help you decide on the best location. Keep in mind water needs, rotational grazing patterns, and efficient movement of both livestock and machinery. When a location is selected, a fence line should be cleared of brush and trees so that a vehicle can be driven through after the fence is completed.

Wire fencing materials are sold by the rod. One rod equals 16.5 feet; 320 rods equal one mile. Barbed wire is sold in 80-rod spools (1/4 mile). Woven wire is generally available in 20-rod rolls. To completely enclose a 40-acre field will require 4 spools of barbed wire (320 rods). If the fence is to have four strands, 16 spools will be needed. Calculate the number of line posts needed for the distance to be covered. Line posts are generally 15 to 20 feet apart, with shorter distances for smaller diameter posts.

Since labor usually represents one-third or more of your total costs of building a fence, it is worthwhile to pay the added cost for good materials that should add years to the life of the fence. Posts are an example. Untreated wooden posts are cheapest, but you must count on replacing them often. Soft woods may last only 2 to 7 years; white oak posts from 5 to 10 years. After pressure treatment, these same posts can last 25 to 30 years. Surface application of preservative is not recommended, since there will not be enough absorption of the material. Steel posts are most expensive, but they are easiest to set and will last at least 25 years, and possibly much longer.

Line posts should be a minimum of 3½ inches in diameter; corner and gate posts, a minimum of 8 inches across the top; and brace posts should have a 5-inch top diameter. Larger diameter posts add considerable strength. A 4-inch post has twice the strength of a 3-inch post; a 5-inch post, 4 times more. Line posts

LIFE EXPECTANCY FOR WOOD POSTS (YEARS)		
Variety	Untreated	Pressure Treated
Osage orange	25-30	—
Red cedar, black locust	15-25	—
White oak	5-10	25-30
Southern pine, hickory, red oak, sycamore, poplar, cottonwood	2-7	25-30

measuring 6 to 6½ feet are usually recommended, though length will depend on how deeply they can reasonably be set. Depth will be determined in large part by conditions of the soil. If possible, set line posts 2 to 2½ feet deep.

Specifications for fencing wire are important when making the purchase. Barbed wire is usually available in 12½ to 14 gauge. (Smaller gauge numbers mean heavier wire.) The lighter gauges stand up best in dry areas where there is less deterioration. You can also buy high tensile barbed wire, which is stronger and more durable. For example, 13½ gauge H.T. wire has a breaking point equal to 12½ gauge standard wire. Nine-gauge coated wire is recommended for reinforcing brace assemblies.

Thickness of the galvanized coating is classified into three categories: Class I, II, and III, with Class III being the thickest. An aluminum coating is available on some wire. Aluminum coating will usually resist corrosion 3 to 5 times longer than galvanized of the same thickness.

Backbone of the fence is the corner post and brace assemblies. Installation of these assemblies often takes up to half of the total construction time. Construction aspects of these brace assemblies are shown below.

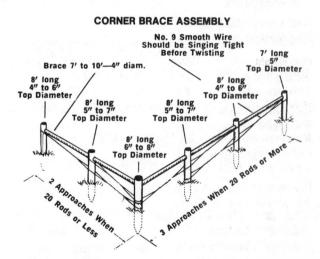

CORNER BRACE ASSEMBLY

When corners are more than 80 rods apart (less in uneven terrain), braced line post assemblies should be constructed for stretching. These assemblies are the same as a single-span braced corner, except that a diagonal brace wire is used to take

149

fence pull in the opposite direction. For bracing, use two loops (4 strands) of 9-gauge, coated wire and draw tight by twisting with a lever.

As a guide to setting line posts, stretch a cord or wire between corner and brace assemblies. Once line posts are set, begin stretching and installing wire by working in sections running from one corner or brace post assembly to another. Stretch wire with care. It's easy to ruin a fence by overstretching, and it can also be dangerous. Stretch woven wire only enough to pull the line wire humps out approximately halfway. With barbed wire it is more difficult to tell the correct tension. Stretch it tight enough to be springy when touched with a hammer handle or stick.

Be systematic when stringing wire. Always work from the top down. Install the top wire first, then the next highest, etc. This helps assure that the tension on all wires will be uniform when the fence is completed. Attach wire to the sides of posts nearest to livestock being fenced, except where appearance is important.

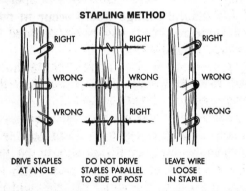

STAPLING METHOD

RIGHT · RIGHT · RIGHT
WRONG · WRONG · WRONG
WRONG · RIGHT · WRONG

DRIVE STAPLES AT ANGLE · DO NOT DRIVE STAPLES PARALLEL TO SIDE OF POST · LEAVE WIRE LOOSE IN STAPLE

Method of stapling wire to posts is important to fence life. Minimum staple size should be 1½ inches; use longer ones in soft wood posts. Driving the staples tight against the wire is a common mistake. This weakens the wire and does not allow the fence to expand and contract. The illustration shows the correct method.

To join ends of barbed wire, use a simple wrap splice. Take several wraps around the opposing wire in each direction. Don't loop the ends by doubling them back on themselves. For extra strength, make a split strand "western union" splice. When splicing woven wire, leave about 6 inches of wire beyond the vertical stays. Place the stays together and wrap the free ends behind the opposing stays.

At the corner where the fence is being stretched, wrap each line wire around the post and back onto itself. This avoids the tendency of the post to twist, as would occur if tension were held

by staples. Start fastening the center wires on a woven wire fence and proceed toward the top and bottom. With barbed wire, one method is to cut and unravel one of the strands. Wrap the strand around the post and back on itself. This lets the stretcher continue to hold the wire tight. Then, cut and attach the second strand the same way.

Select a fence design that meets your needs. Woven wire is seldom needed for cattle, but is used to confine sheep and hogs. Generally, a 4-strand barbed wire fence is sufficient for cattle and horses, though 5 strands are sometimes used in border fences for maximum protection. Three strands are used primarily for intermediate or cross fences.

BARBED WIRE SPACING

10″
10″
10″
10″
12″

10″
10″
10″
10″
51″
16″

16″
16″
16″
16″

Combination fences use barbed wire strands above woven wire to keep larger animals from reaching over and breaking down the fencing. A typical combination fence that can be used for cattle, horses, sheep, and hogs has an overall height of 54 inches. Woven wire is 939 (9 line wires, 39 inches high) and is topped by two strands of barbed wire. A 32-inch woven wire fence with 1 barbed strand next to the ground is often used for hogs.

Suspension fencing is a lower-cost design used in the West and where the terrain is mostly level. With this type of fence, line posts are spaced 80 to 120 feet apart and twisted wire stays are inserted every 10 to 16 feet to keep the four barbed wires spaced evenly. This fence will spring back and forth in the wind and when touched by animals. This action helps to discourage animals.

Corner bracing is especially important in a suspension fence, since the wire must be kept taut. Wires are stretched so that there is no more than a 3-inch sag between posts. Metal strips are used to hold wires to posts, allowing free movement. Standard wire clips can be used with steel posts.

On-Farm Livestock Research

Even with the vast number of livestock experiments being conducted at various experiment stations, there may be times when you will want to run a test of your own.

Conducting an experiment is an exacting science, but it is possible to do an excellent job on your own farm. Six basic steps must be followed when performing a livestock feeding, management or housing experiment.

Determine the problem. Decide exactly what is to be tested. Write down the purpose of the trial. This helps you to keep your objectives in mind.

Next, lay out the experiment. Usually, it is best to set aside two groups of animals—one control and one test. Treat both groups exactly alike, except for the practice to be tested. Then determine what facilities will be needed. Make sure the labor requirements will fit into your present working pattern. It is impossible to conduct an experiment without an accurate set of scales for weighing the animals and measuring feed or product.

Selecting the animals. Since you are making this test to determine the desirability of changing, it is wise to use small numbers. This way any poor results won't hurt your total profit picture. However, you should have enough animals to eliminate individual differences. For cattle or hogs, 8 to 12 animals in each group will usually be enough.

Start with a uniform group of animals. Select animals of equal condition, weight and age. If at all possible, the breeding background should be similar. Select animals raised under the same program before the experiment. If you can't meet these two requirements, try to select even numbers of similar animals so the variations will be about the same in each group.

Once the entire group is selected, it must be broken down into control and test groups. To eliminate bias, divide the animals at random. Assign each animal a number and choose the numbers from a hat. If you have different types of animals, randomly divide each type separately. Thus, each type will be equally represented in both groups.

Some experiments are designed to test differences between various types of animals. In these cases, you don't have to randomly divide the animals. However, the two groups should be as much alike as possible with respect to all other factors than the one to be studied.

Conducting the experiment. The purpose of an experiment is to evaluate the effect of one change. Therefore, all other factors must remain constant. Both groups should be treated the same and have equal facilities. Studying one group under a certain set of circumstances and comparing the test group with the rest of your animals is not an adequate test.

The conditions of the test should match normal operations. The only difference in the test should be in the size and scale of operation.

If your experiment involves a drastic dietary or environmental change for the experimental group, you may get a sudden reduction in growth or production. If the experimental practice could be worked smoothly into your regular operation, you should allow time for the animals to recover from the initial reaction before starting the experiment. But if this drastic change would occur in normal practice, these reactions should be included when you're evaluating the results.

Any preventive medicinal treatments should be the same for both groups. If possible, they should be administered at the same time.

Minor details, such as the source and availability of water, must be identical for both groups. The housing facilities should be in the same location and of the same size. Each group should be subject to the same environmental factors, such as weather, shade, and humidity.

Keeping records. Before, during and after the experiment, records provide the basis for evaluation. The worth of the study is tied closely to accurate, complete records. Keep notes of your observations throughout the project. Eating habits, temperament, appearance and any unusual activities during the experiment may provide answers to unexpected differences between the groups.

Keep accurate records on feed used in the experiment. Record not only feed placed in the feed bunk, but any feed wasted. This provides an accurate record of feed actually consumed.

Animal production or weights should be recorded at the beginning and end of the study. Since animals react differently to various changes, take measurements at regular intervals during the experiment. Some feed additives, for example, result in large gains in production or weight at first and then fall off. Others may produce a gradual increase in production or gains. It is important to recognize these patterns and their effect on the final decision.

If an animal becomes sick, or dies during the experiment, determine the cause of the illness. If it is not directly or indirectly associated with the experiment, then the animal should be removed from the test data. If the illness is connected with the experiment, then include the stricken animal.

Measuring the results. The results of a livestock study are measured in terms of feeding, management or environment.

Daily gain or production can be calculated by simply recording the beginning and ending weights or the production over the test period. Records taken during the study will show any patterns associated with the change.

Feed efficiency is an important measure for deciding if a change would be beneficial. This measure may be calculated by dividing the total feed used during the test by total production or weight gained during the study.

$$\frac{\text{total feed used}}{\text{total pounds gained}} = \frac{\text{feed required per}}{\text{pound of gain}}$$

Applying the cost of the feed to the feed efficiency figures gives the feed cost per unit of gain or production.

Economic feasibility of a new practice may be determined by totaling the cost of feed, labor, facilities and management. This total is divided by the total production or gain, giving the cost per unit. This provides the most important measure for evaluating the proposed practice.

Each test will have special features requiring special analysis. One of the keys to successful experimentation lies in determining these special problems and measuring and evaluating them.

Drawing conclusions may be a difficult problem area of "on location" testing. It's one thing to measure differences, but entirely another matter to properly evaluate their significance. If the study results vary widely between the two groups, it is rather easy to reach a conclusion. However, the differences are often rather small and could be due to inaccurate measuring procedures or experimental error. In such cases, you may not be able to make a final decision by merely observing the test results and studying the experimental notes.

When there is doubt about the test differences, the results should be analyzed statistically. Under these circumstances, have the analysis run by a qualified person to insure reliable information. Failure to do this could be costly if a wrong decision is made.

The two biggest factors affecting statistical significance are size of group and individual animal differences. The larger the group, the smaller the importance of one animal. However, regardless of the group size or the care exercised in selecting a uniform group of animals for the test, variations caused by factors other than the specific thing being tested will still exist.

The results of an example experiment shown in the table, illustrate how statistical comparisons can be helpful in evaluating test results. Notice that statistical difference has been calculated for average daily gain and feed efficiency for each of the groups of animals in two different tests. The significant difference in average daily gain for the control group in Test A was plus or minus 1.15 pounds. This means that this much variation in individual performance from the average of the group can normally be expected outside the realm of differences which might result from the factor being tested.

EXPERIMENTAL RESULTS
(with statistical measures)

	Test A		Test B	
	Control 2 steers	Test 2 steers	Control 10 steers	Test 10 steers
Average daily gain, pounds	2.50	2.75	2.40	2.75
Significant difference	±1.15	±1.20	± .25	± .30
Feed efficiency, pounds per cwt. gain	850	795	830	790
Significant difference	± 90	+100	± 50	± 60

In the control group of Test A, average daily gain of an individual animal can range from 1.35 to 3.65 (2.50 plus and minus 1.15), without being significantly different. The average performance of the test group falls within this range, so their performance is not considered to be statistically different from the control animals.

When more animals were tested (Test B), the amount of difference which can be expected outside of that caused by the test decreased for both groups. The average daily gain between the test and control animals was significantly different. The average daily gain of 2.75 was outside the range of 2.15 to 2.65 pounds per day permitted in the control group (2.40 plus and minus 0.25). However, the feed efficiency is still not significantly different, even though it appears to be.

Beef Herd Selection Principles

Guidelines for making selection decisions in beef breeding can help you improve your herd. Careful record keeping is essential for identifying the superior animals.

Genetic improvement is made by selection. If you allow only superior animals to reproduce, each succeeding generation will be better than the last. But, failing to accurately identify the superior animals will cut the potential for herd improvement. That's why modern selection practices utilize performance testing and records in addition to visual appraisal and judgment.

Herd selection and testing go hand in hand. Performance records are more accurate, they're not biased, and they let you systematically sort out a variety of factors. By measuring and recording individual growth rate, conformation and reproductive ability, you establish a basis for: (1) identifying high producing cows; (2) culling low producers; (3) choosing replacement heifers; and (4) evaluating bull performance.

FACTORS IN SELECTION

Understanding the principles behind good selection programs will help you do a better job of planning your own approach to herd improvement. Since breeding is the basis for improvement, genetic principles underlie good practices.

Heritability indicates how strongly a given performance trait is influenced by parents. If the trait has a high heritability, expression of that trait in the offspring is influenced to a large degree by the genetic makeup of the parents. Low heritability traits are less influenced by the parents' makeup and depend more on environmental factors. The table gives heritability estimates for important traits in beef cattle.

Rate of improvement depends on the heritability of traits and also on the number of traits for which you select. If breeding stock is chosen on the basis of several traits, then less selectivity can be made for any single trait. This slows the rate of improvement for any single measure of performance.

How fast you move toward improvement goals depends on the performance level of your herd at the start, how rigidly you cull, how well replacement heifers are selected and the superiority of the bull used.

TRAITS TO SELECT

Beef cattle improvement goals have undergone marked shifts in past years. Today, however, emphasis is directed to traits which are associated with performance, efficiency and economic worth. This means that traits which should receive major consideration are: reproductive efficiency, maternal ability, growth rate, feed efficiency, longevity, and carcass quality.

Although the heritability of reproductive performance is low, its economic impact is so great that it must be a primary trait for which you select. The cow's maternal ability is determined mainly by her milk production. Since milk production is the biggest factor in calf growth, maternal ability is principally measured by the calf's weight at weaning.

Growth rate can be easily measured by weights taken at weaning, yearling age or in the feedlot. Growth rate has a high heritability, so it can be steadily improved by selection. Since beef is sold by the pound, growth is very important economically. Feed efficiency is an economic trait that is difficult to measure in normal production situations. However, a high correlation between the two traits means that a breeder who is improving growth rate is also increasing feed efficiency.

HERITABILITY ESTIMATES

Traits	% Heritability
Fertility	10
Birth weight	40
Cow maternal ability	40
Preweaning gain	40
Weaning weight	30
Conformation score at weaning	30
Post-weaning gain in feedlot	57
Post-weaning gain in pasture	45
Yearling weight	60
Efficiency of gain in feedlot	40
Carcass Items:	
Dressing percent	45
Carcass grade	45
Thickness of fat	40
Loin eye area	70
Tenderness	60
Retail yield	60

Traits which influence carcass quality are highly heritable and of considerable economic importance. The USDA Carcass Data Service gives herd owners the opportunity to obtain complete carcass data by identifying their calves with special ear tags.

HOW TO START

First, each cow must be individually identified by some positive means. Ear tags are popular and easy to read. Brands and tattoos are the most permanent identification, but to read them often requires restraining the cow.

Mark all calves at birth to positively relate them to their dam. Birth date, sex and sire can be recorded in the same record with the cow. These steps aren't complicated, but they are essential to effective selection programs and management of the cow herd.

Help in herd testing and selection is available from a large number of sources. Record forms and electronic processing and analysis of test information are offered by beef improvement associations in most states, working with universities. Performance Registry International and most breed associations offer testing and recordkeeping programs.

ADJUSTING WEIGHT RECORDS

The formula shown is used to adjust calf weaning weights to a 205-day basis. Weights should be taken between 180 and 240 days of age. In calculating the adjusted weight, assume a 70 pound birth weight if actual weight isn't known.

$$\frac{\text{Actual weaning wt. - actual birth wt.}}{\text{weaning age, days}} \quad \times \quad 205 \quad + \quad \text{actual birth wt.}$$

Adjusting for sex has been done in various ways, usually by adjusting all calves to the same basis. One method is to adjust each heifer's weight by the amount that the average weight of your heifers differs from the average weight of your steers. Another is to assume that heifers are 5% lighter and bulls are 5% heavier than steers at weaning.

Adjustment for dam compensates for the lower maternal ability of younger and older cows.

Various systems of adjusting for the effect of the dam have been used in the past. The Beef Improvement Federation now recommends you use standards set up by the breed association for your own breed. Use the guidelines below if more breed-specific adjustments are not available.

ADDITIVE FACTORS, POUNDS

Age of Dam	Male	Female
2 years	60	54
3 years	40	37
4 years	20	18
5-10 years	0	0
11+ years	20	19

To use these adjustment factors, first compute the 205-day weaning weight using the formula above. Then, use a factor from the table to further adjust this figure in order to compensate for age of the dam and sex of the calf. For example, a 205-day weight of 400 pounds for a heifer calf from a 3-year-old cow will yield an adjusted weaning weight of 437 pounds.

Yearling weight. Research has shown that yearling weight has a high degree of heritability and is a better criteria for selecting animals than is weaning weight. Yearling weights are computed on a 365-day basis and should be taken at least 160 days after weaning. This formula is used by BIF to compute adjusted yearling weights.

$$\text{Adj. 365 day wt.} = \frac{\text{Actual final wt. - actual wn. wt.}}{\text{Number days between weights}}$$
$$\times 160 + \text{wn. wt. (205 days) adj. for age of dam}$$

MANAGEMENT DECISIONS

Ordinarily you should keep about 40% of your heifers just to maintain herd size. You will cull some of these based on yearling weights and others because of breeding problems later. If you are going to expand the herd, you should hold back more than 40%.

Cows producing the poorest calves or with poor reproductive records should be culled. The bull responsible for the greatest number of light calves can be sifted out. From your records you will also be able to identify the most important traits you should look for in selecting a replacement bull.

Selecting Herd Bulls

Using genetically superior bulls is the most efficient means of upgrading the beef herd. About 85% of a calf's genetics are determined by the last three generations of bulls used.

Though a bull contributes only half the genetic make-up of a given calf, he has more impact on cow herd returns than this. It's a matter of multiplier effect. One bull can breed 25 to 35 cows per season; double this annually if you're operating a split fall calving and spring calving herd.

The bulls' dominant role in contributing new genetic material into the herd is particularly apparent if viewed over a period of several years. A good bull that stays in service several years imparts his improving capabilities directly to that many calf crops. In addition, the genetic capabilities are further passed on through heifer offspring selected for replacements and moved into the herd.

Impact of bull selection will depend on the characteristics for which the bull was chosen in the first place. For example, estimates show that weaning weights are about 30% heritable while mature weight is about 85% heritable.

Important carcass characteristics range from 70% heritable for the loin-eye area down to 30% for carcass grade and 25% for conformation scores at weaning.

Further, as the general level of the performance ability of the herd advances both in gain capability and grade, the more difficult it becomes to make additional improvements. In very high performing herds you may backslide unless you're very careful.

Select performance tested bulls, even though this practice is not foolproof. Many examples have illustrated that bulls of similar mature appearances can have vastly different productive capabilities when put in service. This can occur even between closely related animals.

The importance of using selection principles can easily be seen over a period of a few generations. Herds in which bull selection is intensively practiced will show far more improvement than those in which the females alone are selected. If two or three generations of superior bulls have been used in the herd, there will be considerable compounding of genetic improvement capability in the female replacements, even though specific selection was not made on the females.

Evaluating bull improvement capability is rather difficult for all characteristics, but you can make a fair estimate on the basis of weaning weight. This example makes no allowance for possible grade score improvement.

Assume that a bull is selected with a weaning weight base that is 100 pounds heavier than the average weaning weight of your current sire's offspring. This 100 pounds is then added to the cow herd's index (or capability) of increasing offspring weight and divided by 2. In this example it's assumed that the cow herd has zero capacity for improving weaning weights.

This produces a 50-pound base to be multiplied by a 30% heritability factor. The higher weaning weight bull should then add 15 pounds to the average weaning weight of offspring when introduced into the herd. The table below shows the potential income increase through three calf crops, presuming 25 calves produced annually and two different calf sale prices. Higher prices would further increase income potential.

Increase in live weight sale value from original herd. Twenty-five calves from new selected sire. Twenty sold. Five heifers kept for replacement.

1st year	15 pounds increase in weaning wt. per calf.	
	300 lb.	300 lb.
	40¢	50¢
	$120	$150
2nd year		
	300 lb.	300 lb.
	40¢	50¢
	$120	$150
3rd year		
	300 lb.	300 lb.
	40¢	50¢
	$120	$150
Total	$360	$450

Offspring boost weights beyond the original herd average if bred to a sire of comparable productivity. Based on the introduction of the original improved bull, the weight increase to be expected was, as indicated, 15 pounds. In the second generation, his heifers should produce calves 12.5 pounds heavier than the herd average. A third generation would have calves 10.8 pounds heavier; fourth generation, 9.2 pounds heavier; and a fifth generation, 7.8 pounds heavier.

If you fail to continue selection for improved bulls in subsequent years, you'll backslide from the position established by the one improved bull. To get fair economic analysis of the value of the bull he must be credited at least with the increased gain created in the first generation heifers.

The second illustration indicates the added value of introduction of five head of the improved bull's heifers into the herd annually for three years. These heifers are assumed to remain in the herd for a five-year period. Prices for calves are the same as in the first table. The combined increases indicate that such a bull, at 50¢ calf prices, will boost income about $926 over a seven-year period.

Income will be increased more if replacement daughters are bred to calve at two years rather than at three as shown in this example.

INCREASE IN LIVE WEIGHT VALUE FROM OFFSPRING OF REPLACEMENT DAUGHTERS*

1st year	5 daughters x 12.7 lb. =	63.5 lb.	63.5 lb.
		40¢	50¢
		$25.40	$31.75
2nd year	10 daughters x 12.7 lb. =	127 lb.	127 lb.
		40¢	50¢
		$50.80	$63.50
3rd year	15 daughters x 12.7 lb. =	190.5 lb.	190.5 lb.
		40¢	50¢
		$76.20	$95.25
4th year	15 daughters x 12.7 lb. =	190.5 lb.	190.5 lb.
		40¢	50¢
		$76.20	$95.25
5th year	15 daughters x 12.7 lb. =	190.5 lb.	190.5 lb.
		40¢	50¢
		$76.20	$95.25
6th year	10 daughters x 12.7 lb. =	127 lb.	127 lb.
		40¢	50¢
		$50.80	$63.50
7th year	5 daughters x 12.7 lb. =	63.5 lb.	63.5 lb.
		40¢	50¢
		$25.40	$31.75
	Total	$381.00	$476.25

*Assumes five daughters per year for three years until fifteen daughters in herd. Daughters start producing at three years of age and continue to produce for five years.

Yearling weight and gain efficiency are more highly heritable than weaning weight. These factors are equally important in bull selection to develop a better picture of total performance of bulls. This is particularly important if you're feeding out your own cattle.

If you're not feeding out your cattle, these factors are still important, because growability, up to 1,000 pounds, and feed efficiency are the watchwords of modern cattle feeders. Increasing emphasis will be put on this in the future. If your cattle fill the bill, they'll have higher marketability. In other words, they'll become "reputation" cattle—the kind of cattle feeders will come looking for.

WHEN AND WHERE TO BUY BULLS

Buying service age bulls is a common practice among most cattlemen. However, unless you're buying bulls that have already been on performance testing programs, you should buy at weaning

Ingredient	Percent
Ground ear corn	35
Cottonseed meal	10
Whole oats	10
Wheat bran	10
Molasses	5
Cottonseed hulls	20
Alfalfa hay (chopped)	10
	100

OKLAHOMA STATE

age. If you buy at weaning, buy several more than you need as breeding replacements. Then you can conduct your own winter feeding and weighing trials to determine the relative merit of the young bulls. The table shows a ration used for 150-day self-feeding trials by Oklahoma researchers. This is not a full-feed program but should promote rapid growth on young bulls from weaning age up to yearling weight.

Where to buy bulls is a question of personal choice. Many states have established bull testing stations where purebred breeders may put bulls on feed to establish their doing ability. You can get a reasonable comparison of the breeding from these tests since the environmental conditions are the same. The breed associations also have similar testing setups.

Comparing privately tested herds from different areas when you're not sure of the comparability of rations, starting weights and health programs is a touchy subject.

When you're not sure of the conditions, you'll have to rely on the breeder's reputation, or buy on the basis of an in-herd comparison. To a certain degree you'll have to rely on the old eyeball method of judging the respective bull's qualities in relation to the needs of your herd to make your final decision. Then calculate what you can afford to pay for the improvement you feel you'll gain. In an industry fraught with inexactness, bull selection is still, perhaps, the most inexact portion of the science.

Be Confident of Bull's Breeding Ability

To have confidence in a bull's ability, check him for physical soundness and fertility and be sure he is properly conditioned for breeding.

A bull you select as a herd sire might be thoroughly evaluated on the basis of pedigree, appearance, and performance tests, but he is worthless if he can't do his job–breed cows. Moreover, his value is less than nothing if you discover this problem too late. By the time his inadequacy shows up in the next calf crop, many dollars of potential profits are lost, leaving only maintenance expenses for open cows to show for your trouble.

Bull fertility problems may be more common than you think. In a survey of nearly 11,000 bulls, Colorado State University researchers found that 20% (one bull in every five) did not get satisfactory ratings as potential breeding bulls. Results of the survey are shown below.

BULLS CLASSIFIED AS QUESTIONABLE OR UNSATISFACTORY

Reasons	Number of Bulls	% of Total
Semen quality was questionable or unsatisfactory	1,832	16.7
Defects of the testis	1,931	17.6
Defects of the penis	388	3.5
Defects of the epididymis or vas deferens	112	1.0
Defects of limbs and feet	597	5.5
Abnormalities found by rectal examination	547	5.0

Other tests show a tremendous variation in breeding performance of bulls during a 90-day breeding season. You can vastly reduce the chances of using an infertile or subfertile bull by careful observation, by having a breeding soundness examination performed, and by managing the bull properly.

To perform his duties, a bull must be able to move about freely, have adequate senses of sight and smell, be free of disease, and be conditioned to work for the length of the breeding season. He must have a reproductive system capable of delivering normal sperm to the female reproductive tract and have a strong desire to do so (libido).

PHYSICAL EXAMINATION

You can make a preliminary "eyeball" evaluation of breeding bull prospects. Reject any bull which has poor feet and legs and those with undersized or misshapen testicles. A complete breeding soundness examination will probably be conducted by a veterinarian or someone trained in livestock anatomy and reproduction.

Normally, bulls are given a physical examination 30 to 60 days before the start of the breeding season to allow time for replacement if any are found to be unsatisfactory. The evaluation should start from the ground up.

First, watch the bull walk. Look for signs of lameness, pigeon toes, splay feet, or cocked ankles. The rear legs are especially important since they must support weight while breeding. "Post legs" (rear legs too straight) is a common defect that causes bulls to stifle more easily. Check feet for swelling, overgrown hoofs, corns, or cracks.

In addition to assessing the general condition and appearance of the bull, look for a sound set of teeth and eyes that are clear and free of pinkeye scars or cancer eye.

The reproductive system should be observed carefully, beginning with the penis and sheath. Note any discharges from the prepuce. Check for swelling or blood clots of the penis that may indicate injuries or a broken penis. Some bulls suffer from a "tie" or adhesion on the penis, making it difficult or impossible to extend for breeding. While this can be corrected surgically, it is an inherited defect.

Testicles should be of the same size and firmness and should hang vertically. They should slide freely within the scrotum and not cause pain when examined. Occasionally, a bull with a hernia is found during an examination of the scrotum. The epididymis, which carries sperm from the testicle, should be seen at the bottom of the testicle and can be palpated for any abnormalities.

Size of a bull's testicles is related to fertility and has become an important aspect of breeding evaluation. Look for large testicles. For measurement to be a reliable indicator, the bull should be at least a year of age. The distance around both testicles should be at least 34 cm. in a yearling bull; mature bulls should measure 36 to 40 cm.

Veterinarians generally will follow up their examination of the external reproductive system with an examination of the accessory sex glands via the rectum.

Semen evaluation is an important part of a fertility examination. Samples averaging 2 to 4 ccs can be collected by electroejaculation or by having the bull serve an artificial vagina. A good sample will have a milky or creamy appearance. Under a microscope, a drop of the semen will have the appearance of boiling or rolling with the activity of millions of sperm. Often a specimen is stained and further evaluated for percentage dead and abnormal sperm cells.

While semen testing is very valuable from the standpoint of determining semen deficiencies, use some caution in applying the results. It is not a reliable means of classifying the fertility level of bulls. Don't cull a bull on the basis of one semen test, since the first sample can be misleading.

From the time sperm cells begin to form in the testicles, it is 40 to 60 days before they are ejaculated. Some bulls experience temporary periods of poor semen quality due to stress. Higher than normal temperatures caused by climate or infection are the most common cause. Thus, a second semen test within 30 to 60 days is advised.

Desire to mate is an aspect of the bull's breeding qualifications that cannot be checked during a physical exam. Low sex drive can be a problem in an otherwise sound breeding bull and there is large variation in mating desire among bulls. Presently, the only way to detect these bulls is to watch them with a cow in heat and see if they have the desire and ability to mount and serve.

Some bulls will refuse to mate in the first few days at a new location. Allow a new bull some time to become accustomed to his new surroundings before assessing his mating behavior.

MANAGING FOR FERTILITY

Try to have bulls in moderate condition at the start of breeding season. Overfat bulls are lazy and tend to have a reduced desire to mate. On the other hand, bulls that are too thin lack the stamina to maintain activity over the length of the breeding period. Research has also shown that underfeeding during a bull's growth phase reduces sperm-producing capability.

Mature bulls in good flesh can be maintained on the same ration as the cow herd, but will require 50% to 75% more feed. If necessary, grain can be added to condition them prior to the breeding season. Young bulls from yearling age to 3 years need extra energy, since they are still growing. After the breeding season, a young bull should be fed a few pounds of grain to support growth and condition him for the following season.

Don't overwork bulls. Too many cows per bull during a limited breeding season lowers calving percentage. The table provides a guide to the number of bulls you'll need for a 60-day season.

NUMBER OF COWS FOR ONE BULL

Age of Bull	Pasture Breeding	Pen Breeding
15-20 months	10-15	10-20
2 years	15-20	25-35
Mature	25-30	35-50

Bull fertility is greatest between the ages of 2 and 4, then tends to decline with advancing age. Most producers begin using bulls at 2 years, but yearling bulls can be used on a limited number of cows by the time they are about 15 months of age and weigh 1,100 to 1,200 pounds.

A young virgin bull should have some initial experience before being turned in with the cow herd. It is a good idea to turn him in with a couple of heifers beforehand. This gives him some experience at mounting and breeding and usually insures a favorable first breeding experience.

Stress can lower fertility because reproduction is one of the first body functions affected when the animal is subjected to adverse conditions. Control heat stress by providing shade. In one study, Angus bulls with access to shade had approximately 25% greater semen motility and percent normal sperm. Stress from periods of sickness may slow or stop sperm production temporarily.

Extremely cold weather can be harmful, too. Though not usually a problem, it is something to be concerned with during bitterly cold weather with a rapid wind chill. The scrotum and even the testicles can freeze in extreme conditions.

Prepare the bull by taking care of some of the routine chores a few weeks before breeding. Feet are often neglected and this can result in lameness only a short time into the breeding season. Trim excess growth early enough to allow soles to toughen. Trim twice if hoofs are extremely long. Also provide some exercise well in advance to prepare bulls for the rigors of breeding.

Treat for lice and worms before the breeding season. Test for tuberculosis, brucellosis, and other diseases that might be a threat in your locality. Check with your veterinarian for recommended vaccinations. Generally, these include IBR, leptospirosis, and vibriosis.

Cattle Identification Systems

Identification is important in beef production as a prerequisite to record keeping, performance testing and certain disease testing procedures.

Cattle are identified both to establish ownership and as a means to discern one animal from another. Without the ability to identify and record specific information on individual animals, strict selection of breeding animals and close management of the herd are impossible. Once a good identification system is established, it may mean only an additional 20 to 30 minutes per animal in actual applied time.

COW IDENTIFICATION

This is the first step in establishing performance testing programs. Numbers used will relate the cow and calf through the record keeping system, but markings need not be the same. In fact, some operators will find it easier to use temporary systems on the calves, at least until replacement heifer selections are made.

On the cows, permanent identification is best. This means that cows should be either tattooed or number branded.

Most typical procedure is to tattoo cows to insure permanent records, then use a second marking system for easier, faster identification. In this respect, either eartags, neck chains or number brands can be used. In large herds, visible marking of bulls is desirable. Registered bulls will carry ear tattoos for permanent I.D., but brands, either permanent or temporary, are best since they can be read easily while observing breeding performance.

Tattooing is recommended as a permanent marking system. This means numbering cattle inside their ears. It's a nuisance to positively identify cattle since you must catch them to read the number. Registered cattle must be tattooed. If you're in the business to sell to outside customers, you'll usually want to keep other markings to a minimum. This is why, for registered cattle, either eartags or neck chains are recommended rather than branding.

Neck chains are used primarily on purebred cows, but there are drawbacks to using them. They're the most expensive type of secondary marking system. Losses can be a problem with neck chains, especially in brushy country. Cows frequently pull the chains off over their heads or links break. In addition there is some danger of animals hanging themselves. Neck chains aren't practical for calves.

Earmarking is primarily restricted to general herd rather than individual animal identification. In many states an earmark is registered along with an ownership brand. It has been used extensively in hogs for identification, however, and could be applied. It isn't a handy system and is rather unsightly if a number of marks must be made. In addition, cattle hair grows long enough to make small ear notches indistinct unless you have the animal in a chute where you can check it.

Crop . . . .
Overslope . . . .
Underslope . . . .
Swallow Fork . . . . .
Steeple Fork . . . . . .
Oversharp . . . .
Undersharp . . . .
Split . . . .
Bit, Under or over . .

The illustration shows the standard type of cattle earmarkings and the name of each. Earmarks have been used as a backup means of proving ownership, but could be used for a variety of other purposes. Various marks could serve as a code to designate birth months, sires if cows are artificially bred, or birth years for heifers to be kept for breeding.

Eartags are available in a wide variety of shapes and colors and are relatively easy to attach. They can be purchased with numbers preprinted by the manufacturer, or can be printed on the ranch. Ease and flexibility have led most ranchers to use them for calf and cow identification. Because of their contrasting colors and placement in the ear, they are relatively easy to read.

The drawback to eartags is simply that they can be pulled out and lost. However, with the new plastic types this is not a serious problem. Experience has shown that flexibility is the key to good eartag retention. The best tags are those that are free-swinging and flexible enough to resist getting caught. It should also be attached in the more flexible area near the end of the ear.

In using the eartag, a straight numerical code on the calves is all that's needed. These can be related to the permanently marked cow. Later, after selections have been made, replacements can be branded for an easily read, permanent marking.

If you've used artificial insemination or maintained separate sire groups, use different colors to designate different bulls' offspring if sire comparisons are part of the records.

Branding with a hot iron is one of the oldest and most permanent methods of identifying cattle. Registered brands are recognized as a legal symbol of ownership and are helpful in preventing cattle theft. The technique is also used for individual identification using numbers or letters.

The technique of freeze branding also produces permanent and readable markings, but in many states it is not accorded the same legal status as a hot brand. Freeze branding is also slower and requires special equipment.

Branding is the most foolproof identification system. In many areas cattle carry both a registered ranch brand and an individual branded number. However, branding has shortcomings. If you use a hot brand there is an eventual loss due to hide damage. For newborn calf identification, the system isn't convenient or recommended.

Branding with dye has been used successfully by some operators for identifying newborn calves. But temporary branding is most often used in marketing channels or in feedlots. Ranchers generally require more positive markings.

brands. Biggest advantage to either system is that only one straight bar branding instrument is required. Various combinations of straight lines are used to code numerals from one to nine.

Besides the convenience of needing only one tool, brands produced using these systems are usually much clearer. The curved figures of ordinary numbers such as '0' and '8' often produce difficult to read brands.

Numbering or coding system used in the herd is largely a matter of personal preference, except where a particular system is required by a registry association. Your system of numbering animals should be as simple as possible while still permitting easy identification. While a variety of information can be coded on the marking, this usually serves to complicate the code. Much of this information can easily be recorded in the books. Generally not over four numbers and letters are recommended. Three are even better.

A popular method of coding represents the year of birth as the first number. The numbers following it represent the number assigned to the particular animal. For example: 599—The 99th animal born in 1975. If over 100 animals are to be coded it is advisable to use a letter to represent the second 100 and so on. 5A33—The 133rd animal born in 1975. 5B1—The 201st animal marked in 1975.

For commercial producers the year of birth designation is not so important. This can be kept on records. Up to 234 animals can be coded using only one alphabetical letter and one number (A3). If another letter is added to the end of the code (A3C), approximately 6,000 animals can be coded. More animals can be coded if the position of numbers and letters are switched.

With the advent of computerized testing and record keeping procedures it becomes necessary to plan your coding system so that it is compatible with the computer. It's a good practice even though this may not presently be a concern.

Some procedures use a system which numbers the calf the same as its mother. Since the computer can't tell a calf from a cow, this system would require modification. Additionally, the computer cannot distinguish between a 10-year old cow born in 1972 and a new calf born in 1982, since both numbers could be the same. A method of correcting this would be to expand each year number to 82 or 72 when it is entered onto computer forms. Don't use symbols the computer can't handle.

CODING SYSTEMS

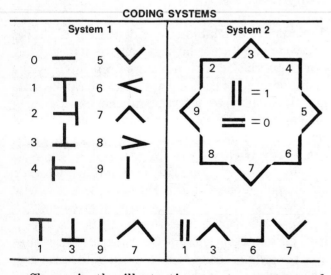

Shown in the illustration are two systems of coding numbers for individual indentification

Beef Cattle Crossbreeding

A mapped-out strategy is needed for good crossbreeding results.
Look at both the pros and cons of a crossing program.

The search for hybrid vigor and the continued immigration of new breeds into this country are making crossbreeding even more important in the beef business. Still the important question confronting producers is: Will it increase profits in the commercial herd? Most studies of crossbreeding say yes, with some qualification. Crossbreeding should fit the producer's needs. It must be done systematically and according to plan. It is not a cure-all for poor management.

Deciding to crossbreed involves such considerations as: what breeds to cross, the breeding system and whether to use artificial insemination. To answer these questions, weaknesses in the herd and goals for improvement need to be well understood.

Advantages of crossbreeding are: (1) combining breeds to obtain a more desirable animal and (2) increasing performance through hybrid vigor. These two factors are distinct. Some of the advantages from crossbreeding are due to one factor and some are due to the other.

Crossing or combining breeds can produce a compromise between important traits in each breed, and perhaps produce a more desirable animal overall. The aspect of hybrid vigor (heterosis) has been used in agriculture for years. Simply stated it means that the offspring receive an extra boost from the mating of genetically unlike parents. The advantage may show up in earlier puberty, increased fertility, less death loss, increased birth weight, increased weight gains and added milk production.

Indications are that heterosis has the most effect on reproductive traits; intermediate effect on growth rate; and the least effect on carcass traits. Research indicates that hybrid vigor from the two-breed cross produces a 3% to 5% boost in growth rate and number of calves weaned. Crossing the F_1 female to a third breed adds another 3% to 5% nudge to production. The accumulative improvement amounts to between 19% and 25% increased production from the three-way cross when compared to straight breds.

Performance of Crossbred and Straightbred Calves Produced by Straightbred Dams

Trait	Straightbred Index	Crossbred Index
Survival to weaning	100	103
Weaning weight	100	105
Yearling weight	100	106
Age at puberty	100	110

Performance of Crossbred and Straightbred Dams Producing Crossbred Calves

Trait	Straightbred Index	Crossbred Index
Conception at first service	100	110
Pregnancy rate	100	106
Weaning weight	100	106
Pounds of calf weaned per cow maintained	100	120

Crossbreeding can't take the place of following good selection practices. Research shows that hybrid vigor has the greatest effect on those traits which are most difficult to improve by selection programs. This means the requirement for selecting high-quality breeding stock will remain just as great, but crossbreeding will pay an extra dividend.

Management problems. Many operators will find their management must be upgraded in order to take advantage of crossbreeding. One problem is that cattle have overlapping generations which may require the use of more than one breeding pasture. Calves may have less uniformity and, chances are, record keeping will need more emphasis.

The problem of difficult births is associated with crossing to a larger breed. Even if the calves are saved, it can take longer to get the cow rebred, since time is required for healing. Calving problems are lower in the larger breeds of cows, but maintenance costs will be higher.

Artificial breeding is highly compatible with crossbreeding. Conversion to AI does require some modification from a natural breeding program, but it will help solve problems associated with bull rotation and maintaining separate breeding pastures. AI offers a better selection of bulls, including exotic breeds, and the genetic traits of a top bull are available to your herd.

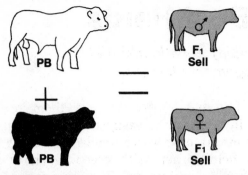

STRAIGHTBRED HERD. Crossbred calves can be produced by crossing a straightbred cowherd with a bull of a different breed. This system does not take the most advantage of hybrid vigor in reproductive performance. However, F₁ females can be sold to an operator using the next system.

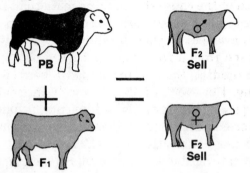

CROSSBRED F₁ FEMALES. This sytem takes advantage of hybrid vigor in the cows and makes the most use of the crossbreeding advantage.

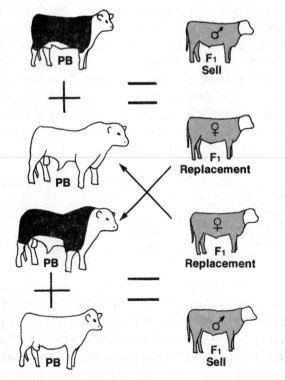

TWO-BREED CRISSCROSS. The advantage of keeping replacement heifers is retained with this system, but it will require a few years to work into. Maternal hybrid vigor will be about 67% of that obtained with a first cross cow.

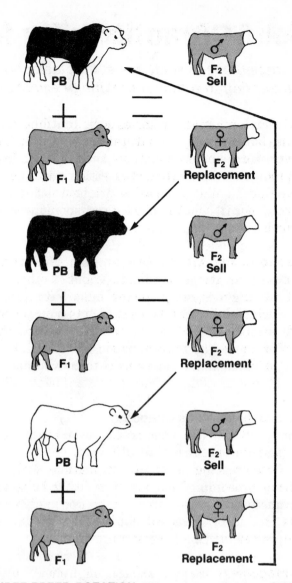

THREE-BREED ROTATION. This sytem retains about 87% of the maximum maternal hybrid vigor. As with the two-breed system, it will take several years to fully work into.

Crossing systems. Since hybrid vigor has its greatest influence on reproductive traits, the use of the F₁ female gives the biggest boost to total production. The F₁ cow is a better mother, but a need to purchase replacements is a built-in disadvantage. Rotational and crisscross breeding systems retain some hybrid vigor in the cows while enabling replacements to go back into the herd.

Modifications can be made, or other systems can be planned which will use crossbreeding to advantage. With an understanding of crossbreeding and a plan for improvement, striking results can be achieved. On the other hand, indiscriminate crossing produces a variety of results and soon loses its advantage.

A.I. Is Practical For Many Beef Herds

In frozen semen you have a wide selection of high quality genetic material, but shifting to artificial breeding requires some management changes.

Artificial insemination solves some breeding problems, but without the natural services of a bull, several drawbacks must be overcome to keep reproduction at an efficient level. To judge the net benefit or liability from using A.I., you should first take a look at what is needed to make it work in your herd.

Reasons for A.I. By breeding artificially, a rancher has access to bulls he couldn't otherwise afford. Higher-quality, tested bulls with proven producing ability can be used. Another important side benefit is control of venereal diseases that may be spread by natural mating.

During a short breeding season A.I. insures that there is plenty of bull power available while eliminating the costs and problems associated with keeping bulls. Cows can be mated to a wide selection of bulls, or the genetics of a single top bull can be passed to the entire herd.

Crossbreeding is highly compatible with artificial breeding. Problems of rotating bulls and maintaining separate breeding groups in different pastures are eliminated. Availability of "exotic" breeds has increased the attractiveness of A.I.

Management Needs. Depositing semen in the cow's reproductive tract should be viewed as only one step in the overall artificial breeding program. Other management factors that surround the actual insemination may have the greatest influence on success. Most cattlemen point to good advance planning and a commitment to make A.I. work as key factors in achieving good results.

Positive Identification of all cows and heifers is needed for heat detection and herd records. Ear tags work well because they are easy to read while checking heat. But, it's helpful to have a backup means of I.D. such as brands or tattoos in case ear tags are lost.

Facilities Required can vary according to your operation. Analyze the farm layout. You'll want to use more confined pastures for easier heat detection and handling of animals.

Good breeding facilities are important. Don't try to get by with "thrown up" corrals and breeding chutes. Present chutes and headgates may

work fine, but it's best to have them located so cows in heat can be easily moved to them. Ideal locations are near water, shade, or bedding areas.

A holding pen with breeding chute is the minimum facility needed. This basic facility is improved by installing a roof over the breeding chute and providing two pens, one for cows found in heat in the morning and the other for evening cows. Width of the chute should be no more than 24 to 26 inches, with a side door for inseminator access. Cows are held in place by sliding bars and can be released from a front gate or backed out.

Breeding Season for most A.I. herds is in the spring. However, A.I. can fit nicely into fall calving programs. Cows calved in the fall will be winter fed in closer confinement when breeding begins, so closer attention is possible.

Whatever the program, a short breeding season is best. Long breeding periods complicate management in almost every area. A breeding period lasting 45 days is ideal, but to achieve it takes careful attention. Normally, cows won't return to heat until about six weeks after calving. This leaves another six-week period to get them bred so they will calve on schedule the following year.

Heifers need more time to get back in shape for breeding after their first calf (see table below). So, to get their later calving to coincide with the rest of the herd you'll need to breed them about two months early for their first calf.

WHEN COWS SHOW HEAT AFTER CALVING							
Days from calving:	40	50	60	70	80	90	100
Older cows (5 years and over)	55%	70%	80%	90%	90%	95%	100%
Younger cows (2-3 years old)	15%	30%	40%	65%	80%	80%	90%

After two heat periods have passed and all cows have been bred at least once, a "clean up" bull may be turned in with the herd. Then, by pregnancy testing about three months after the close of the breeding season, open cows can be identified and sold.

Nutrition Level of the herd has a marked effect on the percentage of cows coming into heat and conceiving during the early part of the breeding season--so much so that it's one of the most important factors in the success of A.I. Poorly fed cows make heat detection more difficult, and settling rate is lower.

Energy seems to be the single most important item in efficient reproduction. Cows should be gaining weight prior to and during the early part of the breeding season. Other nutrients closely involved in reproduction are: protein, calcium, phosphorus, and vitamin A.

Records Help You Manage the breeding program. When you shift to A.I. you'll probably find that records automatically get more attention. Among other things, they help you anticipate heat periods in cows and to match cows with the proper bulls at breeding. They also help you determine where you are going and your progress in herd improvement.

The people involved in the breeding effort are important too. With each step from heat detection to insemination so important to success, reliable people are needed to make it work. It is known that a person with a good mental attitude and the ability to handle cattle can make a sizable difference in conception rates.

Net Results From A.I. should be favorable in a great many herds. On the whole, breeding costs will be comparable with those where natural service is used, even though a much higher-priced bull is being used artificially. A study of several Wyoming ranches revealed that A.I. costs were slightly higher than natural breeding, but the increase was more than offset by the higher value of the calves produced.

Low conception rate can have a serious effect on overall cost of A.I., but with good management there is no reason for conception to be below what you would expect from natural mating. Some operators have consistently settled 90% of their herd in a 45-day breeding season.

Timing Is Critical. Once breeding season begins, timing activities to the cow's reproductive schedule is fundamental to success. Cows should be observed at the most opportune time to catch them in heat. Then they should be moved to the breeding pen, and inseminated during the optimum period for conception.

Best Heat Detection Periods are early in the morning and late in the evening--the cooler parts of the day. Check heat at least twice a day, from daybreak to about 8:30 a.m. and 4:00 p.m. to dark.

Experience in watching cows brings success at detecting heat. You'll develop your own cues and methods of checking cows. Some operators use pressure sensitive strips mounted over the tailhead which show the cow has been ridden, but they are no substitute for personal observation. Surgically altered spotter bulls are also used to some extent.

Standing to be ridden is the surest sign of heat, but if this cue alone were used, about 25% of the cows would be missed. Other strong signs of heat are a clear mucous discharge from the vagina and a reddened and swollen vulva. In the hours both before and after standing heat, cows are nervous and may attempt to ride other cows, but will not stand to be ridden themselves.

Chances For Conception are best during a 10-hour period at the end of standing heat. That's why so much emphasis is placed on heat detection and timing the insemination. The chart shows when breeding should take place in relation to the cow's heat cycle.

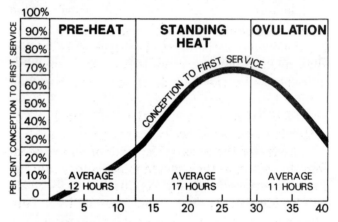

The tried and tested rule of thumb says that cows first observed in standing heat in the morning should be bred in the evening. If in heat in the evening, they should be bred the following morning. Breeding times may need to be adjusted somewhat for a small percentage of cows that have either very long or short heats.

Who Will Inseminate? You may do the breeding yourself or place a capable employee in charge, or hire an experienced inseminator. The technique of inseminating can be learned, and like any other skill, you improve with practice. If you or an employee will do the breeding, get proper training. It will pay off in higher conception rates.

Artificial breeding schools are held at various locations by A.I. companies. Sessions are generally three to five days in length. There are commercial breeding schools offering courses that last one to two weeks. In addition to insemination technique, the schools teach semen handling and storage, and other important herd management practices.

Winter Feeding Beef Cows

Proper nutrition over winter is essential if a cow is to produce a healthy, heavy-weaning calf every year.

Costs of feeding your beef cow herd through the winter months are generally the heaviest of the year. But, a stingy winter feeding program could save one dollar for you now and cost two more later in lower production for the year. That's why your goal in wintering should be to minimize feed costs while meeting the cow's nutritional needs for good production.

Both underfeeding and overfeeding decrease productivity. Idea is to bring cows through the winter in thrifty condition to calve, rebreed on time, and wean heavy calves.

Nutrient requirements of the cow will depend on her condition at the start of winter and whether she is lactating. After a cow calves, her protein requirements for the first four months of lactation are double. Energy needs jump about 50%. Her ability to rebreed is one of the first functions to suffer if these needs are not met.

The fatter the cows at the start of winter feeding, the less gain they should make before calving. Pregnant cows in fleshy condition should make only small winter gains, or even lose slightly. Thin cows may need to gain 100 to 150 pounds by calving time, while cows in medium condition need to gain only the weight of their calf (60 to 80 pounds) over the winter.

Where herd size is large enough, sorting into groups is recommended. Pregnant cows can be fed according to their condition, or, if the herd is pregnancy checked, fed in groups according to anticipated calving date. Even more important, however, is separating replacement heifers, bred heifers, and lactating cows so they can be fed differently.

Feeding young stock properly over the winter is very important for proper development. Long-term studies at the Fort Reno Experiment Station in Oklahoma show that the three most critical nutritional periods for good lifetime production of the female are her first two winters as a heifer, and the period following her first calf, until she is rebred.

The studies showed that heifers should gain 75 to 100 pounds or three-fourths to one pound per day during their first winter as weaner heifers. Bred yearlings or young cows should make some gain up to calving, preferably 50 to 100 pounds. After calving and early lactation, they will have lost about 100 pounds, but can recover this weight during the grazing season.

Meeting protein requirements. A dry beef cow's daily protein needs can be met by:

- Four to seven pounds of good quality legume hay.
- Full feed of mixed hay that is about half legume.
- One pound of 40% supplement with grass hay or silage.
- One and one half to two pounds of 40% supplement or its equivalent with low-quality roughages such as ground cobs or cotton seed hulls.
- Two hours grazing on small grain pasture every other day.

Protein supplement can be self-fed by mixing salt with soybean or cotton seed meal to control consumption. Consumption of self-fed protein will stabilize at around one pound per day, if a mixture of one part salt to two parts meal is provided. One part salt to three parts supplement will give about two pounds per day of protein consumption.

Start out feeding the salt mixture in a ratio of one part salt to four to five parts meal. Increase the percentage of salt as the cows become accustomed to the supplement. Be sure plenty of drinking water is available or the high salt intake could be harmful.

Hand feeding protein requires more labor, but tests have shown that feeding every other day is adequate. Doubling the daily intake for alternate day feeding allows timid cows a better chance to get their share. Even longer periods between feedings may be possible, but probably won't give you the opportunity to check cows often enough.

Supplements containing urea must be consumed often to avoid the possibility of their being toxic. Also, recent tests have shown that urea is of less value for cows wintering on low energy roughages.

Vitamins and minerals. Special attention should be given to Vitamin A in winter feeding. Green feeds are high in this vitamin, but dry, weathered forages and grains are deficient.

Pregnant cows consuming roughages deficient in Vitamin A should receive 30,000 I.U. of Vitamin A daily; nursing cows 40,000 I.U. Vitamin A can be supplemented by feeding five to six pounds of good quality legume hay, feeding alfalfa pellets or meal, adding a Vitamin A supplement to the grain or protein, or by using a commercial fortified supplement.

Principal minerals needed by wintering beef cows are: calcium, phosphorus, salt and iodine. Most rations can be adequately supplemented by a free-choice mineral mixture of equal parts iodized salt, and either bone meal or dicalcium phosphate. Additional block or loose salt should be available. Trace mineralized salt will provide insurance against deficiencies, but generally is not needed unless you're in a trace mineral deficient area.

Use cheap roughages and utilize home grown forage for wintering cows. That's the key to controlling costs. Then, round out the diet by supplementing protein, vitamins and minerals, and if necessary, by adjusting energy levels. In times of roughage scarcity, grain may be a cheaper source of energy than purchased roughage.

In many areas heavy use is made of lower-cost roughage sources and harvest leftovers, including corn stalk grazing, husklage, corn stalk silage, ground corn cobs, sorghum or milo harvest residue, soybean straw, small grain straw, stockpiled annual forages and small grain grazing.

Grazing harvest residues in the field is the cheapest and lowest labor method. In an open winter as little as two acres of good corn stalks will winter a cow. She probably won't need any protein the first 30 days. Later, legume hay will supplement both protein and energy. Or, protein can be fed alone with grain or silage fed to supplement energy.

More cows can be wintered on corn or sorghum residue if the material is stacked or chopped and ensiled. This works well on many farms, but requires more labor and is higher in cost. Other feeds such as straw, corn cobs and cotton seed hulls will supply roughage needs and have economic advantages when forage supplies are short.

Suggested rations in the tables are shown in pounds. They are designed for cows weighing from 900 to 1,100 pounds and in average condition. With the rations using low-grade roughages, it may be necessary to add grain to keep cows in proper condition. Grain should be ground, crushed or rolled.

When using low grade roughages, add one-half pound of 40% supplement and five to six pounds of grain to the ration after calving. Increase Vitamin A to 40,000 I.U. for lactating cows.

RATIONS USING GOOD-QUALITY ROUGHAGE (pregnant cows)

Ration (lbs./day)	1	2	3	4	5	6
Legume hay, good	5	--	6	--	--	--
Grass hay, good	13	18	--	10	--	--
Corn silage, good	--	--	30	--	40	--
Sorghum silage	--	--	--	--	--	55
Legume silage	--	--	--	30	--	--
Protein suppl. (40%)	--	3/4	--	--	1	1
Mineral mix	--	+	--	--	+	+

RATIONS USING LOW-QUALITY ROUGHAGE (pregnant cows)

Ration (lbs./day)	1	2	3	4	5	6
Corn cobs or cotton seed hulls	14	12	14	14	--	--
Corn stalks or straw	--	--	--	--	Free Choice	Free Choice
Corn silage	--	--	--	--	--	20
Alfalfa meal, dehyd.	--	1-1/2	--	--	--	--
Legume hay, good	6	--	3	--	8	--
Protein suppl. 40%	1/2	1	1-1/4	2	--	1-1/2
Molasses	--	--	1	2	--	--
Ground shelled corn	--	3	--	--	--	--
Vitamin A*	--	--	+	+	+	+
Mineral mix	+	+	+	+	+	+

*30,000 I.U. per cow daily

RATIONS FOR FIRST 4 MONTHS OF LACTATION

Ration (lbs./day)	1	2	3	4	5	6
Legume hay, good	20	--	--	10	8	--
Grass hay, good	--	20	--	--	--	10
Corn silage	--	--	65	50	--	30
Sorghum silage	--	--	--	--	50	--
Legume silage	--	--	--	--	--	--
Ground shelled corn	6	7	--	--	3	5
Protein supplement	--	1	2	--	--	1
Vitamin A*	--	+	+	--	--	+
Mineral mix	--	+	+	+	+	+

*40,000 I.U. per cow daily

THUMB RULES FOR WINTER FEEDING.

1. Begin feeding before cows lose too much weight.
2. If possible, feed herd in groups according to nutritional needs.
3. Feed best roughage to calves, first calf heifers and lactating cows.
4. Feed approximately two pounds of dry roughage for each 100 pounds of body weight.
5. One pound of hay equals about 2-1/2 pounds of corn silage, or 3 pounds of sorghum silage in energy value.
6. When roughages are scarce, grain may be a cheaper energy source than hay.
7. Replace only one-third to one-half of the hay ration with grain. Watch for digestive upsets on high grain levels.
8. One pound of grain is equal in energy to two to three pounds of hay depending on hay quality.
9. Save better roughage for later in the winter.
10. Provide plenty of fresh water at all times.

Feeding Crop Residues To Beef Cow Herds

Salvaging residues that might otherwise go to waste can help to reduce wintering costs. The material is better utilized if it is stacked or baled.

Crop residues are mainly energy feeds for cattle. They need to be supplemented by protein, vitamins and minerals. Mature pregnant dry cows utilize harvest leftovers the best and may receive all their winter energy needs from salvage feeds. Stocker cattle and heifers will need additional energy to make satisfactory gains.

Feeding methods range from straight field grazing to completely mechanized harvesting and feeding. As more complete utilization is made of residues, equipment and labor needs rise. Some feeding guidelines are given here, but you should develop your own program based on available feeds and the needs and limitations of your operation.

Grazing corn stalks in the field is common. It's the cheapest and lowest labor way to harvest residues. During most winters an acre of stalks will give 40 to 50 cow days of grazing (two acres per cow gives 80 to 100 days grazing) in Iowa.

Cows select only the best feed, but the method is inefficient. Probably only 20% to 30% of the available feed is recovered by grazing. Feed quality also varies. If the field has a large percentage of downed ears, cows will sometimes founder. Later only less desirable feed remains. If snow covers the ground additional feed must be provided.

Corn husklage, discharged from the rear of the combine during grain harvest, consists of husks, cobs and a small amount of grain. A convenient method of collecting husklage is by using a Foster Harvest Master, consisting of a blower mounted on the rear hood of the combine and a trailing dump wagon.

Husklage yield is normally around one ton of dry matter per acre. The material can be dumped in the field or rechopped and ensiled. If ensiled, moisture usually must be added to reduce spoilage. Dumps to be left in the field can be tripped as the combine turns at the end of the row with very little loss of time. Dumps are then fenced and fed as needed.

Harvesting husklage improves residue utilization. In Iowa comparisons a combination of grazing and husklage dump feeding increased capacity to 75 to 95 cow days per acre. Husklage dumps pro-

vide feed during periods of snow cover, but feeding should be controlled with temporary fence or feeding panels to minimize waste and get good cleanup.

Corn stalklage is material left in the field after combining that can be picked up with forage harvesting equipment. A flail-type cutter is commonly used to harvest the material, which can then be ensiled, left in field stacks or stored next to confined feeding areas.

Big package forage equipment is also becoming popular for stalklage harvest. Stack wagons such as the Hesston Stakhand, equipped with a flail pickup can be used. Some farmers disconnect the straw spreader, then harvest only the two rows behind the combine, which will contain a higher percentage of husk. Large balers are also used to harvest stalks. Excessive spoilage occurs unless you wait until moisture in stalks is under 40%.

Self feeding stacks and bales of stalklage require management. Cattle will trample and bed on the material unless controlled. Use feeding panels or adjust temporary fencing to control feeding.

AVERAGE COMPOSITION OF RESIDUES

	Dry Matter	Crude Protein	TDN
Corn: Leaf	76%	7.0%	58%
Husk	55	2.8	68
Cob	58	2.8	60
Stalk	31	3.7	51
Husklage	78	3.7	65
Stalklage	60	4.0	50
Milo: Leaf	66	10.0	56
Stalk	25	3.6	57
Stover	40	4.7	54
Soybean: Stalk	88	4.0	35
Pod	88	6.1	51
Stover	87	4.3	40
Barley Straw	88	2.5	42
Oat Straw	88	2.5	45
Wheat Straw	90	2.5	40
Wheat Chaff	89	3.0	43

Soybean residues yield fewer nutrients per acre than corn or milo, but have proven valuable in cow wintering programs. Material that ends up as tailing behind the combine contains the most nutritious parts of the plant residue. Dried stems are only about 30% digestible--leaves about 60%.

Pods are higher in protein and are the best part of the residue.

Plant parts highest in nutritive value are difficult to collect after combining. However, trailing dump wagons can collect about 1,800 pounds dry matter of this material per acre. A Stakhand following a 5-row combine with the straw spreader removed collected 1,500 pounds of material in one trial.

Wintering trials have shown good results where tailing dumps were provided in addition to stubble grazing. Cows maintained their weight over a 100-day period on 2.5 acres per head. Consumption of 32% liquid supplement averaged two pounds per day.

Grain sorghum stubble lends itself well to grazing since the stalks stand upright and are more leafy than corn or soybean residues. During periods of snow cover the standing stalks have particular advantages. However, grazing sorghum stalks does require some caution because of the risk of prussic acid poisoning.

Usually several days of grazing can be obtained after harvest before new tiller shoots have developed enough to cause problems. The stover can then be safely grazed again, starting three days after a killing frost.

Ensiling sorghum stalks is not a common practice, but can be easily done without adding water since leaves and stalks retain their moisture several weeks after grain harvest. The material is easier to chop and pack than corn stalks.

Stacking or baling the stubble offers the advantage of stockpiling residue, but requires more labor and expense. In some areas stalks will not dry sufficiently for storage unless they are mowed, windrowed and field dried.

In tests under Midwest conditions, milo stubble provided 65 cow days per acre of winter grazing (1.5 acres per cow for a 100-day period). Combined head residue was provided in dumps, but was not well utilized even when access was controlled.

Small grain residues have potential for wintering beef cows and are used extensively in some Plains areas. TDN content of straw is 40% to 45%, but digestible protein is under 1%.

Using straw as a hay stretcher or hay replacer works best. Cows will select only the hay if offered both, so a good method is to allow cows access to straw all day and feed hay in the evening.

Best quality feed is the tailings collected behind the combine during grain harvest. Both protein and digestibility are higher in this "chaff."

Supplementing crop residues. Crop residues are low in three key nutrients: protein, phosphorus and Vitamin A. Free choice mineral in a weather proof feeder, is recommended for cows on residues. A simple mineral mix including Vitamin A consists of 50% trace mineral salt, 30% bonemeal or dical, and 20% Vitamin A (5,000 I.U. per gram). Vitamin injections can also be given.

Daily protein requirements of dry cows on crop residues can be met with .35 pounds of crude protein per head per day. It appears that a supplement based completely on urea will not give optimum performance.

Legume hay is an excellent supplement for residues. Five to seven pounds of good legume hay will meet protein and vitamin needs, although additional phosphorus will be needed.

Dry cows on stalk fields can usually get by without protein supplement for the first 30 days, since they selectively graze the best feed. When feed quality declines, supplement will be needed to maximize performance. Cows being fed chopped residues cannot sort out better parts. Iowa tests show the chopped stalklage and husklage fed as a complete feed should contain two pounds of cracked corn and one pound of molasses in order to get sufficient intake to maintain cow weights.

Soil considerations and costs of crop residue harvest are subject to individual conditions. With complete removal of crop residue you should replace nutrients as you would on ground cropped for silage. For example, a ton of corn stalks contains about 15 pounds of nitrogen, 5 pounds of phosphate, and 15 pounds of potash.

Erosion and the loss of soil tilth-building material are worrisome to some farmers. Loss of tilth has not proven to be too great a problem unless complete removal of residues is practiced over a period of years, or unless soils are compacted or poorly drained. Erosion can be a problem depending on soil structure and erosion potential.

The costs of the more complete programs of residue removal and feeding can go quite high in some operations. If you already own the needed equipment, residue harvest is one method of spreading machinery costs over more tonnage. But you may have to look beyond recovery of residues to justify substantial new machinery investments.

Producing More Beef From Pasture

As feed costs rise, so does the value of pasture land.
Advantages to adding more pounds of beef on pasture increase.

Overall, nearly 80% of the total feed used to produce a pound of beef is made up of pasture and roughage. Although higher levels of forage mean somewhat more production time is required, economics favor more roughage when feedgrains are expensive. Backgrounding steers and heifers to heavier weights on pasture can reduce production costs. Beef can be finished by feeding grain on pasture, using less grain than is normally required in the feedlot.

BACKGROUNDING ON GRASS

Taking cattle to heavier weights on pasture is most advantageous during periods of high grain prices. Even though pasture gains become less efficient at increasingly heavier weights, they still compete favorably with high costs in the feedlot. Also, when grain is expensive cattle feeders pay relatively higher prices for well-grown cattle.

Managing cattle for grazing, or purchasing them in the proper condition prior to the pasture season is important to a successful backgrounding program. Systems designed to make maximum use of pastures have shown that the level of gain through the winter can be critical.

If calves are wintered before going to pasture, they should gain at a level between .75 and 1.25 pounds per day. Although cattle make good compensatory growth when wintered at lower levels, it is generally not economical since costly winter feed is poorly utilized. On the other hand, if wintered to arrive on grass in fleshy condition, gains on pasture will suffer. Upper limit of winter growth appears to be 1.5 pounds per day if the cattle are to make good use of pasture.

Average weight gains per day on good pasture range from 50% to 75% as large as those made by cattle on a full feed of grain. Best performance usually occurs during June and July, when the highest quality grass is produced. Earlier spring growth is often too high in moisture to allow the best gains, while grass later in the summer becomes dry and less digestible. Since it isn't easy to obtain an optimum balance between pasture production and stocking rates for the full season,

the best approach lies in striking a happy medium between low rates of gain when grass is retarded and letting forage go to waste when pasture growth is lush.

On pastures with abundant forage, yearling steers will usually gain 1.25 to 1.5 pounds per day. Two year olds should gain 1.5 to 2.0 pounds. Improved pastures in the Midwest produce 200 to 300 pounds or more of gain per acre during a grazing season. Irrigated grass pastures often produce 650 to 750 pounds per acre, with irrigated alfalfa pastures making up to 1,800 pounds gain per acre.

Management suggestions for backgrounding on grass:

- Use your best quality pastures for backgrounding. Cattle won't gain efficiently on low quality roughage.
- Have cattle in light to moderate flesh for going to grass. Fleshy cattle make poor use of pasture. However, avoid cattle that are light because of chronic sickness.
- Establishing legumes in grass pastures is advantageous. Fertilization requirements are reduced, while the legumes support rates of gain, particularly during the midsummer.
- Implanting growing cattle can boost gains by 10% to 15% during the grazing season.
- Supply a good mineral-free choice through the season, along with salt and plenty of water. Use of sprays, dustbags or backrubbers is also important since flies reduce gains and contribute to eye problems.
- Worm cattle if needed before going to pasture and complete all operations such as castrating and dehorning. Consult a veterinarian for vaccinations recommended locally.
- Supply a bloat suppressing agent if pastures contain more than one-half legumes.

Grass finished beef can be a profitable system for some producers, primarily in the Southeast. But, true grass finishing (Good and Choice grades on grass only) is difficult for most cattlemen. In order to reach finish, grass-fed cattle must weigh at least as much as comparable grain-finished cattle. This can add up to an extra year to age at slaughter and may increase total production costs due to the longer ownership and inefficient gains on grass at heavy weights.

The problem of yellow-colored fat in the carcass is another drawback to strict grass finishing. While fat color has nothing to do with quality or eating characteristics, it isn't welcomed by most beef buyers. Commonly, heavy grass-fed yearlings are fed grain in drylot for as little as 60 days, which helps to raise carcass grade and reduce fat coloring.

GRAIN ON GRASS

Feeding grain to cattle on pasture is a sound option for many farmers with permanent pasture available. Yearling cattle can be finished to the Good and Choice grades directly off of pasture while consuming less grain than would be required in drylot. Several experiments have shown that savings of 100 pounds of grain or more can be made for each 100 pounds of animal gain. Other advantages of grain on pasture include lower overhead cost and labor required; no need to handle manure; and increased return per acre of pasture.

Plenty of good quality grass and the right kind of cattle are needed if cattle are to be finished by the end of grazing season. Cattle should be in moderate flesh and of sufficient quality in order to reach the Choice grade. Yearling steers should weigh at least 600 to 700 pounds by the beginning of good grazing.

Self-feeding on pasture is the preferred method of getting grain to the cattle. Consumption is more even when cattle have continual access to a self-feeder, and gains for self-fed cattle usually surpass those that are hand fed twice daily. Grain can either be full-fed or limit-fed through a self-feeder. Choice is pretty much up to the desires of the manager and the gains required for the cattle.

In tests covering four grazing seasons at Purdue University, yearling steers were fed whole shelled corn on well fertilized birdsfoot trefoil-bluegrass pastures. Feeding rates were one-third, two-thirds and a full feed of grain (approximately 0.5, 1.0 and 1.5 pounds of grain per 100 pounds of body weight). Average daily gains were 0.95, 1.85 and 2.95 pounds respectively, and produced 497,924 and 1,973 pounds of beef per acre of pasture.

A summary of 12 years of grain on grass tests at North Carolina indicated that limiting grain intake to 0.8 to 1.0 pound per hundred pounds of body weight produced the best returns. Intake was controlled to this level by feeding a mixture of 90% ground shelled corn and 10% salt or animal fat. Yearling steers were marketed off of grass-ladino clover pastures at 1,000 to 1,050 pounds.

Some farmers feed no grain until pastures mature in the summer, then full-feed for the remainder of the grazing season. Another alternative is to limit feedgrain from the beginning of grazing, switching to a full feed when pastures become scant and coarse.

Optimum stocking rates vary according to the productivity of the pasture and the level of grain fed. Rates should be fairly heavy to make good use of the grass. For yearling cattle full-fed grain on good grass-legume pasture, stocking rate will range from four to six head per acre. If pasture is not as high in quality or if cattle are limit-fed grain, reduce rate to one to three head per acre.

Protein savings is another advantage of a grain on grass system. Most research has shown that supplemental protein is not required when pastures are green and growing. A lick tank supplement or dry biuret didn't improve performance on green pasture in Purdue tests. However, when grass is coarse or dry as in drouthy periods, extra protein will be beneficial. Cattle most likely to be deficient in protein are those on a full feed when pastures are scant, since they are not consuming enough green forage to meet their needs.

Carcass grades of cattle coming off pasture depend on several factors. In general, however, grades are no more variable than those of cattle similarly finished in drylot. Genetic ability and length of time on concentrates are the most important factors. Use these guidelines in planning your own program: Assuming good pasture and well grown yearlings, steers fed grain at 1% of their body weight for the season should grade mostly Choice. If steers receive a full feed of grain on grass, figure that 60 to 80 days of grain feeding should produce Good grade cattle. A full grain feed for about 120 days will be needed to yield mostly Choice carcasses.

Management suggestions for feeding grain on grass:

- Manage pastures to keep plenty of green forage available. In some cases extra fencing may be required to allow rotation for better pasture utilization and quality.
- Limit pasture size so cattle won't get too far away from the feeder.
- Supply a free-choice mineral continually. A good mixture consists of two parts bonemeal or dicalcium phosphate and one part salt. Other salt should be provided separately.
- Implant cattle with an approved product and follow recommendations on subsequent implants during the season.
- Provide backrubber or use sprays or dustbags to control flies.
- Locate feeder near water and next to shade.
- Provide three to four inches of feeder space per head.
- Never allow self-feeder to run empty. Avoid sudden changes in feed, such as switching from ground shelled corn to whole shelled corn.
- Use an antibloat agent if pastures are over one-half legume.

Beef Growing and Finishing Rations

Standard rations outlined on this page will meet the nutrient requirements established by the National Research Council. Alterations can be made to include other available feedstuffs.

Ration suggestions shown in the tables have been prepared by Missouri beef specialists. Substitution of other feeds can be made in the rations by recomputing the nutrients supplied and shuffling the pounds of ingredients, if necessary, to meet animal requirements.

RATION CONSIDERATIONS

Cost per unit of protein should be your primary guide in selecting protein supplements. Protein provided from the oil meals—soybean meal, cottonseed meal and linseed meal—is approximately equal in value for cattle feeding. Commercial protein supplements contain vitamins and minerals which should be considered when making price comparisions.

Urea and other non-protein nitrogen compounds can replace part of the protein in beef rations. However, energy level is the key factor in urea utilization. All of the supplemental protein may be supplied by urea in high energy rations. In low energy rations, urea may need to be limited to half of the supplemental protein. Liquid and dry supplement appear about equal in protein value.

For purposes of comparing prices, figure that six pounds of corn and one pound of urea are equal in both energy and protein to seven pounds of 44% oil meal supplement.

Major minerals that require supplementation are calcium, phosphorus and salt. These can be added to a complete mixed ration or offered free choice. Deficiencies of trace minerals sometimes occur when using common feedstuffs, so trace mineralized salt is recommended as insurance.

Calcium deficiency is most likely to occur with a high concentrate ration, while a shortage of phosphorus is most likely on a high roughage diet. As a rule of thumb, beef rations should contain about 0.5% salt, and 0.3% each of calcium and phosphorus on a dry matter basis. Maintain the calcium to phosphorus ratio between 1:1 and 2:1.

Cattle synthesize several vitamins in the rumen. Thus, Vitamins A, D, and E are usually the only ones that need to be considered in ration formulation. Cattle housed in confinement may be short of Vitamin D, but it is usually adequate in

GROWING AND FINISHING RATIONS
(Amounts per head daily—as fed basis)

Wintering Rations for Calves to Go to Pasture
(1 lb. daily gain)

Feedstuff	Ration 1	Ration 2	Ration 3
Silage	25-35 lbs.	20-30 lbs.	
Hay (legume)		5 lbs.	
Hay (1/2 legume)			12-15 lbs.
Protein (44%)	1 lb.		
Mineral mix (free-choice)*			
Trace mineral salt	1 part	1 part	1 part
Dicalcium phosphate	1 part	1 part	
Monosodium phosphate			1 part

Growing Rations for Calves to Be Finished Shortly
(1.5 lbs. daily gain)

Feedstuff	Ration 1	Ration 2
Silage (full-fed)	30-50 lbs.	
Hay (at least 1/2 legume)		10 lbs.
Grain (1 lb./100 lbs. body wt.)		4-6 lbs.
Protein (44%)	1-1/2 lbs.	1/2 lb.
Mineral mix (free-choice)*		
Trace mineral salt	1 part	1 part
Dicalcium phosphate	1 part	1 part
Monosodium phosphate		1 part

Finishing Rations

Feedstuff	Ration 1	Ration 2	Ration 3	Ration 4
Shelled corn (1-1/2 lbs./100 lbs. body wt.)	8-15 lbs.			
Shelled corn		full-fed	full-fed	full-fed
Protein (44%)	1-1/2 lbs.	1-1/2 lbs.	1-1/2 lbs.	1 lb.
Silage	full-fed	5-10 lbs.		
Legume hay (good quality)				4-6 lbs.
Grass hay			4-6 lbs.	
Mineral mix (free-choice)*				
Trace mineral salt	1 part	1 part	1 part	1 part
Limestone	1 part	2 parts	2 parts	
Dicalcium phosphate	1 part	1 part	1 part	1 part

*You may substitute bonemeal for dicalcium phosphate, and tripolyphosphate for monosodium phosphate.

animals exposed to direct sunlight. No consistent benefit from supplemental Vitamin E has been found.

Vitamin A is a primary consideration in cattle feeds. Supplementing 15,000 to 30,000 I.U. of Vitamin A per head daily is usually ample for cattle fed in drylot.

Substitution of some feeds can be made freely in rations. Mixed legume-grass hay can substitute pound for pound with legume hay. Hay and haylage are interchangeable on an equal dry matter basis. Substitute high moisture corn for dry corn on the basis of dry matter content.

Milo can be substituted freely for corn, though

171

its value in the ration can vary widely depending on the variety and processing method used. Wheat is an excellent feed and can substitute for up to 50% of the grain in finishing rations. In order to receive its full value, barley should not be used as the only grain in a finishing ration. Oats should be limited to 30% of a finishing diet.

FEEDING PROGRAMS

Drylot growing rations can be separated into two types. Rations for wintering calves that will go back to grass should produce gains in the area of .75 to 1.0 pound per day. Faster gains would limit pasture gains later and likely reduce overall growth efficiency. On the other hand, slower winter growth may reduce total gain for the year.

Rations that will produce more rapid growth are justified for cattle which will be finished without going to pasture. Daily gains of 1.5 pounds are typical of this type of growing program.

Calves fed primarily roughages will eat nearly 2.5% of their body weight in air dry feed daily. If grain is provided it is generally fed at a level of 0.5% to 1.0% of body weight. Provide 15 inches of bunk space for growing cattle.

Cattle on finishing rations generally gain faster and need less feed per pound of gain when fed high energy feeds. Gain cost, however, will depend on relative price for feedstuffs. Animals eating 1.5% of their weight in grain daily are considered to be on a full feed of grain. However, they may consume up to 2.5% if little roughage is provided.

If cattle have been receiving some grain previously, they can be brought onto a full feed of grain by increasing grain by one-half pound daily. Increases should be made only if they clean up their feed. Observe cattle carefully as they approach full feed.

If animals are not accustomed to eating grain, this schedule can be used: Feed one to three pounds of grain mixed with five pounds of hay or equivalent silage on the first day. Then, increase grain one pound per head daily until they are receiving one pound per hundred pounds of body weight. When all cattle are consuming this level, increase grain one-half pound per day for heavy feeders and one-half pound every second day for light feeders, until they are consuming a full feed. Roughage level will be reduced as grain increases, but make sure cattle have all they want to eat at all times.

All-concentrate rations have been used to some

extent, but in most practical situations at least 5% roughage is needed in the ration. This amounts to about 1.5 pounds of hay or five pounds of silage per head daily. In such high concentrate rations, whole shelled corn appears equal or slightly superior to ground corn. If roughage level is above 20%, ground corn is preferable.

As a guide for figuring feed needs, assume cattle on finishing rations will eat 2% to 2.5% of their body weight in grain and supplement plus 0.5% to 1.0% in air dry roughage daily. Allow 18 inches of bunk space for finishing yearling cattle.

COMPLETE MIXED RATIONS (MIXTURE FOR 100 POUNDS—AS FED BASIS)

Ration A: Corn, Soybean Meal, Alfalfa Hay

| Ingredient | Ration Number | | |
	No. 1 lbs.	No. 2 lbs.	No. 3 lbs.
Ground shelled corn	50.42	64.70	68.58
Soybean meal (44%)	--	--	4.00
Alfalfa hay	49.00	34.80	27.00
Dicalcium phosphate	0.21	0.13	--
Limestone	--	--	0.02
Salt (trace mineral)	0.37	0.37	0.40
	100.0	100.0	100.0
Composition, dry matter basis	%	%	%
TDN	72.50	77.50	82.50
Protein	14.40	13.00	12.80
Ca	0.72	0.52	0.47
P	0.33	0.33	0.33
Salt	0.45	0.45	0.45

Ration B: Corn, Soybean Meal, Corn Silage

Ingredient	No. 1	No. 2	No. 3
Ground shelled corn	4.80	17.46	38.00
Soybean meal (44%)	3.20	4.00	5.23
Corn silage	91.60	78.00	56.00
Dicalcium phosphate	0.12	0.08	--
Limestone	0.12	0.27	0.52
Salt (trace mineral)	0.16	0.19	0.25
	100.0	100.0	100.0
Composition, dry matter basis	%	%	%
TDN	72.50	77.50	82.50
Protein	12.00	12.50	12.80
Ca	0.44	0.44	0.44
P	0.33	0.33	0.33
Salt	0.45	0.45	0.45

Ration C: Corn, Soybean Meal, Urea, Timothy Hay

Ingredient	No. 1	No. 2	No. 3
Ground shelled corn	47.62	63.23	78.80
Soybean meal (44%)	0.38	--	--
Urea (281 protein equiv.)	0.89	1.00	1.00
Timothy hay	50.00	34.54	18.85
Dicalcium phosphate	0.33	0.22	0.10
Limestone	0.38	0.61	0.85
Salt (trace mineral)	0.40	0.40	0.40
	100.0	100.0	100.0
Composition, dry matter basis	%	%	%
TDN	72.50	77.50	82.70
Protein	12.00	12.35	12.60
Ca	0.44	0.44	0.44
P	0.33	0.33	0.33
Salt	0.45	0.45	0.45

Beef Herd Health

A systematic health program stressing disease prevention will improve your cow herd and increase your profits.

Disease organisms, viruses and bacteria are always present. Insects, birds, air, water, soils, other animals and man all can pass organisms to cattle.

Your objective in a herd health program should be to maintain or gain immunity from the effects of infection and disease. The results will be faster growth; better feed efficiency, production and reproduction; and/or lower treatment costs and death losses.

Unnatural conditions or stress weaken natural body defenses. In turn, the ability of disease organisms to invade and attack life systems increases as natural resistance and immunity are lowered or when injuries or surgery break the barrier of protective cell tissue. Therefore, cattle should be carefully handled and fed to reduce stress. If practical, time procedures such as vaccinating and weaning at intervals to avoid compounding stress at any one time. Use of sterile methods cannot be overemphasized. Always clean and disinfect vaccinating needles, knives and other instruments after use on each animal.

Isolate all cattle brought in from outside sources for a quarantine period of at least three weeks unless you have positive proof they are free of communicable diseases. It takes about seven days for diseases to incubate, so healthy looking cattle are not necessarily disease-free on arrival. Isolate all sick cattle. Isolation pens should be separated from other pens and corrals by several feet.

Sanitation is the best scours preventive. Enteritis or inflammation of the intestine that results in scours is the single biggest preweaning problem of calves. Several treatments are available, but are not effective against the broad spectrum of scours-causing organisms. Your best bet is to prevent calves from becoming infected from either carrier animals or infected premises. Calve in a clean area. Feed hay from racks or bunks and move calf and cow to a less confined area within three days.

Parasites spread disease organisms and put stress on cattle. Some veterinarians say worming cattle is the most important thing you can do to protect them. You can't vaccinate or give other treatments effectively until worms are controlled.

Feed deficiencies and toxicities, which may be locally or seasonally prevalent, should be corrected. Grass tetany is related to low magnesium levels in early season grass. Tetany can result in serious losses unless it is recognized quickly and magnesium supplementation is provided.

Excessive molybdenum in forage and hay is a localized problem, as is selenium deficiency. Know your area and source of hay with regard to these minor element balance problems so proper corrective measures can be used.

Vaccination is usually a practical secondary or backup defense and in some cases the only defense against a disease. Most vaccines contain protein substance antigens that, when introduced into the body, stimulate the production of disease-resisting antibodies. This is the same type of immunity that may develop in an animal during recovery from an infection or disease.

In using vaccines, remember that they do not produce instant immunity. It usually takes 7 to 14 days for the antibodies to build up enough to cope with typical challenge exposures to disease-producing organisms. Antitoxin vaccines are available for immediate, but temporary, protection (usually for 10 to 14 days) against some diseases.

Rate of success varies among beef animals. A vaccine that gives protection to 75% to 85% of recipients is considered good.

Vaccines may lose their effectiveness if improperly handled. To insure good results, buy from a reliable source, keep properly refrigerated, read the label instructions and administer as recommended by the manufacturer or veterinarian. Discard unused portions.

Injections are made primarily by one of two methods. Subcutaneous (beneath the skin) injections are used for most of the clostridial vaccines. The shortest needle possible is the best and use it only as long as it remains sharp. A blunt or hooked needle invites infection by doing too much damage to the skin. Short-pointed needles are generally preferable since they won't "hook" as readily as needles with long points.

An intramuscular injection should be placed into a muscle and is the method commonly used for antibiotic placement. It requires a longer needle, often with a larger bore than the one used for subcutaneous injections. Slap the site of injection a couple of times so the animal won't "start" at unexpected pain.

Preconditioning may be a part of your animal health program if you're a feeder calf producer. If you're doing a good job with a systematic, planned animal health management program, probably you're also doing most of the things that normally fit in a preconditioning program.

One common aspect of preconditioning that does not necessarily fit in with the animal health aspects is preweaning. Most feedlot operators put this high on the list since they want the calves ready to eat and start gaining immediately when they come into the feedlot. Of course, this is a chore that many ranchers would just as soon not perform, since it necessitates a certain amount of feeding and handling that would normally not be done on the ranch.

An efficient record system is the key to a sound preconditioning program. You should be able to show the buyer what practices you have performed and when. Some helpful things to include in your records are: Castration and dehorning dates (along with the methods used), immunization dates (include the types of vaccines used), parasite control practices and the nutritional program you have followed. Show the date if calves have been preweaned.

HEALTH MANAGEMENT PROGRAM

The following checklist is based on University of Nebraska recommendations, and will provide guidelines for setting up your individual program. Timing of some vaccinations may vary with the vaccine or combination you are using. Ask the supplier or veterinarian for specific recommendations.

REPLACEMENT HEIFERS

- Between 30 and 60 days before breeding, vaccinate for vibriosis, leptospirosis, IBR (rednose), PI3, and BVD. (Consult a local veterinarian about lepto and BVD vaccines.)
- Six weeks and three weeks before calving give enterotoxemia toxoid (types C and D).

COWS

- Vaccinate annually for vibrio and lepto 30 days before breeding. (Can be given to pregnant cows at weaning or when pregnancy testing.)
- Annual booster shot of entotoxemia toxoid should be given three to six weeks before calving.
- Give vitamins A, D, and E before breeding if ration was deficient.
- Be sure the cow is in breeding condition. It takes 40 to 60 days of good nutrition to prepare the system for the reproductive process.
- Pregnancy check 60 to 90 days after the close of the breeding season. Treat nonbreeders if possible—cull those that won't breed.

CALVES

- Castrate bull calves early. (Best if done at birth.)
- At about two months of age give 2-way blackleg vaccination.
- At two to six months of age vaccinate heifer calves for brucellosis.
- If calves are worked 30 days before weaning, give both steers and heifers PI3, IBR (nasal type), and pasturella vaccines.
- At weaning if calves have been given the above treatment 30 days before, give second injection of pasturella, plus 4-way blackleg.
- If calves are worked only at weaning, give IBR-lepto combination and 4-way blackleg vaccines.
- If you prewean, do so 30 days before shipment and teach calves to drink and eat from troughs and bunks.

ENTIRE HERD

- Maintain fly control program with dust bags, oilers, sprays or powders throughout the fly season.
- Treat for grubs during the appropriate period for your section of the country. Treatment may need to be repeated during the winter for good control of lice.
- Hold new cattle in isolation for 30 days and vaccinate against diseases that are prevalent in the area before turning them in with the herd.
- Consult a local veterinarian when setting up your herdwide vaccination program. He may recommend other specific vaccinations based on his knowledge of local disease conditions.

Reproductive Diseases of Cattle

Reproductive problems in the herd can be complex and difficult to identify. These specific diseases are often responsible for abortions and infertility.

Probably the most common disease resulting in open cows and reduced conception rates is vibriosis. Leptospirosis might rank second and rednose (IBR) third. In California, foothill abortion (EBA) is most prevalent. Brucellosis is still a potential cause of abortion and should be considered. Although rare, trichomoniasis is classified as a true venereal disease of cattle, along with vibrio. Other diseases such as BVD and listeriosis are commonly linked with abortion.

Vibriosis is an infectious disease of the genital tract and is spread by breeding. Although common in the West, it has been increasing in eastern states in recent years. The disease is caused by a bacterium, *Vibrio fetus,* and shows up in the herd as fertility problems and occasional abortion. Signs may be a low herd calving rate or a calving period that suddenly spreads out over several months. The small number of abortions that occur may not be alarming and may be overlooked.

Primary effect of vibriosis is temporary infertility. Conception may be delayed 3 to 8 months in infected cows. Only a few bulls become infected, but bulls can carry the organism from cow to cow. Except for a few cows that become carriers, most older animals will eventually throw off the infection. The disease can be maintained in herds for years by replacement heifers that continue to become infected and by carrier cows.

Positive diagnosis of vibrio is not easy and usually requires some detective work based on herd breeding records and laboratory samples taken from the genital tracts and aborted fetuses. Luckily, vibriosis is preventable through vaccination and currently available vaccines will provide maximum protection if used correctly.

No really effective treatment is available for infected herds.

Massive doses of streptomycin have been used, but are not considered practical. Vaccination of the herd is the most effective practice and will generally provide a boost to conception rates. Use of artificial insemination will stop the spread of the disease. Most infected cows usually develop immunity and eventually become pregnant.

Trichomoniasis is also a venereal disease of cattle, but is much rarer than vibriosis. Outwardly, signs of the two diseases are very similar; repeat services and a strung-out calf crop. Abortion usually occurs early in gestation. Females may show a discharge from the genital tract, while bulls generally show no symptoms. Bulls are permanently infected, but cows can recover in three to four heat cycles if left unbred.

The organism, *Trichomona fetus,* is found in the genital tracts of both male and female and can be identified through a microscope. Since there is no vaccine, prevention rests with keeping the disease out of the herd through cautious selection of replacement bulls. The disease is treated by taking advantage of the self-limiting nature of the infection in females. Infected cows are given 60 to 90 days of sexual rest. Artificial insemination should be used to prevent infecting a susceptible bull. In most cases, infected bulls should be slaughtered.

Leptospirosis affects all domestic animals, much wildlife and man. It is caused by small, spiral-shaped bacteria called *Leptospira.* Many strains of Leptospira have been identified, but important ones in the U.S. are: *L. pomona, L. Harjo, L. grippotyphosa, L. canicola,* and *L. icteroheamorrhagiae.* The first three are most common.

Actually, there are two forms of lepto. The acute form is often seen in younger animals and causes high temperature, depression, bloody urine and sometimes death. Older animals in breeding herds seldom show the acute form; in these cases the first symptom usually is abortion. The situation is often described as an "abortion storm" in beef herds. In dairy cows, initial symptoms may be a sudden drop in production and thick, blood-tinged milk.

Abortion usually occurs 2 to 3 weeks after infection. All infected cows don't abort, but abortion is most likely in the last third of pregnancy. Leptospira are passed out in the urine, infecting other cattle primarily through contaminated water. In some cases, it may be transmitted by breeding and artificial insemination.

Consult your veterinarian for lepto vaccination recommendations. While vaccines are available for all five common strains, a trivalent vaccine is normally recommended in areas where the disease is a threat. Antibodies do not supply cross-protection, so a vaccine for the specific strain present must be used. Other preventive methods include: controlling rats, fencing cattle from potentially contaminated streams and ponds and separating cattle and hogs.

Treating infected cattle with streptomycin will effectively stop the shedding of the organism. Recovered animals have immunity, and the future breeding value of herds which have experienced the disease is usually normal.

Brucellosis is one of the oldest known causes of abortion. Although its incidence has been greatly reduced by the national eradication program, a small number of herds are still infected. The most obvious sign of brucellosis is abortion during the last half of pregnancy. Retained placentas and enlarged testicles also are symptoms in infected herds.

Proper vaccination of heifers with Strain 19, coupled with caution in purchasing herd replacements, is the best preventive. Age at vaccination is important since heifers may show positive blood tests if vaccinated too late.

Rednose or IBR is produced by a virus of the Herpes group and as such can cause a variety of symptoms. Cattlemen are aware of the respiratory symptoms. However, IBR can also infect the fetus, causing fetal death and abortion. Abortion can occur at any stage, but is most common late in pregnancy. Still another reproductive form of the disease is an inflammation of the vulva and vagina.

Modified live virus vaccines provide good immunity and should be used routinely on heifers between weaning and breeding age. Intramuscular vaccines may cause abortion in pregnant cows, while internasal types appear safe during pregnancy. If IBR is diagnosed, vaccination of the entire herd is recommended.

Other diseases that produce various symptoms in nonpregnant animals can also infect the fetus during pregnancy, causing abor-

tion. BVD (bovine virus diarrhea) can infect pregnant cows without causing diarrhea, but can cause abortion, stillbirth, or calves born with a loss of hair and with brain damage. Listeriosis (circling disease) also can produce abortions. Normally, symptoms are nervous disorders caused by an inflammation of the brain. This disease is transmitted from other animals, including rodents, and is also associated with moldy roughages, especially silage.

A vaccine is available to provide good immunity to BVD and may be given annually to all replacement heifers. Occasional unfavorable reactions occur with live virus vaccines, so consult your veterinarian. There is no vaccine against listeriosis. Supportive treatment with antibiotics and sulfas is sometimes helpful until the infection clears up.

Various toxins and nutrient deficiencies can also be associated with abortion or breeding problems. Among these are mycotoxins (mold toxins in feed) and ration deficiencies of phosphorus, calcium, energy, protein and vitamin A. Feeds or water that contain high levels of nitrate have also been implicated.

Prompt diagnosis should be the first priority if problems occur in your herd. Any abortion should not be taken lightly. It is a sign that something went wrong during pregnancy. It may be confined to the individual cow, or it could be a herd problem requiring a management change or medical treatment.

Length of gestation	Description of fetus
2 mos	size of a mouse
3 mos	size of a rat
4 mos	size of a small cat
5 mos	size of a large cat
6 mos	size of a small dog (hair around eyes, tail, muzzle)
7 mos	fine hair on body and legs
8 mos	hair coat complete, incisor teeth slightly erupted
9 mos	incisor teeth erupted

Be prepared to assist your veterinarian in finding the cause of reproductive failures. If abortion occurs, isolate the cow from the rest of the herd. Put the fetus and placenta in a plastic bag and preserve it by refrigerating (do not freeze). Reproductive records, ration ingredients, a history of herd vaccinations and the identity of any new animals in the herd may provide helpful clues. The table above provides a rough guide for estimating the age of aborted fetuses.

DISEASES CAUSING ABORTIONS IN CATTLE

Disease	Organism	How spread	Stage of gestation at abortion	Samples needed for diagnosis	Vaccination	Remarks
Vibriosis	Bacteria (Vibrio fetus venerealis)	Venereal disease spread by infected bulls.	Early abortion (sporatic)	Vaginal mucus from cow; fetus; washing from bull.	Killed vaccine 30-60 days before breeding.	High incidence of repeat breeding and open cows.
Trichomoniasis	Protozoa	Venereal disease spread by infected bulls.	2-4 months	Preputial washings from bulls; uterus from cull cow; fetus	None	Treatment: sexual rest for 60-90 days; A.I.; cull infected bulls.
Leptospirosis	Bacteria (At least five serotypes)	Infected urine or aborted fetus.	Any stage, usually 6-9 mos.	Blood sample 10% of herd.	Annually-more often if needed.	Laboratory should determine serotype.
Brucellosis	Bacteria (Brucella abortus)	Aborted fetus	6-9 months	Blood sample from cow; fetus; placenta.	Dairy heifers: 3-6 mo. Beef: 3-10 mo.	Infected animals are culled.
Foothill abortion (EBA)	Unknown	Suspect spread by tick	6-9 months	Fetus; blood sample; placenta.	None	Aborting animals usually immune.
Red nose (IBR)	Virus	Infectious from cow to cow.	6-9 months	Fetus; placenta; blood samples.	Live vaccine.	Abortion may or may not occur.
Virus diarrhea (BVD)	Virus	Contagious from cow to cow.	Variable, usually early in gestation	Two blood samples, 3 weeks apart.	Vaccinate animal after 8 mos. of age.	Calves may be born with brain damage.
Listeriosis (circling disease)	Bacteria	Other animals; rats; moldy feed.	Variable	Fetus; placenta; blood from cow.	None	Uterine infection; illness in cattle.

There's No "Best" Hog Housing System

The type of hog raising facility you build can affect number of pigs weaned, rate of gain and feed efficiency, as well as labor and capital requirements.

The choice of housing and facilities is often perplexing, especially since no one system is superior on every farm. A good manager can make almost any housing system work. However, the type of facility will often dictate the number of farrowings per year and management practices to be used. Normally, in selecting housing, you will trade some advantages for disadvantages. That's why final selection must be considered carefully in light of your individual situation.

Types of housing range generally in steps from complete pasture production to totally enclosed, environmentally controlled buildings for all stages of production. Confinement systems featuring partial environmental control fall somewhere in between those extremes with various combinations of housing types being used. Such a unit may have a solid floor central farrowing house and open front buildings for nursery, finishing, and gestation.

SYSTEMS COMPARED

It is often said that increased confinement substitutes capital for labor. More accurately, the trend toward higher-cost confinement housing has permitted operators to spread their labor and management over many more hogs, make more intensive use of facilities and shift production to a year-round basis. Slotted floors have encouraged the shift to confinement by easing manure handling requirements. Animal performance has generally benefited, but it isn't always true that the more expensive the facilities, the better the performance that can be expected.

Farrowing facilities. Confinement of the farrowing operation is the first step in intensifying hog production since it does away with seasonal farrowing. The higher initial investment for confinement permits continuous hog production and reduces labor requirement per hog produced.

Three types of farrowing houses located on the same farm were studied by Missouri University researchers: (1) Enclosed confinement building with a solid concrete floor; (2) enclosed confinement building with partially slotted floor; and (3) individual portable houses with pens in front.

The least economical unit appeared to be the solid floor confinement building, due to high labor requirements for manure handling. Labor was reduced considerably in the slotted floor structure.

FARROWING HOUSE COMPARISON

	Type of farrowing house		
	(1)	(2)	(3)
Live pigs born per litter	10.94	10.14	9.51
Pigs saved per litter	9.71	9.32	8.64
Percent death loss	11.2	8.1	9.1
Daily labor per litter (min.)	10.0	1.7	1.5
Fixed costs per sow and litter	$ 7.29	$13.82	$5.43

Initial investment and fixed costs were lowest for portable houses, but lower production tended to offset that advantage. Nearly one more pig per litter was weaned in the confinement buildings than in the portable houses.

Under favorable climatic conditions, portable farrowing houses on pasture can be profitable. They are particularly well suited to operators with limited capital, lower-cost land, and the need for flexibility. On the other hand, confinement farrowing houses have definite advantages in harsh climates and on valuable cropland; but slotted floors are necessary to justify long-term investments in confinement farrowing.

Growing and finishing. Pigs eat less in hot temperatures to minimize body heat. In a cold environment they eat more to acquire the added energy needed to maintain body temperature. As a result, protection afforded by housing can affect performance significantly.

Summer performance studies in Illinois showed that pigs did better in open front buildings with concrete pads in front than they did in dirt lots. Improvements of about 10% for both rate of gain and feed efficiency were recorded for hogs housed in the buildings.

OPEN BUILDINGS VERSUS DIRT LOTS (Summer)

	Open Front	Dirt Lots
Space/pig (sq. ft.)	10	180
Avg daily gain (lb.)	1.56	1.41
Feed/pound gain (lb.)	3.30	3.69

ILLINOIS

In winter, hogs in ordinary open front buildings did significantly poorer than hogs in either a modified open front structure or in an environmentally regulated house in Nebraska tests. Pigs were finished from 40 to 230 pounds in 119 days in both of the more controlled buildings. Pigs in the open front structure required an additional 22 days and 95 pounds of feed to reach market weight.

Modified open front buildings were then compared to totally enclosed environmentally regulated buildings. The MOF buildings housed hogs totally under roof on partially slotted floors. During winter the exposed side could be closed. Environmentally regulated buildings were fully insulated, heated and mechanically ventilated.

PERFORMANCE IN TWO FINISHING HOUSES

	Modified Open Front	Environmentally Regulated
Fall and Winter Performance		
(Cold)		
Avg. daily gain (lb.)	1.68	1.62
Feed/pound gain (lb.)	3.06	2.88
(Zone Heat)		
Avg. daily gain (lb.)	1.54	1.54
Feed/pound gain (lb.)	3.23	3.22
Utility cost/pig/day	2.24¢	2.46¢
Summer Performance		
Avg. daily gain (lb.)	1.58	1.52
Feed/pound gain (lb.)	3.06	3.13
Utility cost/pig/day	--	0.36¢

NEBRASKA

Comparison of pig performance during the summer showed only a small difference in favor of the MOF building. During winter the colder environment of the MOF building resulted in poorer feed conversion. However, when catalytic heaters were installed to supply zone heat, performance of pigs in the MOF and ER buildings was equal. Although a climate significantly different from that in Nebraska could change the results, these relationships should apply to any area of the U.S. with a moderately cold winter.

Initial investment cost per square foot was calculated to be $7.50 for the MOF building; $9.33 for the ER building, and $5.00 for the open front house. Assuming an area of eight square feet per hog, initial cost per animal is about $15 cheaper for the MOF than for the ER building. Building costs were lowest for the open front building, but total cost of gain was highest due to poorer efficiency and slower rate of gain.

Manure disposal. The type of facilities and nearness to neighbors may dictate the waste system which must be used. Solid waste handling is not being designed into most new building systems since it is not well adapted to mechanical handling and has high labor requirements.

With slotted floors, you have several choices. Manure can be stored in the pit and hauled out or drained to another holding area such as a lagoon at intervals. Some systems allow overflow to drain to a lagoon continuously. Another newer system uses recycled lagoon water to frequently flush manure from beneath the slotted floors.

Some problems with lagoons are that odors can be a problem unless the system is correctly designed and well managed. A large part of the fertilizer nutrients are lost and some method of moving manure to the lagoon will be needed.

LABOR AND FEED REQUIREMENTS

Sizing a new hog enterprise correctly is particularly important when you are planning to produce hogs to take advantage of feed and labor available on the farm. Labor requirements in the table are the estimated hours of direct production labor needed under three housing systems.

Approximate Direct Labor Requirements in Hours per Sow per Year--15 Market Hogs Produced

		Confinement	
Stage of life cycle	Portable pasture	Solid floor	Slotted floor
		hours	
Breeding herd	6.5	6.0	3.5
Farrowing (to 4 weeks)	9.0	8.5	5.0
Nursery (4-8 weeks)	6.0	3.0	1.5
Growing-finishing	14.5	16.0	9.5
Total	36.0	33.5	19.5

Slotted floor housing has a big impact on labor, reducing requirement per pig by about 40%. Highest amounts of labor are usually absorbed by pasture production systems. Even so, there is a large variation between farms with the same facilities. Some highly automated confinement operations report labor need as low as 15 hours per sow (about one hour per finished hog).

FEED REQUIREMENTS (Farrow to Finish)

	Avg. per 220-pound hog sold, lbs.
Sows, dry and gestating	124
Sows, lactating	49
Boars	4
Starting (up to 40 pounds)	50
Growing and finishing	630
Total	857

Feed requirements shown above can be used in planning. Of the total feed requirement, about 25% will be used to raise the pig to feeder weight. Also, figure that 20% of the total 857 pounds of feed will be supplement, leaving about 12.2 bushels of corn needed to produce a finished hog.

Swine Selection Guidelines

Selection of replacements based on sound genetic principles can improve your herd. Production records, visual appraisal and live or carcass measurements are useful tools.

Selection is the basis for any swine herd improvement. Simply stated, it is a decision as to which animals are better. The decision isn't always easy, but its accuracy is critical to herd progress. Once the chosen animals are mated, the influence of that mating will show up in many future generations, affecting the rate of genetic advancement.

A sound selection program should emphasize only important economic traits. Sow productivity, soundness, feedlot performance and carcass merit include the important factors that determine productive efficiency.

Productivity of the sow is perhaps the most important trait. Her ability to settle, the number of pigs she farrows and weans, and total litter weight are measurable indications of her reproductive efficiency.

Physical soundness can affect production and is determined primarily by visual appraisal. Since teat development is heritable, it should be considered in selecting both male and female breeding stock. Straight and strong feet and legs are even more important now that most hogs are raised on concrete. Stress susceptibility has become a significant problem and is reason to disqualify any animals from breeding. Other blemishes and abnormalities, especially those which are genetically derived, should be culled out.

Rate of gain and feed efficiency are the principal measures of productivity from weaning to market. Weight gains are easiest to measure. Measurement of feed efficiency is expensive, but luckily, leanness and growth rate selections, together, correlate well with improvement in efficiency of gain.

Common carcass measurements are: thickness of backfat, loin eye area, length, and yield of lean cuts. In the live animal, the simplest and most common measurement is the backfat probe. More elaborate electronic devices such as the Sonoray and Scanogram make carcass estimates in live animals. Measurements taken after slaughter help predict carcass merit in close relatives.

The table below gives selection guidelines for breeding animals. Although all of the figures are attainable in practical swine operations, you may have to settle for replacement animals with slightly lower qualities. However, these figures should represent at least a minimum goal.

SUGGESTED GUIDE FOR SELECTING BREEDING STOCK

	Boars	Gilts
Litter size	8 or more	8 or more
Teats on underline	12 or more	12 or more
Feet and legs	wide, correct stance; adequate bone	wide, correct stance; adequate bone
Age at 220 pounds	170 days or less	180 days or less
Pounds of feed per cwt. of gain	less than 320	less than 340
Probed backfat at 220 pounds	1 in. or less	1.2 in. or less
Carcass length at 220 pounds	29.5 in. or more	29.5 in. or more
Loin eye area at 220 pounds	4.5 sq. in. or more	4.5 sq. in. or more
Percent lean cuts (liveweight) (carcass wt.)	36% or more 52% or more	36% or more 52% or more

Heritability information. Variations in livestock are due to both heredity and environment. The heritability figures shown in the next table are estimates of how much of the difference between hogs is due to inheritance.

HERITABILITY ESTIMATES FOR SWINE

Level of heritability	Trait	Average percent
High	Carcass length	60
	Percent ham (based on carcass weight)	60
	Backfat thickness	50
	Loin eye size	50
Medium	Percent lean cuts (based on carcass weight)	35
	Feed efficiency	35
	Growth rate (weaning to market)	30
Low	Weaning weight	15
	Number farrowed	10
	Number weaned	10
	Birth weight	5

If a trait has a high heritability percentage, improvement can proceed at a faster rate than for a trait with a low figure. Remember, however, that the reverse is also true. An animal that is very poor in a highly heritable trait can bring about a quicker decline in herd performance.

A basic selection rule is that the more traits selected for, the slower the progress on any one trait. This means that most attention should be focused on highly heritable traits. Characteristics with lower heritability can't be ignored, but too rigid selection for them will slow the overall rate of progress. Good management calls for identifying basic herd improvement needs and placing major selection emphasis on those characteristics.

Basic tools needed in swine selection are not extensive. Good records, a set of scales, and a steel backfat rule should be considered essential items.

Identification of each animal is required. As pigs grow under the same management condition on the farm, production records will help make reliable comparisons between individuals. Visual appraisal, available carcass information, and measurements taken at normal market weights will provide solid information for making selection decisions.

JULIAN CALENDAR

	Jan.	Feb.	Mar.	Apr.	May	June	July	Aug.	Sep.	Oct.	Nov.	Dec.
1	001	032	060	091	121	152	182	213	244	274	305	335
2	002	033	061	092	122	153	183	214	245	275	306	336
3	003	034	062	093	123	154	184	215	246	276	307	337
4	004	035	063	094	124	155	185	216	247	277	308	338
5	005	036	064	095	125	156	186	217	248	278	309	339
6	006	037	065	096	126	157	187	218	249	279	310	340
7	007	038	066	097	127	158	188	219	250	280	311	341
8	008	039	067	098	128	159	189	220	251	281	312	342
9	009	040	068	099	129	160	190	221	252	282	313	343
10	010	041	069	100	130	161	191	222	253	283	314	344
11	011	042	070	101	131	162	192	223	254	284	315	345
12	012	043	071	102	132	163	193	224	255	285	316	346
13	013	044	072	103	133	164	194	225	256	286	317	347
14	014	045	073	104	134	165	195	226	257	287	318	348
15	015	046	074	105	135	166	196	227	258	288	319	349
16	016	047	075	106	136	167	197	228	259	289	320	350
17	017	048	076	107	137	168	198	229	260	290	321	351
18	018	049	077	108	138	169	199	230	261	291	322	352
19	019	050	078	109	139	170	200	231	262	292	323	353
20	020	051	079	110	140	171	201	232	263	293	324	354
21	021	052	080	111	141	172	202	233	264	294	325	355
22	022	053	081	112	142	173	203	234	265	295	326	356
23	023	054	082	113	143	174	204	235	266	296	327	357
24	024	055	083	114	144	175	205	236	267	297	328	358
25	025	056	084	115	145	176	206	237	268	298	329	359
26	026	057	085	116	146	177	207	238	269	299	330	360
27	027	058	086	117	147	178	208	239	270	300	331	361
28	028	059	087	118	148	179	209	240	271	301	332	362
29	029		088	119	149	180	210	241	272	302	333	363
30	030		089	120	150	181	211	242	273	303	334	364
31	031		090		151		212	243		304		365

Age at 220 pounds is a convenient method of expressing growth rate. The Julian Calendar above shows the number of each day in the year and can be used to quickly calculate age in days. Computation is made by weighing the pigs at as close to 220 pounds as possible and determining days of age. Adjustments are then made for poundage varia-

tions by adding one day for each two pounds under, or subtracting one day for each two pounds over 220 pounds actual weight.

Adjusted backfat measurements are particularly useful for prospective breeding stock. Three probes are made, then adjusted to a 220-pound basis using the table below. Measurements are taken at the following points: behind the shoulder, above the front elbow, and back about one inch; at the last rib; and halfway between the last rib and the base of the tail. All probes are made 1-1/2 inches to the side of the midline.

CONVERTING BACKFAT TO A 220 LB. EQUIVALENT

3 Probe Total	WEIGHT RANGE								
	240 238 242	235 233 237	230 228 232	225 223 227	220 218 222	215 213 217	210 208 212	205 203 207	200 198 202
1.5	.42	.44	.46	.48	.50	.52	.54	.56	.58
1.6	.45	.47	.49	.51	.53	.55	.57	.59	.61
1.7	.49	.51	.53	.55	.57	.59	.61	.63	.65
1.8	.52	.54	.56	.58	.60	.62	.64	.66	.68
1.9	.55	.57	.59	.61	.63	.65	.67	.69	.71
2.0	.59	.61	.63	.65	.67	.69	.71	.73	.75
2.1	.62	.64	.66	.68	.70	.72	.74	.76	.78
2.2	.65	.67	.69	.71	.73	.75	.77	.79	.81
2.3	.69	.71	.73	.75	.77	.79	.81	.83	.85
2.4	.72	.74	.76	.78	.80	.82	.84	.86	.88
2.5	.75	.77	.79	.81	.83	.85	.87	.89	.91
2.6	.79	.81	.83	.85	.87	.89	.91	.93	.95
2.7	.82	.84	.86	.88	.90	.92	.94	.96	.98
2.8	.85	.87	.89	.91	.93	.95	.97	.99	1.01
2.9	.89	.91	.93	.95	.97	.99	1.01	1.03	1.05
3.0	.92	.94	.96	.98	1.00	1.02	1.04	1.06	1.08
3.1	.95	.97	.99	1.01	1.03	1.05	1.07	1.09	1.11
3.2	.99	1.01	1.03	1.05	1.07	1.09	1.11	1.13	1.15
3.3	1.02	1.04	1.06	1.08	1.10	1.12	1.14	1.16	1.18
3.4	1.05	1.07	1.09	1.11	1.13	1.15	1.17	1.19	1.21
3.5	1.09	1.11	1.13	1.15	1.17	1.19	1.21	1.23	1.25
3.6	1.12	1.14	1.16	1.18	1.20	1.22	1.24	1.26	1.28
3.7	1.15	1.17	1.19	1.21	1.23	1.25	1.27	1.29	1.31
3.8	1.19	1.21	1.23	1.25	1.27	1.29	1.31	1.33	1.35
3.9	1.22	1.24	1.26	1.28	1.30	1.32	1.34	1.36	1.38
4.0	1.25	1.27	1.29	1.31	1.33	1.35	1.37	1.39	1.41
4.1	1.29	1.31	1.33	1.35	1.37	1.39	1.41	1.43	1.45
4.2	1.32	1.34	1.36	1.38	1.40	1.42	1.44	1.46	1.48
4.3	1.35	1.37	1.39	1.41	1.43	1.45	1.47	1.49	1.51
4.4	1.39	1.41	1.43	1.45	1.47	1.49	1.51	1.53	1.55
4.5	1.42	1.44	1.46	1.48	1.50	1.52	1.54	1.56	1.58
4.6	1.45	1.47	1.49	1.51	1.53	1.55	1.57	1.59	1.61
4.7	1.49	1.51	1.53	1.55	1.57	1.59	1.61	1.63	1.65
4.8	1.52	1.54	1.56	1.58	1.60	1.62	1.64	1.66	1.68
4.9	1.55	1.57	1.59	1.61	1.63	1.65	1.67	1.69	1.71
5.0	1.59	1.61	1.63	1.65	1.67	1.69	1.71	1.73	1.75
5.1	1.62	1.64	1.66	1.68	1.70	1.72	1.74	1.76	1.78
5.2	1.65	1.67	1.69	1.71	1.73	1.75	1.77	1.79	1.81

To take a backfat measurement, make cuts in the skin at right angles to the back with a knife wrapped three-eighths inch from the tip to avoid cutting too deeply. Insert the rule downward toward the center of the animal, through the fat to the top of the muscle. After taking readings, locate the three probe total in the table and find the adjusted measurement under the appropriate weight column.

Swine Breeding Guidelines

Herd breeding programs must be managed according to the specific sexual patterns and reproductive characteristics of hogs. These guidelines are the result of extensive research.

Sexual activity in swine usually begins at between five and eight months of age. Once females reach puberty, estrus or "heat" periods reoccur at approximately 21-day intervals until they are bred.

Maximum reproductive efficiency isn't reached until several months after puberty. Compared with the first heat period, gilts will shed one or two more eggs by the third heat. Number of pigs born and weaned increases until about a sow's fifth litter, then gradually declines thereafter. A boar's sexual drive and semen quality may decline after he reaches about three years of age.

REPRODUCTIVE CHARACTERISTICS OF HOGS

Gestation period	114 days (range 109-220)
Interval between heat periods	21 days (range 18-24)
Heat occurs after weaning pigs	5 days (range 2-10)
Length of heat period	2-3 days (range 1-5)
Best time to breed in heat period	1st and 2nd day
Number of services per sow	Two at 12 to 20 hr. intervals
Gilts:	
Age to breed	8 months
Weight to breed	250-300 lbs.
Boars:	
Age at puberty	5-6 months
Minimum age to breed	7 months

Breeding gilts. Normally, you should wait until the third heat period. Gilts should be eight months of age and weigh at least 250 pounds by that time. While some advantage is gained by inducing earlier puberty and breeding younger, it isn't yet practical for most commercial operations.

Delayed puberty has become more common in confined operations, with some gilts not coming into heat until 9 to 12 months of age. The cause of this problem isn't well understood, though confinement conditions are involved. Several practices will help induce puberty. Sexual stimulation from contact with a nearby boar is probably most helpful. Gilts kept in a pen adjacent to the boar came in heat 40 days earlier in one university test. Moving gilts to pasture or a new location will help induce puberty. Short periods of stress from moving or hauling often cause a large percentage of gilts to come into heat four to six days later.

Flushing gilts is recommended to improve litter size. Increase feed to 6 to 8 pounds about 10 days before breeding. Be sure to reduce feed afterward to keep gilts from getting too fat and to minimize fetal death during pregnancy.

After weaning, sows usually come into heat within five days when pigs are weaned at four weeks of age or older. If sows are in good condition, rebreed them at this first heat. When lactation lasts less than four weeks, the return to estrus in a group of sows is scattered over a longer period of time. Also, fertility at the first heat is generally impaired, so breed at the second heat.

Signs of estrus can usually be observed well before the sow actually comes into heat. Swelling and coloring of the vulva may begin two to six days before actual estrus. The sow becomes restless, frequently sniffs at the genitals of others, and utters typical grunts. Mounting of other sows may begin the day before actual receptivity to a boar.

Sows will accept a boar during a period of about 56 hours. Ovulation occurs about 40 to 42 hours after standing heat begins. As shown in the diagram, the period of peak fertility begins some 14 hours after the onset of heat and generally corresponds to the period a sow will stand to pressure applied to the haunches. However, only about 80% of the sows and half of the gilts will respond to haunch pressure in the absence of a boar.

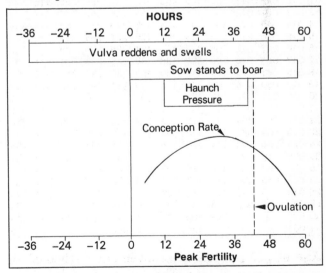

In practice, best conception is usually obtained by breeeding about 20 hours after the sow will stand to the boar, followed by a second mating 12 to 18 hours later. If only one mating is made, wait until about 30 hours after the sow first enters standing heat.

Boar reproductive records show that one out of every 12 untried boars has a reproductive problem causing him to be sterile or subfertile. Using one of these "problem" boars can set your production schedule back badly.

Every new boar should be test mated during the last 30 days of his isolation period from the herd. Using a gilt in heat, observe his aggressiveness and desire to mate. Give some assistance and training if needed during the first service or two, and check his ability to enter and mate normally.

Watching for heat in the gilts 18 to 21 days later will determine if they are pregnant. However, to gain the most confidence in the boar's ability to settle, you should also have a semen sample evaluated.

RECOMMENDED BREEDING LOAD PER BOAR

Age of boar	Number of services		Number of females
	Daily	Weekly	Pen mating (21-day period)
Young (7-9 mos.)	—	2	—
Young (9-12 mos.)	1	7	8-10
Mature boar	2	10	10-15

Proper boar power is determined by the number of times a boar can successfully mate during a given period. It's best to think in terms of services per day or week rather than number of sows per boar. The table shows recommended number of services for boars of different ages.

The table also lists the number of sows you should expect a boar to pen breed efficiently, provided heat periods are rather evenly spaced. If periods are closely synchronized, more boar power is needed. Use young, untried boars sparingly until they are familiar with their duties. Don't pen mate young boars under nine months of age.

When pen breeding, rotate boars in pens at intervals to minimize the effects of a boar that is sterile or subfertile. Breeding by hand takes more labor, but advantages are that it reduces stress on boars and assures you that mating has occurred. Breeding twice at the recommended intervals pays. Research shows that two breedings will improve conception rate 10% and hike litter size one pig compared to breeding only once.

Seasonal effects on reproduction can be fairly dramatic. Fewer females come into heat during the hot summer months and conception rate and litter size are often smaller. High temperatures during the first and the last three weeks of pregnancy are most critical. Semen quality of boars can be reduced for four to six weeks following high temperatures.

In order to keep farrowing facilities full in November and December, an adequate number of females must be bred during July and August. Evaporative cooling, shade and foggers will help reduce the effects of temperature on breeding. Some producers also remove boars from breeding pens during the heat of the day. Still, it's best to expose 10% to 15% more females to boars during hot weather breeding.

SWINE GESTATION TABLE (114 DAYS)

Bred	Jan.	1 2 3 4 5 6 7 8 9 10 11 12 13 14 15 16 17 18 19 20 21 22 23 24 25 26 27 28 29 30 31	Jan.
Farrow	April	25 26 27 28 29 30 1 2 3 4 5 6 7 8 9 10 11 12 13 14 15 16 17 18 19 20 21 22 23 24 25	May
Bred	Feb.	1 2 3 4 5 6 7 8 9 10 11 12 13 14 15 16 17 18 19 20 21 22 23 24 25 26 27 28	Feb.
Farrow	May	26 27 28 29 30 31 1 2 3 4 5 6 7 8 9 10 11 12 13 14 15 16 17 18 19 20 21 22	June
Bred	March	1 2 3 4 5 6 7 8 9 10 11 12 13 14 15 16 17 18 19 20 21 22 23 24 25 26 27 28 29 30 31	March
Farrow	June	23 24 25 26 27 28 29 30 1 2 3 4 5 6 7 8 9 10 11 12 13 14 15 16 17 18 19 20 21 22 23	July
Bred	April	1 2 3 4 5 6 7 8 9 10 11 12 13 14 15 16 17 18 19 20 21 22 23 24 25 26 27 28 29 30	April
Farrow	July	24 25 26 27 28 29 30 31 1 2 3 4 5 6 7 8 9 10 11 12 13 14 15 16 17 18 19 20 21 22	Aug.
Bred	May	1 2 3 4 5 6 7 8 9 10 11 12 13 14 15 16 17 18 19 20 21 22 23 24 25 26 27 28 29 30 31	May
Farrow	Aug.	23 24 25 26 27 28 29 30 31 1 2 3 4 5 6 7 8 9 10 11 12 13 14 15 16 17 18 19 20 21 22	Sept.
Bred	June	1 2 3 4 5 6 7 8 9 10 11 12 13 14 15 16 17 18 19 20 21 22 23 24 25 26 27 28 29 30	June
Farrow	Sept.	23 24 25 26 27 28 29 30 1 2 3 4 5 6 7 8 9 10 11 12 13 14 15 16 17 18 19 20 21 22	Oct.
Bred	July	1 2 3 4 5 6 7 8 9 10 11 12 13 14 15 16 17 18 19 20 21 22 23 24 25 26 27 28 29 30 31	July
Farrow	Oct.	23 24 25 26 27 28 29 30 31 1 2 3 4 5 6 7 8 9 10 11 12 13 14 15 16 17 18 19 20 21 22	Nov.
Bred	Aug.	1 2 3 4 5 6 7 8 9 10 11 12 13 14 15 16 17 18 19 20 21 22 23 24 25 26 27 28 29 30 31	Aug.
Farrow	Nov.	23 24 25 26 27 28 29 30 1 2 3 4 5 6 7 8 9 10 11 12 13 14 15 16 17 18 19 20 21 22 23	Dec.
Bred	Sept.	1 2 3 4 5 6 7 8 9 10 11 12 13 14 15 16 17 18 19 20 21 22 23 24 25 26 27 28 29 30	Sept.
Farrow	Dec.	24 25 26 27 28 29 30 31 1 2 3 4 5 6 7 8 9 10 11 12 13 14 15 16 17 18 19 20 21 22	Jan.
Bred	Oct.	1 2 3 4 5 6 7 8 9 10 11 12 13 14 15 16 17 18 19 20 21 22 23 24 25 26 27 28 29 30 31	Oct.
Farrow	Jan.	23 24 25 26 27 28 29 30 31 1 2 3 4 5 6 7 8 9 10 11 12 13 14 15 16 17 18 19 20 21 22	Feb.
Bred	Nov.	1 2 3 4 5 6 7 8 9 10 11 12 13 14 15 16 17 18 19 20 21 22 23 24 25 26 27 28 29 30	Nov.
Farrow	Feb.	23 24 25 26 27 28 1 2 3 4 5 6 7 8 9 10 11 12 13 14 15 16 17 18 19 20 21 22 23 24	March
Bred	Dec.	1 2 3 4 5 6 7 8 9 10 11 12 13 14 15 16 17 18 19 20 21 22 23 24 25 26 27 28 29 30 31	Dec.
Farrow	March	25 26 27 28 29 30 31 1 2 3 4 5 6 7 8 9 10 11 12 13 14 15 16 17 18 19 20 21 22 23 24	April

Sow Herd Management

Breeding herd profits revolve around reproductive performance. Thus, management should focus on maximizing the number of pigs farrowed and weaned per sow.

Many opportunities exist to improve potential profits in hog operations. The greatest opportunity, however, is through improvement of general performance of sow herds.

High conception rates are essential to profitable farrowing operations. The factors affecting conception are primarily nutrition, health and breeding timing. This is well understood by anyone in the hog business. However, the differences of management in these areas are more frequently reflected in litter size than in overall conception percentage, assuming, of course, that these are not great nutritional deficiencies or disease problems.

The impact of low conception at any given breeding time has further been minimized by the trend to multiple farrowing. Sows that fail to conceive can be rebred with a group scheduled for the next 30 to 60 days without a great loss of time.

Should a sow fail to settle with the second group, she should be removed from the herd.

Nutrition is important for maintaining a high level of reproductive performance. Tight management of the feeding program is needed, since the quality of feed and the quantity must be controlled. Sows will consume energy far above their needs if allowed free access to grain. Feed intake must be limited during gestation, while maintaining protein, vitamins and minerals at proper levels.

Feeding programs for the breeding herd are discussed elsewhere. However, here are the feeding recommendations for gilts and sows that are maintained under drylot or confined conditions.

FEEDING RECOMMENDATIONS

	Percent Protein		Av. Daily Feed, lbs.	
	Gilts	Sows	Gilts	Sows
Pre-breeding	15-16	14	5-6	4-6
Breeding season (flushing)	15-16	14	6-8	6-8
Gestation, early	14	14	4-5	4-5
Gestation, late (last 30 days)	14	14	5-7	5-7

Health programs are important in successful hog production. Past history of disease in the herd will determine individual program needs. In this regard, consult your local veterinarian. There are general guidelines, however.

Vaccinations should be made two to three weeks prior to breeding. The same is true of worming. In some cases these treatments can be made the last two to four weeks of gestation. But sows and gilts should not be wormed or vaccinated during the first two-thirds of the gestation period.

Feeding antibiotics has been extensively researched. The results show considerable variation. However, there have been significant improvements made in litter size where herd history showed high disease levels and litter size was low. Research designed to specifically stress sows at given periods of their pregnancy has shown that embryo loss is quite high when stress occurs in the first two weeks following breeding.

For this reason, antibiotic feeding is frequently recommended for the two weeks prior to breeding and for two to three weeks afterward. Commercial premixes are available that will supply the recommended 250 grams of antibiotic per ton of feed. If your herd has a past history of reproductive organ infections, antibiotic feeding for one to two weeks before and after farrowing is advisable.

Sanitation is a key element in maintaining herd performance and preventing disease. This includes both good housekeeping and management so that diseases are not brought into the herd. The majority of swine diseases are passed by infected carrier animals. Extreme caution is needed when introducing new stock into the herd. Know the health status and background of the herd from which new breeding stock originates. Make sure an adequate vaccination program has been carried out and keep new stock isolated for at least 30 days. Restrict visitors from the breeding herd.

Sanitation of buildings starts with complete removal of all manure, dirt and debris after each group of hogs is removed. Next, a chemical disinfectant should be used on all equipment and buildings. After it is disinfected, the building should remain idle for a week or longer before a new group is moved in to it.

Breeding procedures are frequently at fault when litter size is low. Don't mistake size for maturity in gilts. Gilts should be at least eight months old before they're bred. Ovulation is greater on the second and third estrus cycles. Breeding too early may cost you two to four pigs per litter.

Basically the same thing applies to rebreeding mature sows following early weaning. If pigs are weaned at three to four weeks, both conception rates and litter size will be improved by bypassing the first estrus cycle. Sows' reproductive organs need time to recover from the previous pregnancy and farrowing. When pigs are weaned later, first cycle breeding should result in suitable conception rates and litter size.

BREEDING INFORMATION

Age to breed gilts	8 months
Weight to breed gilts	250-300 lbs.
Length of heat period	2-3 days (range 1-5)
Best time to breed in heat period	1st and 2nd day
Number of services per sow	2 services at 24 hour interval
Interval between heat periods	21 days (range 18-24)
Heat occurs after weaning pigs	5 days (range 2-10)
Gestation period	114 days (range 109-120)

Breeding timing has become an important factor in management with the increasing practice of hand mating. Where labor is available to check sows regularly, hand mating is the preferred procedure. It definitely extends the servicing capacity of a boar. With hand mating the boar should successfully breed 20 to 30 sows.

Double breeding sows has not materially improved litter size, but it has increased overall conception where hand mating is practiced. Sows normally release eggs during the latter part of the heat period. If double mating, breed on both the first and second days of heat. If single breeding is used in your program, heat detection is critical. Breeding on the morning of the second day seems to be the best policy.

When using a pen breeding system, sows should be divided into groups of 10 to 12, with one boar per pen. One mature boar should be able to breed this many sows during a three-week breeding period. Rotating boars between pens is a good practice since it helps minimize the consequences should a boar be sterile.

Facilities alter management methods to a large degree. The trend in the hog business is toward total confinement, even of the sow herd. Still, many large operations are equally successful using "old-fashioned" pasture systems.

Regardless of the basic system used, there are several consistent goals. Space allowances should not be minimized. In confinement, sows need 20 to 35 square feet per head. In dirt lots, allow at least 150 to 200 square feet. On pasture, stock at the rate of 10 to 12 head per acre.

Tie stalls in confinement systems are gaining popularity. The illustration below shows two types and dimensions. Sows remain tethered at all times. This system reduces activity, thereby reducing injuries and possibly, feed costs.

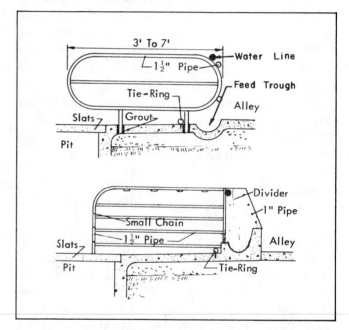

The economic advantages of a tie stall system are difficult to define. However, in operations using this system, producers find that the sow herd can be managed more closely. Individual feeding and treatment of sows are exact and generally, fewer sows are culled under tethered conditions than under pasture systems.

Usually little time is required to adapt sows to tethers. They often quit fighting ties within two to four hours. Temperament of sows in the herd can make a difference in their adaptation to ties. In Canadian operations an initial 20% of the sows failed to adjust. They remained nervous and some did not come into heat. After three generations of selection, this was no longer a problem.

184

Feeding Sows and Gilts

Rations fed from breeding to farrowing affect pig size, vigor and the number of pigs born and weaned. Tight control of both feed quality and quantity is essential.

Of the total number of fertilized eggs shed by the breeding herd, a third or more do not survive and produce a live pig. Both overfeeding and underfeeding will push the proportion higher, but with modern rations most females are overfed on energy. Fat sows have a higher percentage of embryonic deaths during pregnancy and experience more problems at farrowing. Furthermore, overfeeding can increase feed costs by as much as 75% during gestation.

BEFORE BREEDING

If you're selecting gilts from market hogs, pull them out no later than 200 pounds. Some operators know enough about genetic background to make this selection at 125 pounds. You want fast growth without fat accumulation on gilts. By reaching sexual maturity early, gilts can go through more heat periods before breeding at eight months. They seldom should weigh more than 250 pounds at this time. By gaining one pound daily through gestation, they will weigh 350 to 375 by farrowing.

Developing gilts properly requires special attention. Overfeeding is just as common as underfeeding. Replacement gilts should be limit-fed a sow gestation ration to gain around one pound per day. A finishing ration should not be used for gilts which are hand-fed on a restricted intake, since finishing rations are designed to be full-fed. Mineral and vitamin levels will likely be inadequate and may result in poor bone and skeletal development in the gilts.

Hand feeding is usually best for gilts since bulking the ration with ground cobs or alfalfa meal takes more labor and is only partially effective. If gilts are on good pasture, only two to three pounds of feed per day should be adequate. In drylot, figure on four to five pounds—slightly more in rough weather.

Flushing before breeding is recommended for gilts to increase the number of eggs shed. Increase the concentrate ration to six to seven pounds per day about two weeks before breeding to increase litter size. Sows seldom need flushing because they have been on lactation rations with the previous litter. When sows are bred on the first heat period there is no value in flushing. Apparently, weaning pigs has a flushing effect on sows. Most sows will come into heat within four or five days after pigs are weaned. Sows on a restricted diet that haven't been bred for two or more heat periods after pigs have been weaned should benefit from a flushing diet of six to eight pounds of feed for about a week prior to breeding.

BREEDING TO FARROWING

Sows should gain 60 to 70 pounds during gestation, or the weight lost in the previous farrowing and lactation period. Gilts should gain no more than 115 pounds. Gestation rations must furnish the nutrients to maintain the sow's or gilt's body and to develop the unborn litter. Gilts need some additional feed for growth.

Adjust the grain portion of the ration to control growth, but don't sacrifice on ration quality. If a sow receives less than a normal amount of a standard gestation ration to control her weight, she may easily be shorted on key amino acids, vitamins and minerals needed for development of her unborn litter.

Pre-Gestation and Gestation Rations

Ingredient	14% protein (limit fed)		
	No. 1	No. 2	No. 3
Ground milo or corn	1,554 lb.	--	--
Ground ear corn	--	1,553 lb.	--
Ground oats	--	--	1,749 lb.
Soybean meal (44% protein)	300 lb.	353 lb.	159 lb.
Dehydrated alfalfa meal (17% protein)	50 lb.	--	--
Ground limestone	6 lb.	11 lb.	10 lb.
Dicalcium phosphate	58 lb.	51 lb.	50 lb.
Salt (iodized)	10 lb.	10 lb.	10 lb.
Trace mineral premix	2 lb.	2 lb.	2 lb.
Vitamin premix	20 lb.	20 lb.	20 lb.
	2,000 lb.	2,000 lb.	2,000 lb.

After being bred, sows and gilts can be maintained during the first 75 days of gestation on three to five pounds of a 14% supplement such as the three examples shown in the table. During the last third of pregnancy, most of the development of the unborn litter takes place. Beginning about the 75th day of gestation, increase feed to six pounds per head per day.

Methods of feeding to restrict feed intake during gestation include: hand feeding, self-feeding and interval feeding. Hand feeding is recommended because it permits better control of the nutrient intake of each animal. If feeding stalls are used, amounts of feed can be adjusted individually.

Feed intake has proven difficult to control with self-feeding. Sows often become too fat. To control intake, large amounts of bulky materials must be added to the rations. This requires labor and often extra expense.

Allowing sows access to feeders at spaced intervals has been successful in some operations. A common system permits access to feeders for a period of eight hours every third day. Though no decrease in reproductive performance is seen, the main drawback is that sows are not observed as frequently as you might like.

Management systems used on your farm will affect the level of ration needed. On good pasture during the summer, only one to two pounds of concentrate feed may be required. Supply a mineral supplement free-choice to insure an adequate mineral intake. A mixture can be made by combining dicalcium phosphate, limestone and trace mineralized salt in a 2:2:1 ratio.

If silage is fed, sows will eat about 10 to 14 pounds daily and gilts about 8 to 12 pounds. Add 1-1/4 pounds per head daily of a 40% supplement containing adequate vitamins and minerals. Added grain may be needed, depending on the level of grain in the silage.

When hogs glean corn fields in the fall, added nutrients are necessary to balance out their nutritional needs. Feed about three-fourths pound of protein supplement fortified with vitamins. Also provide a free choice mineral mixture.

AT FARROWING

A few days before farrowing, replace about a third of the sow or gilt ration with wheat bran or middlings. This bulky feed is a laxative, preventing constipation during extreme confinement at farrowing. Some operators cut off all feed about 12 hours before a sow is likely to farrow; others idle her along on a few handfuls of bulky feed like bran or ground oats. Water is more important than feed at this stage.

After farrowing, appetite normally returns in a day. Use the same bulky feed as before farrowing, working sow or gilt up gradually. Increase until she is getting a full feed of 15% lactation ration in about a week. As a general rule a lactating sow will eat 2-1/2 to 3 pounds of feed for each hundred pounds of body weight. Another guide is to feed according to the number of pigs nursing. One pound of feed per pig is a rule of thumb.

Lactation Rations

Ingredient	15% protein (full fed)		
	No. 1	No. 2	No. 3
Ground milo or corn	1,263 lb.	--	1,257 lb.
Ground ear corn	--	1,553 lb.	--
Ground oats	--	--	302 lb.
Soybean meal (44% protein)	349 lb.	373 lb.	347 lb.
Dehydrated alfalfa meal (17% protein)	100 lb.	--	--
Ground dried beet pulp	200 lb.	--	--
Ground limestone	4 lb.	12 lb.	12 lb.
Dicalcium phosphate	52 lb.	50 lb.	50 lb.
Salt (iodized)	10 lb.	10 lb.	10 lb.
Trace mineral premix	2 lb.	2 lb.	2 lb.
Vitamin premix	20 lb.	20 lb.	20 lb.
	2,000 lb.	2,000 lb.	2,000 lb.

With three to five week weaning, you have only a brief period of time to get pigs off and growing right. Self-feeding in the farrowing crate or stall, or frequent hand feedings and observation to make sure sows are eating well, is fully justified. About twice as much feed is needed during nursing as during gestation.

Water needs are vital throughout lactation, since milk is over 80% water. This can mean as much as five gallons of water per lactating sow to yield up to 1-1/2 gallons of milk daily. Constant access to clean water will help prevent udder problems and maintain high nutrition demanded at this time.

Antibiotics are sometimes fed at breeding time. They are most effectively used to combat specific problems in the herd. In some herds with histories of breeding troubles, the use of oral antibiotics at therapeutic levels has increased litter size. If antibiotics are fed, they are usually started a week before breeding and discontinued by two to three weeks after breeding.

BOAR FEEDING

Hand feeding boars the same rations used during the gestation period for sows and gilts is a good idea. Young boars in breeding condition usually grow well on six pounds of feed during the first breeding season, and are maintained well on four pounds of feed when not in service. The tendency is to overfeed. However, a boar may become temporarily or permanently sterile if a deficient ration is fed over a period of time.

Baby Pigs—Birth to Weaning

Pigs require close management from birth to weaning. Weaning large litters of healthy, heavyweight pigs is a key factor in swine herd profits.

The three to six weeks from birth to weaning is the shortest but most critical time period in your entire hog program. It takes the right kind of attention, supplemental heat, fortified starter feeds and sanitation to save 90% of pigs farrowed. Set your sights on 35-pound pigs in 35 days to get the most out of capital, management and labor.

Concentrate efforts on (1) saving every healthy pig born, (2) maintaining health and rapid growth, and (3) keeping sows in best condition possible for milking and rebreeding.

Steps to saving pigs start with good gestation rations, farrowing quarters sanitation and pre-farrowing vaccination against diseases such as TGE (transmissible gastroenteritis).

Disease precautions during post-weaning are especially critical. Keep alert to disease problems in your area, and keep visitors away from the farrowing quarters if possible.

When farrowing starts, every pig must breathe normally within minutes and get to the sow for the early colostrum milk to survive. The mothering sow, through this colostrum, provides the newborn pigs with nutrients for early growth and antibodies for combating stress. Pigs have "built-in" ability to absorb these antibodies early in life. But this ability drops about 50% every three hours after the pig has been farrowed; in 12 hours the ability may be totally lost. The resistance acquired by the pig is only against the diseases the sow has been exposed to, and the immunity begins to wear off rapidly within a week. The pig's own disease resistance develops early and exceeds that from sow's milk in about four weeks.

Need for sow-sitting is still highly controversial. Some top operators place their confidence in sow nutrition, crossbred vigor, controlled farrowing environment and farrowing crates on slotted floors without bedding. With considerable management skill, they get big litters without checking sows at night. Other operators similarly equipped still stay with every sow as she farrows, especially the gilts.

Emergency measures to save extra pigs at birth include artificial respiration by use of a plastic funnel inverted over the pig's snout with rhythmic blowing of air into the pig's lungs, and a combination of warmed cow's milk and sugar fed through a small tube inserted in the pig's throat.

Soon after farrowing, pigs should be dried off if chilling is possible, their eye teeth clipped to prevent injury and infection to other pigs or the sow's udder, and their navel cords treated. Pinch rather than cut the navel cord, to avoid bleeding. Apply a weak solution of tincture of iodine, using a new cotton swab for each pig to protect against tetanus. Operators who don't stay with sows feel swabbing or dipping is a waste of time since infection already would have entered. They rely more on antibiotics.

Castration, tail docking and ear notching should be completed within the first three days. Performing these operations early reduces stress and the possibility of infection.

Anemia prevention requires iron injections within three days after farrowing, and a second injection if pigs aren't eating enough creep feed. Inject an iron dextran compound containing 150 mg. of iron into the neck muscle. Repeat at two to three weeks if necessary. Use plastic disposable syringes, or sterilize them to avoid abscesses.

Sow's milk is relatively low in iron and in confinement housing no other natural source of iron is available. If pigs are anemic they grow more slowly and require stronger measures to ward off disease. In addition to shots, iron paste or pills can be given and iron "spools" can be attached to the side of the pen for small pigs.

Don't expect sows to provide all the pigs' nutritional needs until weaning. Peak milk flow is reached about four weeks after farrowing, while pigs' greatest needs come earlier.

Boost early pig growth by giving five-pound pigs a good taste of pre-starter feed. In terms of response, these early feeds can be less costly than growing-finishing rations. Less feed is needed to produce a pound of gain—as little as one pound feed per one pound gain. Early growth rate and thriftiness help later pig performance.

CREEP AND STARTER RATIONS

ingredient	Pigs 10-25 lbs. 1	2	Pigs 25-50 lbs. 3	4
Ground yellow corn	1,151	937	1,383	1,169
Dried skim milk		200		200
Soybean meal (44%)	776	647	561	433
Sugar		100		100
Stabilized fat		50		50
Ground limestone (38% Ca)	11	8	12	8
Dicalcium phosphate	46	42	28	24
Salt	5	5	5	5
Trace mineral premix	1	1	1	1
Vitamin premix	10	10	10	10
Selenium premix (in deficient areas)	1	1	1	1
	2,000	2,000	2,000	2,000
Calculated Analysis				
Protein	22.1	21.7	18.4	18.0
Calcium	0.8	0.8	0.6	0.6
Phosphorus	0.8	0.8	0.6	0.6

Creep and starter rations let pigs get off to a fast start if properly formulated. Optimum protein percentage is about 22% for creep diets and 18% for starter. The trend in recent years has been toward more simplified pre-weaning diets. Diets based on corn and soybean meal plus minerals and vitamins have proven entirely satisfactory.

Baby pigs will perform somewhat better if given milk protein in their diet rather than protein from plant sources. But, common feed ingredients such as dried skim milk may not be available and are often high priced. Research has shown that pigs recover growth deficit soon after weaning.

In most cases an antibiotic or combination of antibiotics should be added to creep and starter rations. The choice and amount to be added to the feed will depend on the disease level on the farm.

Physical environment of baby pigs is important for health and performance. Litter and sow should not contact other sows and pigs for at least one week. Litters may be paired in three weeks. Avoid drafts on pigs; supplemental heat should provide 85° to 90° F. temperature in sleeping area the first week. Shiver mechanism in the pig can't do the job until he's two weeks of age. Withdraw heat source about 5° per week by raising heat lamps.

Transferring pigs to even up litters or to provide mothers for orphan pigs can be successful, pro-

vided the two sows farrow within 48 hours of each other. Before transferring extra pigs to another sow, allow them to nurse. Runts should be destroyed. Spraying a disinfectant on the litter and transferred pigs is helpful in masking odors and getting the sow to accept the pigs. Painting with vanilla extract has also been effective.

Vaccinating pigs is sometimes delayed until eight weeks to avoid added stress with three to six weeks' weaning. Boar pigs shouldn't be castrated and vaccinated at the same time. It is usually a better practice to castrate earlier. Pigs less than six weeks old may not be able to develop immunity when challenged by vaccination.

FEEDING THE MILKING SOW

Sows nursing a litter are often underfed. Lactation rations should be limit-fed during the first few days after farrowing with a light feeding on the first day. Increase daily feed gradually up to nearly full feed by seven to ten days after farrowing. Substitution of up to 20% wheat bran for corn in the ration starting three to five days before farrowing will help prevent constipation. Ground wheat or milo may be substituted pound for pound for corn in the ration.

SOW LACTATION RATIONS

	Rations 1	2	3	4
Ground yellow corn	1,574	1,190	1,226	1,417
Oats		400		
Alfalfa meal (17%)				200
Soybean meal (44%)	359	344	308	322
Wheat bran			400	
Ground limestone (38% Ca)	30	30	30	23
Dicalcium phosphate	21	20	20	22
Salt	5	5	5	5
Trace mineral premix	1	1	1	1
Vitamin premix	10	10	10	10
Selenium premix (in deficient areas)	1	1	1	1
	2,000	2,000	2,000	2,000
Calculated Analysis				
Protein	14.8	15.2	15.0	15.0
Calcium	0.85	0.85	0.85	0.85
Phosphorus	0.50	0.50	0.65	0.50

A good milking sow will lose weight during lactation even though she is self-fed. If you use hand feeding, feed her all she will clean up twice daily. Normally, a lactating sow will eat 2-1/2 to 3 pounds of feed per hundred pounds of body weight. Another guide is to feed according to the number of pigs nursing. About one pound of feed per pig is a rule of thumb.

Feeding Hogs for Market

Management during the growing and finishing phases
should center on making the most economical conversion of feed to pork.

Feeding out the weaned pig for market avoids many of the complexities involved in managing a breeding herd. Thus, efforts during this period can focus on bringing the pigs to sale weight quickly with a minimum of expense. Aim for marketing hogs (210 to 240 pounds) by the time they reach 5-1/2 months of age.

Impact of feed efficiency on potential profits is important since feed costs can amount to three-fourths or more of all costs in a growing-finishing operation. If pigs are to increase their weight by 180 pounds, an average of 630 pounds of feed and a period of four months will be required. Approximately 80% of the feed requirement is grain; nine to ten bushels of corn, or the equivalent, are needed to bring the average pig to market.

Lighter weight pigs make highly efficient gains. But, as shown in the table, each additional pound of gain requires larger amounts of feed, since more feed is required just for maintenance. Feed conversions of 3.2 pounds of feed per pound of gain over the complete period are within reach for many producers, but conversions of 3.5 or 3.6 are probably closer to average. Potential savings by achieving the more efficient rate amount to about one bushel of corn per hog marketed.

Approximate Age	Av. Live Weight	Av. Daily Feed Intake	Av. Daily Gain	Approximate Av. Feed Per Lb. Gain
(days)	(lbs.)	(lbs.)	(lbs.)	(lbs.)
50	30	2.0	1.0	2.0
80	70	4.3	1.6	2.7
97	100	5.5	1.8	3.1
117	140	6.8	2.0	3.4
145	200	8.3	2.1	4.0

Complete mixed rations do the best job of producing rapid growth and low cost of gain. Typical research shows that when a complete ration is compared with free choice corn and supplement, a 3% reduction in feed use and 4% improvement in daily gain are observed. Other advantages of complete rations include better control of supplement consumption and more uniform pigs.

One method of mixing complete rations is to include a commercial supplement with ground grain. Mixing can be done commercially or with a grinder-mixer. A second method, more popular with medium and large sized operations, is to build a ration from the ground up as outlined in the ration formulation tables on this page. Choice of method should be evaluated from the standpoint of cost and convenience, as well as ability to do a good job in feed preparation.

Form of feed provided can affect wastage and feed utilization. Pigs up to 50 to 75 pounds make best use of fine ground feeds. For heavier pigs, however, there is no advantage in fine grinding, and pigs will waste more feed. From a practical standpoint, medium grinding is best (three-eighths to one-half inch screen). Milo should be cracked.

Pelleting hog rations generally proves beneficial by both controlling waste and improving efficiency. On the average you might expect feed savings of 5% to 10% when feed is pelleted. Producers who buy complete feeds should consider pelleting, using the added level of costs required to determine if it is feasible.

Adjust self-feeders to keep waste down. Key is to keep the level of feed in the trough low. If pigs can work agitators just enough to get the feed they want, performance will not be affected. Watch feeders closely since excessive wastage is often difficult to detect. Tests have shown that improper feeder adjustment can account for 3% to 12% of the feed being wasted.

Formulating rations is primarily a problem of supplementing protein, vitamin and mineral ingredients to correct deficiencies in the grain. The following tables showing complete rations and fortified supplements are based on average analyses of ingredients. Use actual analyses if available. Feeds should be mixed carefully for even distribution of all ingredients.

New pigs stressed by weather or shipping should be given a ration with added bulk for about 10 to 14 days after arrival. An excellent starting feed can be made by replacing corn in the ration with 5% to 15% oats. The diet should also contain a high level of broad-spectrum antibiotics.

The fortified protein supplements shown can be mixed with grain for a complete feed. Add supplement according to the level of protein desired. For example, to mix rations containing 16%, 14% or 13% protein, you would add 491, 350 or 281 pounds respectively of the first supplement (37.5% protein) for a ton of complete feed. To achieve the same protein levels using the second (36.2%) supplement, you would add 517, 368 or 294 pounds to make a ton. The free choice supplement shown is designed to be fed along with shelled corn to pigs between 75 pounds and market weight.

COMPLETE MIXED RATIONS FOR GROWING-FINISHING HOGS

Ingredient	50 to 75 pounds		75 to 125 pounds		125 to 220 pounds	
Yellow corn	1,591		1,623		1,654	
Grain sorghum		1,464		1,595		1,624
Soybean meal (44%)	358	487	326	357	295	327
Limestone (38% Ca)	17	18	17	18	17	18
Dicalcium phosphate	22	19	22	18	22	19
Salt	5	5	5	5	5	5
Trace mineral premix	1	1	1	1	1	1
Vitamin premix	6	6	6	6	6	6
	2,000	2,000	2,000	2,000	2,000	2,000
Calculated analysis						
Protein	14.90	18.10	14.30	15.80	13.80	15.30
Lysine	0.70	0.83	0.66	0.66	0.62	0.62
Methionine + cystine	0.50	0.50	0.49	0.43	0.47	0.42
Tryptophan	0.17	0.23	0.16	0.19	0.16	0.18
Calcium	0.60	0.60	0.60	0.60	0.60	0.60
Phosphorus	0.50	0.50	0.50	0.50	0.50	0.50
M.E. kcal/lb.	1,586	1,586	1,587	1,588	1,587	1,588

FORTIFIED PROTEIN SUPPLEMENTS

Ingredient	For Pigs Weighing:		Free Choice Supplement
	40 to 125 lbs.	125 lbs. to Market	
	Pounds per ton		
Soybean meal (44%)	1,705	1,615	1,225
Meat and bonemeal (50%)	--	--	400
Ground legume hay or alfalfa meal (17%)	--	--	200
Ground limestone	50	50	
Dicalcium phosphate or defluorinated rock phosphate	160	250	90
Salt	40	40	40
Trace mineral premix	5	5	5
Vitamin premix	40	40	40
	2,000	2,000	2,000
Analysis: Crude protein, %	37.5	36.2	38.6
Calcium, %	2.9	3.6	2.9
Phosphorus, %	2.0	2.5	2.0

PURDUE

Protein quality in hog diets is more important for efficient growth than the precise level of protein. The real purpose is to provide proper levels of amino acids such as lysine, tryptophan, and methionine + cystine which are deficient in most feedgrains. Complete mixed rations shown in the table have been formulated by a computer to meet amino acid requirements. This accounts for the variations seen in total protein contents.

Cost of protein should be used to determine whether some animal protein should be included with plant protein in the diet. Contrary to what was once believed, soybean meal can supply all of the hogs' amino acid needs. So let cost per pound of protein be your guide.

Grain substitution can reduce feeding costs at times when alternative grains are competitively priced. Wheat can replace corn or milo pound for pound in the ration. Due to its better protein quality, wheat may have a slightly higher value than corn on an equal weight basis. Barley has a value about 90% that of corn, but will reduce gains somewhat if fed as the only grain in the ration. Oats, with about 80% to 85% of corn value, should be limited to no more than 30% of a growing-finishing ration because of its high fiber content.

Vitamins and trace minerals will help to balance out the diet. Shown below are Purdue premix compositions which will balance needs for the mixed rations and supplements shown in the tables on the left. Be sure to check the composition of premixes you are using and adjust the amount in the rations accordingly. Your premix might contain half the level of vitamins as in the premix shown. In that case, double the level in the ration, or feed according to manufacturer's recommendations.

VITAMIN AND MINERAL PREMIXES

Vitamin	Per pound of premix	Trace mineral	% of premix
Vitamin A	400,000 I.U.	Copper	1.0
Vitamin D	40,000 I.U.	Iodine	0.04
Vitamin E	1,000 I.U.	Iron	10.0
Vitamin K	300 mg		
Riboflavin	400 mg	Manganese	4.0
Pantothenic acid	1,600 mg	Zinc	10.0
Niacin	2,400 mg		
B12	2 mg	Selenium premix[1]	

[1]In selenium deficient areas a commercial premix containing 0.02% selenium can be fed at the rate of one pound per ton of complete feed (1 part per million). Otherwise Vitamin E levels should be doubled.

PURDUE

Response to antibiotics varies widely depending on stress and disease level, season of the year and other environmental factors. However, gains are sometimes improved 10% or more and efficiency increased 5%. Young pigs show the biggest response. In practical feeding programs, antibiotics are often fed at the rate of 200 to 250 grams per ton in the growing phase, then reduced to 0 to 50 grams during finishing. Since disease organisms may build resistance to an antibiotic, alternating the kind of antibiotic used is recommended. Follow label recommendations of feeding and withdrawal levels before slaughter.

Managing a Hog Health Program

Probably no swine herd is free of disease. The goal is to avoid introducing new disease organisms and to manage so that problems do not appear. This requires daily attention to detail.

Approximately one-third of all pigs farrowed do not survive to weaning. Losses other than death are difficult to measure, but they are substantial–abortions, poor conception, reduced growth and efficiency. Medication and treatment costs are direct costs to the producer.

Preventing exposure to disease organisms, maintaining animals' resistance, and managing the immune system to increase immunity to common diseases are the key aspects of a herd health program. To accomplish them, a planned program must be set up and followed on a routine basis.

Protection against exposure to disease organisms is the first defense against health problems. Strict sanitation in facilities also dramatically reduces the dose exposure to organisms already present. Thoroughly clean and disinfect the premises and provide a rest period before introducing new animals. Wash sows and clean their udders before putting them in the farrowing house. Clean drinking water is a necessity.

Visitors of various kinds carry diseases. Restrict entry to the facilities and insist that anyone entering wear disinfected footwear. Provide a tray or bucket, along with a brush and disinfectant. Furnishing boots and clothing for off-farm visitors is recommended. Trucks servicing the operation should be required to load and unload outside the production area. Because they can transmit diseases to hogs, dogs and other animals should be kept out with fencing. Control rats around the farmstead.

Take special precautions when bringing in new breeding stock, since this is a primary pathway for disease transmission. New stock should be tested for brucellosis, leptospirosis, and pseudorabies, and purchased from a reputable source. Buy stock early enough to allow at least a 30-day isolation period. Boars should be purchased at least 60 days before using. After an initial 30 days of isolation and observation, retest for the above diseases.

Controlled exposure to common organisms is recommended. Following the boar's 30-day isolation, there should be some cross-exposure between the boar and the herd. This can be done by allowing fenceline contact with sows or by feeding manure. Penning a couple of cull gilts with the boar exposes him to organisms present in the herd and also provides some initial sexual training.

The purpose of cross-exposure between animals is to create a common pool of immunity by controlled exposure to organisms during a noncritical time in the production cycle. For example, by allowing sows and gilts to contact each other at least 3 weeks before entering the farrowing house, they develop some immunity before farrowing. Feed fresh boar manure to gilts at least 30 days before breeding and again 5 days later.

Suggested vaccinations, shown on the back of this page, will vary by region and specific herd. While not all apply to every herd, they demonstrate a routine timetable for vaccinations that is essential to a good health program.

Follow the advice of a local veterinarian in deciding which vaccinations to give. Leptospirosis and erysipelas vaccines have become nearly routine. Others may depend on your particular situation. Your veterinarian may recommend an autogenous bacterin, using the particular strain of organism present on your farm. An example is the oral milk vaccine for *E. coli* scours.

Control parasites. Periodic fecal examinations will determine which types of worms are present and the most effective dewormer. The worming schedule, shown in the following table, should be linked with other practices aimed at preventing the buildup of worm eggs. Rotate pastures and lots, disk lots, and clean and disinfect houses.

If mange is present, the intensive spraying program listed should be followed. Lice are easier to control, and once eliminated, the number of sprayings can be reduced or perhaps stopped.

Preventative medications. Prevent iron deficiency anemia with a commercial iron product at 2 to 4 days, and follow up in 2 weeks with another injection or provide an oral supplement.

Feed additives such as antibiotics and other medications are routinely used to reduce clinical and subclinical infections and to improve growth and feed efficiency. Antibiotics are typically fed in starter and grower rations, up to 75 pounds, and in sow farrowing rations. Chemical residues in slaughtered hogs, particularly from sulfa products, have become an increasing concern. Follow all label instructions and withdrawal times.

Reducing stress improves herd health, since stressful conditions lower the animals' ability to fight off infections and may allow subclinical infections to become full-blown diseases. Provide the recommended space allowance per animal. Limit pens to 20 to 30 animals and don't resort hogs once pens are established. Feed a balanced ration and avoid sudden ration changes. Temperature, poor sanitation, and improper ventilation greatly increase the level of stress. An isolation area should be provided for sick animals.

Disease diagnoses are a key part of the herd health program. Should a disease outbreak occur, consult your veterinarian for a complete diagnosis. In fact, a postmortem examination by your veterinarian should be performed on all dead pigs to ascertain the cause of death. Routine postmortem examinations help detect chronic, slow-moving diseases before they become established in the herd. A devastating disease may be prevented by early vaccination or treatment.

Many producers periodically have slaughter checks made of several hogs to help them monitor the disease level of the herd. If scheduled ahead, this can be done by a veterinarian at the plant. Otherwise, your veterinarian may be able to check the carcasses at a local slaughter facility. Several diseases and health-related conditions can be picked up by these slaughter examinations.

HEALTH MANAGEMENT TIMETABLE

Time (age)	Vaccination and parasite control	Management and breeding
GILTS		
6 months	Deworm; spray for lice and mange; feed fresh manure from boars and sows. Repeat in 1 week. Commingle with cull sows and initiate fenceline contact with boars.	Select gilts with well-developed external genitalia and at least 12 well-spaced nipples (not inverted). Reduce feed intake to about 6 pounds/day until bred.
7 months	Leptospirosis (lepto) (5 serotypes), erysipelas.	—
8 months	—	Breed on 2nd or 3rd heat period (at least twice to different boars).
9 months	—	Pregnancy check (35-60 days postbreeding).
10 months	—	
6 weeks prior to farrowing	Clostridium toxoid. Spray for lice and mange.	—
4 weeks prior	Transmissible gastroenteritis (TGE). Oral *E. coli* milk vaccine or *E. coli* bacterin, atrophic rhinitis (rhinitis). Spray for lice and mange.	—
2 weeks prior	TGE, rhinitis, clostridium, *E. coli* bacterin. Spray for lice and mange, and deworm.	Include feed additive for scours control or sulfa for rhinitis control.
1 week prior	—	Include bulk (e.g., wheat bran 30%, Epsom salts 1%, or potassium chloride .75% of ration). Wash sows with detergent before entering farrowing house.
Farrowing	3rd *E. coli* bacterin (or 1-week postfarrowing).	Record litter and sow information.
4 weeks postfarrow	Lepto and erysipelas. Spray for lice and mange.	Wean. Provide comfort, sanitation, and proper diet.
BOARS		
4-6 months	—	Bring to farm at least 60 days prior to breeding. (Boars are ready for limited use at 8 mos.)
First 30 days following purchase	Retest for brucellosis, lepto, and pseudorabies. Spray for lice and mange, and deworm. Rhinitis.	Isolate for 30 days. Feed unmedicated feed, and observe for diarrhea, lameness, pneumonia, and ulcers.
Second 30 days following purchase	Vaccinate for erysipelas, lepto, and rhinitis.	Feed manure from herd. Commingle with cull gilts, and observe desire and ability to breed. Provide fenceline contact with gilts and sows to be bred.
Every 6 months	Revaccinate for lepto, erysipelas, and rhinitis. Deworm.	—
Every 3 months	Two sprayings at 7-10 day intervals for lice and mange.	—
PIGS		
1-2 days	Iron injection.	Clip needle teeth. Dock tails. Ear notch.
7 days	Rhinitis, pasteurella.	—
2 weeks	Iron (injection or oral).	Castration.
4 weeks	Rhinitis, pasteurella, erysipelas.	Wean.
Weaning + 10 days	Spray for lice and mange.	—
Weaning + 20 days	Spray.	—
Weaning + 30 days	Spray, deworm.	—
4 months	—	Withdraw all feed medication.
5-6 months	—	Slaughter check 10 market hogs.

PORK INDUSTRY HANDBOOK

Chapter 8

Dairy Production

Today's commercial dairy farms differ greatly in many different characteristics including size of herd, level of production and acres of cropland. A given operation in one area might fully and profitably utilize available land, labor and capital, while an entirely different combination of resources might be required to achieve the same objective in another area.

All profitable dairy operations are characterized by high milk production per cow, lower than average feed costs and an above average volume of business.

High production per cow is achieved through a sound breeding and feeding program. An analysis of DHI herd summaries indicates that a herd producing an average of 15,000 pounds of milk annually might reasonably return double the income-over-feed cost that can be expected from a herd averaging about 10,000 pounds.

A sound breeding program requires that you be familiar with the genetics and the desirable traits required for high production. These traits include desirable conformation, size and efficiency, and reproductive efficiency. Another desirable characteristic is a long productive life. The longer a cow can be productively maintained within the herd, the lower the cost will be since there will be less need for purchasing or raising replacement heifers.

A good recordkeeping system is essential for a profitable dairy operation and a sound breeding program designed to continuously upgrade the production of your herd. Records supply the information needed to determine how your herd is progressing and they allow you to continually evaluate individual cows. A good recordkeeping system should be simple, accurate, complete, up-to-date and easy to keep. Individual cow records should include the following information: Birth date and ancestry; weekly and monthly production and total production for each lactation; breeding and calving information; health and veterinary data; periodic milk fat test and lactation fat yield and feed consumed.

Dairy recordkeeping programs are well organized through the National Cooperative Dairy Herd Improvement Program. Several recordkeeping programs are operated through the organization. These programs are as follows:

Official Dairy Herd Improvement Program (DHI) is the most widely used and best developed recordkeeping program. A supervisor visits each enrolled farm each month. He records each cow's production for two consecutive milkings and sends a sample to the laboratory for a fat test.

Owner Sampler (O-S) program ranks second to DHI. Essentially it provides the same information as DHI; however, the records are not considered official. The information on milk yield and sample for testing is obtained and recorded by the dairyman or his employees.

Dairy Herd Improvement Registry Program (DHIR) is sponsored by the breed associations. Records are obtained in accordance with official DHI rules plus a supplemental set of rules, which impose certain restrictions adhered to by the breed associations.

Weigh-a-Day-a-Month (WADAM) is a program which allows dairymen to obtain management information at a somewhat lower cost than official DHI or O-S programs and without the aid of a DHI supervisor.

Alternate AM-PM Plan is operated in several states as an unofficial plan which again supplies the same basic information as DHI and O-S programs. The major difference is that milk weights and samples are taken from one milking each month rather than two consecutive milkings.

The biggest single advantage of recordkeeping programs has been the information they have supplied, making it possible to thoroughly evaluate the genetic merits of dairy sires available through the Artificial Insemination (AI) program. It also has helped each individual producer to select and breed on this basis.

Feed costs comprise more than half the total cost of producing milk. Consequently, it is important to feed for maximum efficiency and production. Dairymen with profitable herds feed around 2 to 2.5 pounds of forage per 100 pounds of body weight daily. Amount of concentrate fed per cow per year may most profitably range from 5,000 to 6,000 pounds. However, from a nutritional standpoint, it is not as much a matter of how much you feed a cow as it is in feeding the proper amount at the right stage of lactation. Nutritional needs vary greatly with the cow's stage of lactation.

Feeding dairy cows no longer has a hit-or-miss approach. Use of computer programs enables a dairyman to tailor his ration to the needs of the individual cow and to formulate the least-cost ration from available feeds.

Methods of feeding, housing and milking may need to be altered as you enlarge your business to increase your production and income.

Planning Dairy Facilities

The trend in dairy facilities is toward larger, more specialized units, mainly to achieve greater labor efficiency. As a result, rather rapid changes are occurring in design and mechanization.

Many benefits are possible from the new innovations taking place in dairying. Milking parlors have increased labor efficiency on many farms, and now the use of free stall housing and automated feeding are further reducing the labor requirements per cow. Liquid manure systems are redistributing labor needs throughout the year.

Careful planning is of utmost importance when combining the many available labor saving innovations into a dairy operation. Your goal should be to arrive at the best labor-capital combination for your particular situation. Because dairying is not a high margin business, investments need to be made wisely, especially since costs other than feed represent from one-fourth to one-third of total costs.

EFFICIENT COW TRAFFIC

Movement of cows into and out of the milking parlor is a bottleneck in many operations. Alleys should be at least 12 feet wide for cow herds of between 30 and 40 head. Larger herds will require even wider alleys for smooth cow movement. Using loose housing allows about 50 square feet of barn space per cow.

Cow traffic should be routed in a circular pattern as shown in the illustration. Animals should come from the rest area into the holding area, through the parlor and back to the rest or feeding area. Cows should enter and exit the parlor in a straight line, without hindrance from steps or slopes.

Every dairy complex should have a premilking holding pen. It reduces herding time and in most cases can be automated with a moving gate to push cows toward the parlor. In some situations a holding pen for cows already milked helps to save labor. Holding areas should provide about 20 square feet per cow.

It is desirable to provide for isolation pens just beyond the milking parlor. Arrange them so you can easily divert cows into them as they leave the parlor. Pens should have stanchions for securing the cows, and one pen should contain several stanchions for holding cows for breeding and pregnancy testing. A good rule is to provide one pen for each ten cows in the herd.

Building new facilities, rather than remodeling, will usually allow you greater freedom in designing your operation to achieve maximum use of space and labor. Topography and existing structures may pose some problems. However, various studies indicate that new facilities will usually require only a few more years to pay for themselves than remodeled facilities.

Even though some present facilities might be made part of the expanded complex, the reduction in initial capital required may be small compared to the increased labor efficiency possible in a new setup. Old facilities may fit other areas of the operation better than they could be incorporated into the milk cow complex.

EXAMPLE OF COW, MANURE AND FEED HANDLING DESIGN

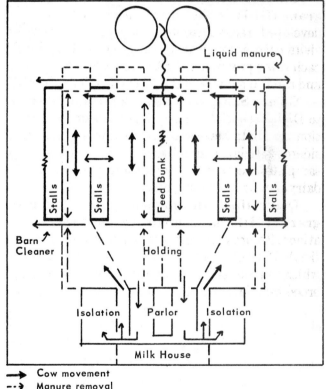

→ Cow movement
--→ Manure removal

Adding a parlor to a stanchion barn can be profitable, but careful planning is necessary to achieve the full benefits which are possible through this investment. Research on Connecticut farms turned up a wide variation in the labor efficiency which was achieved by adding a milking parlor to a stanchion barn. The average milking rate achieved on these farms was only 25 cows per hour. This compares with 35 to 40 cows per hour using a herringbone system coupled with free stalls.

The major problem encountered on these Connecticut farms was wasted time in moving cows to and from the stanchions. Holding pens are essential with stanchion-milking parlor setups. It's preferable to have pens for holding animals both on the way in and out of the parlor.

A pipeline or portable dump station can also be added to a stanchion barn for reducing labor needs. A dump station can be installed for considerably less than a complete pipeline. These units save time, but the dump station still requires lifting heavy buckets, and limits labor efficiency.

It may be more profitable to mechanize feeding and manure removal than to either build a parlor or add an around-the-barn pipeline. A number of systems with varying degrees of mechanization can be used.

PLAN EASY MANURE REMOVAL

Facilities should allow for straight-line pushing of manure from rest, feeding and holding areas. This may require several outlets, and it may mean more than one manure holding pit. Consider a mechanical gutter cleaner for moving manure from dunging areas to the storage or spreader unit.

Avoid pushing manure from wide alleys into narrow alleys. Make long sweeps with the scraper or pusher. Build curbs high enough to avoid spillover into stalls and alleys and locate pits outside cow traffic areas where possible to reduce investment in manure storage. Reinforced concrete lids often make up over half the investment in manure storage.

Alleys and floors should slope toward manure outlets, unless rainfall will create overflow problems. If you make alleys wide enough for easy cow movement you'll generally have sufficient space to maneuver manure removal equipment. Proper selection of implements, blades and buckets is necessary.

THE FEEDING SYSTEM

The feed distribution system should be included in your facility plans, but it shouldn't take precedence over design features for efficient cow traffic and manure removal.

The type of feed distribution system will depend to a large extent on the forage being fed. Hay feeding systems can be worked into free stall milking parlor systems at little disadvantage. Limit-fed animals need 24 inches of space at the manger per cow, while self-fed cows or those getting feed three or more times per day will only need about six inches per animal.

Feed storage units should be easily accessible for filling as well as removal of feedstuffs. Investment in extra conveying equipment can eliminate problems which may exist.

FLEXIBILITY FOR THE FUTURE

While specialization tends to limit the flexibility of many dairy facilities, much of this freedom can be retained through advanced planning. In the illustration, expansion is possible by adding on to either side of the present structure. Additional space for storage of forage can be built at the end of the barn, either in a clump or strung out along the upper side of the barn.

Another parlor might be added to one side of the existing parlor. Additions to the barn itself can be made on either side, using the same milking parlor and isolation units. The initial parlor might be made large enough to permit adding additional stalls at any time. Allowing plenty of holding area would also permit you to add automatic washing stalls at a later time.

Noncritical factors include cold versus warm housing, construction materials, type and size of feed storage, bedding versus mats and type of manure handling. Though important to your total success, these should be secondary to and not interfere with the four critical factors which have been discussed.

Complete Dairy Rations and Group Feeding

Complete all-in-one rations, fed outside the milking barn, can save labor and offer certain nutritional advantages. In many herds, group feeding can provide further benefits.

Group feeding and complete rations are not synonymous. Milk production efficiency is improved in larger herds where cows can be grouped according to production level and fed complete rations. In smaller herds, where separating cows into groups isn't feasible, the convenience and laborsaving aspects of complete feeds have advantages.

COMPLETE FEEDS

Blending the concentrate and roughage portions of the ration together has several advantages. First, cows eating a complete feed no longer consume individual feedstuffs according to preference. Each bite of a complete feed provides balanced nutrition. Further, complete feeds help solve the serious problem of getting enough energy consumption into high producing cows. Grain consumption isn't limited by time in the milking parlor.

Laborsaving may be the primary advantage in many herds. Feeding can be automated to a greater degree, and most operators have experienced a substantial labor reduction when they changed to complete feeds. Cows can be milked faster and there is less dust and manure in the milking barn.

More flexibility of ration ingredients is another key benefit. Complete feeds permit easier use of computer and least-cost formulations. By-product feeds can easily be included, and major ration adjustments can be made without digestive upsets. Since cows consume the ration more frequently and in smaller amounts, urea and other NPN supplements are utilized more effectively.

Milk production on complete rations has been at least as good as traditional feeding systems. In one California trial, cows fed complete rations produced 3.1 pounds more milk per day than other cows fed the same roughages and concentrates supplied separately. Fat test was unaffected, but solids-not-fat was slightly higher for the complete ration group.

Cow movement into the milking parlor is commonly considered a major problem with a complete feeding system. However, experience has shown that most herds can adapt readily when no grain is offered during milking. Some herdsmen report that after an initial training period, cows are actually more calm and relaxed during milking. Parlors such as individual side opening types may cause more difficulty, however, since cows do not enter them in groups.

Some operators prefer to feed a minimum level of grain in the parlor, but that increases labor and equipment needs.

Feed mixing equipment is needed to thoroughly blend feedstuffs and prevent cows from sorting ingredients. A mixer wagon equipped with load cells to weigh ingredients can be used to feed cows at several locations. It is most efficient in a drive-through feeding setup. Stationary mixers mounted on scales can be used in other feeding systems.

A complete feeding system doesn't adapt well to long hay or bales. Hay must be shredded or coarsely chopped for complete mixing. If cows are grouped, additional facilities or building modifications may be needed. These factors make some operations much easier to adapt to complete feeds than others.

Correct ration formulation is highly important in a complete feeding program since cows can't select among ingredients. Precise specifications for complete feeds haven't been fully researched. However, basic guidelines shown in the table are being used successfully, and are suggested by California dairy specialists.

COMPLETE RATION GUIDELINES*

Roughage (min. %)	50.0
Crude fiber (min. %)	17.0
Crude protein (min. %)	13.0
Calcium (min. %)	0.6
Phosphorus (min. %)	0.4
Nonprotein nitrogen (max. %)	0.45

*Air dry basis (90% dry matter).

Salt should be provided free-choice or included as 0.5% of the ration. Concentrate level between 30% and 50% of the feed will meet requirements for most levels of milk production. When all milking cows are fed a single complete ration, a ratio of 40% concentrates to 60% roughage has been very successful.

Fiber content needs special attention in complete feeds. Inadequate fiber can depress rumen function, causing low fat tests and digestive problems. Include 17% fiber as a minimum in the feed and maintain adequate roughage particle size.

Feedstuff analysis is recommended for control of feed composition and cost efficiency.

GROUP FEEDING

Group feeding results in more efficient conversion of feed to milk than when all cows in the herd are fed the same ration. Usually, little difference is seen in milk production between group and non-group fed herds, but feed cost per cwt. of milk sold consistently favors those fed in groups.

Feeding in groups permits high producers to receive enough energy to produce milk at maximum efficiency. At the same time, lower producers are more efficient since they are not allowed to convert excess energy into body fat.

It's best to divide the herd into two or more groups if possible, and feed different rations. Often the housing type and facilities will determine how easy it is to switch to group feeding. The number of cows needed to justify group feeding will vary in individual herds, but generally two or more groups of 30 to 40 cows are needed. This often limits group feeding to medium or large sized dairy operations.

Grouping by production is the most common system. Either two or three groups of milking cows are maintained separately and fed feeds containing different levels of energy. Dry cows are separated from the milking herd, and first calf heifers are either fed separately or included in the high or medium producing groups.

Cow groupings should be determined from the range in production levels of cows in the herd. For a two-group system, a common breaking point between groups is the 50 pound per day production level. One three-group system breaks cow groupings into those below 55 pounds; those above 55, but below 80 pounds; and those above 80 pounds.

The group of highest producing cows in the herd should receive maximum concentrates (about 50% of the ration on a drymatter basis). The medium group will receive from 30% to 40% concentrates, and the low producing group, including cows during late lactation, will get 10% to 25% concentrates in the mixed feed. The table gives suggested drymatter composition of rations fed to low, medium and high producing cow groups.

SUGGESTED TOTAL RATION COMPOSITION

	Production Level			Dry cows
	High	Medium	Low	
	(% of dry matter)			
Crude protein	16-17	15-16	14-15	12-13
Total digestible nutrients	72+	68-72	65-68	60-65
Fat	2	2	2	2
Calcium	0.7-0.9	0.7-0.9	0.7-0.9	0.7-0.9
Phosphorus	0.4-0.5	0.4-0.5	0.4-0.5	0.4-0.5
Magnesium	0.2	0.2	0.2	0.2
Potassium	0.8-1.1	0.8-1.1	0.8-1.1	0.8-1.1
Salt	0.5	0.5	0.5	0.4
Sulfur	0.2	0.2	0.2	0.2
Iron (ppm)	100	100	100	100
Cobalt (ppm)	0.1-10	0.1-10	0.1-10	0.1-10
Copper (ppm)	10	10	10	10
Manganese (ppm)	20	20	20	20
Zinc (ppm)	40-80	40-80	40-80	40-80
Iodine (ppm)	0.6	0.6	0.6	0.6

CORNELL UNIVERSITY

Objections to grouping cows according to production center on the stress caused by shifting cows between groups. Most groups are reshuffled monthly on the basis of DHIA tests. Once cows enter a new group, a new order of social dominance must be established. However, research at Ohio State University has shown that the effect of transferring cows to another group is minimal. Production levels of new cows in the group fell 1.5 pounds only during the first day after moving. There was no effect on other cows in the group.

Lactation stage groupings can also be used and they overcome the need to shift cows between groups. In this system cows stay in the same group throughout lactation. Cows are placed in the group as they freshen. At some point one group is closed and a new group is begun.

Forage and concentrate levels of the rations for each of the groups must be adjusted as the lactation proceeds and milk production falls. To be practical, herds using this grouping system should be large enough to have at least two groups of fresh cows containing 40 to 60 cows each.

Electronic feeders are being used to allow high producing cows access to extra grain while others consume only the complete feed balanced for their needs. Cows can adapt themselves rather easily to the feeders, but a high level of management appears to be needed in order for the system to work satisfactorily. Boss cows are a problem and may bully the high producers away from the feeders. The system works best if cows have been grouped to eliminate bossy cows as much as possible.

Dairy Herd Sire Selection

Making the best use of the genetic advantages offered by artificial breeding requires a careful analysis of sires selected for use in the herd.

The bull has a tremendous impact on production progress in a dairy herd. He contributes 50% genetically to each new generation. Since 70% to 100% of all heifers born must be saved for replacements, he may contribute over 90% of the genetic makeup of your herd in four generations.

HERITABILITY VARIES

The variation in the heritability rate for different traits makes some more important to your breeding program than others. Selecting a sire with a poor record for a highly heritable trait will pull your herd downward in a hurry. Yet, traits with a lower heritability rate must be considered regularly as they are more difficult to improve. A longer term program is necessary to improve these less heritable factors.

HERITABILITY OF DAIRY COW TRAITS

Trait	Heritability Value %
Length of teats	75
Percent butterfat content	55
Disposition (temperament)	40
Diameter of teats	35
Udder attachments:	
fore udder	30
rear udder	16
Milk production	25
Butterfat production	25
Dairy character score	25
Final type score	25
Mastitis resistance	25
Speed and ease of milking	24
Mammary system score	20
Size and shape of udder	14
Feet and legs	12

The overwhelming importance of milk and butterfat production per animal in dairy herd profit demands that these two traits receive top priority in any breeding and sire selection program. Fortunately, as you can see in the accompanying table, both of these are inheritable at about the same level, and usually they both go the same direction.

Butterfat and protein content of milk are also important. Specialized markets may pay premiums for high test milk, and at least 3% butterfat content is needed for whole fluid milk nationally. This factor may get second priority.

SELECT FOR OTHER TRAITS

Other factors are also of economic importance to the dairyman. Studies show that cows with high first lactation production typically stay in the herd longer, and 40% of cows culled annually are due to low production. But you still must have a solid animal to gain longevity. For instance, udder problems cause about 14% of cow culling. Size and shape of udder and teats and ease and speed of milking are important.

The cow's feet and legs, pelvic region, dairy character and mastitis resistance are also important to a long, productive and profitable life. Cows that last the longest are usually the cows with higher type scores. Look for high production first and then the body and mammary system traits that allow a longer life.

The primary limitation is that the more traits on which you base selection, the lower the progress for any one given trait. For instance, if you are selecting for milk production, but decide to add equal selection for one other trait, you slow progress in improving milk production to about 70% of that possible. If you select for three or four traits, progress slows to 60% or 50% of that possible with only one trait. You should select highly heritable traits which will give you the best return on each dollar invested.

The economic advantages of artificial insemination versus keeping a bull on the farm are such that dairymen should be using AI almost exclusively. It's no longer a matter of which costs more. Rather, it's a matter of the improvements possible via each route—and there is no question that AI offers the greatest possible improvement on an individual cow basis.

DAIRY SIRE SUMMARIES

The tool that has really made the big difference between the economics of natural versus AI service is the dairy herd sire summary now available on most AI bulls. This summary gives you the true genetic value of each bull and the amount of improvement you can expect.

The predicted difference of a sire is a measure of his transmitting ability to his daughters. The value given is the expected production difference between his daughters and their herdmates in herds with average production for the breed. This difference is obtained by comparing the sire's daughters with other animals which freshened during the same period of the year, with the production figures adjusted for age and geographic region of the country.

The figure itself is based on the breed average production, so if your herd is above or below the breed average, your actual predicted difference would vary. A rule of thumb is for every 1,000 pounds of milk your herd differs from the breed average, you should change the predicted difference figure given by 100 pounds. If you are above the breed average you would subtract 100 pounds from the predicted difference given, but if below you should add 100 pounds.

Applying this rule of thumb, you can see that more rapid progress can be made with high P.D. bulls in herds that are below the average production for the breed. For example, a herd that is producing 2,000 pounds higher than the average would need a bull with a P.D. of plus 200 pounds of milk just to stay even. The same bull used in a herd 2,000 pounds below the average would be expected to improve production approximately 400 pounds per lactation in his daughters.

The repeatability figure for a sire is a statistical measure and tells you approximately how much you can depend on the particular bull to transmit the given amount of production improvement shown. It is based on the number of daughters on which records have been kept, the number of herds they were in and the number of records kept per daughter being used in his daughter-herdmate comparison. The greater the number in each of these categories, the more reliable the predicted difference of the bull will be. A repeatability of 70% or greater is considered high, although some popular and well-proven bulls can reach 99%. A repeatability of 30% or less is considered low.

When using the predicted difference and repeatability figures, you should balance them out in your herd breeding program. Select bulls with high predicted differences—certainly not bulls with a negative predicted difference. Depend on bulls with high repeatability. At least 70% of your herd should be bred to bulls with 70% or higher repeatability.

You can use bulls with less than 30% repeatability on up to 10% of your herd, but use several bulls rather than just one. This improves your chance of getting high quality offspring while giving young bulls a chance to prove themselves. The other 20% of your herd can be bred to bulls with between 30% and 70% repeatability figures.

Other factors to consider. Older bulls should be discounted about 50 pounds of predicted difference for each year they are older than the younger bulls with which they are being compared. The older bull naturally has a higher P.D. because the herdmates his daughters were compared with in making his record were less productive than the herdmates of the younger bulls now being tested.

Another important factor is the percent of first lactation records not completed. It can be used as a guide to the number of daughters that did so poorly they were culled early. There is considerable variation between bulls on this factor since some bulls have up to 25% incomplete first lactation records. Avoid bulls with more than 10% to 12% incomplete first lactation records.

Information available from A.I. firms that market semen from particular bulls should give specific data on the physical traits passed on to daughters. Use traits such as disposition, ease of milking, udder shape, and soundness of feet and legs in your selection program, particularly when you have a deficiency in any given trait.

Your bull selection program may vary somewhat according to the specific needs of your herd and other management factors. However, these general guidelines should be followed in most herds:

● Breed 70% to 80% of your herd including heifers to proven bulls shown to be reliable in increasing production. Use bulls with at least a 500-pound improvement for milk production, and a repeatability of at least 70% for holsteins—60% for other breeds.

● Pick a few sires with the highest P.D. and select from among them the bulls that can improve one or two traits that are most in need of improvement in your herd.

● Breed at least 20% of your herd to carefully selected young sires that are in the process of being proved.

Raising Dairy Replacements

On the average, half to three-quarters of all heifers born must be saved to replace culls and maintain herd size. Proper care of this young stock is fundamental to future herd prospects.

The primary goal in raising dairy herd replacements is to produce a heifer for the lowest possible cost and at the same time maintain the quality of the heifer. A better calf makes a better cow, and therefore the best place to begin a program for improving your herd is with the replacement heifers. With the right combination of breeding, feeding and management you'll be able to control your costs while bolstering your milking herd.

THE NEW CALF

For several reasons, it's very important that the calf get colostrum early. First, it is highly concentrated with both fats and solids-not-fat, but they diminish rapidly during the first 24 hours. Second, the first milk contains disease fighting antibodies which are absorbed directly through the calf's stomach walls into the bloodstream during the first few hours. And third, colostrum contains vitamin A which also helps reduce disease problems in young calves.

The calf should be provided with a dry stall that is free of drafts, but well ventilated to prevent high humidity. Individual stalls work best for the first two months of the calf's life since they prevent contact with other calves and sucking. Slotted floors and wire bottomed stalls keep the calf dry without need of much bedding and with less frequent cleaning.

Daily feeding schedule given in the table can be followed during the first two months. Feed whole milk or colostrum for the first three days. Feeding milk or milk replacer longer than two months is uneconomical since the calf can do as well on grain and good hay. Getting calves off milk early is also helpful in reducing scours. Calves may be weaned as soon as the calf is eating 1 to 1-1/2 pounds of grain per day—usually at about four to five weeks.

Milk replacers can be worked into the ration beginning at three days. The normal mix is one to nine pounds water, but follow the directions. Overfeeding is a major problem with young calves. Heavy breeds should be fed no more than 10% of body weight daily and light breeds no more than

8%. Signs of digestive problems mean you should cut back on the amount fed for a few feedings.

SUGGESTED DAILY FEEDING SCHEDULE FOR DAIRY CALVES

Age in days	Milk		Replacer		Grain	Hay	
	Breed Size		Breed Size			Breed Size	
	Large	Small	Large	Small		Large	Small
	Pounds						
0 to 3	8	6	0	0	0	0	0
4 to 5	8	6	0	0	0	0	0
6 to 10	8	6	.9	.6	*	0	0
11 to 20	9	7	1.1	.7	.6	*	*
21 to 30	8	8	1.2	1.0	1.0	.4	.2
31 to 40	6	7	.9	.9	1.3	.7	.3
41 to 50	5	3	.5	.7	1.7	1.0	.6
51 to 60	2	4	.2	.5	2.2	1.4	.9

*Some offered, but amount eaten is usually very small.

The practice of feeding soured colostrum until weaning or until the supply runs out has increased in herds during recent years. The "first milk" is easily stored and cuts down on early feeding cost. It is also more easily digested and apparently aids in the prevention of scours. Calves should receive about four pounds of sour colostrum per day, diluted with the same amount of warm water.

Calf starter can be offered free choice as early as five to seven days of age. Encourage calves to eat by placing a small amount in their mouths or letting them suck it from your fingers. The feed should contain 16% to 18% protein with molasses added to encourage consumption.

If you prepare your own starter, add 1% each of dicalcium phosphate and salt. Use a natural protein supplement with coarsely ground grain. About 30% of the ration can be rolled oats. Provide about 0.5% antibiotics in the ration unless they are being supplied in the milk replacer, but be sure antibiotics are used during the first two months. Adding vitamins A and D is recommended.

THE GROWING CALF

Consumption of starter feed will increase rapidly once the calf is weaned. Calves should continue to receive three to five pounds of starter plus good quality hay until they are seven to eight weeks old. Don't feed over six pounds of grain since intake of hay needed to get the rumen functioning will be decreased.

By three months of age calves will grow normally on grain and good hay or silage. Provide 12% to 13% protein in the total ration plus salt and minerals. Two to four pounds of grain are usually sufficient. By nine months of age growth can usually be maintained on silage or good quality forage. Extra energy is needed only with low quality roughages.

Feed requirements needed to raise a two year old dairy heifer are approximated in the following table. Feeding these amounts should give you heifers that can be bred at 15 months of age and will be ready to freshen at 24 months.

APPROXIMATE FEED REQUIREMENTS FOR DAIRY HEIFERS

Months of age	Milk** lbs.	Holstein Grain lbs.	Hay lbs.	Milk lbs.	Jersey Grain lbs.	Hay lbs.
1 and 2	300	80	45	200	55	30
3 and 4	0	190	200		168	110
5 and 6	0	180	425		155	315
7 and 8		125	600		125	415
9 and 10		*	880		*	585
11 and 12		*	1,050		*	695
Total to 1 year	300	575	3,200	200	500	2,150
13 and 14	0	*	1,180		*	800
15 and 16			1,280		*	870
17 and 18			1,400		*	900
19 and 20			1,500		*	920
21 and 22			1,590		*	965
23 and 24		300	1,350		300	995
Total 1 to 2 years		300	8,300		300	5,450
Total: Birth to 2 years	300	875	11,500	200	800	7,600

*Two to four pounds of grain daily will be necessary with low quality forage.
**25 pounds of milk replacer can be substituted for most of the milk.

Either individual or group pens and stalls can be used from two months old to pasture age. Again, slotted floors are proving to be desirable. Humidity and drafts must be controlled so facilities should be well ventilated and kept dry and clean.

Your choice of pasture or confinement growing from six months of age until freshening will depend on pasture availability and cost. Note that grain should be fed through eight months and again during the two months prior to freshening. Also, you may want to feed grain during the 13 to 16 month period to get animals bred. Improved mechanization of feeding and manure removal are making confinement growing profitable.

Prevention of disease should be a fundamental part of all calf programs. Most calves have some immunity that is provided by the colostrum until four to six months of age. However, this immunity is of little value if poor environmental conditions are not eliminated. Studies show that housing density of young calf quarters and damp, poorly ventilated conditions can contribute greatly to disease outbreaks. Provide a clean, dry environment and properly sanitize feeding utensils for young calves. When a calf becomes sick, always isolate it from the others and then provide treatment.

Use the advice of your veterinarian for vaccinations needed locally. Normally, heifers should be vaccinated for IBR between six and twelve months of age. BVD vaccine should be given between eight and twelve months of age; at least two months before breeding. Calfhood vaccination for brucellosis should be given between two and six months of age.

VARIETY OF GROWING PROGRAMS

Research points up one fact—calves must be fed close to the schedules shown or they will be slow growers, slow breeders and late fresheners. Arizona research has revealed that size is more important than age for early breeding and early freshening. Holstein calves used in the research grew rapidly without fat, and were bred at nine to ten months of age, weighing 650 to 750 pounds. These heifers freshened at 19 to 21 months and had few problems. Calving problems and rebreedings were normal. Udders were more poorly shaped, but they outgrew this problem.

NORMAL HEART GIRTH AND WEIGHT OF HEIFERS

Age in Months	Holstein Inches	Pounds	Jersey Inches	Pounds
Birth	31	96	24-1/2	56
2	37	161	32-1/2	102
6	50	396	44-1/2	277
9	57	559	51-3/4	409
12	62-1/2	714	56-1/2	520
15	65-1/4	805	59	585
21	71-1/2	1,025	64	740

It does not pay to go beyond 27 months at first freshening. Your profits will be highest by freshening at 23 to 26 months, even though first lactation production may be slightly less than for older animals. More milk production over the heifer's lifetime will result from getting the animals into production quicker, and most dairymen will realize lower growing costs by reducing freshening age. Feed costs will be about the same regardless of the program used if breeding is scheduled at 15 months. Waiting until the heifer is 24 months of age to breed means much higher feed costs.

Dairy Reproductive Management

Breeding problems can eat into dairy profits in a hurry.
Careful, systematic management is needed to keep breeding efficiency high.

Low breeding efficiency can be one of the most serious and frustrating problems dairy managers face. Since milk is a by-product of the reproductive process, problems with reproduction cause serious declines in herd production. Top cows are often culled because of poor reproduction; treatment and breeding costs mount up quickly; and the loss from fewer calves can be sizable.

Dairy breeding economics show that one calf per cow every 12 to 13 months results in the greatest net return. Make that schedule your goal in herd management. While arguments can be made for management practices which would lengthen the breeding schedule, they will not add to overall herd profits.

Gearing the breeding program to a one-year calving interval means drying off cows after 10 months of lactation. This allows at least 60 days rest before calving. Cows are rebred after 60 days of their new lactation.

A systematic approach to managing herd reproduction is needed for good results. As with most other areas of management, reproduction interlocks with other herd practices: herd health, nutrition, dry cow management, housing, etc.

A good approach is to first identify the factors that are critical to maximum reproductive performance. A written-out program for your herd that specifies routine daily and periodic tasks can be very helpful.

Then, translate the program into action. Make record keeping, heat detection, breeding, pregnancy testing and health practices part of your regular working routine. Assign particular responsibilities to yourself and other workers. For instance, one person should be ultimately responsible for getting cows settled.

Heat detection is probably the biggest roadblock to efficient reproduction, particularly in herds using artificial breeding. A Minnesota study found that 90% of the cows that were not detected in heat had actually been cycling. Only 10% of those missed were not ovulating due to abnormalities.

Time spent watching for heat may be more profitable than any other chore. Still, heat detection is easily slighted in a busy farming operation. Convenient times to check heat are often the poorest times for detection. Feeding time is one of the worst. On the other hand, the first thing in the morning and the last thing in the evening are good times.

Normal cows show several signs of heat and most dairymen are alert for these signals. Still, some are better than others at catching cows in heat. A general rule is to know your cows and be alert to changes in behavior. Below are some guidelines:

- Watch cows closely that are standing together at the edge of a larger group.
- Bellowing or attempting to ride other cows may indicate heat is approaching.
- Restlessness, frequent urination and fence walking are signs.
- Appetite and milk production may be reduced.
- Milking pattern may change. Let down may be slower or faster.
- Standing to be ridden is the surest sign the cow is in heat.
- Mud or ruffled hair over the tail can indicate a cow has been ridden.
- The lips of the vulva often become flabby and wet.
- Clear strings of mucous may be discharged from the vulva. This may be the best signal for cows that show no other signs.
- Some cows show a bloody discharge about two days after heat occurs. Although it's too late for breeding, this is a good indication of when heat occurred.

Cows should be watched for signs of heat at least three times a day for several minutes. Using heat detection aids such as a gomer bull equipped with a chin ball marker or other devices that show the cow has been ridden may prove useful.

Proper timing of breeding is a very crucial factor in obtaining good reproductive results. Breed during the middle or toward the end of the heat period. Breeding too early or too late lowers conception rate, but breeding early is probably the most common fault. The first six hours of heat is too soon.

According to the rule of thumb, cows first observed in standing heat during the morning should be bred late the same day. Cows first in standing heat during the afternoon should be bred the following morning. The graph shows the best breeding period in relation to the beginning of standing heat.

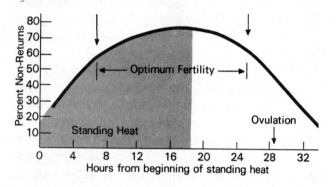

Note that breeding should take place a few hours before ovulation occurs. Since the time of egg release cannot be predicted exactly, timing of breeding should be based on the time when standing heat began. However, some cows complicate the picture by having longer or shorter heat periods. Average duration is 18 hours, but can range from 3 to 28 hours. For good results, cows that do not fit the normal pattern may need to be bred a few hours earlier or later than usual.

Records are indispensable in a good breeding program. Record items important to reproduction; breeding and calving dates, heats, health problems and other observations.

Keeping records of heat periods is one of the first steps in improving herd breeding performance. Perhaps the biggest help from records is in improving your ability to anticipate heat periods. Close observation when the cow is due to be in heat will increase the chance of detection. Also, records reduce the chance of the cow not being bred because someone thought she hadn't been fresh long enough. Records help detect failure to cycle or erratic cycles sooner, so treatment can begin quickly. Good records are also a valuable aid to your veterinarian. Check records every morning.

Replacement heifers are important to overall herd efficiency. The key to maximizing a heifer's contribution to the herd is breeding at an early age. Calving at 24 months of age is the most profitable. Although production will be lower for the first lactation, rearing costs are less and heifers will be more profitable over their lifetime in the herd.

Early reproduction requires good growth. Feed heifers so that they meet the minimum breeding weights and ages shown in the table. This means heifers should be gaining continually, but should not get fat. Don't reduce energy in the ration as breeding time approaches, as it may cause them to stop cycling.

Minimum Age And Weight Of Dairy Heifers At Time Of Breeding

Breed	Minimum Age	Minimum Weight
Ayshire	13 mos.	600 lbs.
Brown Swiss	15 mos.	750 lbs.
Guernsey	13 mos.	550 lbs.
Holstein	14 mos.	700 lbs.
Jersey	13 mos.	500 lbs.
Milking Shorthorn	14 mos.	650 lbs.

Detecting heat in heifers requires extra care. Virgin heifers may not show typical signs of heat and often have shorter heat periods. It's best to check heifers often, and keep good heat records. For good udder development, heifers should not be bred before their third heat period.

Nutrition and health play important roles in reproduction and can't be overlooked in a good breeding program. It's important to realize, however, that feed and health aspects get blamed for a multitude of breeding troubles when management is the limiting factor.

Certain diseases and general herd health can severely limit reproductive capability. However, under most conditions, cystic ovaries or infections after calving cause the majority of reproductive problems. Early treatment by a veterinarian will reduce lost time and get the cow bred back as soon as possible. Have the vet check all cows that have not cleaned properly after calving, show an abnormal discharge, or have not been in heat by 60 days after freshening. Cows that have not settled after two services should be checked and treated. If a veterinarian makes regular pregnancy tests, he will be able to keep an eye on herd health and reproductive problems.

Measures of Reproductive Efficiency

	Good	Average
Calving interval (mos.)	12-13	13.5-15
Days open	100	120 or more
Services per conception	1.4	1.8 to 2.2
Services per calf born	1.6	2.0 or more
Non-return rate	75% or more	65%-75%
Open after 3 services (%)	10%-12%	15%-18%

Controlling Mastitis

Mastitis is the dairyman's most costly disease. Total management can control economic losses from discarded milk, lower production and high culling rates.

Mastitis costs dairymen a large chunk of their potential income each year. Average dollar losses are estimated at $30 to $60 per cow. Milk loss following treatment of clinical cases mounts rapidly. Discarding milk for two to three days means as much as $15 to $20 in production lost for just one treatment in early lactation.

The number of clinical mastitis cases represents only the tip of the iceberg. For every clinical case found there are nine or ten subclinical mastitis problems. By the time you spot clinical cases in the strip cup, production is already suffering up to 20% in the infected quarter.

A higher culling rate is typical of mastitic dairy herds, too. Some cows are shipped after bad cases and cows are culled for udder problems as well as low production later, possibly due to the mastitis problems. Tissue lost to mastitis scar also reduces the cow's production capacity.

TOTAL MANAGEMENT APPROACH

The only way to conquer mastitis and its economic consequences is to tackle the problem on a total management basis. Slight any area, and your mastitis problem will be greater and more costly.

The management package consists of (1) proper milking time management, (2) properly functioning equipment of sufficient capacity to do the job, (3) a screening and treatment program, (4) routine dry cow treatment, (5) properly designed facilities and (6) good general herd management.

Milking time management is very important since mastitis is 90% man-made. At milking time the dairyman must put machines and methods together for an efficient harvest of the milk.

Wash hands before milking to reduce outside bacteria. Clean clothes also help. The first step in the milking procedure is to strip two or three squirts of milk into the strip cup. Do this before stimulating, being sure not to push milk from the teat cistern up into the udder. It may contain a high concentration of bacteria. Check the strip cup for flaky, chunky or stringy milk. If found, treat the cow and don't sell the milk.

Udders should then be washed with a warm sanitizing solution using an individual towel for each cow. A gentle wash stimulates milk letdown. Then dry with another paper towel. Wait about one minute—not more than two—before you attach the milker unit. Attach teat cups gently, but squarely, with as little vacuum loss as possible.

Milk flow rate and milk out time vary between cows, but should not differ by more than two to six minutes. To stay within this range each operator should run from two to four milker units, depending on the milking setup and his other duties. Machine stripping is not necessary since neither production nor leukocyte count is affected, but if you machine strip, be sure the teat cups do not crawl up the teat. When this happens the annular ring, teat sphincter and walls of the teat cistern take a beating, causing irritation and mastitis.

To remove the teat cup, press in on the teat just above the teat cup, while stopping the vacuum to the cup. In some cases you'll be able to turn off the vacuum to the whole claw before removing the teat cups. Don't let cups touch the floor or they'll pick up dirt and germs.

Dip teat cups in a sanitizing solution after each cow, but don't let the dipping solution get dirty. When this happens you increase rather than decrease the problems of sanitation. Dip cups deep enough so that the throat of the teat cup is dipped as far as possible.

Dipping teats in an iodine or chlorophine solution after milkout is important in mastitis control. Dipping doesn't control current problems, but will help prevent new cases from occurring.

In University of Wisconsin research, teats were dipped on the right sides of cows' udders and not on the left sides. Infections were identified from milk samples. Over a 13-month period, the right quarters had 53.2% fewer cases of mastitis infections than the untreated left quarters. About 20% fewer clinical mastitis treatments were required for the treated quarters.

Bacteria on teat ends are destroyed by dipping. Also, milk film is removed, thereby depriving new bacteria of a growth medium. Since the sphincter muscle of the teat is relaxed after milking, germs have a good opportunity to enter the streak canal and udder.

Use only recommended chemicals at proper strength to avoid irritation or chapping of the teat. It is usually simplest to use one of several commercial products that are available. Dip or spray at least the lower half, making sure the bottom of the teat gets good coverage.

Properly functioning equipment of sufficient capacity to do the job is the next element in the management package. New systems should be built to the manufacturer's recommendations, with a little excess capacity if possible. Both cubic feet per minute (CFM) capacity of the pump and pipeline size are important. They are affected directly by the number of units and length of the pipeline from which units operate.

Equipment should be checked regularly or milk losses will occur. Improper vacuum capacity and fluctuating vacuum levels are major contributors to the problem. The vacuum relief valve, vacuum line and stallcocks should be cleaned monthly.

A qualified person should clean and check pulsators every other month. The vacuum pump should be flushed and the oil changed every three months. Check inflations frequently for cracks, and change them at least three times a year. Twice each year the pump capacity and vacuum level should be checked. Valves and gaskets should be looked at twice a year, and all rubber parts should be replaced annually.

Screening and treating cows are very important steps in the total mastitis control program. The strip cup is good for twice daily checking, but don't forget you're losing at least 20% of milk production when you can detect mastitis in the strip cup. These cases should be treated with an antibiotic product containing an anti-inflammatory agent. Milk must be discarded following treatment, but getting right at the problem by treating reduces the long-term costs of mastitis.

In addition to the strip cup you should use a test like the California Mastitis Test (CMT) regularly. It is easy to run at cowside and tells the degree of inflammation or infection present. Recording the history of these readings over a period of time is valuable in proper treatment and total management of mastitis.

Samples showing positive CMT readings should be sent to a culturing and sensitizing laboratory for further analysis. The culture tells what kinds of bacteria are present and the sensitivity test shows what treatment is best for that cow. Both of these tests are important to proper treatment in future cases that show up in the strip cup.

Routine dry cow treatment is somewhat controversial. However, research shows that most dairymen should be infusing all quarters with an approved dry cow product at the time when cows are dried off. Treating only selected cows may be adequate in some herds which maintain very low cell counts.

Treatment during the dry period is the most effective way to eliminate existing infections, since dry treatments contain a higher dosage with a longer-acting base. Presence of a long-acting antibiotic can also prevent new infections which are relatively high during the early dry period. Studies show that perhaps half of all cows have some infection when turned dry and the level of infections increases unless treated. Treatment, combined with attentiveness to signs of udder inflammation during the dry period, are very important to the success of the overall control program.

Properly designed facilities are a prerequisite to mastitis control. Stall size, curb height, alley width, space at the manger, size of holding and loafing areas and concrete surface all play an important part in herd health. Minimum udder manure contact reduces the presence of bacteria on the udder and teats. Put all facilities on one level of cow traffic and avoid sharp corners to reduce injuries. Calves, on colostrum particularly, should have individual stalls and should not be allowed to suck at any time.

General herd management must be excellent. Nutritional needs must be met to reduce stress as well as to take advantage of problem-free cows. Herd health must be maintained to keep the leukocyte count low. The cow is under enormous stress early in lactation, so these factors are most important during peak production. The cell count usually increases during late lactation. Stress from the weather or environment can also increase the leukocyte count.

Dry Cow Management

The way you manage the cow during the dry period affects her health and level of milk production during the following lactation.

A dairy cow needs a rest from lactation to rejuvenate milk-producing cells in her udder. In research comparing groups of twin Holstein sisters, milk production in the group with no dry period dropped to 75% of that of the control group which was dried off normally. During the third lactation, production dropped still further, to 62%.

If handled properly during their dry period, cows will be in the best body condition to withstand the stresses of calving and early lactation. The dry period also affords a convenient opportunity for herdsmen to treat and care for cows while they are non-productive.

Length of the dry period should be neither too long nor too short. Short dry periods won't optimize production in the following lactation, while long periods are needless and reduce total production.

Most cows should be dry for a period of six to eight weeks. Many dairymen shoot for an eight-week period and average about seven weeks. But without good records it's easy to misjudge when a cow should be turned dry.

Either DHIA records or barn records will predict the expected calving date. Average gestation is 283 days. Turning a cow dry about 55 days before her expected due date should be optimum for the majority of the herd. First and second lactation cows benefit from a few extra days, while older cows can get by on 40 to 45 days. Cows milking heavy during late lactation are likely to show more profit from a shorter dry period.

Drying off can be done several ways. Your goal should always be to dry off as rapidly as possible without injuring the udder. When turned dry, pressure in the cow's udder stops milk secretion and the remaining milk is eventually absorbed. The faster the transition, the better for the cow.

For most cows the best drying off method is to remove the cow from the milking herd, eliminate grain feeding and feed limited forage and water for two to three days. Then stop milking abruptly. Her udder should be watched closely for two to three weeks. Extremely high producers or cows with a history of mastitis may require several milkings to relieve udder pressure.

FEEDING DRY COWS

Dry cow feeding can be divided into two phases. The first is primarily a forage feeding phase, lasting until two to three weeks before freshening. The second phase is a gradual shift in the cow's nutrition to prepare her for production.

Feed dry cows to get them in proper condition and then to maintain it. Never overfeed since it can increase problems around freshening time. Weight gain from late lactation to calving shouldn't be more than 100 to 200 pounds. Figure that an extra 100 pounds of body weight is needed during this period for energy reserve. Also, the calf will gain about 40 pounds during the last eight weeks of lactation.

Cows that go into the dry period in good condition can be maintained at less expense. Cows in late lactation replace body fat at 70% to 75% efficiency, compared to 58% during the dry period, according to USDA research. Conditioning thin cows with extra grain during late lactation is beneficial.

The table shows the daily nutrient requirements for dry cow maintenance and development of the rapidly growing fetus. Since two to three-year old cows are still growing, they need additional nutrients.

DAILY NUTRIENT REQUIREMENTS*

Nutrient	Dry cow	Lactating cow (50 lbs./day)
Protein—(%)	9	15
TDN—(%)	53	65
Net Energy—(M-cal /lb.)	.50	.73
Fiber—(%)	15	15
Calcium—(%)	.35	.47
Phosphorus—(%)	.26	.35
Vitamin A—(IU/lb.)	1,450	1,450
Vitamin D—(IU/lb.)	300	300

*100% dry matter basis.

Hay, grass silage and pasture often contain enough energy to maintain cows in good condition. Thin cows will need some grain. Two to five pounds of grain with a hay ration should be adequate to condition most cows.

If fed alone, corn silage should be limited to about 50 pounds per day, because of its high energy content. Hay is recommended to maintain fiber level, and the quantity fed does not need to be limited. Grass hay is preferred to legume hay for a better calcium and phosphorus balance. If hay and corn silage are fed together, a good ration consists of about half and half on a dry matter basis. For a typical Holstein cow, this would be about 10 pounds of hay and 40 pounds of corn silage.

Minerals and vitamins. A shortage of phosphorus is common during the dry period. Since little or no grain is fed, phosphorus in the feed is low. If legume hay is fed, its high calcium level tends to throw the calcium-phosphorus ratio further out of balance. Generally, alfalfa hay should be limited to 10 pounds per day, and a mineral mixture containing about two parts calcium to one part phosphorus fed free-choice. If a high level of legume hay is fed, provide either sodium tripoly phosphate or monosodium phosphate. A simple method is to provide equal parts of trace mineral salt and mineral supplement free-choice.

If your cows have a history of milk fever, be especially cautious of legumes and high calcium levels. Recent research has shown that maintaining phosphorus levels while feeding a calcium deficient ration during the latter part of the dry period is beneficial.

Include 30,000 units of vitamin A, 5,000 units of vitamin D, and 30 units of vitamin E with the daily ration if there is any question of the vitamin content of roughages. Or, you can supply A-D-E in an intramuscular injection two weeks before calving.

Feeding before freshening. Shifting to a moderate level of grain feeding two to three weeks before freshening will condition bacteria in the cow's rumen and adjust the energy level to prepare for concentrate feeding during lactation.

Increase grain gradually. Since the cow is already going through many changes associated with preparing for calving and lactation, a rapid shift from all forage to large amounts of concentrates can cause digestive upsets at a critical time. Cows also need this period to adjust to urea, if it is included in the milking ration.

The practice of "lead feeding" to reach high grain levels just prior to freshening has been shown to be inefficient and a potential cause of digestive problems. A more moderate approach to grain feeding before freshening is recommended.

Start with about four pounds of grain per day. Increase grain slowly until cows are consuming from 0.5% to 1% of their body weight daily. Thus, for a 1,400-pound cow, the limit would be 14 pounds per day. Maintain forage intake at a minimum of 1% of body weight on a dry matter basis (about 16 pounds of hay or 42 pounds of silage).

Displaced abomasum (twisted stomach) is related to reduced muscle tone in the digestive system, associated with high-grain, low-fiber and all-corn silage rations. To avoid the problem, limit grain intake and avoid extremely fine-chopped silages and low-fiber roughages. Limit corn silage to about 40 pounds per day and maintain hay at five to ten pounds.

Udder edema appears to be related to salt levels more than any other feed factor. If edema is a problem, exclude salt from the grain mix which is fed prior to freshening.

GENERAL MANAGEMENT

Facilities for dry cows make managing easier. Moving cows out of the milking herd aids in drying off and also reduces milking time since dry cows don't enter the milking barn. Separate facilities permit you to feed a controlled ration. Grouping dry cows with bred heifers works well if all animals are able to get their fair share of feed.

Exercise during the dry period is important. Free access to pastures and lots helps maintain good muscle tone and adequate blood circulation. If cows are kept in stanchions, turn them out for a few hours each day.

Maternity pens are justified on most farms because they provide safe and comfortable conditions for cows. Calving in a restricted space such as stanchions or free-stalls is uncomfortable and can be dangerous. Square maternity pens are preferred, containing about 150 square feet of floor space per pen.

Udder infusion of all cows at the last milking with an approved dry cow mastitis treatment is recommended by most researchers. Treating only selected cows is not advisable unless the herd maintains a very low cell count. One study showed that half of all cows have some infection at drying off, and if left untreated the level of infections increased to 60% during the dry period. Most new mastitis infections occur during the first two weeks of the dry period. Old infections are most easily and effectively treated during this time.

Always practice extreme sanitation after treating dry cows. Dip the teat after each treatment. Check udders daily, especially during the first few weeks after drying off. Monitor health and body conditioning and watch cows close to calving.

208

Producing Dairy Beef

Calves of dairy breeds produce high quality beef and provide flexible growing and feeding programs on many farms.

Feeding dairy steers for beef was once primarily a sideline to the dairying operation. Now, it's a substantial business in its own right, helping to meet growing consumer demand for beef. Increasing emphasis on feeding out dairy steers has been caused by the steady decline in the number of calves killed as veal, together with the widespread use of artificial insemination which makes more calves available for feeding.

Comparing beef versus dairy breeds shows that, overall, dairy calves compare favorably. Holsteins consistently make faster gains on feed, but since they eat more feed, efficiency of gain is usually slightly poorer.

Differences in the way beef and dairy breeds convert feed to beef are most obvious after slaughter. The table below shows a Michigan State University summary of several research comparisons of Holstein and beef-type steers. Notice that dressing percent is lower for dairy steers—primarily due to their substantially leaner carcasses. Cutability, or yield of lean meat, is improved over beef steers, also because of this lack of fat.

BEEF TYPE VS. DAIRY TYPE STEERS[1]

Performance Trait	Beef	Holstein	Difference
Average daily gain	2.38	2.60	.22
Feed per lb. of gain	8.16	8.19	.03
Daily feed consumption (% of body weight)	2.42	2.6	.18
Dressing percent	61.1	58.2	2.9
Carcass grade[2]	11.9	9.2	2.7
Marbling[3]	15.5	13.4	2.1
Fat thickness	.61	.22	.39
Cutability	49.1	51.3	2.2

[1]Summarized from several research trials.
[2]Good: 9, 10, 11; Choice: 12, 13, 14.
[3]Small: 13, 14, 15; Modest: 16, 17, 18.

Even more apparent is the final grade difference between beef-type and dairy steers. Shown in the table, beef carcasses averaged low Choice; Holsteins low Good. However, only part of this spread in grades is caused by a smaller degree of marbling in dairy beef. Differences in body conformation also account for much of the grade separation. Had the dairy steers possessed a beef-type conformation, they would have been able to qualify for the high Good and low Choice labels on the basis of their marbling scores.

Responses of taste panelists comparing the eating qualities of steaks from dairy and beef steers indicate that, on the average, "beef" steaks were slightly preferred on the basis of flavor, juiciness, and overall acceptability. But, panelists preferred "dairy" steaks for tenderness.

Management flexibility in producing dairy beef makes it possible to fit dairy steers into a variety of farm operations. Calves will have been reared on a milk or milk replacer diet, plus a starter ration. By the time they are 16 to 18 weeks old, they should weigh around 350 pounds. By that age a decision must be made either to keep the calf on a high-energy diet for rapid growth or to use forages and limit daily gains. Here are some common ways of handling dairy calves:

● Place the calf on pasture and grow out to 700 to 800 pounds, then feed out or sell. Usually grain is fed during the growing phase to equal 1% of body weight daily.

● Feed the calf in confinement on a high-roughage, limited grain ration, then full feed from approximately 800 pounds to market.

● Full feed the calf on a high-energy or all-concentrate program and market for slaughter at 900 to 1,000 pounds.

● Feed out to slaughter using all roughage or roughage plus limited grain.

Feeding dairy steers is fundamentally no different than feeding beef breeds. Nutritional requirements are no different at the same weight and stage of maturity. However, since most dairy steers will fall into a grade range from high Standard to high Good, more latitude is available to feeders in the use of roughages or concentrates.

The next table shows two high-roughage methods of finishing dairy beef. Steers fed roughages alone will gain from 1.7 to 2 pounds per day, 2.3 to 2.5 pounds per day if they receive added concentrate feeds to equal 1% of their body weight. If fed roughages alone, though, they will require 30 to 50 days longer to reach weight.

HIGH ROUGHAGE METHODS FOR FINISHING DAIRY BEEF

	Roughage		Roughage + grain	
	Corn silage + alfalfa hay	Corn silage	Corn silage + alfalfa hay	Corn silage
Initial weight (lb.)	700	700	700	700
Final weight (lb.)	1,000	1,000	1,000	1,000
Gain (lb.)	300	300	300	300
Days on feed	170	150	125	120
Average daily gain (lb.)	1.8	2.0	2.4	2.5
Average daily feed consumption (lb.)				
Ground corn	---	---	7	7
44% protein supplement	1	2	1	1.5
Alfalfa hay	5	---	5	---
Corn silage	40	55	25	40
Total consumption (lb.)				
Ground corn	---	---	875	840
44% protein supplement	170	300	125	180
Alfalfa hay	850	---	625	---
Corn silage	6,800	8,250	3,125	4,800

Dairy calf feeding tests in Minnesota show the effects of various proportions of concentrates to roughages. Although gain differences were not particularly large, higher energy feeds gave faster gains. Beef produced per pound of feed also increased with the "hotter" rations. Both dressing percent and grade rose slightly for the somewhat fatter steers on the higher concentrate feeds.

FEEDLOT COMPARISON
Performance of Holsteins on varying concentrate to roughage ratios

Item	11:1a	3:1a	1:1a
No. cattle.	35	27	26
Av. initial wt., lb.	427	409	419
Av. final wt., lb.	1005	1015	967
Av. daily gain, lb.	2.41	2.46	2.30
Total feed/cwt. gain, lb.	707	747	778
Carcass data			
Rib eye area, sq. in.	10.5	10.0	10.0
Fat cover, in.	0.32	0.27	0.20
Marbling score[b]	5.4	5.0	5.1
Grade[c]	7.6	7.5	7.0
Dressing %	62.1	60.7	60.0

a Parts by weight of concentrate to roughage.
b Marbling score: slight, 4; small, 5; modest, 6.
c Carcass grades: high Standard, 6; low Good, 7; av. Good, 8; high Good, 9.

In recent years, feeding dairy calves from weaning to around 1,000 pounds on all-concentrate rations has given good results and is now a growing practice. Feeders generally find dairy steers can utilize all-concentrate rations with fewer digestive upsets. Also, without roughage, steers do not develop a "paunchy" appearance. Trials in California showed that Holsteins started at around 200 pounds, implanted with a hormone and self-fed all concentrates will gain about 2.75 pounds per day. They will produce a pound of gain on about 6.5 pounds of feed and will grade Standard and Good at 1,000 pounds.

In those trials, calves were weaned slowly to a dry feed. At about 200 pounds they were placed on ration 1 (shown in the table). When they weighed 500 to 600 pounds they were implanted and switched to ration 2 until slaughtered at about a year of age, weighing 950 to 1,050 pounds.

Feed	Ration 1	Ration 2
Rolled barley	1046	1446
Rolled corn	200	--
Beet pulp	200	200
Cottonseed meal	200	--
Molasses	200	200
Dehydrated alfalfa meal	100	100
DiCalcium phosphate	20	20
Urea	20	20
Salt	10	10
Vitamin A	4	4

Feeding economics of dairy beef show up best when fed cattle prices are within a narrow range from Choice down to Standard. If bought, fed and marketed well, dairy steers often show a better profit than beef steers.

Both high-roughage and high-concentrate feeding programs have certain advantages for feeders. Price differences between low and high grades of feeder and slaughter cattle, plus forage and concentrate costs will help determine which feeding system is most profitable. High-concentrate feeding for fast gains and improved carcass characteristics will be shown to its best advantage when grain prices are low in relation to beef prices.

Handling dairy calves requires firm management to reap maximum profits. Here are some important points:
● Feed dairy beef as you would beef-type animals. Follow a planned feeding and marketing program.
● Bring dairy calves on feed carefully after the stress of weaning.
● Separate calves according to size. If small and large calves are mixed, riding will occur, injuring or slowing up smaller cattle.
● A few dairy calves don't respond well to feeding. Don't hang on to them—cull early.
● Don't try to overfinish dairy calves to reach a higher grade, since grade is determined by body conformation as well as finish.
● Most dairy calves should be finished by 15 months of age, at around 1,000 pounds.

Chapter 9

Livestock Feeds and Feeding

Efficient and economical feeding can mean the difference between profit and loss in a livestock program. The rate of gain, level of production and health of livestock are highly dependent on the feeding program. The modern livestockman needs to make full use of the new developments and the increased knowledge in the area of basic feeds, feed additives, drugs and feed handling equipment. To do this, he should have a sound working knowledge of principles of nutrition, livestock feed requirements and up-to-date feeding methods.

Value and composition of feeds must be known so a producer can match available feeds with the nutrient requirements of the animal. Top animal performance requires that rations contain recommended levels of each of the following feed components:

- protein
- carbohydrates
- fats
- minerals
- vitamins
- water

Two general groups of feeds and their specific characteristics must be taken into account when balancing cattle and sheep rations.

Concentrates—feeds low in fiber and high in total digestible nutrients. Such feeds include grain, protein meals and molasses.

Roughages—feeds high in fiber and low in total digestible nutrients. Examples of these feeds are pasture grasses, silages and hay.

211

A certain amount of roughages are required by ruminants to provide bulk in their diet. However, concentrates make up almost the entire ration in single stomach animals (hogs) and poultry.

A number of feedgrains can be substituted for each other in livestock rations, either in total or in part. Prices vary and at times a local condition may make it profitable to buy a different type of grain than you normally feed. It is also advisable to vary the proportion of grain to roughage as the relative price shifts between the two groups of feeds. Feed substitution tables can help when figuring how much of a given feed can be substituted and in determining possible savings.

Your substitution possibilities are not limited to grains and roughages alone. Several synthetic proteins including urea, biuret and diammonium phosphate can be used to supply a portion of the animal's protein requirements. However, unlike feeds which are high in protein, these substitutes provide no energy. Therefore, protein substitutes become economical to feed only when their cost plus the cost of the extra grain required to provide the additional energy is less than the cost of the same amount of protein purchased as meal.

Plan feed requirements well in advance of your needs. Part of a successful livestock program is planning for a good supply of feed throughout the year or feeding period. This is especially true for roughage. Since roughage is bulky, most growers prefer to produce roughage on the farm. By referring to standard feed requirements, you can figure about how much hay, silage and grain will be used during the feeding season. If feed must be purchased, you are able to determine how much and when it is needed. This will help you to estimate and provide for your storage needs, such as bulk hoppers, bins and silos.

Make use of feed additives that boost livestock growth and promote better health and disease control. These include hormones, antibiotics, tranquilizers and other drugs and medication, plus vitamin and mineral premixes.

Complete mixed rations can help you boost feeding efficiency. The efficiency with which livestock converts feed depends on many factors other than a balanced ration. The form in which feeds are fed is one of these factors. Feeding tests indicate that complete mixed rations will often produce faster gains with less feed per pound of gain than feeding free choice. Completely mixed rations are also easier to feed, especially with confinement and drylot feeding systems.

If you feed completely mixed rations, you must either invest in mixing equipment and do it yourself, or have it custom mixed. Your decision should be based on the size of your feeding operation, composition of the ration you feed, the investment required in milling and mixing equipment and how profitably you can use your labor elsewhere in the business. It may be advisable to buy some of the more complex rations already mixed unless you are highly trained in livestock nutrition.

Those who hire their rations custom mixed may find it advantageous to use the "grain bank" system. Grain is delivered to the elevator and the operator then fortifies, mixes and delivers a completely mixed ration to the farm as needed.

Feeding high moisture grain has been beneficial for some large operators. This method of feeding allows them to harvest their corn and grain sorghum while it's still high in moisture. It cuts field losses and reduces the risk from bad weather late in the fall. This system also eliminates the need to artificially dry grain for safe storage. Both airtight and conventional tower silos, properly reinforced, work well for storage. Corn can be ensiled as high moisture shelled corn or as crushed or chopped ear corn. Some grain sorghum growers have found that the entire chopped grain head makes good silage.

Warm weather feeding of high moisture grains presents some problems. Feed only an amount that animals will clean up in a short time. This prevents spoilage and waste. However, it may be necessary to feed more frequently during the day.

Once you start feeding a group of animals high moisture grain, be sure to avoid a sudden change to ordinary grain. Switching from high moisture to dry grains can throw animals "off feed," slowing gains until they adjust to the change.

Advances in feed handling and processing methods, which include pelleting of feeds, automatic feed unloaders, conveying equipment, etc., offer ways for increasing feeding efficiencies. Look at your overall feed handling operation when choosing equipment that will fit your operation.

Feed Ingredient Analysis Tables

Use these tables, prepared from National Research Council data, to calculate the nutrient content in feedstuffs. All figures are given on an "as fed" moisture basis.

ROUGHAGES (as fed)

Material	Dry Matter %	Crude Fiber %	TDN %	Digestible Energy Kcal/lb.	Crude Protein %	Digestible Protein %	Calcium %	Phosphorus %	Carotene mg./lb.	Vit. A Equiv./lb. 1,000 I.U.
FRESH ROUGHAGES										
Alfalfa, mid bloom	24.2	6.7	15	295	4.9	3.9	.49	.07	*	*
Bermuda grass	30.9	7.9	19	372	3.5	2.3	.17	.06	39.4	65.6
Bluegrass, Kentucky	35.7	9.9	25	493	5.3	3.7	.16	.14	*	*
Clover, alsike	22.6	5.7	15	303	4.0	2.8	.29	.07	*	*
Clover, crimson	17.7	5.0	11	237	3.0	2.1	.29	.06	*	*
Clover, ladino	18.7	2.7	13	258	4.7	3.3	.25	.07	27.0	45.0
Clover, red	23.6	5.7	15	302	4.3	2.8	.42	.07	19.7	32.5
Fescue	30.6	8.7	17	354	4.4	3.1	.15	.08	*	*
Johnsongrass	24.8	7.4	16	327	3.6	2.5	.23	.06	22.4	37.3
Lespedeza	31.7	9.8	20	363	5.1	4.3	.36	.10	*	*
Orchard grass	24.9	6.9	16	319	3.2	2.2	.13	.13	36.0	60.0
Rye (plant)	20.3	5.2	15	295	4.3	3.4	.11	.09	31.4	52.3
Ryegrass	24.1	5.6	15	295	3.9	2.8	.16	.08	43.6	72.7
Sorghum, sudan grass	20.8	5.7	14	286	2.9	2.1	.10	.09	17.3	28.9
Sugar beet tops	15.9	1.7	10	186	2.8	2.0	.16	.04	2.5	4.2
Sugarcane	27.1	8.0	16	313	1.5	.8	.13	.05	*	*
Sweet clover	24.8	7.3	16	321	4.4	3.5	.33	.07	30.2	50.4
Timothy	27.6	7.4	18	363	3.5	2.1	.16	.10	28.1	48.8
Wheat (plant)	25.9	5.9	19	400	4.1	3.0	.08	.08	44.5	74.2
SILAGES										
Alfalfa, average	30.4	9.2	17	340	5.4	3.6	.49	.12	12.4	20.7
Alfalfa, wilted	36.2	10.9	21	420	6.4	4.3	.51	.12	8.5	14.3
Bermuda grass, average	25.7	8.5	15	286	3.0	1.7	.13	.08	22.7	37.9
Clover, ladino	24.9	5.3	17	345	5.9	4.4	*	*	*	*
Clover, red	27.7	8.3	15	305	3.8	2.2	.43	.06	24.6	41.0
Corn, immature	23.6	5.8	15	315	2.3	1.2	.12	.07	11.9	19.8
Corn, average	25.6	6.4	16	327	2.1	.9	.08	.06	5.3	8.8
Corn, stover	27.2	8.7	14	280	2.0	.8	.10	.05	*	*
Oats, plant	31.7	10.0	19	374	3.1	1.7	.12	.10	17.2	28.6
Orchard grass	29.5	10.5	19	390	4.2	2.9	*	*	22.7	37.8
Peas, field	24.4	7.9	14	277	3.2	2.0	.42	.07	14.3	23.8
Sorghum with heads	28.9	7.3	19	381	2.3	1.2	.10	.06	4.8	8.0
Sugar beet tops	22.5	2.8	12	240	2.9	1.8	.22	.05	*	*
Sweet clover	30.1	9.8	17	330	5.7	4.4	.40	.06	4.0	6.6
Timothy	34.0	12.0	20	404	3.6	2.0	.20	.10	12.2	20.3
DRY ROUGHAGES										
Alfalfa, early bloom	90.0	26.8	51	1,028	16.6	11.4	1.12	.21	52.0	86.7
Alfalfa, mid bloom	89.2	27.6	51	1,036	15.2	10.8	1.20	.20	22.4	37.3
Alfalfa, full bloom	87.7	29.7	48	1,000	14.0	10.0	1.13	.18	14.7	24.5
Barley straw	88.2	37.4	40	725	3.6	.4	.30	.08	*	*
Bluegrass, average	90.6	27.4	53	1,063	10.5	5.8	.35	.24	112.0	186.7
Brome, smooth, early bloom	89.7	28.4	47	1,035	11.0	5.9	.39	.25	*	*
Bermuda grass, average	91.2	26.8	45	909	7.2	3.4	.37	.19	40.1	66.9
Clover, alsike	87.9	28.1	48	1,057	12.9	8.2	1.15	.22	74.5	123.9
Clover, crimson	87.4	25.8	55	1,051	14.8	10.3	1.24	.16	*	*
Clover, ladino	91.2	17.5	60	1,151	20.9	13.2	1.26	.36	66.5	110.8
Clover, red	87.7	26.4	48	1,036	13.1	7.8	1.41	.19	14.6	24.3
Clover, white	90.7	22.0	54	1,080	17.0	10.7	1.70	.29	25.3	42.1
Corn, dry plant, ears & husks	82.4	21.3	53	1,073	7.3	3.4	.41	.21	1.6	2.7
Corn, stalks only	87.2	32.4	51	1,030	5.1	1.9	.42	.08	1.4	2.3
Fescue, average	88.5	27.6	55	1,100	9.3	5.3	.44	.32	*	*
Johnsongrass	90.7	30.2	50	1,017	7.0	3.1	.73	.28	*	*
Lespedeza, early bloom	93.0	27.0	53	1,085	14.5	9.7	1.15	.23	19.3	32.2
Oats hay	88.2	27.3	54	1,078	8.1	3.9	.23	.21	4.0	6.7
Orchard grass	88.3	30.0	50	1,008	8.6	5.1	.40	.33	13.4	22.3
Prairie grass	91.8	30.6	44	909	6.2	2.0	.38	.11	13.4	22.3
Rye hay	92.2	35.7	43	827	7.0	3.0	.32	.26	*	*
Soybean straw	87.5	38.8	37	740	4.5	1.3	1.39	.05	*	*
Sweet clover	91.3	27.4	53	1,072	15.0	10.2	1.54	.23	49.0	81.7
Sugar beet tops, dry	89.3	13.2	54	1,081	11.6	7.1	*	*	*	*
Timothy, average	87.7	29.6	45	1,000	6.8	4.0	.36	.17	5.5	9.2
Wheat straw	90.1	37.4	43	866	3.2	.4	.15	.07	0.9	1.5

*No figure available.

FEED INGREDIENTS (as fed)

Ingredient	Dry Matter %	Fiber %	TDN %	ENERGY Digestible (Cattle) Kcal/lb.	Digestible (Swine) Kcal/lb.	PROTEIN Total %	Digestible (Cattle) %	Digestible (Swine) %	Calcium %	Phos-phorus %	Vit. A Equiv./lb. 1,000 I.U.
Alfalfa leaf meal (dehydrated)	92.0	21.0	56	1,034	996	20.0	15.8	13.0	1.5	0.25	113.3
Alfalfa meal (17% dehy.)	93.0	25.0	50	1,155	652	17.0	14.0	8.3	1.30	0.23	121.7
Alfalfa meal (15% dehy.)	93.0	27.0	50	1,138	652	15.0	11.8	7.0	1.20	0.22	76.6
Barley	89.0	6.0	78	1,480	1,400	11.0	8.7	8.2	0.08	0.40	--
Barley (Pacific Coast)	89.0	6.5	79	1,462	1,426	9.0	7.3	7.5	0.05	0.40	--
Beans (Navy)	90.0	4.0	78	1,496	*	21.0	20.2	*	0.10	0.45	--
Beet pulp (dried)	91.0	20.0	62	1,313	1,300	9.0	4.1	3.7	0.65	0.10	--
Blood meal	91.0	1.0	60	1,180	1,220	80.0	56.0	62.3	0.30	0.20	--
Bone meal (steamed)	95.0	2.0	--	304	300	12.0	8.2	9.4	28.0	13.5	--
Brewers dried grains	92.0	16.0	66	1,216	860	26.0	19.1	20.4	0.25	0.50	--
Citrus pulp (dried)	90.0	14.0	75	1,389	902	6.5	3.5	2.7	2.0	0.10	--
Corn (white)	88.0	2.3	80	1,604	1,551	8.6	6.5	6.9	0.04	0.27	.3
Corn (No. 2 yellow)	89.0	2.5	80	1,623	1,640	8.8	6.7	7.1	0.03	0.27	1.4
Corn (popcorn)	89.8	2.0	83	1,650	1,662	10.0	8.6	9.2	0.01	0.30	--
Corn & cob meal (yellow)	87.0	8.5	73	1,569	1,412	7.6	4.0	5.8	0.04	0.25	1.6
Corn cobs	90.4	33.0	45	851	145	2.5	--	--	0.10	0.04	.5
Corn distillers grain	92.0	13.0	82	1,549	*	24.0	21.2	*	0.20	0.50	--
Corn distillers grain w/solubles	92.0	9.0	87	1,622	*	27.0	21.5	*	0.09	0.37	2.8
Corn distillers solubles (dried)	93.0	4.0	78	1,640	1,500	27.0	21.0	16.1	0.30	1.30	.5
Corn gluten feed	90.0	8.0	75	1,615	*	25.0	21.8	*	0.45	0.70	--
Corn gluten meal (41%)	91.0	4.5	81	1,532	*	42.0	35.7	*	0.15	0.40	--
Cottonseed meal (41%)	94.0	12.0	73	1,469	1,337	41.0	33.2	34.9	0.15	1.10	--
Cottonseed meal (41%) (solvent)	91.5	12.0	66	1,909	1,233	41.0	34.8	34.8	0.15	1.20	--
Cottonseed meal (36%)	93.5	15.7	75	1,723	1,424	36.0	33.2	34.9	0.15	1.10	--
Cottonseed hulls	90.3	44.0	44	742	*	4.0	.2	*	0.10	0.10	--
Feathers, hydrolyzed poultry	91.0	3.2	63	*	1,240	85.0	*	60.2	0.20	0.70	--
Fish meal (mehaden)	92.0	1.0	58	*	1,419	61.0	*	56.4	5.4	2.8	--
Fish meal (anchovy)	93.0	1.0	70	*	1,360	66.0	*	60.7	4.5	2.8	--
Hominy feed (yellow)	90.6	5.0	84	1,725	1,634	10.5	7.2	8.5	0.05	0.50	7.0
Linseed meal (old process)	91.0	9.0	76	1,477	1,540	35.0	31.0	31.8	0.40	0.80	.2
Linseed meal (solvent)	91.0	9.0	70	1,385	1,349	35.0	30.9	31.6	0.40	0.80	--
Meat meal (55%)	93.5	2.5	68	1,424	1,368	55.0	48.6	52.0	8.0	4.0	--
Meat & bone meal (50%)	94.0	2.3	65	1,356	1,299	50.0	46.1	45.0	10.0	4.8	--
Meat meal tankage	92.0	2.0	68	1,456	1,125	60.0	54.5	37.1	6.0	3.10	--
Millet grain	90.0	8.0	65	1,389	1,316	12.0	7.4	8.8	0.06	0.30	--
Milo	89.0	2.0	82	1,426	1,569	11.0	6.3	7.8	0.04	0.28	--
Molasses, beet	77.0	--	61	1,373	*	6.7	3.8	*	0.15	0.02	--
Molasses, cane (blackstrap)	75.0	--	63	1,367	1,120	3.2	1.8	*	0.8	0.08	--
Molasses, wood	66.0	--	56	1,164	1,084	0.7	--	--	1.4	0.05	--
Oats	89.0	11.0	68	1,355	1,300	12.0	8.8	9.9	0.1	0.35	--
Oats, western	91.2	11.0	72	1,407	*	10.0	6.7	*	0.1	0.35	--
Oat groats (hulled oats)	91.0	3.0	85	1,695	1,477	16.0	11.7	14.0	0.07	0.45	--
Oat meal, feeding	91.0	4.0	84	1,677	1,459	16.0	10.8	13.3	0.08	0.40	--
Oat hulls	93.0	27.0	30	745	460	4.0	2.0	3.2	0.10	0.15	--
Peanut meal (solvent)	92.0	13.0	77	1,419	1,549	47.0	42.7	44.5	0.20	0.60	--
Poultry by-product meal	93.0	2.0	74	*	1,483	58.0	*	47.1	3.0	1.7	--
Rice bran (solvent)	90.0	12.0	52	1,045	1,082	14.0	9.1	*	0.06	1.8	--
Rice polishings	90.0	3.0	78	1,605	1,780	12.0	7.7	10.3	0.05	1.4	--
Rice hulls	92.0	40.0	10	200	*	3.0	.2	*	0.08	0.06	--
Rye	89.0	2.0	75	1,516	1,500	11.5	9.4	9.6	0.05	0.30	--
Safflower meal (solvent)	92.0	32.0	50	531	*	21.4	17.2	*	0.4	1.3	--
Skim milk, dried	94.0	0.2	82	1,600	1,720	33.0	30.1	32.8	1.3	1.0	--
Soybeans	90.0	5.0	82	1,695	1,840	38.0	34.1	31.0	0.25	0.6	--
Soybean meal (expeller)	90.0	6.0	74	1,533	1,580	42.0	37.3	39.4	0.25	0.6	--
Soybean meal (44%) (solvent)	89.0	6.0	72	1,444	1,500	44.0	39.0	41.7	0.30	0.65	--
Soybean meal (50%)	90.0	2.8	75	1,511	1,547	50.0	45.8	46.3	0.26	0.62	--
Sunflower seed	93.0	30.0	76	1,572	1,528	16.0	*	*	0.20	0.50	--
Wheat, hard	89.0	3.0	80	1,571	1,625	13.0	10.2	11.9	0.05	0.4	--
Wheat, soft	90.0	2.5	79	1,587	1,659	11.0	8.5	9.9	0.08	0.30	--
Wheat, Durum	87.0	2.5	77	1,508	1,594	13.0	10.6	12.4	0.15	0.40	--
Wheat bran	89.0	10.0	60	1,248	1,141	16.0	12.5	12.2	0.10	0.10	--
Wheat middlings	89.0	2.0	80	1,623	1,460	18.0	13.0	16.0	0.1	0.5	--
Wheat shorts	90.0	5.0	75	1,551	1,440	18.0	13.2	15.4	0.11	0.8	--
Wheat mill run	90.0	8.0	72	1,460	1,440	15.0	10.4	12.2	0.10	1.00	--
Whey, dried	94.0	0.1	78	*	1,560	14.0	*	12.6	1.3	1.0	--
Yeast, brewers, dried	93.0	3.0	70	1,453	1,398	45.0	41.0	39.2	0.12	1.40	--
Yeast, torula, dried	93.0	2.0	66	1,490	1,285	48.0	43.9	39.6	0.55	1.60	--

*No figure available. --No value.

Nutrition Requirements for Beef and Hogs

Tables are condensations of the National Research Council's nutrient recommendations for various classes of beef cattle and hogs.

NUTRIENT REQUIREMENTS OF SWINE

Liveweight class Pounds		Growing and finishing					Bred gilts and sows; young and adult boars	Lactating gilts and sows
		10-25	25-45	45-75	75-135	135-220		
Feed intake	lb	1.1	2.2	3.3	4.4	6.6	4.0	9-12
Daily gain	lb	.66	1.1	1.3	1.65	2.0	—	—
		Percentage or amount per pound of diet[a]						
PROTEIN AND ENERGY								
Digestible energy[b]	kcal	1,591	1,532	1,536	1,540	1,543	1,546	1,543
Metabolizable energy[b]	kcal	1,546	1,436	1,443	1,450	1,452	1,455	1,452
Crude protein[c]	%	20	18	16	14	13	12	13
INDISPENSABLE AMINO ACIDS								
Lysine	%	0.95	0.79	0.70	0.61	0.57	0	0.40
Arginine	%	0.25	0.23	0.20	0.18	0.16	0.15	0.25
Histidine	%	0.23	0.20	0.18	0.16	0.15	0.37	0.39
Isoleucine	%	0.63	0.56	0.50	0.44	0.41	0.42	0.70
Leucine	%	0.75	0.68	0.60	0.52	0.48	0.43	0.58
Methionine + cystine[d]	%	0.56	0.51	0.45	0.40	0.30	0.23	0.36
Phenylalanine + tyrosine[e]	%	0.88	0.79	0.70	0.61	0.57	0.52	0.85
Threonine	%	0.56	0.51	0.45	0.39	0.37	0.34	0.43
Tryptophan[f]	%	0.15	0.13	0.12	0.11	0.10	0.09	0.12
Valine	%	0.63	0.56	0.50	0.44	0.41	0.46	0.55
MINERAL ELEMENTS								
Calcium	%	0.80	0.65	0.60	0.55	0.50	0.75	0.75
Phosphorus[g]	%	0.60	0.55	0.50	0.45	0.40	0.60	0.50
Sodium	%	0.10	0.10	0.10	0.10	0.10	0.15	0.20
Chlorine	%	0.13	0.13	0.13	0.13	0.13	0.25	0.30
Potassium	%	0.26	0.26	0.23	0.20	0.17	0.20	0.20
Magnesium	%	0.04	0.04	0.04	0.04	0.04	0.04	0.04
Iron	mg	63.7	36.4	27.3	22.7	18.2	36.36	36.36
Zinc	mg	45.5	36.4	27.3	22.7	22.7	22.72	22.72
Manganese	mg	1.82	1.36	.91	0.91	.91	4.55	4.55
Copper	mg	2.73	2.27	1.82	1.36	1.36	2.27	2.27
Iodine	mg	.064	.064	.064	.064	.064	.064	.064
Selenium	mg	.068	.068	.068	.068	.045	.068	.068
VITAMINS								
Vitamin A	IU	1,000	795	590	590	590	1,818	909
or Beta-Carotene	mg	4	3.2	2.4	2.4	2.4	7.3	3.6
Vitamin D	IU	100	100	100	68	57	90	90
Vitamin E	IU	5	5	5	5	5	4.6	4.6
Vitamin K (menadione)	mg	.9	.9	.9	.9	.9	.9	.91
Riboflavin	mg	1.4	1.4	1.2	1	1	1.4	1.4
Niacin	mg	10	8.2	6.4	5.5	4.6	4.6	4.6
Pantothenic acid	mg	5.9	5	5	5	5	5.5	5.5
Vitamin B_{12}	mcg	10	6.82	5	5	5	6.8	6.8
Choline	mg	500	409.1	318.2	250	181.8	568.2	568.2
Thiamin	mg	.59	.5	.5	.5	.5	.455	.455
Vitamin B_6	mg	.68	.68	.5	.5	.5	.455	.455
Biotin[h]	mg	.045	.045	.045	.045	.045	.045	.045
Folacin[h]	mg	.272	.272	.272	.272	.272	.273	.273

[a] Requirements reflect the estimated levels of each nutrient needed for optimal performance when a fortified grain-soybean meal diet is fed. Concentrations are based upon amounts per unit of air-dry diet (i.e., 90% drymatter).

[b] These are not absolute requirements but are suggested energy levels derived from diets containing corn and soybean meal (44% crude protein). When lower energy grains are fed, these energy levels will not be met; consequently, feed efficiency would be lowered.

[c] Approximate protein levels required to meet the need for indispensable amino acids when a fortified grain-soybean meal diet is fed.

[d] Methionine can fulfill the total requirement; cystine can meet at least 50% of the total requirement.

[e] Phenylalanine can fulfill the total requirement; tyrosine can meet at least 50% of the total requirement.

[f] It is assumed that usable tryptophan content of corn does not exceed 0.05%

[g] At least 30% of the phosphorus requirement should be provided by inorganic and/or animal product sources.

[h] These levels are suggested. No requirements have been established.

215

NUTRIENT REQUIREMENTS OF BEEF CATTLE (PER ANIMAL DAILY)

Body weight (lbs)	Daily gain (lbs)	Minimum drymatter (lbs)	Roughage (%)	Total protein (lbs)	Digestible protein (lbs)	NEm (Mcal)	NEg (Mcal)	TDN (lbs)	Ca (g)	P (g)	Vitamin A (1,000 IU)
Growing–finishing steer calves and yearlings												
220	1.1	6.4	70-80	0.79	0.53	2.43	0.89	4.0	14	11	6
	1.5	6.0	50-60	0.88	0.62	2.43	1.27	4.4	19	13	6
	2.0	6.2	25-30	1.00	0.73	2.43	1.68	4.6	24	16	7
440	1.1	12.8	80-90	1.25	0.77	4.10	1.49	7.5	14	13	12
	1.5	12.6	70-80	1.34	0.86	4.10	2.14	7.9	18	16	13
	2.0	10.8	35-45	1.34	0.88	4.10	2.82	8.2	23	18	13
	2.4	10.1	15	1.39	0.95	4.10	3.52	8.6	27	20	13
660	2.0	17.9	55-65	1.78	1.10	5.55	3.82	11.9	22	19	16
	2.4	16.8	20-25	1.80	1.14	5.55	4.78	12.3	25	22	16
	2.9	15.6	15	1.83	1.19	5.55	5.77	13.2	29	23	16
880	2.2	20.7	45-55	1.91	1.19	6.89	5.33	15.0	21	20	19
	2.6	18.7	20-25	1.91	1.19	6.89	6.54	15.4	23	21	19
	2.9	19.0	15	1.98	1.23	6.89	7.16	16.1	25	22	19
1,100	2.0	23.1	45-55	2.09	1.23	8.14	5.60	16.5	19	19	23
	2.4	22.9	20-25	2.11	1.25	8.14	7.01	17.8	20	20	23
	2.6	21.2	15	2.11	1.28	8.14	7.73	18.1	21	21	23
Growing–finishing heifer calves and yearlings												
220	1.1	6.6	70-80	0.81	0.55	2.43	.99	4.2	14	11	6
	1.5	6.4	50-60	0.92	0.64	2.43	1.44	4.6	19	14	6
	2.0	6.6	25-30	1.06	0.75	2.43	1.92	5.1	24	17	7
440	1.1	13.2	80-90	1.28	0.77	4.10	1.66	7.7	14	13	13
	1.5	13.2	70-80	1.34	0.86	4.10	2.42	8.4	18	16	13
	2.0	11.7	35-45	1.36	0.88	4.10	3.23	8.8	22	17	13
	2.4	11.0	15	1.41	0.95	4.10	4.09	9.5	25	19	13
660	1.1	16.3	80-90	1.47	0.88	5.55	2.25	9.9	14	14	16
	1.5	14.6	55-65	1.47	0.88	5.55	3.37	10.4	16	15	16
	2.0	15.0	35-45	1.54	0.97	5.55	4.37	11.5	19	17	16
	2.6	15.9	15	1.74	1.10	5.55	6.16	13.7	24	20	16
880	1.1	18.7	70-80	1.72	0.95	6.89	2.79	11.9	15	15	19
	1.5	19.2	55-65	1.74	1.01	6.89	4.06	13.2	16	16	19
	2.0	18.5	20-25	1.74	1.03	6.89	5.43	14.3	17	17	19
	2.4	18.3	15	1.78	1.08	6.89	6.88	15.9	19	18	19
Pregnant yearling heifers–last 3-4 months of pregnancy												
770	0.9	15.2	100	1.34	0.77	6.23	0.65	8.1	15	15	19
	1.3	19.6	100	1.72	0.99	6.23	1.60	10.3	19	19	25
	1.8	22.0	85-100	1.94	1.12	6.24	2.63	12.9	22	21	28
880	0.9	16.5	100	1.43	0.84	6.89	0.71	8.7	16	16	21
	1.3	21.4	100	1.85	1.06	6.89	1.76	11.3	19	19	27
	1.8	25.6	85-100	2.22	1.25	6.89	2.90	14.0	22	22	33
940	0.9	17.2	100	1.52	0.88	7.21	0.74	9.0	16	16	22
	1.3	22.3	100	1.94	1.10	7.21	1.84	11.7	19	19	28
	1.8	26.7	85-100	2.31	1.32	7.21	3.03	14.6	22	22	34
Dry pregnant mature cows–middle third of pregnancy												
880		13.4	100	0.79	0.37	6.89		7.3	11	11	17
1,100		15.9	100	0.92	0.44	8.14		8.6	13	13	20
1,320		18.3	100	1.08	0.51	9.33		9.8	15	15	23
Dry pregnant mature cows–last third of pregnancy												
880	0.9	15.4	100	0.97	0.46	8.4		8.7	14	14	21
1,100	0.9	17.9	100	1.12	0.53	9.7		10.0	15	15	24
1,320	0.9	20.3	100	1.25	0.59	10.9		11.2	17	17	27
Cows nursing calves–average milking ability–first 3-4 months after calving												
880		19.4	100	1.78	1.06	9.9		10.4	25	25	21
1,100		21.6	100	1.98	1.17	11.1		11.7	27	27	24
1,320		24.2	100	2.22	1.30	12.3		13.0	28	28	27
Cows nursing calves–superior milking ability–first 3-4 months after calving												
880		23.8	100	2.57	1.52	13.0		13.5	45	41	34
1,100		26.0	100	2.84	1.67	14.2		14.8	46	43	38
1,320		28.4	100	3.10	1.83	15.5		16.1	46	44	43
Bulls, growth and maintenance (moderate activity)												
660	2.2	19.4	70-75	1.98	1.21	5.6	3.8	12.3	27	23	34
1,100	1.5	26.9	80-85	2.35	1.36	8.5	3.7	16.5	22	22	48
1,540	0.7	28.4	90-100	2.38	1.32	11.0	2.0	17.0	23	23	50
1,980	0	25.1	100	2.18	1.21	13.3	0	13.9	21	21	44

Nutrition Requirements for Dairy and Sheep

RECOMMENDED NUTRIENT CONTENT OF RATIONS FOR DAIRY CATTLE*

Nutrients (Concentration in the feed drymatter)	Cow Wt (lb) ≤880 1,100 1,320 ≥1,540	<18 <24 <31 <40	18-29 24-37 31-46 40-57	29-40 37-51 46-64 57-77	>40 >51 >64 >77	Dry Pregnant Cows	Mature Bulls	Growing Heifers and Bulls	Calf Starter Concentrate Mix	Calf Milk Replacer	Maximum Concentrations (All Classes)
Ration No.		1	2	3	4	5	6	7	8	9	Max.
Crude protein,%		13.0	14.0	15.0	16.0	11.0	8.5	12.0	16.0	22.0	—
Energy											
NE$_l$,Mcal/lb		.65	.69	.74	.78	.61	—	—	—	—	—
NE$_m$,Mcal/lb		—	—	—	—	—	.55	.57	.86	1.09	—
NE$_g$, Mcal/lb		—	—	—	—	—	—	.27	.55	.71	—
ME, Mcal/lb		1.07	1.15	1.23	1.31	1.01	.93	1.01	1.42	1.72	—
DE, Mcal/lb		1.26	1.34	1.42	1.51	1.21	1.12	1.21	1.61	1.91	—
TDN,%		63	67	71	75	60	56	60	80	95	—
Crude fiber, %		17	17	17	17	17	15	15	—	—	—
Acid detergent fiber, %		21	21	21	21	21	19	19	—	—	—
Ether extract, %		2	2	2	2	2	2	2	2	10	—
Minerals[2]											
Calcium, %		0.43	0.48	0.54	0.60	0.37	0.24	0.40	0.60	0.70	—
Phosphorus, %		0.31	0.34	0.38	0.40	0.26	0.18	0.26	0.42	0.50	—
Magnesium, %[3]		0.20	0.20	0.20	0.20	0.16	0.16	0.16	0.07	0.07	—
Potassium, %		0.80	0.80	0.80	0.80	0.80	0.80	0.80	0.80	0.80	—
Sodium, %		0.18	0.18	0.18	0.18	0.10	0.10	0.10	0.10	0.10	—
Sodium chloride, %[4]		0.46	0.46	0.46	0.46	0.25	0.25	0.25	0.25	0.25	5
Sulfur, %[4]		0.20	0.20	0.20	0.20	0.17	0.11	0.16	0.21	0.29	0.35
Iron, ppm[4,5]		50	50	50	50	50	50	50	100	100	1,000
Cobalt, ppm		0.10	0.10	0.10	0.10	0.10	0.10	0.10	0.10	0.10	10
Copper, ppm[4,6]		10	10	10	10	10	10	10	10	10	80
Manganese, ppm[4]		40	40	40	40	40	40	40	40	40	1,000
Zinc, ppm[4,7]		40	40	40	40	40	40	40	40	40	500
Iodine, ppm[8]		0.50	0.50	0.50	0.50	0.50	0.25	0.25	0.25	0.25	50
Molybdenum, ppm[9,10]		—	—	—	—	—	—	—	—	—	6
Selenium, ppm		0.10	0.10	0.10	0.10	0.10	0.10	0.10	0.10	0.10	5
Fluorine, ppm[10]		—	—	—	—	—	—	—	—	—	30
Vitamins[11]											
Vit A, IU/lb		1,455	1,455	1,455	1,455	1,455	1,455	1,000	1,000	1,727	—
Vit D, IU/lb		136	136	136	136	136	136	136	136	273	—
Vit E, ppm		—	—	—	—	—	—	—	—	300	—

[1]It is difficult to formulate high-energy rations with a minimum of 17% crude fiber. However, fat percentage depression may occur when rations with less than 17% crude fiber or 21% ADF are fed to lactating cows.

[2]The mineral values presented in this table are intended as guidelines for use of professionals in ration formulation. Because of many factors affecting such values, they are not intended and should not be used as a legal or regulatory base.

[3]Under conditions conducive to grass tetany, should be increased to 0.25% or higher.

[4]The maximum safe levels for many of the mineral elements are not well defined; estimates given here, especially for sulfur, sodium chloride, iron, copper, zinc, and manganese, are based on very limited data; safe levels may be substantially affected by feeding conditions.

[5]The maximum safe level of supplemental iron in some forms is materially lower than 1,000 ppm. As little as 400 ppm added iron as ferrous sulfate has reduced weight gains (Standish et al., 1969).

[6]High copper may increase the susceptibility of milk to oxidized flavor.

[7]Maximum safe level of zinc for mature dairy cattle is 1,000 ppm.

[8]If diet contains as much as 25% strongly goitrogenic feed on dry basis, iodine provided should be increased two times or more.

[9]If diet contains sufficient copper, dairy cattle tolerate substantially more than 6 ppm molybdenum.

[10]Maximum safe level of fluorine for growing heifers and bulls is lower than for other dairy cattle. Somewhat higher levels are tolerated when the fluorine is from less-available sources, such as phosphates. Minimum requirement for molybdenum and fluorine not established.

[11]The following minimum quantities of B-complex vitamins are suggested per unit of milk replacer: niacin, 2.6 ppm; pantothenic acid, 13 ppm; riboflavin, 6.5 ppm; pyridoxine, 6.5 ppm; thiamine, 6.5 ppm; folic acid, 0.5 ppm; biotin, 0.1 ppm; vitamin B12, 0.07 ppm; choline, 0.26%. It appears that adequate amounts of these vitamins are furnished when calves have functional rumens (usually at 6 weeks of age) by a combination of rumen synthesis and natural feedstuffs.

*Reproduced from Nutrient Requirements of Dairy Cattle, 5th edition, 1978, page 36, with the permission of the National Academy of Sciences, Washington, D.C.

NUTRIENT CONTENT OF DIETS FOR SHEEP (Nutrient Concentration in Diet Drymatter)*

Body Weight (lb)	Daily Gain or Loss (lb)	Daily Drymatter Per Animal (lb)	% Live Wt	Energy TDN (%)	DE[2] (Mcal/lb)	ME (Mcal/lb)	Total Protein (%)	DP[3] (%)	Ca (%)	P (%)	Vita-min A (IU/lb)	Vita-min D (IU/lb)
EWES[4]												
Maintenance												
110	.02	2.2	2.0	55	1.09	.91	8.9	4.8	.30	.28	580	126
132	.02	2.4	1.8	55	1.09	.91	8.9	4.8	.28	.26	632	138
154	.02	2.6	1.7	55	1.09	.91	8.9	4.8	.27	.25	676	147
176	.02	2.9	1.6	55	1.09	.91	8.9	4.8	.25	.24	713	155
Nonlactating and first 15 weeks of gestation												
110	.07	2.4	2.2	55	1.09	.91	9.0	4.9	.27	.25	527	115
132	.07	2.9	2.1	55	1.09	.91	9.0	4.9	.24	.22	535	116
154	.07	3.1	2.0	55	1.09	.91	9.0	4.9	.23	.21	580	126
176	.07	3.3	1.9	55	1.09	.91	9.0	4.9	.22	.21	618	135
Last 6 weeks of gestation or last 8 weeks of lactation suckling singles												
110	.39	3.7	3.3	58	1.18	.96	9.3	5.2	.24	.23	1,136	75
132	.40	4.2	3.2	58	1.18	.96	9.3	5.2	.23	.22	1,220	80
154	.41	4.6	3.0	58	1.18	.96	9.3	5.2	.21	.20	1,288	84
176	.42	4.8	2.8	58	1.18	.96	9.3	5.2	.21	.20	1,405	92
First 8 weeks of lactation suckling singles or last 8 weeks of lactation suckling twins												
110	-.06	4.6	4.2	65	1.32	1.09	10.4	6.2	.52	.37	920	60
132	-.06	5.1	3.9	65	1.32	1.09	10.4	6.2	.50	.36	1,008	66
154	-.06	5.5	3.6	65	1.32	1.09	10.4	6.2	.48	.34	1,082	70
176	-.06	5.7	3.2	65	1.32	1.09	10.4	6.2	.48	.34	1,189	78
First 8 weeks of lactation suckling twins												
110	-.13	5.3	4.8	65	1.32	1.09	11.5	7.2	.52	.37	805	53
132	-.13	5.7	4.3	65	1.32	1.09	11.5	7.2	.50	.36	892	58
154	-.13	6.2	4.0	65	1.32	1.09	11.5	7.2	.48	.34	966	63
176	-.13	6.6	3.7	65	1.32	1.09	11.5	7.2	.48	.34	1,030	67
Replacement lambs and yearlings[5]												
66	.40	2.9	4.3	62	1.23	1.00	10.0	5.8	.45	.25	446	58
88	.26	3.1	3.5	60	1.18	.96	9.5	5.3	.44	.24	552	72
110	.18	3.3	3.0	55	1.09	.91	8.9	4.8	.42	.23	644	84
132	.09	3.3	2.5	55	1.09	.91	8.9	4.8	.43	.24	773	101
RAMS												
Replacement lambs and yearlings[5]												
88	.55	4.0	4.5	65	1.32	1.09	10.2	6.0	.35	.19	429	56
132	.44	5.1	3.8	60	1.18	.96	9.5	5.3	.31	.17	504	66
176	.33	6.2	3.5	55	1.09	.91	8.9	4.8	.28	.16	552	73
220	.22	6.2	2.8	55	1.09	.91	8.9	4.8	.30	.17	690	90
265	.11	5.7	2.2	55	1.09	.91	8.9	4.8	.33	.18	892	116
LAMBS												
Finishing[6]												
66	.44	2.9	4.3	64	1.27	1.05	11.0	6.7	.37	.23	267	58
77	.48	3.1	4.0	67	1.36	1.09	11.0	6.7	.34	.21	290	63
88	.55	3.5	4.0	70	1.41	1.14	11.0	6.7	.31	.19	290	63
99	.55	3.7	3.8	70	1.41	1.14	11.0	6.7	.29	.18	307	67
110	.48	4.0	3.6	70	1.41	1.14	11.0	6.7	.28	.17	322	70
121	.44	4.2	3.5	70	1.41	1.14	11.0	6.7	.26	.16	335	73
Early-weaned[7]												
22	.55	1.3	6.0	73	1.46	1.18	16.0	11.5	.40	.27	644	51
44	.60	2.2	5.0	73	1.46	1.18	16.0	11.5	.36	.24	773	60
66	.66	3.1	4.7	73	1.46	1.18	14.0	9.5	.36	.24	828	65

[1]To convert drymatter to an as-fed basis, divide drymatter by percentage of drymatter.

[2]1 lb TDN = 2.0 Mcal DE (digestible energy). DE may be converted to ME (metabolizable energy) by multiplying by 82%.

[3]DP = digestible protein.

[4]Values are for ewes in moderate condition, not excessively fat or thin. Fat ewes should be fed at the next lower weight, thin ewes at the next higher weight. Once maintenance weight is established, such weight would follow through all production phases.

[5]Requirements for replacement lambs (ewe and ram) start when the lambs are weaned.

[6]Maximum gains expected. If lambs are held for later market, they should be fed as replacement ewe lambs are fed. Lambs capable of gaining faster than indicated should be fed at a higher level. Lambs finish at the maximum rate if they are self-fed.

[7]A 90-lb early-weaned lamb should be fed the same as a finishing lamb of the same weight.

*Reproduced from Nutrient Requirements of Sheep, 5th edition, 1975, page 44, with the permission of the National Academy of Sciences, Washington, D.C.

Analyzing Grains and Roughages

Analysis of feedstuffs permits you to utilize feed nutrients more efficiently and to do a more precise job of formulating rations.

Obtaining an analysis of certain feeds should be beneficial for most dairy and beef producers, and is often desirable for hog producers. By pinpointing the value of feeds precisely, feeding programs can be managed more efficiently. Thus, the advantages of having feeds tested increase as feed costs rise.

Feed tables list average nutrient analyses. By feeding on the basis of these averages, animal performance will be reduced if the actual content of the feed is below average. On the other hand, if the feed is better than average, you might feed unneeded levels of supplemental nutrients. Either way, potential profits are lost.

Systematic analysis of feeds can also be useful to the farmer feeder in evaluating the effects of soil fertility, time of harvest, curing and storage methods. Test results also may provide guidelines for pricing feeds for sale or inventory. Moisture level is particularly important in setting a value for feed, and protein level is being used increasingly as a pricing factor.

Large variations in quality occur in feeds for several reasons. Especially in forage crops, there are quality differences due to growing, harvest, weathering and storage conditions. The ratio of legumes to grasses also affects nutrient composition. Drymatter content of both forages and grains varies greatly.

The following table gives an example of the differences that exist in moisture and protein contents. Feeds were grown on Michigan farms during 1974. To further illustrate these wide differences, 21 corn silage samples tested in 1975 ranged between 4.4% and 7.6% protein, all below the average listed for the previous year.

VARIATION IN FEEDSTUFFS (Dry Basis)

Feed	No. of samples	Dry matter % Range	(Avg.)	Crude Protein % Range	(Avg.)
Legume-grass hay	15	81.4-92.8	(88.5)	7.3-18.2	(12.5)
Legume-grass silage	20	27.1-72.5	(40.0)	6.7.18.6	(13.6)
Corn silage	22	25.4-55.0	(36.2)	5.7-10.8	(8.3)
Corn silage (w /NPN)	20	30.1-50.3	(36.1)	8.8-15.9	(11.8)
Shelled corn	7	63.9-78.8	(73.1)	9.3-10.9	(10.1)

Since forages vary more widely in nutrient analysis than grains, forage testing is particularly important in dairy and beef herds where large amounts are fed. Testing of roughages is strongly recommended for dairymen, since nutrients lacking in the forage must be supplied in the higher-cost grain feed. For beef finishing operations, grain analysis is more useful since grain is the major ingredient in the ration.

EVALUATING FEEDSTUFFS

The basic method of feed evaluation has been in use for a number of years. The procedure, called "proximate analysis," fractions the feed into water, crude protein (CP), crude fiber (CF), ether extract (fat), ash, and nitrogen free extract (NFE). Total digestible nutrients (TDN) can be calculated mathematically from values determined for these six fractions.

Though the test has some limitations, it is widely available from various testing laboratories. Cost varies considerably among laboratories, but you should be able to have a complete proximate analysis run for $15 to $20 per sample.

In most feeding situations, testing for moisture content, crude protein and fiber may be all that is needed to evaluate feed quality adequately. That doesn't require that a full analysis be run. Therefore, the cost will be less.

Moisture. Testing laboratories may report results on a wet "as received" basis, or on a "drymatter" basis. You will need to know the feeding value on a drymatter basis for most ration balancing work.

To convert from a wet to a dry basis, first subtract the percent moisture from 100 to get the percent drymatter. Then, divide the test results by the percent drymatter and multiply by 100.

For example, suppose your haylage tested 55% moisture and contained 9% crude protein on an "as received" or wet basis.

$$100\% - 55\% = 45\% \text{ drymatter}$$

$$\frac{9\%}{45\%} \times 100 = 20\% \text{ crude protein}$$

Your haylage would contain 20% protein on a dry basis. The same method is used to convert other test values such as fiber or energy level.

To convert from a dry to a wet or "as fed" basis, multiply the percent present in the drymatter by the percent drymatter and divide by 100.

Crude protein content is important since it is an expensive nutrient to supplement and is not adequate in many feeds. The amount of protein is determined by measuring the nitrogen present in the feed and multiplying by 6.25. That factor is used because, on the average, feed proteins contain 16% nitrogen.

A crude protein analysis may not give a true picture in all situations, since it doesn't determine how much of the total protein is digestible by the animal. Direct determination of protein digestibility is more costly and complicated, and usually not done by the testing labs. Fiber content of the forage will provide a guideline, however, since higher protein digestibility is normally related to a lower fiber content.

Energy content of forage crops can be quite variable. Grains are more stable in energy level, thus an analysis for the amount available is less useful. If a proximate analysis is obtained on your feed sample, an energy value may be calculated and included with the results.

TDN values calculated from a proximate analysis may tend to overestimate the energy value of forages. A newer method, called "acid detergent fiber" (ADF), is available from some labs and is a more accurate measure of feed energy. This test identifies the more fibrous portion of the drymatter that will be broken down and utilized by the animal.

If an energy value for your forage sample is not obtained, you still may estimate it if you know the crude fiber. The following formula can be used for grass and legume forages. Since grain levels vary, it can't be used for silages containing grain.

$$\text{Est. TDN} = 78.7 - (\text{crude fiber} \times 0.8)$$

Crude fiber must be on a drymatter basis before using this formula. For example, if your hay tested 30% crude fiber on a drymatter basis, the formula gives an estimated TDN content of 54.7%, also on a drymatter basis.

Mineral and vitamin tests are available for grains and roughages. But, before having these analyses run, you should consider their cost relative to the cost of supplementation. In most cases, these tests will not be practical. For example, the cost of supplementing calcium is very low and typical management practices usually insure adequate amounts of vitamins. The cost of phosphorus supplementation, however, may make phosphorus determination desirable in some cases.

SAMPLING FEEDS

Poor sampling may lead to greater error than using average analysis. To obtain a representative sample, follow these procedures:

Hay samples should be taken by a core sampler from several bales or various locations in a stack. Another method is to take representative slices of hay, then chop or finely grind. After thoroughly mixing all samples together, about one quart should be retained for analysis. Wait at least two weeks after hay is stored before taking samples.

When testing silage, allow at least 30 days after filling the silo before sampling. Sample only the feedable, unspoiled material. In silos that have been opened, take 15 double handfuls of material from several locations on the new face. If sampling from the unloader on a tower silo, take the samples near the end of its operation. Mix samples well and retain about two quarts for analysis.

Grain samples should be obtained from at least five locations in the truck or bin. A grain probe is convenient for taking samples. Mix thoroughly and save about a pint as a final sample.

Ration sampling can be useful in checking formulation and uniformity. Take ten or more samples as the feed is being unloaded into the feed bunk, and retain about a quart for analysis.

Handle the sample to insure that it does not become contaminated or deteriorate before it is tested. Plastic bags are ideal containers for feed samples. Milk cartons or insulated paper bags can be used as outer containers for shipping. Laboratories may provide their own sample bags.

To prevent moisture loss, seal the container immediately. If the sample is wet, freeze it to prevent deterioration. Mail samples immediately or carry them to the laboratory.

Testing laboratories in your area should not be difficult to locate. Many state universities offer feed testing services to farmers. County farm advisors and feed dealers should be able to provide information on testing services. When using commercial labs it is a good idea to contact one or more to compare prices and services.

Other chemical tests on feedstuffs may be desirable in certain situations. For hog producers, a lysine analysis of corn samples can help reduce supplement costs. Tests can also be made for the presence of nitrates, various toxins and the presence of feed additives.

Minerals for Beef Cattle

*Deficiencies of key minerals can cause serious declines in beef production.
Cattle should have access to minerals throughout the year.*

Mineral deficiencies are not readily apparent. Effects are usually subtle and show up in slower gains, poorer feed utilization, lowered reproduction and reduced milk production. Except where there is an acute deficiency, death losses, skeletal deformities or thin, gaunt animals are rare.

The table lists the major minerals and trace minerals that are required in the diets of cattle. However, under most conditions a cattleman will need to be concerned with only a few of these.

Besides salt, the major minerals that are usually deficient in beef cattle feeds are calcium and phosphorus. Under certain conditions sulfur, magnesium and potassium may require supplementation. Certain trace minerals are deficient in some areas of the country.

MINERAL REQUIREMENTS OF BEEF CATTLE[a]

Mineral	Growing and Finishing Cattle	Dry Pregnant Cows	Breeding Bulls and Lactating Cows
Sodium, %	0.06	0.06	0.06
Calcium, %	0.18-1.04	0.18	0.18-0.44
Phosphorus, %	0.18-0.70	0.18	0.18-0.39
Magnesium, %	0.04-0.10	—[c]	0.18
Potassium, %	0.60-0.80	—[c]	—[c]
Sulfur, %	0.10	—[c]	—[c]
Iodine, ppm	[b]	.05-0.10	.05-0.10
Iron, ppm	10.0	—[c]	—[c]
Copper, ppm	4.0	—[c]	—[c]
Cobalt, ppm	0.05-0.10	0.05-0.10	0.05-0.10
Manganese, ppm	1.0-10.0	20.0	—[c]
Zinc, ppm	20-30	—[c]	—[c]
Selenium, ppm	0.10	0.05-0.10	0.05-0.10

NRC Nutrient Requirements of Beef Cattle, 1976.
[a]In % of ration dry matter or parts per million.
[b]Very small, but unknown.
[c]Unknown. Suggest using the level for growing and finishing.

Salt consumption satisfies needs for sodium and chlorine in the animal's diet. Most rations should contain 0.25% to 0.5% salt on a drymatter basis. Iodized salt is recommended in iodine deficient areas, and trace mineralized salt should be fed if no other source of trace minerals is furnished.

If salt is supplied free choice, cattle will consume more than their actual needs. More loose salt will be consumed, but the block form is adequate. Consumption varies among individual animals, but cows will average between 1.5 and 2.5 pounds per month, or about 25 pounds of salt per year.

Calcium and phosphorus are important in mineral supplements since one or both usually are deficient in ordinary rations. Grains and concentrates tend to be deficient in calcium. Forages are usually deficient in phosphorus.

Supplemental calcium is needed in high grain rations and corn silage. Phosphorus is usually needed in growing diets and beef cow rations containing mostly roughages. Lower quality roughages such as crop residues may require both calcium and phosphorus supplementation.

The desired ratio of calcium to phosphorus in the diet is between 1:1 and 2:1. An imbalance in this ratio can cause poor absorption of both minerals. However, it is relatively easy to stay within the recommended range in most situations. Generally, phosphorus is the most expensive and is the most variable in feedstuffs.

Trace minerals are needed in very small amounts, but are, nonetheless, important to the overall performance of the animal. Feeds grown in certain regions are recognized to be deficient in specific trace minerals. Trace mineral salt or mineral premixes either can be added to the ration or fed free choice to protect against deficiencies. A common practice is to ignore trace mineral content of the feed when supplementing trace minerals.

The Great Lakes regions and most of the northern U.S. are subject to iodine deficiency. In that area iodized salt is recommended unless a trace mineral salt or premix containing iodine is supplied. Areas of Florida and the eastern U.S. are deficient in cobalt. Cobalt supplementation also appears advisable for beef cows wintered on low quality roughages. Adding one ounce of cobalt chloride or cobalt sulfate to 100 pounds of free choice mineral mixture is recommended if the mixture is made with plain salt.

Selenium deficiencies are known to exist in some areas of the Midwest and the East and West Coasts. In contrast, selenium toxicity has been reported in many areas of the Great Plains. Currently, adding selenium to cattle rations is not approved. Injections containing selenium are the most common alternative. Adding selenium to pasture fertilizers has also been helpful.

SUPPLEMENTATION METHODS

The surest way to fulfill an animal's mineral requirements is to add proper levels of deficient minerals to a complete mixed ration. Another method is to add minerals to the protein supplement that is fed with the ration. A third method is to feed minerals free choice in a salt mix.

Self feeding of a salt mix is satisfactory under most conditions and is the most convenient method for cattle on pasture. Consumption of the free choice mixture won't be the same for all animals, so cattle won't meet their needs exactly. Also for complete preciseness, many different mixtures would be required to adjust for the variety of feeds offered.

Fortunately, a reasonable range in mineral allowances is permissible. Based on the major types of feedstuffs being fed, one of the free choice mixtures shown in the table below can be used on the majority of farms. Mineral-salt mixtures should be provided in weatherproof feeders located in areas that cattle frequent.

FREE CHOICE MINERAL MIXTURES

Mixture 1 — For rations containing mostly grass hay or pasture

	Amount	Calcium	Phosphorus
Dicalcium phosphate	100 lbs.	22.2%	17.9%
Trace mineral salt	100 lbs.	—	—
Total	200 lbs.	11.1%	9.0%

Mixture 2 — For rations containing mostly legume or legume-grass hay.

	Amount	Calcium	Phosphorus
Monosodium phosphate	100 lbs.	—	21.8%
Trace mineral salt	100 lbs.	—	—
Total	200 lbs.		10.9%

Mixture 3 — For corn silage and other rations low in calcium.

	Amount	Calcium	Phosphorus
Feeding limestone	100 lbs.	35.9%	—
Dicalcium phosphate	100 lbs.	22.2%	17.9%
Trace mineral salt	100 lbs.	—	—
Total	300 lbs.	19.4%	6.0%

Mixture 4 — For high grain rations.

	Amount	Calcium	Phosphorus
Feeding limestone	200 lbs.	35.9%	—
Trace mineral salt	100 lbs.	—	—
Total	300 lbs.	23.9%	

Using common mineral ingredients, mineral levels in these mixes can be adjusted, or commercial mineral mixes that contain the indicated amounts of calcium and phosphorus can be used instead of these mixtures. If the commercial mixture contains trace minerals, plain salt can be used.

Tables giving average feed analysis or actual feed test results will help you to correct deficiencies of major minerals in a complete mixed ration. Trace minerals could be provided in the protein supplement, in a premix or in trace mineral salt added to the ration.

COMMON MINERAL INGREDIENTS

	Calcium %	Phosphorus %	Sodium %	Sulfur %	Magnesium %
Beta-tricalcium phosphate	19.6	38.1	—	—	—
Bonemeal, steamed	29.0	13.6	0.5	—	—
Dicalcium phosphate	22.2	17.9	—	—	—
Limestone	35.9	—	—	—	—
Monosodium phosphate	—	21.8	32.3	—	—
Phosphate, defluorinated	33.0	18.0	4.0	—	—
Phosphoric acid	—	23.7	—	—	—
Sodium sulfate	—	—	32.4	22.5	—
Sodium tripolyphosphate	—	25.0	31.3	—	—
Magnesium sulfate	—	—	—	—	18.9
Magnesium oxide	—	—	—	—	60.0

SPECIAL CONDITIONS

Grass tetany can develop when pastures are short of magnesium. The condition is most prevalent in the spring and fall when weather is cool and is most common in older cows after calving.

Adding magnesium to the animal's diet is the surest way of preventing the problem. Magnesium oxide can be added to the mineral mix during high risk periods. Special mineral blocks or liquid supplements also will provide protection. If symptoms of tetany occur, an injection containing magnesium should be given immediately.

Magnesium oxide is unpalatable, so it should be mixed with other ingredients. A common mixture consists of equal parts of trace mineral salt, magnesium oxide, and either dried molasses, ground corn, cottonseed meal or alfalfa meal.

Sulfur is contained in the protein component of the daily diet. Rations utilizing natural protein will supply adequate sulfur. However, if high urea supplements are fed, extra sulfur will be required. About three to four pounds of sulfur should be fed per 100 pounds of urea.

Additional potassium may be beneficial to cattle grazing tall grass pastures during the January-March period. Leaching during this period apparently causes levels in forage to drop below requirements. Some tests have shown potassium supplementation during this period improved cow weights and increased calf survival. Including 20 to 25 pounds of potassium carbonate in 100 pounds of free choice salt-mineral mixture should fill this late-winter need.

Protein Alternatives for Hogs

Several feeding alternatives are available, but keep in mind your hogs' requirements for high quality protein.

Adding soybean meal to a cereal grain feed is a common way of meeting hogs' protein requirements. However, there are several options available which may help you shave protein feeding costs as prices change, shifting the relative value of various feed ingredients.

When you shift to an alternative form of protein, you must be concerned with the quality of protein, not just the total protein level. Most nutritionists agree that hogs have no requirement for protein as such. Their real need is for the component parts, called amino acids. Once the specific requirements for amino acids are met, the ration should be adequate regardless of protein content.

High quality protein feeds are those which contain the correct balance of amino acids to supply the hogs' requirements. Ten amino acids are essential in swine diets, but only three are likely to be limiting in most practical swine rations. The dietary requirements for these—lysine, tryptophan, and methionine—are shown in the table.

REQUIREMENTS FOR COMMONLY LIMITING AMINO ACIDS (PERCENT OF DIET)

Amino Acid	Grower	Finisher	Gestation	Lactation
Lysine	0.74	0.60	0.42	0.60
Tryptophan	0.11	0.07	0.07	0.13
Methionine	0.50	0.30	0.28	0.36

Requirements shown in the table differ somewhat from those listed by the National Research Council, since they reflect amino acid levels used by many universities in making feeding recommendations. Notably, a lysine level of 0.6% in the finishing diet has been found to optimize both rate of gain and lean to fat ratio in the carcass.

Lysine is the most limiting amino acid in most feeds. For example, approximately the last 100 pounds of soybean meal must be added to corn in a ton of finishing ration, solely to supply the proper lysine level. Methionine, once considered the most limiting amino acid has been shown in recent research not to be as serious a problem as once thought. Also, approximately one half of the requirement for methionine can be met by another amino acid, cystine.

PROTEIN ALTERNATIVES

Keeping in mind swine's need for protein quality, you can choose between several alternatives based on ingredient prices, the flexibility afforded by your operation, and your personal preferences. Here's a list of your basic protein supplementation options:

- **Commercial supplement.** This is the simplest method of supplementing your grain, and should also supply vitamin, mineral and additive requirements.
- **Soybean meal.** By following recommendations for each class of hogs based on percent of total protein, soybean meal will meet amino acid requirements. Price comparisons with commercial supplements should include the cost of vitamin premix, minerals and additives.
- **Alternative feeds** to replace soybean meal. You must be careful to meet amino acid requirements for the class of hogs you are feeding and observe limitations on the alternate feeds. Common ingredients that can replace part, or in some cases all, of the 44% soybean meal in the ration are:

Cottonseed meal — Normally limited to less than 10% of the diet. Gossypol content poses problems. Low in lysine.

Linseed meal — Low in lysine and can be laxative if used at high levels.

Corn gluten meal — High in protein, but low in both lysine and tryptophan. Usually limited to 10% of the diet.

Dried distillers solubles — Comparatively lower quality. Low in lysine and tryptophan.

Dehydrated alfalfa meal — Normally limited to about 5% of the finishing ration. Low in lysine and methionine.

Fish meal — Excellent quality. May be expensive.

Meat and bone meal — Can be variable in quality. Low in tryptophan. Limit to less than 10% of the diet. High levels can cause excessive calcium in diet.

Blood meal — Excellent quality, but due to its lower palatability, should be limited to less than half of the supplement.

Dried skim milk — Contains fair amounts of limiting amino acids. Especially useful for young pigs.

	Total Protein	Lysine	Methionine	Cystine	Trypto-phan
Grains					
Barley	11.0	.42	.17	.19	.16
Corn, yellow	8.8	.24	.18	.16	.07
Corn, high lysine	10.8	.42	.13	.16	.11
Milo	11.0	.27	.10	.20	.09
Wheat	13.0	.34	.24	.26	.15
Protein Feeds					
Soybean meal	44	3.0	.65	.67	.63
Cottonseed meal	41	1.7	.52	.64	.52
Linseed meal	33	1.2	.6	.66	.48
Corn gluten meal	62	1.0	1.9	1.1	.3
Dist. solubles, dried	27	.8	.6	.34	.20
Alfalfa meal	17	.73	.28	.18	.45
Fish meal, menhaden	61	4.6	1.7	.5	.6
Meat & bone meal	50	2.75	.65	.60	.29
Blood meal	80	6.90	1.0	1.4	1.05
Dried skim milk	33	2.57	.9	.4	.43

● **Amino acid supplements** to replace meal in the ration. Complete replacement of protein supplements by crystalline amino acids probably should not be considered until more research experience is achieved. However, when natural protein supplements are high priced, feeding economics may favor the use of synthetic lysine in particular.

If synthetic lysine is favorably priced, it can be used to replace 100 pounds of soybean meal in a ton of feed. Figure that 2.75 pounds of pure lysine, 97.25 pounds of corn, will replace 100 pounds of meal. Replacement beyond this level will cause a deficiency of other amino acids.

● **Modified protein grains.** High lysine corn (Opaque-2) can sharply reduce requirements for protein supplementation. However, since high lysine corn can be quite variable in amino acid content, it should be analyzed.

Average lysine content of high lysine corn is approximately 0.42% compared to normal corn at 0.25%. Assuming an average lysine content, you can use this rule of thumb in feeding high lysine corn. For every 100 pounds of high lysine corn used in the ration, decrease soybean meal by six pounds.

● **Whole cooked soybeans** to replace protein meal. Whole beans contain about 18% oil, compared to bean meal with only about 0.5%. Thus, beans are higher in energy, but lower in protein than meal. Protein content of whole beans is about 38%—meal, 44%. As a rule of thumb, figure that six pounds of whole cooked beans are equal to about five pounds of 44% meal. The higher energy content of the cooked beans may also improve feed efficiency by about 5%.

● **Legume pasture** to reduce the amount of supplementary protein needed. Midwestern research shows protein levels for all ages of hogs can be reduced by 2% from drylot recommendations when hogs are on good legume pasture. Bred sows will do well on legume pasture without any additional protein, if they receive two to three pounds of grain per day and a mineral supplement.

● **Reducing protein levels.** This may be justified when supplements are very high priced. However, you should do it carefully, after considering the alternatives. Remember, when protein levels are reduced from standard recommendations, optimum amino acid levels will not be met and performance will decline. The table shows minimum protein levels that can be used without seriously affecting performance.

MINIMUM PROTEIN LEVELS (%)

	Standard Recommendations	Reduced Levels
Gestation	15	12
Lactation	15	14
Starter	18	18*
Grower (40-125 lbs.)	16	15
Finisher (125-Market)	14	12

*No change

Going below the recommended minimum for finishing rations will sacrifice leanness, particularly in meatier hogs, and reduce gains and feed efficiency significantly.

FINISHING RATION EXAMPLES

Ingredients-lbs.	1	2	3	4	5
Yellow corn	1,660		1,598	1,757	1,755
High lysine corn		1,790			
Soybean meal (44%)	300	170		200	120
Whole soybeans			362		
Blood meal					80
L-Lysine				2.75	
Ground limestone	10	10	10	10	15
Dicalcium phosphate	20	20	20	20	20
Trace mineralized salt	10	10	10	10	10

Vitamin mixture and antibiotic as desired.

Substituting protein sources and adjusting rations will be successful if you pay close attention to the nutrient needs of your hogs. The basic alternatives shown on this page can help you to adjust to price fluctuations and problems of feed ingredient availability.

When revising rations, remember that you may have to adjust vitamin and mineral supplement levels. Refer to tables listing the nutrient requirements of swine, plus tables showing feedstuff analysis in order to determine these needs.

Processing Grain for Beef

Several processing methods increase the value of grains and make the conversion of grain to beef more efficient.

Processing methods that give more efficient feed utilization have important cost-saving aspects since feeding a beef animal to market weight requires 40 to 50 bushels of grain or more, depending on efficiency.

Processes that change the physical structure of the grain kernels have been found to increase efficiency by making them more digestible by animals. Until a few years ago, grain processing was simply breaking or crushing the kernel. Recently, newer techniques have been developed which add the forces of heat, moisture and pressure.

No test comparisons are available for all the processing methods described on this page, but newer processes using heat or moisture increase the value of most grains significantly over straight milling. Equipment costs for some processes, however, may limit their use to larger operations.

Grinding and rolling have been popular methods of processing various dry grains. For grain sorghum in particular, coarse grinding is necessary for good utilization. One disadvantage has been the dustiness and small particles, which cause lower animal acceptance of the feed. Where dustiness is a problem, rolling is preferred over grinding.

Grinding is not always necessary. Ground corn offers no advantage over shelled corn in high concentrate rations. At roughage levels of 20% or more, grinding may improve the value of corn. High moisture milo should be ground before feeding, but there is no advantage to grinding high moisture corn in rations with less than 15% roughage.

Steam flaking is common in larger feeding operations of the West and Southwest, particularly where large amounts of milo are being used. Equipment costs for boilers and processing machinery have prevented many smaller feeders from flaking. Flaking gives the greatest improvement in feeding value to milo, with corn second. Less benefit occurs from flaking wheat and barley.

Flaking is a refinement of the steam rolling process. For flaked grain the kernels are steamed for a longer period (15 to 30 minutes), then rolled to very flat, thin flakes. Quality of the flakes produced is quite important to their feeding value. Thinly flaked grain is the most desirable. Proper operation of the equipment is important, and quality control of the flakes is a critical aspect of the process. Rollers are usually maintained to produce flakes 1/32 inch thick.

Flakes coming from the rollers are generally 18% to 20% moisture, too high for storage in conventional bins for any period of time. In most cases, the flakes are dried to around 15% moisture after being rolled.

Due to the better digestibility of steam flaked grains, daily gains of fed cattle are usually increased by about 6% and feed efficiency improved by approximately 10%. Benefits are most apparent in high concentrate diets.

Roasted corn is processed by heating in a roasting machine to approximately 300 degrees. Dry heating results in a moderate expansion of the kernel and changes the texture of the grain. A nut-like flavor is produced that is highly palatable to cattle.

The reason for improvement from roasting is not completely known, but it is apparently affected somewhat by a partial gelatinization of the grain starch, making it easier to digest. Studies have shown that, although cattle will consume approximately the same amount of roasted grain as they do raw grain, both daily gains and feed required per pound of gain are considerably improved from roasting. Tests at both Purdue and Iowa showed roasting improved gains 6% to 12% and feed utilization 10% to 14%. Roasting shows promise since cost of roasting equipment may be lower than that of some other processes.

Popped grain sorghum is produced in fundamentally the same way as you pop corn at home. Kernels are heated to approximately 300 degrees, where they pop and expand. Milo is reduced in weight from approximately 49 pounds per cubic foot to 6 pounds per cubic foot by popping. In developing the process, one problem has been the number of "old maid" kernels left unpopped.

In Texas tests, cattle fed popped milo showed a marked reduction in the amount consumed, probably due to the bulkiness. Since smaller amounts were eaten, daily gains were depressed, but feed efficiency was improved 17% over cattle fed regular milo.

A variation of the popping process is a system called Jet-Sploder. Grain is dry heated to a critical temperature, then fed into rollers where it pops and then is flaked. Drying of the popped flakes isn't necessary for storage.

Micronizing of grain sorghum is accomplished by heating the grain with infrared waves emitted by a gas-fired generator. The name micronizing comes from the microwaves that do the heating. Grain is heated without popping, then put through a cutting type of roller which produces a dry, uniform product similar in appearance to flaked grain.

More research in Texas has shown that micronizing has approximately the same feeding value as steam flaked milo. Processing costs, however, appear to favor micronizing and may make the process appealing to smaller feeders.

Exploded grain represents a unique moist heat and pressure process. In a commercial exploding unit, grain is metered into a chamber where steam is added under 200 to 400 p.s.i. pressure. Once the steam has penetrated the grain, the chamber is suddenly lowered to atmospheric pressure, resulting in the rapid expansion or "exploding" of the kernels. Quality control with this process is of less concern since nearly 100% of the grain is exploded. All types of grains can be exploded, but again, milo shows the greatest improvement in feeding value.

Density of the milo is reduced from 56 pounds per bushel to approximately 10 pounds. This makes it desirable to run the grain through a roller to reduce bulk and improve its handling qualities. Equipment installation costs about the same as for a steam flaking system.

Extrusion is a process that produces a ribbon-like product which breaks into small flakes of various sizes and shapes depending on the kind of grain and its moisture content. In the extruder, grain is crushed by a spiral screw and forced out through a small hole. Pressure on the grain escaping from the hole heats it to a temperature of approximately 200 degrees. No drying of the extruded grain is generally needed for storage.

To date, research with extruded grain has been limited and results variable. However, extruded milo appears to be nearly equal to steam flaked milo. Tests so far with corn have not shown its value improved as much as by steam flaking.

Reconstitution of feed grains is a simple process that is available to many smaller feeders. Reconstitution simply brings dry grain to a high moisture level by adding water. By adding water, the feeding value of the grain is improved, making it comparable to normal high moisture grain. Feeding efficiency is improved by as much as 10%.

Water is added to grain to raise the moisture content to 25% to 30%. The grain is then ensiled and allowed to ferment for about 21 days. This gives it handling and storage characteristics similar to grain harvested in the high moisture state.

For many feeders, the drawback to reconstituted grain is that it should be ensiled. For others, reconstituted grain has the advantage of permitting more efficient use of their silo structures. More than one filling of high moisture grain can be made after harvest in a single structure by reconstituting dry stored grains.

Commercial equipment is available for reconstituting grain. Another method is to simply pour or spray water over the grain before it goes into the silo. If grain is watered and then augered up into a vertical silo, the mixing action and pressures exerted in the auger improve moisture absorption. The higher the auger, the more pressure that is applied. Heating the water to about 160 degrees also increases the rate of absorption.

Reconstituting grain, then allowing it to ensile, is thought to bring about a partial germination of the kernel. The conversion of starch to simpler sugars in the process appears to cause an easier breakdown in the animal's rumen. Tests have shown that grain should be reconstituted and stored whole. Grinding or rolling the grain would aid in water uptake, but apparently destroys the ability of the grain to partially germinate. If desired, grain can be processed after coming out of storage for feeding.

Results of feeding tests using reconstituted high moisture corn and milo have indicated rather consistent advantages. Improvement for wheat and barley is less pronounced and results of feeding trials are more variable.

Feeding High Moisture Corn

Feeding high moisture grains provides an excellent option for many feeders, but proper storage and handling is important.

Grain with a moisture level between 22% and 30% is normally considered high moisture for feed uses. However, most feeders try to hold moisture at 26% to 28% for best storage and feeding results. Wet grain should be ensiled for a period of at least 21 days before feeding to allow for fermentation. Exception is acid treated grain which does not require tight storage and does not ferment.

Several storage methods for high moisture corn can be used satisfactorily. Whole ear or shelled corn can be ground and stored in trench or bunker silos. Spoilage losses are kept to a minimum by tight packing and sealing with a plastic cover. Concrete stave silos can be used, but may need added reinforcement due to the extra weight. Care must be taken to seal the stave silo, especially when storing whole shelled corn. Oxygen limiting silos give good results for all types of high moisture corn. Acid grain preservatives allow corn to be stored in a variety of structures without spoilage by blocking fermentation of the grain.

BEEF CATTLE FEEDING

There are advantages to feeding high moisture corn to beef cattle. Acceptability is generally improved over dry grain and cattle can be kept on feed with less difficulty. Tests indicate that high moisture corn has a greater feed value than dry corn when figured on a dry matter basis.

Several feeding trials at Purdue University indicate good results from high moisture shelled corn, ensiled either whole or ground. Purdue researchers believe that, on the average, high moisture corn will give approximately 10% better feed conversion.

At Iowa State University, a four year study showed high moisture whole shelled corn stored in a stave silo and in a sealed silo to be equal. Both gave slightly faster gains and 9% better feed efficiency than dry corn.

An advantage of 9% was also found for high moisture corn in Nebraska trials. However, processing and storage methods made significant differences in the final feeding value. The best feed was whole kernel high moisture corn stored in a sealed structure and fed whole. Second best was corn that was rolled before feeding. Corn that had been rolled before going into the silo and acid treated corn rated no better than dry corn in feeding value.

Overall, research seems to indicate somewhat better efficiency from corn that has been properly ensiled in the whole kernel.

Acids produced in high moisture corn ground before storage may have a tendency to reduce dry matter intake of cattle on high grain rations. Feeding 10% to 15% roughage on a dry basis will prevent this problem. Feeding some dry corn with the wet corn is also effective.

Adding urea and minerals at the time the corn goes into the silo will help to correct protein and mineral deficiencies. It also has been effective in buffering some of the acids produced in ground high moisture corn. Here's a simple additive mixture.

HIGH MOISTURE CORN ADDITIVE MIXTURE	Pounds or percent
Urea, 45% nitrogen	40
Limestone, feed-grade	33
Salt, trace-mineralized	27
	100

This mixture should be added at the rate of 0.4 pound per ton of corn for each percent dry matter in the corn. For example, a ton of 26% moisture corn would get 29.6 pounds of additive. If urea is used alone, a rate of 0.16 pound for each percent dry matter should be used.

Ground ear corn makes a good feed when ensiled at moisture levels of 24% to 30%. Since the cob makes up 20% of the material, no other roughage need be fed. Shelled corn added during the later finishing period will increase energy. In a summary of 14 tests, the high moisture ground ear corn increased gains 3% and feed efficiency 10% over dry ground ear corn. Apparently high moisture storage increases the feed value of the cob portion of the material.

High moisture milo gave good results in Kansas, Oklahoma and Texas tests. In many cases, high moisture storage improves the value of milo more than it does corn. High moisture milo that was stored whole gave gains similar to dry milo but averaged 10% more efficient. Milo ground for storage in a trench silo was 6.5% more efficient.

DAIRY CATTLE AND HOGS

Dairy cows and hogs can make good use of high moisture grains. Research has shown, however, that performance is as good, but generally no better than it is on dry grains. High moisture storage for hog and dairy operations should be justified by advantages other than improved feeding value.

No more than a day's supply of ensiled corn should be prepared for feeding because of spoilage. Corn treated with acid shouldn't spoil and can be used in self feeders. Complete mixed feeds work best for hogs as they often won't eat enough self-fed supplement.

Equal milk production on either dry or high moisture corn is the general conclusion after several dairy tests. Although some trials have shown a decrease in fat level, this is avoided when roughage is kept at adequate levels.

PRESERVING QUALITY

By harvesting and storing high moisture corn you may be able to save a higher percent of nutrients than you could if the grain were dry. But, good management of the grain is needed to preserve its ultimate value as livestock feed. Proper storage is the biggest factor in preserving quality. This includes careful control of moisture levels, uniform distribution in the silo, and proper packing and sealing of the structure.

High moisture grain storage should be sized according to the amount of feed that will be used. Rate of removal of the high moisture grain is particularly important for silos that are not air tight. Once feeding begins, enough material must be removed daily to prevent spoilage on the open face. Generally two to four inches should be removed from the top of a stave silo—somewhat more from the face of a trench silo. To prevent spoilage of the grain after it has been removed from the silo, feeding within 4 to 10 hours is usually required.

Adjustments for moisture. A common error in feeding high moisture grain is not making ade-quate adjustment for a lower dry matter content than in dry grain. Multiply the weight of high moisture grain by the factors in the table below to adjust it to a 15.5% moisture basis. You can also use these factors when purchasing high moisture grain. If you are buying on a 15.5% moisture basis, multiply the gross weight of the high moisture grain by the appropriate moisture factor. The answer will be the correct pay weight.

FACTORS FOR CONVERTING HIGH MOISTURE GRAIN TO A 15.5% MOISTURE BASIS

Moisture %	Multiplier	Moisture %	Multiplier
21	.935	26	.876
22	.923	27	.864
23	.911	28	.852
24	.899	29	.840
25	.888	30	.828

RECONSTITUTION

By using reconstitution, silos can be refilled with high moisture grain anytime of the year by simply adding water to dry grains. Also, water can be added to equalize the moisture contents of high moisture grains so no adjustments for dry matter variations need be made later when feeding the grain.

AMOUNT OF WATER TO BE ADDED IN ENSILING HIGH MOISTURE GRAIN

% Moisture In Grain	% Moisture Desired						
	30	29	28	27	26	25	24
	Gallons of water to be added per ton						
29	3.5	--	--	--	--	--	--
28	7.0	3.5	--	--	--	--	--
27	10.5	7.0	3.5	--	--	--	--
26	14.0	10.5	7.0	3.5	--	--	--
25	17.5	14.0	10.5	7.0	3.5	--	--
24	21.0	17.5	14.0	10.0	7.0	3.5	--
23	24.5	21.0	17.5	13.5	10.0	7.0	3.5
22	28.0	24.5	21.0	17.0	13.0	10.0	7.0
21	31.5	28.0	24.0	20.5	17.0	13.0	10.0
20	35.0	31.5	27.5	24.0	20.0	17.0	13.0
19	38.5	35.0	31.0	27.5	23.5	20.0	17.0
18	42.0	38.5	34.5	31.0	27.0	23.5	20.0
17	46.0	42.0	38.0	34.0	30.5	26.5	23.5
16	50.0	46.0	42.0	37.5	34.0	30.0	26.0

Water should be mixed with the grain before it goes into the silo rather than sprinkled on after the silo is filled. The table shows the amount of water to be added per ton of grain to bring moisture to desired level.

Feeding results from properly reconstituted high moisture grain are comparable to corn that is harvested wet. Grain should be reconstituted whole for optimum feeding results.

Urea and Minerals for Corn Silage

Adding urea and/or mineral supplements to silage before storage helps correct nutrient deficiencies and can also enhance the fermentation process.

On good land, more pounds of beef or milk can be produced per acre with corn silage than with any other crop. It is a high-energy feed containing 60% to 70% TDN dry matter basis. But on a net energy basis, corn silage rates relatively lower than grain. It contains more energy for maintenance than for production. This makes it an excellent winter feed for beef cows and growing cattle where maintenance requirements are a large percentage of total energy needs.

SUPPLEMENTING SILAGE WITH UREA

Protein deficiency is the most serious limitation of corn silage. At a normal moisture content of 70%, it contains 2.5% protein or less. On a dry matter basis, it contains about 8% protein.

Protein deficiency can be corrected economically with urea at time of ensiling. Feed grade urea is usually 45% nitrogen—equivalent protein content is 281%. But urea contains no energy and must be balanced with energy and minerals before nitrogen can be utilized by an animal in the synthesis of amino acids and protein. Corn silage, with its high-energy content, is a natural "carrier."

Adding 10 pounds of feed grade urea (45%) to a ton of 30% dry matter corn silage raises the protein content to 12.7% on a dry matter basis. Including urea with corn silage adds only protein—the major deficiency. Too, all cattle get a uniform amount of urea. If mixed in the concentrate mixture, the animals consuming the most concentrates will get the heaviest dose. Generally, if concentrates are limited, or not fed at all, the addition of 10 pounds of urea per ton of silage will bring the protein level up to near requirements for growing and finishing beef cattle, growing dairy heifers and maintaining dry dairy cows. Urea treated silage is acceptable at the 10-pound-per-ton rate.

Dry matter content of silage should not be much less than 30% or more than 40% if urea is added. A dry matter content around 35% is best. In wet silage, much of the urea would be lost to excessive seepage, while urea may escape as ammonia if the silage is too dry. Also, high ammonia levels may make the silage unpalatable to livestock.

High levels of urea added to silage can decrease performance. While levels of 20 pounds per ton have given good feeding results, a common recommendation is to limit urea to no more than 2% of the dry matter in a ton of silage. Using this guide, up to 14 pounds of urea could be added to silage containing 35% dry matter.

ADD UREA TO SILAGE AT TIME OF STORAGE

Adding urea to silage as the silo is filled avoids mixing later as each batch of silage is fed. Urea also enhances fermentation during the ensiling process and apparently improves silage quality. Additions of either urea or limestone, or a combination of the two, increase the production of organic acids, particularly lactic acid, in the silage.

Incorporating urea into the silage at filling time can be done in several ways. It's easiest when using a blower to fill the structure, since the action of the blower helps mix in the urea. One common way, when filling uprights, is to simply spread the urea over a wagonload of chopped silage. The unloading and blowing process mixes the urea into the silage satisfactorily. Another approach is to rig a fertilizer box from a corn planter to the blower, to meter urea into the stream of material. Weigh one or two average loads of silage to get proper proportion.

Adding urea to bunker or trench silos is a little more difficult. When a good mixer wagon or truck-mounted unit is used to feed the silage from a bunker, adequate mixing occurs before the silage gets to the feed bunk. Two common ways to distribute the urea in the silo are using a hand operated seeder as the silo is being filled, or dissolving the urea in water and distributing it uniformly over each load or layer.

Utilizing urea-corn silage. There are any number of combinations of ingredients that could be used in ration formulation with urea-corn silage. The rations presented in the next table are taken from Iowa State recommendations and will meet the energy and protein needs for the various types of animals at the performance level indicated. The rations are based on the assumption that iodized salt and a simple mineral will be provided on a free choice basis. Also, vitamin A supplementation is recommended for finishing beef.

EXAMPLE RATIONS WITH UREA-CORN SILAGE

Ration Ingredients		Protein, lbs.	TDN, lbs.
Rations for wintering 400 to 500 lb. calves or dairy heifers to gain 1.6 lbs. per day			
Urea-corn silage	25 lbs.	.95	5.0
Ground ear corn	3 lbs.	.22	2.2
Supplement (44%)	.75 lbs.	.33	.6
		1.50	7.8
Urea-corn silage	25 lbs.	.95	5.0
Alfalfa hay	5 lbs.	.75	2.5
		1.70	7.5
Rations for finishing 400 to 600 lb. calves as short yearlings to gain 2.25 lbs. per day			
Urea-corn silage	30 lbs.	1.14	6.0
Ground ear corn	5 lbs.	.44	3.6
Supplement (44%)	.5 lbs.	.22	.4
		1.80	10.0
Rations for finishing yearling cattle, 800 lbs., to gain 2.6 lbs. per day			
Urea-corn silage	35 lbs.	1.33	7.0
Ground ear corn	10 lbs.	.73	7.4
Supplement (44%)	.5 lbs.	.22	.4
		2.28	14.8
Urea-corn silage	39 lbs.	1.48	7.8
Ground shelled corn	8 lbs.	.71	6.4
Supplement (44%)	.25 lbs.	.11	.2
		2.30	14.4
Rations for 800 to 1,000 lb. dairy heifers			
Urea-corn silage	60 lbs.	2.28	12.0
Ration for wintering 1,000 lb. pregnant beef cows			
Urea-corn silage	25 lbs.	.95	5.0
Mixed hay	4 lbs.	.52	1.9
Straw or cobs	6 lbs.	--	2.7
		1.47	9.6

IOWA STATE

ADDING MINERALS TO CORN SILAGE

Limestone is generally added to corn silage to increase the content of organic acids and improve the nutritional value of silage. While the addition of limestone raises calcium levels, there has been considerable variation in the feeding benefits derived from using limestone in the silage. Generally, the addition of limestone has been shown to improve both gains and efficiency in beef cattle, but there has been little or no benefit shown for lactating dairy animals.

Other mineral additives can be used to round out deficiencies in the silage. In addition to calcium, these include phosphorus, sulfur and other trace minerals. The addition of proper amounts of these minerals and urea at filling time should mean no other supplementation will be needed in a high-silage growing program.

A "complete" corn silage can be produced by adding a dry urea-mineral mixture or adding a commercially available liquid, such as Pro-sil. Composition of the urea-mineral mixture is shown below. Finely ground shelled corn is included in the mixture to prevent caking, since it tends to attract moisture.

UREA-MINERAL MIXTURE FORMULATION

Ingredient	Percent	Pounds Per Ton
Urea (45% N)	30.35	607
Dicalcium Phosphate (20% Ca, 18.5% P)	6.80	136
Sodium Sulfate (22.5% S)	6.05	121
Trace Mineral Salt (High Zn)	6.80	136
Finely Ground Shelled Corn	50.00	1,000
Total	100.00%	2,000 lbs.

Pro-sil is a liquid silage additive, composed of anhydrous ammonia, molasses and minerals, that was developed and tested at Michigan State University. Use of either of these silage treatments is intended to meet the protein and mineral needs of cattle that are full fed on silage, provided shelled corn isn't fed in excess of 1% of the animal's body weight per day.

APPLICATION RATE FOR TREATING CORN SILAGE

Percent Dry Matter of Corn Silage	Pounds of Pro-Sil Per Ton of Silage	Pounds of Urea-Mineral Per Ton of Silage	Pounds of Urea Per Ton of Silage
28%	36	33	11
30%	39	35	11
32%	41	38	12
34%	44	40	12
36%	46	42	13
38%	49	45	14
40%	51	47	14
42%	54	*	*
44%	57	*	*

*Do not treat silage above 40% DM with urea or urea-mineral mixture.

Adding either of the treatments containing minerals according to the application rates shown above will boost the nutrient content of silage to approximately the following levels on a dry matter basis: 12.5% crude protein; 0.40% calcium; 0.30% phosphorus; and 0.45% trace mineral salt. Sodium sulfate should be included at the rate of one pound of sulfur for each 15 pounds of nitrogen in the supplement.

Grinding, Measuring and Mixing Feed

The heart of any farm feed plant is the process of grinding, measuring and mixing. As equipment in this area constantly improves, your range of choices widens.

Hammer mills will grind any type of feed from small grains to hay, one at a time or all at once, and in a variety of grinds from very fine to coarse. The only exception is the small electric blender-grinder which handles up to four different grains or supplements at once, but no roughage.

CAPACITY OF SMALL MILL
by type of livestock fed

	Pounds Per Day Per Animal	1/2 Hour No. Fed	1 Hour No. Fed	2 Hours No. Fed
Dairy or beef	20.00	45	100	200
Beef feeding (grain sup.)	10.00	90	200	400
Laying hens	.30	3,350	6,700	13,400
Broilers (10 weeks)	.24	4,100	8,300	16,500
Heavy hogs	7.50	135	270	540

MIX MILL, INC.

Capacity of any mill will vary, depending on fineness of grind, moisture of ingredients, kind of material, number of hammers, and power available. An average range for a hammer mill is from 600 to 1,200 pounds per horsepower-hour. For many operations, the 2 to 5 hp mills are adequate. The table above will give you an indication of how many head of livestock can be fed per day with a small, automatic electric mill. Where greater mill capacity is needed, larger hammer mills are used. Shown are conservative estimates of mill capacity with 20 to 30 hp available.

CAPACITY OF LARGE HAMMER MILL
(pounds per hour)

Screen	Baled Hay	Oats	Shelled Corn	Ear Corn
Fine	1,000 & up	5,700 & up	12,400 & up	11,300 & up
Medium	2,000 & up	9,000 & up	16,900 & up	14,700 & up
Coarse	3,000 & up	10,200 & up	20,300 & up	15,800 & up

SIZE OF SCREEN

Fineness of Grind	Hay	Oats	Shelled Corn	Ear Corn
Very fine to fine	1/2"	1/8"	1/8"	1/4"
Fine	3/4"	1/4"	1/4"	1/2"
Medium	1"	1/2"	3/4"	1"
Coarse	1-1/2"	1"	1-1/2"	2"

H. C. DAVIS SONS MFG. CO., INC.

Number hammers, 80; diameter of rotor with hammers extended, 24 inches; total granulation area, 840 square inches; speed under load, 2,400-2,800 rpm; power, 20 hp electric, 2-plow tractor or 30 hp electric, 3-plow tractor.

While many hammer mills handle both hay and grain, some are built as individual hay grinders where baled hay must be chopped and often mixed into a ration. Both stationary and mobile pto models are available. A typical hay grinder has a capacity of about seven tons per hour and will cost around $2,500, including conveyors, shafts, etc.

Roller mills have an average capacity of 900 to 1,800 pounds per horsepower-hour, depending greatly upon size and type of roll. Given in the table is a typical range of capacities for available power. Expect the lowest capacity when rolls have 14 or 15 corrugations per inch of roll, and highest capacity when rolls have 5-1/2 or 6 corrugations per inch.

If you plan only to crush or crack shelled corn, a roller mill with fewer corrugations per inch allows

Roller Mill Capacity*

Horsepower	Capacity, lbs./hr.
2	3,000 to 5,000
5	7,000 to 17,000
10	10,000 to 33,600
20	20,000 to 84,000
25	84,000

*Based on pounds of shelled corn.

you to get highest capacity per horsepower. But if you plan to roll one or more small grains such as barley or milo, select a roller mill with about 14 or 15 corrugations per inch to get a uniform product.

Some roller mills have several sets of rolls, one for each grain. One make has two sets of rolls to handle more than one type of grain at a time. Grain goes through both sets of rolls to get a fine enough grind for hogs, although most roller mills are used for preparing cattle rations where a cracked, crushed, rolled or crimped product is required. Roller mills produce a more uniform product than most hammer mills, with fewer fines.

Burr mills will do a uniform job of grinding ear corn and all types of grain. A 25 hp burr mill will produce 18,000 to 21,000 pounds of ground ear corn, or 33,000 pounds of ground shelled corn per hour. This is about 800 pounds of ear corn and 1,300 pounds of shelled corn per horsepower-hour. Most of them are operated by tractor pto.

MEASURING

Weight measuring in batches is most accurate, but you generally lose the advantage of continuous flow. Scales are accurate to a fraction of 1%, using either electronic types or the conventional arm type, although the latter is more subject to human error. Dial types are often preferred because the operator can anticipate "cut-off" of feed flow. Here are five basic ways to measure feed by weight:

(1) Weigh ingredients into a truck or trailer-mounted mixer unit using a platform scale.

(2) In place of a platform scale, electronic load cells are used on trucks and ingredient weights are read on a dial console. They are battery powered. This system works well when feed sources are scattered.

(3) The ration is weighed by a hopper-bottom bin mounted on a scale. Feed then flows into a grinder and onto a mixer.

(4) The mixer is mounted on scales and ingredients are delivered to it from the grinder or storage.

(5) The dump-type meter is semicontinuous, and operates on the counterbalance principle. When one of two compartments are filled, the unit flips over so the second fills while the first empties. A counter records the number of trips made. Error is less than 5%.

Volumetric meters generally have an error rate of less than 5%, which is considered adequate for concentrates. Several meters are now on the market for adding extremely small portions of ingredients to the ration.

The auger meter is one of the most accurate. When the metering rate is controlled by regulating the speed, it has an accuracy of 98% or better.

The vibrator meter is also very accurate. Recent designs have been tested at 98% accuracy. It operates without a motor by using an electric vibrator attached to the bottom of a metal trough and box. Output is measured with an adjustable gate or by adjusting the current in the vibrator coil. It is inexpensive, and is not easily plugged by trashy or limpy material.

A belt-type blender is also used in automatic blender-grinders, as well as auger meters. The height of each spout over the belt is adjusted to give the correct ratio of ingredients. These are also very accurate.

Another type is the rotating table meter with capacity regulated by adjusting the height of the grainspout centered above the disk. Accuracy was acceptable but some tendency for clogging was noted. Newer models may have solved this problem, however.

The metal belt meter with a strike-off gate is slightly more expensive than some others, but it tends to do a better job of metering nonfree flowing materials. Fluted wheel meters are similar to those used in grain drills. It is accurate and operated by sliding the fluted wheel in and out of a well at the bottom of the feed hopper.

Roughage meters for silage and for haylage and silage in a continuous flow system are available. As material flows through the meter, a press wheel transmits electrical impulses to a counter dial unit.

MIXING

For complex rations there are two types of batch mixers—vertical and horizontal. Small electric grinder-mixers blend the ingredients together, eliminating the need for a separate mixer.

Vertical mixers use an upright inverted cone tank with a vertical auger in the center. These are the least costly and capacities range from 1/2 ton to 3 tons. Ceiling height may be a limiting factor when installing one. A 3-ton mixer may be 20 feet tall. Often, two smaller mixers are used. Most portable grinder-mixers are equipped with vertical mixers. These units handle all grains, supplements, premixes and roughages, and molasses in dried form.

Horizontal mixers are equipped with paddles, augers, or a combination to do the mixing. Power requirements are much higher than for vertical mixers. A 1/2-ton mixer needs 5 to 10 hp while 3 to 5 ton mixers take 30 to 50 hp. The horizontal is best adapted for mixing coarse roughages such as silage and is preferred for liquid molasses.

Method of Feed Distribution

Once you can justify mechanized feed handling, you must choose the system that will be the most economical and efficient for your operation.

Basic systems of mechanized feed distribution can be classed into three categories.

● Continuous flow from silo or bin storage to mechanized bunk. It can be fully automated and ingredients are generally proportioned on a volumetric basis. Equipment is available to deliver separate rations to different lots automatically.

● Batch mixing and proportioning and mechanized bunk delivery. Batch system allows use of weighing for accurate ingredient control— best for careful ration preparation.

● Batch mixing and proportioning and delivery in batch to fenceline bunks using side-unloading wagon, pto grinder-mixer or side unloading auger wagon that mixes ration. Again, ration is prepared by weight, but more labor is required for delivery.

Flexibility is essential. Plan for easy expansion and for higher resale value if you don't expand. Can you change enterprises with minimum modification? Also, apply these factors to your choice of a distribution system: Arrangement of current facilities; size, number of head; type, beef, dairy or diversified; number of rations; control desired over formulation and delivery; size of feed area and distance from storage; indoor or outdoor feeding; and available labor.

MECHANICAL BUNK DELIVERY

The trend is away from auger bunks toward feeders using belts, chains and slats, and trays. With more farmers feeding roughage-concentrate mixtures, most auger systems tend to separate fine and coarse particles, depositing more fines near the head of the bunk, coarse ones toward the end.

With augerless feeders, particle separation is minimized. They also have much lower power requirements, allowing you to use longer feed bunks. Capacity is also greater, they don't wear as fast and are less noisy than augers.

When you convey concentrates only, an auger is generally best. Chain and slat types tend to ride over concentrates, and belts allow material to worm underneath.

Small, uniform particles handle most efficiently. Haylage is hardest of all. It's important to cut it as fine as possible.

A good bunk feeder delivers feed with little in-gredient separation, but it must first receive a ration that is properly metered and mixed. It should come in a steady, uniform flow. This depends on good silo unloaders, which are available, and on good metering and proportioning devices. Various types are on the market, but further development is needed for accurate metering devices in a continuous flow system that are low cost and easy for recordkeeping.

Many types of feeders are on the market. The revolving tube is shown in Drawing A. It is open on the top. When material reaches the end, the entire tube rotates and drops feed in the bunk down the length at the same time and to either side.

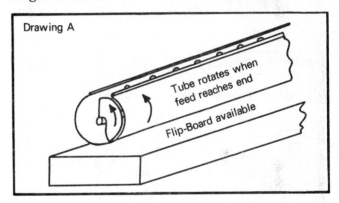

Drawing A

Tube rotates when feed reaches end

Flip-Board available

Drawing B illustrates a tray on a chain system. Each tray carries a load of feed until it is dropped in the bunk.

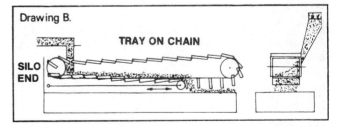

Drawing B.

TRAY ON CHAIN

SILO END

A chain and slat type is shown in Drawing C. Feed drops onto the apron at point C. The traveling apron, A, drops feed on one-half of the bunk length and then reverses direction and fills the other half. A one horsepower motor can handle 225 feet of bunk and flow rate may be more than 300 pounds per minute.

Drawing D shows a belt with a plow arrangement to divert feed to either side of the bunk. One company uses a revolving brush to sweep feed off the belt that is reversible.

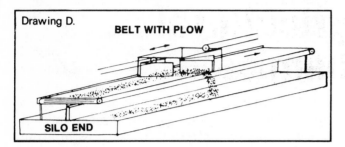

Drawing D.
BELT WITH PLOW
SILO END

Another unit uses chain and slats over a tapered board. Board is wide near the silo end and tapers the length of the bunk. The tapered system allows feed to drop into the bunk down its entire length at the same time. Another type is the revolving chain. It works like a gutter cleaner.

Consider these factors: ● Judge merits of feeder types as they apply to your setup. Check their design flexibility. ● Ability to handle heavy and light flow of any ingredient and coordinates easily with unloaders, metering, and proportioning equipment. ● Service policies of dealer and manufacturer. ● Installation costs.

BATCH DELIVERY

Both the bunk feeder wagon and auger mixer wagon are used for outdoor fenceline feeding and sometimes for indoor bunk distribution.

Bunk feeders are usually powered by pto, side-unloading boxes. They deliver forage-based rations to bunks and do some mixing during unloading. Capacities range from 100 to over 700 cubic feet. A chain and slat bottom moves material forward. At the front, two or three beaters, mounted one over the other, mix and kick it onto the cross-conveyor for discharge in the bunk.

Many bunk feeders have reversible bed conveyors—a handy feature for rear end gate or rear side unloading. Some feeders unload from only the left or right front side and on some the cross-conveyor is reversible for either side—you may find this flexibility desirable.

Besides feed bunk discharge, these wagons are used for hauling freshly chopped forage and unloading into the blower. This makes a wagon's discharge features critical. Discharge height and distance from the wagon are important, too.

Maximum delivery heights range from four to five feet. Conveyor extensions help compensate for unsuitable heights. Chain and slat cross-conveyors are easily extended. Auger cross-conveyors can be fitted with extensions too, but they won't handle bales. Check options.

Usually, one beater for each two feet of box height is used. They will break up chunks and mix ingredients when layers of grain or supplement are placed on the load.

For power, the larger wagons should be pulled by at least a 60 hp tractor, depending on weight and softness of the ground.

Auger mixer wagons, mounted on a wagon or truck, can thoroughly mix, and sometimes weigh, any type of ration. Electronic load cells under the box can weigh ingredients as they are added or you can use platform scales. Large augers (24-inch diameter) or ribbons can mix the ration enroute to the bunk. Most employ a "V" type steel box with about three mixing shafts running lengthwise. Capacity ranges from 200 to 500 cubic feet. They excel in thorough mixing, accurate weight control, easy recordkeeping and dependability. They are versatile and can be used for other materials such as fertilizer, seed grain and harvest grain.

The large units mounted on wagons or trucks have side unloading for bunks. Some smaller ones are mounted on trailers and may have a single auger in the "V" bottom that delivers material to a vertical unloading auger—they are most favorable for grain. Mixing members can be added.

Chapter 10

Agricultural Chemicals

Chemicals are playing an increasingly important role in the production of both crops and livestock.

Correct use of chemicals can result in greater and more economical production from healthier animals. It can result in higher yields of improved quality crops. On the other hand, incorrect use of chemicals can be disastrous as well as unprofitable. You must use proper dosages or rates of application. Time of application, stage of crop maturity and other conditions must be considered when using agricultural chemicals.

Observe caution in chemical use. Before using any chemical make sure its use has government approval. Regulations are strict, and will likely become more so, concerning residues found in crops, meats or milk. Don't end up with a product you can't market. Follow all label recommendations. Chemical labels have special significance. They are prepared after extensive testing by the manufacturer. Then they must be approved by the Environmental Protection Agency. Take precautions to avoid injury to crops, livestock or the operator. Keep equipment clean to prevent contamination and well calibrated to prevent applying more or less than the prescribed rate.

To prevent crop damage, be sure to use only recommended chemicals. Be sure that the one selected won't carry over and affect the crop the following year. Also, be careful of drift.

CHEMICALS HAVE MANY USES

There are several major classes of agricultural chemicals. Choose a chemical within a given class which will do the job most effectively, economically and without creating unnecessary environmental problems.

Chemical drugs are used in the treatment and control of livestock diseases and parasites.

Antiseptics and disinfectants are used for maintaining general health, sanitation and disease prevention.

Chemical synthetics are used in fertilizers and livestock feeds.

Pesticides are materials or mixtures of materials used to kill unwanted plants, animals or insects. Types of pesticides are insecticides, fungicides, herbicides and rodenticides. All these names end with "cide," which means "killer."

Pesticides receive more widespread attention and closer management than the other classes of agricultural chemicals.

Insecticides are classed according to the way they enter the body or tissues of the organism they affect.

- Stomach poisons are those eaten by the pest. They enter its digestive system.
- Contact poisons enter the pest through its skin or outside tissue.
- Fumigants enter as gases through the breathing passages (sometimes the skin).

Insecticides are available in various forms, including dust, granules and liquid or gas. The physical form affects the method and equipment needed for application. They may be sprayed, applied in a furrow, banded, applied as a fumigant, etc.

Herbicides are best classified on the basis of how they are applied, how they act and what they kill.

Postemergence or foliage herbicides are applied over the top growth of the crop, or directed to the base of the crop to avoid excessive contact with the plants. They may be divided into two major groups.

- Contact herbicides give quick kill of weed parts that are covered with the material. Effects usually appear within a few hours

after treatment. They are particularly helpful where a quick kill of green vegetation is desired and where soil herbicide residues need to be avoided. A good example is paraquat applied to sod for no-tillage cropping. The dead sod becomes a mulch to conserve moisture. Used in combination with a residual herbicide (one that remains in the soil to give longer control), weed growth is inhibited over an extended period.

- Translocated herbicides are those that are absorbed by the plant and eventually kill it by moving into the buds, root tips and growing points.

Soil applied herbicides are those that are taken up by the plant from the soil either through the roots or by contact of the emerging seedling shoot with the soil. These types are referred to as preplant or preemergence herbicides, since they are applied before the crop comes up. These herbicides persist in the soil for several weeks or months—others even longer. Herbicides having a long residual life must be carefully chosen and used since they may cause some injury to certain succeeding crops.

Use chemicals economically. As with anything else, it's possible to go overboard in the use of chemicals. This may not always be profitable in every case. The use of chemicals requires investment in materials, equipment and labor. Regardless of how effective any particular chemical is, it's a bad buy unless the returns are greater than the costs. Before deciding to use any chemical, the smart farm manager will know the answers to these questions:

- What additional equipment will be required, what will it cost and how long will it last?
- What does the chemical cost and how effective is it?
- How much labor will be required?
- What are the dangers involved?
- Will the chemical have undesirable after-effects?
- How much will production or quality of the crop be improved?
- Is this the most economical way to handle the problem?

236

Herbicide Formulations

To properly select and use herbicides, it is important to know the various forms in which they are sold and to understand the label directions on their mixing and application.

Herbicides are formulated as wettable powders, solutions, emulsions, granules or pellets. Any of these, except granules and pellets, may be applied as a spot treatment, broadcast, banded over the row, or directed to a specific part of the plant.

Most organic chemicals used for herbicides are not soluble in water. To be useful, therefore, they must be prepared so they can be conveniently and uniformly spread over the weed or crop at rates as low as one-eighth pound per acre.

Solutions consist of one or more chemicals dissolved in water or other carriers. In a solution the ingredients lose their separate identity. Most water solutions can be seen through easily. Sugar or salt in water and amine salts of 2,4-D, for instance, form true solutions.

Emulsions are formed when one liquid is mixed with another liquid, but each retains its separate identity. Emulsions can be either oil-in-water or water-in-oil. Oil-in-water emulsions consist of small oil droplets surrounded by water. If the oil droplets are large, the emulsion will separate rapidly unless agitated.

Water-in-oil emulsions consist of small drops of water surrounded by oil. Mayonnaise is an example. Water-in-oil herbicide emulsions are known as invert emulsions.

Emulsions are usually formulated when the organic chemical is soluble in oil, but not in water. When the proper emulsifying agents are added, an emulsion can be made that is suitable for spraying.

Wettable powders are frequently prepared when the active ingredient is insoluble in both oil and water. Wettable powder formulations form suspensions consisting of solid particles dispersed in either oil or water.

Granules and pellets are manufactured by either sticking the active ingredients to clay granules or combining them into pellets. Granules of clay are usually light and difficult to handle in the wind. Applicator shields will reduce blowing. Pellets are quite dense and relatively easy to spread under windy conditions.

Chemical structure of a given material largely determines its suitability for use in granular formulations. Generally, the more volatile and soluble a chemical, the more suitable it is for granular use.

LABEL TERMS

To accurately follow label directions for herbicide application, commonly used label terms should be clearly understood. A *carrier* is the liquid or solid material added to the chemical compound to facilitate its application in the field. *Diluent* is any liquid or solid material serving to dilute an active ingredient in the preparation of a formulation. An *emulsifying agent,* often added to liquid formulations, is a surface active material which facilitates the suspension of one liquid in another. A *surfactant* is a material which facilitates and accentuates the emulsifying, dispersing, spreading, wetting or other surface modifying properties of herbicide formulations. *Wetting agents* help to achieve more thorough contact of the spray solution with the plant surfaces. A *suspension* is a mixture of very finely divided solid particles dispersed in a solid, liquid or gas, usually a liquid.

Compounds are said to be *compatible* when they can be mixed and applied satisfactorily. *Miscible liquids* are those capable of being mixed and remaining mixed under normal conditions. A compound is *volatile* when it evaporates or vaporizes (changes from a liquid or solid to a gas) at ordinary temperatures on exposure to the air. *Vapor drift* is the movement of herbicidal vapors from the area of application. The movement of airborne spray particles from the intended area of application is *spray drift.*

HERBICIDE CONCENTRATION

Recommended rates of application from various states are often given in terms of an acid equivalent or active ingredient. From a practical standpoint, these terms are synonymous and indicate the amount of herbicidal material contained in the formulation.

The recommended rates shown on the labels of commercial products are given in terms of total material. For instance, a state recommendation for atrazine might call for 1.6 pounds per acre of active ingredient. The commercial formulation, AAtrex 80W, is a material containing 80% active ingredient in the form of a wettable powder. This is indicated by the "80W." The state recommendation of 1.6 pounds active ingredient would require application of two pounds of commercial formulation (AAtrex 80W). This is calculated by dividing 1.6 by .80.

Application rates of herbicides formulated as liquid are also frequently given in pounds. A recommendation for alachlor might be two pounds per acre. The commercial formulation, Lasso, is a liquid containing four pounds of active ingredient per gallon. This recommendation would translate to one-half gallon or two quarts per acre.

SURFACTANTS

Addition of a surfactant, as its derivation from "surface active agent" implies, can increase the effectiveness of foliar applied herbicides. It improves plant coverage, removes air films between the spray and leaf surface and increases the foliar absorption of the herbicide within the plant.

Surfactants are used only when the herbicide will be applied to weed foliage. Thus, there is no reason for their addition to solutions to be applied preplant or preemergence.

Some postemergence solutions are formulated with the surfactant already included in the product; other formulations of the same herbicide may require the addition of a surfactant at time of application. It is important that label directions are followed regarding the specific herbicide recommended and its use. If a surfactant is added to a formulation already containing one, crop damage might result. Poor weed control is likely if a surfactant is recommended, but not used.

CHEMICAL MIXTURES

Combinations of two or more herbicides applied as a single treatment can broaden control and adaptation, reduce persistency and combine modes of action. Combinations may be purchased as a packaged formulation or separately and mixed in the spray tank.

Another form of herbicide combination is the overshot or overlay method. This is where one herbicide is broadcast preplant or preemergence, followed by a band application of another herbicide at, or immediately after planting. This is best used where the broadcast herbicide will control most of the weed species present. For an overshot application, the herbicide used is normally specific. Purpose is to control one or two weeds not controlled by the broadcast application.

There is no real problem in using prepackaged mixtures. They must have federal clearance to be sold and there is no doubt about the compatibility of the materials.

Tank mixes of various herbicides are a different matter. The mixture of two or more herbicides must have federal label clearance by at least one of the manufacturers of the products. Previous to congressional passage of the amended FIFRA (the pesticide law), farmers could legally use unlabeled tank mixes by assuming responsibility for any illegal residues in food and feed products. Now it is illegal for a farmer to use a pesticide in any manner inconsistent with the label directions.

Practicality of tank mixtures depends on a number of factors. Placement, timing and distribution of each component of a tank mix must be checked to be sure the restrictive requirements of all the components are met. Some pesticides need to be placed on the surface while others require incorporation. Distribution requirements for fertilizers are not as exacting as for herbicides. Compromising one requirement may limit the usefulness and safety of the mixture.

One of the biggest problems with tank mixes is failure of components to remain uniformly dispersed. Some of the causes are inadequate agitation, insufficient spray volume, or lack of a suitable emulsifier. Wettable powders and water-dispersible liquids require good agitation to keep them dispersed. Suspensions require one to two gallons of spray carrier per pound of product to maintain good dispersion.

Correct mixing procedures are vital for a satisfactory blend. Never put a pesticide in an empty spray tank. Always partially fill the tank with water before adding the pesticide. Wettable powders should be mixed with water to form a slurry before they are added to the spray tank. Emulsifiable concentrates should be pre-emulsified in water before they are added to a fluid fertilizer. Wettable powders should be added before emulsifiable concentrates.

Factors Affecting Herbicide Performance

The effectiveness of herbicides in controlling weeds is influenced by a multitude of factors, including herbicidal properties, weather, method of application and soil.

The properties of a given chemical largely determine how it should be applied, how it kills and what weeds it will control. From an applicator's point of view, it is important to classify herbicides on this basis.

Foliage sprays are applied to the top growth of plants. Applied in this manner, herbicides function in one or both of two possible ways. Contact herbicides give a quick kill of plant parts that are covered with the spray. Effects usually appear within a few hours after treatment. They are particularly helpful where a quick kill of green vegetation is desired and where residue from a soil applied herbicide would be undesirable. A good example is paraquat applied to sod for no-till cropping. The dead sod becomes a mulch to conserve soil moisture. Combined use of a contact and a residual herbicide can provide both immediate weed kill and season long weed control.

Translocated herbicides are absorbed into the plant. They move to buds, root tips and other growing points. Regardless of their classification, some herbicides kill by disrupting chlorophyll development or interfering with the formation of pantothenic or amino acid. Others prevent plants from producing or using glucose, sucrose or more complicated carbohydrates.

Soil applied herbicides are taken up by the plant from the soil either through the roots or by contact of emerging seedlings with treated soil. All preemergence herbicides are of this type, as are soil sterilants.

While it has long been assumed that preemergence herbicides were taken up through the root of the plant, recent greenhouse experiments indicate this is not necessarily the case. It is possible that the majority of the herbicide is absorbed by the seedling shoot as it pushes through the soil surface. Because the emerging shoot is in a very moist microclimate and not well developed, it is easily affected by soil applied herbicides. This would explain why, with some herbicides at least, moderate rainfall after application gives better weed control than a heavy rain. Moderate rainfall moves the chemical into the soil a little and pro-

vides sufficient moisture for uptake by the seedling. Excessive rainfall may move the more soluble herbicides past the shoot zone, reducing their effectiveness.

Selectivity is an inherent characteristic of all herbicides. Each chemical is rather specific in the weeds it best controls and the crops on which it can safely be used. Among the reasons for differences are plant structure, method by which the herbicide is absorbed, whether or not the chemical is translocated within the plant after uptake, and the life function of the plant.

When selecting a herbicide, match the chemical, or a combination, with the particular crop and weed problem, taking other considerations into account. A weed map for each field of the farm can be useful in tailoring a chemical program to achieve maximum benefit. Equally important is selecting according to cost, method of application, available application equipment, residual activity of the chemical and label restrictions.

Plant differences account for much of the variation in herbicide selectivity. For example, corn produces an enzyme that destroys atrazine before it damages the plant. The herbicide 2,4-DB can be used to control broadleaf weeds in legumes because they convert inactive 2,4-DB to 2,4-D, whereas legumes do not.

Using a directed spray is another way to achieve selectivity in a crop for controlling certain weeds when it may not otherwise be suitable. This method of application permits taking advantage of differential height between the crop and the weeds. For example, it is possible to direct a spray so that it covers weeds less than one inch tall in the row while avoiding contact with a crop which may be substantially taller. Additionally, some plants resist herbicides because of a waxy coating or protection at some stage of growth. Both factors can work together. Cotton, for example, has a thick bark in addition to a waxy coating on the shank of the young plant. Until the bark begins to crack, naphtha can be applied at the base of the plant to control small weeds. Once the bark cracks, the naphtha will cause injury to the cotton plant.

Soil persistence, or the time a herbicide remains active, varies widely due to the chemical, soil and climatic factors. Some herbicides will give effective season long control, others may lose their effect sooner. Other herbicides may carry over into the following season causing possible damage to a succeeding susceptible crop.

Some of the processes that reduce the persistence of herbicides are listed below.

● Volatility is the tendency to evaporate into the air. This process is associated with the vapor pressure of a chemical which increases with temperature. Photo-decomposition is the breakdown of a herbicide by ultraviolet light from the sun.

● Absorption by soil particles occurs with some chemicals. The herbicide is bound to clay and organic matter particles within the soil. Rates of those chemicals which are highly absorbed by the soil need to be adjusted according to soil type.

● Leaching occurs when a herbicide is dissolved in water and moves down through the soil profile. A small amount of leaching of a surface applied chemical may be desirable to move it into the top one or two inches of soil where most weed seeds germinate.

● Plant uptake by weeds and crops has the effect of reducing the chemical concentration within the soil. This is particularly true if the herbicide is metabolized by the plant or if the top growth is harvested and removed.

● Decomposition of a herbicide can be caused by soil microorganisms and chemical reactions. Various soil microorganisms utilize a herbicide as a source of food or energy. Susceptible herbicides persist longer under dry, cold conditions that are less favorable for the growth of microorganisms. Chemical breakdown as a result of hydrolysis, oxidation, reduction or hydration is usually influenced by these same factors.

WEATHER AND APPLICATION METHOD

Several instances have already been discussed whereby the effectiveness of herbicides can be influenced by weather, including rate of movement into the plant and persistence. Aside from these influences, the method of application is tied to the weather and its effect on herbicide activity.

Herbicides can be applied before planting the crop, after the crop is planted but before it comes up, and after the crop is up—otherwise referred to as preplant, preemergence and postemergence. A postemergence application is made in the form of a foliage spray. The material enters the plant through the leaf surface. After entry, many herbicides move to other parts of the plant by translocation. This process is most rapid under conditions favoring fast growth.

Preemergence herbicides are applied to the soil surface. To be effective, they need to be mixed with the soil by either mechanical means or rainfall. Though it has been stated that rainfall activates a herbicide, this is not the case.

Soil type and organic matter content can affect herbicide performance. Some herbicides are tied up by clay and organic matter within the soil. The higher the clay and organic matter content of a soil, the higher the rate will need to be to achieve effective control.

The toxicity of a herbicide is related to its concentration in soil water. An excessive amount of soil moisture may tend to dilute a given herbicide rate and reduce its weed killing ability. In a dry soil, on the other hand, it becomes more difficult for plants to absorb water, consequently they do not absorb as much herbicide either. Also, there is a tendency for some herbicides to be absorbed by clay and organic matter as the soil dries.

Using Herbicides Effectively

To minimize problems and achieve best results there are a number of factors you should consider when mixing and applying herbicides.

Herbicide combinations may control a broader spectrum of weeds with less risk of crop injury or carryover than from use of a single herbicide applied at a higher rate. However, proper procedures must be followed when tank mixing two or more chemicals. Specialists offer these suggestions.

Compatibility problems, or the failure of chemicals to remain uniformly mixed, may be caused by inadequate agitation, improper mixing procedures, or lack of a stable emulsifier in some emulsifiable concentrates.

Good mechanical or hydraulic jet agitation is required to maintain uniform dispersion of wettable powder or water-dispersible liquid suspensions. By-pass agitation is not sufficient to maintain good dispersion. These suspensions require about 1 to 2 gallons of spray carrier per pound or quart to maintain good dispersion. Liquid fertilizer has a higher density than water. Used as a carrier, it maintains better dispersion of these materials than does water.

Check compatibility of chemicals before mixing in a sprayer. Testing procedure is as follows:

• Calculate spray volume per acre and volume or weight of pesticide per acre. Convert quarts and pounds of pesticide per acre spray volume to amounts per pint of spray. One pound of wettable powder per 25 gallons is approximately 1 to 1-½ teaspoons per pint and one quart per 25 gallons is approximately 1 teaspoon per pint.

If you have a gram scale and milliliter pipette, you can convert to metric measurements. One pint equals 473 milliliters; one tablespoon, 14.7 milliliters; one teaspoon, 4.9 milliliters; and one pound, 2.3 grams. Roughly, one level teaspoon of a wettable powder equals 2 to 3 grams. One pound per 25 gallons equals 2.3 grams per pint and 1

quart per 25 gallons equals 4.7 milliliters per pint.

• In each of 2 quart jars, place 1 pint of carrier to be used (water or liquid fertilizer).

• Add one-third teaspoon of a compatibility agent (3 pints per 100 gallons) to one jar and mark "A." Mark the other jar "B."

• Add the proper amount of each pesticide to each jar in the proper sequence (discussed later under "Proper Mixing Procedures").

• Close the jars and shake or invert to mix thoroughly.

• Observe the mixtures after 5 minutes and again after 60 minutes.

If jar B shows no sign of precipitation, aggregation, separation, or oil scum formation within 5 minutes, or if slight separation occurs but readily mixes again with shaking, the materials are compatible and can be mixed without using a compatibility agent, provided good agitation is maintained.

If jar A with the agent stays mixed while jar B does not, the materials are compatible provided you add the agent at 1 to 3 pints per 100 gallons of carrier before adding the pesticides to the spray tank.

If both jars show signs of incompatibility, you may be able to correct the situation when a liquid fertilizer is used as the carrier by premixing the pesticides with water, as described later. However, you will need to run the compatibility test again. If this premixing doesn't overcome the problem, don't apply the materials together.

After the jar sets for 60 minutes separate layers may appear. If these can be resuspended by shaking, application is possible.

Proper mixing procedures prevent problems that can occur when using several chemicals together. Here are the suggested steps to follow.

• Fill the sprayer tank one-half to two-thirds full before adding any adjuvant or herbicide.

• Start the agitation system and continue operation through the mixing process.

• When a compatibility agent is used, add it ahead of the herbicides. Some emulsifiable concentrates may be unstable in salty solutions, such as liquid fertilizers. Some manufacturers have special fertilizer formulations containing salt stable emulsifiers, whereas others suggest that you check emulsion stability and when needed, add an agent such as Compex, Sponto 168, Uni-Mix, Unite, or Triton QS 44. These are usually added at the rate of 1 to 3 pints per 100 gallons of spray solution.

• When different herbicide formulations are used, add them to the spray tank in this order: Wettable powders, water dispersible liquids (sometimes called liquids or flowables) and surfactants, and lastly emulsifiable concentrates. Be sure each product is well mixed before adding the next one. Preemulsify emulsifiable concentrates by mixing them with an equal volume of water before adding to the tank.

Proper mixing is especially important when using wettable powders and emulsifiable concentrates together.

• Premix all herbicides in water before adding to a fluid fertilizer, if more than one herbicide is to be used. Premix wettable powders at the rate of 5 pounds of product per gallon of water. Pour the material into the water and allow it to stand until the powder sinks below the water surface. Stir the mixture, then slowly add it to the fertilizer. Premix liquids and emulsifiable concentrates at the rate of 2:1 to 1:1, herbicide to water, before adding to a fluid fertilizer. This procedure is especially important for emulsifiable concentrates.

• Finish filling the tank while maintaining agitation. Mix only the amount of spray solution that can be sprayed in a day. Otherwise, thorough agitation will be required to resuspend "settled out" material. Sometimes the mixture will not resuspend. Empty and clean tanks often to prevent accumulation of material in the tank.

Practicality of tank mixtures or package mixes depends on proper timing and placement of each chemical in the mixture, so use only those registered for a given method of application and follow label directions. Some chemicals should be preplant incorporated; others, surface or foliar applied.

Use of herbicides with fluid fertilizer requires label clearance also. When using fluid fertilizer as a carrier, remember that it is desirable to incorporate most fertilizers, which may or may not be the case with the particular herbicides used. Poor weed control will result if herbicides are incorporated too deeply and more uniform application is required for herbicides than for fertilizer. Timing can be a factor too, since fertilizer is often applied early in spring, whereas herbicides should not be applied too early. Avoid overlapping or skips.

Additives or surfactants are sometimes warranted for specific types of application or when compatibility problems arise. However, do not use them indiscriminately, since they may not improve herbicide performance and may, in fact, reduce weed control or cause crop injury. Each herbicide contains its own special blend of additives which the manufacturer has determined as being best for the product and which will mix, handle, and perform well under a wide range of conditions.

In some instances, though, an additive may be best applied by the applicator. This is usually specified on the label. For example, when a herbicide may be applied either to the soil or postemergence, the addition of crop oil to the postemergence spray is an applicator option.

Incorporation

Some herbicides must be incorporated to reduce surface loss caused by volatilization or photodecomposi-

tion. Those that are highly volatile should be incorporated immediately. Incorporation with the soil may reduce dependence of some herbicides on rainfall. Soil moisture may be sufficient to activate them.

Depth and thoroughness of incorporation depend on soil texture and soil moisture, type of equipment, and depth and speed of operation. Ideally, most of the herbicide should be incorporated in the top 1 to 2 inches of soil where weeds germinate. Deeper incorporation may cause crop germination problems. Dilution may reduce effectiveness of a herbicide if it is incorporated too deeply. Incorporation may be poor in wet soil.

Incorporation equipment is varied, but some tools achieve more uniformity, both vertically and horizontally, than others. Each incorporation tool should be operated at its optimum speed and depth.

Tandem Disks (light to medium weight) incorporate herbicides to about one-half to two-thirds of the operating depth, though the portion that is mixed in the upper 2 to 3 inches of the soil rises as speed is increased from 4 to 6 mph. Two diskings are necessary to achieve optimum incorporation.

For best results, the second disking should be perpendicular to the first. If the herbicide is sufficiently covered on the first pass, the second pass can be delayed until final seedbed preparation.

Heavier Disks with blades of 20 to 22 inches or more in diameter with 8 inches or wider spacing are not as suited for incorporation, though spacing of the disks has more to do with effectiveness than size of the disks. When operated at a depth of less than 4 inches, the blades do not properly invert the soil. When operated at 6 inches or deeper some of the herbicide is incorporated more deeply than desired. Consequently, large disks incorporate best at the 4 to 6 inch depth, though distribution is not as uniform as when a lighter disk is used for this purpose.

Field Cultivators will produce the best results when operated at a rather shallow depth and at 5 to 7

mph. Two passes are required to obtain adequate incorporation, though using a disk for one of the passes may achieve better distribution. Second pass with the field cultivator should be angled to the first pass. If the rear row of shanks is allowed to operate more deeply than the forward rows, untreated soil may be brought to the surface. Mount a drag or harrow behind the field cultivator to level ridges and to give a light mixing.

Do-Alls, according to Illinois tests, can provide uniform, shallow mixing in a single pass, with peak concentration in the top 2 inches of soil, regardless of speed or operating depth. Operated at 4 mph and 3 inches deep, 87% of the herbicide was incorporated in the top 3 inches of soil; at 5.5 inches, 77% was fairly well distributed in the top 3 inches. Horizontal uniformity is decreased when operating speed exceeds 4 mph–sweeps tend to windrow the herbicides. For cotton and soybeans, which require somewhat shallower incorporation than other crops in order to prevent injury, operate at 4 to 5 mph at about 3 inches deep.

Roterras produced more horizontally uniform distribution than either a disk or Do-All in Illinois tests. Most uniform distribution was obtained at a speed of 4.5 mph, an operating depth of 3.5 inches, and a rotor-tine speed of 333 rpm. At this operating depth, peak vertical concentration was obtained at 1 to 2 inches; 2 to 3 inches at a 5-½ inch depth.

Rolling Cultivators can be particularly valuable tools for incorporating a herbicide that has been applied to a bed. With a high forward speed and a large angle on the cultivator sections, good soil mixing to a shallow depth is possible. However, extra care should be taken to keep the sections from windrowing herbicides if large angles are used.

Rotary Tillers can do a good job of incorporating herbicides, but they are an expensive tool if used just for this purpose, and they require more power. The rotary tiller thoroughly mixes herbicides to the entire operating depth.

Herbicide Incorporation

Several factors affect the distribution of a herbicide in the soil—type of soil, soil moisture, cropping and tillage system, incorporation equipment used and how well it is operated.

Some herbicides must be incorporated into the soil. Highly volatile herbicides escape into the air if left on the soil surface. Others are decomposed by sunlight.

Incorporation is optional for some herbicides. You may apply them preemergence to the soil surface, or preplant incorporate them into the soil.

Incorporated treatments generally perform more consistently over a period of years, especially in seasons when the soil is dry in the early weeks after planting—a time when weed control is critical. Incorporation places the herbicide where more moisture is available, increasing the likelihood that emerging weeds will absorb the chemical. Also, thorough incorporation improves control of some tough to kill weed species.

Herbicide distribution can be very uniform when applied to the soil surface. If application is followed by a timely rain, weed control can be extremely good. Under these circumstances incorporated treatment won't be as good as surface application of those herbicides that can be applied either way. Some uniformity of distribution is sacrificed in return for incorporating the herbicide into the soil where it will have a greater opportunity to control weeds when rainfall is limited. The objective, therefore, should be to distribute the herbicide as uniformly as possible to reduce skips and streaks of weeds, and to avoid "hot spots" and crop injury.

Particular attention should be given to your overall tillage and cropping system, soil condition and moisture, herbicide rate, depth of incorporation, and proper selection and operation of tillage tools used to incorporate the herbicide.

Conservation tillage systems save time and fuel, and protect the soil from erosion by leaving the surface covered with crop residue, but they place a greater burden on herbicides to control weeds. At the same time, achieving good herbicide incorporation under these conditions presents a greater challenge. Soil conditions and the presence of crop residue on or near the soil surface are less suited to incorporation. Clods and crop residue may interfere with incorporation. Clods that are not broken down during tillage may later "melt down," leaving untreated weedy areas. Further, incorporation is impossible with a no-till system.

Tilling sufficiently to incorporate herbicides properly often results in loss of the erosion control benefits of reduced tillage. Farmers willing to make only two spring tillage passes are concerned whether they should apply the herbicide to the rough surface and then incorporate twice, or to first level the ground and then apply and incorporate the herbicide with only one pass. More answers are needed, but a possible solution may be to apply the herbicide between the front and rear gangs of a tandem disk on the first tillage pass.

Soil condition should be taken into account regardless of the tillage implement used. Uniform vertical and horizontal distribution is highly dependent on good soil tilth. There may, in fact, be more variation in incorporation due to soil type and moisture than to differences in equipment. For instance, a powder-dry soil will often flow like water—it will not mix, pitch, or throw. So, it is impossible to get proper incorporation. Conversely, a wet soil, particularly one that is high in clay, is heavy and sticky. A disk may merely slice through the soil without mixing it. Other implements may not properly dig in and mix the soil, and when using a field cultivator or power-driven horizontal tillers, the soil may not adequately fall in behind the tines to achieve proper vertical placement.

Depth of incorporation should be sufficient to protect the chemical from surface losses and to place it where there is enough moisture for absorption by germinating weeds. Ideal placement is about 1½ to 2 inches for most annual and broadleaf weeds. Some specialists have suggested that deeper incorporation may be required for good control of some of the larger seeded weeds that have the ability to germinate and emerge from a deeper soil depth, or those weeds that also reproduce vegetatively by underground rhizomes or bulblets. However, recent research indicates that uptake of the herbicide by a weed is not limited to its root system—that effective control of most weeds is achieved through uptake by the shoots as they push up through the soil.

Placing a herbicide deeper than necessary simply dilutes it and makes it less effective. Aside from dilution, the performance of some incorporated herbicides may be reduced somewhat due to adsorption of part of the chemical by the organic matter and clay colloids in the soil. Therefore, a somewhat higher rate (closer to the maximum recommended rate) may be advised when the herbicide is to be incorporated.

Planting depth relative to placement of the herbicide in the soil is another factor to consider, especially if the margin of crop tolerance is relatively narrow. Under these circumstances, seed ordinarily should be placed below the incorporated herbicide. Where possible, select a crop-tolerant herbicide which allows placing seed at the most appropriate depth for good, vigorous emergence without concern of herbicide injury.

Most incorporation equipment now in use was designed primarily for tillage, but much of it will provide adequate incorporation in a variety of soil types and conditions, if operated properly. The method of incorporation used should mesh as closely as possible with the overall tillage and planting system.

Disks are most widely used for incorporation, but effectiveness depends on kind of disk used and how it is operated. Finishing disks (those having spherical rather than conical blades no more than 8 inches apart and no greater than 20 inches in diameter) consistently provide the best horizontal and vertical distribution. Operated at 5 to 6 mph and 4 to 6 inches deep, the bulk of the herbicide is incorporated at one-half to two-thirds the depth of operation. Two passes, preferably with the second pass at a different angle from the first, are recommended to improve horizontal distribution.

Using some of the more soluble herbicides where a light incorporation is optional, a single pass may be sufficient to achieve adequate distribution with any of the incorporation implements. However, there is a greater risk that a single pass may result in areas of high and low chemical concentrations that cause weed streaking and crop injury. In some cases, farmers who have been successful using single pass incorporation for several years run into problems because of different soil and weather conditions in a given season.

Large cutting disks (those with blades more than 8 inches apart and greater than 20 inches in diameter) are less desirable. When operated at less than 4 inches deep, the blades do not properly invert the soil and very little soil mixing occurs. Operated at 6 inches or more, the blades incorporate some of the herbicide too deeply. However, cutting disks having 22 inch spherical blades spaced 9 inches apart can provide adequate incorporation if operated at the proper depth. Specialists caution against using wide disks for incorporation, unless you are assured of good depth control on the wings.

Field cultivators provide best results when operated 3 to 5 inches deep and 3 to 5 mph. Two passes are required, and to avoid streaking, the second pass should be angled across the first pass. Sweeps or shovels often provide better incorporation than chisel points, as they slice and lift the soil more. Field cultivators tend to move the soil laterally, though some vertical incorporation occurs as the soil flows back into the slot behind the tines. Consequently, the herbicide is uniformly distributed within the upper few inches of soil. A light drag or harrow mounted behind the cultivator can help to level the ridges and give a light mixing. Operating a field cultivator faster than 5 to 6 mph tends to windrow the herbicide between the points or sweeps.

Operate a field cultivator level. If the rear row of shanks is operated deeper than the forward rows, untreated soil may be brought to the surface. Some farmers believe they can achieve a more uniform seedbed by using a disk on the first pass, followed by a field cultivator.

Power-driven tillage tools, either horizontal or vertical tillers, have potential for one pass incorporation. The vertical tillers, commonly referred to as rototillers, provide nearly perfect mixing of the herbicide, both vertically and horizontally, to the depth of operation. Major precaution is to properly maintain the correct rpm relative to ground speed. Major drawbacks are the cost of the equipment, slow operation, and power requirements.

The vertical tillers, which till the soil with oscillating or rotating vertical tines, provide excellent horizontal distribution, but regardless of operating depth most of the herbicide is placed within top 2 inches of soil. Some examples of this kind of equipment are the Roterra, Vicon, Rotaspike, and Niemeyer.

Seedbed conditioners, often called "do-alls," use two or three rows of spring teeth spaced 6 to 9 inches apart followed by a reel-type chopper-mixer, and behind that four or five rows of spike teeth on close spacing, often trailed by a spring-loaded leveling board. For maximum effectiveness, these tools should be operated at relatively high speeds in soils having good soil tilth. Vertical placement may be concentrated in the upper 2 inches. You may want to remove the board when incorporating to keep from destroying incorporation uniformity within the soil.

Rolling cultivators can be used to incorporate herbicides, especially when it is necessary to incorporate in a band or on beds that need to retain their shape. A similar tool that can be used for incorporating in a band is the Ro-Wheel.

When incorporating on a bed, gangs need to be set to match the bed's contour. With high speeds of 5 to 7 mph and large angles on the cultivator sections, good soil mixing to a rather shallow depth is possible. If you use large angles, be careful to keep the sections from windrowing the herbicide, though. To obtain thorough mixing two passes may be necessary–one pass in one direction to throw soil to one side, then in the other direction to throw the soil back. In any instance, however, the angle of the gangs is critical for proper soil mixing of the herbicide.

Listers, used in some instances to throw up beds after broadcasting a herbicide, may achieve sufficient incorporation, while saving a trip over the field. Success is dependent on soil type and moisture after planting, so check this practice for your area before you try it.

Other incorporation methods that are somewhat incidental include rotary hoeing and herbigation. A rotary hoe can give shallow incorporation and might improve the effectiveness of herbicides applied preemergence. With low rainfall this method can help to control the first flush of weeds and the herbicide may be more effective against succeeding weed growth.

Herbigation can be used to apply a herbicide with irrigation water and sometimes can substitute for mechanical incorporation. When managed properly, you can regulate the depth to which the herbicide is moved in the soil.

Preventing Herbicide Injury

The objectives of a herbicide program should be to achieve good weed control without causing injury to the crop and to minimize carryover of the more persistent herbicides.

Herbicide injury can be caused by chemicals that have a close crop tolerance. Use of a herbicide combination may improve crop tolerance and reduce carryover.

Application rates for some herbicides vary greatly with soil type and organic matter. For example, the triazines, such as atrazine, Princep, or Milogard, are absorbed by soil clay and organic matter. The lower the organic matter and/or the coarser the soil, the lower the application rate should be to prevent crop injury. Check labels for specific recommendations. Some herbicides are not recommended for use on soils having less than a certain amount of organic matter or on coarser textured soils.

Calibrate equipment carefully, after you have made sure all nozzles are the same size and all deliver a uniform application rate. A worn nozzle will deliver a higher rate than an unworn one. Calibrate in the field at the speed and pressure you will be using. If you have to change speed or pressure, you will need to recalibrate. Adjust boom height and spray pattern to give uniform application.

Accurate, uniform application requires additional care aside from careful calibration. Here are some suggestions:
● Be sure the herbicide is mixed well in the tank. Problems sometimes occur when mixing herbicide combinations that include emulsifiable concentrate formulations and wettable powder or water dispersible liquid formulations. To help avoid mixing problems, fill the tank at least half full with water or liquid fertilizer before adding the herbicide. When mixtures are used, wettable powders should be added to the tank before emulsifiable concentrates. Preemulsify an emulsifiable concentrate by mixing it with an equal volume of water before adding it to the tank. Empty and clean tanks often.

Most triazines, for example, require some agitation in the tank to keep the herbicide in suspension. If it is necessary to stop and shut off the sprayer, allow time for proper mixing when you restart.

Water and acceptable fertilizer solutions will provide similar weed control with preplant or preemergence herbicides. Postemergence application of herbicides with fertilizer solutions (except for some chemicals that may be put on as directed sprays) should be avoided. The activity of the herbicide applied postemergence may be increased two to four times when mixed with a fertilizer solution rather than water.

Non-pressure nitrogen solutions or complete liquids can be used, but suspensions may create more compatibility problems. Polyphosphate combinations help to improve the suspension of wettable powders and water dispersible liquids such as AAtrex 4L. Be sure the herbicide you use is compatible with and cleared for use with a fertilizer solution. Some herbicides and fertilizers require compatibility agents. Most labels for herbicides cleared for use with liquid fertilizers explain how to run a compatibility test.
● Use some type of marking system to avoid skips or overlaps.
● When incorporating a herbicide, use equipment that will achieve uniform distribution. The tandem disk is most widely used. It incorporates to about half the depth at which it is operated. A field cultivator can be used for incorporation, but streaking may occur unless a drag-harrow is pulled behind and the operation is performed twice in different directions across the field. Some of the power tillage tools appear to provide one-pass incorporation, if conditions are satisfactory.

Incorporation should be part of normal seedbed preparation in order to prevent excess tillage which can intensify soil crusting, leading to delayed emergence and possible crop injury. Speed and depth are important for all equipment–incorporating too deep will reduce herbicide effectiveness.
● Contact with the crop must be limited for some postemergence sprays. Others can be applied over the top if timing is correct.
● Shut off the applicator when turning on field ends. Do not overlap or make double applications.
● When filling the sprayer tank, avoid overflow or spilling.
● Avoid drift by using low pressure nozzles and/or drift inhibitors. Don't spray on windy days.

Weather conditions can alter the effect of the herbicide and the tolerance of the crop to it, so crop injury can sometimes occur even though you may follow all possible precautions. Under cool, wet stress conditions, the metabolism of the crop is reduced and the plant grows slowly. The herbicide taken into the plant may not be detoxified as rapidly as normally, resulting in injury to the crop.

Under warm, humid conditions the plant may take up the herbicide more rapidly. In the case of postemergence application, the plant tissue may be more susceptible to contact injury. Hot, dry stress conditions can also influence the effect of the herbicide.

Some cropping practices can help you reduce the chances of crop injury due to adverse weather. Prepare the soil properly, select vigorous varieties and seed, follow a good fertilization program and seed at the proper depth. All of these practices will help to get the crop up fast and give vigorous growth, thereby reducing the possibility of herbicide injury.

Avoid planting too deep. This could mean that the growing point of the seedling would be in contact with the herbicide longer.

Herbicide Carryover

Most precautions discussed for preventing crop injury in the season the herbicide is used will help to reduce the chances of herbicide residue being carried over and injuring the succeeding crop. However, herbicides break down more slowly in dry and/or cool seasons, meaning there is a greater possibility of carryover into the following season. If the following spring is wet and/or warm, though, additional breakdown will probably occur before planting, especially for later planted crops.

Chances of carryover are greater on soils or areas in a field that have a high soil pH, unless herbicide use is managed to take this condition into account. Breakdown of some herbicides proceeds more slowly as soil pH increases, and crop tolerance may be reduced. In Iowa tests, soybeans planted following corn treated with atrazine showed only a minimum of injury when the soil had a pH of around 7 or lower, but severe injury and a sharp yield reduction occurred when the soil was limed to a pH of 7.3 or above.

Soil may have a higher pH in areas of a field adjacent to a limestone rock road (100 to 200 feet from the road) or where drain tile has been installed recently. Such areas may not require liming or the pH may be higher than desired for the prevention of herbicide injury. This sometimes explains why herbicide injury is more severe in one area of a field than another.

Persistent herbicides create the greatest carryover concern--the triazines, such as atrazine, Milogard, and Princep, and the dinitroanilines, such as Treflan, Tolban, and Cobex.

Atrazine may carry over enough to cause injury to crops such as small grains, flax, forage legumes and grasses, soybeans, sunflowers and sugar beets. Princep is more persistent than atrazine.

The dinitroanilines used on soybeans and dry beans normally do not carry over sufficiently to affect succeeding crops, but injury to corn, sorghum, small grains and sugar beets is possible following a dry season and reduced tillage.

Simple crop tests can be run to determine if carryover will be a problem with the crops you plan to plant. Make a pass with a grain drill ahead of planting, seeding wheat or oats, to see if any injury shows up. If injury occurs on these test plants, you can suspect herbicide residues in the field.

For more accuracy, you may choose to run a bioassay test as outlined by Illinois agronomists. They recommend making the test as close to planting as possible, but you will probably want to test early enough to permit making decisions concerning tillage, cropping rotation and herbicide selection.

• Take soil samples from several areas in the field. Field ends, high knolls, areas adjacent to limestone roads and areas in the vicinity of newly laid drain tiles may need to be sampled separately, as discussed earlier. You will need about a gallon of sample soil for each test.

• You should have some untreated 'check' soil to use for comparison. If you don't have similar untreated soil, you can create a check by inactivating the herbicide in a sample. Mix the soil with activated charcoal, using a 0.5 gram capsule of charcoal per quart of soil. Most drugstores have these capsules.

• Plant two or three pots each of treated and 'check' soil so that you can note any variability in growing plants and avoid drawing the wrong conclusions.

• Use pint or quart cans, cardboard cartons or greenhouse flats. Put holes in the bottom for drainage. Place the pots in a warm location having plenty of sunlight.

• Select the seeds to plant on the basis of the herbicide you test.

Different levels of triazine residue can be determined by planting annual ryegrass or bluegrass, oats, and soybeans in each of three pots—both in treated and check soil. The small grasses are the most likely plants to show symptoms; soybeans, the least.

Different levels of dinitroaniline residue can be determined by planting annual ryegrass, sorghum or sudangrass, wheat and corn. The annual ryegrass is most likely to show symptoms; corn, the least.

• Symptoms from triazine residue will usually occur in two to three weeks. On the grasses, it will show as leaf burn from the tip to the base of the leaf. Soybean injury will appear as browning or mottling of the unifoliate or first trifoliate leaves. Severe injury will kill seedlings.

Dinitroaniline residue symptoms will show up as the seedlings emerge. Symptoms may include stunted plants, poor secondary root development and failure of the leaves to unroll properly. With severe injury, seedlings may fail to germinate and emerge.

Corrective action may be necessary to prevent crop injury from herbicide carryover, if indicated by the tests. If injury to the test plants is slight, Illinois specialists say that you can minimize potential injury in the field by thoroughly mixing the soil. That could mean plowing rather than disking, chisel plowing or using one of the reduced tillage systems, or plant a less sensitive crop. If severe symptoms occur, you may have to plant the same crop as the previous season.

Avoid using a herbicide that has an additive effect with the residue of the carried over herbicide. For example, should triazine injury occur to the test oats, but not to soybeans, you may want to avoid using Sencor or Lexone if you plant soybeans. Sencor or Lexone can be safe for use with beans, but the combined effect of these herbicides with atrazine residue could result in severe injury, particularly if the soil pH is high.

The method and time of application are other factors to consider in minimizing carryover of persistent herbicides into the following season. At equal rates, preplant or preemergence application will produce less residue than postemergence application. Late season application can increase carryover, too. Iowa specialists advise that you not plant crops other than corn or sorghum the next year if atrazine is applied after June 10.

Herbicide Spray Equipment

Most crop sprayers you can purchase today have well balanced components and are versatile enough that, with attachments and adjustment, they can be used for any field spraying job.

Most farmers purchase manufactured sprayers ready to mount on the tractor rather than buy components separately and "engineer" their own as was common in the past. You avoid the problems of balancing the components (tank, pump, nozzles, etc.) for the job, but there are a number of options which you should consider for accurate herbicide application. This page discusses nozzles and spray patterns. Pumps and other components will be covered in subsequent pages.

The heart of any sprayer is the pump; the business end of the sprayer is the nozzle tip. Other necessary components are the tank, hoses and/or boom, valves, gauges and strainers. The nozzle tip determines the rate of chemical distribution at a particular pressure. Flow rate is influenced to a lesser extent by pump pressure--thus changing pressure is a poor way to regulate volume.

Desirable pressure for herbicide application is between 10 psi and 40 psi (pounds per square inch), depending on the type of nozzle tip used. Below 10 psi the spray pattern falls apart. Above 40 psi the spray material is atomized too finely and drift becomes a problem. With insecticide or defoliant spraying higher pressures--60 psi to 125 psi--are desirable to penetrate crop foliage and create a finer droplet for better coverage. Usually the same tank, pump and other sprayer components can be used for both jobs by changing nozzles and configuration of the sprayer.

TYPES OF SPRAYS

A hollow cone spray is one in which most of the liquid is concentrated in the outer edge of a conical pattern. It breaks up into small droplets and is used mostly for insecticide application.

Flat spray nozzle tips produce a narrow elliptical spray pattern which delivers less material on the outer edges of the pattern. Several nozzles mounted on a boom give uniform distribution over broad areas by overlapping the tapered edges of individual spray patterns. Most common use is broadcast application of herbicides.

Even flat spray nozzle tips give a pattern similar to flat spray except concentration of droplets is uniform across the pattern. They are used for band spraying of herbicides, either behind the planter

press wheels or for postemergence application.

Flooding nozzle tips produce a flat spray with a very wide angle at pressures as low as 10 psi. Flooding nozzles are most often used for liquid fertilizer application, but have found increasing usage in the application of preplant herbicide from a boom mounted in front of a disk. Each nozzle can cover a width of 40 to 80 inches, depending on height above the ground.

Other nozzles are designed for application requiring special spray patterns, but 99% of herbicide application will be with flat, even flat, or flooding nozzle tips.

Spray Nozzle Assemblies usually have four parts: the nozzle body, the strainer, the tip and the cap. The assembly illustrated below is the Spraying Systems Co.'s TeeJet Spray Nozzle. Nozzle tips are interchangeable--you don't have to change the entire nozzle assembly to change capacity or spray pattern. In fact, with few exceptions nozzle tips of one manufacturer will fit nozzle assemblies of another manufacturer.

Type TT Male body   Type T Female body   Strainer   Cap   Flat Spray Tip

Nozzles are made of either brass, aluminum, nylon, stainless steel or hardened stainless steel. Hardened stainless steel is the best--and the most expensive, followed by stainless steel. Aluminum nozzles' main advantage is that they are lightweight and are used principally in aerial application. Many sprayers come from the manufacturer equipped with brass nozzles and these are sufficient for non-abrasive materials such as emulsions. Neither brass nor aluminum is suitable for applications of wettable powder formulations, suspensions or other abrasive materials. These will quickly erode the nozzle tip orifice, distorting the spray pattern and increasing the volume of material applied. In addition some materials, principally liquid fertilizers, are corrosive to brass and aluminum. The only advantage to brass is that it is cheap in the short run.

Nylon nozzles are corrosion and erosion resistant and as cheap as brass. They are nearly as wear resistant as stainless steel. One disadvantage is that orifice size is sensitive to temperature change—output can vary as much as 10% between low and high temperatures.

You can arrive at a good compromise between cost and durability by using nozzle bodies and caps of cheaper material with nozzle tips and strainers of stainless steel.

SELECTING THE PROPER NOZZLE TIP

With herbicide application you are going to be spraying broadcast from a boom, a band over the drill area at planting, or, for postemergence, either broadcast or band.

You would use a flat spray tip for boom mounted nozzles, and possibly flooding tips for applying incorporated materials in front of a disk. For band and most postemergence applications you would use even flat spray tips.

It's at this point that you consult the nozzle manufacturers' catalogs. There are three principal manufacturers of spray nozzles and accessories: Century Engineering Corp., 221 Fourth Ave., S.E., Cedar Rapids, Iowa 52401; Delavan Manufacturing Co., 811 Fourth Street, West Des Moines, Iowa 50265; Spraying Systems Co., North Avenue at Schmale Road, Wheaton, Illinois 60187. Your local spray equipment dealer will probably handle one or more of the lines and will have catalogs.

The table reproduced at the right is an example of the information contained in the catalogs. It is the Spraying Systems Co.'s TeeJet 80° Series Flat Spray Tip. Century and Delavan catalogs contain the same information for their nozzle lines.

The 80° refers to the angle of spray as it leaves the nozzle, which determines the width it will cover when the nozzle is a given height above the ground. Flat Spray Tips are also available in 65° and 73° angles, and flooding nozzles go as high as 147°.

In the table the first column gives the nozzle number, the gallons per acre delivered at 30 psi and 4 miles per hour, and the density of the nozzle strainer, either 100 mesh or 50 mesh.

The second column gives various pump pressures and the third column shows the capacity of one nozzle in gallons per minute at those pressures. The columns on the right of the table show gallons applied per acre at various speeds.

Assume that you want to apply 20 gallons per acre of total spray solution at 30 psi with travel speed of 7.5 miles per hour. Going down the 7.5 mph column, you come to 21 at 30 psi with a No. 8006 tip. Note that as speed of travel increases or as pressure is reduced, gallons per acre decline.

Output changes much faster with changes in speed, so to get your 20 gallons per acre output, increase speed slightly above 7.5 mph.

Pump Capacity can also be determined from the table. Using the same example, note in column 3 that at 30 psi the 8006 tip delivers .52 gallons per minute. Say your boom is 20 feet or 240 inches and has 12 nozzles. 12 x .52 = 6.24 gallons per minute total. If you are using jet agitation you need 50% of the pump volume going back to the spray tank. Thus, you need a pump capable of delivering at least 12.5 gallons per minute.

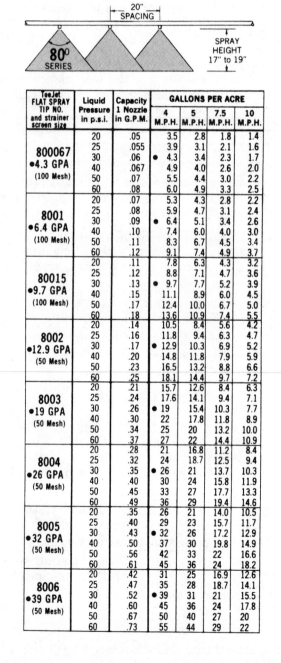

TeeJet FLAT SPRAY TIP NO. and strainer screen size	Liquid Pressure in p.s.i.	Capacity 1 Nozzle in G.P.M.	GALLONS PER ACRE			
			4 M.P.H.	5 M.P.H.	7.5 M.P.H.	10 M.P.H.
800067 •4.3 GPA (100 Mesh)	20	.05	3.5	2.8	1.8	1.4
	25	.055	3.9	3.1	2.1	1.6
	30	.06	• 4.3	3.4	2.3	1.7
	40	.067	4.9	4.0	2.6	2.0
	50	.07	5.5	4.4	3.0	2.2
	60	.08	6.0	4.9	3.3	2.5
8001 •6.4 GPA (100 Mesh)	20	.07	5.3	4.3	2.8	2.2
	25	.08	5.9	4.7	3.1	2.4
	30	.09	• 6.4	5.1	3.4	2.6
	40	.10	7.4	6.0	4.0	3.0
	50	.11	8.3	6.7	4.5	3.4
	60	.12	9.1	7.4	4.9	3.7
80015 •9.7 GPA (100 Mesh)	20	.11	7.8	6.3	4.3	3.2
	25	.12	8.8	7.1	4.7	3.6
	30	.13	• 9.7	7.7	5.2	3.9
	40	.15	11.1	8.9	6.0	4.5
	50	.17	12.4	10.0	6.7	5.0
	60	.18	13.6	10.9	7.4	5.5
8002 •12.9 GPA (50 Mesh)	20	.14	10.5	8.4	5.6	4.2
	25	.16	11.8	9.4	6.3	4.7
	30	.17	• 12.9	10.3	6.9	5.2
	40	.20	14.8	11.8	7.9	5.9
	50	.23	16.5	13.2	8.8	6.6
	60	.25	18.1	14.4	9.7	7.2
8003 •19 GPA (50 Mesh)	20	.21	15.7	12.6	8.4	6.3
	25	.24	17.6	14.1	9.4	7.1
	30	.26	• 19	15.4	10.3	7.7
	40	.30	22	17.8	11.8	8.9
	50	.34	25	20	13.2	10.0
	60	.37	27	22	14.4	10.9
8004 •26 GPA (50 Mesh)	20	.28	21	16.8	11.2	8.4
	25	.32	24	18.7	12.5	9.4
	30	.35	• 26	21	13.7	10.3
	40	.40	30	24	15.8	11.9
	50	.45	33	27	17.7	13.3
	60	.49	36	29	19.4	14.6
8005 •32 GPA (50 Mesh)	20	.35	26	21	14.0	10.5
	25	.40	29	23	15.7	11.7
	30	.43	• 32	26	17.2	12.9
	40	.50	37	30	19.8	14.9
	50	.56	42	33	22	16.6
	60	.61	45	36	24	18.2
8006 •39 GPA (50 Mesh)	20	.42	31	25	16.9	12.6
	25	.47	35	28	18.7	14.1
	30	.52	• 39	31	21	15.5
	40	.60	45	36	24	17.8
	50	.67	50	40	27	20
	60	.73	55	44	29	22

Herbicide Spray Equipment—Pumps

A broad selection of reasonably priced, well-engineered pumps for field sprayers is available. The trick is in selecting the right one for the job.

The pump is the heart of the field crop sprayer, but it can be chosen only after you have determined total volume requirements of the sprayer with the largest capacity nozzles you are likely to use, plus a sufficient volume for tank agitation. Most pumps used for pesticide application are either roller pumps or centrifugal pumps. Gear pumps, piston pumps and diaphragm pumps have high initial cost in relation to capacity.

Roller pumps

In the past, roller pumps have been the most commonly used pump for crop sprayers. They are designed for direct drive from the tractor power-take-off and are available for either 540 or 1,000 rpm pto speed. Depending on size, roller pumps can produce pressures to 300 psi and output of 8 to 30 gallons per minute.

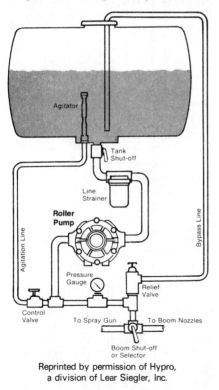

Reprinted by permission of Hypro, a division of Lear Siegler, Inc.

The primary problem with roller pumps is that, as it wears, its output is reduced until it can no longer meet the requirements of the sprayer. However, roller pumps are cheap enough ($50 to $100) that they can be replaced after one or two seasons.

Chemicals formulated as wettable powders are a problem for roller pumps in two respects. First, wettable powders are abrasive to the rollers, greatly accelerating wear compared to chemicals formulated as liquids. Second, unless they receive constant and considerable agitation wettable powders will settle out in the sprayer tank, resulting in variability in rates of active chemical ingredient applied.

Paddle wheels in the bottom of the tank powered by a separate battery-driven electric motor do a good job of agitation. Hydraulic agitation by a bypass or special agitator line directly from the pump is simpler and more practical. Hydraulic agitation using a roller pump is satisfactory on a small spray rig. But as spray rig size has increased along with greater capacity tanks, only the largest capacity roller pumps are able to supply enough volume to provide sufficient tank agitation for wettable powders.

Centrifugal pumps

Centrifugal pumps have very low wear characteristics; therefore they are well suited to handle abrasive materials. Their high capacity (30 to 130 gallons per minute) provides plenty of volume for hydraulic agitators in the tank. Centrifugal pumps do not build pressure as high as roller pumps, but are capable of pressures of 75 psi and higher.

Centrifugal pumps must be operated at something over 3,000 rpm and if the pump is to be run by the pto, a step-up mechanism is needed. The most common step-up is a belt and pulley assembly. Another method is to drive the pump from the tractor fan or generator belt, utilizing a magnetic-clutch similar to those used to drive automobile air conditioners. Magni-Clutch is available from Scienco, Inc., 3093 Bellbrook Center Dr. E., Memphis, Tennessee 38116.

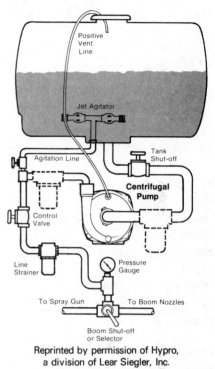

Reprinted by permission of Hypro, a division of Lear Siegler, Inc.

Some centrifugal pumps are built with an integral planetary gear arrangement. The gears are completely enclosed and mount directly on the pto shaft. Comparing belt-driven to gear-driven pumps, the belts are subject to wear and eventual breakage, while the gear drive can be expected to have longer repair-free life at a substantially higher initial cost.

Hydraulic motor-driven centrifugals offer the advantage of a high-speed power source which has less dependence on tractor engine speed than pto driven pumps. With a pto driven centrifugal, the tractor must be run at a fairly high throttle to keep pto rpm high enough to operate the pump. When pump rpm drops below 3,000, output falls off steeply. The hydraulic system of most modern tractors produces considerably more output than is needed by the spray pump's hydraulic motor; thus, pump speed is not directly dependent upon engine rpm. The result is that the tractor can be operated at half throttle rather than wide open with considerable fuel saving.

Selecting the right pump

Suppose you are purchasing a new field sprayer or buying a new pump for your present rig. How do you decide the kind of pump to buy?

Questions to be answered are: What is the volume requirement of the sprayer in gallons per minute? Will the sprayer be used a little or a lot? Will a significant amount of your spraying be with wettable powder materials?

Pump output should be a least 40% greater than nozzle requirements if mechanical tank agitation is used and twice the nozzle requirements if hydraulic tank agitation is used to keep wettable powders in suspension. Thus, if nozzle requirements are five gallons per minute, your pump should deliver at least seven gpm with mechanical agitators and ten gpm with hydraulic agitation.

Referring to pump manufacturers' specifications, a small roller pump will meet those requirements only if hydraulic tank agitation is unnecessary. With tank agitation, you would need a medium to large capacity roller pump. Since capacity requirements can be met with a roller pump in this situation, even if half of your spraying is done with wettable powder formulations, the roller pump is a good choice. Rollers can be replaced after each season's use or the entire pump replaced every two or three years.

The large roller pumps are practical when nozzle requirements are 10 to 15 gpm and most of your spraying will be liquid or non-abrasive formulations. But if you are using a considerable amount of wettable powders or using the rig to spray several hundred acres a year, you should definitely consider going to a centrifugal pump. Price of the larger roller pumps is close to $100 and you can get a centrifugal which will last longer with no worry about abrasives or agitation requirements for $125 to $150.

Drive Source—direct through the pto or indirect through a hydraulic motor— is a tough decision.

There are limitations with hydraulic motor pumps as to the tractor you can use. Many pre-1960 vintage tractors do not have a large enough hydraulic system. While some older tractors might meet the requirement, the hydraulic systems were not built for continuous operation and do not have sufficient capacity to cool the hydraulic fluid.

Second, on some of the newer large tractors the output at the remote outlet can be too much for the pump motor. This is the case for tractors having open-center hydraulic systems with remote outlet output in excess of about 13 gallons per minute. With open-center tractor hydraulic systems the pump motor bypasses excess hydraulic fluid through a needle valve back to the tractor reservoir. But it cannot be adjusted to bypass more than a certain gallonage per minute. If tractor capacity is too high, heat builds up in the fluid which can burn up the pump motor or damage the tractor's hydraulic system.

Before buying a hydraulic motor-driven pump you need to check the tractor hydraulic system output at the remote outlet. If it is an open-center system with an output over 13 gpm, check the pump's specification to be sure it can handle that output. Generally, these high capacity hydraulic systems are on large tractors which are not normally used as spray rig platforms.

Tractors using closed-center hydraulic systems supply only as much fluid as is needed to operate the motor. Hydraulic motor-driven pumps use a metering orifice to regulate the flow; consequently where closed-center systems are used there is no problem with over-heating.

Here's a general guide on the types of hydraulic systems used by tractors. It is up-to-date as of 1975. Don't depend completely on this since later models may have different systems.

All IH, AC, Case, David Brown, Deutz and Ford models have open-center systems. All post-1960 John Deere models have closed-center systems except the 830 which is open-center. Most pre-1960 model John Deeres have open-center systems, but may not have enough capacity for this use. For Massey-Ferguson, Minneapolis-Moline and Oliver, check with the dealers as some models are open and some closed-center systems.

There is one disadvantage of hydraulic motor pumps that should be noted: When you slow the tractor (perhaps for rough field conditions) the pump continues to deliver the same amount of spray through the nozzles. This results in an increase in the rate of material applied per acre. With a pto driven centrifugal pump, as tractor engine speed and ground speed decrease, spray pump output decreases almost proportionately. Therefore, once it is calibrated, the pto driven pump will deliver approximately the same rate per acre as tractor speed varies within normal operating ranges.

Pump manufacturers

Most retail sprayer and many agricultural supply outlets carry one or more lines of spray pumps. The following companies are the principal manufacturers: Ace Pumps, 1650 Channel Ave., Memphis, Tenn. 38113—roller and centrifugal pumps.

Century Engineering Corp., 221 Fourth Ave., S.E., Cedar Rapids, Iowa 52401—roller and centrifugal pumps, sprayers, nozzles and accessories.

Delavan Mfg. Co., 811 Fourth St., West Des Moines, Iowa 50265—roller and centrifugal pumps, spray nozzles and accessories.

Hypro, 375 Fifth Ave., N.W., St. Paul, Minn. 55112—roller and centrifugal pumps and pump accessories.

General Hydraulics, 301 Charles St., South Beloit, Ill. 61080—roller pumps.

If you cannot find what you need from local suppliers, a note to any of the above companies should bring information quickly.

Herbicide Sprayer Arrangements

A detailed discussion of the application methods and equipment designs you can use for effective preplant, preemergence and postemergence weed control.

Your herbicide sprayer can be arranged in several different configurations to provide desired placement of the herbicide for the job to be done. Usually, the same basic sprayer--tank, pump, gauges, hoses, etc.,--can be used for broadcast spraying, band spraying, directed sprays and topical applications by changes in the number, type, and placement of nozzles.

Broadcast spraying for preemergence treatment is usually done with a series of nozzles spaced equidistant along a boom as shown in Figure 1. Boom height above the ground or weed foliage is determined by the spacing of nozzles along the boom and the angle of the spray pattern from nozzle tips.

Figure 1

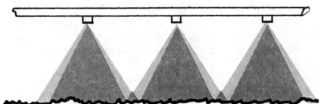

Most boom sprayers come equipped with 80° spray angle tapered edge flat spray tips spaced 20 inches apart. Boom height of 17 to 19 inches allows the outer edge of the pattern of each nozzle to over-

Figure 2

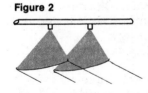

lap the pattern of the adjacent nozzle. Since the volume of spray delivered on the outer edges of flat spray tip patterns is less than the volume delivered in the center one-half of the pattern, overlap assures uniform distribution across the width of the boom (Figure 2). To prevent adjacent patterns from intercepting, nozzle tips should be rotated 12° to 15° so the patterns are slightly offset.

Flat spray nozzle tips are available with 65°, 73° and 80° spray angles. With the smaller angles, the boom will have to be higher to achieve the desired overlap at nozzle spacings of 20 inches, or the nozzle spacings will have to be reduced while holding the boom height constant.

For preplant materials applied broadcast from a disk or other tillage implement, an arrangement similar to the one shown in Figure 3 is popular. It is an alternative to mounting a boom under the belly of the tractor, which might prove awkward. Flooding nozzle tips or hollow cone nozzles, which deliver a comparatively high volume at a very wide

Figure 3

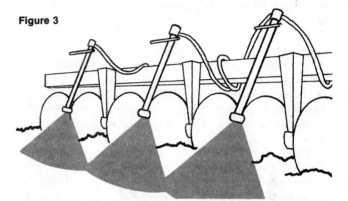

spray angle, allow nozzle placement close to the disk and close to the ground. The large orifice size of these nozzles reduces the incidence of clogging in the usually dusty conditions encountered. Both flooding and hollow cone tips produce adequate volumes at low pressure (10 to 20 psi) to produce coarser droplets and minimize drift. Also, their wide spray angle reduces the number of nozzles needed. Nozzles with flooding tips should be pointed straight down, but hollow cone tips must be pointed at a forward angle, as shown in Figure 3, to prevent the round pattern from hitting the disk.

Preemergence band spraying in conjunction with the planting operation is common. The most

Figure 4

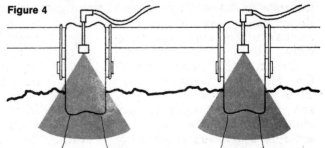

precise placement method is to attach the spray nozzle directly behind each planter unit as shown in Figure 4. Even flat spray tips which deliver a uniform rate of material across the entire width of the spray pattern are used for band spraying.

A flexible hose from the pump, rather than a hollow boom, should be used for delivery to the nozzles, since each planter unit is independently suspended from the planter tool bar. A boom rigidly attached to the tool bar will result in constant variability of band widths and herbicide concentrations with even small changes in individual row heights. This same problem occurs when the herbicide is applied in a separate operation immediately after planting. Many farmers prefer a separate operation for preemergence application so as not to delay planting with sprayer calibration, tank filling, etc., but there is a trade-off of precision for expediency.

POSTEMERGENCE APPLICATIONS

Basically, there are four distinct methods of applying postemergence herbicides: broadcast over-the-top (topical), band topical, semi-directed band and directed band application.

The easiest method, broadcast over-the-top from a boom, can be used with only a few herbicides. One or more of three factors often make topical broadcast application of postemergence herbicides unfeasible: (1) Selectivity of the material--application of some herbicides to the foliage and particularly to the terminal bud of the crop plant damages or kills the crop; (2) dense crop foliage intercepts the spray, preventing sufficient coverage of small weeds; (3) cost--if middles can be cultivated, materials cost can be significantly reduced by band application to the drill area only.

Topical application means that the herbicide can be applied to the crop foliage with little or no danger of crop damage at the recommended application rate. When crops are small, application of the herbicide from a boom, either broadcast or banded over the drill area, will give good results. Remember that with broadcast application you should use tapered edge flat spray tips; with band application switch to even flat spray tips.

When the crop is larger, creating an "umbrella," you will get better weed control with a three nozzle per row arrangement similar to Figure 5. As shown, the top nozzle is directed into the crop foliage to kill large weeds as tall or taller than the crop. The two side nozzles provide coverage of the mid-portion area of the foliage and under the base of the crop. This arrangement is

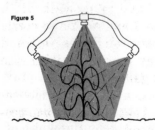
Figure 5

needed in only a few situations such as a heavy foliaged crop of soybeans where weeds are large, using a herbicide to which the crop is very tolerant. This is a good arrangement for application of Basagran at mid-season to soybeans where cocklebur is a problem. If the weeds are not as tall as the crop, you won't need the top nozzle. It is important with this or any arrangement using more than one nozzle per row, to remember that nozzle tips with smaller capacities than a one nozzle per row arrangement should be used.

Directed spray application means that the spray should be directed to the base of the crop plants, avoiding contact with the crop foliage. This is accomplished by mounting nozzles on a platform skid or gauge wheel so that the spray is delivered to the same area in relation to the crop, regardless of changes in row elevation. At least two nozzles, one on each side of the drill, are necessary to give coverage across the drill and under the foliage of the crop. Many farmers prefer four nozzles per row with two nozzles directed to the rear to cover the row shoulder as shown in Figure 6. Various modifications and improvements of the design illustrated here are available from several manufacturers of specialized spray equipment.

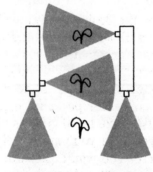
Figure 6

Semi-directed spray application can be employed with many herbicides which cause slight damage to the crop from foliage contact, but possibly significant damage if they contact the terminal bud or growing point of the crop. Figure 7 shows the nozzle placement that should be used. Note that it is different from Figure 5 in that the spray is directed to cover only the lower stalk of the crop, not the foliage. Absolute precision is not necessary with this application, so drop nozzles from a boom type applicator can be used to obtain desired coverage. The nozzles also can be mounted on a cultivator frame to combine application with cultivation of the middles.

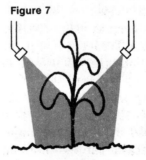
Figure 7

Calibration Of Herbicide Sprayers

Accurate application of herbicides is important, but sprayer calibration can be vexing.
This method lets you avoid most of the arithmetic and requires a minimum of measuring.

All you need to calibrate a sprayer is this sheet, a pencil, a watch with a sweep second hand, a tape measure and a pint container.

With preemergence spraying, there are two factors that you don't want to change very much: (1) Tractor speeds--below three and above seven miles per hour are usually impractical. (2) Spray pressure--above 40 psi excessive drift results and below 20 psi preemergence spray nozzles won't operate properly. You have to quadruple pressure to double spray volume, therefore only small changes in spray volume should be attempted by changing pressure.

The best way to deliver the desired amount of material per acre is to mix the recommended amount of herbicide in the number of gallons per acre the sprayer is applying. Most herbicide labels call for a certain amount of product in 10 to 20 gallons or 20 to 40 gallons of water per acre; e.g., 1-1/2 pounds of AAtrex 80W in 20 to 40 gallons of water. With calibration you find your sprayer is applying 23 gallons per acre. You would therefore mix 1-1/2 pounds of AAtrex per 23 gallons of water in the tank. If the tank holds 200 gallons you would divide 200 by 23=8.69 x 1-1/2 pounds =13 pounds of AAtrex with each tankful.

Now assume that the recommendation is the same, but calibration shows you are applying only 9 gallons per acre. This is outside of the desired range. While it may be possible to increase output by slowing ground speed and/or increasing engine rpm, this method is usually inefficient. It's better to go to higher capacity nozzle tips.

Nozzle tips will deliver a certain gallonage per minute at various pressures. A TeeJet 8003 tip, for instance, will deliver .30 gallons per minute at 40 psi, which results in 22 gallons per acre at 4 miles per hour. A TeeJet 80015 tip will deliver only .15 gallons per minute at 40 psi--11.1 gallons per acre at 4 mph. Catalogs published by the three major nozzle manufacturers contain tables showing capacities of various nozzles. Check with your dealer or write the manufacturers for their catalogs: TeeJet Spraying Systems Company, North Avenue and Schmale Road, Wheaton, Illinois 60187; Delavan Manufacturing Company, 811 Fourth Street, West Des Moines, Iowa 50265;

Century Engineering Corp., 221 Fourth Avenue S.E., Cedar Rapids, Iowa 52401.

Broadcast calibration. Before going to the field be sure the spray pump works, all hoses are in good shape, nozzles and filters are clean. Put some water (no chemical) in the tank, run the pump and adjust the bypass valve until the pressure gauge shows that the pressure is where you want it--30 psi or 40 psi. Measure 200 feet in the field. Have the tractor up to desired speed before you enter the course, run sprayer over the 200 foot course at the speed you want to travel, and mark the throttle.

Mark the time it takes on Scale No. 1 of the nomograph on the back of this sheet. On Scale No. 2 mark the total spray width of your rig. Draw a line between the marks on Scale No. 1 and Scale No. 2 and extend it to the Turning Line.

Next, with the tractor out of gear, open the throttle to your mark. Check the pressure gauge to be sure pressure is the same as when the tractor was moving. If it is not, adjust the throttle slightly until it is the same. Catch a pint of water from one nozzle and record the number of seconds it takes on Scale No. 6. (At this point, catch a pint from each nozzle and record the time. Replace any nozzle which varies more than 10% from average.)

Draw a line from your mark on Scale No. 6 through Scale No. 5 (number of nozzles) and extend it through Scale No. 4 (total pumping rate, gpm). Then, a line drawn between your mark on Scale No. 4 and your mark on the Turning Line will cross Scale No. 3 which shows your application rate.

For broadcast spraying, mix the recommended per acre amount of material in the number of gallons per acre application rate.

Band application. Proceed as with broadcast calibration, marking speed and total swath width of the sprayer on Scales No. 1 and No. 2 and nozzle capacity and number of nozzles on Scales No. 5 and No. 6 of the nomograph. Say your application rate found on Scale No. 3 is 10 gallons per acre.

That's total field acres, not the acreage actually covered in the band. That is where some people get confused. Just remember that *the recommended amount of herbicide on that portion of* the field actually sprayed in the band is the same as the broadcast rate. So you have to calculate the proportion of the row which is in the sprayed band.

Say row width is 38 inches and you're spraying a 14 inch band. The proportion banded would be 14/38. Assume the broadcast rate is 2 pounds of material per acre. 2 x 14/38=28/38 or about 3/4 pound of material for each 10 gallons of water.

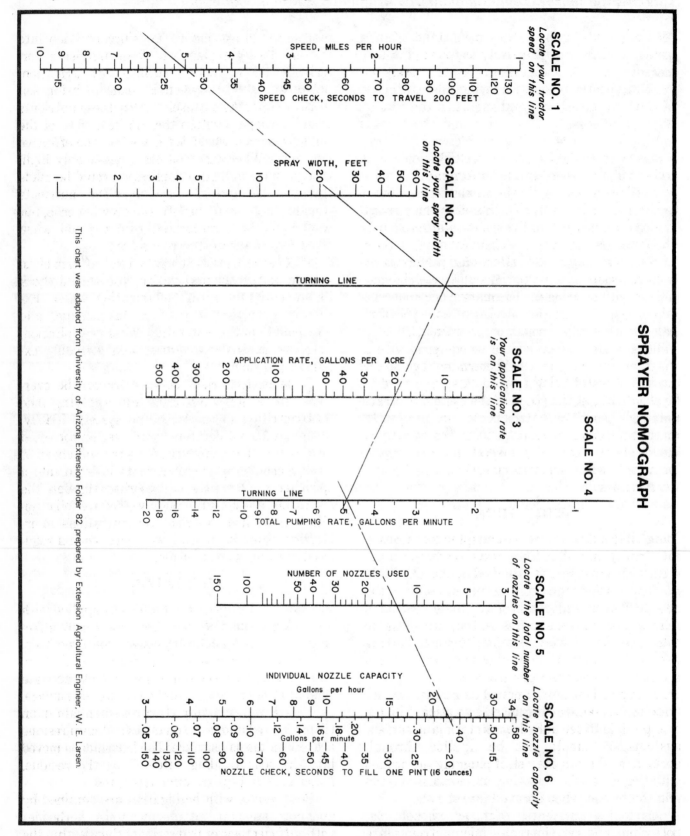

SPRAYER NOMOGRAPH

This chart was adapted from University of Arizona Extension Folder 82 prepared by Extension Agricultural Engineer, W. E. Larsen.

Applying Chemicals With Sprinkler Irrigation

This practice offers an efficient way of putting on some fertilizers and herbicides.
A well-designed and properly managed irrigation system is required.

Fertilizer, herbicides, and, in some instances, other pesticides can be effectively applied through center-pivot and linear-move sprinkler systems. Advantages of this practice include the saving in trips over the field and reductions in the cost of labor and energy.

A sprinkler system must be well designed and properly operated to obtain uniform application—an absolute necessity for the success of this practice. For instance, a 20% variation in the amount of water applied within the system will result in a like variation in the rate of chemical applied. Such an error may not greatly affect crop performance, from a moisture standpoint, but it can be disastrous with a herbicide. The margin between crop injury, adequate weed control, and poor performance can be small, so accuracy is essential.

A sprinkler system should be equipped with a water meter so you can determine the exact amount of water being applied. Also, you need to be able to adjust the speed of the system to a rate that will permit you to put on an acceptable amount of water in relation to the chemical you are applying. Carefully inspect for and repair leaky gaskets, malfunctioning sprinkler heads, and worn nozzles.

FERTIGATION

The mobile nutrients are best adapted for injection into irrigation water. They move readily into the soil solution and are not absorbed by the soil. These nutrients include nitrogen, sulfur, and some of the chelated micronutrients. Since these nutrients readily move into the root zone, they are available to crops soon after application. Further, putting these nutrients on during the growing season helps to minimize losses through leaching.

Nitrogen is usually applied as ammonium nitrate or urea-ammonium nitrate solution. Though it is possible to use anhydrous ammonia in surface systems, it should not be applied through sprinklers. You run the risk of plugging the nozzles with precipitated salts. Also, ammonia is volatile and can be lost when sprayed into the air.

Immobile nutrients, such as phosphorus, potassium, and some inorganic micronutrients, are best suited to application and incorporation into the soil ahead of planting. These nutrients normally would be applied too late with irrigation, unless an early irrigation is made to bring soil moisture up to field capacity. Also, these nutrients would be tied up within the top inch or so of the soil surface and would not move into the effective root zone. Where the soil tests reasonably high, though, a maintenance application could be made through the sprinkler system. The nutrients wouldn't necessarily benefit the growing crop, but they would be incorporated with the soil when tilled for the succeeding year's crop.

If phosphorus is to be applied in the form of an ammonium phosphate solution, you should check its compatibility with the irrigation water. Excessive quantities of calcium, magnesium, and bicarbonate in the water may cause precipitation, plugging screens and nozzles and corroding exposed equipment.

Some micronutrient deficiencies can be overcome in a growing crop by applying the micronutrients in the irrigation system. Ideally, though, a known deficiency can best be corrected by applying the micronutrient to the soil ahead of time. Some of the micronutrients injected into a sprinkler system may be absorbed through the leaves, but it is not a thoroughly effective foliar application method. Nutrient concentrations in irrigation water are much lower than when a regular foliar treatment is made.

HERBIGATION*

Preplant or preemergence herbicides applied with a sprinkler system often control weeds more effectively than when applied by conventional methods. The water incorporates those herbicides that require mixing with the soil or may help to activate those that are normally applied to the soil surface. Herbigation is especially effective when minimum tillage is used and large quantities of crop residue are left on the soil surface. The herbicide is moved into the soil, avoiding "tie-up" by the residue. Skips and overlaps are eliminated, too.

Best results with herbigation are obtained by applying preplant or preemergence herbicides with sufficient water to distribute them within the top 2 inches of soil, advise Nebraska specialists. Generally, this is achieved by applying the herbicide with about 0.5 inches of water on sandy soils and 0.75 inches on fine-textured soils.

A problem can arise if highly volatile herbicides, such as Eradicane or Sutan+ (those that require immediate incorporation), are applied to soils that are already wet. For best results, apply these herbicides to dry soil. Also, do not apply herbicides through sprinklers when the wind exceeds 10 mph. Strong winds can cause uneven application, and the herbicide may drift.

Herbigation must be properly timed to fit into your tilling and planting schedule. Best performance is obtained by applying herbicides very soon after planting. Usually, the herbicide should be put on within 5 days after final tillage–before the weeds germinate. A good procedure is to till and plant one-half of the center-pivot circle, then start to herbigate while tilling and planting the other half of the circle.

In many instances, the same injection pump can be used for applying both fertilizer and herbicides through the sprinkler system. However, using the same pump usually requires that the herbicide be mixed with a fairly large quantity of water in a supply tank. Consequently, if a wettable powder formulation is used, it will be necessary to keep the chemical agitated so that it will not settle out of solution. A sprayer tank with an agitation system works well as a supply tank for this purpose. Or, an auxiliary pump can be rigged up to do the job. An alternative is to use a low-volume injection pump to inject either a concentrated herbicide formulation or low-volume mixtures.

A number of preplant or preemergence herbicides are now labeled for application through sprinkler systems. Among those labeled for use on corn, for instance, are atrazine, Bicep, Dual, Dual + atrazine, Eradicane, Eradicane + atrazine, Lasso, and Lasso + atrazine. You can also legally apply other preplant or preemergence herbicides in this manner if they are cleared for use on a specific crop, if the label does not prohibit their use in a sprinkler system, and if all other conditions on the label can be met. For example, a herbicide is cleared for use on a crop and the label does not state that it cannot be applied through a sprinkler system, but the label does say the herbicide must be incorporated into the soil using mechanical means. The latter requirement would rule out the use of the herbicide in a sprinkler system. You must accept all responsibility for the use and the

*"Herbigation" is a registered trademark of Stauffer Chemical Company.

performance of any herbicide that is not specifically labeled for herbigation.

SAFETY DEVICES

Sprinkler irrigation equipment must be properly equipped with safety devices to prevent possible pollution of ground water.

Mechanical or electrical failure could shut off the irrigation pumping plant while the injection equipment continued to operate. The entire irrigation pipeline could be filled with the chemical mixture. To prevent this from happening, the irrigation pumping plant and chemical injection pump must be interlocked so that one will be shut off if the other stops. Where an internal combustion engine is used, the injection pump can be belted to the drive shaft or an accessory pulley of the irrigation engine. Where an electric motor is used to power the irrigation pump, the injector pump could be driven by another electric motor that is interlocked with the pump motor.

Check and vacuum relief valves (anti-siphon devices) are needed in the irrigation pipeline to prevent solutions from siphoning back into the well. These valves should be installed between the irrigation pump discharge and the point where the chemical is injected into the pipeline. A check valve is also needed in the chemical injection line to prevent backflow into the supply tank.

CALCULATING APPLICATION RATES

The rate of chemical application per acre is quite critical, especially with herbicides. You need to accurately calibrate or match the injected volume to the area covered by your center-pivot system.

Here's a sample calculation to show how you can determine injection rate for a herbicide.

● Assume that you want to apply 5¼ pints of a herbicide per acre using a center-pivot system that covers 132 acres.

● Multiplying 5¼ by 132 gives a total of 693 pints, or 86.6 gallons, needed. Supposing that you have a 300-gallon supply tank, you would need to add sufficient water to fill the tank.

● You determine that it takes 20 hours for your center pivot to complete one revolution while applying ½ inch of water. Dividing 300 gallons of solution in the supply tank by 20 hours means that you would need to inject 15 gallons per hour, or ¼ gallon per minute, into the irrigation pipeline.

● Set metering pump according to manufacturer's directions. Check delivery rate of the injection pump to make sure it is correct.

Chapter 11

Buildings, Equipment and Machinery

Investment in buildings, equipment and farm machinery can pay a high rate of return through greater livestock gains, higher crop yields and lower labor costs. Before making a major investment, though, consider a number of questions. Will the investment permit you to operate more effectively, produce a better product, reduce labor requirements, and/or increase your net income?

Investing too much in buildings, equipment and machinery can be as unwise as not investing enough. It's not advisable to tie up capital that could be used more effectively for other purposes, such as fertilizer, pesticides or livestock. An alternative may be to hire custom work or lease machinery and equipment.

Design efficient buildings. Buildings are essential for operating an efficient farm business, even though the overhead costs of depreciation and upkeep often appear to be burdensome. Your buildings should perform one or more of the following functions: Provide controlled environment for your livestock, provide the shop area necessary for maintaining equipment, serve as the nerve center or hub of your operations, enable you to store supplies which can be bought advantageously in bulk or large quantities, or provide crop storage.

Farm buildings should be designed with the following objectives:

• Economic per unit cost of construction.

- Adequate strength and size to do the job desired.
- Durability to keep replacement and upkeep costs at a minimum.
- Handy, efficient use provided by well-planned farmstead layout.

Surveys show that replacement of farm buildings is a major problem for most farmers. If you are going to construct a new building, decide whether it should be built to exactly suit your enterprise or to fill a more versatile roll should your farming plan change over the years.

Take space requirements of livestock, crop or machinery into account. Also, determine what mechanical equipment is to be used in the building. Construction site should be well chosen. All principle buildings should be accessible from the central area of the farmstead. The court area should be 100 to 120 feet wide and paved or graveled where practical. The type of material you use can greatly affect the life and cost of the building, and you will want to give the appearance some thought as well.

Match buildings and equipment. Methods of livestock production are changing. The trend toward more confinement systems of livestock production is increasing capital requirements for building equipment. Investment in such equipment may represent as much or more capital than the buildings themselves, so it is necessary to plan your buildings to make efficient use of the equipment. Plan well in advance of building construction or remodeling such things as type of feeding operation, method of manure handling, feedlot paving and method of feed handling.

When planning grain storage and the space necessary, have your future feeding programs well in mind. Will you feed grain as high moisture or dry? Will you feed a complete ration, pellet your feeds or wafer your hay? For example, if you should shift to feeding high moisture grain rather than dry grain, you would need completely new storage facilities. High moisture grain storage requires well-constructed, airtight or conventional silos rather than bins or cribs.

Invest wisely in machinery. There are two kinds of costs involved in owning and operating any piece of machinery. These costs are classified as follows: *Fixed costs* include depreciation, taxes, insurance and interest on the investment. These costs will go on whether you use the machinery or not. *Variable costs*, sometimes called operating costs, include repair bills, maintenance, gas, oil and/or lubrication and general upkeep. These costs are involved in the actual operation.

Where fixed costs are high, it may be advisable to rent machinery or hire a custom operator. It becomes overly expensive to equip a farm with high cost machinery which may be used only a few days and then lie idle the rest of the year. Do as much as possible to keep machinery investment down by keeping it in good repair and selecting and buying wisely.

Wise selection of machinery for a particular farm depends on:
- Size and type of the farming operation.
- Soil types and topography.
- Labor available.
- Capital available.
- Service you can expect from the dealer, including his stock of replacement parts in case of a breakdown.

A sound purchase decision can be made only by the farm operator. Pertinent information, such as test results, is helpful, but only as an aid in making your decision. Maintenance and repair must be approached systematically if expenses are to be kept low and machinery maintained at a trouble-free level. Breakdowns are costly, both in terms of time wasted and reduced crop production.

Farmers must continue to lower their production costs and increase their farm efficiency. Mechanization may be one way to accomplish this objective, provided the investment in machinery is kept in balance with the size of the operation.

Farm Building Economics

Farm buildings are an economic necessity in the growing trend to intensify crop and livestock production on farms.

Today, livestock production and crop conditioning systems include refined handling equipment, assorted facilities and buildings.

Adding building improvements means planning and financing an operational system, not just a building. Buildings are important in modifying environmental conditions to make a system work, but, in terms of costs, they are only incidental.

SYSTEM BUDGET ANALYSIS

Pre-budgeting all income and expenses is important when developing new systems for livestock and poultry production. What should you expect in returns from a heavy investment in buildings and system improvements? If the estimated annual adjusted gross income pays off the total capital investment in 10 years or less, it is a sound business venture. The more desirable rate of payoff is six to seven years or less.

To find annual adjusted gross income, estimate income and subtract all variable costs—labor, feed, building and equipment maintenance, taxes, insurance, interest on investment and other operating expenses.

BUILDING SELECTION

Selection of individual building components is the final step in the planning and development of an enterprise system. The building places a "cap" on the complete system and ties it all together. It may be the final stage in a plan, but it is not the least important.

Decisions on buildings are based on three facts: What type of building? What is the cost? What production efficiencies will it generate?

As components of production systems, buildings represent a high initial investment normally comprising 50% to 60% of the total system capital input. But, on an annual production cost basis, they will represent only 11% to 13% of the total production costs. Don't do any drastic cost cutting on buildings—$400 or $500 may stretch purse strings in initial investment, but will reflect little change in annual cost and could materially affect production performance.

Another approach is a cost analysis of individual building ownership. From records and experience, it is concluded that the annual cost of a farm building normally ranges from 15% to 19% of the original cost. Cost distribution is as follows:

Depreciation .... 5% to 7%
Maintenance & repair.............. 2% to 3%
Taxes, insurance & misc............ 2% to 3%
Interest (12% on 1/2 of investment)... 6%

This represents an annual dollar cost of $150 to $190 per $1,000 investment. Determining the production use value of a building is difficult because of the variables. Judgment and limited research can be used to determine what the building will provide in increased product value and production efficiency compared to having no building.

Building types. Decisions on the type of building to purchase are not easy. There is a wide choice of building designs, materials and prices.

Currently there are pros and cons for open, naturally ventilated buildings versus enclosed, insulated and mechanically ventilated buildings. Research has established that modified environment buildings (closed-insulated) increase efficiency in poultry and hog production, but still are questionable for cattle.

It is estimated that the additional investment cost for insulated and ventilated buildings for poultry and hogs will be returned in about four years through feed savings, rate of gain and management efficiencies.

Justification of such buildings for cattle cannot be confirmed at this time. Cattle need shelter, but not totally controlled environment.

BUILDING FEATURES

Clear span interiors, particularly for narrow building widths, will be more flexible and workable.

Costs for interior columns versus trussed construction will be comparable to widths of 50 feet to 60 feet. Over 60 feet, cost will favor column supports. Expect about an 8% to 10% increase per square foot of building cost for each 10 to 15 feet of width over 60 feet.

Wood or steel framing. Choice of steel, pole or stud frame will depend on a combination of factors such as size, design, use, price and availability of the particular building you think will best fit your needs. Before buying, get information on more than one design and compare competitive features and prices.

Pole structures have price advantages over steel when there is up to 40 feet clear span widths. For widths over 40 feet, steel becomes very competitive. Steel will be more competitive in all cases where a concrete floor and footings are to be installed, because it eliminates the advantage of poles acting as footings in pole type construction.

Roofing and siding choices. Steel, aluminum and shingle for roofing and steel, wood and aluminum for siding are popular in the order listed, with steel well in front in footage used in current farm construction. Other building materials such as concrete, composition and compressed panels and plastics are available.

Color in siding and roofing panels is growing rapidly in use. Cost is more per square foot of material than galvanized or aluminum sheets. However, pre-color coating will add about five to seven years of service life and attractiveness to the farmstead.

Insulation and ventilation provide a more uniform building environment for livestock. High density of livestock and poultry in confined system buildings increases need for wall, ceiling and roof insulation and for a mechanical ventilation system.

Insulation needs are influenced by climate, type of construction and methods of heating and/or cooling. For all practical purposes, the insulation needs for livestock and poultry buildings are based on minimum levels by climatic zones. A builder or materials supplier should be able to advise you on the minimums for the zone in which you are located.

Insulation value of materials is measured by the resistance of heat transfer through material, designated as the "R" value. The chart shows the "R" values for various common building materials.

Adequate ventilation systems for all insulated livestock and poultry buildings are a must and should be designed into the buildings on the basis of the type, number and density of animals or birds to be housed. Ventilation systems should be designed for maximum and minimum airflow needs during summer and winter periods.

MATERIALS	"R" VALUE
Plywood, 1/2″	0.63
Wood-fir or pine, 25/32″	0.98
Asbestos-cement board, 1/8″	0.03
Wood fiber board, 1″	2.00
Mineral wool blanket, 1″	3.70
Expanded polystyrene, 1″	3.50
Urethane, rigid, 1″	6.70
Mineral wool, fill type, 1″	3.33
Vermiculate, expanded, 1″	2.08
Concrete block, 8″	1.11

Don't cut costs on insulation and ventilation. For assurance of needs, check with your state university extension engineers.

PACKAGE BUILDINGS

Building manufacturers and fabricators are offering more and more preengineered, packaged buildings on the market. The buildings are designed and packaged to meet specific production operation needs on the farm. Packages include all the building and equipment components that can be assembled on site by builder contractors or with the use of local or farm labor. With the increasingly complex nature of livestock buildings and systems, it may mean savings for you in time and money to contract complete materials and erection of buildings by experienced builders.

You may save on cost per square foot of building if you build yourself with farm labor, but a builder can complete the job in one-third to one-half the time it will take inexperienced labor.

Packaged buildings will normally have some price advantages. There will be less choice of materials and options of design and equipment, but you'll be buying an operational building unit that has been planned and tested.

If you want to see detailed plans for a wider choice of materials and designs, plans and engineering assistance are available from the state university agricultural extension service and from materials suppliers.

Livestock Building Insulation and Ventilation

*Providing a proper environment for animals confined in buildings
demands careful attention to ventilation and insulation requirements.*

Ventilation and insulation work together to control building environment. Ventilation helps control temperature, humidity and odors, and provides the air change necessary for optimum animal health and production. Building insulation provides a barrier against heat exchange, and helps control moisture condensation. Heat is exhausted in summer and conserved in winter.

INSULATION REQUIREMENTS

Materials differ greatly in their insulating qualities and since many types are available, the only fair comparison between them must be made on the basis of their "R" value, or resistance to heat passage. Heat resistance values for common materials are shown in the table at right.

Some manufacturers quote "R" values for their insulation on an "installed" basis. This is not a true value for the material alone, but includes values for other assumed components used in normal construction. Compare materials on the basis of the value specified for the insulation only.

The amount of insulation needed varies depending on the prevailing range of temperatures. Refer to the map to determine recommended amounts of insulation needed.

RECOMMENDED INSULATION

Climate Zone	Total Resistance(R)	
	Walls	Ceilings
Mild	9	12
Moderate	9-14	16
Cold	14	23

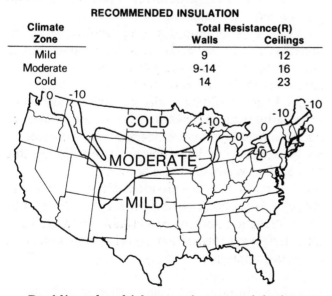

Doubling the thickness of a material also approximately doubles its "R" value. A total "R" value can be computed by totaling values for the various materials and thicknesses for ceilings and walls. Insulating the perimeter of a concrete slab floor is also helpful if floor heat is used.

INSULATION VALUES OF COMMON MATERIALS

Materials	Thickness (Inches)	"R" Value
Fiberglass or Mineral Wool Batts	1	3.7
Wood Fiber	1	4.0
Paper or Pulp Products	1	4.15
Expanded Polystyrene	1	3.8
Urethane Foam	1	6.25
Concrete	1	.08
Plywood	.375	.47
Insulating Sheathing	.78	2.06
Single Glass	.125	.89
Concrete Block	8.0	1.92
Light Weight Concrete Block	8.0	2.88
Fir or Pine Boards	.75	.98
Asphalt Shingles		.44
Air Space (3/4" or larger)		.90

Vapor barriers are necessary in confined livestock buildings since animals release large amounts of moisture into the air. If this moist air is allowed to seep into insulation and contact the cooler outer surface, condensation will occur. Wet insulation loses its value and deteriorates rapidly. To counter this, impermeable materials such as a polyethylene film or foil are installed directly over the interior surface of the insulation.

VENTILATION REQUIREMENTS

During warm weather, ventilation is needed primarily to control temperature. In cold weather the primary function is to remove moisture from the building. Minimum air flow in winter may be only 1/25 of that needed during warm temperatures, so summer conditions set the maximum air change capacity needed.

Livestock release large amounts of moisture. A sow and litter may release as much as three gallons per day into the air. Heat produced by the animals raises the temperature and moisture-holding capacity of the air. However, air inside the building usually is not able to hold all the moisture produced, especially in cold weather. To prevent condensation and damp conditions, moisture must be removed.

In winter, moisture-laden air is vented from the building and replaced by cold, drier air which then expands, and picks up additional moisture. The result is a movement of moisture from the building. However, some heat loss is unavoidable in the exchange of air. Cold weather ventilation must be a compromise between the minimum amount needed to control moisture and the maximum that can be permitted to control temperature.

Relative humidity. As shown in the table below, when air temperature is 60 degrees, condensation will begin on walls and ceiling if their temperature is 50 degrees at 70% relative humidity; 46 degrees at 60%; and 41 degrees at 50%. To stop condensation, it is necessary to insulate so that interior walls and ceiling don't fall below the condensation temperature.

TEMPERATURE AT WHICH CONDENSATION BEGINS

Inside Air Temperature	Relative Humidity		
	70%	60%	50%
	Condensation Temperature		
40°F.	32°F.	28°F.	24°F.
50	41	36	33
60	50	46	41

The concentration of animals, outside temperatures, and the amount of inside heat conserved by insulation determine the relative humidity at any given time. With these conditions set, ventilation is used to expel moist air and keep relative humidity under the condensation point. However, in very cold temperatures, often a higher rate of ventilation will not be helpful, since the colder the air, the less moisture it will carry. Under these conditions, it is difficult to maintain dry conditions without the use of supplemental heat.

Ventilation systems must supply an adequate volume of air, distributing it evenly to avoid damp corners and drafty areas in the building. The system should also be able to adjust to the range of climatic conditions to be encountered.

In "cold confinement" buildings, a minimum ventilation system will include adjustable wall panels to utilize natural air circulation. Roof insulation and ridge ventilators are added to control humidity and condensation. In some buildings a pressure fan is installed to overcome the lack of dependable air circulation in cold weather.

"Warm" buildings are completely insulated and may require supplemental heating and cooling. Ventilation is supplied by a coordinated system of inlet and outlet ducts, with mechanical air movement.

Mechanical ventilation is accomplished on either pressure or exhaust principles. Pressure systems push air through the building, exhaust systems pull air through. In both types, an axial-flow, propeller type fan is commonly used. Fans should be rated in cubic feet per minute capacity in order to be correctly designed into either system.

System design. One single-speed fan, sized to operate continuously at low outside temperatures is generally used. This can be coupled with one or more additional fans, set to start when temperature inside the building increases to certain levels. A similar effect can be produced by operating a larger fan, and adjusting air flow by changing the position of louvers on intake ducts.

RECOMMENDED VENTILATION RATES

Animal	Units	Minimum Winter	Fall & Spring	Minimum Summer
Swine				
Farrowing	cfm/sow & litter	20	80	210
Nursery	cfm/pig	2	15	36
Grow & Finish				
40 - 100 lbs.	cfm/pig	5	20	48
100 - 150 lbs.	cfm/pig	7	25	72
150 - 210 lbs.	cfm/pig	10	35	100
Gestation	cfm/hog	12	40	180
Beef	cfm/1,000-lb. animal	15 (draw from pit if on slats)	100	200 Plus pit fans
Dairy				
Stanchion or Freestall	cfm/1,000 lbs.	25-37	75	150
Poultry	cfm/lb.	1/2	3/4	1-1/4*

*Multideck houses require more--up to two air changes per minute.

Location and type of ducts depends on the particular building design. It's important that ducts be correctly sized and well disbursed for good air distribution. In an exhaust system for example, the area of inlet ducts should be in a ratio of one square inch for every four cfm of fan capacity. Area of outlets in a pressure system should be one square inch per seven cfm of fan capacity.

A common exhaust system uses fans mounted in the walls. Incoming air passes through a baffled slot under the eaves. Position of the baffle allows air to warm before reaching livestock in winter. In summer, slot width can be widened.

In one pressure system, a ceiling-mounted fan uses baffles to distribute air horizontally. Air is mixed before escaping through several spaced outlets in walls. Another pressure system distributes air in the building through a perforated plastic tube. Still another, used in farrowing houses, delivers air via individual tubes to each farrowing crate during warm weather.

Planning Your Farmstead

A good farmstead pays off in many ways. It can provide better living, increased work efficiency and greater farm production.

Few farmers have the opportunity to build a new, ideal farmstead. Usually, changes must be made in the existing plan. Often these changes are made without adequate planning for present and future needs. Study your present farmstead and decide what changes are necessary to develop a more workable arrangement. Then proceed in a step-by-step manner. Some of the objectives to keep in mind when making plans are as follows:

Building needs depend on the crops and livestock produced. The farmstead should be planned around properly servicing these buildings and strategically locating them in relation to the other farmstead facilities.

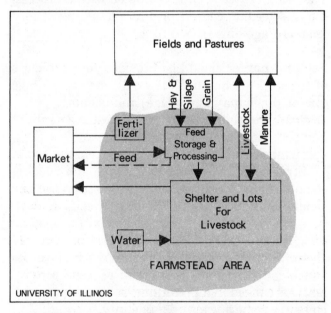

Efficiency of labor and machinery is greatly improved through well-arranged buildings, lots, and fields. The high production per man hour that is facilitated through a well-arranged farmstead will help to boost profits. A modern farmstead arrangement can eliminate miles of walking and endless wasted hours. Buildings should be designed and arranged so that livestock and equipment do most of the work, eliminating much manual effort.

Flexibility should be built into any farmstead arrangement. Allow for possible shifts in enterprises if markets or your operation should suggest a need to alter your present enterprise combination.

Allow for expansion as well. Don't neglect your major enterprise, however, and plan around it.

ADAPT PLAN TO LOCATION

Consider such factors as drainage, prevailing winds, sunlight, snowfall and other natural forces when planning your farmstead. The building arrangement should be designed to take advantage of these natural conditions while minimizing their adverse effects.

Good drainage sites should be selected for buildings, service areas and lots. Provide for good drainage away from the farmhouse and yard to carry off surface water and allow for adequate sewage disposal.

A gently sloping farmstead greatly helps natural drainage. A high spot or knoll is an ideal location. However, it may be necessary to change slope or drainage by grading. It may be easier and better to change farmstead topography by using earth moving equipment than it is to try to arrange buildings to fit natural conditions.

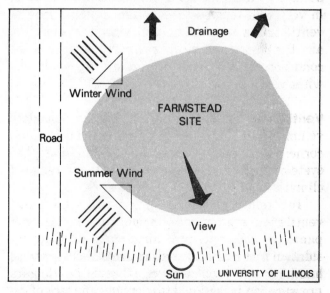

Prevailing winds and sunlight can be used to your advantage when buildings are properly laid out. Summer winds are usually from the southwest and winter winds from the northwest. Construct the farmstead to take advantage of the cooling effects of summer winds, yet in such a way that the buildings will protect work and livestock areas from cold winter blasts. Locate the fronts of the buildings to the south or east, if possible, and group them so they form a wind barrier. South fronts let sun in during the winter. This helps to dry out bedding and reduces moisture problems.

Use wind breaks on northern and western edges of the farmstead to protect against winter winds. In snowfall areas, windbreaks and proper building placement will help control drifting and save on snow removal.

SERVICE AREA

A farm service yard is the hub or center of the farmstead. It reduces the distance between buildings, yet provides reasonable fire protection and allows room for moving machinery about. Shape is not fixed—it can be square, rectangular or L-shaped. However, provide plenty of space for turning machinery and big trucks. Use gravel or crushed rock to make an all-weather drive to major buildings. Other areas of the yard should be planted in grass.

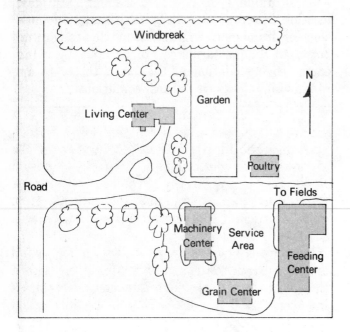

Central machinery center is more desirable than storing machinery in several buildings. Repairs are easier to make and attachments and mounting brackets are less apt to be mislaid or lost. Machinery storage building and shop should be easily accessible from traffic lanes and fields.

Allow plenty of space for maneuvering machinery. Use space in the service yard whenever possible. If the machine shed has doors on both sides, allow for turning on the back. If the back doors are

rarely used, they could open directly into a pasture or field and the building could be lined up with the service yard fence.

Machine sheds are sometimes built along the lane to fields. In this case allow room to get machinery in and out. Leave room for expansion.

Face big doors, which are often left open, away from the house and road for a neater farmstead appearance. Ice and snow problems can be partly eliminated by facing doors to the south and east.

Grain storage center is usually situated at the farmstead unless portable equipment is used for storing where it will be fed later. A spot in the service yard is the best location, preferably near one side so that there is enough room for the elevator and for driving trucks and wagons in and out.

Various types of storage buildings are suitable. The size and type depend on farm needs. Plan to use mechanical loading and unloading equipment. The grain center may be combined with a processing and feeding center for direct handling of feed from storage bins to livestock.

Feeding center should be provided for each class of livestock produced. This would include storage for roughage (hay and silage) and bedding.

Arrange buildings to give livestock sunlight and maximum protection from winter winds. Summer winds should carry odors away from the house.

Structures for storing hay, silage and bedding should be easily reached from the service yard and should be adapted for mechanical or self-feeding.

LIVING CENTER

A well-planned farmhouse should fit into its farmstead surroundings, as well as have conveniently arranged living, working and sleeping areas. Here are some suggested guidelines.

- Build the house at least 100 feet from the road. This cuts down on noise and dust and it increases privacy.
- Locate the driveway close to the main entrance of the house.
- Locate the kitchen so the driveway and service area can be easily viewed from the kitchen window.
- Build the garage attached or adjacent to the house. Avoid facing the garage toward the road, since open doors are unattractive.
- Provide sufficient parking space for your own cars and trucks and for those with whom you will be doing business.

Wind and Snow Control

In many areas, a system of wind control will reduce problems with drifting snow, cut heating costs in buildings, and improve animal performance in outside lots.

Controlling wind and snow on the farmstead involves employing any of several methods to change wind direction and velocity. When wind speed is reduced, snow and dust settle out in a fairly predictable pattern. But, because wind speed and direction are constantly changing, no method of control is foolproof.

Your wind and snow-control system should be based on the *prevailing* winds in your locality, usually from the north or northwest in winter, shifting to the south in summer.

Windbreak fences reduce wind velocity and cause snow to drop before reaching the area being protected. The action of a windbreak depends on its construction. For example, a solid fence will cause the wind to deposit snow on both sides in deeper drifts than will a porous fence.

The distance snow is deposited downwind is roughly proportional to the height of the fence. With solid fences, wind drops snow for a distance of about five times the fence height. You can also expect significant wind reduction for a distance of about 15 times the height of a solid fence.

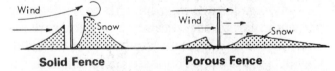

Solid Fence   **Porous Fence**

A fence with 25% to 50% open space is more effective in controlling wind, according to Canadian studies. Also, it drops more snow than does a solid fence but creates shallower, longer drifts. This speeds snow melting and makes snow removal easier. Generally, the major snow drop is confined to a distance of ten times the fence height downwind of an open fence. Wind protection is usually adequate for a distance of 20 times the fence height.

Fence openings should be 2 to 2½ inches wide, running either vertically or horizontally. Openings wider than 6 inches are ineffective.

Windbreak fences of both the solid and open type should be mounted off the ground to allow wind to continually sweep snow downwind and away from the fence, increasing its effectiveness. Mount solid fences about 4 inches above the ground; open fences, 1 foot above the ground. Sturdy construction is important, especially for solid fences that take the wind's full force.

Shelterbelts consist of trees planted in several rows on the windward side of the farmstead. In general, you can expect significant wind reduction for a distance of about 20 times the maximum tree height. Snow will be deposited within the belt and for a distance of five to ten times tree height, or about 150 feet downwind.

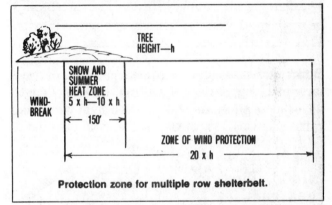

Protection zone for multiple row shelterbelt.

Shelterbelts are most effective if located about 150 feet upwind from the area to be protected. This allows snow to settle out before reaching buildings and also provides sufficient air movement for natural building ventilation. Shelterbelts should also extend approximately 150 feet to either side of the protected area to minimize the swirling effect of the wind as it goes around the ends of the belt.

Windbreaks save energy. Studies in high-wind areas, such as the Northern Plains, have shown that properly placed windbreaks can reduce heating costs 20% to 30%. This is because wind velocity is reduced, thereby decreasing air infiltration into the building. A solid row of dense shrubs planted around the base of a building creates a dead-air space and helps insulate the foundation or basement.

In summer, a properly located shelterbelt can channel air currents to remove heat by increasing wind velocity around the house and farm buildings. Also, a dense tree area has a substantial cooling effect. This is more than just the shade provided. Leaves produce an evaporative cooling effect.

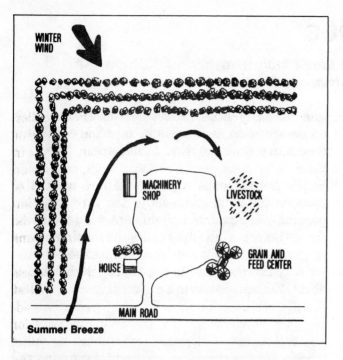

WINTER WIND

MACHINERY SHOP

LIVESTOCK

HOUSE

GRAIN AND FEED CENTER

MAIN ROAD

Summer Breeze

Building drafts can be a serious problem, particularly in a long, narrow, open-front building (length 2½ or more times its width). Even mild winds can cause excessive lengthwise drafts within the build-ing. Several remedies can be helpful. First, construct a "swirl chamber" measuring at least 16 feet by

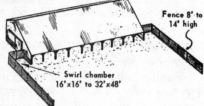

Fence 8' to 14' high

Swirl chamber 16'x16' to 32'x48'

16 feet on the upwind side of the building (see il-lustration). The chamber is made of porous fence, and ideally, should be as high as the building eave. *Never connect a windbreak fence to a corner of the building.* This will funnel wind and snow into the building.

Another solution to lengthwise drafts is to build solid partitions inside the building at about 50-foot spacings. Partitions should reach the rear of the building but need not be higher than the open front. Or, close the first 16 feet of open sidewall at each end of the building. *Never close only the center section of an open-front building.* This will increase draft problems.

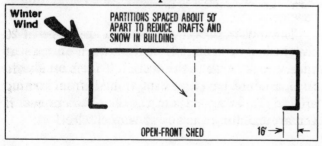

Winter Wind

PARTITIONS SPACED ABOUT 50' APART TO REDUCE DRAFTS AND SNOW IN BUILDING

OPEN-FRONT SHED   16'

Wind passing over the roof of an open-front building causes a slight vacuum and may draw wind and snow into the open front. One remedy is to leave a small opening near the top of the rear wall. The size of this opening should be equal to the size of the ventilation opening at the roof ridge in a gable roof building. Drafts can also be deflected by installing a 2-foot-high solid panel running just under the eave on the open side.

Building location can cause wind and snow prob-lems. For example, adjacent silos located upwind of a feedlot can create a swirling motion and in-crease wind velocity in the lot. Best solution is usually a 10-foot-high porous fence extending at least 30 feet on each side of the silo. Tall buildings located on the downwind side can divert wind back into the lot. While this is usually not too serious, it should be considered when planning the lot.

Buildings, such as silos located downwind of the open-front side of a building, can deflect drafts and snow into the structure. *Never locate the open-front side of a building within 60 feet of an upright silo or other building.*

Buildings located too close together can create a wind-tunnel effect as currents blow through the passageway. It's best to arrange buildings at least 50 feet apart. For an existing situation, the best solution is to install a windbreak fence or stack hay bales across the passageway.

Buildings located in rows with their long axis perpendicular to the prevailing wind can cause heavy snow loads on roofs. Separation of the build-ings by 150 feet will eliminate the problem. Com-monly, however, roofs are simply designed to take the heavier load.

Roads and lanes can be shielded from snow if you recognize how snow is deposited. When a road is cut through a hill, wind blowing across the depres-sion slows and drops a drift. One solution is to place a porous snow fence about 60 feet upwind of the area. You should also create gentle side slopes. Sharp edges create more drifting.

Roads bordered by trees, shrubs, and even woven-wire fencing can create drifting. If a border of trees or shrubs is desired, it should be located downwind and set back from the roadway. In heavy-snowfall areas, locate roads along the top of ridges, where possible, because wind velocity in-creases slightly there and will not drop snow. Elevating the roadway 1 to 2 feet above the sur-rounding terrain will serve the same purpose.

266

Cattle Handling Facilities

Well designed handling facilities permit better use of labor and minimize stress and injury to both livestock and handlers.

Once working corrals have been constructed, a bottleneck or flaw in the design can seriously damage their usefulness, causing poor and inefficient movement of cattle through the structure.

Designing the working corral is essentially a problem of organizing the different parts into a working unit that fits the site and needs of your livestock program. The component parts of the system are: holding pens, crowding pen, working chute, squeeze chute or head gate, and loading chute. If needed, the system can also include a scale, spray pen, cutting gates or dipping vat.

Start by preparing a scale drawing. Lined graph or chart paper works well. Ordinarily you will want to keep the design fairly simple, while still meeting your handling requirements. But consider other aspects—safety, flexibility, and convenience. Keep in mind the habits and preferences of cattle while you are planning, and prepare several designs before making your final decision.

Select a location for the corral near an all-weather road for loading and unloading, and make it as convenient as possible to your pastures. Pay particular attention to good drainage at the site and consider prevailing winds in orienting the corral layout. If possible, position the facilities so that cattle moving through the chutes will be heading back toward the direction from which they came. This aids movement by taking advantage of the animals' desire to return to a familiar area.

Pens and lots should be built to contain the required number of cattle and provide for efficient movement through the working area. A minimum of two holding pens is needed; one for holding cattle before working, and one for cattle after they have been worked. Use the specifications shown in the table to size holding pens for the number of cattle you expect to process in one group.

In larger herds you'll need holding space for all the cattle from one pasture. If cattle will be held in pens over night, increase the size of the holding pens to allow 40 to 60 square feet per head and provide watering facilities.

Gates should be located in the corners of pens, constructed so they are free-swinging and will not sag. Normally gates should close in the direction cattle are moving, but gates used for cutting or crowding must swing in either direction. Fences in the holding pens can be five feet high, but should be six feet in areas where cattle are worked or crowded. Shape of the holding pen is of little importance, except that tight corners should be avoided. Keep in mind how additional holding pens might fit into the layout if later required.

Position the crowding pen for direct access from holding pens into the working chute. Most layouts utilize a funnel-shaped or circular crowding area to make use of a free-swinging gate for pushing the cattle forward into the working chute.

Size of the crowding area will determine the number of cattle that can be worked in one group. Pen size should be 150 square feet or larger if you want to be able to work a full truckload at a time. If desired, the crowding pen can also do double duty as a spray pen or sorting area.

DATA SUMMARY

Space Requirements:	Below 600 lbs.	600-1,200 lbs.	Over 1,200 lbs.
Holding area (per animal)	14 sq. ft.	17 sq. ft.	20 sq. ft.
Crowding pen	150 sq. ft. or space for 1 truckload		
Working chute (vertical sides)			
Width	18 in.	22 in.	26 in.
Desirable length (min.)	20 ft.	20 ft.	20 ft.
Working chute (sloping sides)			
Width at bottom	15 in.	15 in.	16 in.
Width at top	20 in.	24 in.	26 in.
Desirable length (min.)	20 ft.	20 ft.	20 ft.

Loading chute (all weights of cattle)	
Width	26-30 in.
Length	8 ft. (min.)
Rise	3-1/2 in./ft.
Height	
Gooseneck trailer	15 in.
Pickup truck	28 in.
Van-type truck	40 in.
Tractor-trailer	48 in.
Double deck	100 in.

Beef cow operations should use dimensions for over 1,200 pounds. Large exotic breeds may require another two inches in chute width—bulls an extra four inches.

The working chute should be a minimum of 20 feet in length to handle four or more animals at once. Proper width is essential. The chute should be narrow enough to prevent animals from turning around. Tapering sides of the chute works best if you are handling various sizes of cattle.

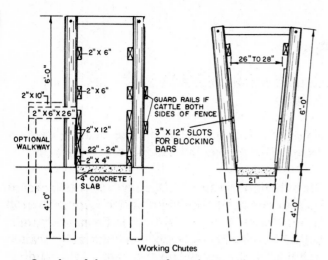

Working Chutes

Overhead bars spaced at intervals across the top of the working chute help keep animals from

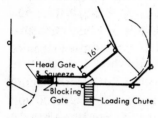

Simplified diagram showing working area and funnel-shaped crowding area. Layout can be expanded to include needed holding pens.

rearing up and prevent the problem of an animal going over on its back in the chute. A blocking gate or blocking bars inserted through the chute can be used to restrain the animal and prevent backing up. A sturdy head gate is required for restraint at the end of the chute. For several types of operations such as branding, a squeeze chute is also needed. One access door the width of the chute will be needed behind the head gate or squeeze to provide access to the rear of the animal. Additional doors may be useful.

Location of the loading chute should allow cattle to be loaded without going through the area of the head catch or squeeze, since animals may associate

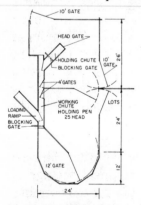

Layout shows main features of a medium-size handling facility. Basic design can be scaled up or down as needed. Plan doesn't lend itself well to expansion as additional pens would not lead to crowding area. However, this could be remedied by providing a cutting alley adjacent to the working area.

this area with discomfort and be inclined to balk. The height of the loading chute generally determines its required length, but it should be no shorter than eight feet. Keep the rise to 3-1/2 inches per foot of length or less. Heights required for loading various trucks are listed in the table.

Provide a stair-stepped floor in the loading chute, or one rough enough for good footing. Constructing the chute so it is adjustable to different heights will make it much more usable.

Construction features in the working facility can make it more functional. Elevated man walkways along both sides of the working and loading chutes are desirable. Paving is needed in key areas. Scored concrete makes a good floor for crowding areas and working chutes and should be sloped for good drainage. A floor and a roof over the working area provide all-weather use.

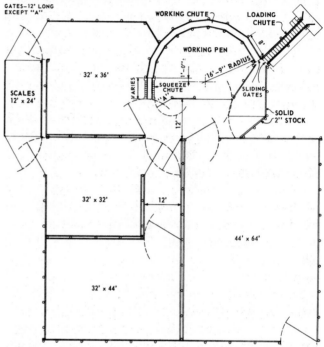

The larger facility shown here makes use of platform scales and features a curved working chute for efficient cattle movement. Location of the loading chute allows cattle to be loaded without going through the working chute. This corral could handle around 400 feeders.

Four-inch top diameter posts should be set on six-foot centers for working fences. Set treated posts three feet in the ground. Set steel posts in concrete. Fencing can be made from a variety of materials; wood poles, pipe, wire cable, sucker rod or two-inch treated planks.

Posts should extend six feet above ground in the working area. Use five six-inch planks, positioning the top of the first plank 16 inches above ground level. Use eight-inch planks in small, crowded areas. Where cattle are on both sides of the fence, use a 40-inch high guard rail. Cable fences for working areas should have seven strands beginning 16 inches above ground.

Study several layouts before selecting a final plan. Sketches shown here demonstrate the key elements and are helpful in analyzing cattle movement through the corral. Other sketches should be available from the Agricultural Engineering Department at your State University.

Efficient Corral Systems

These curved corral systems take advantage of cattle's behavior patterns to make working and sorting easier and more efficient.

A well-designed and built working corral is an important management tool. To make modern identification and breeding systems work you have to be able to sort cattle easily.

The working corrals depicted on the back of this sheet make use of two key aspects in the behavior of cattle. By following a curved path through the corral facilities, cattle are unable to see where they are going until nearly there; thus, they move easier. The curved design also permits easier sorting since animals can move back in the direction they came from–a natural tendency.

The curved construction makes an explanation of these corrals somewhat difficult to follow, but careful study will show how efficient movement of cattle can be achieved. The corral systems in Diagrams 1 and 2 on the back utilize the principle of gathering cows in a large round pen, then working and sorting them in curved alleys and diagonal pens. Groups of cattle from the large gathering pen are brought up into the curved reservoir lane. From this curved lane the animals are sorted back into the diagonal pens (Diagram 1). The animals will move easily into the diagonal pens because they will be going back in the direction from which they came.

The curved sorting reservoir lane can be used for many sorting functions, such as sorting for mass A.I., separating cows from calves, and sorting calves. When the corral system is being used to separate cows and calves, one of the diagonal pens (Diagram 1) is used to allow the cows to pass through into the holding pen. This ensures that there will be enough space for holding the calves in the remaining diagonal pens.

The curved sorting reservoir lane is also used to hold animals that are waiting to go to the squeeze chute, A.I. chute, or loading ramp. The scale is located alongside the curved lane (Diagram 1). Cattle pass from the diagonal pens across the scale and into the curved lane. The curved lane will hold one full diagonal sorting pen of cattle.

The curved reservoir lane terminates in a round crowding pen in Diagram 1 and in a funnel-shaped crowding pen in Diagram 2. The sides of the crowding pen, single file chute, and the loading chute should be completely solid to prevent the cattle from being spooked by outside distractions.

The loading chute in Diagram 1 is positioned so that both rear end loading and side loading tractor trailer trucks can use it. The chute must extend out far enough so that a side loading tractor trailer will not hit the scale. The approach to the loading chute is curved to prevent the cattle from seeing the truck until they are part way up the ramp.

On one side of the loading chute, before the beginning of the ramp, there is a 6-foot gate that can be swung inward for loading low stocktrailers. This is a handy feature.

In both Diagrams 1 and 2, a gate is positioned in front of the squeeze chute to allow you to sort animals as they leave the chute. By flipping a 14-foot gate located in the side of the first diagonal pen, animals leaving the squeeze chute can be sorted a third way, if needed (Diagram 1).

Economical System

There is a difference between the total capacity of all the pens and the practical working and sorting capacity of a corral. Practical capacity is usually one-half or less of total capacity.

To be able to sort cattle you must gather the animals in one pen, then sort them into other pens. The corrals in Diagrams 1 and 2 are designed to be economical to build, and permit a large number of cattle to be handled in a relatively small space. The corral in Diagram 1 can handle 300 pairs or 400 cows in a space measuring 200 by 300 feet. The corral in Diagram 2 has a working and sorting capacity of 100 cows. It occupies a space measuring 120 by 150 feet. Within these dimensions, the animals can be gathered and sorted, and still remain in the systems.

These systems are also designed to use the least number of gates and the least lineal footage of fence and still have the capability for easy sorting. There are fewer gates and less lineal footage of fence in these corrals than in square layouts.

A.I. Chutes

If you plan to use artificial insemination, it is recommended that you use a separate chute for breeding. A cow often associates the squeeze chute with pain, and if the cow becomes agitated during insemination she is less likely to conceive. Many ranchers install a dark-box A.I. chute instead of using a conventional squeeze.

A dark-box is simply a narrow chute with solid sides, front, and top. After the cow enters, a chain is fastened behind her to prevent her from backing out. A burlap cloth is then draped down over her back so that the inside of the chute is completely dark. Even a nervous cow usually will stand still in the dark-box. If you have a problem persuading

your cows to enter the dark-box, cut a 6-inch by 12-inch window in the front gate.

If your cattle are very wild, build an extra long dark-box and put a pacifier cow in front of the cow to be bred. The bred cow is released through a side gate. Use a pacifier cow that isn't in heat.

On operations where synchronized A.I. is used, dark-box chutes can be built in a row on a 60° angle, as shown in Diagram 3. Four cows are turned in at once. The multiple A.I. chute can be used with the corrals in Diagrams 1 or 2 instead of the single animal A.I. chute shown.

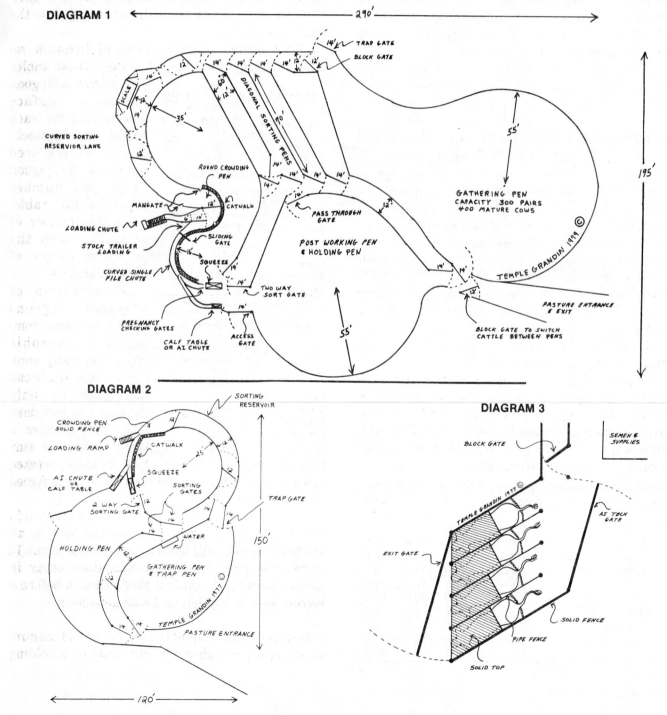

Manure Systems Planning Data

Since waste handling facilities are now an integral part of livestock operations, proper sizing of the system is fundamental to good planning.

The information given is for use in planning manure disposal facilities. The estimates of manure production, storage requirements, and other helpful tables are based on research conducted at universities in several states.

Manure quantity. Guidelines for estimates of the amount of manure that will be produced by different animals are listed in the table on the back. Figures are approximations.

In figuring waste volume, use 7.5 gallons for each cubic foot of manure. There are about 34 cubic feet to a ton of manure.

Manure storage requirements can be determined by multiplying the manure produced per day by the number of days in the required storage period. This figure is multiplied by the number of animals, to arrive at the total amount of manure that will be present at the end of the holding period.

To handle manure in liquid storage pits or tanks, extra space is required since water must be added to further dilute the manure for proper storage and handling. The table on the next page gives the amount of storage capacity needed per animal for various retention periods. Estimates are 1-1/2 times the volume of manure to provide for extra liquids and unusable space.

In planning, figure that moisture content for efficient pumping of liquid manure should be around 90%. To irrigate with liquid wastes, moisture content should be about 95%. The table below shows amounts of additional water needed to raise moisture to various levels.

INCREASING MANURE MOISTURE CONTENT WITH WATER

1 cu. ft. (7.5 gal.) Moisture	Changed to Moisture	Cu. Ft.	Gal.	Gallons Added
84%	87%	1.23	9.2	1.7
	90	1.60	12.0	4.5
	95	3.10	23.3	15.8
80%	85%	1.33	10.0	2.5
	90	2.00	15.0	7.5
	95	4.00	30.0	22.5
75%	80%	1.25	9.3	1.8
	85	1.66	12.4	4.9
	90	2.50	18.7	11.2
	95	5.00	37.5	30.0

Sizing pits and tanks. To calculate the capacities of manure holding structures, use the formulas and tables on the next page.

Sizing waste lagoons. Whether a manure lagoon is aerobic (using oxygen) or anaerobic (without oxygen), it should be large enough to provide sufficient water in which bacteria can decompose the waste material.

Wastes from different kinds of livestock require varying quantities of water. These tables give minimum lagoon volume or surface area needed for each pound of livestock. The total required volume of the lagoon equals the number given in the table, times the number of animals, times the maximum weight of each animal.

Water volume for anaerobic lagoons

	Volume per pound of animal
	cu.ft.
Poultry	3
Swine	2
Cattle	1

Surface area for naturally aerobic lagoons*

	Surface area per pound of animal
	sq. ft.
Poultry	4.5
Swine	2.5
Dairy cattle	1.5
Beef cattle	1.5

*Max. depth 6 ft., 3 to 4 ft. preferred.

Water volume for mechanically aerated lagoons (Long-term detention)

	Volume per pound of animal
	cu. ft.
Poultry	0.75
Swine	1.00
Dairy cattle	1.25
Beef cattle	0.75

Construction of anaerobic lagoons should be deep compared to aerobic types. Naturally aerobic lagoons are broad and generally only three to five feet deep since they require a large amount of surface exposed to the air. Mechanically aerated lagoons require less surface area since air is forced into the liquid.

Over a period of time sludge will accumulate in the bottom of a lagoon. Hog wastes held in an anaerobic lagoon will build up at a rate of about 12 inches per year. Lesser accumulations occur in aerobic lagoons. A settling pond or basin before a lagoon reduces loading and sludge buildup.

Sizing of ponds. Liquid runoff from solid manure handling systems should be diverted into a holding pond, or a combination of a settling basin and a holding pond. To size a pond to the expected amount of runoff, figure that one acre of drainage will produce 3,600 cubic feet (27,000 gallons) from each one inch of rain. The first pond or settling basin should have the capacity for one inch of runoff. The detention or holding pond should be sized to meet your state's anti-pollution requirements, or be built large enough to hold all runoff until it can be conveniently emptied.

Nutrients in manure. The last table shows the average amounts of N, P and K contained in fresh animal manure. Dilution with water will reduce this nutrient content.

Not all nutrients in manure can be returned to the plants. Estimates of nitrogen losses in liquid manure are as high as 50%. Amount of nutrients retained depends on how the manure is handled. Liquid manure systems retain more nutrients. Heavy losses can occur from solid waste systems through leaching and runoff of the liquid.

The land area necessary for final spreading or dispersion of manure will vary. Maximum rates are being studied and differ due to factors such as soil type and climate. Current Illinois recommendations for maximum annual application rates from liquid manure holding pits are:

Cattle............ 20-30 tons/acre

Hogs............. 10-15 tons/acre

Poultry .... 4- 8 tons/acre

CAPACITIES OF RECTANGULAR LIQUID MANURE TANKS

Wide x long x deep in feet	Total Capacity	
	Cu. ft.	Gallons
10 x 30 x 10	3,000	22,500
12 x 30 x 10	3,600	27,000
14 x 30 x 10	4,200	31,500
16 x 30 x 10	4,800	36,000
18 x 30 x 10	5,400	40,500
20 x 30 x 10	6,000	45,000
25 x 30 x 10	7,500	56,250
30 x 30 x 10	9,000	67,500

CAPACITIES OF EARTHEN STORAGE PITS WITH 1:2.5 SLOPING SIDES*

Wide x long x deep (feet)	= Capacity (cu. ft.)	Wide x long x deep (feet)	= Capacity (cu. ft.)
50 x 50 x 10	8,300	100 x 125 x 10	77,000
50 x 75 x 10	14,500	100 x 150 x 10	96,000
50 x 100 x 10	20,800	125 x 125 x 10	102,000
50 x 125 x 10	27,000	125 x 150 x 10	127,000
50 x 150 x 10	33,000	150 x 150 x 10	158,000
75 x 75 x 10	27,000	100 x 100 x 20	66,000
75 x 100 x 10	39,600	100 x 125 x 20	91,000
75 x 125 x 10	52,000	100 x 150 x 20	116,000
75 x 150 x 10	64,000	125 x 125 x 20	129,000
100 x 100 x 10	58,000	125 x 150 x 20	166,000

*Slope of sides will depend on soil conditions.

Rectangular Storage
Width x Depth x Length x 7.5 = gals. capacity

Circular Tanks
Diameter x Diameter x Depth x 5.86 = gals. capacity

CAPACITIES OF ROUND LIQUID MANURE TANKS

Diameter x depth in feet	Total Capacity	
	Cu. ft.	Gallons
20 x 10	3,140	23,550
24 x 10	4,520	33,900
27 x 10	5,660	42,450
30 x 10	7,065	52,980
20 x 12	3,770	28,275
24 x 12	5,429	40,717
27 x 12	6,871	51,532
30 x 12	8,483	63,622

APPROXIMATE DAILY MANURE PRODUCTION

Animal	Cu. Ft./Day Solids & Liq.	Percent Water	Gallons/ Day
(10) head of hogs			
50 lbs.	2/3	75	5
100 lbs.	1-1/3	75	10
150 lbs.	2-1/4	75	17
200 lbs.	2-3/4	75	20-1/2
250 lbs.	3-1/2	75	26
1,000 lb. cow	1-1/2	80-90	11
1,000 lb. steer	1	80-90	7-1/2
1,000 lb. horse	3/4	65	5-1/2
(10) head of sheep	1/2	70	4
(1,000) 5 lb. layers	3	55-75	22-1/2

LIQUID MANURE STORAGE*

Animal & Weight	Per animal storage capacity needed for					
	90-days		120-days		180-days	
	cu. ft.	gals.	cu. ft.	gals.	cu.ft.	gals.
Beef Cattle						
500 lbs.	101	759	135	1,013	203	1,519
750-1,000 lbs.	135	1,013	180	1,350	270	2,025
Dairy Cattle						
500 lbs.	85	640	115	850	170	1,280
750 lbs.	125	950	170	1,265	250	1,900
1,000 lbs.	170	1,275	225	1,700	340	2,550
1,200 lbs.	180	1,375	245	1,825	360	2,750
1,400 lbs.	215	1,625	290	2,160	430	3,250
Hogs						
Weaning-60 lbs.	8.1	60.8	10.8	81.0	16.2	121.5
Weaning-100 lbs.	17.6	131.8	23.4	175.5	35.1	262.9
100-200 lbs.	36.5	273.8	48.6	364.5	72.9	546.7
Sow	72.9	546.8	97.2	729.0	145.8	1,093.5

*Based on 1-1/2 times the total excrement to allow for nonusable space and addition of liquid.

FERTILIZER VALUE OF LIQUID MANURE

Animal	Lbs. of Nutrients Per Ton of Manure		
	Nitrogen	Phosphorus	Potassium
Dairy cattle.........	11	2	10
Cattle	14	4	9
Swine............	10	3	8
Horses	14	2	12
Sheep............	28	4	20
Poultry	31	8	7

Gutter Flushing for Swine Buildings

Gutter flushing is a relatively recent innovation in swine waste handling. This discussion will help you to determine if such a system will fit into your building plans.

If you are planning a new swine building or remodeling or renovating an old building, you should consider a gutter flushing system. Here's an outline of what is involved and what you can expect from a flush system. For actual design specifications, consult a farm building engineer or contractor. Also, you may wish to discuss gutter flushing with operators already using the system.

Frequent removal of wastes by automatic flushing is the principle behind the system's growing popularity. A small-capacity pump brings water continuously from a lagoon to a tank located at the high end of a sloped, shallow gutter. Periodically, the tank discharges enough water to scour and float waste material out of the building.

Two types of gutters are used: Open-gutter flushing has been used successfully in finishing buildings and on open, paved lots. Under-slat flushing is best used in farrowing, nursery and confined gestation buildings.

In open-gutter systems, flushing does more than wash away wastes. The flushing action actually trains hogs to dung in the gutter. When properly working, the system reduces odors and keeps houses quite clean, though the pen design and frequency of flushing will affect cleanliness.

Pigs will dung in damp, drafty areas and sleep where it is dry. To keep them dunging in the gutter, it should be flushed a minimum of every 2 hours. Length of pens should be less than three times their width in flush buildings. Floors should slope five-eighths inch per foot toward the gutter. Solid pen dividers are used except across the gutter where wire panels are used.

Gutter flushing fits best in farrow through finish operations where all manure is handled as a liquid, since there is little possibility of disease transmission by pigs brought in from an outside source. A feeder pig producer may find gutter flushing less advantageous because of the lower volume of wastes handled. Open-gutter flushing may not be suitable for finishing purchased feeder pigs because of the possibility of disease transmission.

A flushing system increases the volume of material by 10 to 100 times, so water and storage needs will increase greatly unless flush water is recycled. Normally water from the second stage of a two-stage lagoon is recycled through the gutter.

Advantages of gutter flushing. Construction costs for an open-gutter flush building are as much as 30% lower than for a comparable building with a deep pit. However, this advantage is reduced by the lagoon requirement. The average two-stage lagoon (based on 450 cubic feet per finishing hog) will reduce the savings to about 10% to 15%. A building with under-slat flushing costs about the same as a deep pit building.

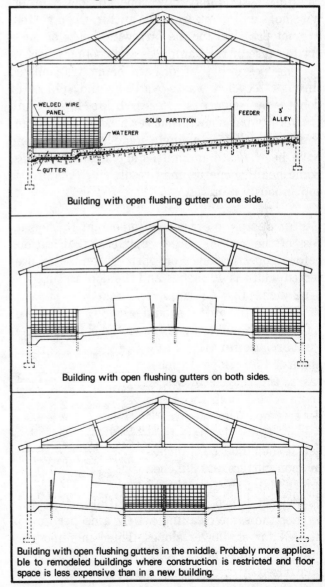

Building with open flushing gutter on one side.

Building with open flushing gutters on both sides.

Building with open flushing gutters in the middle. Probably more applicable to remodeled buildings where construction is restricted and floor space is less expensive than in a new building.

Properly managed, a gutter flushing system reduces odors and gases in the building. Less frequent waste disposal is needed. Spreading from the lagoon can be reduced to once or twice a year and can be applied through irrigation equipment.

Construction flexibility is another advantage. An older building such as a poultry house with a dirt floor may be converted more easily to a flush system than to a deep pit system. For new construction, the roof can be erected first.

Disadvantages. Wastes treated in a lagoon lose more nutrient value than those in a deep pit. The lagoon may require four to six times more area than the building. While only two mechanical components are needed (pump and flush tank), they are subject to breakdowns.

If medicated drinking water is being provided, the flush system may have to be shut down, otherwise hogs will drink from the gutter. Open gutters are not practical for the farrowing house or nursery because of the dampness and cooling effect.

The possibility of disease being transmitted through recycled waste water is the subject of debate by scientists. Research at Iowa State University has shown that certain types of organisms can survive in a single-stage lagoon, but none have been found in multi-stage lagoon systems. Some health benefits may result since manure is continuously removed.

Gutter design is extremely important to the success of the system, so get complete specifications before construction. For open gutters, the preferred width is 40 inches and the depth usually is 3-1/2 inches (2 x 4 form).

Slope of the gutter should provide a flow rate of 2 feet per second or faster down the channel. Open gutters generally have about a 1.5% slope. In most cases, the release of water from the flushing tank determines the depth of water flow. Initial flow depth should be 1-1/2 inches in open gutters and 3 inches under slats. Gutters should be at least 1 inch deeper than initial flow depth.

Minimum Flushings Per Day*		
Building	Under slats	Open gutter
Farrowing	2	—
Nursery	4	—
Finishing	6	12
Gestation	4	6

*More flushes per day will reduce odors.

For the same cleaning action, a deeper flow is needed for shallower slopes. Thus, in remodeled buildings, construction and grading problems are minimized by constructing a deeper channel (2 x 6 forms) and creating a flow depth of 3 to 4 inches.

A sump pit is located at the lower end of the gutter to allow flush water to pass through the gutter without backing up.

Flushing tanks are of three basic types. All dump automatically, with the frequency depending on how rapidly they are filled. The siphon tank is filled gradually until the siphon is activated, releasing the contents suddenly. Siphon tanks are available commercially and have the advantage of no moving parts. Tipping bucket and trap door tanks are activated by the weight or volume of water. Both provide rapid dumping, but their moving parts mean mechanical problems are possible.

Design of lagoons is the same for a flush building as for conventional swine buildings. The table shows volume requirements.

Lagoon Volumes Required Per Pound of Live Animal

Type of lagoon	Once-a-year dewatering	Twice-a-year dewatering
	cu. ft./lb. liveweight	
Two-stage lagoon		
First stage	1.25	1.25
Second stage	1.15	0.75
One-stage lagoon	2.15	1.75

A two-stage lagoon is recommended since recycled water has undergone more treatment. Less salts are present in this water to clog pumps and piping, plus the potential for disease organisms is reduced. Single-stage lagoons can be improved by adding a settling tank to receive wastes from the flushing gutters. Install inlet pipes below the surface to prevent freezing.

Pumps and pipes. The pump used to fill the flush tanks can be quite small. For example, a 10 gallon per minute pump will fill two 300 gallon tanks and dump them hourly. Electrical usage by such a small pump will be fairly low.

A self-priming, centrifugal pump with semi-enclosed impellers is preferred, since it is least likely to clog. The motor should be rated for continuous use and large enough to drive the pump at its recommended speed. Slower pumps cost more initially but last longer.

Replacement seals and impellers should be kept on hand, along with a spare motor. Often a separate pump is installed on a bypass in case the first pump fails. Pumps with metal impellers or metal parts in contact with the waste water should not be used because salts form deposits on metal and eventually plug the pump. PCV pipelines should be used for the same reason.

Grain-Drying Energy Management

Here are several ways you can modify your grain-drying system and/or manage your drying operation to conserve fuel and electricity.

Major objective with any drying system should be to dry grain only enough to safely maintain its condition and quality under your particular climatic conditions until it is marketed or fed. Overdrying is costly and wastes energy.

Given below are moisture contents at which grain can be safely stored in aerated, well-managed storage, though this will vary somewhat by area.

SAFE STORAGE MOISTURE FOR AERATED GOOD QUALITY GRAIN

Shelled corn and sorghum	
Fed during winter	18%
Dried for safe holding into early spring	16-17%
Sold as no. 2 grain by spring	15½%
Stored up to 1 year	14%
Stored more than 1 year	13%
Soybeans	
Sold by spring	14%
Stored up to 1 year	12%
Wheat	13%
Small grain	13%
Sunflowers	9%

Drying grain below the levels suggested increases drying costs, and the additional shrinkage discounts the price you receive for the grain, as shown for corn.

COSTS OF DRYING CORN BELOW 15.5%

Moisture content	Extra drying costs	Extra shrinkage costs	Total overdrying costs
	cents/bu		
14%	2.6	4.4	7.0
13%	4.3	7.2	11.5
12%	6.2	9.9	16.1
11%	8.2	12.6	20.8

Based on shelled corn at $2.50/bu, propane at 70 cents/gal, and electricity at 5 cents/kWh.

Energy requirements for drying grain to safe storage levels vary widely among drying systems. Comparisons of energy requirements and costs for various methods are shown in the table below. At the assumed costs of propane and electricity, the cost of drying corn from 25.5% to 15.5% is only about half as much for natural air drying as for a high-speed dryer with in-dryer cooling. Though fast drying methods greatly speed up drying, they use more energy. On the average, high-speed batch or continuous flow drying systems require 2,000 to 3,000 BTUs per pound of water removed; batch drying in a bin, 1,500 to 2,000 BTUs; and in-bin drying, 1,000 to 1,500 BTUs per pound of water.

Modification of drying systems, or the planning of new drying facilities should involve consideration of partially drying grain with a high-temperature dryer (where used), then drying the rest of the way with a low-temperature drying system. A complete shift to low-temperature drying may be another alternative. Shifting a greater share of the drying load to low-temperature drying methods can usually save substantial energy. However, savings should justify the cost of modifications.

Efficiency of continuous flow and batch dryers can be increased somewhat by adjusting drying temperature. Increasing drying temperature within limits required to maintain grain quality will improve drying efficiency, as illustrated in the table. Decreasing airflow will do likewise, but it is difficult to do and grain may not be uniformly dried. Several continuous flow dryers are now designed to recirculate cooling air and a portion of the drying air, thus recovering and recycling valuable exhaust heat. Energy savings usually amount to 15% to 20%.

HEAT ENERGY REQUIREMENTS FOR BATCH OR CONTINUOUS FLOW DRYERS

Drying temperature °F	Airflow (cfm/bu)				
	40	50	60	70	80
	Heat energy required (1,000 BTU/bu)				
130	18.8	21.0	23.0	25.5	27.8
165	17.2	19.1	21.0	23.0	25.2
200	15.3	16.9	18.5	19.8	21.1
235	14.0	15.3	16.3	17.2	18.2

Heat energy to dry corn from 25% to 15% moisture. Assumes air temperature of 50°F and 75% relative humidity.

Dryeration can save about 25% of the energy required for complete drying with a high-temperature dryer. Corn is dried within 2 percentage points of desired final moisture, transferred without cooling to a special dryeration bin to temper, then cooled. Since the process removes about 2 percentage points of moisture, grain can be moved to final storage without further drying. It's in the final drying stages where kernel stress occurs. Dryeration eliminates drying during this stage, so higher temperatures can be used.

Grain is allowed to temper in the bin for about 8 to 10 hours. Then a fan delivering one-half to 1 cfm per bushel of airflow is started to cool grain over an 8 to 12-hour period.

In-storage cooling can be used in place of cooling grain in a high-temperature dryer. The cooling reduces moisture by about a percentage point. Probably the biggest advantage of in-storage cooling is increased drying capacity. The cooling cycle of a batch dryer can be eliminated, or the cooling section of a continuous flow dryer

COMPARATIVE ESTIMATES OF ENERGY REQUIREMENTS AND DRYING CAPACITIES WHEN DRYING CORN FROM 25.5% TO 15.5%*

Drying method	Propane/100 bu		Electrical energy/100 bu		Total energy cost/100 bu	Increased high-speed dryer capacity
	Gallons	Cost**	kWh	Cost**		
High-speed drying with in-dryer cooling	20	$14.00	10	$0.50	$14.50	—
Dryeration	14.5	10.15	7	.35	10.50	60%
In-storage cooling	17.5	12.25	8	.40	12.65	35%
Combination drying	8	5.60	70	3.50	9.10	300%
Natural air drying	—	—	140	7.00	7.00	—

*Comparisons are made on the basis of 100 bu of corn at 15.5 percent moisture content. If comparisons are made on actual 56 lb. bushels at the reduced moisture contents, the fuel and electrical requirements would be higher.

**Energy costs assumed were 70¢/gal propane and 5¢/kWh of electricity.

can be converted to full heat. A tempering period is not recommended, as condensation occurs.

Combination drying involves the use of a high-temperature dryer to reduce grain moisture to around 20% to 22%, followed by in-storage cooling and low temperature. Fuel savings of 50% or more are possible when corn is dried from around 26% to 21% in a high-temperature dryer, then finished with low temperature. Though electrical requirements are increased, this method generally uses less than 1 kWh per bushel. Total net energy requirement can be substantially reduced. Combination drying also allows you to double or triple your high-speed dryer capacity. It eliminates stress cracks in grain and allows safe handling of wetter grains. A perforated floor and drying fans must be installed in all storage bins.

Low-temperature drying is a process that slowly dries grain with natural air, or air is heated only a few degrees in the bin in which it is stored. Usually from 2 to 7 degrees of supplemental heat are added, with about 2 degrees provided by the fan motor. Success depends on adequate airflow and perhaps supplemental heat. Grain must be sufficiently dried within an allowable period of time to prevent spoilage. Where bins are filled rapidly it is difficult to deliver enough air to satisfactorily dry corn containing more than 22% to 23% moisture using natural air.

MAXIMUM INITIAL MOISTURE CONTENTS FOR A FAST-FILL PROCEDURE

Airflow rate (cfm/bu)	Harvest date		
	Early	Mid-season	Late
0.75	20.0%	20.0%	20.0%
1.0	21.0	21.5	21.5
1.25	21.5	22.0	22.0
1.5	22.0	22.5	22.5
2.0	23.0	23.5	24.0
3.0	24.0	25.0	26.0

Bin filled within a period of a few days.

Combination drying is more feasible for corn containing more than 21% to 22% moisture. Since allowable drying time decreases and the amount of water to be removed increases with moisture content of the grain, the required

airflow rises rapidly with moisture content, particularly with a fast fill rate. Much the same is true for unseasonably warm falls.

Be careful not to pile corn deeper than the airflow will handle for a given depth and moisture. Also, avoid filling too fast in unseasonably warm weather. Much higher airflow rates are required under these conditions. A 10-degree higher than normal temperature will cut allowable drying time in half. For this reason it is desirable to design a low-temperature system for sufficient airflow and heater size to provide backup drying capacity when needed. Where combination drying is used, grain can be dried to safer levels with the higher temperature dryer.

Fan horsepower requirements can be minimized by limiting grain depth. However, a higher investment in bins may result. About twice as much fan horsepower is required to deliver the necessary airflow with corn piled 22 feet, compared with 16 feet.

FAN HORSEPOWER PER 10,000 BU CORN

Airflow rate (cfm/bu)	Depth of corn				
	8 ft	12 ft	16 ft	20 ft	24 ft
0.75	0.8	1.9	3.7	6.3	9.5
1.0	1.5	3.8	7.4	12.6	19.3
1.25	2.4	6.3	12.6	21.7	33.1
1.5	3.7	9.5	18.9	33.1	—
2.0	7.5	19.8	39.7	—	—
3.0	19.8	52.0	—	—	—

Calculated horsepower per 10,000 bu of corn based on a fan efficiency of 50%.

Whether or not you add supplemental heat partially depends on how you plan to use the corn and/or how long you will keep it in storage. Fall weather in the Midwest is usually favorable enough to dry corn to 15.5%.

If grain is to be fed throughout the winter, there is no need to dry it below 18% in the fall. For longer storage, a natural air system can be designed to finish drying to a lower moisture level the following spring. However, if you want to add insurance and finish drying in the fall, you may want to add some 3 degrees or so to supplemental heat. To maximize energy use, use heat only during inclement weather.

Effects of auxiliary heat on energy use and comparative drying

time are illustrated in the table. The example is for 24% moisture corn piled to a depth of 16 feet in a bin having an airflow of 2 cfm.

EFFECTS OF AUXILIARY HEAT ON LOW-TEMPERATURE DRYING

Electric heat added (°F)	Final moisture (percent)	Drying time (days)	Energy use (kWh/bu)
0	15.2	37	2.0
1	14.7	34	2.4
3	13.7	29	3.0
5	12.9	26	3.4
7	12.2	22	3.7

Solar drying, though new, is expected to increase rapidly. Farmers are incorporating collectors into the walls and roofs of new or existing structures. Though solar drying appears best adapted to low-temperature drying systems that take advantage of the relatively slow rate at which solar energy can be collected, some installations with large surface collection areas are capable of producing temperature rises of 30 to 40 degrees at midday.

The costs shown in the table provide an idea of the drying cost that might be associated with a solar collector. Costs include initial investment in a collector, plus 10% interest. They are based on a capacity of 6,000 bushels of corn and a collector size that equates to about 1 square foot per 4 bushels of corn. This will provide a couple of degrees temperature rise under central Iowa conditions. Assumed airflow is 1.3 cfm per bushel.

COLLECTOR COST PER BUSHEL OF CORN

Initial Cost ($ per sq ft)	Useful life (years)					
	2	3	5	10	15	20
	(Cents)					
.50	5.1	3.6	2.4	1.5	1.2	1.0
.75	7.7	5.4	3.6	2.2	1.7	1.5
1.00	10.2	7.2	4.8	2.9	2.3	2.0
1.50	15.4	10.8	7.1	4.4	3.5	3.0
2.00	20.5	14.4	9.5	5.8	4.6	4.0
3.00	30.7	21.6	14.3	8.8	6.9	6.0
4.00	40.9	28.8	19.0	11.7	9.3	8.0

Ammonia treatment of corn permits you to extend drying time, and may make it possible to take advantage of warmer temperatures that prevail during early harvest. You may get by with somewhat less airflow and/or supplemental heat. EPA has approved treatment for corn to be fed on the farm.

Year-Round Management of Stored Grain

Storing grain for extended periods makes it even more important that you understand what is needed to keep the grain in proper condition.

Grain that is *dry, cool,* and *clean* will store successfully over an extended period. Management steps needed to assure success center around these key aspects: Making sure that grain goes into storage at a safe moisture level and is relatively clean; using aeration properly to cool grain and equalize temperature differentials; and preventing damage caused by insect infestations.

Moisture content of grain as it goes into storage generally sets a limit on how long it can be stored safely. Under most conditions, you should assume that grain in bins equipped for low rates of aeration will not undergo further drying. Thus, grain must be at the desired moisture level before it enters long term storage.

Grain must be drier to be stored through the warm summer months than if it is to be removed in the spring or early summer. And, if it contains a lot of broken kernels, chaff, and other material, it would need to be even lower in moisture to resist mold growth and insect infestation. Normally, corn can be stored at 15% to 16% moisture if removed in the spring. It will store for 1 year at 14% moisture under good conditions.

To provide for less than ideal conditions and allow a margin of safety, you should assume that for year-round storage corn, wheat, and grain sorghum should be dried to 13% moisture and soybeans to 12% moisture.

Get grain in the bin and conditioned for storage as soon as possible after harvest. Grain has a limited storage life, as shown in the table below.

If a large portion of the grain's storage life is used up during fall and winter, it may not keep through summer. That percentage of its life can't be recovered, even though it is further dried and cooled later. The number of days grain is held at a given moisture and temperature, divided by its allowable storage period, gives the percentage of life used up. The same grain at new moisture and temperature levels will have used up the same percentage of its new storage life.

Maximum Allowable Storage Time*

Grain Temp. (Degrees F.)	Grain Moisture (%)					
	16	18	20	22	24	26
	Days Storage					
35	670	265	112	74	49	37
40	500	200	85	56	38	28
45	385	150	64	42	28	21
50	290	115	48	32	21	16
55	215	86	36	24	16	12
60	165	65	28	18	12	9
65	125	49	21	14	9	7
70	93	37	16	10	7	5
75	70	28	12	8	5	4

*Data were developed for shelled corn. They can be applied to all grains.

Before filling a bin, thoroughly clean it and treat with an approved residual insecticide. These steps are especially important for long storage periods since opportunities for insect development are greatly increased.

Don't cone the grain up under the bin roof unless you plan to remove this excess at the earliest possible time. Peaking the grain tends to increase moisture migration problems and makes it impossible to get into the bin to properly inspect the grain during storage.

Aeration

Aeration is used almost exclusively to maintain grain temperatures at desired levels. Problems develop in the bin when unequal temperatures in the grain mass cause slow circulation of air from warm grain to cold. As they pass through the warm center of the grain, these small convection currents pick up moisture and deposit it in the cold layer at the top. The result is an area of spoiled, crusted grain on the surface at the top center of the bin, which is often mistaken for a roof leakage problem.

The aeration system must be properly designed. Bins should be provided with a minimum of 1/10 cfm of air movement for each bushel of storage capacity. Thus, a 10,000 bushel bin requires a minimum of 1,000 cfm of aeration capacity.

Faults in the design of the system will reduce the efficiency of air movement. Common design errors are: a connecting duct from the fan too small to handle the airflow; too small a perforated area where air enters grain; and ducts not arranged properly. Here are guidelines from Purdue University engineers that will allow you to check the adequacy of a planned or existing system.

Connecting ducts should be large enough so the velocity of airflow does not exceed 1,500 feet per minute (fpm). For example, a bin designed for 1,000 cfm of aeration capacity will need a minimum of 0.66 square feet of duct entrance area. (1,000 cfm ÷ 1,500 fpm = 0.66 square feet.)

Provide enough perforated surface area so air will enter the grain no faster than 30 fpm. Unless you are using a full perforated floor, you may need to check this by totaling the square feet of the perforated area. (Use only 80% of the area of full round perforated ducts lying directly on the floor.) Divide the aeration capacity of the bin by 30 to find the area required. Example: 1,000 cfm ÷ 30 = 33 square feet of perforated area needed.

In flat storage buildings or large diameter bins, perforated ducts should be arranged so that the distance between ducts is not greater than the depth of the grain. Distance from the nearest duct to the wall should not exceed one-half the depth of the grain.

Horsepower required to operate the aeration fan can be determined from the next table if you know the grain depth and surface area of the bin floor. For example, assuming a bin is designed for 1/10 cfm per

Fan Horsepower Requirements for Aerating Shelled Corn

Corn Depth	Aeration Air Flow Rate (cfm/bu)				
	1/10	1/4	1/2	3/4	1
	Horsepower per 100 sq ft*				
10	.015	.04	.01	.02	.03
15	.025	.06	.24	.54	1.0
20	.034	.10	.48	1.2	2.3
25	.05	.21	1.0	2.3	4.3
30	.07	.36	1.7	4.3	
40	.14	.83	4.3		
50	.26	1.6	8.8		

*Fan horsepower per 100 square feet of bin floor or cross-sectional area.

bushel and grain depth is 20 feet, the table shows that .034 hp is needed per 100 square feet of floor area. If the bin diameter is 30 feet, it contains 706 square feet of floor area. Thus, .034 times 7.06 equals .24 or one-fourth hp.

Floor Areas of Common Round Bins

Bin Diameter (ft)	Floor Area (sq ft)
18	250
21	346
24	452
27	572
30	706
33	855
36	1,017
40	1,256
42	1,385
48	1,808

Operating the fan. The important point to remember is that it takes several days to cool (or warm) grain using airflow rates typical for aeration. Grain cools in a moving zone, not uniformly throughout the bin. Thus, if the fan is operated for a few hours only, there will be a layer of cool grain near the ducts. Temperature difference between the cool layer and the rest of the grain will be greater than if the fan had not been run at all.

Once the fan is turned on, it should be operated long enough to cool all the grain in the bin to a uniform temperature. For bins equipped for 1/10 cfm, about 160 hours (nearly a week) is required to accomplish this. At higher airflow rates, the time required is proportionately shorter.

After filling a bin, turn on the fan and cool the grain to below 60°F. This is especially important if the grain was binned during hot

weather or has been artificially dried and its temperature is above the average outdoor day-night temperature. Grain put in the bin on a sunny fall day is usually much too warm for storage.

Operate the fan again during late fall or early winter to reduce grain temperature to between 30° and 40°F.–close to average winter temperature. Do not freeze the grain, however, since you may have problems in the spring when aeration is used again to warm the grain.

Don't become overly concerned about undoing what you have already accomplished when operating the fan during relatively short periods of unfavorable weather. Small amounts of moisture are added to the grain on damp days, but this usually will be removed before the cooling process is completed. It is more important to keep the cooling front moving through the grain unless a warm rainy spell lasts for a week or longer. Once the grain has cooled, don't operate the fan until spring unless problems develop.

Warming of grain in the spring is a controversial practice, but its value is questionable only if the grain will be removed before the warm summer months. Grain in long term storage that will stay in the bin over summer should be aerated to warm it. Otherwise, the cool grain and warm outside temperatures are likely to cause reverse moisture migration that can result in a layer of wet, moldy grain 2 to 3 feet below the surface.

Continuous fan operation is particularly important during the warming process, since the warm moist conditions that develop in the grain, if the warming front is stopped are ideal for spoilage. The goal is to uniformly warm the grain to about 50°F. In the Corn Belt, this is usually done in March or April.

Summer aeration is not recommended unless hot spots or other problems develop in the grain. During the summer, the fan can be operated for periods of less than an hour to check the condition of the grain. Odor of exhaust air gives an early clue to spoilage.

If an infestation of insects develops in the bin before late summer, it will be necessary to fumigate. If possible, hire a professional for this job because the chemicals used can be quite hazardous.

Light insect infestations that show up later may be controlled by cooling the grain again with aeration. Insect development is very slow below 60°F. and insects go dormant or die during extended periods of 35° F. or below. However, if not killed by fumigation, insects may be only dormant. They will be present in a marketing sample and will become active as soon as the grain warms.

Inspect grain regularly. Grain conditioning specialists recommend that you check grain in the bin at least every other week, and more often if there are indications that a problem is developing. Get into the bin. Probe, feel, smell, and look at the grain. Remember, you are trying to spot problems before they become serious, so watch carefully for any changes that take place. Hot spots, insect infestations, and other problems start in the grain mass and soon migrate to the surface. Probe the grain for crusting under the surface. Check the surface for damp, warm, and musty spots. Inspect for insects and mold in areas where fines and broken kernels have accumulated.

Long Term Storage Management

FALL ● Clean and treat bin. ● Dry grain to proper moisture for long term storage. ● Bin and cool grain as soon as possible. ● Aerate continuously for 1 week (1/10 cfm). ● Check grain routinely.

WINTER ● Aerate grain in late fall—early winter to bring grain temperature near the winter norm. ● Do not freeze grain. ● Keep check on grain condition.

SPRING ● Warm grain by continuous aeration to about 50°F. if grain will be held over summer. ● Inspect grain regularly.

SUMMER ● Do not aerate unless problems develop. ● Fumigate the bin if insect infestation develops. ● Check regularly for insects and mold.

Harvest Losses in Corn and Soybeans

Harvest losses are a direct profit loss to a farming operation. By following a systematic procedure you'll spend no more than ten minutes estimating these losses.

Conditions occur when harvesting losses are unavoidably high. But even then, you can be certain you're doing the best job under the prevailing conditions. For top harvest efficiency you must know three things: (1) what overall losses are, (2) where they are occurring and, (3) what to do machine-wise to avoid them. This page will discuss the first two factors in detail. Some suggestions will be made on machine adjustments, but consult your operator's manual for further details.

Soybean combine loss analysis. Ohio agricultural engineer D.M. Byg recommends the following technique for checking losses. Make a rectangular frame that encloses 10 square feet and be sure it's equal in width to the header of your combine. The table shows the frame length for various header widths to make up the necessary 10 square feet. Byg suggests a length of plastic clothesline with wire pins taped to the corners for a portable frame. For larger width combines you may want to double the frame length shown. This will give you a 20 square foot frame.

Header Width (feet)	Frame Length (inches)
10	12
12	10
13	9-1/4
14	8-1/2
15	8
16	7-1/2
17	7
18	6-11/16
19	6-5/16
20	6
22	5-7/16
24	5

To make a loss check after preliminary adjustment, pick a spot in the field that is generally representative of the field. Then stop, and as quickly as possible shut off the machine and back up one combine length.

First place the frame across the swath harvested at the rear of the combine. Count all beans in the frame and divide this number by 40 for the total bushel per acre loss. If you use a 20 square foot frame to determine loss per acre, divide number of beans found in the frame by 80.

Next, to pinpoint where these losses are occurring, check the uncut beans in front of the header to see what the preharvest loss is. Be sure to count both loose beans on the ground and beans in pods lying loose on the ground. Early in the season, it may be zero. Later on after wetting and drying it can be substantial. Divide this by 40 for bushels per acre. Subtracting this preharvest loss from the total loss tells how much of the loss is machine loss.

Determine gathering unit losses by laying the frame down in front of the cutter bar where you've just cut. Then go through and pick out free beans—count two splits as one bean and determine the bushel per acre loss. (Be sure to subtract the preharvest loss so you don't double-count this.) Then count beans on cut-off stems and do the same. Follow this by counting beans on uncut stalks, and finally count beans in pods remaining on uncut portions of stems. Add all these gathering unit losses together, subtract from the machine loss and you have cylinder and separation loss.

You now have pinpointed losses in this order—preharvest, shatter, loose stalk loss, lodged stalk loss, stubble loss and cylinder and separation loss. If these total 2 to 2.5 bushels in dry beans, with a moisture content of 12% to 14%, you're in good shape. If they are above this, and preharvest shatter can't be blamed, then you should be able to lower losses by proper adjustment.

Pinpointing adjustments. Knowing the kind of loss problem you have, you can make adjustments specifically geared to the loss. If there are too many free beans ahead of the combine, then it is probably reel adjustment that's at fault. Speed should be about 34 rpm if travel speed is close to 3 mph. Ohio suggests a reel speed of 1.25 times ground speed. If you have equipped your combine with a floating or flexible cutter bar, the reel axle should be set about eight inches ahead of the cutter bar.

If the main gathering loss is uncut lodged stalks, you may have to compromise. By setting the reel lower and farther forward, you may bring these stalks in, but at the same time this could increase the number of cut stalks thrown on the ground by reel carryover and increase reel shatter. Adjust until you get the optimum situation.

If main gathering loss is pods left on stalks, or

"slobber" (cutting through pods), your best bet is to set the cutter bar lower. Both hydraulic platform control and flexible cutter bars are helpful.

SOYBEAN HARVEST LOSS AS AFFECTED BY COMBINE HEADER CONTROL.*

Type of Loss	Finger Height Control	Floating Cutterbar	Floating Cutterbar and Finger Height Control
	percent	percent	percent
Preharvest loss	2.22	1.53	1.95
Shatter loss	3.59	3.91	3.70
Stubble loss	.19	.07	.03
Lodge loss	.11	.01	.06
Stalk loss	2.59	1.59	1.91
Total header loss	6.48	5.59	5.70
Threshing loss	.30	.56	.51
Total loss	9.00	7.67	8.16
	bushels	bushels	bushels
Total yield per acre	49.57	50.27	49.90
	inches	inches	inches
Stubble height	3.49	2.42	2.18

*Percent loss is based on the percent of total yield and is an average of data from Hark, Beeson, and Galland Varieties.

WISCONSIN UNIV.

Cylinder and separation loss may be hard to diagnose with a shredder installed. Should these losses seem excessive, make a fast machine stop by turning off the key. Then examine material on chaffer and pull some stalks off walkers. If you find unthreshed pods, especially if conditions are damp, then increase cylinder speed and examine chaffer to see if openings are too close. Don't do this if combine is powered by a turbo diesel.

You should vary ground speed according to the conditions. Generally, speed should be between 2.6 and 3 mph.

CORN HARVEST LOSSES

Corn harvest losses can go all over the map. Ohio engineers found losses varying all the way from 2.3 bushels per acre up to 30 bushels per acre during three years of field surveys. This includes ears, kernels and imperfect shelling.

For combines, the average loss is between six and seven bushels per acre. Corn pickers have a better record, but they still average 4.5 bushels per acre left in the field.

Measuring losses. You should check for ear loss and kernel loss. First, select a number of areas at random over the field for checking. Count the number of kernels in a 10 square foot area and the number of ears in 1/100 of an acre. Each three-fourths pound ear equals one bushel per acre loss (or three one-half pound ears equal two bushels per acre)—two kernels per square foot equal one bushel per acre.

ROW LENGTH IN FEET PER 1/100 ACRE

Row Width (inches)	One Row	Two Rows	Three Rows	Four Rows	Six Rows	Eight Rows
	Distance 1/100 Acre					
20	262	131.0	87.3	65.5	43.6	32.7
28	187	93.5	61.3	46.7	31.1	
30	174	87.0	58.0	43.6	29.0	
36	145	72.5	48.3	36.2		
38	138	69.0	46.0	34.5		
40	131	65.5	43.6	32.7		
42	124	62.0	41.3	31.0		

OHIO STATE UNIV.

The table at right gives the dimensions for test areas at different row widths.

Avoiding losses. First step in a clean harvest is to get in the field on time. The Ohio researchers have found that as moisture goes down, field losses shoot up sharply.

Length For Ten Square Foot Frame

Row Width (inches)	Row Length (inches)
20	*
28	51.5
30	48
36	40
38	38
40	36

*Use same frame as for 40 inch rows, but place frame over two rows at a time.

OHIO STATE UNIV

Optimum moisture for best combine harvest is 26% to 27%. This means you need to get in the field before this to keep the average moisture near the optimum level. Around 30% is the practical limit for beginning harvest—kernel damage and tipping mount rather sharply above this level.

Go slowly, generally 2.5 to 3 mph is the most practical speed. In Ohio studies, ear loss almost tripled when speed was increased from 2.26 to 3.10 mph. Ear loss is usually the greatest single source of loss in corn harvest. Researchers say that a good combine operator can keep ear losses to one bushel per acre.

Coordinated row spacing of the harvesting and planting units is important. A slight mismatch with a two-row head can be tolerated, but as the head gets wider—six or eight row equipment—a precise match-up is critical.

Badly lodged corn presents a special problem with a corn combine, sometimes called the "cone of loss." Ears lying directly in the row are missed because corn heads don't have gathering chains below the snapping rolls and there isn't as much lift in a combine roll. Solution is to keep the header as close to the ground as possible and depend on the stone trap to prevent possible machine damage.

How To Use Nebraska Tractor Tests

These standardized reports contain valuable information that can be used to compare performance and economy of various brands and models of tractors.

Performance and economy aren't the major reasons certain tractors are more popular than others. Farmers often list price, dealer service and trade-in value as reasons for buying a particular brand. Yet, performance and economy are built into these other attributes, and thus are important factors in tractor choice.

The most unbiased data on horsepower and economy of tractors sold in the United States are the Nebraska Tractor Tests. They are available on a subscription basis from the University of Nebraska, shown in condensed form in the Red Book—a reference most farm equipment dealers have available—and published by Doane's Agricultural Report in slightly condensed versions.

POWER TAKE-OFF TESTS

Shown below is the portion of an official test report that deals with power take-off performance. This particular example illustrates several points that can be used in tractor selection.

POWER TAKE-OFF PERFORMANCE

Hp	Crank- shaft speed rpm	Fuel Consumption Gal per hr	Lb per hp-hr	Hp-hr per gal	Temperature Degrees F Cooling medium	Air wet bulb	Air dry bulb	Barometer inches of Mercury

MAXIMUM POWER AND FUEL CONSUMPTION

Rated Engine Speed—Two Hours (PTO Speed—665 rpm)								
62.47	2000	4.195	0.465	14.89	191	65	76	28.693
Standard Power Take-off Speed (540 rpm)—One Hour								
54.62	1624	3.624	0.460	15.07	196	65	75	28.930

VARYING POWER AND FUEL CONSUMPTION—TWO HOURS

54.95	2070	3.529	0.445	15.57	184	65	76	....
0.00	2183	1.070	....	....	173	66	76	....
28.29	2132	2.152	0.527	13.15	177	67	78	....
62.91	2000	4.226	0.465	14.89	196	64	75	....
14.35	2161	1.615	0.780	8.89	181	69	82	....
41.90	2104	2.767	0.458	15.14	185	69	82	....
Av 33.73	2108	2.560	0.526	13.18	183	66	78	28.703

The first line under the heading, "maximum power and fuel consumption," shows the tractor's maximum power; its fuel use in gallons per hour; and horsepower-hours produced per gallon of fuel, an indication of overall fuel efficiency. This particular model is a little below average for a diesel. Average for 54 tractors recently tested is 15.35.

The next line gives maximum power at standard pto speed, and may or may not be important to you. Some tractors, and this is one of them, produce standard pto speeds of either 540 or 1,000 rpm

at less than full rated engine speed. In this case, at standard pto speed, maximum power produced by the engine is only 54.62, off sharply from the 62.47 produced at rated rpm. It's something to consider if you're buying for heavy pto use and feel you'll need the maximum output of the engine.

You can also determine characteristics of the engine at less than full throttle when the pto test reflects a lower rated rpm to obtain the standard pto speed. Several of the larger models will show very little horsepower reduction when the throttle setting is cut back to reach 1,000 pto rpm. In some instances fuel consumption will drop rather sharply. This indicates that you can obtain significant fuel savings by operating at the lower rpm.

In the next series of tests, "varying power and fuel consumption," the final line is an average of those tests and is a good indication of average hourly fuel consumption throughout the year. In this case, overall, 2.560 gallons were used per hour. You'll find this figure multiplied by the number of hours of use per year will just about hit gallons of fuel needed for the tractor.

The horsepower-hours per gallon is again a good indication of overall fuel efficiency. As mentioned, this tractor was a little under at maximum power, but its 13.18 horsepower-hours per gallon average beats the 54-tractor average of 12.67.

DRAWBAR PERFORMANCE

Shown in the next column is a portion of an official test reflecting drawbar performance under different loads. It's important to check speed at which these tests were made. In this case, speed under heavy pull was around 5.5 mph. This may not be the speed you'd use for heavy tillage. If not, glance down to the test under "maximum power with ballast" and pick the speed you'd prefer. If, for example, 4.5 mph suits you better, you can get an idea of power developed, drawbar pull in pounds and wheel slip.

Back to the upper portion of this test, the section, "maximum available power," reflects what the tractor will do in horsepower, pounds pull, fuel consumption and fuel efficiency under heaviest pull before engine rpm begins to fall below rated rpm. In this situation, fuel efficiency is slightly under the 54-tractor average of 13.27, but it's a good performance.

DRAWBAR PERFORMANCE

Hp	Draw-bar pull lbs	Speed miles per hr	Crank-shaft speed rpm	Slip of drivers %	Fuel Consumption Gal per hr	Lb per hp-hr	Hp-hr per gal	Cool-ing med	Air wet bulb	Air dry bulb	Barometer inches of Mercury
VARYING DRAWBAR POWER AND FUEL CONSUMPTION WITH BALLAST											
Maximum Available Power—Two Hours—4th Gear (4 Lo)											
90.77	6158	5.53	2100	5.19	6.956	0.531	13.05	182	61	78	28.785
75% of Pull at Maximum Power—Ten Hours—4th Gear (4 Lo)											
72.35	4669	5.81	2180	3.91	5.734	0.549	12.62	188	66	78	28.484
50% of Pull at Maximum Power—Two Hours—4th Gear (4 Lo)											
50.89	3186	5.99	2213	2.32	4.487	0.611	11.34	178	61	83	28.760
50% of Pull at Reduced Engine Speed—Two Hours 5th Gear (1 Hi)											
50.49	3157	6.00	1707	2.37	3.802	0.522	13.28	179	61	82	28.720
MAXIMUM POWER WITH BALLAST											
75.26	13116	2.15	2177	14.75	1st Gear (1 Lo)			184	59	81	28.720
90.29	11072	3.06	2105	11.07	2nd Gear (2 Lo)			180	50	63	28.910
93.70	7808	4.50	2103	6.83	3rd Gear (3 Lo)			180	51	65	28.910
91.45	6210	5.52	2099	5.11	4th Gear (4 Lo)			179	50	64	28.910
91.49	4703	7.29	2106	3.74	5th Gear (1 Hi)			178	48	59	28.910
88.36	3201	10.35	2098	2.41	6th Gear (2 Hi)			176	50	59	28.910

VARYING DRAWBAR PULL AND TRAVEL SPEED WITH BALLAST 4th Gear (4 Lo)

Pounds Pull	6210	6855	7325	7469	7553	7445
Horsepower	91.45	90.32	84.73	75.55	65.46	54.60
Crankshaft Speed rpm	2099	1893	1669	1463	1255	1062
Miles Per Hour	5.52	4.94	4.34	3.79	3.25	2.75
Slip of Drivers %	5.11	5.98	6.29	6.44	6.60	6.60

TRACTOR SOUND LEVEL	dB(A)
Maximum Available Power 2 Hours	88.5
75% of Pull at Max. Power 10 Hours	89.00
50% of Pull at Max. Power 2 Hours	90.5
50% of Pull at Reduced Engine Speed 2 Hours	89.00
Bystander (8th gear)	90.0

The second line shows the same conditions but drawbar load has been cut to 75% of the maximum. This is a good test for judging overall fuel consumption and efficiency under day in, day out heavy tillage operations.

The next two lines, "50% of pull at maximum power" and "50% pull, reduced power," provide good information if you're planning to buy a large tractor but plan to use it on light drawbar loads a considerable amount of time. In this case, shifting up to 5th gear (1 Hi) and reducing throttle setting to 1700 rpm developed about the same pull and horsepower as under full throttle in a lower gear on this light load. You'll note, though, that hourly fuel consumption dropped from 4.487 gallons to 3.8 gallons. Fuel efficiency also rose.

The "varying pull and travel speed" test is a guide to how well the tractor copes with an overload. In this case, additional load was gradually added until peak pull of 7,553 pounds was reached at 3.25 mph compared to 6,210 pounds at maximum power. This tractor's engine has excellent torque characteristics. In fact, there's almost an on-the-go range shift in the engine. For instance, at 3.25 mph it's pulling almost as much, 7,553 pounds, as it did in 3rd gear in the maximum drawbar pull test when a pull of 7,808 pounds was achieved.

Note that in 3rd gear, speed was 4.5 mph and horsepower developed was 93.7. When pulled down in 4th gear, pull was nearly the same, speed was less and horsepower produced was only 65.46.

Some of the larger models will show very little horsepower reduction when pull is increased to achieve a moderate reduction in the rpm of the engine. If this is the situation, it would indicate that somewhat less than full throttle operation would achieve about as much real work as operating at maximum throttle. Wear and tear would be reduced, and fuel consumption is usually less.

SOUND LEVEL

"Tractor sound level" is a recent addition to tractor test reports. This tractor showed sound levels around 90 dB(A) in all tests. That's about average. With a cab some models may drop below 80 dB(A). Many tractors without cabs will be up around 100 dB(A). That's a big difference since an increase of 10 dB(A) will just about double the loudness to the human ear.

Sound levels will become more important in the future. Under the new job safety standards that are going into effect, you can expect a noise standard to be developed for agricultural equipment. It will probably be in the 90 dB(A) area or lower, since tests have shown that hearing damage occurs if you're subjected to higher levels of sound than this for long periods of time.

TIRES, BALLAST AND WEIGHT

This portion of the official test is briefly summarized in Doane's. It gives you an idea of the tire equipment used and the weight added. Here's an example where a large tractor was tested with dual rear tires. If weights used for the ballasted tests are substantially more than you would add, then you'll have to recognize that you won't utilize as much horsepower as is potentially available. Again, compare the test speeds for drawbar pull, tire equipment and weighting. It's logical to use higher field speeds pulling less load to produce the power as long as safety isn't endangered.

TIRES, BALLAST and WEIGHT		With Ballast	Without Ballast
Rear tires	—No, size, ply & psi	Four 18.4-38; 8; 18	Four 18.4-38; 8; 16
Ballast	—Liquid	1113 lb each	None
	Cast iron	1116 lb each	None
Front tires	—No, size, ply & psi	Two 11.00-16; 6; 28	Two 11.00-16; 6; 28
Ballast	—Liquid	None	None
	Cast iron	60 lb each	None
Height of drawbar		21 inches	23 inches
Static weight with operator—Rear		18275 lb	9360 lb
Front		4350 lb	4230 lb
Total		22625 lb	13590 lb

NEBRASKA TRACTOR TEST 1173 – MASSEY-FERGUSON 1805 DIESEL

POWER TAKE-OFF PERFORMANCE

Hp	Crank-shaft speed rpm	Fuel Consumption Gal per hr	Lb per hp-hr	Hp-hr per gal	Temperature Degrees F' Cooling medium	Air wet bulb	Air dry bulb	Barometer inches of Mercury
MAXIMUM POWER AND FUEL CONSUMPTION								
Rated Engine Speed—Two Hours (PTO Speed—1013 rpm)								
192.65	2800	13.030	0.468	14.79	188	61	75	88.857
Standard Power Take-off Speed (1000 rpm)—One Hour								
191.60	2765	12.975	0.469	14.77	187	61	75	28.855
VARYING POWER AND FUEL CONSUMPTION—Two Hours								
167.49	2865	11.277	0.466	14.85	178	60	75	....
0.00	3036	4.117	....	....	169	59	74	--
86.69	2969	7.485	0.598	11.58	176	60	75	....
191.26	2801	12.985	0.470	14.73	190	61	76	....
44.12	3011	5.565	0.873	7.93	172	60	75	....
127.98	2918	9.444	0.511	13.55	178	61	75	....
Av 102.92	**2933**	**8.479**	**0.570**	**12.14**	**177**	**60**	**75**	**28.853**

DRAWBAR PERFORMANCE

Hp	Draw-bar pull lbs	Speed miles per hr	Crank-shaft speed rpm	Slip of drivers %	Fuel Consumption Gal per hr	Lb per hp-hr	Hp-hr per gal	Temp Degrees F Cool-ing med	Air wet bulb	Air dry bulb	Barometer inches of Mercury
VARYING DRAWBAR POWER AND FUEL CONSUMPTION WITH BALLAST											
Maximum Available Power—Two Hours 5th Gear (Lo 3 Std)											
162.95	12763	4.79	2798	6.70	12.767	0.542	12.76	179	44	53	28.950
75% of Pull at Maximum Power—Ten Hours 5th Gear (Lo 3 Std)											
131.41	9743	5.06	2888	4.46	10.586	0.558	12.41	177	61	68	28.322
50% of Pull at Maximum Power—Two Hours 5th Gear (Lo 3 Std)											
90.28	6464	5.24	2952	3.11	8.379	0.642	10.77	177	60	70	28.695
50% of Pull at Reduced Engine Speed—Two Hours 8th Gear (Hi 1 Ov'D)											
90.77	6480	5.25	1772	2.92	6.122	0.467	14.83	177	71	73	28.615
MAXIMUM POWER WITH BALLAST											
155.20	18781	3.10	2794	14.66	3rd Gear (Lo 2 Std)			181	43	54	28.900
167.55	16145	3.89	2798	9.05	4th Gear (Lo 2 Ov'D)			179	44	57	28.895
167.06	13082	4.79	2800	6.66	5th Gear (Lo 3 Std)			179	42	53	28.880
167.59	11017	5.70	2808	5.17	6th Gear (Lo 3 Ov'D)			179	42	53	28.880
170.17	9187	6.95	2800	4.22	7th Gear (Hi 1 Std)			180	43	55	28.910
166.62	7582	8.24	2800	3.41	8th Gear (Hi 1 Ov'D)			179	44	55	28.890

VARYING DRAWBAR PULL AND TRAVEL SPEED WITH BALLAST— 5th Gear (Lo 3 Std)

Pounds Pull	13082	13982	14951	16108	16755	17226	17171	16432
Horsepower	167.06	160.74	150.62	139.46	123.42	104.40	84.12	60.93
Crankshaft Speed rpm	2800	2538	2242	1954	1677	1395	1124	847
Miles Per Hour	4.79	4.31	3.78	3.25	2.76	2.27	1.84	1.39
Slip of Drivers %	6.66	7.22	8.18	9.51	10.17	11.06	10.94	10.42

TRACTOR SOUND LEVEL (with cab)

	db (A)
Maximum Available Power 2 Hours	86.5
75% of Pull at Max. Power 10 Hours	86.5
50% of Pull at Max. Power 2 Hours	86.5
50% of Pull at Reduced Engine Speed 2 Hours	82.5
Bystander 11th Gear (Hi 3 Std)	93.0

TIRES, BALLAST AND WEIGHT

			With Ballast	Without Ballast
Rear Tires	—No., size, ply & psi		Two 23.1-30; 8; 16	Two 23.1-30; 8; 16
Ballast	—Liquid		1570 lb each	None
	Cast iron		97 lb each	None
Front Tires	—No., size, ply & psi		Two 23.1-30; 8; 16	Two 23.1-30; 8; 16
Ballast	—Liquid		530 lb each	None
	Cast iron		195 lb each	None
Height of Drawbar			20 inches	20 inches
Static weight with operator	—rear		9500 lb	6160 lb
	front		13290 lb	11840 lb
	total		22790 lb	18000 lb

Department of Agricultural Engineering **Dates of Test:** April 3 to April 23, 1975 **Manufacturer:** MASSEY-FERGUSON INC., DETROIT, MICHIGAN

FUEL, OIL AND TIME Fuel No 2 Diesel Cetane No 51.7 (rating taken from oil company's typical inspection data) **Specific gravity converted to 60°/60°** 0.8314 **Weight per gallon** 6.922 lb **Oil SAE** 30 **API service classification** SB/SE-CA/CC (MS-DM) **To motor** 3.225 gal **Drained from motor** 1.603 gal **Transmission and final drive lubricant** Massey-Ferguson Permatran **Total time engine was operated** 59 hours

ENGINE Make Caterpillar Diesel 3208 **Type** eight cylinder vee **Serial No** 90 N 6966 **Crankshaft** Mounted lengthwise **Rated rpm** 2800 **Bore and stroke** 4.5″ x 5.0″ **Compression ratio** 16.5 to 1 **Displacement** 636 cu in **Cranking system** 12 volt electric **Lubrication** pressure **Air cleaner** dry type with replaceable paper element with automatic dust unloader **Oil filter** full flow with two replaceable screw-on paper cartridges **Oil cooler** engine coolant heat exchanger **Fuel filter** replaceable pleated screw-on cartridge **Muffler** upright muffler **Cooling medium temperature control** two thermostats

CHASSIS Type four wheel drive **Serial No** 9C 003752 **Tread width rear** 68″ to 88″ **front** 68″ to 88″ **Wheel base** 120″ **Center of gravity** (without operator or ballast, with minimum tread, with fuel tank filled and tractor serviced for operation) Horizontal distance forward from center-line of rear wheels 45″ Vertical distance above roadway 41″ Horizontal distance from center of rear wheel tread 0″ to the right/left **Hydraulic control system** direct engine drive **Transmission** selective gear fixed ratio **Advertised speeds mph** first 2.1 second 2.5 third 3.6 fourth 4.2 fifth 5.0 sixth 5.9 seventh 7.1 eighth 8.4 ninth 12.0 tenth 14.1 eleventh 16.9 twelfth 19.8 reverse 1.4, 1.6, 5.3 and 6.3 **Clutch** single dry disc operated by foot pedal **Brakes** internal expanding shoe actuated hylraucially by a foot pedal **Steering** hydrostatic **Turning radius** (on concrete surface without brake) right 204″ left 204″ **Turning space diameter** (on concrete surface without brake) right 431″ left 431″ **Power take-off** 1000 rpm at 2765 engine rpm.

REPAIRS AND ADJUSTMENTS: During the break-in the shifting fork lock screw came loose and the transmission was locked in second gear. This was corrected and test continued. During the Maximum gear run one of the bolts holding the exhaust pipe to the left exhaust manifold broke. A new bolt and gasket was installed and test continued.

REMARKS: All test results were determined from observed data obtained in accordance with SAE and ASAE test code or official Nebraska test procedure.

The tractor did not meet manufacturer's claim of 183.6 estimated drawbar horsepower.

First and second gears were not run as it was necessary to limit the pull in third gear to avoid excessive wheel slippage.

Bystander sound test was run in 11th gear as tractor engine did not reach maximum rpm during acceleration in highest gear.

Fuel temperature at injection pump return was 146 degrees F.

We, the undersigned, certify that this is a true and correct report of official Tractor Test **1173**.

L. F. LARSEN
Engineer-in-Charge

G. W. STEINBRUEGGE, Chairman
W. E. SPLINTER
D. E. LANE
Board of Tractor Test Engineers

POWER TAKE-OFF PERFORMANCE

Hp	Crank-shaft speed rpm	Fuel Consumption Gal per hr	Fuel Consumption Lb per hp-hr	Hp-hr per gal	Temperature Degrees F Cooling medium	Temperature Degrees F Air wet bulb	Temperature Degrees F Air dry bulb	Barometer inches of Mercury
MAXIMUM POWER AND FUEL CONSUMPTION								
Rated Engine Speed—Two Hours (PTO Speed—1002 rpm)								
125.88	2200	8.090	0.446	15.56	189	61	75	29.133
VARYING POWER AND FUEL CONSUMPTION—TWO HOURS								
111.41	2293	7.640	0.476	14.58	186	62	76	....
0.00	2392	2.747	....	....	178	60	73	....
56.75	2335	5.096	0.624	11.14	183	61	74	....
127.22	2200	8.206	0.448	15.50	191	61	75	....
28.64	2357	3.943	0.956	7.26	179	61	75	....
84.36	2316	6.396	0.527	13.19	187	61	75	....
Av 68.06	2315	5.612	0.579	12.13	184	61	75	29.127

DRAWBAR PERFORMANCE

Hp	Draw-bar pull lbs	Speed miles per hr	Crank-shaft speed rpm	Slip of drivers %	Fuel Consumption Gal per hr	Fuel Consumption Lb per hp-hr	Hp-hr per gal	Temp Degrees F Cool-ing med	Air wet bulb	Air dry bulb	Barometer inches of Mercury
VARYING DRAWBAR POWER AND FUEL CONSUMPTION WITH BALLAST											
Maximu Available Power—Two Hours—7th Gear (B2)											
104.99	7211	5.46	2196	7.07	8.116	0.536	12.94	187	59	77	28.790
75% of Pull at Maximum Power—Ten Hours—7th Gear (B2)											
87.70	5578	5.90	2314	4.69	7.331	0.580	11.96	182	62	70	28.895
50% of Pull at Maximum Power—Two Hours—7th Gear (B2)											
60.76	3738	6.10	2357	3.36	5.975	0.682	10.17	182	46	54	29.080
50% of Pull at Reduced Engine Speed—Two Hours—8th Gear (C2)											
61.06	3760	6.09	1985	3.31	5.020	0.571	12.16	178	54	66	29.045
MAXIMUM POWER WITH BALLAST											
94.83	12032	2.96	2297	14.94	3rd Gear(A3)	....	183	59	74	28.990
103.64	9279	4.19	2200	9.65	5th Gear(B1)	....	186	52	66	28.880
103.54	7657	5.07	2198	7.60	6th Gear(C1)	....	185	54	68	28.880
107.63	7388	5.46	2200	7.17	7th Gear(B2)	....	187	55	69	28.800
108.46	6185	6.58	2201	5.81	8th Gear(C2)	....	186	56	71	28.860
108.44	5597	7.27	2200	5.08	9th Gear(B3)	....	188	58	75	28.860

VARYING DRAWBAR PULL AND TRAVEL SPEED WITH BALLAST—7 G(B2)

Pounds pull	7388	8053	8605	8998	8843	7553
Horsepower	107.63	104.29	98.92	89.93	75.53	54.59
Crankshaft speed rpm	2200	1970	1764	1546	1319	1097
Miles per hour	5.46	4.86	4.31	3.75	3.20	2.71
Slip of drivers %	7.17	7.87	8.70	9.52	9.25	7.60

TRACTOR SOUND LEVEL (with Sound-Gard cab) dB(A)

Maximum available power 2 hours	82.5
75% of pull at max. power 10 hours	82.5
50% of pull at max. power 2 hours	82.0
50% of pull at reduced engine speed 2 hours	82.0
Bystandar 16th gear (D4)	87.5

TIRES, BALLAST AND WEIGHT

		With Ballast	Without Ballast
Rear tires	—No., size, ply & psi	Two 18.4-38;8;20	Two 18.4-38;8;20
Ballast	—Liquid	1085 lb each	None
	Cast iron	750 lb each	None
Front tires	—No., size, ply & psi	Two 11L-15;6;28	Two 11L-15;6;28
Ballast	—Liquid	None	None
	Cast iron	20 lb each	None
Height of drawbar		20 inches	20½ inches
Static weight with operator—Rear		11640 lb	7970 lb
Front		3420 lb	3380 lb
Total		15060 lb	11350 lb

Department of Agricultural Engineering
Dates of Test: October 5 to October 13th, 1972
Manufacturer: JOHN DEERE WATERLOO TRACTOR WORKS, WATERLOO, IOWA

FUEL, OIL AND TIME Fuel No 2 Diesel **Cetane** No 54.5 (rating taken from company's typical inspection data) **Specific gravity converted to 60°/60°** 0.8342 **Weight per gallon** 6.946 **Oil SAE** 30 **API service classification** John Deere Torq-Guard or CD-SD **To Motor** 4.023 gal **Drained from motor** 3.735 gal **Transmission and final drive lubricant** John Deere Special 303 Oil **Total time engine was operated** 41 hours

ENGINE Make John Deere Diesel **Type** 6 cylinder vertical with turbo-charger **Serial No** 6404TR-09 34145OR **Crankshaft Mounted** lengthwise **Rated rpm** 2200 **Bore and stroke** 4.25" x 4.75" **Compression ratio** 14.7 to 1 **Displacement** 404 cu in **Cranking system** 12 volt electrical (two 6 volt batteries) **Lubrication** pressure **Air cleaner** precleaner and two dry type in series with replaceable treated paper elements **Oil filter** full flow with replaceable paper cartridge **Oil Cooler** engine coolant heat exchanger for crankcase oil and radiator for transmission and hydraulic system **Fuel filter** sediment bowl with screen and replaceable paper primary and secondary filter elements **Muffler** was used **Cooling medium temperature control** thermostat

CHASSIS Type standard **Serial No** 4430H-003931 **Tread width rear** 60.0" to 90.1" **front** 48.0" to 68.0" **Wheel base** 106.7" **Center of gravity** (without operator or ballast, with minimum tread, with fuel tank filled and tractor serviced for operation) Horizontal distance forward from center-line of rear wheels 33.4" Vertical distance above roadway 41.5" Horizontal distance from center of rear wheel tread 0.5" to the left **Hydraulic control system** direct engine drive **Transmission** selective gear fixed ratio with partial range syncro-mesh and power shift **Advertised speeds mph** first 2.0 second 2.6 third 3.4 fourth 4.3 fifth 4.7 sixth 5.5 seventh 5.9 eighth 7.0 ninth 7.7 tenth 8.5 eleventh 9.1 twelfth 9.8 thirteenth 10.8 fourteenth 11.6 fifteenth 14.0 sixteenth 17.8 reverse 3.2, 4.1, 7.5, 8.8, 11.2 **Clutch** wet multiple disc operated hydraulically **Brakes** wet disc hydraulically power actuated by two foot pedals that can be locked together **Steering** hydrostatic **Turning radius** (on concrete surface with brake applied) right 146" left 146" (on concrete surface without brake) right 158" left 158" **Turning space diameter** (on concrete surface with brake applied) right 292" left 292" (on concrete surface without brake) right 316" left 316" **Power take-off** 540 or 1002 rpm at 2200 engine rpm.

REPAIRS AND ADJUSTMENTS: No repairs or adjustments.

REMARKS: All test results were determined from observed data obtained in accordance with SAE and ASAE test code or official Nebraska test procedure. First and second gears were not run as it was necessary to limit the pull in third gear to avoid excessive slippage. Fourth, tenth, eleventh, twelfth, thirteenth, fourteenth, fifteenth and sixteenth gears were not run as the test procedure requires only six travel speeds. During maximum drawbar run in 3rd gear the transmission came out of gear twice making it necessary to hold the shift lever in place to complete the run.

We, the undersigned, certify that this is a true and correct report of official Tractor Test 1110.

L. F. LARSEN
Engineer-In-Charge

G. W. STEINBRUEGGE, Chairman
W. E. SPLINTER
D. E. LANE
Board of Tractor Test Engineers

Tractor Transmissions

Just as with automobiles, the options that are available today on a new tractor are much greater than they were a few years ago.

Without getting into a highly technical discussion of the various types available, here's a quick run-down of commonly available transmissions.

Spur gear transmissions are the simplest and transfer engine power to rear wheels with the least loss due to friction, etc. They have been around for many years, consist of straight cut gears that mesh with each other to transmit power in the various gears. Their advantages are simplicity, high efficiency, sturdiness and low cost. A disadvantage is that they cannot be shifted quickly. They also tend to be noisier than other types of transmissions. This is a factor if a cab is installed since it is apt to pick up gear noise and amplify it.

Constant mesh helical gear transmissions are very similar to automobile or truck transmissions. In these units the gears are cut at an angle and operate in mesh all the time. The angle cut reduces noise level. Since they are meshed at all times shifting is accomplished by a collar which engages the gear with the shaft. These collars can be equipped with synchronizer clutches to make shifting easier.

Auxiliary range shifts can be of two types. Quite common on smaller utility type tractors is a simple "crash box" range shift that doubles the speeds available from the regular transmission. It cannot be shifted on the go. Also available on some of these models is a "fast reverser" which is a shuttle type arrangement that is popular when the tractor is used with a front-end loader.

The other type which is available from most manufacturers is an on-the-go range shift. This unit, usually located ahead of the main transmission, allows the operator to shift down and for one company it goes up and down without stopping. Usually, the speed reduction is about 20% for large tractors.

Power shift transmissions use a series of planetary gear sets and hydraulically operated clutches to produce 8 or 10 speeds forward. Most of these have a clutch pedal like inching control to ease handling when hitching to implements or operating in close quarters.

Hydrostatic transmissions are practically taking over in the small suburban tractor market. They are also available on several combines, forage harvesters and swathers. However, only one manufacturer offers a line of hydro farm tractors. The principal advantage of the hydrostatic is that speed is infinitely variable from stationary to full speed. However, most units will have a simple transmission to improve efficiency over the entire range of speeds.

The basic principle of the hydrostatic transmission is that an oil pump, powered by the engine, pumps oil to a hydraulic motor which may either be attached to a normal final drive train or installed in the wheel itself. Generally, driving the rear wheel through a normal final drive train has achieved higher efficiencies than actually installing the motor in the wheel itself.

Summary: The simpler the transmission the more efficiently it will transmit horsepower. However, efficient transfer of horsepower through the gears of the transmission and final drive train is not the principal objective of a tractor owner. He's primarily concerned with the work that can be accomplished at the drawbar. This introduces many additional factors into the situation such as tire size, singles or duals, weighting, hitching methods and heights. Therefore, undue concern over a couple of percentage points of loss in transmission efficiency becomes insignificant.

COMPARISON OF TRACTOR TRANSMISSIONS

Type	Load Matching	Efficiency	*Added Cost, %
Conventional	Base	1.0	
Single planetary	Better	0.95-1.0	4-5
Full power shift	Much better	0.86-0.99	8-10
Hydrostatic	Ideal	0.74-0.77	15.5

*Added cost as percent of a standard diesel tractor.   MO. UNIV.

TRANSMISSION SELECTION

The main thing to keep in mind in the selection

process is to recognize that it's not the efficiency with which power is transmitted that is of greatest importance in the final analysis. The important criterion is how much drawbar work can I get done?

The two charts below illustrate this principal. Two John Deere 4020's were compared: one a power shift, the other syncro-range. In sandy soil, draft load was light until plowing depth reached nine inches. There was no need to shift so the syncro-range model did more work on less fuel. In the clay sod, it was a different story. By being able to shift when needed the power shift model did more work per hour and this made up for the loss in efficiency of the transmission so that fuel consumption per acre was no more and in some situations a little less than the syncro-range equipped model.

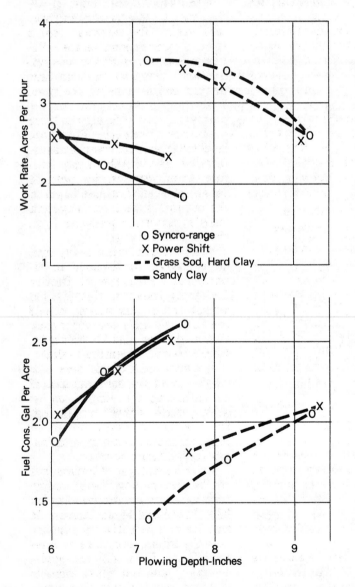

For the smallest tractors, those under 35 pto hp, the most inexpensive transmission is usually the best buy. These will most often be utility tractors. They are lowest in cost and the extra cost of a more sophisticated transmission is probably not a good buy. However, there is an exception. If the tractor is to be used regularly with a front end loader and service will be fairly heavy, it's a good idea to investigate options such as shuttle transmissions.

In larger models, say up to 60 hp, a more thorough investigation of transmission options is in order. First of all, in this horsepower range you'll generally be power short on most field work. This means that an on-the-go range shift or a power shift transmission will often increase work effectiveness when doing heavy tillage or pto work. In the horsepower ranges an on-the-go downshift usually reduces forward speed by one-third.

High horsepower tractors. One school says you'll generally have a surplus of power anyway, and will size equipment to fit the tractor, therefore, you really don't need to go to the extra expense of buying the more costly transmission. This makes sense under some circumstances. For instance, where a wheatland type tractor is being used with tillage tools such as rod weeders, chisel plows, etc., where drawbar requirements are quite predictable and change primarily as a function of depth, the simple transmission fills needs quite satisfactorily.

The other school of thought is that high horsepower tractors, especially in the Corn Belt, are not used only for heavy tillage operations. Hence the widest range of forward speeds, with the greatest amount of flexibility, makes them much more useful. Further, they have engines that are efficient over a much broader engine rpm range and the more gears available the greater the economy on low horsepower work. Heavy duty pto work, of course, makes the most flexible transmission available a good buy. For instance, in the grain swathing areas large pto combines, when used with an automatic or hydrostatic transmission tractor, perform almost as efficiently as do SP units.

Trade-in important. If on-the-go range shifts are almost "standard," then the trade-in value could be adversely affected if you don't buy this type.

Traction and Weighting

Soil condition, tire configuration, speed, slippage, ballast, and drawbar position will all affect tractive performance.

Efficient operation of farm tractors is extremely important, particularly as the cost of inputs to power them continues to rise and you are faced with the need to get maximum output from these machines in the field.

The most important factor affecting the performance of the tractor is the soil itself. Unfortunately, you are often faced with less than ideal conditions. A summary of the effects of soil conditions is shown in the table.

EFFECT OF SOIL CONDITION

Soil condition	Usable hp as % of max pto hp
concrete	86.0%
firm	62.5%
tilled	55.6%
soft	47.6%

The reduction in usable power is due to two factors–slippage of the drive wheels, and rolling resistance encountered by the tractor as it moves through the field. On extremely soft soils, rolling resistance is highest, since the tractor is continually "climbing" out of a rut.

Optimum efficiency requires the proper use of weight and tire size under all operating conditions. For a given soil, the most important factor affecting the performance at the drawbar is the weight the tire carries.

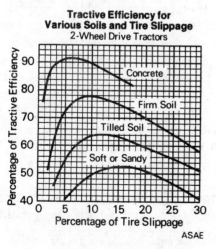

Tractive Efficiency for Various Soils and Tire Slippage
2-Wheel Drive Tractors

ASAE

The graph shows that maximum efficiency usually occurs when slippage is between 10% and 15%. Reducing slippage to less than 10% results in increased rolling resistance and soil compaction. Usable horsepower is further reduced. Slippage greater than 15% cuts output and causes excessive tire wear.

Advances have been made in traction theory, but two factors continue to have the most effect on traction. They are the load to power ratio and the speed of travel.

The speed of travel is a major consideration. Operating at higher speeds increases output and cuts wear on the transmission. Research by Case Tractor Company shows 9½ times more strain on a transmission when a tractor is operating at continuous load at 2 mph than when it is operating at 6 mph. Slower speeds at full load will increase the torque (strain) on the power train. Field conditions also determine speed, since rough conditions dictate slower speeds. However, field operations should be in the 4.5 to 5.5 mph range, minimum.

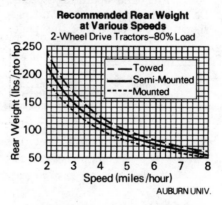

Recommended Rear Weight at Various Speeds
2-Wheel Drive Tractors–80% Load

AUBURN UNIV.

A summary of load to power ratios is given in this graph. For firm soils, subtract 10 pounds per hp. For soft soils, add 10 pounds. As an example, a 150 pto hp tractor, disking at 5 mph in sod, would require about 90 pounds of rear weight per pto hp, or 13,500 pounds rear weight.

Weighting can also be based on total tractor weight. The following guidelines are from the University of Nebraska.

POUNDS TRACTOR WEIGHT PER PTO HP FOR FIRM AND TILLED SOILS

For light draft, high speed (6 mph)	110-130 lbs
For average draft, average speed (5 mph)	130-155 lbs
For heavy draft, slow speed (4 mph)	155-200 lbs

UNIV. OF NEBRASKA

Using these recommendations, the same 150 pto hp tractor would require between 19,500 pounds and 23,250 pounds total weight.

What about tires? First of all, they must be able to carry the tractor's weight. The maximum load a tire can carry depends on the inflation pressure. Usually the load rating and inflation pressure are printed on the side of the tires. These ratings do not take into account maximum efficiency at lower pressures, however. Firestone research shows that lower pressures increase traction. One study indicated maximum traction with 14 psi on the inside dual and 12 psi on the outside. A table of maximum loads at minimum pressures is on the back of this page.

Duals are usually less costly than large singles, particularly at replacement. Research at Purdue University indicates that if total weight on the rear wheels is held constant, the duals are better than singles on loose soils. On firm soils, there's no real advantage to duals.

A tractor with single tires will receive about the same advantage by ballasting the singles as by adding duals without weight, but the unballasted duals will cause less compaction. Duals with ballast provide maximum traction.

Major advantages of tripling are reduced compaction, lower rolling resistance and greater stability on hills. There can be an increase in traction and reduction in slippage with the triples, according to Firestone tests. It is still uncertain, however, whether these results stemmed from higher static weights with the triples versus the duals.

287

Radials are also a consideration. Research at Auburn, Alabama, indicates that the radial has its biggest advantage on firm soils. The softer the soil, the less the advantage. Other tests concluded that the radial tires gave from 6% to 18% greater traction at 15% slip in five of seven soil types. The longer and narrower load surface of radials also reduces rolling resistance.

For 4-wheel drives, the same basic principles apply, with the exception of slightly different weighting techniques.

Since 4-wd tractors have all four wheels pulling, weight distribution under load should be equal on all four wheels. The load transfers weight to the rear wheels, however, which means that the front weight should be greater under static, no-load weighings. An estimate of the total weight for the 4-wd can be made by consulting the following graph. Do not exceed the maximum manufacturer's weight recommendation posted in the cab, however. The same principles on slippage apply to 4-wheel drives as to 2-wheel drives.

Consider a tractor that has 300 engine horsepower. Using the .86 factor, this would equal about 258 pto hp. Operating at 5 mph would require 115 pounds per pto hp, or 29,670 pounds total weight. This

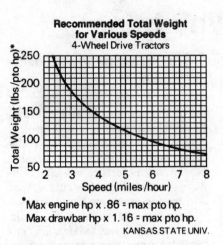

Recommended Total Weight for Various Speeds
4-Wheel Drive Tractors

*Max engine hp x .86 = max pto hp.
Max drawbar hp x 1.16 = max pto hp.
KANSAS STATE UNIV.

should then be checked against the maximum allowable weight by the manufacturer.

Distribution of static weight is best at about 60% on the front axle and 40% on the rear. With transfer under load, this will provide a 50/50 weight distribution. Drawbar positions are also important. Higher drawbar positions result in more weight being transferred to the rear axles. Generally, if tractor static weight is concentrated on the front axle, you should use the higher drawbar positions.

To check your tractor, initially ballast it according to the graphs, depending on the maximum pto horsepower and operating speeds. Do not exceed the tire ratings shown at the bottom of this page,

however. Determine the weight needed. Check the weight of the tractor, and then add cast iron or liquid weight based on the capacities given in the table.

To measure slippage, pick operating conditions which will be typical for the tractor. Mark a tire with chalk and mark the starting point. Then operate in the field for 20 revolutions of the wheel, at the speed and load you intend to use. Mark the finish. Raise the tillage tool and retrace your path to the starting point, counting the revolutions of the wheel. Each revolution less than 20 needed to retrace the route indicates 5% slippage. If it takes the wheel 17 revolutions unloaded to retrace the distance, the slippage is 15%.

Remember that slippage should be in the 10% to 15% range, depending on the soil condition. If it's less than 10%, weight should be removed. If more than 15%, weight should be added. Before adding weight to the tractor, check the table to be sure the tires will not be overloaded. If tires will be overloaded, you'll have to move to larger ones or duals. Tires in dual or triple configurations should be loaded only to 90% of the rated capacity. This protects them from overloads which may occur momentarily in multiple tire applications.

LOAD CAPACITIES, INFLATION PRESSURES, AND LIQUID BALLAST CAPACITIES[a]

Tire size	Single		Dual		Capacity gal of water at 75% fill	lb CaCl$_2$[c]	Ballast lbs water and CaCl$_2$[b]
	Minimum recommended pressure psi	Maximum load capacity at minimum pressure lbs	Minimum recommended pressure psi	Maximum load capacity at minimum pressure lbs			
15.5-38	14	3160	12	2540	56	196	663
16.9-30	16	3900	—	—	63	221	746
16.9-34	16	4140	12	3080	70	245	829
16.9-38	16	4380	12	3260	77	270	912
18.4-30	16	4680	—	—	77	270	912
18.4-34	16	4970	12	3700	85	298	1007
18.4-38	16	5250	12	3910	94	329	1113
20.8-34	16	6010	12	4470	109	382	1291
20.8-38	16	6360	12	4730	120	420	1421
23.1-26	16	6280	12	4670	109	382	1291
23.1-30	16	6700	12	4980	123	431	1457
23.1-34	16	7110	12	5290	136	476	1610
24.5-32	18	8180	12	5680	146	511	1729
28.1-26	18	7800	12	5410	134	469	1587
30.5-32	18	9770	12	6780	186	651	2202

[a]Based on Tire and Rim Association standards. All figures are given for individual tires. [b]Liquid ballast capacities and weights are based on a solution of 3½ pounds CaCl$_2$ per gallon water. The resulting solution is slush free at −12°F. [c]Based on Type 1 (77%) calcium chloride. If type 2 (94%) calcium chloride is used, reduce the number given in the table by 25%.

Sizing Field Equipment to Tractors

These guidelines, combined with a little experience, will help you to more accurately match field equipment to tractors.

Proper matching of implements to tractors improves field performance while reducing operating costs, repairs, fuel consumption, and possibly, initial capital outlay. Understanding the basic principles of soil resistance, usable power, slippage, and speed can help in the selection of tractor/implement combinations.

Typically, soil resistance, commonly referred to as implement draft, will affect field performance more than other factors. Here, we are referring primarily to implement functional draft, rather than the draft associated with rolling resistance of the tractor and implement. The rolling resistance of the tractor will be compensated for by adjusting horsepower ratings and we assume the rolling resistance of the implement to be only slight, since most equipment is operated with little weight on the carrier wheels.

Operating depth, speed of travel, soil type, and moisture content all interact to determine the draft of an implement. Increasing the depth of tillage or the speed of travel will tend to increase draft. Deep tillage implements, such as moldboard plows, will be more drastically affected by these factors, as shown in the following graph.

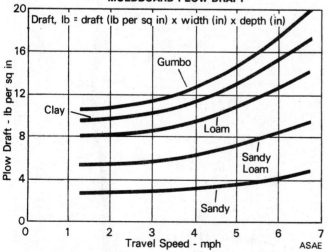

MOLDBOARD PLOW DRAFT

Draft, lb = draft (lb per sq in) x width (in) x depth (in)

Soil moisture also can affect draft. A 1% increase in soil moisture can decrease the moldboard draft 10%, according to American Society of Agricultural Engineers (ASAE) research.

When sizing tillage implements, usable power ratings, rather than maximum pto, engine, or

other ratings, must be used. Since slippage and rolling resistance will undoubtedly occur, pto and engine power estimates will tend to result in improper implement sizing. Also, pto ratings do not take into consideration the power lost in power trains and final drives, typically about 10%, but sometimes as high as 25%. Still other tractors do not have a pto, and consequently, no accurate estimation of pto horsepower.

The following table, adapted from work done by Wendell Bowers, Agricultural Engineer at Oklahoma State University, gives a fairly accurate method of estimating usable horsepower. It uses an .86 factor in converting from one rating to another, and takes into account the effect of various soil conditions on usable power.

USABLE HORSEPOWER FACTORS

From To	Maximum				Usable Drawbar Horsepower		
	En- gine	PTO	Con- crete	Firm Soil	Firm Soil	Tilled Soil	Soft Surface
Max Hp							
Eng	—	1.16	1.35	1.57	1.83	2.12	2.47
Pto	0.86	—	1.16	1.35	1.57	1.83	2.12
Concrete	0.74	0.86	—	1.16	1.35	1.57	1.83
Firm soil	0.64	0.74	0.86	—	1.16	1.35	1.57
Usable Hp							
Firm soil	0.55	0.64	0.74	0.86	—	1.16	1.35
Tilled soil	0.47	0.55	0.64	0.74	0.86	—	1.16
Soft surface	0.40	0.47	0.55	0.64	0.74	0.86	—

OKLAHOMA STATE UNIV.

Here's an example of how to use the factors in the table to find the usable power of a tractor with 300 engine horsepower operating on firm soil. From the table, the conversion factor is .55. Thus, a good approximation of the available power will be 300 ehp x .55 = 165 drawbar horsepower. In tilled soil, multiply drawbar horsepower by the .86 factor from the table–165 db hp x .86 = 142 usable horsepower on tilled soil. Note that usable power on firm soil is 86% of maximum power available. This allows you some reserve power for getting through the tough spots in fieldwork.

The next step in sizing equipment is to determine proper implement width. Horsepower needed will be determined by the interaction of speed and total draft. Here, total draft is the product of draft per foot of width times width of the implement. Increasing the speed will require a reduction in the draft, either by working shallower depths or narrower widths. The formula, drawbar horsepower = total draft (pounds) x speed (mph) ÷ 375, gives the relationship.

Here's how to use the above formula to determine maximum equipment width: Width (ft) = [usable hp x 375] ÷ [speed (mph) x draft (lbs/ft)]. Assume you want to pull a heavy tandem disk harrow 5 mph with the 300 ehp tractor. From the soil resistance table on this page, you can see that average draft will require 325 pounds per foot of width. The 300 ehp tractor has 165 usable hp on firm soil. Plugging these figures into the formula, you'll find that for these conditions, the tractor should be sized to a 38 foot disk.

Increasing the speed of travel would increase the power requirement. Operating at 6 mph, the width of the implement would have to be reduced to about 32 feet to maintain the same total draft.

A handy reference nomograph has been developed by Bowers to estimate the interaction of speed, soil resistance, width, and horsepower. As long as any three are known, you can accurately determine the fourth. Plotted on the chart are the assumptions used in the formula example above. Beginning on the chart at usable (drawbar) horsepower of 165, a line is drawn through the operating speed of 5 mph, indicating (on the turning line) that total draft of 12,500 can be pulled. If the tandem disk will have 325 pounds of draft per foot of width, the optimum width needed will be about 38 feet.

When sizing field equipment, field speeds should be in the 4.5 to 5.5 mph range, minimum. Also, slippage should be checked and, where possible, maintained within 10% to 15% to minimize transmission wear, tire wear, and rolling resistance, with maximum horsepower output and fuel economy.

DRAWBAR HORSEPOWER FOR TILLAGE TOOLS

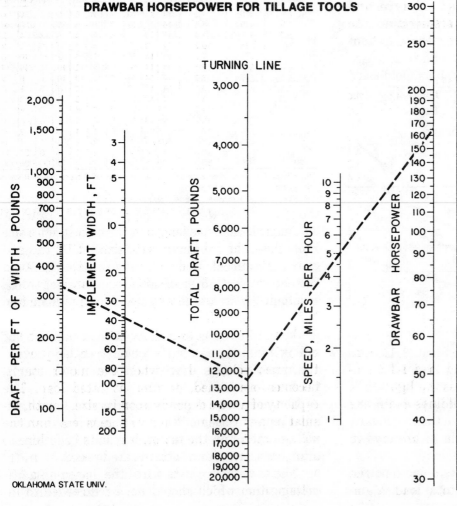

OKLAHOMA STATE UNIV.

Operation	Pounds of Draft/ Foot of Width	Typical Speed, mph
SOIL RESISTANCE		
Plowing (8 inches deep)		
Gumbo	1,250	4.0
Clay	1,050	4.0
Loam	950	4.5
Sandy loam	700	5.0
Sand	350	5.0
One-way Disk		
Heavy draft	400	4.0
Medium draft	300	5.5
Light draft	200	7.0
Chisel Plowing (8 inches deep)		
Hard, dry	800	4.0
Medium clay loam	500	5.0
Sand, sandy loam	200	6.0
Offset or Heavy Tandem Disk		
Heavy draft	400	4.0
Medium draft	325	5.0
Light draft	250	6.0
Tandem Disk Harrow		
Heavy draft	300	4.0
Medium draft	200	5.0
Light draft	100	6.0
Field Cultivator		
Heavy clay soils	650	4.0
Clay loam	450	5.0
Sandy loam	300	5.0
Sand	150	6.0
Spike Tooth Harrow		
Heavy draft	60	4.0
Medium draft	40	5.0
Light draft	20	6.0
Land Plane		
Heavy draft	800	4.0
Medium draft	550	5.0
Light draft	300	6.0
Subsoiling		
Sandy loam	70-110 lbs/in depth	5.0
Medium clay loam	100-160 lbs/in depth	3.0
Planting		
Corn, soybeans, cotton	250-450 lbs per row	3.0-6.0
Grain drill	30-100	2.5-6.0
		ASAE

Planning Electric Power Needs

Modernizing a farm's electric system requires careful planning prior to installation to assure safety and efficiency.

Any electrical system modernization plan should start with a calculation of probable load demand. Figure total load in amperes at 230 volts, even though all equipment may not operate at once. Plan ahead by adding an allowance for future expansion. Next, calculate the permissible voltage drop on the circuit.

Remember that the main service entrance wires and equipment are based on computed load for the entire system. Building service entrance wires and equipment are based on computed load in buildings and feeder wires to and between buildings are based on calculated maximum demand.

Calculating probable load demand. To find total computed or connected load for a building, total the full load in amperes for large or permanently connected equipment. Multiply full load current of the largest motor by 1.25. This increases the amperes full load above rating to assure adequate wire size and correct fuse selection needed to handle a starting overload. Example:

FEED ROOM REQUIREMENTS

Motor*	HP	Amperes Full Load
Silo unloader	5	28 x 1.25 = 35.0
Feed mill	1	6.5
Feed mixer	2	12.0
Auger	1/2	3.7
Auger	1-1/2	9.2
Total amperes at 230 volts		66.4

*Amperes full load for electric motors are listed in the "Wire Sizes" table in the next column.

Convenience Outlets:
   2 outlets at 1-1/2 amperes each = 3 amperes at 115 volts
Lighting Load:
   1-1/2 amperes at 115 volts
Total Load:
   4-1/2 amperes at 115 volts
   4-1/2 ÷ 2 = 2.25 amperes at 230 volts
   66.4 + 2.25 = 68.65 amperes full load at 230 volts

Figure each convenience outlet load 1-1/2 amperes at 115 volts. Figure lighting load 1-1/2 amperes per outlet at 115 volts, unless the lighting is for a special purpose such as buildings requiring high wattage lamps.

Be certain to estimate probable future load in all cases.

Add total amperes at 230 volts to one-half the total amperes at 115 volts for the total load in am-

peres at 230 volts.

From these calculations, wire sizes, switches, etc., can be determined. Although this page includes tables for wire types and sizes for electric motors, it does not provide all the answers for complete farm wiring. Consult your power supply company for complete information on all types of installations. Additional information is available in the booklet, "Agricultural Wiring Handbook," at $3 per copy from the Farm Electrification Council, 909 University Ave., Columbia, Mo. 65201.

Wiring sizes and voltage drop. In farm buildings all general circuits should be at least 20-ampere capacity and wired with No. 12 wire.

WIRE SIZES FOR INDIVIDUAL SINGLE-PHASE MOTORS, BASED ON 3% VOLTAGE DROP ON FULL-LOAD CURRENT

Motor Horse-power	Volts	Approx. Full Load, Amperes	Length of Run, in Feet									
			100	200	300	400	500	600	700	800	900	1000
1/4	115	4.6	14	12	10	8	8	6	6	6	6	4
1/3	115	5.1	14	12	10	8	8	6	6	6	4	4
1/2	115	7.4	12	10	8	6	6	4	4	4	4	2
3/4	115	10.2	12	8	6	6	4	4	2	2	2	2
1/4	230	2.3	14	14	14	12	12	12	12	10	10	10
1/3	230	2.6	14	14	14	12	12	12	10	10	10	10
1/2	230	3.7	14	14	14	12	12	10	10	8	8	8
3/4	230	5.1	14	14	12	12	10	10	8	8	8	8
1	230	6.5	14	14	12	10	10	8	8	8	6	6
1-1/2	230	9.2	14	12	10	8	8	6	6	6	6	4
2	230	12.0	14	10	10	8	6	6	4	4	4	4
3	230	17.0	10	10	8	6	6	4	4	4	2	2
5	230	28.0	10†	6	6	4	2	2	2	1	1	0
7-1/2	230	40.0	8*	6	4	2	2	1	0	0	00	00
10	230	50.0	6†	4	2	2	1	0	00	00	000	000

†Type RH or RHW in cable or raceway; all types in air. For other types of wire in cable or raceway use next size larger.
*For wires in cable or raceway, use next size larger.

INDUSTRY COMMITTEE ON INTERIOR WIRING DESIGN

Regardless of the length of the circuit, wire size must meet the minimum safe size set by the National Electrical Code to prevent too great a voltage drop. A drop of 5%, for example, would result in a 17% loss in any lighting appliance and 10% loss in any heater.

Motor wiring is especially critical because the circuit must furnish sufficient current to prevent too much voltage drop when the motor starts, becomes overloaded, or runs at rated load. The capacity of a wire depends upon its size, length, insulation and voltage. When voltage is less than the voltage rating on the motor, it results in failure to start, accelerate and attain rated speed.

The table above lists wire sizes based on a 3% voltage drop which should not be exceeded to insure satisfactory operation. Since these figures are for copper wire only, aluminum wire must be one size larger. It's lighter and costs less per foot. However there's some concern that aluminum wiring may be hazardous under some conditions.

Types of wires. Use non-metallic sheathed cable for most inside wiring—type NM for dry areas and NMC whether conditions are damp or dry. Do not use non-metallic sheathed cables in service entrances, poured concrete, or haymows.

For service entrance cable, use SE or ASE. It must be enclosed in suitable metal raceways or fuse controlled before it enters a building.

Use moisture-resistant, covered wiring for outside, overhead service to buildings. Types RW, RHW, TW and THW may be used. "R" denotes rubber insulation, "T" thermoplastic, "H" heat resistant and "W" moisture resistant.

ALLOWABLE CURRENT-CARRYING CAPACITIES

| AWG Wire Size | Conductors in Cable, Raceway, or Buried | | Single Conductors in Free Air | |
	Type R, RU, RUW, RW, T, TW	Type RH, RHW, THW	Type RHW, THW	Type TW, RW
	amperes		amperes	
14	15	15	---	---
12	20	20	---	---
10	30	30	40	40
8	40	45	65	55
6	55	65	95	80
4	70	85	125	105
2	95	115	170	140
1	110	130	195	165
1/0	125	150	230	195
2/0	145	175	265	225
3/0	165	200	310	260
4/0	195	230	360	300

PACIFIC NORTHWEST COOPERATIVE EXTENSION

From this table, the wire size for outside conductors can be determined once the load demand on the circuit is known. These are limiting capacities beyond which excessive temperatures may damage the insulation. No. 10 is minimum permissible in overhead spans up to 50 feet. Over 50 feet, No. 8 is minimum.

Direct burial wiring for underground distribution requires type USE for services, feeders, and branch circuits; but type UF can be used only for feeders and branch circuits.

Multiple conductor cable is used as the neutral conductor for overhead distribution.

Conduit and tubing protect wiring from injury, moisture and vapor. Electrical metallic tubing, EMT, is used for either exposed or concealed work inside buildings. Use flexible metal conduit where rigid conduit cannot be used. If the area is wet get the waterproof type.

Service entrance panels are generally available in 30, 60, 70, 100, 150 and 200 ampere sizes. Provide capacity enough for the total building load plus at least one spare circuit. For most buildings with more than one circuit, the 60 amp size is the smallest used.

Each panel should have circuit breakers, pull-out fuse blocks, or switches, so the power can be shut off. The National Electric Code requires that not more than six switches or circuit breakers can disconnect the main service.

Grounding. All electrical equipment should be grounded according to NE code for safety. A one-half inch solid copper weld bar ten feet long, driven eight feet into the earth, makes a good grounding electrode. Water pipes can be used, but not plastic pipes or plastic fittings.

Provide grounding type outlets for portable type equipment. A motor frame must be grounded for safety in case an ungrounded wire should contact it.

Where fuses are used for protecting circuits of 30 amps or less, they should be the plug type rather than cartridge type because the cartridges are harder to use and higher in price.

Where fuses are used to protect branch circuits, feeders, or motors, it is recommended that they be the time delay type to prevent needless blowing on motor starting currents. Such fuses will not provide running overload protection to a motor unless the circuit serves only one motor and fuses are rated according to the motor full-load current.

SINGLE OR THREE-PHASE DISTRIBUTION

Single-phase, 60-cycle, 115-230 volt, grounded neutral electric service to farms is generally accepted as standard. Motors on single-phase lines are usually limited to 5 or 7-1/2 hp maximum.

Motors of 10 hp capacity and up are often supplied with 440-volt, three-phase service, when available, since this service is more efficient and economical for large power requirements. Smaller motors with heavy starting loads, such as silo unloaders, should be served with three-phase service when possible. Since it is not always available within an economical distance from the farmstead, the power company should be consulted first. Single-phase power can be supplied from a three-phase line.

292

Electric Motor Selection and Use

Thanks to recent developments in electric motors and improvements in rural electric service, farmers can utilize motors of just about any type and horsepower.

In the past, electric power companies have limited electric motors to about 7-1/2 hp on rural lines, forcing the use of tractor power for many jobs. Today you can utilize electric motors that produce more mechanical power than the largest tractor on the market. Developments in motors and rural service have made this possible.

Irrigation, liquid manure pumping, grain drying, forage blowing and feed grinding are some of the heavy jobs where high horsepower motors are needed. Advantages are the ability to match load requirements with motor size; servicing and maintenance costs are lower than for any power source; automatic operation is possible with no refueling problem; fire hazard is minimum and the noise level is low.

MOTOR SELECTION

If you're replacing an old or burned out motor, try to determine the reason for failure—you may need either a larger or heavier duty motor. Standards for insulation have changed and a new motor of the same size may, as a result, be smaller in physical size, forcing you to modify the

If you'd need this size* internal combustion engine	. . . You'd use this size** electric motor
20- 23 hp	15 hp
27- 30	20
33- 38	25
40- 50	30
53- 60	40
67- 75	50
80- 90	60
100-113	75
133-150	100

*"Brake" or "Dynamometer" rating
**Nameplate rating

mounting brackets to install it. Also, the old one may be a repulsion type motor and the new one a capacitor type. A higher starting current may call for new wiring.

To replace an internal combustion engine with an electric motor you have to match horsepower rating and speed. The table shows how to match horsepower. A rule of thumb is that an electric motor should be rated at two-thirds to three-fourths the rating of the internal combustion engine. A given motor is available in four or more rpm categories. If none of these match the speed requirements of the equipment, use electronic devices or belts and pulleys.

CONSULT POWER SUPPLIER

Your power supplier has regulations on how much electric demand you can place on single-phase lines. The supplier's representatives can help you determine this amount, plus any improvements needed in the farm electrical system and in the size and type motors best for the job. Often the farm's wiring is too small. Remember that a 10% undervoltage will give a 7-1/2 horse motor the characteristics of a 6.1-horse motor with 21% greater slip and 18% less torque.

Some power companies are beefing up their primary lines so that you can use large motors safely. Many are now permitting 10-horse, single-phase motors on rural lines and some are extending three-phase service or supplying converters to any farmer in their area.

SINGLE-PHASE MOTORS

It isn't the running current or horsepower that limits the size of electric motors, but the short duration starting surge. Most single-phase motors draw five to six times the running current for starting. To overcome this disadvantage, "soft start" motors are coming on the market with only 2-1/2 to 3 times greater current draw for starting, which means you can use motors up to about 40 hp.

Because of low starting current draw, a soft-start motor is designed for operating loads that can be started at no-load or partial load, such as forage blowers, irrigation pumps and dryer fans. Acceleration time is a few seconds longer than with other motors, but it operates as a standard capacitor type single-phase motor at full rated speed. Cost compares with a three-phase rotary transformer converter, up to about 20 hp. Beyond that, the single-phase motor is considerably cheaper. However, more than one motor can be operated from the converter.

The trend in single-phase motors is away from the repulsion type toward capacitor type motors for any load from light to heavy. Repulsion-induction motors (wound rotor and squirrel cage) serve best where the load is heavy and varies widely.

Some are still being used for silo unloaders. While they draw the lowest starting current, a repulsion motor costs more and requires more maintenance because of brush and commutator wear.

Capacitor motors are simple in construction, having no wound rotor or brushes. Current relays, autotransformers and capacitors are used. Capacitors (condensers) are used to provide better starting torque. A second capacitor may be added to the running winding to add more efficiency after starting. These capacitor-start-capacitor-run motors are replacing many of the heavy load jobs of repulsion motors. Use them on barn cleaners, silo unloaders, manure pumps, irrigation, feed augers, and crop dryers. Capacitor motors are designed much like the split-phase motor, but split-phase motors require six to eight times more current for starting than they do at full load. These are the fractional horsepower motors commonly used for building fans and small conveyors.

THREE-PHASE

Instead of a single coil for single-phase, three coils in the armature of a generator allow current to be taken from three points on its periphery, giving you three "kicks" per revolution instead of one—this is three-phase. Because these motors start with such a low amount of current, motor size is limited only by the power supply. They cost less, maintenance is less and life is generally longer than for other motors. Greatest obstacle is getting three-phase service to your farm. Where demand in a farming area is great enough for it, the power companies can provide it economically, but possibly at a higher rate. If you can't take advantage of three-phase power and your horsepower requirements are too great for single-phase motors, a phase converter may be installed.

Phase conversion. A phase converter can change single-phase power to a form that three-phase motors can use. Motors of 75 hp are being used safely with phase converters, with the most popular size about 15. At least a 200 amp service is best for motors of 15 and 25 hp, but it is better to have more, possibly 600. Manufacturer and power company should help select the type converter and adapt it to your operation.

One type is the static converter often used with irrigation pump motors, where motor size will fall between 1 and 60 hp with little variation in size. One method supplies current to a single motor and another can service several motors, but total horsepower in use at one time is limited.

Another type is the rotary transformer, economical for operating several three-phase motors. These units consist of a bank of condensers and a three-phase motor with the shafts cut off so that no load can be attached to it. It serves as the rotating transformer. Motors of varying sizes can be operated from it, so long as the largest doesn't exceed the unit's capacity. A drawback to this type is that it must be running before other motors can be started. This idle time adds to your operating costs and wear on your motor.

MOTOR PROTECTION

Remember that circuit protection will not protect the motor. Some motors have built-in overload protection of the thermal type. They are automatic or manual reset. Other motors can be purchased with thermal protection devices attached for a small cost of around $10. They cut the motor off when it overheats, to protect it from burnout. Time delay fuses are also suitable for motor protection.

SIZE OF TIME DELAY FUSE TO USE

Motor Full Load Running Current (from motor nameplate)	Time Delay Fuse Size	Motor Full Load Running Current (from motor nameplate)	Time Delay Fuse Size
ampere		ampere	
1.81 to 2.25	2.50	7.31 to 9.25	10
2.26 to 3.00	3.20	9.26 to 11.00	12
3.10 to 3.60	4.00	11.10 to 14.00	15
3.61 to 4.00	4.50	14.10 to 18.00	20
4.10 to 4.55	5.00	18.10 to 22.00	25
4.56 to 5.70	6.25	22.10 to 28.00	30
5.71 to 7.30	8.00		

UNIV. OF MN.

Enclosures. The National Electrical Manufacturers Association, NEMA, has standards for correct enclosures for electrical controls which are vitally important to you. In simplified terms, the protective housing for such controls as switches and fuses should comply with NEMA standards when installed. For instance, the enclosure used in a swine building or milking parlor might call for a NEMA Type 4 enclosure which is watertight and dusttight. A NEMA Type 3 would be used outdoors since they are dusttight, raintight and sleet resistant. Enclosures will protect your controls.

Chapter 12

Water and Irrigation Management

The water system is a permanent and important part of any well-planned farm operation. Management problems may be classified into two broad groups: The control of water or drainage, and water supply and use.

Develop a drainage system that will effectively handle your problem. Don't think this problem will take care of itself. A properly developed system can increase crop yields, eliminate wet spots, reduce erosion and improve labor use.

There are two major types of water control—surface and sub-surface drainage. Each type has advantages in certain situations. Surface drainage systems may make use of several types of land forming. These types include terraces, diversion ditches, waterways, open ditches and dams. Sub-surface systems make use of tiling and mole drains.

Plan the water supply to allow for the needs of the home, livestock, miscellaneous farm uses (cleaning and general sanitation), supplemental or complete irrigation and fire protection. Water requirements should be based on needs during years of low rainfall rather than average years. Tables of daily home and livestock needs, as well as crop irrigation requirements, can be used as a guide.

Wells, reservoirs, lakes or ponds, and streams are all possible sources for water. These sources will vary from area to area. When choosing or developing the source, consideration should be given to requirements, reliability, periods of the year when needs are greatest, and where the water is to be used. It is important to consider how far water must be transported from source to point of use. Remember, the greatest water demands are usually during the periods when supplies are lowest.

The water supply for the home, and to a lesser degree for livestock, should be checked by health authorities to make sure it is safe. Steps should be taken to prevent contamination and pollution. Locate the water source to avoid these problems as much as possible.

Surface waters may contain three types of contaminants—undissolved solids, dissolved elements, and bacteria. Undissolved solids can usually be removed by proper treatment and filtration. Objectionable or harmful dissolved chemicals can sometimes be removed by chemical reaction, filtration, oxidation or a combination of these. Bacterially contaminated water can often be purified by chemical treatment. The types and amounts of undesirable or objectionable materials present determine the type and amount of treatment involved.

Water treatment consists of three basic steps. These steps are: Sedimentation to remove many of the undissolved solids; filtration to remove the remaining undissolved solids; and purification to kill harmful bacteria. In addition, some water may contain substances requiring additional treatment facilities or processes.

Irrigation is being practiced by an increasing number of farmers to eliminate moisture shortages during the growing season. However, an irrigation system will not necessarily assure that the user will profit from its use by protecting his crops from drouth and increasing his yields. Before any system is installed, some solid answers to the following five questions are needed:
- Will it pay me to irrigate?
- How much water will it take?
- Where will the water come from?
- What are the labor requirements?
- Which system is best?

Irrigation systems can be classified into three basic types.

Sprinkler systems:
- Multi-sprinkler (hand moved, tractor moved, self-moved, self-propelled)
- Single-sprinkler (hand moved, tractor moved, self-propelled)
- Boom-sprinkler (tractor moved, self-propelled)
- Solid-set

Surface systems:
- Level-systems (level border, contour levee, level furrow)
- Graded-systems (graded border, contour ditch, graded furrow, corrugation, contour furrow)

Subsurface systems:
- Open ditch
- Underground conduit.

Selection of an irrigation system must be based on many factors including cost, water supply and the land to be irrigated. There are certain situations which rule out the choice of some systems. These include the following:
- A thin soil over an impermeable subsoil requires a sprinkler system. It would be impossible to level the land without cutting away much of the top soil.
- Very sandy soils require sprinkler irrigation so the amount of water applied can be closely matched to the intake rate of the soil.
- Excessive slopes, over 2%, do not lend themselves to gravity or surface irrigation.
- A limited water supply gives a slight advantage to a sprinkler system in most cases. However, a reuse reservoir can improve the efficiency of a surface system.
- Limited labor supply usually shifts the advantage to one of the more mechanized sprinkler systems.

Extra time in working out a well-designed system will be profitable. As in surface drainage, land forming to prepare fields for water control and to facilitate further mechanization is important. Irrigation should not be installed merely as insurance against drouth. The costs are too high. To really pay off it should be used whenever soil water content is not high enough for maximum crop production.

A complete water system should be planned so all parts fit together, work together and contribute toward a desired goal. The costs involved in the development or improvement of a farm water system must not be overlooked. Questions to ask are—will the costs of carrying out the proposed plan be balanced by increased production and efficiency? Will it lead to better living?

Farm Water Systems

An efficient water system is an important element in any farming operation.
It should be clean, convenient, and be able to supply enough water for future needs.

A water system is inadequate when two or more faucets are turned on and the pressure drops; the pump runs continuously; or animals have to wait for water.

Figure your water needs in gallons per day. Increase this total 25% to 50% for future demands. Your water system should be capable of producing one-half this amount per hour so that the pump does not run more than one to three hours per day.

WHICH TYPE PUMP?

Two types fulfill most farm requirements, the submersible and the jet pump. Most popular is the submersible pump.

Submersible pumps. For shallow or deep wells, it has become the favorite for farm water systems. Although more expensive, submersible pumps have significant advantages. They require little or no maintenance and there's no pump house to build. Motor, centrifugal pump and impellers are enclosed in a unit that fits down inside the well casing several feet below water drawdown level.

SUBMERSIBLE PUMPS		
HP*	Lift** Feet	Gallons Per Hour
1/4	20	420
	100	200
1/2	20	520
	280	110
1	20	1,630
	500	210
5	40	5,100
	440	840
10	40	7,500
	440	2,280
15	120	9,480
	760	2,040
20	160	9,600
	1,000	2,160
40	28	38,100
	2,308	1,980

*Pumps available at horsepower sizes between those listed.
**Approximate range. Does not include friction and valve loss.

Enough stages are built in to generate the required head feet. Stages are keyed to the pump shaft and consist of impellers and diffusers. Submersible pumps require a well diameter of at least four inches. They push the water up and make no noise, even sizes over 300 hp. Magnetic starters are often supplied for submersible pumps with three-phase motors. If phase converters are used to obtain three-phase power supply, the manufacturer may not extend warranty on the pump.

Jet pumps. A jet pump can be located away from the well to eliminate the need for a pump house or pit. They are easy to service and installation costs are low, especially in high water tables or shallow wells. You can get jet pumps that are convertible from shallow to deep wells.

There are two basic styles of jet pumps, the horizontal and the vertical. These are further divided into shallow well and deep well variations.

A shallow well pump has one suction pipe, not exceeding 25 feet, since this is the maximum depth at which you can depend on atmospheric pressure to force water to the pump. For deeper wells, a second pipe returns a portion of the water to an injector in the well creating a velocity that carries the water up to the pump impeller. In shallow well jet pumps, the injector is located at the entrance to the impeller. The vertical type can fit directly over the well head and may incorporate several impeller stages for increased capacity.

CONVERTIBLE SINGLE STAGE JET PUMPS*				
	Shallow Well		Deep Well	
HP	Lift Feet	Gallons Per Hour	Lift Feet	Gallons Per Hour
1/2	15	570	30	795
			130	150
3/4	15	875	30	990
			170	100
1	15	1,350	30	1,140
			170	110
1-1/2	15	1,850	30	1,620
			170	260

*Discharge pressure approximately 40 psi for all pumps except deep well 1/2 and 3/4 hp at 30 psi.

LIFTING POWER

The vertical distance from well drawdown level to the pump and the pressure desired at the outlet are the two main factors needed in determining "total head." Manufacturers normally indicate the GPH (gallons per hour) or GPM (gallons per minute) their pumps can produce at various pumping distances and discharge pressures.

Total head is expressed in feet. Pressure (psi) can be converted to feet by multiplying by 2.31. A pressure of 40 psi is equivalent to 92 feet. A vertical lift of 100 feet plus 92 feet makes a total head of 192 feet. Loss of pressure due to friction of water flowing through pipe and fittings also adds to the total head, but if pipes are sized properly the loss is negligible. Pump lift capacity is usually stated for sea level. Reduce this by one foot for each 1,000 feet of elevation.

FARM WATER REQUIREMENTS

	Gal./Day
Beef steer or cow	1-1/2/100 lbs. wt.
Sheep	2/sheep
Horse	10-15/horse
Sows	4-5/hog
Market hogs	2/hog
Cleaning	1/hog
Liquid feeding	1-2/hog
Liquid manure	1/4-1/hog
Milk cow (drinking)	35/cow
Dry cow	15/cow
Calf	12/cow
Cow washer	10/cow
Hosing floors	15/100 sq. ft.
Liquid manure	3/cow
Cleaning milk equipment	2/cow
Livestock waterers	5 gal./min.
Chickens (drinking)	5/100 birds
Turkeys (drinking)	18/100 birds
Cleaning cages and pens	2/100 birds

HOME WATER REQUIREMENTS

Each person for all purposes	50 gal.
Automatic washer	30-50/load
Dishwasher	5-15/load
Shower or tub	20-50/ea.
Hose and nozzle	200-300 gph
Lawn sprinkler	120 gph

Outlet pressure. New water systems should have at least an average of 40 psi. Livestock operations often need more for cleaning. In this case, a booster pump can be installed for pressures upward of 75 psi.

PRESSURE TANKS

A pressure tank will eliminate frequent pump starting and stopping, save electricity and pump wear. It also holds a reserve supply of water for a limited time and eliminates water hammer. Many pressure tanks have a cushion of air under pressure over the water. The amount of water and air gets out of balance and waterlogging results.

To keep the proper balance, several types of automatic air devices are used. One is a disk or diaphragm separating the air and water inside the tank. They can be installed in existing tanks, and most new tanks have them. Submersible pumps may have air drawn into the discharge pipe through a snifter valve when the pump stops. Air is forced into the pressure tank when the pump starts and an air unloader takes care of excess exhausts.

PRESSURE TANKS

Tank Size, Gal.	GPH at 40 psi*
42	340
82	660
120	970
220	1,760
315	2,550
525	4,260
1,000	8,100

*GPH (gallons per hour) capacity at average pressure of 40 psi.

Another type, called the Hydrocel, eliminates the need for air volume controls. They can be used with any type pump and can be placed anywhere on the pump discharge line. They have no need for air. An elastic cell inside a small steel tank expands as water is pumped into it, placing water under pressure similar to air in a balloon.

WATER SYSTEM PROBLEMS

Check your system for these deficiencies:

1. Well too shallow. A deeper well may be all that's needed.

2. Well casing too small. A large pump on a small diameter well limits output. Well diameter should be at least four inches.

3. Pump too small. Compare output of your present pump against current water needs.

4. Distribution pipes too small. If you have adequate pressure at the pump but insufficient pressure at distant points, run a larger line. Never install a distribution line of less than 1-1/4 inch steel pipe or its equivalent.

5. Pump worn out or needs repair. Often only the well screen needs cleaning, or valves and jets are plugged.

Always consult your local Department of Public Health for regulations. If you store or prepare chemicals or fertilizers any closer than 150 feet from the well, contamination can result.

Source of Contamination	Minimum Distance (feet)
Waste disposal lagoons	300
Cesspools	150
Livestock and poultry yards	100
Privies, manure piles	100
Silo pits, seepage pits	150
Milkhouse drain outlets	100
Septic tanks and disposal fields	100
Gravity sewer or drain not pressure tight	50
Pressure-tight gravity sewer or drain	25

Planning an Irrigation System

Determine the irrigation capacity required of your irrigation system, then choose equipment to efficiently deliver the water to your crops.

Understanding the requirements for an efficient irrigation system can be helpful when working with an irrigation engineer in sizing up and designing a system. Careful planning of a total irrigation system can eliminate many of the unnecessary and costly problems which may rise from piecemeal or poorly designed systems. Some of these problems may include failure to meet crop moisture needs during critical periods, mismatched pumps and power units and excessive power costs.

Select and design a system that will fulfill the following objectives:

● System meets the moisture needs of the crop while being suited to the soils and topography of the farm.

● Pump efficiently delivers the required amount of water at the necessary pressure.

● Power unit is sufficiently large to deliver enough power under all conditions of pumping.

Even though the initial installation may be for a field or two, the entire farm must be considered with the idea that expansion in later years is likely.

DETERMINING WATER REQUIREMENTS

A common mistake is trying to cover too much land with too little water. This limits the effectiveness and returns from any system. Soil, crops to be grown, and area of the country all need to be considered when projecting water requirements.

APPROXIMATE AMOUNTS OF WATER HELD BY DIFFERENT SOILS

Soil Texture	Inches of water held per ft. of soil	Max. rate of irrigation Inches per hr. bare soil
Sand	0.5-0.7	.75
Fine sand	0.7-0.9	.60
Loamy sand	0.7-1.1	.50
Loamy fine sand	0.8-1.2	.45
Sandy loam	0.8-1.4	.40
Loam	1.0-1.8	.35
Silt loam	1.2-1.8	.30
Clay loam	1.3-2.1	.25
Silty clay	1.4-2.5	.20
Clay	1.4-2.4	.15

Soils vary widely in water-holding capacity, along with the maximum amount of water they can absorb in an hour. Likewise, each crop has a specific water requirement within a given climate. Almost all states have some information available on the daily peak crop water use rates by various soil groups. Knowing this and the acreage to be irrigated, you can determine the necessary water supply and allow for an acceptable amount of water loss in any system. On the average, daily crop moisture consumption ranges from 0.1 to 0.3 inches.

The system should be designed to properly apply and distribute an adequate supply of water. The following requirements should be met as closely as possible: (1) Peak moisture needs of the crop must be met and applied at a given rate over a specified time; (2) application rate must be kept within bounds so runoff is avoided; and (3) proper nozzle size and spacing must be selected to assure uniform water application.

Soil influences both the amount of water that can be applied at one irrigation and the frequency. Together, these factors determine water supply necessary for delivering the proper amount for any one irrigation. The smaller a soil's capacity to hold water, the lower the rate should be, and the more often water must be applied. Maximum rate is further established by soil absorption rate or amount of water that can be applied without runoff.

Dependable water supply cannot be based on average requirements since the supply would be adequate only about half the time. Consequently, water needs are usually estimated on the basis of probability. High value crops may justify a water supply which is adequate 9 years out of 10. On the other hand, it may not be economical to provide an adequate supply of water for low-value crops in more than 5 of 10 years.

Where the water source will be a well, geologic maps and information about rock formation will provide an approximate idea of its water supplying capacity. It is advisable to sink a test well to eliminate any guesswork. Reservoirs can provide adequate supplies, but since they have little or no inflow during the irrigation period, they should be large enough to store all the water required, plus an allowance for losses from evaporation and seepage. Farm ponds are usually too small. Only about half the water is available for irrigation—you need to have 1.5 to 2.0 acre-feet of water for every acre you intend to irrigate. The problem with relying on small streams and ditches is that these are at their lowest during the dry period when irrigation needs are highest.

Required rate of delivery for the water supply source can be calculated by the following equation:

$$Q = \frac{453 \, Ad}{FH}$$

Q = rate of delivery in gallons per minute
A = acreage of design area
d = gross depth of application in acre-inches per acre
F = number of days allowed for completion of one irrigation
H = number of actual operating hours per day

PUMP AND POWER REQUIREMENTS

Nebraska irrigation engineers report that some irrigation pumping plants use two to three times as much fuel as they should because of poor engineering. Maximum water output and minimum fuel requirements are obtained only when the engine drive, pump and water distribution systems are matched.

Pump horsepower output, or water horsepower, must be matched to the amount of water to be pumped, required lift (means drawdown or pumping level of a well must be known), pressure loss in the lines and pressure at the nozzles. A formula for determining pump horsepower and selecting a pump is outlined by Missouri agricultural engineers.

$$whp = \frac{gpm \times tdh}{3960}$$

whp = water horsepower output
gpm = gallons per minute discharge from the pump
tdh = total dynamic head (total pressure) in feet of water

Total dynamic head (feet) may be determined by adding the following: Difference in elevation from source of supply to point of discharge, friction loss in pipe and fittings, and discharge pressure.

Brake horsepower is the power required by the pump on a continuous basis and is figured using the following formula.

$$\text{Brake Horsepower} = \frac{\text{Water Horsepower}}{\text{Pump Efficiency} \times \text{Drive Efficiency}}$$

Use a pumping efficiency of 75% for new units or existing pumps in good adjustment. Drive efficiency for belts or gears is approximately 95%.

Rating curves that describe operating characteristics of pumps aid in selecting a pump that is efficient within the desired operating range.

Power units, whether electric motors or internal combustion engines, are rated differently. Electric motors are rated by continuous (brake) horsepower. Internal combustion engines normally have SAE ratings—the bare engine is tested for a short period under cool conditions and adjusted to sea level. Use the following table to determine the size of engine needed. If a farm tractor will be used, the horsepower required by the pump should not exceed 75% of the maximum belt or pto horsepower output of new tractors or those having engines in excellent condition; 50% or lower for tractor engines in only fair condition.

HORSEPOWER RATING ADJUSTMENT OF AN ENGINE CONSIDERED FOR IRRIGATION PUMPING

Condition	Divide horsepower required by the pump (bhp) by:
Engine Accessories	.85
Maximum air temperature (degrees)	
110	.95
100	.96
90	.97
Elevation above sea level (feet)	
250	.99
500	.98
1,000	.97
2,000	.94
Continuous service	.80

The nameplate output of an electric motor should be closely matched to the power requirement of the pump when a direct connected drive is used. Allow for motor efficiency of about 90%. If other pump drives are used, then the drive loss should be considered. An oversized electric motor adds to the original investment and does not save on operating costs.

Developing Irrigation Water Sources

A water supply's adequacy and dependability must be assessed before planning an irrigation system.

Whether ground or surface water is used for irrigating, the source must be dependable and the quality of water suitable for this purpose. Without these prerequisites, investment in an irrigation system could be easily jeopardized.

DEEP WELLS

Use of a geologic map and information on the rock formation and water-supplying power of an acquifer, along with logs from wells in your area can provide a good idea of the output which might be expected from a well drilled on your farm. However, it is suggested that a test well be drilled to eliminate the guesswork.

The water bearing characteristics of the formation can accurately be logged by using a test well. Samples should be taken every five feet or so to determine the depth and thickness of each stratum. Further, the nature and size of particles can be examined to aid in well construction.

A test well or wells serve a number of purposes. Besides determining the presence of water, drillers can usually get a good indication of the best location for a well. You also get a good idea of the necessary depth of a well, and can fairly accurately determine whether the water can be developed for your planned irrigation program.

Selecting a reliable well drilling contractor is a must. Since the location, design, construction and development of a well all depend on the results of test drilling, it is advisable that the well contract not be written or agreed upon until information has been collected and analyzed from the test drilling. It may be desirable to have separate contracts for test drilling and for the well.

A contract should detail how the well will be constructed and give an itemized estimate of each appropriate item which will be included in the construction of the well through its completion. Don't automatically accept the lowest bidder, since there are many ways of constructing a cheap well that may not be detected for some time. The efficiency of a gravel pack well hinges in large measure on its construction and development. The flow of water from the acquifer through the intake portion of the well and into the casing should be as unrestricted as possible. This is especially important when the potential yield of the acquifer is about the same to only slightly more than the desired discharge. This means that much attention should be given to well screens and the gravel pack.

The development phase which follows drilling is especially critical. A poor job of developing a well may reduce its capacity by as much as 50%, as well as shorten its useful life.

Well development is basically a cleaning process that follows drilling and it assures that the well produces at its maximum designed capacity. A test pump is used to pump water back and forth through the screen, filter pack and formation around the borehole to remove drilling fluid and other material which may restrict water flow. Pumping starts slowly and the rate is gradually increased until maximum capacity, or a capacity that's about 20% greater than the anticipated use rate is reached. Once developed, the well is tested for output and drawdown characteristics using various discharge rates, ranging from 20% above to 20% below the maximum anticipated use.

Pump selection and design for your system cannot be made until after the well has been developed and tested. The pump must be matched to the amount of water to be pumped, the required lift (which means you must know the drawdown or pumping level of the well), the pressure loss in lines and the pressure at the nozzles.

	QUANTITY OF WATER IN GALLONS PER MINUTE REQUIRED TO IRRIGATE A GIVEN ACREAGE						
Acres to Be Irrigated	Hours of Pumping per Day						
	10	12	14	16	18	20	22
10	170	140	120	105	95	85	75
20	335	280	240	210	190	170	155
30	505	420	360	315	280	255	230
40	675	560	480	420	375	335	305
50	840	700	600	525	465	420	380
60	1,010	840	720	630	560	505	460
80	1,435	1,120	960	840	750	675	610
100	1,680	1,400	1,200	1,050	935	840	765
120	2,015	1,680	1,440	1,260	1,120	1,010	915
150	2,520	2,100	1,800	1,575	1,400	1,260	1,145
200	3,360	2,800	2,400	2,100	1,870	1,680	1,525

SOUTH DAKOTA

Every pump manufactured has a certain rate and pressure head at which it operates most efficiently. Where possible, select a pump that will operate at 80% to 85% efficiency. Performance curves are available for every pump.

Given in the table is water capacity per minute required to irrigate given acreages of crops with daily water requirements falling between 0.2 and 0.3 inch per day. It assumes a 70% efficiency.

SURFACE WATER

Even in areas with a reasonably dependable high level of rainfall, operators are looking for ways to eliminate the severe losses that can occur during short periods of dry weather. In the absence of significant underground water reservoirs or rivers with sufficient flow to meet irrigation needs, the other alternative is to design a supplemental irrigation system around a limited water supply such as a small lake, farm pond, intermittent stream, reservoir or shallow, low yielding wells.

Individual, detailed analysis will be necessary to determine whether it is worthwhile to develop supplemental irrigation from restricted water resources. There are wide differences from one farm to the next in the amount of water that can be developed, the acreage that can be covered, and the type of distribution system which may be most desirable. You need to assess your own situation to determine if water development and installation of a system will be feasible.

Acreage irrigable from surface reservoirs, such as lakes or ponds, depends on the surface area and depth and, over time, the refill rate from the drainage area. For supplemental irrigation, you should rely only on the measured capacity through the summer.

In most areas where supplemental irrigation will be practiced, four to five inches will be enough to complement natural rainfall through the summer months even in an unusually dry year.

When estimating reservoir capacity, figure that only about half the water therein will be available for irrigation. Assume a pond with a surface area of one acre and an average depth of eight feet of usable water. This gives a total of 96 acre inches, of which about 50 inches will be available for irrigation. If the water requirement exceeds rainfall by four acre inches, this reservoir would irrigate only about 12 acres.

Irrigating with low yield wells has real potential, especially if several units can be hooked in a series with one pump. Another alternative is shown.

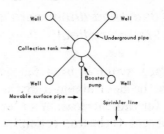

This system pumps from each well into a single collection point. Water is picked up by a booster pump and applied through a sprinkler system. The booster pump would not be necessary if a gravity distribution system were part of the design. However, gravity flow distribution systems aren't well adapted to supplemental irrigation.

The central collect system works best if each well produces 75 to 150 gallons per minute. Four wells of this capacity would allow pumping at the rate of about 450 gallons per minute to the distribution system. This is significant because 450 gpm equals one acre inch each hour of operation. With 20 hours of continuous operation, you could put a one-inch application on 20 acres or cover 100 acres in five days.

Intermittent streams are not reliable sources of water for full-scale or even supplemental irrigation. The majority of states in the Midwest and South are ruled by "riparian" rights. This means a landowner can use water flowing by or through his land for domestic use and domestic animals. Water can also be diverted for "beneficial use" such as irrigation. However, downstream landowners have the same rights and are entitled to have the water flow to them "basically undiminished."

If there is a plentiful stream flow, no particular problem may develop. But when you need the water, an "intermittent" stream will likely be low. If you diverted water for irrigation and it did materially diminish downstream neighbors' water, they could legally stop you from pumping.

In some instances it may be feasible to divert flow from such streams into off-stream reservoirs in the spring. This could be a means of creating a much larger pond than your natural drainage would supply. Frequently such streams have thin water bearing layers out from the stream itself. This is also a potential source for a series of small wells. Even wells that yield only 15 gallons per minute can be used to pump into surface reservoirs. This size flow will produce 24 acre feet of water on a year-round basis.

Irrigation Water Measurements

Correct application of irrigation water is of the utmost importance. Under-irrigating or over-irrigating can severely affect income and erosion control.

The following information is required to calculate the capacities of wells in terms of acreage, reservoir capacities and other facets of irrigation water movement. Obtain competent technical consultation when you develop an irrigation system. Technicians will use the same data given here, but the importance of correct system design cannot be overemphasized. It's too important, and redesign too costly, for you to gamble on making personal errors. This information is primarily intended for your use in cross-checking and for estimates of irrigation potential on your farm.

UNITS OF WATER MEASUREMENT

There are two units used in measuring water—volume and flow rates. The following are the basic units you'll be concerned with:

- 1 acre-inch = 27,154 gallons or 3,630 cubic feet water. This is the amount of water required to cover 1 acre to a depth of 1 inch.
- 1 acre-foot = 325,850 gallons or 43,560 cubic feet of water
- 1 cubic foot = 7.48 gallons or 1,728 cubic inches or 62.37 pounds of water
- 1 cubic foot per second = 448.8 gallons per minute
- 450 gpm = 1 acre-inch per hour (approximate)
- GPM x 0.002228 = cubic feet per second
- $\frac{\text{Pump discharge in gpm}}{450}$ = acre-inches per hour
- $\frac{\text{Total acre-inches pumped}}{\text{No. acres covered}}$ = average depth applied in inches

The above equivalents are used to measure water flow from wells, streams and small pipes. Some of this information has been put into graphic form. The graph on the right converts flow in gallons per minute to acre-inches per hour.

Irrigation efficiency must be considered when making irrigation calculations. This is the amount of water that reaches the root zone stated as a percentage of total water pumped. Losses from evaporation, deep percolation and runoff can be quite high.

There's no exact formula for determining a field efficiency that will work in every instance. Field layout and overall system capacity will alter this from one operation to the next. One of the best approaches is to run tests and determine how much water you must apply to get the necessary quantity of water into the root zone area of your soil. Compare this with the amount of moisture in your soil, using information on water penetration depths and water holding capacities for your particular soil types.

A 75% field efficiency is a practical goal. This means that to get three inches of soil moisture, you must apply four inches of water. Irrigation efficiency must be included in any calculation used to determine the pumping time required to irrigate a field or the capability of the water source in terms of acreage.

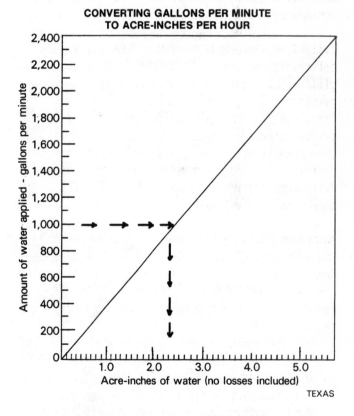

CONVERTING GALLONS PER MINUTE TO ACRE-INCHES PER HOUR

Amount of water applied - gallons per minute (vertical axis): 0, 200, 400, 600, 800, 1,000, 1,200, 1,400, 1,600, 1,800, 2,000, 2,200, 2,400

Acre-inches of water (no losses included) (horizontal axis): 1.0, 2.0, 3.0, 4.0, 5.0

TEXAS

MEASURING PIPE DISCHARGE

Flow discharged through pipes can be meter measured. This is recommended, if it is important that you obtain an exact measurement. The illustration on the next page shows how to take approximate measurements on pipe flows.

303

The top three figures in the illustration show how to measure flow from full pipes, while the bottom figure shows where to measure on a pipe flowing partially full.

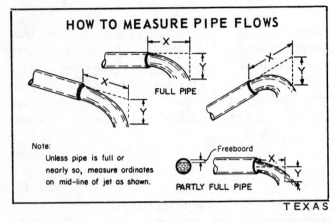

The first table below shows the usual water output in gallons per minute, with a fairly normal vertical distance of 13 inches.

DISCHARGE FROM PIPES FLOWING FULL
In Gallons Per Minute with Vertical Drop "Y" = 13 inches

Pipe Size		Horizontal Distance "X"						
Inside Dia.	Sq. In. Area	12"	14"	16"	18"	20"	22"	24"
2"	3.14	38	44	50	57	63	69	75
2½"	4.91	59	69	79	88	98	108	118
3"	7.07	85	99	113	127	141	156	170
4"	12.57	151	176	201	226	251	277	302
5"	19.64	236	275	314	354	393	432	471
6"	28.27	339	396	452	509	565	622	678
7"	38.48	462	539	616	693	770	847	924
8"	50.27	603	704	804	905	1,005	1,106	1,206
9"	63,62	763	891	1,018	1,145	1,272	1,400	1,527
10"	78.54	942	1,100	1,257	1,414	1,571	1,728	1,885
11"	95.03	1,140	1,330	1,520	1,711	1,901	2,091	2,281
12"	113.10	1,357	1,583	1,809	2,036	2,262	2,488	2,714

NEW MEXICO

APPROXIMATE FLOW FROM PARTIALLY FULL PIPE
Rate of Flow in Gallons Per Minute

Y	Inside Diameter of Pipe "D" in Inches				
D	4	6	8	10	12
0.1	142	334	579	912	1,310
0.2	128	302	524	825	1,185
0.3	112	264	457	720	1,034
0.4	94	222	384	605	868
0.5	75	176	305	480	689
0.6	55	130	226	355	510
0.7	37	88	152	240	345
0.8	21	49	85	134	194
0.9	8	17	30	52	74
1.0	0	0	0	0	0

NEW MEXICO

Flow from partially full pipes is not large. The second table shows approximate discharge from partially filled pipes. "Y" in this instance is measured on the mid-line of the jet of water as illustrated.

DETERMINING IRRIGATION POTENTIAL

Only so many acres can be irrigated from a given water supply. This will be more restricted than you might think, if crops have high and frequent water requirements.

The following formula is used to determine acreage that can be irrigated from a known flow rate of water:

$$A = \frac{GPM \times H \times D \times 60 \times E}{27,154 \times X}$$

A = Acres to be irrigated

GPM = Gallons of water per minute

H = Hours of operation per day

D = Days required to cover

60 = 60 minutes per hour

E = Irrigation efficiency

27,154 = Gallons in 1 acre-inch

X = Inches of water to be supplied

Here's an example of how this formula would work with a 1,000 gpm well, a 10-hour operating day, a 10-day requirement on coverage, 70% efficiency and a 3 acre-inch requirement.

$$A = \frac{1,000 \times 10 \times 10 \times 60 .70}{27,154 \times 3}$$

A = 51.56 acres

Using the same basic data and rearranging the formula you can determine the gallons per minute required to irrigate a given acreage. Consider the gpm requirement for 100 acres under the same time, efficiency and water conditions as those given above.

$$GPM = \frac{27,154 \times X \times A}{H \times D \times 60 \times E} = \frac{27,154 \times 3 \times 100}{10 \times 10 \times 60 \times .70} =$$

1,940 gpm required to irrigate 100 acres

Channel flow in ditches is best measured by a flow meter, though weirs are commonly used. Many different style weirs are available commercially.

Irrigation Scheduling

When you use a well-designed irrigation system, your success as an irrigator depends on how accurately you determine when to irrigate and how much water to apply.

Sufficiently good guides are now available to reduce the guesswork which formerly accompanied irrigating by the calendar or according to fixed rotation schedules.

Irrigating when soil moisture is adequate costs money, fuel, labor and time. It also may leach nutrients from the root zone, is wasteful of water and may result in soil erosion. Conversely, excessive delays in irrigating can reduce yields as much as 25% to 50%.

Effective management of irrigation water hinges on knowing how much water a soil can store and understanding how this amount can vary with changing soil and cropping conditions.

Water-holding capacity of a soil is the amount of water that can be held which is available for crop use. It is that amount of water stored within the limits of field capacity and the wilting point.

Field capacity is the maximum amount of water left in a soil after it has fully drained. The wilting point is the point at which the plant can no longer obtain enough moisture to supply its needs. Thus, the prime objective of irrigation is to maintain soil moisture within these limits.

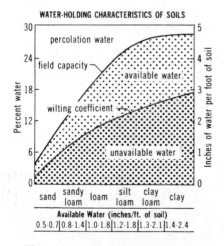

WATER-HOLDING CHARACTERISTICS OF SOILS

| Available Water (inches/ft. of soil) |
| 0.5-0.7 | 0.8-1.4 | 1.0-1.8 | 1.2-1.8 | 1.3-2.1 | 1.4-2.4 |

The amount of available water that can be stored in a soil at a given time depends on soil type and rate of water use by the crop. On fine textured soils, for instance, excess water may drain over a period of 25 days or so. In more humid areas, irrigating beyond field capacity becomes more risky, since there is the chance of rainfall.

During a crop's peak water use period it is possible to apply water in excess of field capacity on fine textured soils. Chances of water being lost through drainage is reduced with the crop rapidly taking up moisture. On shallow, fine textured soils, this may be enough extra moisture to stretch the time between irrigations by a day or two.

Water intake rate of various soils needs to be taken into account when scheduling irrigations. Fine textured soils take up water much less rapidly than coarse soils, so a longer irrigation time is required on fine textured soil to apply a given amount of water. Suggested maximum rate of irrigation on bare soils ranges from .75 inch per hour for sandy soil to .15 inch for clay. However, if a sod or mulch is present, the intake rate may be four times greater than for bare soils.

Intake rate of a soil may be high at the outset, then decline as the soil becomes wet. Applying water at a rate faster than the soil can take it up results in soil compaction, puddling, erosion, and runoff.

The active root zones of crops provide a guide for determining the amount of water to apply per irrigation. The active root zone depends on the crop, the depth of the soil and the stage of growth.

The sketch shows the effective or active rooting depth of a crop. Notice that the upper half of the root zone takes up about 70% of the water requirements of the crop. Soil depth, in some instances, may determine the active root zone. Soils that have less than six feet of loamy sand, finer textured soils overlying sand and gravel, or an impermeable layer, limit the potential root zone of the deeper rooting crops.

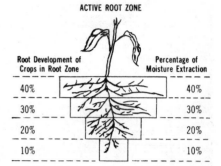

ACTIVE ROOT ZONE

Root Development of Crops in Root Zone		Percentage of Moisture Extraction
40%		40%
30%		30%
20%		20%
10%		10%

Given in the table are the potential and active root zones for various crops when root development is not restricted.

ROOT ZONES OF VARIOUS CROPS

Crop	Potential Root Zone (Inches)	Active Root Zone (Inches)
Corn Sorghum Alfalfa Tomatoes Wheat	72 or greater	48
Sugarbeets Soybeans Field beans Potatoes	60	36
Pasture	36	24
Onions Blue grass lawns	24	18

Evapotranspiration or consumptive water use is another important phase of soil moisture evaluation. It is that quantity of water removed from the root zone of a soil over a given period of time. It includes moisture used by the crop (transpiration) and that lost through evaporation. Rate of use varies widely with the crop grown, time of season, climate, amount of cloud cover, percent of crop cover, wind movement, temperature, etc.

An example of evapotranspiration and how it varies over a season and with weather conditions is shown in the following table. The rates given apply to cabbage, sweet corn, field corn, popcorn, potatoes, snap beans, soybeans, sugarbeets, and tomatoes grown in Ohio. If you are not familiar with the evapotranspiration rate for a given crop in your area, check with your county extension service advisor or Soil Conservation Service. For a given crop, the rate can vary widely from that shown, particularly in arid regions.

EVAPOTRANSPIRATION (Inches Per Day)

| | Weather (Hours of Sunshine) | | |
Dates	Cloudy (0-3)	Normal (4-10)	Bright (11-15)
Apr. 15-30	.05	.07	.09
May 1-14	.07	.09	.12
May 15-31	.09	.12	.15
June 1-14	.11	.14	.18
June 15-30	.14	.17	.21
July 1-14	.15	.20	.24
July 15-31	.16	.20	.25
Aug. 1-14	.15	.19	.24
Aug. 15-31	.13	.17	.21
Sept. 1-14	.11	.14	.18

Decision to irrigate hinges on understanding the relationship between soil water holding capacity and crop use if a method other than that of applying water at predetermined stages of crop growth is used.

The most common rule is to irrigate when about 50% of the available water in the root zone has been used. This takes into account the fact that rate of water use by a crop goes down as the soil water content nears the permanent wilting point. Yield is usually reduced when the crop is stressed during critical growth stages. This rule should be adjusted for soil type and the overall capacity of your system.

Coarse textured soils hold less water than fine ones, but readily release the water to plants over most of the available range. The soil suction remains relatively low until 65% to 80% of the water has been used. On these soils, the grower's main problem is to maintain moisture reserve in case his pump or irrigation equipment fails. This means irrigating when no more than 50% to 60% of the available moisture has been used. Some irrigation specialists recommend applying water when only 35% of available water has been used to provide a wider safety margin.

On finer soils, 60% or more of available water can be depleted, but it is not desirable to go beyond 1.2 to 1.5 bars of soil suction at the 18 inch depth during peak water use. When crop use drops off toward the end of the season, soil suction can be permitted to go higher without causing problems.

A concept known as programmed soil moisture depletion is a departure from the practice of maintaining soil moisture at the levels discussed. The plan is to deplete available soil moisture gradually as the growing season progresses. Irrigation is started when the soil moisture deficit is about one to two inches greater than the amount to be applied. The allowable deficit gradually increases to about 60% to 80% of capacity by the end of the season. The root zone is never completely refilled. Rather, a minimum one to two inch deficit is maintained to allow room for rainfall which might otherwise be wasted.

Resistance blocks, when installed and used properly, are good tools for determining soil moisture. Electrical resistance blocks should be installed early enough in the growing season so crop roots will grow down around them. Place them so they will not interfere with cultivation. Start the hole in the crop row and slope it at about a 60° angle toward the furrow. Backfill the hole with the same texture soil as that in which the block is placed. Make sure the hole is well filled and packed to exclude air. Suggested block placement depths at each station are given in the table for several crops.

SOIL MOISTURE BLOCK DEPTH

Crop	Shallow (1st irr.)	Medium (Other irr.)	Deep
Corn	12"	18"	36"
Grain sorghum	12"	18"	36"
Alfalfa	12"	18"	36"
Soybeans	6"	12"	24"
Sugarbeets	6"	12"	24"
Field beans	6"	12"	24"
Potatoes	6"	12"	24"
Pasture	6"	12"	18"

Approximately four stations should be located about the field. With surface irrigation, place the stations far enough from the ends of the field so they are not influenced by the supply ditch on the upper end or poor drainage on the lower end. With sprinkler irrigation, don't place a station under a point of discharge from a head or in the way of a moving wheel.

Meter readings should be made and recorded about every five days early in the growing season and every three days during the critical growing period. Suggested meter readings at which irrigation should be started are listed below.

The shallow block reading is used to determine when to irrigate the first time. After that, the roots will have penetrated so that the 12 to 18 inch block is used to determine other irrigations. The deep block can be used to monitor root activity as well as depth of irrigation water penetration.

READING FOR FIRST IRRIGATION

| | Shallow Block | | |
Soil Texture	Delmhorst Meter	Bouyoucos Meter	Bars of Tension
Loamy sands and sandy loam	135	80	0.65
Very fine sandy loams and silt loams	120	60	0.85
Clay loams and silty clay loam	80	35	1.2

Field use of electrical resistance blocks requires that special attention be given to a number of details to assure that the readings recorded by the meter accurately reflect the soil's true moisture situation. Here are some tips given by Nebraska irrigation specialists:

● Use average reading to determine soil moisture condition. Discard a reading that is definitely wrong.

● Keep a running record for the entire irrigation season.

● Make adjustments in the hours per irrigation set if poor distribution occurs from upper to lower end of irrigation run in surface irrigated fields.

● Walk down adjacent rows when making readings to prevent compaction in the furrow where stations are located.

● Rodents may cut wire leads at ground level during the summer. Splice if necessary.

● Allow time for water penetration before reading blocks after irrigation. One day for sands and three days for clays.

● Keep a soil probe handy if you are in doubt and want to double check.

Managing For Efficient Use Of Irrigation Water

By careful scheduling of water application rate, you may save water and fuel, make better use of fertilizer and improve crop yields.

Refilling the root zone to field capacity each irrigation can be wasteful in humid and semi-arid regions. Rainfall soon after irrigation can mean that some water and fuel are wasted. Further, the excess water will percolate below the root zone, carrying along with it nitrates and other soluble nutrients.

To achieve maximum use of plant nutrients applied as soluble fertilizers, you must prevent them from being leached during the growing season. For instance, there are more corn roots in the top two feet of soil than in the rest of the root zone. If water can be retained in the upper two feet of soil, nutrients will remain more readily available than if they are leached to greater depths.

Recent irrigation research by Nebraska irrigation specialists shows that limited irrigation can produce corn and sugar beet yields as good or better than when the soil is irrigated to capacity. Nearly half the water and energy used in irrigation can be saved. Tests have shown that under Nebraska conditions only 6.2 to 10 inches of irrigation water is needed most years, with severe drouth being an exception. Yet, the average amount of water pumped for irrigation there is 16 to 20 inches.

CORN YIELDS AT VARYING WEEKLY IRRIGATION RATES

Design Criteria	Amt. of Water per Irrig.*	Total Irrig. Water Applied	Rainfall plus Irrigation	Corn Yield
inch/day	inches	inches	inches	bu./ac.
Check**		0.0	9.45***	102
0.10	0.70	6.2	15.7	159
0.15	1.05	8.0	17.4	167
0.24	1.68	10.7	20.2	156
0.30	2.10	13.2	22.7	158

*The amount of water applied is shown as 100% water application efficiency and a uniformity coefficient of 80. No runoff returned to the field.
**Soil moisture in the root zone was at field capacity at planting time and was refilled by rainfall until June 28.
***Rainfall was 9.45 inches from June 14 to September 20.

Tests with corn were run for four years. While only one year's results are shown in the table, the same irrigation rate gave the highest yield in each of the four years. Application of 1.05 inches of water each week produced the top yield of 167 bushels per acre in 1972. Applying twice as much water reduced yield by nine bushels per acre.

Though Nebraska tests have been limited to corn and sugar beets, researchers say limited irrigation can be used on most crops grown on soils suitable for this practice. Present research suggests that this practice be confined to those soils which are at least five feet deep and having a water holding capacity of 1.5 inches or more per foot of depth. Sandy soils with lower water holding capacity are being tested. Given are the appropriate water holding capacities of various soils.

WATER HOLDING CAPACITIES OF SOILS

	Inches of water per foot of soil
Very coarse textured sands	0.40 - 0.75
Coarse textured sands, fine sands, and loamy sands	0.75 - 1.00
Moderately coarse texture— sandy loams and fine sandy loams	1.00 - 1.50
Medium texture—very fine sandy loams and silt loams	1.50 - 2.30
Moderately fine texture—clay loams and sandy clay loams	1.75 - 2.50
Fine texture—sandy clays and clays	1.60 - 2.50
Peats and mucks	2.00 - 3.00

Programmed soil moisture depletion is an irrigation management concept that has evolved as a result of tests such as those just discussed. This irrigation scheduling procedure requires the application of at least one inch of water each week unless rainfall nearly refills the root zone. Sufficient water storage remains in the soil to take advantage of rainfall.

In the case of corn, one inch of applied water usually penetrates less than a foot into the soil each irrigation during the two to three week period when corn's water use rate is at its peak. If rainfall occurs soon after irrigation the water may penetrate deeper, but the chances of moving below the root zone are slim during this period.

Once corn reaches the milk stage the water applied may satisfy the corn's reduced water use rate. Later on, one inch of water per week will exceed the amount taken up by the corn. As a result, the water will penetrate deeper and soil moisture depleted earlier will be restored as the season progresses. The soil moisture isn't likely to be replenished by the time corn is mature, but fall and spring rainfall will refill the root zone for the next season's crop.

Missouri tests have shown that irrigation can generally be discontinued 45 days after 50% of the silks have emerged from the ear shoots, but there must be a 10 day reserve of moisture in the soil at that time. At that stage of maturity about 90% of total dry matter has accumulated in the kernels.

The milk line in the kernels is another method used by the Missouri researchers for determining when to discontinue irrigation. Water use can be safely terminated when the upper half of the kernels have developed horny endosperm.

Scheduling irrigations is critical to the success of this irrigation method. Depending on soil moisture, more or less than one inch of water per week may be required in a particular irrigation or perhaps an irrigation can be eliminated altogether.

By the start of the season (around June 20) the root zone (top five feet of soil) should be filled to field capacity. Then be ready to start irrigating before the soil moisture deficit exceeds two inches — sooner if the crop is small and shallow rooted. Depending on planting date and rainfall, irrigation should begin about the last week of June.

Start out applying one inch of water each week, but be ready to adjust the rate if stored soil moisture indicates need for a change. Each week you will need to know the following: amount of water you have applied, how uniformly it is distributed over the field, how much rainfall has occurred, the amount of water extracted from the root zone and how deep the roots have penetrated.

Necessary tools for making these determinations include a moisture sampling tube, electrical resistance blocks, rain gauge, and water meter to register the amount of water applied. Unless you know how much moisture has been added to the soil through irrigation and rainfall and monitor soil moisture, there is no way of knowing if adjustment from the one inch rate is necessary.

When using electrical resistance blocks to monitor soil moisture conditions, it is important to place them so you get a good picture of available soil moisture throughout the root zone. A minimum of two blocks per station is advised — one shallow and one deep. Because the programmed soil moisture depletion approach to irrigation is limited to soils which are at least five feet deep, the shallow blocks should be placed 18 inches below the surface as recommended for soils which are four or more feet deep. The deep blocks should be located at 36 inches.

A water meter can often be paid for by the savings in water and fuel. If proper size and type is installed, it can give satisfactory service over a rather long time, but should be checked for accuracy at least once every two years. Sand can be especially destructive to meters. Where a meter is calibrated in acre-inches, the average application in inches is determined by dividing acre inches by the number of acres irrigated.

Irrigation systems, using programmed soil moisture depletion to reduce irrigation requirements, can be designed with limited pumping capacity or full capacity systems can be operated to deliver required water over fewer hours. Shown in the table are various system designs which will deliver the required amount of water within a varying range of operating times.

DESIGN CRITERIA FOR IRRIGATION SYSTEMS

Design Criteria		Capacity of Irrigation System for 130 Acres		
		Operated 100% of time	Operated 75% of time	Operated 50% of time
inches/day	inches/wk.	gal./min.	gal./min.	gal./min.
0.10	0.70	246	328	492
0.15	1.05	365	486	730
0.20	1.40	491	655	982
0.24	1.68	590	786	1,180
0.30	2.10	731	974	1,462

A 900 gallon per minute center-pivot sprinkler system operating on 130 acres has previously been considered a full capacity system. However, a 600 gallon per minute system could be considered full capacity using programmed soil moisture depletion. It would need to be operated only 61% of the time to apply 1.05 inches per week, leaving the system idle about 40% of the time. This would leave sufficient leeway for an irrigator to cooperate with his electrical power supplier in scheduling electrical use to reduce peak loads during a 24 hour period. Provided enough irrigators in an area cooperated, that could mean substantial savings for rural electric districts which pay on the basis of peak electrical loads.

Providing for 25% down time to take care of unexpected interruptions and additional capacity for drier seasons, a center-pivot sprinkler system applying 486 gallons per minute on 130 acres has the capacity to deliver 1.05 inches per week.

Irrigate to Maximize Use of Applied Water

Within the optimum efficiency range of a given system, an operator should try to make the best possible use of applied irrigation water.

An efficient irrigation pumping plant and proper scheduling are essential for producing good crop yields with the least possible water and energy. However, since each system has an inherent level of efficiency between water applied and that which is effectively used by crops, you should try to achieve the maximum efficiency that your system is capable of delivering.

No irrigation system is 100% efficient. Losses within the system occur through such factors as deep percolation, unequal distribution and wind. Therefore, total water applied must be sufficient to overcome these losses plus meeting the demands of evapotranspiration (the water that is used for crop production). Evapotranspiration comprises that water used by the crop in transpiration and that lost from the soil through evaporation.

The average efficiencies of various irrigation systems, as rated by Nebraska specialists, are given in the table. The ratings are based on 900 gallons per minute capacity for each of the systems. Shown in the second column is the number of inches that must be applied to achieve a net application (amount required for crop production) of 14 inches. For instance, to apply a net of 14 inches using a traveling big gun, it would be necessary to apply a total of 20 inches.

Average Efficiency of Various Irrigation Systems

System	Percent efficiency	Water per acre (inches)
Traveling big gun	70	20.0
Center-pivot	80	17.5
Skid-tow	75	18.6
Gated pipe with reuse	75	18.6
Auto-surface	85	16.4

Water application may vary as much as 50% from the averages given in the table, depending on operating conditions and how the irrigator manages the system. For example, a center-pivot sprinkler may operate at only 60% efficiency during the day when the temperature is over 100 degrees and the wind is blowing 15 to 20 miles per hour. At night the same system may operate at 90% efficiency–a result of little or no wind and a high relative humidity.

Another factor which can affect the efficiency of a system is how uniformly it applies the water over the field. For instance, the uniformity could vary from 60% to 90%, depending on design of the system and how it is operated. There could be as much as 50% variability in the amount of water applied.

Following are some practices that can help you maximize the efficiency of your system.

Sprinkler Systems

Sprinkler systems usually apply water rather uniformly. Under most conditions proper nozzling and nozzle spacing insure uniformity, but this can be greatly affected by wind. In some cases wind may cause droplets to drift completely out of the area being irrigated. Normally, the uniformity of non-moving sprinklers is much more affected by wind velocity. Continously moving sprinklers partially overcome wind problems.

Design of center pivot systems is intended to achieve uniform water application over the whole circular area under the towers. The purpose is not only to obtain as high efficiency as possible, but to reduce runoff and erosion. Being circular, the ring under each tower becomes larger toward the outer circumference of the circle, meaning that the farther the towers are from the center, the more water per minute they must apply in order to obtain uniform application. This is achieved in one of three ways:

● Maintain some constant spacing between nozzles and gradually increase nozzle size. ● Maintain the nozzle size and put the sprinklers progressively closer together toward the outer edge of the circle.
● Use spray nozzles.

Spray nozzles permit operating at less pressure than sprinkler heads, reducing power requirements. However, the peak application rate of spray nozzles is five times higher than that of sprinkler heads. This high application rate can cause runoff, but where runoff can be avoided, a 20% to 50% saving in energy is possible.

Heavier water rates per application can help to improve water efficiency, report North Dakota specialists. But, you must be careful not to exceed the water holding capacity of a soil and leave room for some rainfall between irrigations in humid and semihumid areas.

While nothing much can be done about temperature, wind speed and relative humidity, applying more water less often can help to make better use of water. When irrigation specialists compared the efficiency of applying less than one-half inch and three-fourths inch of water in one application, they found that the lighter application gave an efficiency of 71% compared with 82% for the heavier application. At the lower efficiency, almost 2-1/2 inches were needed to get the required 1-3/4 inches. At the higher efficiency, only 2-1/8 inches were needed.

Nozzle operating pressure has a large influence on uniformity of application. Where operating pressure is too low, water is not broken up sufficiently. The result is large droplets which travel rather long distances. Conversely, if the pressure is too high the water is broken up into excessively small droplets which travel short distances.

Nebraska specialists recommend a minimum pivot pressure of 75 psi for constant spacing; 60 psi for variable spacing; and 40 psi for spray nozzles. You may need higher pressures on silt or clay soils and high gallonage systems. Also, spray nozzle pressure should be increased for fields with large elevation differences.

Water evaporation, as well as distribution, is greatly affected by wind. Texas research results shown prove that evaporation losses increase rapidly with wind speed.

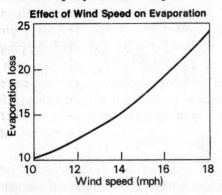

Wind drift can be reduced with solid set sprinkler systems. Nebraska specialists offer these suggestions:

● Reduce head spacing on lateral if winds are persistent. ● Reduce lateral spacing if winds are persistent; otherwise, within the flexibility of the system, reduce lateral spacing under windy conditions to 50% of wetted diameter. ● Taller risers up to 40 inches are considered advantageous. ● Operate sprinkler heads in manufacturer-suggested range. ● To the extent possible, use large nozzle sizes. ● Orient laterals perpendicular to wind.

To reduce wind drift of stationary or traveling big guns follow these suggestions:

● Do not irrigate when wind velocity exceeds 10 mph. ● Orient travel lane direction perpendicular to the prevailing wind. ● Do not irrigate when the wind direction is parallel to the travel direction. ● Distance between travel lanes should be no more than 45% of the no-wind wetted diameter.

Surface Irrigation Systems

To obtain high efficiency with surface systems, a manager must know his soil and irrigate accordingly. He must know how the flow rate in the furrow affects advance of water down the row and the intake pattern along the length of the field. He needs to recognize that intake rate varies during the season and that he must correct for these changes.

Some basics of surface irrigation should be understood in order to manage for maximum efficiency.

Intake rate of a soil is greatest at the start of irrigation and it decreases as irrigation proceeds. The longer water is applied in a furrow the slower it soaks in. When a stream of water is applied in a furrow, the water advances down the row at a non-uniform rate. It tends to run fast at the upper end of the field and slows down near the lower end, as more of the water soaks in and less is available for surface storage in the row.

Recession occurs when the water is shut off. This means that when the flow of water stops at the upper end it continues to flow for perhaps another hour or hour and one-half at the lower end. Opportunity time is the length of time water has to enter the soil at any given point along the furrow.

Ideally, the perfect irrigation pattern is where there is very little deep percolation at the upper end of the field and the root zone is just full at the lower end.

A reuse pit with a properly designed pump to handle all runoff can permit a large flow rate and a shorter time set. This can avoid the type of undesirable application illustrated in the drawing. More uniform water application throughout the field could be obtained at a considerable saving in water and nitrogen fertilizer.

A POOR DISTRIBUTION PATTERN

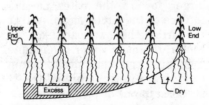

A reuse pit cannot substitute for periodic soil moisture checks, land smoothing and control of furrow flows. Often, land leveling can greatly increase efficiency.

Water distribution may be improved by modifying the irrigation furrow in conjunction with the use of an automatic gated pipe system with reuse capabilities. This applies primarily to some soils with medium to high intake rates and slopes of only 0.2% to 0.3%.

Nebraska conducted tests comparing the use of a conventional ditcher with and without smoothing and packing. The tests were on silty clay loam. Object was to apply 2 inches or less of water as effectively as possible.

Without smoothing and packing, irrigation time was 370 minutes on the upper end of the field compared with 260 minutes on the lower end. Smoothing and packing the furrow resulted in an irrigation time of 360 minutes at the upper end of the field and 315 minutes at the lower end. Use of a Hawkins ditcher tended to smooth and pack the furrow more than a conventional ditcher, thus additional smoothing was of lesser benefit.

Automatic gated pipe systems when properly managed can save 30% to 40% of the water normally applied. Automatic gated pipe systems with tailwater reuse are designed to use maximum allowable stream size for each furrow or border to flow the water across the field as fast as possible without serious erosion. Water should flow through the field in 1-1/2 to 2-1/2 hours with a total irrigation set time of 3 or 4 hours on many soils with slopes of less than 0.5%. Set time on slopes of 1% to 2% may need to be 8 to 12 hours to apply 2 or 3 inches. Application of 1 to 2 inches can be applied to steeper slopes, but you may have to irrigate as frequently as every 5 to 7 days during peak crop use.

A water meter will tell a lot about total seasonal water use in relation to crop needs. A soil probe, field checks of water penetration and observations of how fast the water travels through the field can give clues to possible problems.

Maintaining Irrigation Pump Efficiency

The efficiency of fuel use for irrigation depends on how well you maintain the pumping plant once it has been properly matched to the system.

Many operators in western and more humid areas alike are expanding and relying more heavily on irrigation as a way to produce profitable crop yields in the face of increasing production costs and rising land values. Yet, the cost of energy requires managing irrigation systems as efficiently as possible to hold down on pumping costs.

New irrigators should give careful attention to drilling properly designed wells and matching system and pumping units to the capacity of their wells. Both new and established irrigators should emphasize proper pumping plant maintenance and manage them as effectively as possible to save on fuel and water. Here are some factors to consider.

Pumping plant efficiency is usually expressed as water horsepower-hours (whp-hr) per unit of fuel. Water horsepower can be determined by multiplying the gallons per minute discharged from the pump by the total dynamic head. Then divide by 3,960. No pumping plant, regardless of how well it is designed, is 100% efficient. Energy is lost within the motor or engine. Power is lost between the drive shaft and pump and within the pump itself. However, Nebraska engineers have developed performance standards for various energy powered pumping units (shown in the table).

These standards represent a performance level that can reasonably be obtained by pumps, engines or motors and drives that have average or above efficiency. Units must be properly selected, installed, adjusted and operated to reach these standards. If all components are above average in efficiency, a pumping plant could exceed the standards.

PERFORMANCE STANDARDS FOR IRRIGATION PUMPING PLANTS

Energy source	Performance standards whp-hr/unit of fuel
Diesel	10.94 per gal.
Gasoline	8.66 per gal.
Propane	6.89 per gal.
Natural gas	66.7 per 1,000 cu. ft.
Electricity	0.885 per kw-hr

A unit that obtains less water horsepower hours per unit of fuel or uses more fuel than calculated from the Performance Standard shown is termed "substandard." Based on tests of units

being operated in Nebraska over a seven year period, only 24% exceeded 90% of the standard.

Using the performance standards shown, the amount of energy a pumping plant should use can be determined from total lift and quantity of water to be pumped. This can be done by using the chart developed by Wyoming specialists. The example given in the chart shows that an efficient pumping plant discharging 1,000 gallons per minute (gpm) against a lift of 300 feet should require no more than 86 kilowatt hours per hour of electricity; 6.9 gallons of diesel fuel; 11 gallons of propane; 114 cubic feet per hour natural gas; or 8.8 gallons of gasoline per hour.

Using the performance standards shown, the amount of energy a pumping plant should use can be determined from total lift and quantity of water to be pumped. This can be done by using the chart. The example given shows that an efficient pumping plant discharging 1,000 gallons per minute (gpm) against a lift of 300 feet should require no more than 86 kilowatt hours per hour of electricity; 6.9 gallons of diesel fuel; 10.8 gallons of propane; 8.6 gallons of gasoline per hour; or 1.14 thousand cubic feet per hour natural gas.

Causes for substandard performance are summarized by Nebraska specialists.

● Pump efficiency hinges on selecting a turbine impeller that will lift a particular amount of water to a certain height at a specified speed. If pumping conditions change or if impellers are not matched to existing conditions, the pump will be inefficient. Piping systems not included in the original design will change pumping conditions and plant efficiency. The pump impellers may be out of adjustment. This results in higher than normal engine speeds to deliver the required amount of water. The pump may be operating below or above the designed speed.

● The engine may be overloaded or underloaded. Engines usually work most efficiently when operated at 75% to 100% of their continuous rated brake horsepower at a reasonable speed. Drive ratios may need to be changed. The engine may need adjustment of ignition, timing and carburetion on spark ignition engines; fuel injection timing on diesel engines. The parts may be excessively worn, causing loss of compression. Continuous overloading of an electric motor probably won't seriously affect its efficiency, but will reduce its useful life.

• The drive ratio may be incorrect for matching pump and engine speeds. This causes inefficient operation of the pump or engine or both. Drive misalignment decreases efficiency and reduces drive life.

Pumping plant tests can help you keep operating costs at a minimum. The past results show that the most likely candidates for poor efficiency are old, single stage pumps. But tests also show that any pumping plant, regardless of its age or lift is likely to be operating well below the Nebraska Standard. This means, say Nebraska specialists, that it is costing more to operate the unit than should be expected. They say a good way to determine where you are operating in respect to the Nebraska Standard is to compare your system's past fuel and operating records with the standard. The information needed is pumping lift, delivery pressure gpm, number of hours of operation last year, and the gallons of fuel used. If all that is not known, but you do know the rated load of your pumping plant, the hours of operation and the energy used, you can still get a good idea. Knowing the water horsepower of your plant, you can determine how its efficiency compares with the Nebraska Standard. Multiply the water horsepower by number of hours

of operation. Divide the figure by units of fuel used. Compare the units used with those determined for the Nebraska Standard given in the table. Dividing the units used by your system by those given in the Nebraska Standards gives you the efficiency of your system.

Past results have shown that the average pumping plant in Nebraska operates at about 76% of the Nebraska Standard, so if your plant is no higher than 76% efficient it could stand some improvement. Practical field application of the tests has shown that after adjustment, pumping plant efficiency was increased an average of 10%. Average savings of a medium sized pumping plant (900 gpm, 200 feet total pump lift) was $287 for 1,000 hours of operation.

A water meter and pressure gauge should be a part of an irrigation system. Reading changes in either can alert the irrigator to possible problems in the system. Most water meters provide instantaneous reading of the quantity of water that is being pumped and can provide an early indicator of possible problems in the pumping plant.

A change in meter readings during the season may indicate wear in the pump, change in water levels, wear in sprinkler equipment or some other problem. This reading can also be used with the chart to determine energy requirements. Meters can help you save water by fitting your irrigation rate more closely to the needs of your crops.

Before you can adjust the irrigation rate you must know how much water you are actually applying. Based on the average initial cost of an eight inch meter ($250 to $400) and a well applying 18 inches of water to 90 acres each year, Nebraska engineers calculate the annual cost of the meter to be 66¢ per acre.

A pressure gauge at the pump discharge can serve as a trouble indicator. Change in pressure would suggest that some checking of the system is in order.

The specialists say you should keep three records—water meter readings, pressure gauge readings and quantity of energy used. These can serve as a guide to the irrigator for maintaining the system at top performance and efficiency.

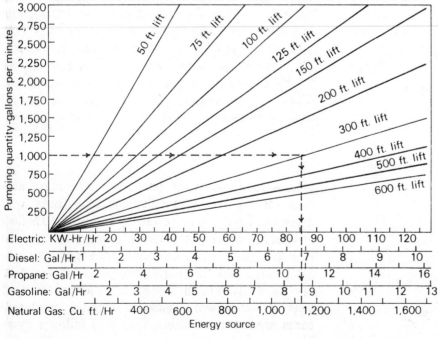

ENERGY REQUIREMENTS FOR AN EFFICIENT IRRIGATION PUMPING PLANT

Chapter 13

Marketing

Marketing is a vital phase of farming. Decisions made in this area of farm management may mean the difference between profit or loss. A farmer's income is determined by not only how much he produces, but also by how much he can receive for his product at the marketplace.

Marketing decisions must be made well in advance of a sale. Decisions actually begin when you decide what crops you are going to grow and how many acres of each crop you will plant. As a result, you need to view the market situation for a given commodity over the long range and try to project what prices will prevail when you are ready to sell your crop or livestock. Perhaps you should set for yourself some price goal at which you would sell your crops or livestock. Then you can make use of various marketing tools to assure that you will receive this price if the market opportunity should arise prior to actual sale.

Prices vary widely. In past years, the right sale time for a given commodity could be fairly well assessed. There was a tendency for crops to follow a seasonal price pattern. The same was true for livestock. Presently, seasonal price patterns are not pronounced. The high price period in one year may turn out to be the lowest price period the next year. However, while seasonal livestock price patterns are less predictable, they still follow a cycle over the years. These cycles can help you establish your long range production plans.

Essentially, prices are determined by the same basic factors as they were years ago—supply and demand. However, these factors are much more subject to volatile changes now than they were in the past. Many more factors go into the makeup of supply and demand, especially since world developments are now playing a much greater role in setting U.S. prices.

Supply may be thought of as the quantity and/or the quality of products being offered for sale at a particular time. Demand relates to the quantity or quality of products which consumers want. Consumers will pay more for a product that is scarce. They are willing to buy more when that product is plentiful and the price is lower. At the same time, farmers are willing to produce more when the price is high. They cut back or shift production to some other commodity when the price is low and offers less chance of making a profit.

Farmers have little control over price in general, even though they can adjust their production over time to take advantage of price shifts between commodities. There are many farmers making their own individual decisions about what to produce for sale. As a result, no one farmer can control the price that he receives at the marketplace. Further, because of many different sizes of operations and cost structures, a price that may return a profit to one farmer may result in a loss for another farmer.

While the farmer does not set the price of the products he sells, the manufacturer sets the price of those things the farmer buys. Why the difference? The reason is that there are fewer manufacturers of what farmers buy than there are farmers producing for their market. Each manufacturer has a similar cost structure. They also have a good idea of how much they can sell for a price that will return a profit. Consequently, they tend to produce only about that quantity which they can sell for a predetermined price.

Know the marketing tools which are available for your use. There are tools available for marketing farm commodities, just as there are tools for producing them. These tools include cash contracts, futures markets, price charts, weather forecasts and on-farm storage.

The use of cash or futures contracts is closely related. Both are tools which can be used to sell and "lock in" a price for a commodity well in advance of the time that the product is ready for sale. When you know what your breakeven costs are for various crops and livestock, you can reduce your risk by using a contract to sell at a price which will cover those costs plus a profit.

You must have market goals. Regardless of the marketing tools you use, they all have their particular advantages and disadvantages. Determine what these are and understand the risks which their use involves. Then, use those tools that best meet your goals. For instance, the goal for most is to make maximum profit. However, assume that you are in a financial bind. Perhaps the only way you can assure a potential creditor that you are a suitable loan risk is to sell your crop or livestock by use of a contract. This will guarantee a profitable price for your product, but it may prevent you from taking advantage of a somewhat higher price at a later time.

Commodity Futures Trading

The futures market can be a valuable marketing tool, but it should be well understood by the producer who uses it to hedge his production.

Futures markets are being used by an increasing number of producers who recognize the vital role this system can perform in the operation of their business. Futures trading, while somewhat complicated, serves a very important function. It is a way of reducing your market risk while assuring yourself a profitable return for the crops or livestock you produce. However, it may not necessarily permit you to sell them at the highest possible price that occurs during the season or marketing period.

A common question is, "How can a person sell something he doesn't have?" You can't, but you can make a contract to deliver something at a future time and place. That is what happens when you sell commodity futures. On the other side of the contract, a buyer agrees to accept delivery of the commodity at some future time and place. However, deliveries are not made on futures contracts. Rather, offsetting contracts are made—you buy back a contract of a like amount as that which you had previously sold. The buyers and/or sellers gain or lose on that specific contract.

Farmers use futures contracts primarily to set a price for their crop in advance of harvest or to set a livestock price while they are being finished for market.

Futures trading offers several advantages over forward cash contracting. You can always find a buyer for a futures contract. Then, if you should decide at some later time not to stay with the contract, you can get out of the deal without any problem by purchasing an offsetting contract. A cash contract, on the other hand, is not as easily reversed. This flexibility is a unique and valuable feature of the futures market.

Futures traders consist of two basic groups—speculators and hedgers. The speculator attempts to make money by correctly anticipating market price movements. If he expects the price to go up, he goes "long"—buys a contract. When he expects the price to fall, he assumes a "short" position—sells a contract. He seldom owns any of the commodity he trades, nor does he have any desire to take or make delivery on a contract.

The hedger, on the other hand, is involved in owning the physical commodity he trades on the futures market. He might be a livestock feeder, a crops farmer, a country elevator manager, or a grain or livestock producer. Any of these people could be hedgers by using futures contracts to offset their position in the cash market. Basically, those people who hedge do so to avoid the risk of unfavorable price movement on the cash market. The speculator is the one who is willing to accept the risk which the hedger seeks to avoid.

A grain production hedge, in its simplest form, involves a sale of a futures contract against the particular grain being produced. The impact of declining harvest prices can therefore be eliminated or at least minimized for grain that must be sold during the harvest season. However, due to a variety of reasons, hedges placed at planting time have not worked out particularly well in recent years. The prices in the spring actually turned out to be lower than those which prevailed during the harvest period which followed. Even so, prices were generally good compared to historical standards and the futures market offered an acceptable return. Also, there was the distinct possibility that a large acreage could have sent prices lower at harvest had not other market factors entered the picture. Further, there have been instances when hedging has worked out well, with the price contracted being higher than harvesttime prices.

When you sell futures you lock in a price between your hedging date and harvest. For that reason, and because no one can consistently pick the top of a market, it is usually recommended that a hedger spread his futures contract sales over several weeks. This will allow you to average out your hedging price and give you additional time to assess the emerging new crop supply-demand balance before committing your entire production. However, this can result in a lost opportunity if prices should turn higher.

When hedging, it is advisable to leave some room for crop problems which might occur. For that reason, you had better not sell futures contracts which would represent more than 75% of "normal" production. Remember that when you sell you must either produce or buy back in order to fulfill the sales commitment you have made in the form of a production hedge. If you sell more than you eventually grow, you are a speculator.

Once a contract is made, the buyer must decide when to lift his hedge by buying back an offsetting contract. To maintain his hedge or price protection for the full period, the producer should maintain his hedge as long as he owns his grain, then close out the futures position on the same day the grain is sold.

TRADING PROCEDURE

Be careful to select a broker of high integrity, so you can be assured that he will carry out your market orders as given. This is especially important since orders are typically given over the phone. A trader should keep a record of all the orders he gives his broker, but he has to trust his broker to execute these orders. Some brokers are more knowledgeable about certain commodities than others. The broker can be a valuable source of information on trading activity and market factors, as well as the rules and regulations on specific contracts, but you should not expect him to make the decision as to when to place or remove a hedge—that is your responsibility.

Once you select a broker, he will ask you to sign a written agreement which gives him the authority to trade commodities for you on the exchange. Among the items in the agreement is a statement which gives the commission agent authority to close out your hedge account if you fail to maintain the prescribed amount of margin in your account. The major portion of the agreement spells out the duties and responsibilities of the commission agent and the authority given to him by you, the hedger.

Cost of futures trading involves the fee or commission charged by the broker to carry out your transactions and the margin requirement. A brokerage fee is charged for each contract bought or sold.

A margin deposit of a prescribed amount must be made by a buyer or seller of a futures contract. The basic purpose of the margin deposit is to assure other traders and the clearing house of the exchange that the trader will be able to pay any losses he might incur in the futures market. The initial deposit made by the trader is often called the "original deposit" and usually represents about 5% of the value of the product. The minimum original deposit required is established by the exchange, but an individual broker may re-

quire a larger original deposit if they deem it necessary for their protection.

Once deposited, the margin must be kept current if it is to continue to provide about the same degree of protection to the exchange and the broker. An adverse price movement of 25% to 30% will bring a call from the exchange to the brokerage firm for "additional margin" to restore the margin account to the original level. This is referred to as a margin call. The hedger must be ready to put a check in the mail immediately. If the broker does not receive the check in about two days, one or more of your contracts will be closed out in order to restore the proper margin balance. Should the price continue to change against your position, you will be called on regularly to bring your margin deposit back up to the required minimum maintenance margin level.

While an increase in the futures market may result in a margin call and necessitate the need to make a further deposit to keep the hedge in effect, the hedger should not necessarily become discouraged and liquidate. The chances are that an increase in the futures market will be reflected in a similar increase in the cash value of the commodity. Thus the hedge is still in force and functioning properly. It is only when adequate financial and mental preparation have not been made that a margin call is a matter of concern. If a portion of the futures account is closed out due to a failure to meet margin call, a true hedge no longer exists unless you immediately sell a similar amount of cash grain.

To prevent liquidation, make certain that both you and your banker understand this important aspect of commodity futures trading. Adequate plans should be made to cover possible margin call in advance of entering into a hedge. A margin call may prompt a review of your initial hedging plan with your broker and banker to determine if a hedge is still desirable.

Another consideration relative to margin deposits is that they do not bear interest if deposited in cash. Therefore, interest should be included in the cost of hedging. It is possible to deposit some types of interest bearing securities rather than cash, but you must check this with your broker to find what is currently acceptable. Also remember that if you have a short hedge in futures against storage and the futures price declines, the additional "paper profit" can be withdrawn from the account.

Using the Grain Futures Markets

By hedging on a futures market, you may be able to lock in an acceptable price for your crop ahead of harvest or while the grain is still in storage.

Grain futures are not new. They have been used by elevators, processors, merchandisers and speculators for years. In fact, futures markets were first put into use in the mid-nineteenth century. Down through the years, farmers have been somewhat reluctant to hedge with the futures markets. In the last few years, though, use of futures by cash grain farmers has been on the increase

WHY USE GRAIN FUTURES?

Grain futures markets, properly used, will inject price stability into the farming business. This is the basic reason for hedging by a farmer—whether it be a cash grain farmer or a feeder. A farmer can guarantee himself, within reasonable limits, a price for his grain he has determined is acceptable.

A farmer might use grain futures markets in one of three ways: (1) to set the price of a growing grain crop any time prior to harvest; (2) to set the price of feed without taking immediate delivery; or (3) to fix the price of grain in storage for deferred delivery.

A fourth way in which a farmer might use the futures markets is to speculate. Farmers do it every day in the normal operation of the business. Storing grain for a price rise is speculation. Placing cattle on feed is speculation. And taking a position in the futures market, gambling that prices will move in such a way that the contract can be liquidated at a profit is speculation. Farmers can, and do, speculate in the futures market every day. But it's important to realize that systematic buying and selling on the futures market is not a part of the farm business operation. A farmer speculating without consideration of the cash grain aspects of a farming operation functions no differently than a lawyer, doctor or a shoe clerk might operate.

UNDERSTANDING THE BASIS

Probably the most important single factor in the successful hedging of grain is a thorough understanding of basis. The term "basis" normally means the difference between the price of cash grain at the delivery point and the nearby future. However, it may be modified to refer to the cash price in relation to a more distant future. For instance, if in June the Chicago basis is termed "two under," this means that cash grain in Chicago is selling for 2¢ less than the July future. By the same token, if the Peoria basis was four under the September, this would mean that cash grain in Peoria is selling 4¢ under the September future.

In theory, the basis at any market should—within a single marketing year—be equal to the costs of storing grain until the delivery month plus the cost of transportation to the delivery point.

In reality, the basis always varies more than the theoretical relationships of storage and transportation would suggest. But as a rule, it follows a more or less consistent pattern and is within a reasonable range of what would be expected from storage-transportation relationships.

Know your local basis. Since the "normal" basis varies considerably between areas, you need to know what is normal on your market. To get at this, you need prices for a number of years. Often, the elevator operator in your community can be of help—he will usually have historical price records.

If you know the normal basis, then a particular futures quote can be translated into an equivalent cash price on your local market at some specified point in time.

HOW TO USE FUTURES

Once the decision is made to hedge on the futures market, the procedure is relatively simple. The customer must contact a broker and ● sign an agreement; ● deposit sufficient funds to guarantee performance on the contract (margin money); and ● instruct the broker as to the trades he wants to transact.

Typically, the margin required will be about 10% of the value of the commodity being traded. The exchange establishes a minimum margin deposit. The broker will usually require more. It may run as low as 5% of the contract value or as much as 20% or more.

Also, you may be asked for additional money for maintenance margin if the market moves adversely—this is the amount below which the total value of the contracts must not be allowed to fall. This minimum may be set at roughly 75% of the initial margin.

A hedging example. Here's the way a cash corn producer might use the futures market to hedge a growing crop.

Assume this grower lives in west central Illinois. He grows 200 acres of corn and can conservatively expect 20,000 bushels production. Typically, a grower would not hedge more than 60% to 75% of expected production. Normal harvest basis is 8¢ to 11¢ under.

In mid-June, with the corn up and growing well, he notes the December corn future at Chicago is trading at $2.01. Subtracting the 11¢ basis, this projects to a local cash corn price at harvest of $1.90. He is willing to take this price for his corn crop. So, in mid-June, he—

> **Sells** 20,000 bushels (four contracts) December corn at $2.01.
>
> In November he harvests his corn crop. Local price is $1.92-1/2. In early November he . . .
>
> **Sells** 20,000 bushels cash corn at $1.92-1/2 . . .
>
> At the same time, to liquidate the futures contracts he . . .
>
> **Buys** 20,000 bushels December corn at $2.03-1/2.

The loss on the futures contract was 2-1/2¢ per bushel or $500. After paying roughly $160 interest on the margin he put down on the futures transaction and $120 commission, he had lost $780 or about 4¢ per bushel on the futures contract.

But he sold his cash corn crop for $1.92-1/2, 2-1/2¢ over the anticipated price of $1.90. Subtracting the $780 loss from the futures transaction from cash sale proceeds leaves a "net" of $1.88-1/2 per bushel.

The above example points up one important characteristic of hedging. HEDGING NOT ONLY INSURES AGAINST UNFAVORABLE MOVEMENT, BUT ALSO PREVENTS GAINS FROM UPWARD PRICE MOVEMENT. In other words, it eliminates both losses from adverse price movement and windfall gains.

In the above example, if prices had moved down rather than up from June to harvest, the farmer in the example would have received roughly the same price for his corn through hedging. But without hedging, the net would have been considerably less.

The procedure in pricing grain ahead that is now in storage is the same as in the above example. Establish a target price near the end of the storage season and sell the appropriate futures. At the end of the storage period, sell the cash grain and buy back the futures contract.

Fixing the cost of feed with futures. A livestock feeder can use the grain futures market to set, within limits, the cost of grain for future use. Often a feeder would be better off to buy his entire season's needs in the fall when prices are lowest. But storage may not be adequate to hold that much inventory.

To hedge feed requirements, a feeder would buy futures in an amount equal to his requirements. As storage space is available, he then buys cash corn and sells a corresponding amount of futures. Profits made on the futures transaction are subtracted from the cash price of corn to get the net feed cost.

Since the cash price gains in relation to the futures, the feeder will end up, in effect, paying storage on his future corn requirements. The advantage to hedging is that it removes the risk of sharp price run-ups in the price of feed.

Some rules of thumb. While there are no hard and fast rules for the use of grain futures in the farm business, here are some basic "do's" for hedging.
● Do keep the size of the futures position no larger than the size of the cash grain position involved.
● Do keep the futures position the opposite of the cash position. If you're holding (or growing) cash grain, sell the futures. If you need cash grain (are "short") then buy the futures.
● Do close out both the cash and futures position simultaneously. When you harvest and sell the corn crop, buy back the futures contract. When you buy cash corn for feed, sell the futures contract. If you stay in the futures position after closing the cash transaction, you're speculating.
● Do acquire the services of a knowledgeable grain broker and ask his help in setting up a hedging plan—then stick to it.

Using Livestock Futures Markets

If the futures markets are used correctly, they can minimize the hedger's risks by shifting them to another party.

There are times when hedging a particular product makes sense. On the other hand, there are times when it's a mistake. A well developed marketing sense and a thorough knowledge of your particular production costs are essential tools to use in selecting the right time to hedge.

The futures market is not a panacea. The fact that it is available for hedging doesn't automatically ease management decisions. In fact, futures markets can make decisions even more difficult by opening new alternatives in the marketing program. Carefully analyze all choices before making your decision.

When you make a hedge sale, you're actually evaluating the market at a future date in relation to the cost of the finished product. This includes the cost of the feeder in the case of cattle or hogs, costs of feeding the animals to market weight and also the selling costs you will have.

The table below shows current contract specifications for most livestock and livestock-related contracts that are now in use on the various exchanges.

A HEDGING EXAMPLE

Here's a hypothetical example of how a hedge might work out for a midwestern cattle feeder who buys yearling feeders in September to finish and sell as Choice steers in Omaha in February.

Laid in cost to the cattle feeder is 40¢ per pound for 112 head averaging 728 pounds. He figures total production costs to market will be 50¢ per pound for an average of 347 pounds per head. Total cost (or breakeven point) then is $52,046.40 or 43.23¢ per pound when the lot is sold in February.

Laid in cost
112 head x 728 lbs. x 40¢ = $32,614.40

Feeding costs
112 head x 347 lbs. x 50¢ = $19,432.00
Total cost $52,046.40

Cost per pound $\left(\dfrac{\$52,046.40}{112 \times 1,075}\right)$ = 43.23¢

Here's how he hedged: In September, the February live cattle contract on the Chicago Mercantile Exchange was trading at 45.22¢ per pound. The "basis" or difference between cash and

BASIC CONTRACT SPECIFICATIONS

	Live Cattle	Feeder Cattle	Live Hogs	Iced Broilers	Fresh Shell Eggs	Pork Bellies
EXCHANGE	Chicago Mercantile Exchange	Chicago Mercantile Exchange	Chicago Mercantile Exchange	Chicago Board of Trade	Chicago Mercantile Exchange	Chicago Mercantile Exchange
TRADING UNIT	40,000 lbs. live steers	42,000 lbs.	30,000 lbs.	30,000 lbs.	22,500 doz.	38,000 lbs.
ROUND-TURN COMMISSION	$51.50	$51.50	$51.50	$50.50	$51.50	$51.50
MINIMUM PRICE MOVE...						
Per unit	2-1/2¢ per cwt.	2-1/2¢ per cwt.	2-1/2¢ per cwt.	2-1/2¢ per cwt.	5/100¢ per doz.	2-1/2¢ per cwt.
Per contract	$10	$10.50	$7.50	$7.50	$11.25	$9
Value of 1¢ move per contract	$400	$420	$300	$300	$225	$380
DAILY TRADING LIMITS						
Above or below previous close	1-1/2¢	1-1/2¢	1-1/2¢	2¢	2¢	2¢
maximum range	3¢	3¢	3¢	4¢	4¢	4¢
TRADING HOURS (central time)	Open 9:05 a.m. Close 12:45 p.m.	Open 9:05 a.m. Close 12:45 p.m.	Open 9:15 a.m. Close 12:55 p.m.	Open 9:15 a.m. Close 1:20 p.m.	Open 9:20 a.m. Close 1:00 p.m.	Open 9:10 a.m. Close 1:00 p.m.
DELIVERY MONTHS	Feb., Apr., June, Aug., Oct., Dec.	Mar., Apr., May, Aug., Sept., Oct., Dec.	Feb., Apr., June, July, Aug., Oct., Dec.	Jan., Mar., May, July, Sept., Nov.	All months	Feb., Mar., May, July, Aug.

futures prices tends to narrow during the last trading days of an expiring contract with the cash and futures prices moving toward each other. The degree that cash and futures move together will vary from year to year, depending on supply-demand or other factors at the time of sale.

However, a study of how the February contract has gone off the board relative to this farmer's local cash markets in past years can give him an "in the ball park" figure. He finds that in February his local cash market averaged 1¢ per pound under February futures at expiration. In September, therefore, the February live cattle contract was offering 1¢ per pound or $1,204 above the computed breakeven price on the finished steers.

IN SEPTEMBER HE

Bought:	Sold:
112 feeders which will cost about 43.23¢/lb. or $52,046.40 to market at 1,075 pounds.	Three February futures contracts at 45.22¢/lb.* Total commission was $150.

IN FEBURARY HE

Sold:	Bought:
The 112 steers at 41.22¢/lb. or $49,628.88 for a loss of $2,417.52 on the total feeding effort.	Three February futures contracts at 42.22¢/lb. for a $1,200 per contract total profit after commission of $3,450.

*Since one live cattle contract on the Chicago Mercantile Exchange totals 40,000 pounds, three contracts closely approximate the 120,400 pounds of live animal weight the farmer expects to market.

This is how the total transaction breaks down. After subtracting feed and other costs on the cash transaction the farmer had:

Costs	$52,046.40
Cash Return	$49,628.88
Net Loss	$ 2,417.52

However, since the futures markets also declined, he made $3,450 on his hedge for a final profit of $1,032.48.

That's on a basis of 1¢ per pound between local cash and February futures at expiration. We've said the basis will vary from year to year. If the basis had gone to 3/4¢ (say with February futures at 41.97¢ rather than 42.22¢), the farmer's profit would have been $3,750 in the futures and $1,332.48 overall, instead of a $2,417.52 loss in a straight cash transaction.

If the basis had moved to 1-1/4¢ (February futures at 42.47¢), the farmer's profit would have been $3,150 in the futures and $732.48 overall.

What if the cash and futures markets had shown strength rather than weakness during the feeding period?

IN SEPTEMBER HE

Bought:	Sold:
112 feeders which will cost about 43.23¢/lb. or $52,046.40 to market at 1,075 pounds.	Three February futures contracts at 45.22¢/lb.

IN FEBRUARY HE

Sold:	Bought:
The 112 steers at 44.22¢/lb. or $53,240.88 for a profit of $1,194.48 on the cash feeding effort.	Three February futures contracts at 45.22¢/lb. for no gain or loss except $150 commission.

In the first case, the hedge turned loss into a profit near the level for which the producer was aiming. In the second, there was no gain on the futures market, but profits still were near the level hoped for when the hedge was initiated.

Of course, if in December or January the farmer had become convinced that prices were moving higher, he could have bought back his futures position before the contract expired. However, whenever a farmer makes this decision he must consider that he will be out his commissions; he probably will have at least a moderate loss in the futures market; he will lose his hedge protection and therefore be vulnerable if prices decline after the hedge is lifted.

Margin requirements. One reason a farmer may vacillate after a hedge is initiated is because he may not understand margin requirements and how they work.

Margin is money the hedger must deposit when the trade is initiated. If the market goes against your hedge, you may be subject to a margin call requesting additional capital.

The important point to remember is that you went into your hedge position satisfied with a specific potential profit based on the likelihood that the cash and futures prices would approach the basis you normally see at your market when a futures contract expires. What you may lose in the cash transaction you should pick up in part or in total in the futures trade.

However, you may have to go through some adversity in your futures account even though you're right in the final analysis. It may require additional margin capital. You should be prepared for this when you place your hedge and so should your banker if he's helping to finance it.

Chart Patterns Are Useful Hedging Guides

Supply and demand are the main price setting forces, but "technical" forces, including chart formations, influence day to day commodity futures price trends.

Anyone engaged in any form of commerce, from marketing wheat or cattle to selling cups of lemonade recognizes the importance of supply versus demand as a price making force. Supply-demand fundamentals are equally important in commodity futures trading. But, the futures markets have another side--often more dominant in determining short term price action.

That other side of the futures market is the "technical" side. The technical market is concerned with people. It's a guide to what traders and hedgers are thinking. Supply-demand statistics play the dominant role in how high or low prices may go, but people determine how prices will achieve that level.

How many times have you heard a neighbor say he missed a good market price, not because he didn't expect it, but because it just took longer to develop than he expected and he gave up on it. As a result, he sold too early.

For every farmer saying that, there are scores of speculators in commodity futures bemoaning the fact they were right about a price move, but actually lost money on "in and out" trades while the market was achieving the anticipated level. In the futures markets there are thousands of people determining prices for thousands of different reasons every day.

How then do we put a finger on the dominant attitude about a market held by those who are participating in it? Futures market price patterns are one indicator.

Chart price patterns. There are people trading in commodity futures markets who say they couldn't care less how much acreage has been planted, what yield prospects are, or how many animals are in the nation's feedlots.

These traders are chartists. The pure price chartist concerns himself only with the daily, weekly and monthly gyrations of commodity chart lines in making his buy and sell decisions.

To farmers and ranchers, who traditionally think in terms of the fundamental or supply-demand aspects of the market, the chartist may sound like a strange breed. In the realm of commodity trading he's not. In fact, all good commodity traders incorporate some technical chart study into every trading decision they make.

A knowledge of the chart formations to which traders pay particular attention can be a vital guide for you in the timing of a hedging operation. If you have a good broker, he's familiar with formations and their possible market ramifications.

We're not going into the myriad of chart formations with which traders work. However, we will discuss a couple to give you a general understanding when your broker talks about this aspect of the technical market.

Prices can move in channels. Possibly one of the most intriguing phenomena of commodity futures charts is the way price patterns often tend to channel themselves. Although they can't accurately be called formations, these uptrending, downtrending or sidewise channels are the most basic and common of the price patterns.

A breakthrough below the uptrend line in a rising market (point A) or above the downtrend line in a falling market (point B) can signal a price reversal.

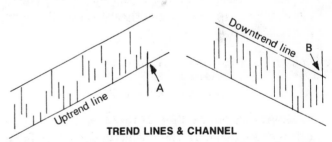

TREND LINES & CHANNEL

Basically, in an uptrending channel there are sufficient sellers at the top and buyers at the bottom to keep prices in the channel. A break below the uptrend line (point A) can indicate that the bears, or sellers, have finally amassed sufficient numbers and power to break the rising market trend--or perhaps more accurately, that some of the buyers in the channel have given up. The break may be temporary, or it could signal the beginning of a sustained move on the downside which may form a channel of its own.

Among numerous formations technical traders watch with special interest are the "Double Top," particularly in cotton, and the "Head and

Shoulders." Both are important because they can signal the end of a major bull move and a subsequent drop to lower price levels.

The double top formation below is a sustained move to higher levels (A); followed by a price decline (B); a move back to earlier highs (C); then downward price pressure which eventually penetrates the lows established on the previous decline (D)--a technical signal to continued lower prices.

Why? Basically for the same reasons we gave in discussing trend lines. Points A and C indicate resistance levels by traders who believe prices are too high; Point B represents a price level where bullish traders collectively took a stand and pushed values up again.

However, once bearish forces muster enough strength to push prices below B, the market can drop dramatically as those who had bought previously give up and "cover" or sell back their long positions. At the same time, traders looking for lower prices are encouraged by the break and pressure the market with additional selling.

DOUBLE TOP FORMATION

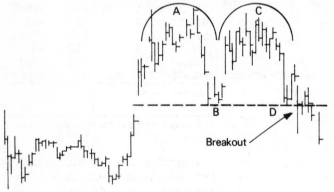

The classic head and shoulders formation has in many past markets signaled the end of a major bull move.

The formation begins with a strong upmove to new contract price highs, as illustrated in the next chart. That move is followed by a downward market reaction which completes the left shoulder before prices again surge to new contract highs.

The highs are followed by another downward reaction which forms the head of the formation; then a move toward, but not to the highs formed by the head. A downward reaction from those levels then completes the right shoulder of the formation.

A line drawn from the low of the left shoulder reaction through the low of the right shoulder reaction depicts the neckline. The formation is completed with price penetration of that neckline.

Head And Shoulder Formation--Nov. 1973 Soybean Contract

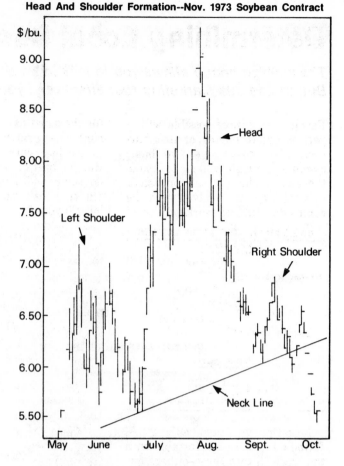

Traders believe that once the neckline of a head and shoulders formation is broken, a downmove at least equal to the distance from the top of the head to the neckline could follow.

Is it hocus-pocus? Maybe so. Certainly it must seem that way to farmers used to thinking in terms of supply and demand. However, chart formations and other technical considerations such as volume and open interest are factors you should be aware of if you plan to use futures markets.

The very fact that speculators tend to believe in these formations can make them happen. Of course, in the end fundamental forces such as production, disappearance, weather, government policy, etc., will dictate market values.

If you are considering a "sell" hedge because:

1. You have studied the market and are fairly certain prices are near the potential highs indicated by fundamental supply-demand forces, and

2. The price being offered by the futures market is good enough to give you an acceptable profit, your main concern becomes the best point at which to place the hedge. With the help of your broker, analysis of chart patterns can be a guide.

322

Determining Local Basis for Storage Hedges

The storage hedge allows you to lock in an acceptable profit before you release your grain. But, to use this marketing tool effectively, you must be able to determine your basis.

Farmers have three possible selling periods: before, during, or after harvest. Also, they have two basic avenues through which to make those sales. They can sell for cash or in some way get involved with the commodity futures markets.

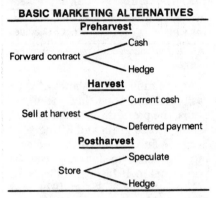

BASIC MARKETING ALTERNATIVES
Preharvest

Forward contract
- Cash
- Hedge

Harvest

Sell at harvest
- Current cash
- Deferred payment

Postharvest

Store
- Speculate
- Hedge

It seems the vast majority of farmers feel most comfortable with the cash alternatives–either forward cash contracting, selling from the field, or storing and speculating that the cash market will rise enough to cover storage costs plus some additional profit. This is unfortunate since the farmer misses one-half of his marketing alternatives when he ignores the futures markets.

In short, hedging allows you to insure a certain price for your crop. If cash prices fall, your profit goal is protected. On the other hand, if prices rise during a storage hedge, your profits will be insulated also. However, the futures market allows you the flexibility to become a cash speculator again anytime you wish by lifting your hedge early.

The key to intelligent hedging is to know your basis or the normal difference between your local cash market and Chicago futures in any given period.

First step is to begin keeping a daily record of your local cash markets relative to Chicago futures. You can take a small notebook and paste in each day's futures prices clipped from the local paper. Then pencil in your local elevator offer

for the same day. By simply referring to last year, you're in a position to see how current bids compare. But for best results, you'll need to do some additional homework by tracking basis relationships back at least 5 years.

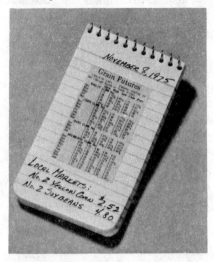

It doesn't have to be a daily tracking. You can select 1 day of the week–i.e., plot your local cash and the futures price for each Monday during past crop years. Then subtract to find the Monday differences between Chicago futures and local cash and plot those differences on a chart for each crop year.

The point to remember is that you will be charting your local prices. We are using St. Louis quotes merely as an example in the following charts.

Basis: St. Louis Cash Corn ± Chicago July Futures 1979-80

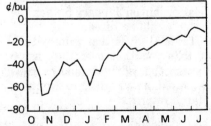

Based on St. Louis cash, the above chart shows how the local cash/July futures basis chart looks for the 1979-80 crop year. We sug-

gest that you make similar charts for your local market for the last 5 or 6 years.

Shortcut to basis history

If the previous example looks like too much work, here's a shortcut method using basis tables which compare cash/futures price relationships for only 2 days out of each past crop year–one for a day during harvest and the other for a day during the later period when you would normally expect to move stored grain to market.

Table A:

OCTOBER 15 CORN BASIS*
CASH ± JULY FUTURES

Crop Year	St. Louis Cash	July Futures	Basis
		Per bushel	
1975-76	$2.70	$3.08	–38¢
1976-77	2.42	2.84	–42¢
1977-78	1.67	2.22	–55¢
1978-79	2.15	2.52	–37¢
1979-80	2.60	3.08	–48¢
1980-81	3.30	3.71	–41¢
Averages	$2.47	$2.91	–44¢
1981-82	$2.57	$3.31	–74¢

*All prices rounded to nearest cent per bushel.

This table tells you that in mid-October, the St. Louis cash basis averaged some 44¢ under July futures during 1975-80. The range was 37¢ under in 1978 to 55¢ under in 1977.

The 1981 mid-October basis was 74¢, cash under July futures, setting up an excellent basis gain opportunity for a storage hedge.

It's that kind of basis which keeps country grain elevators in business. With knowledge of hedging, grain producers can take advantage of it also.

The following table gives further important basis information when used in relation to Table A. For example, Table B tells you that in the past 6 years, the St. Louis cash basis averaged 8¢ under July futures. The range was from 14¢ under to 2¢ over July futures.

JULY 1 CORN BASIS*
CASH ± JULY FUTURES

Crop Year	St. Louis Cash	July Futures	Basis
		Per bushel	
1975-76	$2.91	$2.96	−5¢
1976-77	2.10	2.21	−11¢
1977-78	2.35	2.46	−11¢
1978-79	2.81	2.95	−14¢
1979-80	2.87	2.96	−9¢
1980-81	3.36	3.34	+2¢
Averages	$2.73	$2.81	−8¢
1981-82	?	?	−14¢ to +2¢

*All prices rounded to nearest cent per bushel.

Historically then, Tables A and B show that the St. Louis basis (cash versus July futures) has narrowed an average of 36¢ per bushel from mid-October to July 1. The farmer who stored cash corn and sold July futures in mid-October every year during 1975-80 picked up an average of 36¢ more per bushel (less storage costs) than by selling from the field. The range was from 23¢ (-37 to -14) in 1978 to 44¢ (-55 to -11) in 1977.

Also, Table A shows that the St. Louis cash/futures relationship on October 15, 1981, was offering from 60¢ (-74 to -14) to 76¢ (-74 to +2) per bushel to store corn into July, based on the basis history.

The two tables also tell you that the farmer who stored corn unhedged from October 15 to July 1 in all these years averaged $2.73 versus $2.47 per bushel for those who sold from the field on October 15. Farmers who hedged July futures averaged $2.83 per bushel over the 5-year period.

This is not to say that any one method will be best every year. If you consider 20¢ commercial storage costs from October through June, hedging was most profitable in 3 of the years and storing grain unhedged was most profitable in 2 years. (However, the hedged grain was protected against any dramatic price drop, whereas the unhedged grain was vulnerable.)

The harvesttime sale was least profitable in 5 years. However, a forward cash contract or futures hedge earlier in the summer would have made the early sale most profitable in a couple of the years.

Some additional examples

Suppose you don't care to hold grain into summer. An alternative then would be to pick out a closer futures contract for hedging–March for instance.

The advantage of this is that the bulk of basis change occurs by January. As the market rids itself of the harvest glut, cash and futures prices normally move together quickly through December.

This was determined by building two additional basis tables that you should also consider for your area.

These tables compare the October 15 price to the price around January 5 in the March futures. Table C gives the mid-October basis, cash versus March futures. Table D shows that basis on the closest marketing day to January 5.

Table C:

OCTOBER 15 CORN BASIS*
CASH ± MARCH FUTURES

Crop Year	St. Louis Cash	March Futures	Basis
		Per bushel	
1975-76	$2.70	$3.03	−33¢
1976-77	2.42	2.75	−33¢
1977-78	1.67	2.13	−46¢
1978-79	2.15	2.44	−29¢
1979-80	2.60	2.94	−34¢
1980-81	3.30	3.68	−38¢
Averages	$2.47	$2.83	−36¢
1981-82	$2.57	$3.12	−55¢

*All prices rounded to nearest cent per bushel.

Table C shows that in mid-October, the St. Louis cash basis averaged some 36¢ under March futures during the 1975-80 period. The range was 29¢ under in 1978 to 46¢ under in 1977.

The October 15, 1981, basis was -55¢, some 19¢ below the average. A good hedging opportunity? That depends on cash/March futures basis relationship on January 5 when the hedge would be lifted.

Table D gives that information. It tells you that over the past 6 years, the early-January basis averaged about -10¢, cash under March futures.

Therefore, the cash/March futures basis average during those years moved from -36¢ in mid-October to -10¢ in early January for an average of 26¢. That compares with an average change of 36¢ from October 15 to July 1 in the cash/July basis during the same period.

Table D:

JANUARY 5 CORN BASIS*
CASH ± MARCH FUTURES

Crop Year	St. Louis Cash	March Futures	Basis
		Per bushel	
1975-76	$2.60	$2.69	−9¢
1976-77	2.54	2.62	−8¢
1977-78	2.15	2.22	−7¢
1978-79	2.31	2.29	+2¢
1979-80	2.56	2.87	−31¢
1980-81	3.70	3.78	−8¢
Averages	$2.64	$2.74	−10¢
1981-82	?	?	−31¢ to +2¢

*All prices rounded to nearest cent per bushel.

As the table below shows, if your cash grain market had been St. Louis, the profit difference between selling stored grain and lifting your hedge in July, as opposed to unlocking the hedge in January, was 9¢ per bushel in 1975, 6¢ in 1976, 5¢ in 1977, -8¢ in 1978, 36¢ in 1979, and 13¢ in 1980.

ST. LOUIS CASH/FUTURES BASIS*
CASH/MARCH

Crop Year	October 15	January 2	Change
1975-76	−33¢	−9¢	+24¢
1976-77	−33¢	−8¢	+25¢
1977-78	−46¢	−7¢	+39¢
1978-79	−29¢	+2¢	+31¢
1979-80	−34¢	−31¢	+3¢
1980-81	−38¢	−8¢	+30¢
Averages	−36¢	−10¢	+26¢
1981-82	−55¢	—	—

CASH/JULY

Crop Year	October 15	July 1	Change
1975-76	−38¢	−5¢	+33¢
1976-77	−42¢	−11¢	+31¢
1977-78	−55¢	−11¢	+44¢
1978-79	−37¢	−14¢	+23¢
1979-80	−48¢	−9¢	+39¢
1980-81	−41¢	+2¢	+43¢
Averages	−44¢	−8¢	+36¢
1981-82	−74¢	—	—

*All prices rounded to nearest cent per bushel.

As noted earlier, these examples apply to the St. Louis area only. Cash prices will vary in other areas, sometimes dramatically. That's why it's important that you learn as much as possible about your local situation. Local elevators may be a source of cash data.

The Legal Side of Forward Contracts

*An advance sale contract for grains or cotton will lock
in a price, but be sure you understand the contract terms.*

Forward contracting for the sale of farm commodities has become increasingly popular in recent years. Most grain and staple commodities have commonly been sold at some time following harvest with negotiations, sale, delivery and payment accomplished within a few days. By waiting until after harvest, however, the producer bears the risk that the market price available when the crop is ready to be sold will be different from the price anticipated when the decision was made.

By contracting for the sale of these commodities during the production season or prior to planting, risk of market decline can be avoided. This is especially important to low-equity producers who can least afford to gamble with the market. Also, with price security, they may expand their base for operating credit. Among the other benefits of forward contracting are:

(1) Certainty of time and place for delivery;

(2) avoiding the cost of storage facilities and quality preservation; and

(3) with records of production costs, net crop returns can be projected during the growing season.

On the negative side, the farmer is locked in. If prices rise, he is stuck with his contract price. He's also obliged to deliver a fixed quantity on a specified date. Adverse weather and other unknowns may make it difficult and costly to fulfill the contract obligations.

THE TRANSACTION

Except for the more remote delivery date, forward sales of farm commodities are very much like sales for immediate delivery. Usually, the transaction is quite informal. The parties are generally well acquainted. Either face to face or by phone the producer contacts the buyer to check the current price. If it sounds good, the deal is made. The seller indicates the amount he will deliver, and a delivery date is set.

In some instances the buyer enters the sale in his ledger, noting the commodity, the quality (grade), quantity, price, date of sale and date(s) of delivery. Occasionally, where both parties are present, they may execute a written contract of sale. Very often, however, the deal is closed orally.

ORAL OR WRITTEN AGREEMENT

What happens if the oral negotiations between the farmer and the elevator operator leave the buyer thinking an agreement has been reached while the farmer thinks there are still terms to be resolved? Is the farmer bound? Though oral agreements can in some instances be as binding as written ones, here the farmer is at least partially protected by the Statute of Frauds provisions now contained in the Uniform Commercial Code. The UCC, enacted in every state except Louisiana, provides that contracts for the sale of "goods" which involve $500 or more are legally unenforceable unless they are in written form. Farm products, grain and staples are considered to be goods within the statute.

An informal written memorandum of the transaction should suffice to make the contract enforceable. It need not contain all of the elements of a formal contract but must contain enough to prove that an oral agreement was actually reached. The statute suggests that a paper specifying only the quantity and bearing the signatures of the buyer and the seller is adequate. The courts will imply a "reasonable price" if none is indicated. In addition, even the oral contract may be enforced under the code to the extent that grain has been delivered and accepted or paid for in part.

CONFIRMATION OF GRAIN PURCHASE

To avoid problems of enforcing oral contracts under the statute of frauds and to validate oral contracts, many commodity buyers mail written confirmations of their oral contract of sale. Usually the confirmation sets forth the amount of grain or staple, the quality, the agreed price, delivery date(s), and is signed by the buyer.

If the producer concurs in the terms set forth in the confirmation and signs it, then it is a binding contract. If he immediately rejects the confirmation in writing, no contract exists. But what if the farmer receives the confirmation, sets it aside and does nothing with it? That depends on the court's view of the farmer involved. To enforce the contract, buyers rely on a UCC provision which says that if the transaction is between two merchants, the seller need not sign and return the confirmation in order to be bound by its terms. Clearly the elevator, cotton company or other buyer is a merchant. The question for the courts to decide is whether the farmer-seller is also a merchant. If he is, the written confirmation would make the oral agreement enforceable against him unless he rejects the confirmation in writing within ten days following its receipt.

When an Arkansas farmer failed to deliver soybeans as he had verbally agreed to do, the elevator went to court claiming the farmer was a merchant and since the buyer's confirmation was not rejected in writing within ten days, the farmer was bound by its terms. But the court sided with the farmer, holding that farmers are not merchants and that the statute of frauds was a sound defense despite the elevator's attempt to confirm the deal in writing.

But more recently, courts in Illinois and Ohio refused to follow the Arkansas decision. Instead, they observed that the farmers in question had grown and sold their crops for several years. They kept abreast of the market. Under these circumstances the courts said the farmers should be treated as merchants, bound by the terms of the elevator's written confirmations of sale not rejected in writing within ten days.

What other courts will do with this issue is uncertain. But the uncertainty can be removed if the seller promptly accepts or rejects the written confirmation of sale in writing.

CONTRACT TERMS

Above all, read and understand the contract or confirmation. If the buyers with whom you deal have standard contracts, obtain samples of those forms and take time to discuss their provisions with your attorney before they are signed.

In reviewing such contracts, consider not only your obligations, but those of the buyer as well. Grain sale contracts often provide that if the commodity is not delivered within the specified period, the contract may be extended or cancelled at the buyer's option. Producers are thus at the mercy of the elevator if they're not there with the grain on the date set. But what if the elevator is full and there are no railroad cars available at harvest when you're supposed to deliver? Who pays your storage until cars become available or who pays for the deterioration in quality while the crop stands in the field until the buyer can accept delivery? Many contracts resolve the question by providing that if the elevator is full on the date the seller wishes to make delivery, seller will hold the commodity until space becomes available.

POINTERS

In contracting for future delivery of farm commodities keep the following in mind:

(1) Production cost records are necessary for knowledgeable negotiation of contract price.

(2) Once a price is agreed upon, put the contract terms in writing.

(3) Don't get tied to a very tight delivery schedule. Provide enough flexibility so that you can work around the weather and other unexpected delays and demands upon your time.

(4) Besides price and delivery date, make sure the contract provides:
- the quantity sold (it's vital)
- the point of delivery
- the quality (grade) priced
- what happens if the seller cannot make delivery on time
- what happens if the buyer cannot accept delivery on time.

(5) Don't just disregard written confirmations of verbal agreements. Read and understand their content. See that they are signed by the buyer and make your intentions known by either signing or rejecting the confirmation in writing. If you ignore or do not return the confirmation mailed to you by the buyer, it could be legally binding—just as if you had signed it.

(6) Remember, the failure to have an enforceable contract can work both ways. If the market works down by delivery date, the buyer can rely on the same outs as the seller to avoid his obligation to purchase.

(7) Go over these comments and the contracts or confirmations your buyers use with your attorney. Only he can evaluate the legal aspects of your situation and knowledgeably advise you in your operations.

Forward sale contracts, as discussed in this page, are one means of locking-in a sale price ahead of harvest. Use of the futures market is another technique. Consult a commodity broker or your attorney for the legal aspects of futures contracts.

Cost of Gain Affects Marketing Decisions

Timing of livestock sales for highest profit is affected by both cost of gain levels and current or expected market conditions.

The bigger an animal gets, the more feed it needs for body maintenance, and the less feed it utilizes for added gain. Consequently, more feed is needed for each pound of gain and the cost of gain rises.

Since the body chemistry of livestock works this way, marketing becomes not only a problem of picking a "best" price at which to sell, but also a problem of equating this price to the cost of getting the animal to that point in time when the "best" price occurs. Many times waiting for the top price can actually cost money.

The general loss in feed conversion efficiency when animals are fed to heavier weights is illustrated by the table below, taken from the National Research Council's Reports on "Nutrient Requirements of Domestic Animals."

DAILY FEED REQUIREMENTS AND FEED CONVERSION RATIOS

Body Weight	Daily Feed Requirement	Average Dairy Gain	Feed Per Pound of Gain
(Lbs.)	(Lbs.)	(Lbs.)	(Lbs.)
Finishing Yearling Cattle			
600	17.5	2.6	6.7
800	22.3	2.7	8.3
1,000	25.8	2.6	9.9
1,100	25.8	2.3	11.2
Finishing Lambs			
60	2.7	.35	7.7
70	3.1	.40	7.8
80	3.4	.45	7.6
90	3.7	.45	8.2
100	3.9	.40	9.7
Finishing Hogs			
50- 75	3.7	1.3	2.8
75-125	5.2	1.6	3.3
125-175	6.7	1.7	3.9
175-225	7.8	1.9	4.1

Beef cattle are less efficient users of feed than lambs or hogs. Both feed efficiency and rate of gain become progressively poorer as animals move to heavier weights. As shown in the table, roughly two-thirds more feed is required to put on a pound of gain as the animal nears 1,100 pounds than was required at 600 pounds.

There is little research to show what happens when cattle are fed to weights above "normal" finish of 1,100 pounds. The following chart is taken from Illinois data on efficiency of gain. In these trials, gain data were obtained for successive 28-day periods. The yearling steers went on feed at 688 pounds. One lot came off feed after 140 days at an average weight of 1,114 pounds—the other lot continued to 308 days on feed to 1,442 pounds.

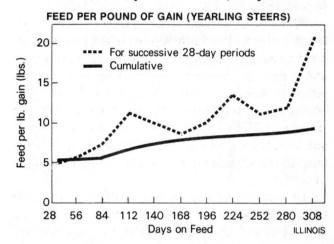

FEED PER POUND OF GAIN (YEARLING STEERS)

In the tests, feed costs showed a progressive rise, paralleling efficiency of gain charted above. Generally, as cattle near normal slaughter weights, the increasingly inefficient use of feed is justified only if there is an increase in the value of the animal due to a higher slaughter grade.

Other economic factors come into play when cattle are fed to heavier than normal weights. It's just about impossible to isolate and weigh precisely the influence of heavier slaughter weights on total cattle markets. But there's no doubt they do have an overall detrimental effect . . . both through the increased tonnage of meat produced and through price discounts on heavyweight carcasses that develop when average slaughter weights increase.

The Illinois trials illustrate one reason why price discounts may be levied against heavy animals. The longer fed steers had a 3% to 4% higher dressing percent and 11% larger loin eye, and graded one-third to one-half grade higher in both quality and conformation. However, these advantages were lost with the wastier carcasses of the heavier animals. The extra fat trim resulted in a 12% lower retail yield, reducing the actual retail value significantly. Another factor is the limited demand for highly finished animals—the market is easily saturated.

Hogs are more efficient users of feed than either cattle or lambs. Still, the same pattern of sharply increasing feed requirements per pound of gain is apparent as the animals move to heavier weights.

The chart below is adapted from North Dakota studies of a few years ago. As the hogs moved to progressively heavier weights, the feed required for each pound of gain moved up sharply. As the animals approached 300 pounds, roughly six pounds of feed were needed for each pound of gain.

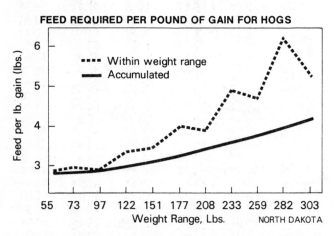

FEED REQUIRED PER POUND OF GAIN FOR HOGS

- ····· Within weight range
- ▬▬▬ Accumulated

Feed per lb. gain (lbs.)

Weight Range, Lbs.　NORTH DAKOTA

55　73　97　122　151　177　208　233　259　282　303

Feeding hogs to excessive weights can have industry-wide implications. Price spreads between weights and grades of slaughter hogs are affected by the relative supply of heavy hogs. Typically, as slaughter weights decline, the price spread narrows between light and heavy hogs. When average weights increase, the spread widens.

COMPOSITION OF CARCASSES BETWEEN 190 AND 250 POUNDS LIVEWEIGHT

Live-weight	Est. carcass weight	Est. lean weight	Est. fat weight	Ten lb. gain composed of:	
				Lean	Fat
190	142.5	74.1	44.5		
200	150.0	77.0	48.5	2.9	4.0
210	157.5	79.7	52.6	2.7	4.1
220	165.0	82.5	56.8	2.8	4.2
230	172.5	85.2	61.1	2.7	4.3
240	180.0	87.8	65.5	2.6	4.4
250	187.5	90.4	70.1	2.6	4.6

PURDUE

One of the primary problems of heavyweight hogs is the question of quality—particularly as it relates to fat-lean ratio. The table shows results of experiments at Purdue University to determine what happens to pork carcasses as hogs move into the heavier weight categories. The research concludes that only about 27% of the increased weight results in additional edible lean meat.

According to USDA's Consumer and Marketing Service, holding hogs from 200 to 250 pounds will ordinarily result in an increase in fatness equivalent to one grade or more, and may reduce the percentage of the four major lean cuts by 3%.

Lambs suffer the same penalties in terms of inefficient and costly gains as other classes of livestock. Note the table on the front. In addition, the price discounts between heavy and lighter lambs can be quite substantial.

With a relatively low level of lamb consumption per capita, the market at retail may fluctuate significantly between heavier and lighter carcasses. Lamb carcasses weighing in the 45 to 55 pound range, grading Choice or above, are usually most acceptable to the trade. Generally, producing carcasses above this weight range is desirable only if buyers will accept them without penalty.

Know your costs and feed efficiencies. There are only general rules as to what may be the most efficient marketing weight for your animals. Too, there may be a conflict between what is best for your own feeding operation and what may be desirable from the long-range viewpoint of the industry. For instance, in a rapidly gaining market, it may be to your advantage to go a little heavy on animals—even at the expense of gain efficiencies. But it's often for this reason that animals are held until they become unduly heavy—and marketed at a subsequent loss when the better market doesn't materialize.

Typically, taking animals to heavier than normal weights involves increasing risk. You are betting markets will strengthen or at least stay steady. Bear in mind, however, that should markets fall, the discount will be applied to the total weight of the animal. While the cost of gain on those final pounds may remain below market price, a discount applied to the total weight can quickly wipe out any advantage to feeding the animal heavier.

Livestock Shrinkage Loss

Shrinkage can be a hidden cost of marketing unless you understand the causes and rates, and can estimate the weight loss of your livestock in transit.

Efficient marketing of cattle and hogs requires an understanding of livestock shrinkage. Distance to be hauled and shrinkage discounts should be considered when choosing the best market for your livestock. The highest price per pound may not be as important as the number of actual pounds reaching market.

TYPES OF SHRINKAGE

Excretory shrinkage is the initial loss of belly fill during the first 12 hour stand. As soon as cattle or hogs are restored to feed and water, much of this loss is replaced.

Tissue shrinkage occurs after prolonged fasting and more extensive traveling. At one point excretory and tissue shrink occur simultaneously, but the longer the shipping time, the more important tissue shrinkage becomes. Since this is an actual loss of tissue weight, it is harder to replace and a loss of carcass weight is maintained by the seller.

It's important for you to estimate shrinkage loss since it is part of your marketing costs. Transporting a longer distance for a higher price may not result in a bigger net profit when you consider the larger weight losses and increased transportation costs. The table at right can help you determine the price you would have to receive to compensate for shrinkage loss due to handling and transportation.

Accurate record-keeping over the years can give you an average shrinkage rate. Past experience helps you estimate the amount of shrinkage to expect and will allow you to bargain with the buyer over discounts. Arbitrary pencil shrink discounts of 3% to 5% may sometimes be higher than the actual loss.

CATTLE SHRINKAGE

Shrinkage occurs whenever cattle are moved, whether for short or long distances. The initial stress of loading and handling causes cattle to lose half as much weight in the first 25 miles as they do in 200 miles. Cattle have been found to shrink 4% in the first four hours of shipping. As the time in transit increases, so does the amount of shrinkage, but at a slower rate than in the first few miles.

NET PRICE WITH SHRINKAGE DEDUCTED

| Offer | Shrinkage of: | | | | |
	2%	3%	4%	6%	8%
$79.00	$77.42	$76.63	$75.84	$74.26	$72.68
78.00	76.44	75.66	74.88	73.32	71.76
77.00	75.46	74.69	73.92	72.38	70.84
76.00	74.48	73.72	72.96	71.44	69.92
75.00	73.50	72.75	72.00	70.50	69.00
74.00	72.52	71.78	71.04	69.56	68.08
73.00	71.54	70.81	70.08	68.62	67.16
72.00	70.56	69.84	69.12	67.68	66.24
71.00	69.58	68.87	68.16	66.74	65.32
70.00	68.60	67.90	67.20	65.80	64.40
69.00	67.62	66.93	66.24	64.86	63.48
68.00	66.64	65.96	65.28	63.92	62.56
67.00	65.66	64.99	64.32	62.98	61.64
66.00	64.68	64.02	63.36	62.04	60.72
65.00	63.70	63.05	62.40	61.10	59.80
64.00	62.72	62.08	61.44	60.16	58.88
63.00	61.74	61.11	60.48	59.22	57.96
62.00	60.76	60.14	59.52	58.28	57.04
61.00	59.78	59.17	58.56	57.34	56.12
60.00	58.80	58.20	57.60	56.40	55.20
59.00	57.82	57.23	56.64	55.46	54.28
58.00	56.84	56.26	55.68	54.52	53.36
57.00	55.86	55.29	54.72	53.58	52.44
56.00	54.88	54.32	53.76	52.64	51.52
55.00	53.90	53.35	52.80	51.70	50.60
54.00	52.92	52.38	51.84	50.76	49.68
53.00	51.94	51.41	50.88	49.82	48.76
52.00	50.96	50.44	49.92	48.88	47.84
51.00	49.98	49.47	48.96	47.94	46.92
50.00	49.00	48.50	48.00	47.00	46.00
49.00	48.02	47.53	47.04	46.06	45.08
48.00	47.04	46.56	46.08	45.12	44.16
47.00	46.06	45.59	45.12	44.18	43.24
46.00	45.08	44.62	44.16	43.24	42.32
45.00	44.10	43.65	43.20	42.30	41.40
44.00	43.12	42.68	42.24	41.36	40.48
43.00	42.14	41.71	41.28	40.42	39.56
42.00	41.16	40.74	40.32	39.48	38.64
41.00	40.18	39.77	39.36	38.54	37.72
40.00	39.20	38.80	38.40	37.60	36.80
39.00	38.22	37.83	37.44	36.66	35.88
38.00	37.24	36.86	36.48	35.72	34.96
37.00	36.26	35.89	35.52	34.78	34.04
36.00	35.28	34.92	34.56	33.84	33.12
35.00	34.30	33.95	33.60	32.90	32.20
34.00	33.32	32.98	32.64	31.96	31.28
33.00	32.34	32.01	31.68	31.02	30.36
32.00	31.36	31.04	30.72	30.08	29.44
31.00	30.38	30.07	29.76	29.14	28.52
30.00	29.40	29.10	28.80	28.20	27.60
29.00	28.42	28.13	27.84	27.26	26.68
28.00	27.44	27.16	26.88	26.32	25.76
27.00	26.46	26.19	25.92	25.38	24.84
26.00	25.48	25.22	24.96	24.44	23.92
25.00	24.50	24.25	24.00	23.50	23.00
24.00	23.52	23.28	23.04	22.56	22.08
23.00	22.54	22.31	22.08	21.62	21.16
22.00	21.56	21.34	21.12	20.68	20.24
21.00	20.58	20.37	20.16	19.74	19.32
20.00	19.60	19.40	19.20	18.80	18.40

Reduce some of the stress caused in shipping by using extra care in loading. Don't prolong loading time unnecessarily. Avoid crowding to reduce bumping, bruising and general congestion which increase nervousness and raise the shrinkage rate. Extreme temperatures, rain, snow and wind can increase shrinkage as well.

Make sure cattle are supplied with fresh water and hay at rest and overnight stops. This will help them regain some of the weight loss from excretory as well as tissue shrinkage. Allowing 24 to 36 hours for resting after long hauls can result in added profits for the seller.

Watch for "double shrink" discounts when your cattle must be shipped to a nearby weighing facility. Even if the scales are within a short distance, shrinkage will be significant because of the heavy weight loss from the initial move. Often a pencil shrink discount of 3% will be made on the weight of the cattle at the weigh-in after they have lost 2% to 3% in the haul to the scales. If cattle are unloaded and not weighed until morning, the seller can expect an additional 2% loss from the overnight stand, even if feed and water are available. In this case, the pencil shrink exaggerates the actual shrinkage.

FEEDER STEER SHRINKAGE

Conditions	Percent Shrink
8-hour drylot stand	3.3
16-hour drylot stand	6.2
24-hour drylot stand	6.6
8 hours in moving truck	5.5
16 hours in moving truck	7.9
24 hours in moving truck	8.9

Differences in shrinkage rates between heifers and steers are variable, but heifers shrink slightly more. There does not seem to be any difference among breeds of cattle.

Pre-conditioning calves is a controversial practice. Some believe calves can shrink excessively if they are weaned, vaccinated and loaded all in the same time period. Pre-weaning and vaccinating can speed recovery of lost weight. However, an Iowa study tends to contradict this advice. Pre-weaned calves in the Iowa test weighed less after transit than they did prior to weaning, while calves that had not been weaned ahead of shipping were heavier than they were 11 days before the shipping date.

Range cattle are not used to crowded pens and shrinkage of 5% or more can result from the stress. Cattle familiar with enclosed conditions may lose only 2% overnight if feed and water are available.

Type of feed alters the amount of shrink. Finished cattle shrink more than feeders in the first 8 to 10 hours, but feeder cattle shrink about 2% more than finished cattle on long hauls—7% to 9% of their total weight. An overnight stand of 12 hours without food and water will cause 4% shrink in cattle fed grass or silage while cattle finished on concentrates may lose only 2.5% to 3%.

HOG SHRINKAGE

Most of the factors that affect cattle also influence the amount of shrinkage in hogs. However, some conditions have more effect on hogs. Special care should be taken when these factors are encountered in transporting.

Hogs are extremely sensitive to temperatures below 20° and above 60°, according to an Indiana study. Temperatures outside this range increase stress and shrinkage in hogs much more than they do in cattle. Heat prostration and death loss can be quite high. Loading and shipping in the cooler parts of the day can sharply decrease the amount of shrinkage.

Handling is very important in reducing hog shrinkage. As with cattle, the hog shrinkage rate is greatest in the first few miles of transit (see table below). Try to keep the excitement and confusion of loading to a minimum to decrease this first shrinkage.

SLAUGHTER HOG SHRINK IN RELATION TO DISTANCE HAULED AND TIME IN TRANSIT

Condition	Percent Shrink
0-35 miles hauled	0.74
36-65 miles hauled	1.37
66-95 miles hauled	1.45
Over 95 miles hauled	1.71
0-75 minutes in transit	0.69
76-200 minutes in transit	1.32
201-400 minutes in transit	1.45
Over 400 minutes in transit	1.95

Overloading should be avoided since it will increase stress and nervousness. However, do not underload and allow hogs too much room to shift around and increase confusion during the haul. Avoid any unnecessary delays or rough handling during shipping.

Allow time for feeding and resting when you get to market so hogs can regain some of the shrinkage loss. This practice may not be economical after short hauls—45 miles or less—according to a Purdue study, but it has proven worthwhile after longer hauls.

Grain Marketing Tables

They'll help you to calculate grain shrinkage and to compare the costs of drying with the moisture discounts applied when you market high moisture grain.

The tables on this page will help you market cash grain. The large table below applies to all grains and gives shrinkage when grain is dried to levels of 13% to 19% moisture. One-half of 1% is included in the table for dry matter shrink.

To figure shrink at levels that may not be included in the table, use this formula:

Shrinkage =

$$100\% - \frac{(\% \text{ dry matter in wet grain})}{(\% \text{ dry matter in dry grain})} \times 100) + 0.5\% \text{ handling shrink}$$

To determine the value of corn shrink, multiply the percentage from the table by the No. 2 corn price. By subtracting this shrink value from the moisture discount, you arrive at the penalty for selling wet corn.

It's important that you know and understand the shrinkage charges that are typically levied in your area. Traditionally, shrinkage charges have been levied at a fixed rate per bushel, per point of moisture—2¢ per point and 3¢ per point have been the most common.

But with higher corn prices, the traditional fixed discounts have gone by the board in many areas. In their place, many elevators are levying a discount as a percentage of the corn price. For instance, a 2% reduction in price of No. 2 corn for each point of moisture over 15.5% has been used in

GRAIN SHRINKAGE TABLE

Initial moisture (Percent)	When Grain Is Dried To These Levels												
	13.0%	13.5%	14.0%	14.5%	15.0%	15.5%	16.0%	16.5%	17.0%	17.5%	18.0%	18.5%	19.0%
	(Percent of Shrinkage)												
15.5	3.37	2.81	2.24	1.67	1.09	--	--	--	--	--	--	--	--
16.0	3.95	3.39	2.83	2.25	1.68	1.09	--	--	--	--	--	--	--
16.5	4.52	3.97	3.41	2.84	2.26	1.68	1.10	--	--	--	--	--	--
17.0	5.10	4.55	3.99	3.42	2.85	2.28	1.70	1.10	--	--	--	--	--
17.5	5.67	5.12	4.57	4.01	3.44	2.87	2.29	1.70	1.11	--	--	--	--
18.0	6.25	5.70	5.15	4.59	4.03	3.46	2.88	2.30	1.71	1.11	--	--	--
18.5	6.82	6.28	5.73	5.18	4.62	4.05	3.48	2.90	2.31	1.72	1.11	--	--
19.0	7.40	6.86	6.31	5.76	5.21	4.64	4.08	3.50	2.91	2.32	1.72	1.12	--
19.5	7.97	7.44	6.90	6.35	5.79	5.23	4.67	4.10	3.52	2.93	2.33	1.73	1.12
20.0	8.55	8.01	7.48	6.93	6.38	5.83	5.27	4.70	4.12	3.54	2.94	2.35	1.74
20.5	9.12	8.59	8.06	7.52	6.97	6.42	5.86	5.30	4.72	4.14	3.55	2.96	2.36
21.0	9.70	9.17	8.64	8.10	7.56	7.01	6.46	5.89	5.32	4.75	4.16	3.57	2.97
21.5	10.27	9.75	9.22	8.69	8.15	7.60	7.05	6.49	5.93	5.35	4.77	4.19	3.59
22.0	10.84	10.33	9.80	9.27	8.74	8.19	7.65	7.09	6.53	5.96	5.38	4.80	4.21
22.5	11.42	10.90	10.38	9.86	9.32	8.78	8.24	7.69	7.13	6.57	5.99	5.40	4.83
23.0	11.99	11.48	10.97	10.44	9.91	9.38	8.84	8.29	7.73	7.17	6.60	6.03	5.44
23.5	12.57	12.06	11.55	11.03	10.50	9.97	9.43	8.89	8.34	7.78	7.21	6.64	6.06
24.0	13.14	12.64	12.13	11.61	11.09	10.56	10.03	9.49	8.94	8.38	7.82	7.25	6.68
24.5	13.72	13.22	12.71	12.20	11.68	11.15	10.62	10.09	9.54	8.99	8.43	7.87	7.30
25.0	14.29	13.79	13.29	12.78	12.26	11.74	11.22	10.68	10.14	9.60	9.04	8.48	7.91
25.5	14.87	14.37	13.87	13.37	12.85	12.33	11.81	11.28	10.75	10.20	9.65	9.09	8.53
26.0	15.44	14.95	14.45	13.95	13.44	12.93	12.41	11.88	11.35	10.81	10.26	9.71	9.15
26.5	16.02	15.53	15.03	14.54	14.03	13.52	13.00	12.48	11.95	11.41	10.87	10.32	9.76
27.0	16.60	16.11	15.62	15.12	14.62	14.11	13.60	13.08	12.55	12.02	11.48	10.93	10.38
27.5	17.17	16.69	16.20	15.71	15.21	14.71	14.20	13.68	13.16	12.63	12.09	11.55	11.00
28.0	17.74	17.26	16.78	16.29	15.79	15.29	14.79	14.27	13.75	13.23	12.70	12.16	11.61
28.5	18.32	17.84	17.36	16.87	16.38	15.88	15.38	14.87	14.36	13.83	13.30	12.77	12.23
29.0	18.89	18.42	17.94	17.46	16.97	16.48	15.98	15.47	14.96	14.44	13.92	13.38	12.85
29.5	19.47	19.00	18.52	18.04	17.56	17.07	16.57	16.07	15.56	15.05	14.52	14.00	13.46
30.0	20.04	19.58	19.10	18.63	18.15	17.66	17.17	16.67	16.16	15.65	15.13	14.61	14.08

some areas. Under this system, with a $2 market, 20.5% moisture corn would be docked 20¢ per bushel.

This change in discounts has been necessary because fixed discounts are unfair as corn prices move higher. When you sell wet corn, you're selling water—the moisture discount should account for this. As corn prices move up, the water you sell in wet corn becomes more valuable, but the fixed discount doesn't change. Hence, the higher the corn price, the less the advantage of drying.

The table at the bottom of this page should prove particularly valuable in transactions between landlord and tenant, for instance, when they want to agree on an equitable price to compensate for the excess moisture in high-moisture corn. From the table, if No. 2 corn price is $2, then 21% moisture corn is worth $1.86 per bushel.

The other table equates high-moisture corn, both in the ear and shelled, to a bushel (56 pounds) of 15.5% moisture shelled corn. Any table that converts ear corn to shelled corn is only an approximation, since the shelling percentage of ear corn varies with the moisture in the kernels and in the cobs, how long it has been stored, size of the ears, hybrid variety, etc. The ratios reflected in the table are from Iowa State University tests and should be about average. Other than using a typical shellout, such as the table is based on, the only way to determine the amount of shelled corn in a lot of ear corn is to shell the entire lot and weigh the shelled corn.

ESTIMATED POUNDS OF CORN AT SELECTED MOISTURE LEVELS TO EQUAL ONE BUSHEL OF SHELLED CORN

Percentage Moisture In Kernels	Pounds of Ear Corn To Equal 56 Pounds 15.5% Moisture Shelled Corn[1]	Pounds of Shelled Corn To Equal 56 Pounds 15.5% Moisture[2]
15.5	68.40	56.00
16.0	68.94	56.62
16.5	69.51	56.96
17.0	70.09	57.31
17.5	70.69	57.65
18.0	71.31	58.01
18.5	71.95	58.36
19.0	72.60	58.72
19.5	73.27	59.09
20.0	73.96	59.47
20.5	74.60	59.84
21.0	75.36	60.22
21.5	76.07	60.61
22.0	76.79	61.00
22.5	77.53	61.39
23.0	78.25	61.80
23.5	79.01	62.20
24.0	79.76	62.61
24.5	80.50	63.03
25.0	81.25	63.45
25.5	82.03	63.88
26.0	82.82	64.32
26.5	83.50	64.75
27.0	84.19	65.20
27.5	84.90	65.65
28.0	85.62	66.11
28.5	86.32	66.57
29.0	87.04	67.05
29.5	87.76	67.53
30.0	88.50	68.01

[1]The ratio of moisture content of kernel and cobs varies considerably. The values in column 2 are based on an average from a large number of samples of different hybrids grown in different years.

[2]One-half of 1% has been included as dry matter loss in column 3.

IOWA STATE

VALUE OF HIGH-MOISTURE SHELLED CORN IN TERMS OF NO. 2 CORN CONTAINING 15.5% MOISTURE ON A DRY MATTER BASIS

Moisture Content	Bushels At 15.5% Moisture	Bushels Shrink Per 1,000 Bu.	Selected Corn Prices (Per Bushel)										
			$1.50	$1.60	$1.70	$1.80	$1.90	$2.00	$2.10	$2.20	$2.30	$2.40	$2.50
16	989.08	10.92	1.4836	1.5825	1.6814	1.7803	1.8792	1.9781	2.0770	2.1759	2.2749	2.3738	2.4727
17	977.25	22.75	1.4658	1.5636	1.6613	1.7590	1.8567	1.9545	2.0522	2.1499	2.2477	2.3454	2.4431
18	965.41	34.59	1.4481	1.5446	1.6412	1.7377	1.8343	1.9308	2.0274	2.1239	2.2204	2.3170	2.4135
19	953.58	46.42	1.4303	1.5257	1.6211	1.7164	1.8118	1.9072	2.0025	2.0979	2.1932	2.2886	2.3840
20	941.75	58.25	1.4126	1.5068	1.6009	1.6951	1.7893	1.8835	1.9777	2.0718	2.1660	2.2602	2.3544
21	929.91	70.09	1.3949	1.4879	1.5808	1.6738	1.7668	1.8598	1.9528	2.0458	2.1388	2.2318	2.3248
22	918.08	81.92	1.3771	1.4689	1.5607	1.6525	1.7444	1.8362	1.9280	2.0198	2.1116	2.2034	2.2952
23	906.24	93.76	1.3594	1.4500	1.5406	1.6312	1.7219	1.8125	1.9031	1.9937	2.0844	2.1750	2.2656
24	894.41	105.59	1.3416	1.4311	1.5205	1.6099	1.6994	1.7888	1.8783	1.9677	2.0571	2.1466	2.2360
25	882.57	117.43	1.3239	1.4121	1.5004	1.5886	1.6769	1.7651	1.8534	1.9417	2.0299	2.1182	2.2064
26	870.74	129.26	1.3061	1.3932	1.4803	1.5673	1.6544	1.7415	1.8286	1.9156	2.0027	2.0898	2.1769
27	858.91	141.09	1.2884	1.3743	1.4601	1.5460	1.6319	1.7178	1.8037	1.8896	1.9755	2.0614	2.1473
28	847.1	152.9	1.2706	1.3554	1.4401	1.5248	1.6094	1.6942	1.7789	1.8636	1.9483	2.0330	2.1178
29	835.2	164.8	1.2528	1.3363	1.4198	1.5034	1.5869	1.6704	1.7539	1.8374	1.9209	2.0045	2.0880
30	823.4	176.6	1.2351	1.3174	1.3998	1.4821	1.5645	1.6468	1.7291	1.8115	1.8938	1.9762	2.0585

IOWA STATE

Moisture Adjustments, Storage and Yield Calculations

Grain is measured on the farm when taking out Commodity Credit Corporation loans and when determining a year end inventory.

The procedures and adjustment factors shown on this page are those used by CCC. They are intended for inventory purposes, not for buying or selling grain.

Figuring volume is the first step needed to determine grain in storage.

Volume of storage structure -- all dimensions in feet.

If square or rectangular -- length x width x height = volume.
Example: Crib 8 feet wide, 32 feet long, 18 feet high.
8 x 32 x 18 = 4,608 cubic feet.

If round and diameter is known --
$1/2$ diameter x $1/2$ diameter x height x 3.14 = volume
Example: Bin 21 feet in diameter, 20 feet high
$1/2$ x 21 x $1/2$ x 21 x 20 x 3.14 = 6,924 cubic feet

If round and only circumference is known --
$$\left(\frac{7 \times circ.}{44}\right) \times \left(\frac{7 \times circ.}{44}\right) \times height \times 3.14 = volume$$

Example: Bin 66 feet in circumference, 20 feet high
$$\left(\frac{7 \times 66}{44}\right) \times \left(\frac{7 \times 66}{44}\right) \times 20 \times 3.14 = 6,924 \text{ cubic feet}$$

After volume is known, bushels of grain are figured by dividing volume by the cubic feet of one bushel of grain. To further refine the estimate of stored grain, corrections can be made for moisture in ear corn and for test weight in shelled corn, sorghum, soybeans and others, as the Commodity Credit Corporation does.

Corn. A bushel of ear corn measures 2.5 cubic feet. It has no more than 16% moisture. Adjust for higher moisture as shown.

Ear corn moisture content (percent)	Adjustment factor (percent)
16.1 to 17.0 both inclusive	98
17.1 to 18.0 both inclusive	96
18.1 to 19.0 both inclusive	94
19.1 to 20.0 both inclusive	92
20.1 to 21.0 both inclusive	90
Above 21.0—no loan	

A bushel of shelled corn must measure 1.25 cubic feet if test weight is 56 pounds per bushel. Adjust for different weights as indicated by the table at right.

For shelled corn testing	Percent
60 pounds or over	107
59 or over, less than 60	105
58 or over, less than 59	104
57 or over, less than 58	102
56 or over, less than 57	100
55 or over, less than 56	98
54 or over, less than 55	96
53 or over, less than 54	95
52 or over, less than 53	93
51 or over, less than 52	91
50 or over, less than 51	89
49 or over, less than 50	88

For soybeans testing	Percent
60 pounds or over	100
59 or over, but less than 60	98
58 or over, but less than 59	97
57 or over, but less than 50	95
56 or over, but less than 57	93
55 or over, but less than 56	92
54 or over, but less than 55	90
53 or over, but less than 54	88
52 or over, but less than 53	87
51 or over, but less than 52	85
50 or over, but less than 51	83
49 or over, but less than 50	82

Wheat. A bushel of wheat must measure 1.25 cubic feet and test 60 pounds per bushel. Make adjustments for different tests according to the table at the right.

For wheat testing	Percent
65 pounds or over	108
64.0 to 64.9	107
63.0 to 63.9	105
62.0 to 62.9	103
61.0 to 61.9	102
60.0 to 60.9	100
59.0 to 59.9	98
58.0 to 58.9	97
57.0 to 57.9	95
56.0 to 56.9	93
55.0 to 55.9	92
54.0 to 54.9	90
53.0 to 53.9	88
52.0 to 52.9	87

For grain sorghum testing	Percent
60 pounds or over	107
59 or over, less than 60	106
58 or over, less than 59	104
57 or over, less than 58	102
56 or over, less than 57	100
55 or over, less than 56	98
54 or over, less than 55	96
53 or over, less than 54	95
52 or over, less than 53	93
51 or over, less than 52	91
50 or over, less than 51	89
49 or over, less than 50	87

Oats. A bushel must measure 1.25 cubic feet and test 32 pounds per bushel. For a different test weight than 32 pounds, use the table.

For barley testing	Percent
50 pounds or over	104
49 or over, but less than 50	102
48 or over, but less than 49	100
47 or over, but less than 48	98
46 or over, but less than 47	96
45 or over, but less than 46	94
44 or over, but less than 45	92
43 or over, but less than 44	90
42 or over, but less than 43	88
41 or over, but less than 42	85

Soybeans. A bushel must be 1.25 cubic feet and test 60 pounds per bushel. To adjust for a different test weight use the table at the left.

Milo. Test weight is 56 pounds per bushel and 100 pounds must measure 2.25 cubic feet. For grain of a different weight, use table.

For oats testing	Percent
40 pounds or over	125
39 or over, but less than 40	121
38 or over, but less than 39	118
37 or over, but less than 38	115
36 or over, but less than 37	112
35 or over, but less than 36	109
34 or over, but less than 35	106
33 or over, but less than 34	103
32 or over, but less than 33	100
31 or over, but less than 32	96
30 or over, but less than 31	93
29 or over, but less than 30	90

Barley. A bushel must measure 1.25 cubic feet and test 48 pounds. Barley of a different test weight can be adjusted according to the table.

DRY MATTER

To find dry matter equivalents of two different feeds, divide the dry matter content of one by the dry matter content of the other. This figure can then be converted to tons, bushels, pounds, etc., by multiplication.

$$\frac{\% \ DM \ (A)}{\% \ DM \ (B)} = \text{equivalent of (B) in DM to (A)}$$

EXAMPLE 1: You have 2,000 bushels of shelled corn at 30% moisture. This is equivalent in dry matter to how many bushels of shelled corn at 15% moisture?

(A) 2,000 bushels corn at 30% moisture = 70% DM

(B) corn at 15% moisture = 85% DM

$$2,000 \times \frac{.70}{.85} = 1,647$$

Therefore, 2,000 bushels of shelled corn at 30% moisture is equivalent in dry matter to 1,647 bushels at 15% moisture.

EXAMPLE 2: You have one ton of hay at 15% moisture which is equivalent in dry matter to how many tons of haylage at 35% moisture?

(A) 1 ton hay at 15% moisture = 85% DM

(B) haylage at 35% moisture = 65% DM

$$2,000 \times \frac{.85}{.65} = 2,615$$

Therefore, one ton of hay at 15% moisture is equivalent in dry matter to 2,615 pounds of haylage at 35% moisture.

MOISTURE VARIATION

In purchasing grain and in changing feeding rations it's often necessary to compare different moisture content materials. The table below shows the pounds of corn at different moisture contents needed to equal one bushel of No. 2 shelled corn.

POUNDS SHELLED CORN OF DIFFERENT MOISTURES EQUIVALENT TO A BUSHEL (56 POUNDS) OF NO. 2 CORN

Moisture	One bushel	Moisture	One bushel	Moisture	One bushel
%	lbs.	%	lbs.	%	lbs.
11	53.17	20	59.15	29	66.65
12	53.77	21	59.90	30	67.60
13	54.39	22	60.67	31	68.58
14	55.02	23	61.45	32	69.59
15	55.67	24	62.26	33	70.63
16	56.33	25	63.09	34	71.70
17	57.01	26	63.95	35	72.80
18	57.71	27	64.82	36	73.94
19	58.42	28	65.72		

PRE-HARVEST YIELD TEST

For a simple, fast, and reasonably accurate method of estimating corn yield in the field, select unit samples of 1/1,000 acre (use table below).

CORN ROW LENGTH EQUIVALENT TO 1/1,000 ACRE FOR DIFFERENT ROW WIDTHS

Row width	Row length		Row width	Row length	
22 in.	23 ft.	10 in.	36 in.	14 ft.	6 in.
24	21	10	37	14	2
26	20	0	38	13	9
28	18	7	39	13	5
30	17	5	40	13	1
32	16	4	41	12	9
34	15	6	42	12	5

Weight of shelled sample. Collect the ears from 10 unit areas. Then weigh the samples and divide by 10 for average weight per unit area. Now weigh enough ears to equal the average weight and shell the sample. After this is weighed you will have the average shelled weight of 1/1,000 acre.

Weight of one bushel shelled corn equivalent to No. 2 corn. First take a moisture sample. Select one ear from each unit area and shell two rows from each ear. Hold sample in a sealed fruit jar to allow moisture to equalize. Test the sample for moisture and find how many pounds of your corn equals a bushel of No. 2 corn, using the table to the left.

$$\text{Bu. per acre} = \frac{\text{wt. shelled sample} \times 1,000}{\text{wt. 1 bu. shelled corn equivalent to No. 2 corn}}$$

SMALL GRAINS YIELD PER ACRE

Yield per acre in the field for small grains such as wheat, oats and barley can be easily figured in three steps using the table at right.

Width of cut	Mark off	Factor
6 feet	400 feet	18.15
7	400	15.56
8	400	13.61
10	200	21.78
12	200	18.15
14	200	15.56
16	200	13.61
18	200	12.10

1. Determine distance to mark off ahead of the combine.

2. Yield of plot in pounds x factor = pounds per acre.

$$\text{factor} = \frac{43,560 \ (\text{square feet per acre})}{\text{plot square feet}}$$

3. Convert to bushels by using the moisture adjustments on front of page. EXAMPLE: You have a field of wheat and a combine with a 12-foot width of cut. Suppose plot yields 150 pounds.

$$150 \times 18.15 = 2,722.5 \ \text{lbs.} \qquad \frac{2,722.5}{60} = 45.38 \ \text{bu. per acre}$$

FARM MANAGEMENT GUIDE INDEX